Venezuela

Krzysztof Dydyński

Venezuela

2nd edition

Published by
   Lonely Planet Publications
   Head Office: PO Box 617, Hawthorn, Vic 3122, Australia
   Branches: 155 Filbert St, Suite 251, Oakland, CA 94607, USA
                   10a Spring Place, London NW5 3BH, UK
                   71 bis rue du Cardinal Lemoine, 75005 Paris, France

Printed by
   The Bookmaker Ltd.
   Printed in China

Photographs by
   Krzysztof Dydyński

   Front cover: Piranhas (A Boccaccio, The Image Bank)

First Published
   October 1994

This Edition
   May 1998

National Library of Australia Cataloguing in Publication Data

   Venezuela.

   2nd ed.
   Includes index.
   ISBN 0 86442 514 7

   1. Venezuela - Guidebooks. I. Title

918.704633

text & maps © Lonely Planet 1998
photos © photographers as indicated 1998

Krzysztof Dydyński

Krzysztof was born and raised in Warsaw, Poland. Though he graduated in electronic engineering and became an assistant professor in the subject, he soon realised there's more to life than microchips. In the mid-1970s he took off to Afghanistan and India and has been back to Asia several times since. In the 1980s a newly discovered passion for Latin America took him to Colombia, where he lived for over four years and travelled throughout the continent. In search of a new incarnation, he has made Australia his home and worked for Lonely Planet as a designer. Apart from this guide he is the author of guides to *Poland* and *Colombia* and has contributed to other LP books.

From the Author

Many friends, colleagues, travellers on the road and the staff of various Venezuelan institutions and agencies have contributed to this book and deserve the highest praise.

Warmest thanks to Nico de Greiff, Pol Acosta, Roberto Andara, Leonor & Alvaro Blanco, Enrique Castro, Gladis Dornheim, Billy Esser, Raquel & Tom Evenou, Mercedes Fonseca Urdaneta, Henry González, Alfredo Jorge, Roberto Marrero, Jesús Morales, Kokyean Segnini, Christina de Tross, and Danka & Tadek Sokołowski. My special appreciation goes to Angela Melendro.

From the Publisher

The editing of this book was coordinated by Craig MacKenzie in LP's Melbourne office. He was assisted by Chris Wyness, Katie Cody and Rebecca Turner. The coordinating designer was Piotr Czajkowski. He was assisted by Marcel Gaston and Jane Hart. Margie Jung designed the cover and Adam McCrow produced the back cover map.

Thanks

Many thanks to the travellers who wrote to us with information and suggestions:

Helena Åhlund, Brian Ambrosio, Vidaz Andersen, Cherie Anderson, Ron Anderson, Fernando Andrade, Nina Andresen, Nicola Ansell, Libby Anstis, Andrea Aster, Guy Atherton, Anna Austin, Ram Avni, Michael Ayling, Christine Badri, Don & Joan Bailey, Neil Bailey, Harry Baker, Françoise Balconi, Tim Barrett, CJ Bayman, MJ Beeston, Friedrich Bellermann, Alexis Bernard, John Beswetherick, René Beuchle, Maarten Biesheuvel, Fabio Biserna, Kate Black, Bonnie Bloch, Gerard Y Bockweg, MJM de Boer, Dirk Bogaert, Alistair Bool, Stéphane Borella, Kris Borring Prasada Rao, Piero Boschi, Peter Brichzin, Sue Brooklyn, Linda Broschofsky, Heather Brown, Philippa Budger, Wun Buesink, Veronica Byrne, A Callegari, Robin Cameron, Geerg Caspary, Wim Ceuppens, Stephen R Chan, Kacie Chang, Kim Chiarchiaro, Catriona Charkin, Pierre Chaux, Thomas Christen, Dale R Christiansen, Pat Coleman, Aaron Corcoran, Catherine Correa, David Cosgrove, Pedro Costa, Jean Côté, Janet Cotter-Howells, Elizabeth M G Court, Maria Courtney, John Crandon, Maralo Crew, Martin Crone, Cameron Curphy, Luca Daffara, Phillip A Dale, João-Geraldo Damasceno, Salee & David M Davis, Amaury Deffontaine, Ric Delaney, Francois Desmeules, Monique Dodinet, Bernard Doyle, Rafael Dreyfus, Audrey & Jack Duchesne, Wendy S Dudelheim, Fedor Dullaert, Cathrine Düscher, Ron Edwardson, Oliva V Eeghem, Eric Eidsmoe, Thomas Eisabach, Herodotos Ellinas, Sally Elvin, Cynthia Esteban, Ruth Evans, Guy Eysseric, A Fachin, Peter Felix Fenéberg, Antonio Ferrada, Chris Fields, Douglas W Fischer, Peter Fischl, Dairne Fitzpatrick, Clyde Flanegan, Marilyn Flax, Richard Fowkes, John C Franklin, Jill Frazer, Johannes & Roswitha Fresner, Erik Futtrup, Ramona Gallo, Nisha Gambhir, David Gerez, Wil & Joyce Gesler, Rita Geysens, Tessa Gibbs, J Kenneth Glass, Peter Goeltenboth, C Gomes, Stuart Neil Gow, Cecilia Graber,

John Grarley, Jorn Grefstad, David P Grill, Lea Grinter, Mark Groves, Michael K Gschwind, Daniel Guerrera, Anna Carin Gustafson, Raymond Haase, Hans-Peter Haberlandner, Robert Hackman, Susanna Hagman, Brian Halliday, P Hamilton, Juanita Hamparsum, Neil Hampton, Lysia Hand, Vagn Asbjørn Hansen, Debbie Harris, Colin Harvey, Boris Hasselblatt, Michelle Hecht, Siegmar & Gerfried Hein, A Henderson, Klaus Henke, Clive Henman, Boris Henn, Kirsten Heuschen, Mark Hewitt, Chuck Hollenbeck, Koosje van der Horst, Armin Howald, Ashley Huggins, Serge G Huguet, David L Huntzinger, Maria Shiguemi Ichiyama, Stéphanie Inglesfield, Richard Lite de Ingunza, Gabrielle Ireland, Louise Jackson, Bruno Jelk, Ken Johannesson, Power Johnson, Ripton Johnson, Kath Jones, Peter Jones, Marilyn Jones-Gotman, David Josephson, Sabine Joyce, N Jrik, Kristine Jürs, Allen Kamen, Paul B Kandell, Georg Karl, Chris Kelley, Jarrod & Cathy Kelly, Jane Kelly, David Kenny, Roger & Rosy Key, Mary Kilpatrick, Rachel Kirsch, Herbert Josef Klein, Brigit Kleymann, Jennifer Klinec, Paul Knøbel, Rainer Knyrim, Steven Koenig, Jacco Konijn, Thilo Kopp, André H Korenhof, Margaret Kostaszuk, Adrie & Jopie Kouwenberg, Ben Krainbrink, Dale & Adrienne de Kretser, Lucy Kunkel, Peter Kunkel, Steven Kusters, P Lack, Andre Lamboo, Mark Laptin, Fernando Lara, Ludovic N Leforestier, Dominique Leon, Nadine Lewin, Andrew Leyland, Yannick Stefano Lusenti, Dikrán P Lutufyan, Hermann Luyken, Ben & Blanche Maartman, Helen Mader, Patrizia Magnani, H F Mann, Jay Mappus, Jane Mardei, Margrit de Marez Oyens, Harry Marieke, Stella Maris, Chris Marks, Alyssa M Martin, Philip B Martin, Gary McCall, Denise & Malcolm McDonough, Twid McGrath, Rachel McGregor, Kathleen McGurk, Don McNeil, Manfred Melchinger, Steve Menari, Ulrike Meyer, Osman K Mian, Burkhard Militzer, Mike Miller, Peter Milton, Adrian Mitu, Rody Moore, Jorge M Moran, Paola Marinoni Morgado, Rohan Morton, Benjamin Moser, Robin Moss, Claudia Mueller, Lori Murphy, Danielle Nadeau, Bruce & Maria Nesbitt, Claire Nichols, Eldon & Susan Nichols, Jan Nielsen, Hans Nieuwenhuis, Eric Noble, Pedro Novak, Ota Novotny, Frédérique Nunero, Mike O'Connor, Betty Odell, Birgit Oehmichen, Felicia Oeystaa, Kristin Offer-Ohlsen, N Okwudili, Antoinette B d'Oronzio, Isaias Ortiz, Dirk van Ostveen, Marcel Ott, Louise Pabe, Markus Pallor, Gary Palmer, Natalie Paganelli, Wim Pannecoucke, Janke Papa, Julie & Spiros Pappas, Beryl & Joel Park, Joseph Parkhurst, Siegrun Päßler, Audrey Patterson, Rhonda Payget, Theon Pearce, Mick Pease, Denise Perreault, Cheryl Petreman, Joaquina Pires-O'Brien, Lucy C Porter, Annette Powell, Julianne Power, Monica Pranzl, Deborah Prhafo, Hans Rasmussen, Brigitte Rauch, Sandra Reami, Bob Redlinger, Judith Rhodes, Thomas Ribisel, Mary Richards, Simon Richards, Randy Riddell, Gunther Riebel, Daniel Filipe Rios, Roman Ritter, Gerry & Janine Rodgers, Willem Roemer, David Rogan, Don Rogers, Ilana Rosenfeld, Laila Rosten, Hans R Roth, Valentina Salapura, Matt Salmon, Anabela Salvador, Volker Sauer, Sigrid Schapitz, Ron Scharis, Marieke Schaube, Arnout Scheltes, Marc Schichs, James Schmidt, Erich Schmitt, Johanne Schulz, Jerome Sgard, Yiftah Shalev, Shaun Shaver, Eran Shayshon, Maria Shrand, Ondrej Simetke, Suzanne Slater, David Smith, Duncan Smith, Charlotte Snowden, Paulo de Sousa Pinto, Steve Souza, Yasmin Spira, Raffa Stefano, Carine Stevens, Michael Stock, Jesse R Struson, María Cristina Suárez, Juli Sutherland, Erik Svane, Helen Rita Sykes, Graham Syrett, Danko Taborosi, Mary Taylor, Olivia Taylor, Marlies Thielpape, Michael Tille, Sara Tizard, Cecilia Topas, Giovanni Tosatti, Don Trask, Marisel Traverzo, Samuel B Trickey, Helen A Tsefuhl, Ingeborg Uitentuis, Bonnie Valentine, Lluis Vallés, Andreá Vannucchi, Michel van Velde, John Versmissen, Manuel Candéa Viana, Rodrigo Fernandes Vieira, Antonio Vizamora, Pam Wadworth, Hans Wagner, Stefani Warren, Jonathan Weber, Jörn Weigle, Maaike van Westen, Dalma Whang, A Wheele, Nick Whittaker, David Williams, Rob Williams, Carol Willison, Anne Wilshin, Ian Wilson, Anne Winchester, Tris Winfield, Thomas Winter, Emanuel & Helgard Wirfel, Joan Wood, Christopher Woods, Dan Workman, Dirk Wütherich, Paul Yale, Alta van Zyl.

Warning & Request

Things change – prices go up, schedules change, good places go bad and bad places go bankrupt. So, if you find things have changed, please tell us and help make the next edition even more accurate and useful.

We value all the feedback we receive from travellers. Julie Young coordinates a small team who read and acknowledge every letter, postcard and email, and ensure that every morsel of information finds its way to the appropriate authors, editors and publishers.

Everyone who writes to us will find their name in the next edition of the appropriate guide and will also receive a free subscription to our quarterly newsletter, *Planet Talk*. The very best contributions will be rewarded with a free Lonely Planet guide.

Excerpts from your correspondence may appear in new editions of this guide; in our newsletter, *Planet Talk*; or in updates on our Web site – so please let us know if you don't want your letter published or your name acknowledged.

Contents

Boxed Asides

Map Legend

BOUNDARIES

▬▬▬▬▬▬▬	International Boundary
─ ─ ─ ─ ─ ─	Provincial Boundary
─── ─── ───	Disputed Boundary

ROUTES

═══════ A25	Freeway, with Route Number
───────	Major Road
───────	Minor Road
═ ═ ═ ═ ═	Minor Road - Unsealed
───────	City Road
───────	City Street
───────	City Lane
┼─┼─┼─●─┼─┼	Train Route, with Station
─┼─┼─Ⓜ─┼─	Metro Route, with Station
╫─╫─╫─╫─╫	Cable Car or Chairlift
─ ─ ─ ─ ─	Ferry Route
─ ─ ─ ─ ─	Walking Track

AREA FEATURES

	Building
+ + + + + +	Cemetery (Christian)
× × × × × ×	Cemetery (other)
	Glacier
	Market
✿	Park, Gardens
	Pedestrian Mall
	Reef
	Urban Area

HYDROGRAPHIC FEATURES

	Canal
	Coastline
	Creek, River
	Lake, Intermittent Lake
»»)) ⇐	Rapids, Waterfalls
	Salt Lake
⊥ ⊥ ⊥ ⊥ ⊥	Swamp

SYMBOLS

✪ CAPITAL	National Capital	✈	Airfield	◪	Mosque
◉ CAPITAL	Provincial Capital	✈	Airport	▲	Mountain or Hill
● CITY	City	∴	Archaeological Site	⛫	Museum
● Town	Town	⊖	Bank	⛤	National Park
● Village	Village	㋐	Beach	←	One Way Street
		🛆	Castle or Fort	🅿	Parking
■	Place to Stay	⌒	Cave	)(	Pass
⚔	Camping Ground	╼┿ 🕇	Church	⛽	Petrol Station
⊞	Caravan Park	⌢⌢⌢	Cliff or Escarpment	✉	Post Office
⌂	Hut or Chalet	⚲	Embassy	🏛	Stately Home
		✛	Hospital	☎	Telephone
▼	Place to Eat	⚑	Lighthouse	❶	Tourist Information
☗	Pub or Bar	✳	Lookout	⊝	Transport
		⚐	Monument	🐘	Zoo

Map Index

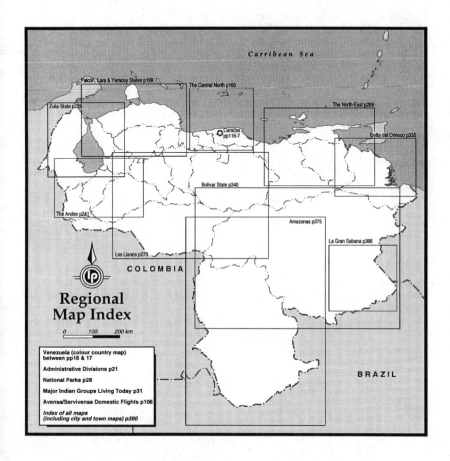

Carribean Sea

Falcón, Lara & Yaracuy States p199

The Central North p160

Zulia State p229

The North-East p289

Caracas pp116-7

Delta del Orinoco p335

Bolívar State p340

The Andes p241

Amazonas p375

La Gran Sabana p366

Los Llanos p273

COLOMBIA

Regional
Map Index

0   100   200 km

Venezuela (colour country map)
between pp16 & 17

Administrative Divisions p21

National Parks p28

Major Indian Groups Living Today p31

Avensa/Servivensa Domestic Flights p106

Index of all maps
(including city and town maps) p390

BRAZIL

Introduction

Venezuela's modern history has been strongly influenced by oil money, which has turned the country into one of the wealthiest nations on the continent. As a result, Venezuela today has some of the best road networks in South America, splendid modern architecture and a well developed tourism infrastructure. Yet deep in the countryside, people live their traditional way of life as if the 20th century got lost somewhere down the road. There are a number of Indian groups unconquered by encroaching civilisation, the most mysterious being the Yanomami, a stone-age culture lost in time along the Venezuela-Brazil border.

The variety of Venezuela's landscapes won't disappoint even the most demanding visitor. The country boasts the northern tip of the Andes topped with snowcapped peaks, and the vast Delta del Orinoco (equal in area

to Belgium), crisscrossed by a maze of natural channels. The southern part of the country is taken up by the legendary wilderness of the Amazon, while the north is bordered for some 3000km by the Caribbean and lined with countless beaches.

Venezuela's most unusual natural formations are the *tepuis*, the flat-topped mountains with vertical flanks which loom over a thousand metres above rolling savannas. Their tops are noted for their moon-like landscape and their peculiar endemic flora. There are about 100 tepuis scattered throughout the south-east of the country; from one of them spills Salto Angel (Angel Falls), the world's highest waterfall (979m) and Venezuela's most famous tourist sight.

To sum up, Venezuela combines some of the best of traditional cultures contained within a beautiful natural setting with decent western-standard tourist facilities – it is, after all, the most Yankeefied country in South America. You can travel smoothly, enjoying familiar comfort, and at the same time experience a kaleidoscope of exotic landscapes, people and wildlife. It's the easy bit of South America, yet it has all you would wish for, from the Caribbean to the Andes to the Amazon it's a perfect introduction to the continent.

In practical terms, Venezuela is a relatively safe and friendly country in which to travel, with fairly inexpensive accommodation, food and domestic transport. Venezuela has South America's cheapest air links with both Europe and the USA, and is thus a convenient gateway to the continent. Don't treat it, however, just as a bridge; give yourself some time to discover this land – it's well worth it.

Facts about the Country

HISTORY
Pre-Columbian Times
Radiocarbon dating of archaeological samples has shown that the first people arrived in what is now Venezuela somewhere around the 14th millennium BC. The oldest examples have been excavated in El Jobo, in the present-day state of Falcón in the northwestern part of the country.

Primitive nomadic groups' cultures evolved from that time on, using rough stone for tools and weapons for hunting. Around the 5th millennium BC, bone and marine shells also came into use. Pottery only began to appear in the 1st millennium BC. Around the same time agriculture began, and this slowly led to the establishment of sedentary settlements. From this stage on, separate groups began to evolve into distinctive cultures.

The more settled way of life resulted in an increase in population growth. It's estimated that by the time of the Spanish conquest about half a million Indians inhabited the region which is now Venezuela. There were isolated communities of various ethnic backgrounds, belonging to three main linguistic families: Carib, Arawak and Chibcha.

The warlike Carib tribes inhabited the central and eastern coast, living off fishing and shifting agriculture. Various Arawak groups were scattered over a large area of western Llanos and north up to the coast. They lived off hunting and food-gathering, and only occasionally practised farming.

The Timote-Cuica, members of the Chibcha linguistic family (the same family to which the Muisca and Tayrona of Colombia belonged) were the most advanced of Venezuela's pre-Hispanic societies. They chose the Andes as their home, where they founded their settlements and linked them by a network of trails. They developed fairly advanced agricultural techniques, including irrigation and terracing where the topography required it.

Venezuela's pre-Hispanic cultures didn't reach the level of architectural or artistic development of the great civilisations of, say, the Maya or Inca. They haven't left behind many significant artefacts, save for some pottery and other simple objects found during excavations. No important samples of their architectural legacy have survived.

Petroglyphs (drawings or carvings on rock), which have been discovered on numerous locations throughout the country, are possibly the most remarkable testimony to the culture of Venezuela's indigenous people. However, exactly when they were done and by whom remains a mystery.

The Spanish Conquest
Christopher Columbus was the first European to set foot on Venezuelan soil – indeed, it was the only South American mainland country Columbus landed on. In 1498, on his third trip to the New World, he anchored at the eastern tip of the Península de Paria, across from Trinidad. At first, Columbus thought he had discovered yet

Columbus Discovers the New World, (1493), by an anonymous artist another island, but continuing along the coast, he found the wide and voluminous mouth of the Río Orinoco – sufficient proof that the place was much more than an island. Astonished with his discovery, he wrote in his diary: 'Never have I read or heard of so much sweet water within a salt ocean', and named the gulf El Mar Dulce, or the Sweet Sea. Today it is called the Golfo de Paria.

A year later another explorer, Alonso de Ojeda, accompanied by the Italian Amerigo Vespucci, sailed up to the Península de la Guajira, at the western extremity of present-day Venezuela. On entering Lago Maracaibo the Spaniards saw the local Indians living in rustic thatched houses on stilts above the water. They called the land Venezuela (literally Little Venice), perhaps with a sarcastic undertone, because it was quite different from the opulence of the Italian city they knew.

The first Spanish settlement on Venezuelan soil, Nueva Cádiz, was established on the small island of Cubagua, just south of Isla de Margarita, in about 1500 (although it was not until 1519 that it was granted a formal act of foundation). The town swiftly developed into a busy port engaged in pearl harvesting, but was completely destroyed by an earthquake and tidal wave in 1541. The earliest Venezuelan town still in existence, Cumaná, on the north-east coast, dates from 1521.

Officially, most of what is now Venezuela was ruled by Spain from Santo Domingo (present-day capital of the Dominican Republic), except for its western part which was governed from Lima. Following the creation of the Virreynato de la Nueva Granada with its capital in Bogotá, in 1717, all of present-day Venezuela fell under the administration of the new viceroyalty. It remained so until independence.

In practice, however, the region was allowed a large degree of autonomy. It was, after all, unimportant and sparsely populated with an uninviting steamy climate, so the Spaniards gave it low priority, focusing instead on Colombia, Peru and Bolivia, which were abundant in gold and silver. In many ways, Venezuela remained a backwater until the oil boom of the 1920s.

Independence Wars

Apart from three brief rebellions against colonial rule between 1749 and 1797, Venezuela had a relatively uneventful history for 300 years after the arrival of the Europeans. All this changed at the beginning of the 19th century when Venezuela gave to Latin America its greatest ever hero, Simón Bolívar. El Libertador, as he is commonly known, together with his most able lieutenant, Antonio José de Sucre, was responsible for ending colonial rule all the way to the Argentinian border.

The revolutionary flame was lit by Francisco de Miranda in 1806, but his efforts at setting up an independent administration at Caracas came to an end when he was handed over to the Spanish by his fellow conspirators. The Spanish shipped him to Spain and he died a few years later in a Cádiz jail. Leadership of the revolution was taken over by Bolívar. After unsuccessful attempts to defeat the Spaniards at home, he withdrew to Colombia, then to Jamaica, until the opportune moment came in 1817.

At the time, events in Europe were in Bolívar's favour. The Napoleonic Wars had ended and Bolívar's agent in London was able to raise money and arms and to recruit over 5000 British veterans of the Peninsular War who were being demobbed from the armies which had been raised to fight Napoleon. With this force of British mercenaries and an army of horsemen from Los Llanos, Bolívar marched over the Andes and defeated the Spanish at the battles of Pantano de Vargas and Boyacá, thus bringing independence to Colombia in August 1819.

Four months later in Angostura (present-day Ciudad Bolívar), a congress was held which proclaimed Gran Colombia, a new state unifying Colombia, Venezuela and Ecuador (though the last two were still under Spanish rule). The liberation of Venezuela was completed with Bolívar's victory over the Spanish forces at Carabobo in 1821, though the royalists continued to put up a desultory rearguard fight from Puerto Cabello for another two years. With these victories under their belts, Bolívar and Sucre went on to liberate Ecuador, Peru and Bolivia, which they accomplished by the end of 1824.

Although both economically and demographically Venezuela was the least important of the areas which made up Gran Colombia, it bore the brunt of the fighting. Not only did Venezuelan patriots fight on their own territory, they also fought in the armies which Bolívar led into Colombia and down the Pacific coast. It is estimated that over a quarter of the population died in these wars.

Gran Colombia managed to exist for only a decade before it split into three separate countries. Bolívar's dream of a unified republic fell apart even before he died in 1830.

After Independence

Venezuela's post-independence period was marked by serious governmental problems which continued for over a century. For the most part, these were times of despotism and anarchy, with the country being ruled by a series of military dictators known as *caudillos*. It wasn't until 1947 that the first democratic government was elected.

The first of the caudillos, General José Antonio Páez, represented the conservative oligarchy and controlled the country for 18 years (1830-1848), though not as president for all that time. Despite his tough rule, he succeeded in establishing a certain political stability and put the weak economy on its feet. He is perhaps the most warmly remembered of the caudillos.

The period which followed was an almost uninterrupted chain of civil wars and political strife, only stopped by another long-lived dictator, General Antonio Guzmán Blanco. He came to power in 1870 and retained it, with few breaks, until 1888. A conservative with liberal leanings, he launched a broad programme of reforms, including a new constitution, compulsory primary education, religious freedom and a package of regulations designed to improve the economy. No

doubt he tackled some of the crucial domestic issues and assured temporary stability, yet his despotic rule triggered wide popular opposition, and when he stepped down, the country plunged again into civil war.

Things were not going much better on the international front. In the 1840s Venezuela raised the question of its eastern border with British Guiana (present-day Guyana). Based on vague pre-independence territorial divisions, the Venezuelan government laid claim to as much as two-thirds of Guiana, up to the Río Essequibo. The issue was a subject of lengthy diplomatic negotiations and led to severe strains in international relations in the 1890s. It was eventually settled in 1899 by an arbitration tribunal, which gave rights over the questioned territory to Great Britain. Despite this, Venezuela continues to claim it to this day. All Venezuelan-produced maps have this chunk of Guyana placed within Venezuela's boundaries, labelled Zona en Reclamación.

Another conflict which led to serious tensions in international relations was Venezuela's failure to meet payments to Great Britain, Italy and Germany, on loans accumulated during the irresponsible government of yet another caudillo, General Cipriano Castro (1899-1908). In response, in 1902 the three countries sent their navies to blockade Venezuelan seaports.

It's worth noting that the independence movement and subsequent governments were almost entirely in the hands of Creoles. They paid little attention to Indians and blacks, and not much more to mestizos or mulatos, who continued to be exploited under conditions similar to or worse than those prevailing under Spanish rule. Although slavery was officially abolished in 1854, in many regions it continued well into the 20th century.

The 20th Century Military Dictatorships

The first half of the 20th century was dominated by five successive military rulers from the Andean state of Táchira, the first of whom was the incompetent Cipriano Castro. The longest lasting and most despotic of the caudillos was General Juan Vicente Gómez, who seized power in 1908 and didn't relinquish it until his death in 1935. Gómez phased out the parliament, crushed the opposition and thus monopolised power, supported by a strong army, an extensive police force and a well-developed spy network. Thanks to the discovery of oil in the 1910s, the Gómez regime was able to stabilise the country and in some ways made it prosperous. By the late 1920s, Venezuela became the world's largest exporter of oil, which not only contributed notably to economic recovery but also enabled the government to pay off the country's entire foreign debt.

Little of the oil-related wealth filtered down to people on the street. The vast majority continued to live in poverty, with little or no educational or health facilities, let alone reasonable housing. Oil money also resulted in the neglect of agriculture. Food had to be imported in increasing amounts, and prices rose rapidly. When Gómez died in 1935, the people of Caracas went on a rampage, burning down the houses of his relatives and supporters and even threatening to set fire to the oil installations on Lago Maracaibo.

Gómez was succeeded by his own war minister, Eleázar López Contreras, and six years later by yet another Táchiran general, Isaías Medina Angarita. Meanwhile, popular tensions rose dangerously, exploding in 1945 when Rómulo Betancourt, the founder and leader of the left-wing Acción Democrática party (AD), took control of the government. He was supported by the majority of the people, including some junior army officers. A new constitution was adopted in 1947, and a noted novelist, Rómulo Gallegos, became president in the first democratic election in the country's history. On the wave of the democratic euphoria, another political party, the conservative Partido Social Cristiano (Copei), was founded by the young activist Rafael Caldera, to counterbalance the leftist AD.

The pace of reforms was too fast, however, given the strength of old military forces greedy for power. The inevitable coup took place only eight months after the election, with Colonel Marcos Pérez Jiménez emerging as leader. Once in control, Pérez Jiménez began ruthlessly crushing the opposition, at the same time ploughing the oil money back into public works, into industries which would help diversify the economy and, particularly, into modernising Caracas. However, spectacular buildings mushrooming in the capital were poor substitutes for a better standard of living and access to political power for the mass of the population, so opposition steadily grew.

Democracy at Last

In 1958 Pérez Jiménez was overthrown by a coalition of civilians and navy and air force officers. Shortly after his fall, the country returned to democratic rule and an election was held, in which Betancourt was elected president. He put an end to the former dictator's solicitous policy towards foreign big business, but was careful this time not to act too impetuously.

Despite some opposition from both communists and right-wing factions, Betancourt enjoyed widespread popular support and succeeded in completing the constitutional five-year term in office – the first democratically elected Venezuelan president to do so. He voluntarily stepped down in 1963. Since then, all changes of president have been by constitutional means, with the two traditional parties, AD and Copei, being the major forces on the political scene. And behind them was oil, the essential factor of Venezuela's political stability. It brought presidents peace of mind or headache, depending on the economic climate of the day.

Presidents Raúl Leoni of AD (1964-69) and Rafael Caldera of Copei (1969-74) had relatively easy and quiet terms, since the steady stream of oil money that flowed into the country's coffers kept the economy buoyant. President Carlos Andrés Pérez of AD (1974-79) witnessed the oil bonanza. Not only did production of oil rise but, more importantly, the price quadrupled following

Faces of Venezuela

Península de
Paraguaná
Curaçao
Bonaire
Peninsula de
la Guajira
Pueblo Nevo
NETHERLANDS
ANTILLES
Archipiélago
Los Roques
Punto Fijo
Golfo de
Venezuela
Golfete
de Coro
La Vela de Coro
Santa
Marta
Riohacha
Maicao
3
Coro
FALCÓN
San Juan de los Cayos
Chichiriviche
San Rafael
Churuguara
4
Tucacas
Puerto Cruz
Maiquetía
Valledupar
Maracaibo
3
Santa Rita
Cabimas
LARA
San Felipe
1
Puerto
Cabello
CARACAS
Los Teques
Rosario
6
17
Carora
YARACUY
Valencia
Maracay
ARAGUA
Cúa
Machiques
Bachaquero
El Tocuyo
Barquisimeto
CARABOBO
San Juan de
los Morros
ZULIA
Lago de
Maracaibo
4
Araure
Acarigua
5
San Carlos
13
El Sombrero
TRUJILLO
Trujillo
Biscucuy
COJEDES
San Carlos
del Zulia
6
1
Valera
PORTUGUESA
Calabozo
El Vigía
Mérida
Guanare
Guanarito
2
Barinas
Pico Bolívar
(5007m)
5
Tovar
MÉRIDA
BARINAS
Libertad
Cúcuta
San Antonio
del Táchira
San Cristóbal
TÁCHIRA
Santa Bárbara
Bruzual
Apurito
San Fernando
de Apure
19
Río Sioca
Mantecal
Guachara
Bucaramanga
19
Guasdualito
Río Arauca
Arauca
Elorza
APURE
Puerto Páez
El Burro
Río Meta
Puerto Carreño
COLOMBIA
Tunja
Puerto Ayacucho
Samariapo
Morganito
BOGOTÁ
San Fernando
de Atabapo

Country Name	República de Venezuela
Area	916,445 sq km
Population	22 million (1997)
Population Density	24 per sq km
Capital	Caracas
Official Language	Spanish
Other Languages	More than 25 Indian languages

San Carlos
de Río Negro

A	B
C	D
E	F

A: Condor
B: Scarlet ibis
C: Paují

D: Jaguar
E: Spectacled cayman
F: Macaws

the Arab-Israeli war. Pérez nationalised the iron ore and oil industries and went on a spending spree. Imported luxury goods crammed the shops and the nation got the impression that El Dorado had finally materialised. Not for long, though.

Political Instability

In the late 1970s, the growing international recession and oil glut began to shake Venezuela's economic stability. Oil revenues started to decline, pushing up unemployment and inflation, and consequently popular discontent increased. Presidents Luis Herrera Campins of Copei (1979-84) and Jaime Lusinchi of AD (1984-89) witnessed a gradual slowing down of the economy.

The 1988 drop in world oil prices cut the country's revenue in half, putting into serious doubt Venezuela's ability to pay off its foreign debt. Austerity measures introduced in February 1989 by the government of President Pérez (elected for the second time) triggered a wave of protests in Caracas, culminating in three days of bloody riots known as the Caracazo which cost over 300 lives. All further measures (which basically consisted of price increases) immediately spurred protests, mostly beginning in universities, and often escalating into riots. Strikes and street demonstrations came to be part of everyday life, as they continue to be today.

To make matters worse, there were two attempted coups d'état in 1992. The first, launched in February by a faction of mid-rank military officers led by Colonel Hugo Chávez, was a shock to most Venezuelans. The president escaped from the Palacio de Miraflores (the presidential palace) minutes before rebel tanks broke in. There was shooting throughout Caracas, claiming over 20 lives, but the government regained control. Chávez was sentenced to a long term in prison.

Another attempt, in November, was led by junior air force officers. The air battle over Caracas, with warplanes flying between the skyscrapers, gave the coup a cinematographic, if not apocalyptic, dimension. The Palacio de Miraflores was bombed and partially destroyed. The army was again called to defend the president, which it dutifully did. This time over 100 people lost their lives.

Both coups failed, as the army commands maintained restraint and gave their support to the president – but will they be so loyal next time? The army is increasingly divided and disillusioned with the economic stalemate which is cutting its income. The two coup attempts have left a clear message – despite nearly 40 years of democracy, the military is ready to take centre stage at any time.

Things became even more complicated when Pérez was accused of embezzlement and misuse of public funds. The Supreme Court examined the issue and, in May 1993, declared that there was enough evidence to charge the president. Pérez was automatically suspended from his duties and Ramón Velásquez was appointed to serve as interim president for the last eight months of the statutory Pérez term. On a continent where the trial of a president is a rare occurrence, it's remarkable that Pérez was eventually sentenced by the court. He was released in September 1996 after 28 months under house arrest.

The 1993 Elections

The December 1993 elections brought Rafael Caldera back as president. He no longer represented Copei, the party he founded, but ran as an independent backed by a coalition of 16 small parties, known as the Convergencia Nacional. He narrowly defeated Andrés Velásquez of the Causa Radical (Causa R), the relatively new but progressive left-wing party founded by unionists. The candidates of the two traditional parties, Copei and AD, were beaten into third and fourth place, respectively.

The election result was a reflection of the social climate of the day. Amid general political instability, and with both traditional parties embroiled in corruption scandals, voters opted for their charismatic former

Simón Bolívar

'There have been three great fools in history: Jesus, Don Quixote and I' – this is how Simón Bolívar summed up his life shortly before he died. The man who brought independence from Spanish rule to the entire north-west of South America – today's Venezuela, Colombia, Panama, Ecuador, Peru and Bolivia – died abandoned, rejected and poor.

The Bolívar family had come to the New World from Spain in 1557. They first settled in Santo Domingo, but in 1589 moved to Venezuela, where they were granted a hacienda in San Mateo, near Caracas. Members of Venezuela's colonial elite, they were well off and steadily extended their possessions. One of their descendants, Juan Vicente Bolívar, acquired a town house in Caracas. He was 47 years old when, in 1773, he married 15-year-old María de la Concepción Palacios y Blanco. They had four children; the second, born on 24 July 1783, was named Simón.

Juan Vicente died in 1786 (Simón was then three years old) and María six years later. The boy was brought up by his uncle and was given a tutor, Simón Rodríguez, an open-minded mentor who had a strong formative influence on his pupil.

In 1799 the young Bolívar was sent to Spain and France to continue his education. After having mastered French, he turned his attention to that country's literature. Voltaire and Rousseau became his favourite authors. Their works introduced him to new, progressive ideas of liberalism and – as it turned out – were to determine the course of his career.

In 1802, Bolívar married his Spanish bride, María Teresa Rodríguez del Toro, and a short time later the young couple sailed to Caracas. Their married life lasted only eight months; María Teresa died of yellow fever. Bolívar never married again, although he had many lovers. The most devoted of these was Manuela Sáenz, whom he met in Quito in 1822 and who accompanied him almost until his final days.

The death of María Teresa marked a drastic shift in Bolívar's destiny. He returned to France, where he met with the leaders of the French Revolution, and then travelled to the USA to take a close look at the new order after the War of American Independence. By the time he returned to Caracas in 1807, he was full of revolutionary theories and experiences taken from these two successful examples. It didn't take him long to join clandestine, pro-independence circles.

At the time, disillusionment with Spanish rule was close to breaking out into open revolt. On 19 April 1810 the Junta Suprema was installed in Caracas and on 5 July 1811 the Congress declared independence. This turned out to be only the beginning; the declaration triggered a long, bitter war, most of which was to be orchestrated by Bolívar.

Bolívar's military career began under Francisco de Miranda, the first Venezuelan leader of the independence movement. After Miranda was captured by the Spaniards in 1812, Bolívar took over command. Over the following decade, he hardly had a moment's rest; battle followed battle with astonishing frequency until 1824. Of those battles personally directed by Bolívar, the forces of independence won 35. Of these, the key strategic achievements were the Battle of Boyacá (7 August 1819), which secured the independence of Colombia; the Battle of Carabobo (24 June 1821), which

president, probably hoping he would repeat his success of the previous term. However, 25 years on, the economic situation was quite different, as was the man himself, 77 years of age by the time of the 1993 election.

Caldera's problems began on the eve of taking office. In February 1994, Venezuela's second largest bank, Banco Latino, collapsed and had to be rescued by a government takeover at an estimated cost of US$2 billion. The domino-like failure of a dozen other banks throughout 1994 cost the brought freedom to Venezuela; and the Battle of Pichincha (24 May 1822), which led to the liberation of Ecuador.

Bolívar's long-awaited dream materialised: Gran Colombia, the unified state comprising Venezuela, Colombia and Ecuador, became reality. However, the task of setting the newborn country on its feet proved to be even more difficult than that of winning battles. 'I fear peace more than war,' Bolívar wrote in one of his letters, aware of the difficulties ahead.

The main problem was the question of the political organisation of Gran Colombia. Bolívar, then the president, favoured a strong central rule, but the central regime was increasingly incapable of governing such an immense country with its great racial and regional divisions and differences. Gran Colombia began to collapse from the moment of its birth.

Bolívar insisted on holding the weak union together, but matters began to slip out of his hands. His impassioned and vehement speeches – for which he was widely known – no longer swayed the growing opposition. His glory and charisma faded.

As separatist tendencies escalated dangerously, Bolívar removed vice-president Santander from office by decree and, in August 1828, assumed dictatorship. This step brought more harm than good. His popularity waned further, as did his circle of personal friends and supporters. A short time later, he miraculously escaped an assassination attempt in Bogotá. Disillusioned and in bad health, he resigned the presidency in early 1830 and decided to travel to Europe. The formal disintegration of Gran Colombia was just months away.

Following Venezuela's separation from Gran Colombia, the Venezuelan Congress approved a new constitution and – irony of ironies – banned Bolívar from his homeland. A month later, Antonio José de Sucre (remembered for inflicting final defeat on Spain in the Battle of Ayacucho on 9 December 1824), the closest of Bolívar's friends, was assassinated in southern Colombia. These two pieces of news reached Bolívar shortly before he was to have boarded a ship bound for France. Depressed and ill, he accepted the invitation of a Spaniard, Joaquín de Mier, to stay at his house, Quinta de San Pedro Alejandrino, in Santa Marta. A bitter remark written in Bolívar's diary at this time reads: 'America is ungovernable. Those who serve the revolution plough the sea.'

Bolívar died on 17 December 1830 of pulmonary tuberculosis. A priest, a doctor and a few officers were by his bed, but none of his close friends. Joaquín de Mier donated one of his shirts to dress the dead body, as there had been none among Bolívar's humble belongings. So died perhaps the most important figure in South America's history.

It took the Venezuelan nation 12 years to acknowledge its debt to the man who won its freedom. In 1842, Bolívar's remains were brought from Santa Marta to Venezuela and deposited in Caracas' cathedral. In 1876, they were solemnly transferred to the National Pantheon, where they now rest.

El Libertador – as he was named at the beginning of the liberation campaign and is still commonly called today – was without doubt a man of extraordinary gifts and talents. An idealist with a poetic mind and visionary ideas, Bolívar's goal was not only to topple Spanish rule but to create a unified America. This, of course, was an impossible ideal, yet the military conquest of some five million sq km remains a phenomenal accomplishment. This inspired amateur without any formal training in the strategy of war won battles in a manner which still confounds experts today. The campaign over the Andean Cordillera in the rainy season was described 100 years later as 'the most magnificent episode in the history of war'.

Voices critical of Bolívar's faults and shortcomings are now almost never heard, yet he was frequently accused of despotism and dictatorship when he ruled Gran Colombia. It was Bolívar himself who once said: 'Our America can only be ruled through a well-managed, shrewd despotism'.

Today Bolívar's reputation is polished and inflated to almost superhuman dimensions. His cult is particularly strong in Venezuela but he is also widely venerated in all the other nations he freed. His statue graces almost every central city square, and at least one street in every town bears his name. One of the final, prophetic remarks in Bolívar's diary reads: 'My name now belongs to history, it will do me justice'. And history has duly done so. ■

government another US$8 billion to pay off depositors. Several other banks failed in 1995. In all, the disaster cost the state coffers the equivalent of 20% of Gross Domestic Product (GDP). Some international experts claim that this was the largest financial collapse experienced by any country in recent times.

Unlike previous free-market-oriented governments, Caldera's opted for a state-controlled economy. By suspending economic rights by decree, the government gave itself power to intervene in any area of economic activity, including price control. It fixed the exchange rate of the local currency and introduced restrictions on the export of foreign currency.

The economic situation, however, continued to worsen. Exports went down, pushing up the budget deficit and eating into already limited state reserves. In December 1995, the government was forced to devalue the local currency by more than 70%, yet it fell even further on the free market, which in turn resulted in galloping inflation.

Facing an economic mess, and without any consistent long-term programme of restructuring the economy, the government turned to foreign creditors for support, but the International Monetary Fund (IMF) demanded hard measures be adopted before any loans could be approved. These had to include a sharp increase in the domestic price of petrol and cuts in public spending. Caldera was reluctant to take such drastic steps, fearing an outbreak of popular protest. But when the president reshuffled his cabinet in March 1996 and appointed Teodoro Petkoff as planning minister, things started moving at a faster pace. A former communist guerrilla leader, Petkoff was one of the founders of the Movimiento al Socialismo party (MAS), created after insurgent forces had been 'pacified' in the early 1970s. The package of measures designed by Petkoff's economic team was approved by the IMF, thus making available about US$3 billion in credit.

The package, introduced in April 1996, included the increase of petrol prices by about 500% and the abolition of exchange controls. Over the following months, inflation soared and consumption fell sharply. Exports (except for oil) were further down and only a third of Venezuela's banks recorded profits.

The lack of economic coherence and direction of Caldera's government cost him a significant loss of credibility and popular support. This was clearly reflected in the results of state elections held in December 1995. Convergencia, the odd agglomeration of minority parties that got together to elect

Caldera, won in just one of 22 states. AD claimed victory in 10 states, and Copei won four governorships, proving that the traditional two-party system, badly shaken in the 1993 elections, was back in business.

Venezuela Today

Throughout 1996 and 1997, Venezuela was plagued by strikes for higher wages by a variety of social groups, including teachers, civil servants and doctors. More than three-quarters of the country's 22 million inhabitants ended 1996 below the poverty line, and unemployment hit a new record of 15%, even though official statistics put it at 12%. An opinion poll carried out in June 1997 showed deep pessimism throughout the nation and a 70% disapproval of the government.

Crime and drug-trafficking have been increasing, and there has been a dramatic expansion of Colombian guerrillas into Venezuela's frontier areas over recent years. The rebels have taken to kidnapping local farmers and cattle ranchers for ransom as a source of financing their activities. In response, Venezuela began to reinforce its border surveillance, and by 1997 had already assembled 30,000 troops in the area.

The potentially explosive issue comes as yet another headache for Caldera's government and could further complicate the long uneasy relationship between the two countries. For tourists, it means an increased risk when travelling in frontier areas.

GOVERNMENT

Venezuela is a federal republic. The president is elected by direct vote for a five-year term and cannot be re-elected for consecutive terms. However, after 10 years (two terms) out of office, a former president can stand for re-election. The elections are held in December and new presidents take office in February of the subsequent year. Note that years given in brackets in the preceding sections refer to the actual presidency period.

The current constitution (in force since 1961) gives the presidency extensive power. Venezuela's president appoints the cabinet,

Administrative Divisions

0   100   200 km

State	Area (sq km)	Capital	State	Area (sq km)	Capital
Distrito Federal	1930	Caracas	Guárico	64,986	San Juan de los Morros
Dependencias Federales	120	–	Lara	19,800	Barquisimeto
Amazonas	177,617	Puerto Ayacucho	Mérida	11,300	Mérida
Anzoátegui	43,300	Barcelona	Miranda	7950	Los Teques
Apure	76,500	San Fernando	Monagas	28,900	Maturín
Aragua	7014	Maracay	Nueva Esparta	1150	La Asunción
Barinas	35,200	Barinas	Portuguesa	15,200	Guanare
Bolívar	240,528	Ciudad Bolívar	Sucre	11,800	Cumaná
Carabobo	4650	Valencia	Táchira	11,100	San Cristóbal
Cojedes	14,800	San Carlos	Trujillo	7400	Trujillo
Delta Amacuro	40,200	Tucupita	Yaracuy	7100	San Felipe
Falcón	24,800	Coro	Zulia	63,100	Maracaibo

the commander-in-chief of the armed forces, and members of the Supreme Court, thus raising the prospect of political interference in the judiciary. There's no prime minister, but planned changes to the constitution include the possible creation of this post.

The Congress is made up of two houses, the 50-seat Senate and the 204-seat Chamber of Deputies. Elections for Congress are held simultaneously with presidential elections and members are elected for five years. Voting is compulsory for citizens over 18 years of age.

There are a number of political parties, of which the major forces are the two traditional movements, the Acción Democrática (AD) and Partido Social Cristiano (Copei), both founded in the 1940s. For more than 30 years, up to the 1993 elections, Venezuelan presidents were always members of one of these two parties.

Over recent years, though, the picture has diversified, with other parties, particularly the Causa Radical (Causa R) and Movimiento al Socialismo (MAS), gaining weight on the political scene.

Administratively, the country is divided into 22 states *(estados)* and the federal district of Caracas. The islands of Margarita, Coche and Cubagua collectively form a state on their own, Nueva Esparta; the remaining 72 islands are all federal dependencies. The states are further divided into municipalities *(municipios)*, 293 of them in all. The states are ruled by governors *(gobernadores)*, elected for a three-year term by direct vote at state elections.

Venezuela is a member of the United Nations (UN), Organisation of American States (OAS), Latin American Integration Association, Organisation of Petroleum Exporting Countries (OPEC), the Andean Pact (trade pact between Bolivia, Colombia, Ecuador, Peru and Venezuela), and the Group of Three (Grupo de los Tres, a trade block of Colombia, Mexico and Venezuela).

The Venezuelan flag, adopted in 1811, has three horizontal belts of equal width: from top to bottom, yellow, blue and red. There's an arc of seven white stars on the blue portion, representing the seven original provinces of Venezuela in 1811.

GEOGRAPHY

With an area of 916,445 sq km, Venezuela is South America's sixth largest country. It's bigger than the UK and France combined, or much the same as Texas and Oklahoma put together. About eight Venezuelas would fit on the Australian continent. Stretching some 1500km east to west and 1300km north to south, it occupies the northern parts of South America. Its neighbours are Colombia to the west, Brazil to the south and Guyana to the east.

In the north, Venezuela is bordered by 2813km of coastline, dotted with countless beaches. Just south of the coast looms a chain of mountain ranges, the Cordillera de la Costa, with a number of peaks exceeding 2000m. This is a structural continuation of the Andes, even though it's separated from the main Andean massif by a lowland. The coastal mountain chain rolls southward into a vast area of plains known as Los Llanos, which stretches as far as the Río Orinoco and the Río Meta. Los Llanos occupies a third of the national territory.

The land south of the Orinoco (which is half of the country's area), called Guayana, can be broadly divided into three diverse geographical regions. To the south-west is a chunk of the Amazon, thick tropical forest, partly inaccessible. To the north-east lies the Delta del Orinoco, a vast swamp crisscrossed by a labyrinth of water channels. Finally, the central and largest part of Guayana is taken over by extensive highlands, with the plateau of open savanna known as La Gran Sabana being its most visited part. It's here that the majority of *tepuis* (table mountains) are located. These gigantic mesas, with vertical walls and flat tops, are all that's left of the upper layer of a plateau which gradually eroded over millions of years. They rise up to 1000m above the surrounding countryside, but reach nearly 3000m above sea level.

The north-western part of Venezuela is another area of geographical contrasts. Here

Río Orinoco

The 2150km Río Orinoco is South America's third longest river (after the Amazon and La Plata), and drains an area of roughly one million sq km of Venezuela and Colombia. Its entire course, from the source to the mouth, lies in Venezuela. Its major left-bank tributaries are Río Apure, Río Arauca, Río Meta, and Río Vichada, while the main right-bank tributaries include Río Caroní and Río Caura.

The Orinoco is also the third most voluminous river on the continent. Its flow and discharge largely depends on the season. The difference between the low and high water levels (in March and August, respectively) can exceed 15m.

The river carries about 50 billion tons of sediment annually and, as a consequence, its delta spreads out into the

Indian dwellings of the Delta del Orinoco, according to a 1599 etching from Sir Walter Raleigh's expedition.

Atlantic. The delta consists of a maze of natural channels which cut a swathe through a predominantly marshy land. The Delta del Orinoco covers an area of about 25,000 sq km, which is not much less than the total size of Belgium. There are more than 40 major mouths, distributed along 360km of the Atlantic coast.

One of these mouths, the outlet of Caño Manamo, was found by Christopher Columbus in 1498, shortly after he landed at the tip of the Paria Peninsula, opposite Trinidad. The Orinoco was thus the first major river discovered in the New World by a European. From that moment on, the river began to draw in adventurers and explorers, mostly because they supposed it was the gateway to the unspecified but legendary El Dorado. In the earliest big expeditions, in 1531, Diego de Ordaz sailed upstream as far as the Raudales de Atures (near present-day Puerto Ayacucho), but the rapids effectively defended the river's upper course from penetration.

Alexander von Humboldt managed to explore some of the upper reaches of the Orinoco in 1800. His major goal was the intriguing Brazo Casiquiare, discovered earlier by missionaries. The Casiquiare is a 220km-long natural channel linking the Orinoco with the Río Negro. It spans the two vast fluvial systems of the Orinoco and the Amazon, and may be the only phenomenon of its kind in the world.

The uppermost reaches of the Orinoco were rarely seen by explorers. This has always been an inaccessible land, and a home to the mysterious Yanomami tribe, who have not been particularly open to outsiders. Actually, it wasn't until 1951 that the exact source of the Orinoco was determined, when a joint French-Venezuelan expedition found the 70m-high cliff of the Cerro Delgado Chalbaud (at an altitude of 1047m), close to the Brazilian border, where the river originates. ∎

---

lies the Sierra Nevada de Mérida, the northern end of the Andean chain. The Sierra is Venezuela's highest mountain range, topped by the snowcapped Pico Bolívar (5007m). Just north of the Andes is the marshy lowland basin around the shallow and brackish Lago Maracaibo. At 13,500 sq km (200km long and 120km wide), it's South America's largest lake, and is linked to the Caribbean Sea by a narrow strait. The basin is the country's main oil-producing area. Northeast of the lake, near the town of Coro, is Venezuela's sole desert, the Médanos de Coro.

The 2150km-long Río Orinoco is by far the longest river in the country. The second longest is the Río Caroní (640km), a tributary of the Orinoco.

Venezuela possesses a number of islands scattered around the Caribbean Sea off the country's northern coast. The largest of these is Isla de Margarita. Other islands and archipelagos of importance include Las Aves, Los Roques, La Orchila, La Tortuga and La Blanquilla.

CLIMATE

Venezuela is close to the equator, so average temperatures vary little throughout the year. They do, however, vary with altitude, dropping about 6°C with every 1000m increase. Since over 90% of Venezuela lies below 1000m, you'll experience temperatures between 22°C and 30°C in most places. The Andean and coastal mountain ranges have more moderate temperatures.

Venezuela has dry and wet seasons. Broadly speaking, the dry season (known as *verano*, or literally summer) goes from December to April while the wet season (known as the *invierno*, or literally winter) lasts the remaining part of the year. There are many regional variations in the amount of rain and the length of the seasons. For example, the upper reaches of the mountains receive more rainfall than the coast and can be relatively wet for most of the year, while you can visit the Coro desert on almost any day of the year and not need to worry about rain. The Amazon has no distinct dry season, with annual rainfall exceeding 2000mm distributed roughly evenly throughout the year.

ECOLOGY & ENVIRONMENT

A short walk along a city street or a bus ride in the countryside will give you an insight into a Venezuelan's attitude towards the environment. Many locals throw away everything they don't need wherever they happen to be. There's an indifference to such behaviour passed on through generations as there is no ecological education. Some cities and many smaller towns don't have sufficient purpose-built refuse heaps, so garbage is simply trucked to the nearest out-of-sight place and dumped. Disturbing as it may be for a visitor, it's only the tip of the iceberg of Venezuela's environmental problems.

A more serious issue is indiscriminate deforestation and the subsequent erosion it promotes. Every year large areas of forest are cleared for agricultural use, pastureland, construction and industrial projects, and for timber. The shrinking forest area affects local wildlife, and an increasing number appear on the endangered species list.

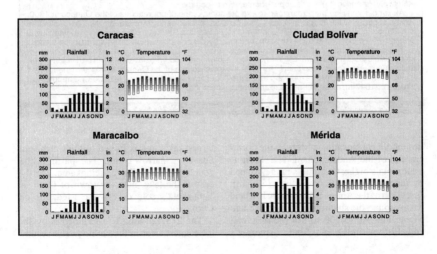

Industry poses a serious threat to the environment. Plants and installations have been built at economically prime locations, with little or no attention paid to the preservation of the ecosystem, and these intruders have introduced long-term sources of contamination.

The Lago Maracaibo has been so heavily contaminated by decades of oil drilling and untreated sewage from the city of Maracaibo, that cleaning it would cost at least US$1 billion. The discovery of oil deposits in the Delta del Orinoco, and the recent commencement of its exploitation, has put at risk the ecological balance of one of the best preserved regions, including the pristine Parque Nacional Mariusa. Right on the edge of the fragile Parque Nacional Mochima, a gigantic cement plant has been built and considerably extended recently. The alleged leak of a chemical from one of the oil refineries in north-western Venezuela in 1996 is thought to be responsible for the death of part of the coral in Parque Nacional Morrocoy. And mercury is widely used in gold and diamond mining in Guayana, polluting rivers and causing health hazards for local inhabitants and the wildlife.

But wildlife is not only threatened by industry. With an amazing variety of exotic species, it's no surprise that legions of poachers comb remote forests in search of rare animals, mostly birds. Today Venezuela is one of South America's major exporters of wildlife, which is smuggled across the border by air and sea.

The lack of conservation of both wildlife and ecosystems is alarming, despite the existence of environmental institutions and legislation. Ironically, Venezuela was at the forefront of Latin America's green movement. The Sociedad Conservacionista Audubon de Venezuela was founded as early as 1970. It is now the leading nongovernmental environment promoter, yet it can't afford to develop a thorough programme.

On the government side, an environmental protection law was enacted in 1975, and three years later the Ministerio del Ambiente (Ministry of the Environment) was created, to become the first ministry of its kind on the continent. In 1992, Venezuela passed a comprehensive environmental law specifying dozens of punishable crimes, including the pollution of soil, water and air, damaging the ozone layer and setting forest fires. This comes complete with a package of detailed technical standards defining protected areas, limits on pollution levels etc.

All this looks highly impressive on paper, yet compliance has been minimal at most. The lack of personnel to enforce the law, a weak judicial system, widespread bureaucracy and notorious corruption, are all drawbacks to the successful prosecution of violators. And the government's current predisposition towards rescuing the crumbling economy at any cost doesn't make things easier.

If there's any redeemable feature of the situation it is that most of Venezuela lacks the population pressures of, say, Brazil, so environmental problems have not yet reached apocalyptic proportions. Nonetheless, if decisive measures aren't implemented promptly, the country's forests and wildlife resources face bleak prospects.

International Environmental Organisations

Many organisations promote the preservation of rainforests and other endangered environments. For more details contact any of the following groups:

Australia
  Friends of the Earth, 312 Smith St, Collingwood, Vic 3066 (☎ (03) 9419-8700)
  Greenpeace Australia Ltd, 24/26 Johnston St, Fitzroy, Vic 3065 (☎ (03) 9670-1633)
UK
  Friends of the Earth, 26/28 Underwood St, London N17JU
  Survival International, 310 Edgeware Rd, London W2 1DY (☎ (0171) 723-5535)
USA
  Rainforest Action Network (RAN), 301 Broadway, Suite A, San Francisco, CA 94133 (☎ (415) 398-4404)
  Conservation International, 1015 18th St, NW, Suite 1000, Washington, DC 20036 (☎ (202) 429-5660)

Cultural Survival, 215 First St, Cambridge, MA 02142 (☎ (617) 621-3818)
Nature Conservancy, 1815 N Lynn St, Arlington, VA 22209 (☎ (703) 841-5300)
Survival International USA, 2121 Decatur Place, NW, Washington, DC 20006
Friends of the Earth, 218 D St, SE, Washington, DC 20003 (☎ (202) 544-2600)
Greenpeace, 1436 U St, NW, Washington, DC 20009 (☎ (202) 462-8817)
Earthwatch, 680 Mt Auburn St, Box 403, Watertown, MA 02272 (☎ (617) 926-8200)
The Chico Mendes Fund, Environmental Defence Fund, 257 Park Ave South, New York, NY 10010
Rainforest Alliance, 270 Lafayette St, Suite 512, New York, NY 10012
Rainforest Foundation Inc, 1776 Broadway, 14th floor, New York, NY 10019

FLORA & FAUNA

As a tropical country with a diverse geography, Venezuela has a varied and abundant flora and fauna. Over millions of years, distinctive biohabitats evolved in different regions, each with its own peculiar wildlife. This wildlife developed here relatively uninterrupted, unlike its counterparts in North America and Western Eurasia, which were affected by the ice ages.

German naturalist Alexander von Humboldt and French botanist Aimé Bonpland were among the first serious explorers dedicated to studying and recording local species, and their work was continued by subsequent expeditions. Although there have been a number of scientific explorations over recent decades, the picture is still very incomplete.

Flora

Generally speaking, Venezuela's plant life is stratified by thermal zones, which means that some particular species are confined to an altitude where they find optimal conditions to grow. Since the country's topography goes from sea level up to 5000m, there's quite a diversity, from rainforest at the bottom end up to boggy highland meadows (páramos) just below the highest peaks.

Rainforest (bosque húmedo) – which still covers nearly a quarter of the country's area – is quite different from the temperate woodlands to which Europeans and North Americans are accustomed. It is home to a diversity and abundance of plants. Even more diversified is cloudforest (bosque nublado), confined to mountain slopes between 1000 and 3000m. It is common to the Andes and upper reaches of the Cordillera de la Costa.

Higher up in the Andes, from about 3300 to 4400m, are the páramos, which are only found in limited mountainous areas of Venezuela and Ecuador, and in Colombia where they are more numerous and diversified. A typical feature of the páramo is the frailejón, or espeletia, a plant with long, down-covered, cream-green leaves arranged in a rosette pattern. It blooms from September to December. There are many species of espeletia, the tallest reaching 10m (in Colombia). The tallest frailejones found in Venezuela are about 3m high.

The flora on the tops of the tepuis is most unusual. Isolated from the savanna below and from other tepuis for millions of years, the plant life on top of each of these plateaus developed independently. In effect, these biological islands have a totally distinctive flora, half of which is considered endemic and typical to only one or a group of tepuis.

The flor de mayo, one of several thousand species of orchid (orquídea), is Venezuela's national flower. The araguaney, known in English as the trumpet tree, is the national tree, and is particularly spectacular at the end of the dry season when it is covered with bright yellow blossoms.

Fauna

Birds There are some 1360 species of birds in Venezuela (more than in Europe and North America combined). There are a number of excellent bird-watching areas, of which the largest and possibly the best is Los Llanos. Parts of the coast, especially those with a developed mangrove ecosystem (Parque Nacional Morrocoy), and cloudforest (Parque Nacional Henri Pittier) are also good territories for bird-watchers.

The bird world ranges from species commonly associated with tropical forests, such as macaw *(guacamayo)*, parrot *(loro)* and toucan *(tucán)*, to a variety of water birds including ibis *(ibis)*, heron *(garza)*, pelican *(pelícano)* and flamingo *(flamenco)*. (Names in italics given above, as well as in the remaining part of this section, are common local names.)

The hummingbird *(colibrí)* is one of the most unusual birds. This colourful little 'helicopter' beats its wings up to 80 times a second as it hovers, producing a characteristic hum, which is where its name comes from. Various species of hummingbird inhabit different climatic zones, including one living high up in the páramo at above 4000m.

Commonly associated with Andean countries, the famous condor *(cóndor)* was wiped out in Venezuela decades ago (apart from those in zoos), but some specimens were introduced in the early 1990s from abroad and let free in the Mérida region. Sadly, only three birds can still be seen; others have allegedly been shot down.

The oilbird *(guácharo)*, a nocturnal fruiteater, inhabits dozens of Venezuelan caves. See the Cueva del Guácharo section for details. The *turpial*, noted for its magnificent yellow, white and black plumage, is the national bird.

Mammals With some 250 species recorded in Venezuela, mammals are well represented. The king of the local forests is the jaguar *(tigre)*, the largest cat in the New World. It had a significant mythological importance in various pre-Columbian civilisations. Today it's an endangered species, threatened by illegal hunting and the shrinking of its natural habitat.

What does abound is the capybara *(chigüire)*, the world's largest rodent, weighing up to 60kg. It's typical of Los Llanos, and you can even find it on the local menu. Also easy to see, even in city parks, are sloths *(pereza)*, invariably hanging motionless from tree limbs. Other mammals to be found in Venezuela include the armadillo *(armadillo)*, the anteater *(oso hormiguero)*, the tapir

(danta), the puma *(puma)*, the ocelot *(ocelote)* and the peccary *(báquiro)*.

Reptiles Possibly the most characteristic Venezuelan reptile is the cayman *(caimán)*, or American crocodile. There are five species of cayman, ranging from the most common, the spectacled *baba*, to the huge *caimán del Orinoco*. The latter inhabits the rivers of the Orinoco basin and can sometimes exceed 5m in length. Its favourite diet is fish, but birds, other reptiles and mammals are a frequent diversion. It has been extensively hunted since the 1920s for its skin, highly valued as leather on local and international markets, and this has put its existence in jeopardy. At present, its population is estimated at between 500 and 1000.

Another giant, the *caimán de la costa*, lives, as its name suggests, along the coast, principally in lower reaches of rivers emptying into the Caribbean Sea and Lago Maracaibo. It can reach 6m from head to tail, and has a rare ability to live in both salt and fresh water.

Snakes include the famous anaconda (the world's longest snake) and the boa, but perhaps the most characteristic Venezuelan snake is the venomous *mapanare*, most of which inhabit Lara state. There are plenty of other venomous snakes, including the rattlesnake *(cascabel)*, though you're unlikely to have many close encounters with them. It's much easier to spot the iguana *(iguana)* which, despite its alarming size, is only a large herbivorous lizard.

Insects This is certainly the most populous wildlife group. Of some 30,000 species so far recorded, butterflies are arguably the favourite of most travellers. There's a great variety of them, including spectacular morphos, which have intensively blue wings spanning up to 15cm.

The insect family comprises less pleasant creatures, such as the commonly called *jején* and *puri puri*. These are small gnats which infest the Gran Sabana and, to a lesser extent, some other regions. Their bites are desperately itchy for days. Also, beware of a large ant, colloquially referred to as the *hormiga 24*. The mysterious number in the name is reputedly due to the fact that the bite of the inch-long ant results in a high fever for a full day, and can be fatal.

Marine Life With some 3000km of coastline and a maze of islands, islets, cays and coral reefs, it's no wonder that submarine flora and fauna are enormously rich. All the multi-coloured fish, starfish, sea urchins, sea anemones and corals, which you've seen in numerous TV documentaries are here, and thriving. There are many good areas for snorkellers and scuba divers – refer to the Activities section in the Facts for the Visitor chapter.

NATIONAL PARKS
The first nature reserve, Parque Nacional Henri Pittier, was established in 1937. It took another 15 years for the next park to be established, but today Venezuela boasts 43 national parks. Between 1987 and 1996, 17 new parks appeared on the map, and several more are expected to be declared shortly.

National parks aside, Venezuela also has an array of 22 other nature reserves called

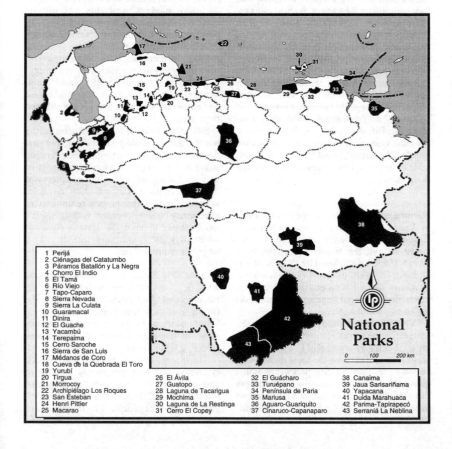

1 Perijá
2 Ciénagas del Catatumbo
3 Páramos Batallón y La Negra
4 Chorro El Indio
5 El Tamá
6 Río Viejo
7 Tapo-Caparo
8 Sierra Nevada
9 Sierra La Culata
10 Guaramacal
11 Dinira
12 El Guache
13 Yacambú
14 Terepaima
15 Cerro Saroche
16 Sierra de San Luis
17 Médanos de Coro
18 Cueva de la Quebrada El Toro
19 Yurubí
20 Tirgua
21 Morrocoy
22 Archipiélago Los Roques
23 San Esteban
24 Henri Pittier
25 Macarao

26 El Ávila
27 Guatopo
28 Laguna de Tacarigua
29 Mochima
30 Laguna de La Restinga
31 Cerro El Copey

32 El Guácharo
33 Turuépano
34 Península de Paria
35 Mariusa
36 Aguaro-Guariquito
37 Cinaruco-Capanaparo

38 Canaima
39 Jaua Sarisariñama
40 Yapacana
41 Duida Marahuaca
42 Parima-Tapirapecó
43 Serranía La Neblina

National Parks

0   100   200 km

monumentos naturales. These are usually smaller than the parks and are intended to protect a particular natural feature such as a lake, a mountain peak, or a cave. The whole system of parks and other reserves covers about 15% of the country's territory.

The Instituto Nacional de Parques, commonly referred to as Inparques, is the governmental body created to run and take care of national parks and other nature reserves. Unfortunately, it seems it only has nominal control over the parks and reserves. Deforestation, contamination, hunting and fishing haven't been eliminated by simply declaring an area a national park, and there's insufficient funds and personnel to enforce protection.

Only a handful of parks have any Inparques-built tourist facilities. Most others are either wilderness or have been swiftly taken over by local private operators, who have built their own tourist facilities and provide transport.

No permits are needed to enter national parks, but some parks charge admission fees. At the time of writing, the list included Los Roques (US$12), the western part of Canaima (US$5), plus half a dozen others, with fees not exceeding US$1.

In theory, you have to pay a fee (usually no more than US$2) for camping in the parks – you do this in regional Inparques offices. However, except for a few parks, you'll probably never be asked to pay.

ECONOMY

Oil is Venezuela's major natural resource and the heart of the economy. The main deposits are in the Maracaibo basin, but other important oil reserves have been discovered and exploited on the eastern outskirts of Los Llanos (in Anzoátegui and Monagas states) and in the Delta del Orinoco.

Since its discovery in 1914, oil turned Venezuela – at that stage a poor debtor nation – into one of the richest countries in South America. Until 1970 Venezuela was the world's largest exporter of oil, and though it was later overtaken by some Middle Eastern countries, its oil production expanded year after year.

As co-founder of OPEC, Venezuela was influential in the fourfold rise in oil prices introduced in 1973-74, which quadrupled the country's revenue overnight. Oil revenues peaked in 1981 with export earnings of US$19.3 billion, representing about 96% of the country's exports. On the strength of this, Venezuela borrowed heavily from foreign banks to import almost everything other than petroleum. As of 1997, Venezuela was OPEC's third largest oil producer, after Saudi Arabia and Iran.

Oil has overshadowed other sectors of the economy. Agriculture, which had never been strong, was largely neglected and only 3% of the country's territory is under cultivation. The major crops include bananas, sugarcane, maize, coffee, cacao, cotton and tobacco. Despite its long coastline, Venezuela hasn't realised the potential of the fishing industry which accounts for only 4% of the total catch of South America, thanks principally to shrimp, sardine and tuna.

Oil apart, Venezuela is rich in natural resources. Iron ore, with huge deposits found south of Ciudad Bolívar, is the most important mineral, followed by extensive reserves of bauxite (from which aluminium ore is extracted), also in Guayana. They gave birth (in 1961) to the establishment and subsequent expansion of Ciudad Guayana, the centre of these industries, as the government attempted to diversify the economy. Other major subsoil riches include gold and diamonds, both in Guayana, and coal near the border with Colombia, north of Maracaibo.

The government also invested heavily in developing manufacturing, such as motor vehicle assembly, chemical, textile, footwear, paper and food industries. Taking advantage of a considerable hydroelectric potential, the gigantic Guri Dam was built (at a cost of US$5 billion) south of Ciudad Guayana. This is the second largest hydroelectric plant in the world, with a potential of 10 million kilowatts. More than half of Venezuela's electricity needs are supplied by hydroelectric power.

In spite of the development of non-oil

sectors, petroleum has remained Venezuela's bread-and-butter industry, generating at least 70% of export earnings. In the early 1980s when global recession struck, oil prices declined. Venezuela's export earnings from oil fell drastically to a low of US$7.2 billion in 1986. This left the country with an unsustainable foreign debt, and forced a 1987 agreement with creditors to 'reschedule' some US$20 billion in repayments. Political uncertainty, the collapse of the major banks and the government's economic mismanagement contributed to what is now Venezuela's worst economic crisis.

In 1996 Venezuela was the only Latin American country whose economy contracted (its GDP shrank by 1.5%), and it had by far the largest inflation in the region (103.2%), four times higher than second-placed Mexico (27.8%). Venezuela's foreign debt in that year reached US$39 billion. In response to workers' demands and countless strikes, in May 1997 the government raised minimum monthly wages by 44% to about US$155, which some analysts viewed as inflationary. Chronic inflation of the past few years has caused the middle class to shrink, while the share of the population living below the poverty level has increased dramatically.

But there may be cause for cautious optimism. As of mid-1997, the long-neglected privatisation programme got underway, the oil sector recorded a steady growth, inflation slowed considerably and currency reserves rose. Yet sustained economic recovery is a long way off.

POPULATION & PEOPLE

As of 1996, the total population was estimated at 22 million, of which over one-fifth lived in Caracas. The rate of population growth stands at around 2.1%, one of the highest in Latin America. Venezuela is a young nation, with over half of its inhabitants under 18 years of age. Yet, at nearly 70 years, average life expectancy is remarkably high.

The mean population density, at about 23

people per sq km, is low, although it varies a great deal. The central coastal region, including the cities of Valencia, Maracay and Caracas, is the most densely populated, while Los Llanos and Guayana are very sparsely populated. More than 75% of Venezuelans live in towns and cities.

Venezuela is a country of mixed races. About 70% of the population is a blend of European, Indian and African ancestry, or any two of the three. The rest are whites (about 21%), blacks (8%) and Indians (1%). Indians don't belong to a single ethnic or linguistic family, but form different independent groups scattered throughout the country.

There are about two dozen indigenous groups comprising some 200,000 people. The main Indian communities include the Guajiro north of Maracaibo; the Piaroa, Guajibo, Yekuana and Yanomami in the Amazon; the Warao in the Delta del Orinoco; and the Pemón in south-eastern Guayana. Venezuela has experienced significant postwar immigration from Europe (estimated at about a million), mostly from Spain, Italy and Portugal, but it nearly stopped in the 1960s and many migrants returned home. From the 1950s on, there has been a stream of immigrants from other South American countries, particularly from Colombia. Venezuela also has some Middle Eastern communities, most notably from Lebanon, which live principally in Caracas and Isla Margarita. According to official statistics, about 600,000 foreigners live in the country today, but unofficial estimates put the number of Colombians alone at some two million. Caracas is the country's most cosmopolitan city.

EDUCATION

The education system has been expanded and modernised over the past few decades to meet the needs of the country's developing economy, yet it has recently suffered budgetary and administrative problems, and has been plagued by strikes by both students and staff. There's compulsory six-year primary education for children who have reached seven years of age. Then comes an optional four-year secondary school education, followed by a one-year preparatory course for university. There are 31 universities in the country, of which the Universidad Central de Venezuela in Caracas is the largest and oldest (70,000 students, founded in 1725) followed by the Universidad de los Andes in Mérida (35,000 students, founded in 1785). Primary education is run by the state and is free, as are some secondary schools as well as government-sponsored universities. The literacy of the population over 10 years of age is about 92%.

ARTS
Architecture

Pre-Hispanic dwellings were built from perishable materials such as adobe, wood and vegetable fibres, and no examples have survived to this day. However, the homes of some remote indigenous communities, whose traditions have continued almost unchanged for centuries, do approximate the form and design of the early Indian homes.

With the arrival of the Spanish, brick and

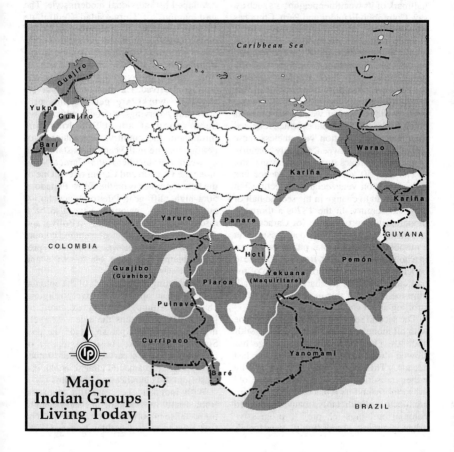

Major
Indian Groups
Living Today

tile made their way into the colony. Following rigid rules established by the Crown, the newly founded towns were laid out on a square grid with streets running at right angles to each other. The Plaza Mayor, cathedral and government house habitually formed the centre, from which towns spread outwards. All buildings – religious, civil and military – were direct reflections of the Spanish style, with only a touch of local colour showing through.

Since the Province of Venezuela was a backwater of the Crown, local architecture never reached the grandeur that was the hallmark of its wealthier neighbours such as, say, Colombia, Ecuador and Peru. Churches were mostly small and unpretentious. Houses followed the modest Andalusian style. They were usually straightforward one-storey constructions, without much external decoration or internal splendour. Only in the last half-century of the colonial era, when there was noticeable economic growth, did a class of wealthier merchants emerge who built residences which reflected their new social position. Nonetheless, these were few and far between, and only a handful of notable examples survive, mainly in Coro.

The first 50 years of independence had little impact on Venezuelan architecture, but things began to change in the second half of the 19th century. In the 1870s a thorough modernisation programme for Caracas was launched by Guzmán Blanco and resulted in a number of monumental public buildings, in a hotchpotch of styles, from neo-Gothic to neoclassical, depending on the whim of the particular architect in charge. You can admire the results of this modernisation while strolling about Caracas' centre.

The second rush towards modernity came with oil money and culminated in the 1960s and 70s. (The pace of urban change has slowed down considerably over the last decade.) This period was characterised by rather indiscriminate demolition of the old urban fabric and its replacement by modern architecture. Predictably, many dilapidated colonial buildings fell prey to progressive urban planners. Accordingly, Venezuela's colonial legacy can be disappointing when compared to that of other Andean countries. On the other hand, Venezuela has some of the best ultra-modern architecture on the continent.

Plenty of international and local architects took part in the transformation of Venezuelan urban centres. Among them, Carlos Raúl Villanueva, who has left behind a large number of projects in Caracas and other cities, is considered the most outstanding Venezuelan architect. He began in the 1930s with fairly classical designs, such as the Galería de Arte Nacional, but soon developed his individual modern style. The vast campus of Universidad Central de Venezuela in Caracas is regarded as one of his best and most coherent designs.

Visual Arts

The visual arts existed long before the Spaniards arrived. The most obvious surviving early works are petroglyphs, predominantly carvings on rock, which have been found at about 200 locations throughout the country. The majority of petroglyphs are in the central coastal region between Barquisimeto and Caracas, and along the Orinoco and Caroní rivers. One of the best examples is on the Cerro Pintado, a 50m-high cliff near Puerto Ayacucho. A number of cave paintings have also been discovered, almost all of them in Bolívar and Amazonas states. The most common colours used by these unknown artists from pre-Columbian tribes were black, white and various tones of ochre.

The painting and sculpture of the colonial period had an almost exclusively religious character. Although mostly executed by local artists and artisans, the style was largely influenced by the Spanish art of the day. Some of that work, consisting mainly of paintings of saints, carved wooden statues and retables (ornamental altar screens), can be seen in old churches and museums.

With independence, painting departed from strictly religious themes and began to immortalise important historical events. The first artist to do so was Juan Lovera (1778-

1841), whose two most famous paintings, *19 April 1810* and *5 July 1811*, can be seen in the Capilla de Santa Rosa de Lima in Caracas.

The most outstanding figure of historical painting was Martín Tovar y Tovar (1827-1902), particularly remembered for his monumental works in Caracas' National Capitol. Other artists who contributed to 19th century Venezuelan painting include Cristóbal Rojas (1857-90) and Arturo Michelena (1863-98). The latter received wide international recognition despite his short life and artistic career. He lived in Paris and his works were exhibited at important salons in what was then the world's art capital. Another Venezuelan living in France, Emilio Boggio (1857-1920) also acquired an international reputation. Influenced by his French colleagues, and by Van Gogh in particular, he became Venezuela's first impressionist.

The epic historical tradition of Tovar y Tovar was continued by Tito Salas (1888-1974), who dedicated himself to commemorating Bolívar's life and achievements and produced a number of paintings on the subject. His best known works are the wall-paintings in the National Pantheon in Caracas.

Modern painting began with Armando Reverón (1889-1954), who made his home in Macuto near Caracas where he executed most of his expressionist works. Another painter who made his mark in the transition from traditional to modern painting was Carlos Otero (1886-1977). Other artists working in the same period include Rafael Monasterios (1884-1961), Federico Brandt (1879-1932), Marcos Castillo (1897-1966) and Manuel Cabré (1890-1984).

Francisco Narváez (1905-82) is commonly acclaimed as Venezuela's first modern sculptor. The art museum in Porlamar (Isla de Margarita), where he was born, has the largest single collection of his works, but there are also a number of his sculptures distributed around Caracas.

The recent period has been characterised by a proliferation of artists representing a wide variety of schools, trends and techniques. One of the most remarkable of these is the painter Héctor Poleo (1918-1989), who expressed himself in a variety of styles, easily switching from realism to surrealism, with some metaphysics in between. Equally captivating is the expressionist painting of Jacobo Borges (born 1931) who by deforming human figures turns them into caricatures.

Other leading contemporary figures in painting and sculpture include Oswaldo Vigas (born 1926), Alejandro Otero (1921-90), Mateo Manaure (born 1926), Alirio Palacios (born 1938), Manuel Quintana Castillo (born 1928) and Marisol Escobar (born 1930).

The No 1 internationally renowned Venezuelan artist of recent decades is Jesús Soto (born 1923), the leading representative of kinetic art (ie art, particularly sculpture, which contains moving parts). He was born in Ciudad Bolívar (where a museum with a collection of his works has been established), and his art has adorned many public buildings and plazas in Venezuela and beyond (Paris, Toronto and New York). Carlos Cruz Díez (born 1923), somewhat overshadowed by Soto's fame, is also noted for his kinetic art.

Literature

There was no written language on the continent before the Spanish conquest, apart from a variety of petroglyphs, the meaning of which is still undeciphered. Accordingly, there wasn't, in the strict sense of the word, a pre-Hispanic Indian literature. Yet there must have been a rich world of tales, legends and stories created, conserved and passed orally from generation to generation. This 'literature' provided invaluable information on the pre-Columbian culture for the first Spanish chroniclers.

The first chronicles narrating the early history of Venezuela include *Brevísima Relación de la Destrucción de las Indias Occidentales* by Fray Bartolomé de las Casas, *Noticias Historiales* (1627) by Fray Pedro Simón, and *Elegías de Varones*

Ilustres de Indias (1589) by Juan de Castellanos. Much more analytical and comprehensive is one of the later and perhaps best chronicles, *Historia de la Conquista y Población de la Provincia de Venezuela* (1723) by José de Oviedo y Baños.

Almost all literature during the colonial period was written by the Spanish, who imposed not only their language but also the cultural and religious perspective of the mother country. A more independent approach emerged with the dawn of the 19th century, with the birth and crystallisation of revolutionary trends. The first 30 years of that century were dominated by political literature.

Among the works of significant historical value was the autobiography of Francisco de Miranda (1750-1816). Simón Bolívar (1783-1830) has left an extensive literary heritage, including letters, proclamations, discourses and dissertations, and also some more literary achievements such as *Delirio sobre El Chimborazo*. As literature, it has strong merits, notably for its expression of ideals and ambitions for the nation as it fought for independence, as well as for its prophetic visions.

Bolívar was influenced by his close friend Andrés Bello (1781-1865), the first important Venezuelan poet. Bello was also a noted philologist, essayist, historian, journalist, literary critic, jurist and translator.

With independence achieved, political writing gave way to other literary manifestations. However, it wasn't until the early 20th century that more mature literature began to emerge. In the 1920s, Andrés Eloy Blanco (1896-1955) appeared on the scene, to become one of the best poets Venezuela has ever produced. This Cumaná-born writer went into exile in Mexico, escaping the persecution of the dictator Pérez Jiménez, and tragically died in a car accident. *Angelitos Negros* is probably the most popular of his numerous poems.

At the same time, several notable novelists emerged, among whom Rómulo Gallegos (1884-1969) was the most outstanding talent and is still, perhaps, internationally the best-

Andrés Bello

known writer in the country's literary history. *Doña Bárbara*, his most popular novel, was first published in Spain in 1929 and since then translated into a dozen languages. Other important novels by this writer, who was also the first democratically elected president in Venezuela's history (in 1947), include *Canaima* and *Cantaclaro*.

Mariano Picón Salas (1901-65) worked in a variety of literary forms, of which essays were possibly his favourite means of expression. A professor, minister and ambassador, he frequently touched on historical and political issues. His extensive literary output includes *El Último Inca* and *Preguntas a Europa*. Miguel Otero Silva (1908-85) was yet another remarkable novelist of the period. He's best remembered for *Casas Muertas*, a best-seller published in 1957.

Arturo Uslar Pietri (born 1906) stands out as an authority in the field of literature. A novelist, essayist, historian, literary critic and journalist, he also has been a prominent figure in politics, having been a minister on various occasions and even a presidential candidate. He's not only the most versatile writer in the country, but also the man with the longest involvement in literature. Since his first important novel, *Lanzas Coloradas*, published in the 1930s, he has written a great deal, and is still active on the literary scene.

Other modern Venezuelan writers of note include Denzil Romero (historical novels), Salvador Garmendia (short forms), Aquiles Nazoa (humour), and Francisco Herrera Luque (historical novels). There's a lot of literary activity among the younger generation, both in poetry and in prose.

Music

There was music in pre-Hispanic times but almost nothing is known about its early forms, functions and instruments. The Spanish, and with them the blacks, introduced new rhythms and instruments and brought diversity to the colony's musical world. European and African traditions gradually merged with one another and with indigenous music, eventually producing what is now Venezuela's folk music. It's not uniform, as different forms have evolved in different regions of the country.

Venezuela's most popular folk rhythm is the *joropo*, also called the *música llanera*, which developed in Los Llanos and gradually conquered the country (see boxed text entitled The Music of Los Llanos in the Los Llanos chapter). The joropo is usually sung and accompanied by harp, *cuatro* (small, four-stringed guitar) and *maracas*. The joropo song *Alma Llanera* has become a sort of unofficial national anthem.

Joropo apart, there are plenty of traditional beats still largely confined to their regions. In the eastern part of the country you'll hear, depending on the particular region, the *estribillo*, *polo margariteño*, *malagueñas*, *fulías*, and *jotas*. In the west, on the other hand, the *gaita* is typical of the Maracaibo region, while the *bambuco* is one of the popular rhythms of the Andes. The central coast echoes with African drumbeats, a visible mark of the sizeable black population.

In addition to locally rooted musical forms, various foreign rhythms have made their way into the country. Of these, salsa and

merengue from the Caribbean basin, and *vallenato* from Colombia have been best absorbed. And, of course, western pop – everything from rock to rap – has become hugely popular among urban youth. All these musical imports fermented the creation of local composers and interpreters of these forms. Oscar D'León is Venezuela's leading *salsero*. Most discotheques now play a cocktail of salsa, merengue and western beats. In city streets you also hear quite a bit of vallenato and joropo. Jazz, except for Latin jazz, is not popular.

As for classical music, it only emerged in the 19th century. The first composers of note include José Angel Lamas (1775-1814) and Cayetano Carreño Rodríguez (1774-1836), both of whom wrote religious music. The beginnings of concert music are accredited to Felipe Larrazábal (1818-73), a pianist, composer and founder of the Caracas Conservatory. The most prominent figure in Venezuela's classical music of that century was Teresa Carreño (1853-1917), another pianist and composer. Born in Caracas, she held her first concert at the Irving Hall in New York at the age of nine. She lived most of her life in Germany, visiting her native country only twice.

The first half of the 20th century hasn't seen any outstanding musical talents, except perhaps for Reynaldo Hahn (1874-1947), another pianist, who lived and composed in Paris, and Juan Bautista Plaza (1898-1965) whose career was tied to Rome.

During the last few decades, Venezuelan musical culture has developed more swiftly. This has been due to both the opening of musical schools and the building of new concert halls. In 1930, the Symphony Orchestra of Venezuela was founded in Caracas, and followed by three other city orchestras.

Dance & Ballet

Integrally linked to music, dance was a part of ritual celebrations and everyday life of the early civilisations, and diversified during colonial and post-colonial times. Dance traditions are possibly most alive among black communities on Venezuela's central coast, where locals rush to dance as soon as home-grown drummers take to their drums, which happens spontaneously, mostly on weekend nights. Elsewhere, folk dance is not part of local lifestyle to that extent, though you can often see amateur dance ensembles in action during some annual feasts.

Folk dance has sown seeds for the creation of professional groups which now promote their musical folklore in a polished form to the general public. The Danza Venezuela, directed by Yolanda Morreno, is the country's prime folk-dance ensemble. It has travelled intensively and pleased audiences on several continents. Some members of the company have formed their own folk groups.

Turning to classical forms, dance and ballet are relatively new on the local scene. Perhaps best known is the Ballet Nuevo Mundo de Caracas, led by Venezuela's most famous ballerina, Zhandra Rodríguez. The Ballet Teresa Carreño, under the artistic direction of Vicente Nebreda, also pursues a classical style. Both groups are based at the Complejo Cultural Teresa Carreño.

Contemporary dance is probably best represented by Coreoarte, directed by Carlos Orta and Noris Ugueto; the Danza Hoy, led by Adriana Urdaneta; and the Ballet de Cámara de Caracas, run by María Barrios. All three companies are based in Caracas.

Theatre
The first theatre, Teatro del Conde, was founded in Caracas in 1784, and since then a theatre tradition has slowly developed. Several theatres opened at the end of the 19th century, in Caracas (Teatro Nacional and Teatro Municipal), Maracaibo (Teatro Baralt), Valencia (Teatro Municipal) and Barcelona (Teatro Cajigal). However, mostly European fare was presented; infrequent local productions mimicked the style and contents of the Old World.

The national theatre was only born a few decades ago, with its major centre in Caracas. Today, there are a few dozen groups, most of them in Caracas. Rajatabla, tied to the Ateneo de Caracas, has been

Venezuela's best known theatre on the international scene. However, since the recent death of its creator and director, Carlos Jiménez, the company seems to have passed through rougher times. Other Caracas-based groups of note include La Compañía Nacional de Teatro and the Teatro Profesional de Venezuela. It's also worth watching out for the Teatro Negro de Barlovento, formed by the black community of the central coast and taking inspiration from its African origins.

Cinema
The first films were publicly screened in Maracaibo in January 1897, only 13 months after the famous show by the Lumière brothers took place in Paris. Venezuela's first short film was shot in 1909; the first silent feature film, La Dama de las Cayenas, was made in 1913; and the first sound film, La Venus de Nacar, was produced in 1932. Venezuela's first international success was La Malandra Isabel, a prizewinner at the Cannes festival in 1951.

It wasn't until the 1970s that local cinematography began to develop at a faster pace, and several thought-provoking films were made. Román Chalbaud, who began his career in that period, is possibly the Venezuelan film director best known internationally. His film El Pez que Fuma (The Fish that Smokes), made in 1977, received some noteworthy critical acclaim abroad. Apart from various theatre works, he made 18 films, including Quema de Judas, La Oveja Negra and the last one, released in 1997, Pandemónium. Other leading Venezuelan directors of the last few decades include Mauricio Wallenstein (La Crónica de un Subversivo Latinoamericano and Macho y Hembra); Alfredo Anzola (Se Busca Motorizado con Moto Propio); Solveig Hoggestein (Macu la Mujer de Policía and Santera); and Josefina Torres (Oriana and Mecánicas Celestes).

On the whole, however, Venezuela's cinematography hasn't reached the artistic quality of some other Latin American nations such as Mexico or Argentina, and hasn't gained much acclaim abroad. Local film production is small, and few domestically produced films reach the screens of commercial cinemas. Public demand for Venezuelan films is low and, accordingly, profits are small. Film distributors prefer foreign movies, which are more likely to realise a profit. Half of the Venezuelan film industry's profit is made in Caracas.

In contrast to cinema, TV production is booming. Venezuelans are great fans of *telenovelas*, or soap operas, and producers and directors do everything they can to meet demand. Over the last two decades Venezuela has become one of the major Latin American producers of that fare, catching up with the two traditional telenovela powers, Mexico and Brazil.

SOCIETY & CONDUCT

Western visitors will probably find Venezuela more accessible than most other Andean countries such as Colombia, Ecuador, Peru and Bolivia. Although Venezuela is a palette of ethnic blends, and traditional culture is still much alive in the countryside, the urban population went through an intensive 'course' of westernisation when oil money hit the nation in the 1960s through to the 1980s. Local shops glittered with all the latest in styles and gadgets, US cars were imported in their thousands and many middle-class Venezuelans travelled regularly to holiday or shop in the USA, principally to Miami. Many western-style facilities were built in Venezuela over that period.

However, although some semblances of western culture are evident, you'll find many local habits, manners and attitudes quite different from those at home. Some of them may be strange or even irritating if you haven't been to this country before.

On the whole, Venezuelans are courteous, polite and hospitable towards guests. They are open, willing to talk and are not shy about striking up a conversation with a stranger. This may vary from a big city to the countryside and from region to region, but wherever you are, you are unlikely to be

alone or feel isolated, especially if you can speak a little Spanish.

You will probably meet many friendly people promising you the earth, but take it easy because that effusiveness often has a short life. Their statements may well gloss over reality, promises can be just wishful thinking, and appointments are often not kept. Few locals will return your phone call after you've left a message, and the passionate friend of one day might hardly recognise you the next. This attitude (common in most of the continent) is largely rooted in the Latin American concept of life *aquí y ahora* (here and now), with little importance given to the future. Don't worry, there will be plenty of new faces and new promises coming your way.

Everyday life is remarkably open and public. One reason for this might be the restricted space of the humble Venezuelan homes, in which a vast majority of the population live. The climate, too, invites the outdoor life. Consequently, much of the family life takes place outside home: in front of the house, in the street, in a bar or the market. And many Venezuelans seem indiscreet about their behaviour or acts in public places. A party in a bar may discuss personal problems at a level allowing all the patrons to follow the conversation. An employee in a bank or travel agency may talk by phone for quite a while about private matters (including love affairs), and doesn't seem embarrassed or ashamed that you're waiting to be served. The driver may urinate on the tyre of his bus after he has stopped for a short break on the road and disembarked along with most passengers. People waiting to use public phones will be squashed up against the person calling. And couples hug and kiss passionately in parks and in the street.

Noise is a constant companion in Venezuela and locals seem to be undisturbed by noise levels many decibels above anything a European could stand. Music blares in restaurants, is pumped into buses, and climaxes at night in discos, taverns and private parties. Powerful portable cassette players are an important part of equipment for beachgoers and holidaymakers. TVs are at full volume, especially during telenovelas and sports transmissions. Some vehicles are as noisy as tanks, and horns are used constantly, even in traffic jams. Street vendors screech at potential customers, and people converse at a volume that would suggest a heated argument.

Like noise, litter is an integral part of Venezuelan life, so be prepared to get used to it. Venezuelans are accustomed to throwing things away wherever they happen to be – in the streets, on the floors of restaurants, hotel rooms, buses, cinemas, in the countryside and also on the beach. Litter bins are virtually nonexistent, except for some in central streets of the major cities. In budget hotels and restaurants you will rarely find an ashtray and asking for one may embarrass the management because they often simply don't have them. It's normal to throw cigarette butts on the floor and nobody pays the slightest attention. In buses, all disposables, including empty bottles, are thrown out the windows.

Venezuelans (like most other Latin Americans) seem to have their own notion of time. Time-related terminology does exist but its interpretation is not necessarily what visitors might expect. For example, *mañana* (literally tomorrow) can mean anytime in the indefinite future. Similarly, the word *ahora* (literally now, or in a moment), often used in its more charming, diminutive forms such as *ahorita* or *ahoritica*, also has a flexible meaning.

If, for example, you're waiting for a bus and ask bystanders when the bus should arrive, their *ahorita viene* ('it's coming') may mean anytime from a minute to a few hours. By the same token, when the driver of the bus waiting at the terminal assures you that *ya nos vamos* ('we are leaving right now'), take it easy – it may still take an hour before the bus departs.

Venezuelans invited to lunch or a party might arrive a few hours late and, by their understanding of time, regard it as normal. The same applies to meetings in the street, cafés, pubs etc. Arriving half an hour later

than arranged may still give you time to read a newspaper before your friends arrive (if they arrive at all). Many offices and institutions have a similarly flexible grasp of their official working hours. Don't expect to arrange anything in an office if you arrive less than half an hour before its statutory lunch break or the end of work in the afternoon.

Some Venezuelans, particularly rural dwellers, also have a different notion of space. If they say that something you're looking for is *allí mismito* (just round here) or *cerquitica* (very close), it may still be an hour's walk to get there.

If you ask for information or directions, don't always expect a correct answer, especially in the countryside. The *campesinos* (country folk), even if they have no idea, may often tell you anything just to appear helpful and knowledgeable. Ask several people the same question and if one answer seems to pop up more frequently than others it may be the correct one. Avoid questions which can be answered by just yes or no; instead of 'is this the way to ...?' ask 'which is the way to ...?'.

Never show any disrespect for Bolívar – he is a saint to Venezuelans. For instance, sitting on a bench in Plaza Bolívar with your feet on the bench, or crossing the plaza carrying bulky parcels (or even a backpack) may be considered disrespectful and police may hassle you.

RELIGION

Most Venezuelans are Roman Catholics. Many Indian groups were converted to Catholicism and only a few, primarily those living in isolation, still practice their ancient beliefs. There are Protestant churches in Venezuela and lately they have been gaining in importance, taking adherents away from the Roman Catholic Church. There are small populations of Jews and Muslims practising their beliefs. One religious curiosity is the cult of María Lionza, today widespread throughout the country (see the Cerro de María Lionza section in The North-West chapter for details).

LANGUAGE

Spanish is Venezuela's official language and, except for some remote Indian groups, all of the population speaks it. There are over 25 Indian languages spoken in the country.

English speakers can be found in large urban centres, but it's certainly not a commonly understood or spoken language, even though it's taught as a mandatory second language in the public school system. What can be said, however, is that it's easier to find somebody speaking English in Venezuela than in, say, Colombia, Ecuador, Peru or Bolivia.

Most of the time you'll be in an exclusively Spanish-speaking environment. You'll probably manage to travel around easily without knowing a word of Spanish, but will miss out on a good part of the pleasure of meeting people. Your experience of the country will be limited as a result.

Spanish is quite an easy language to learn and it's useful in most other Latin American countries as well. It's well worth making some effort to learn at least the essentials before setting off. The Lonely Planet *Latin American Spanish phrasebook* is a worthwhile addition to your backpack. See the Books section in the Facts for the Visitor chapter for suggestions.

Venezuelan Spanish

Venezuelan Spanish is not the clearest or easiest to understand. Venezuelans (except those from the Andes) speak more rapidly than most other South Americans, and tend to drop some endings, especially plurals.

The use of the forms *tu*, 'you' (informal), and *usted*, 'you' (polite), is very flexible in Venezuela. Both forms are used, but with regional variations. Any form you use is OK, though it's best to answer using the same form in which you are addressed. Always use the form *usted* when talking to the police and the guardia nacional.

Note that in Venezuela, as in all Latin American countries, *vosotros* (the plural of *tu*) has almost disappeared and *ustedes* is commonly used in both informal and formal situations.

Greetings in Venezuela are more elaborate than in Spain. The short Spanish *hola* has given way to a number of expressions which are exchanged at the beginning of the conversation. Listen to how the locals greet you and learn some of these expressions in order to keep to the local style.

Although Venezuelans don't seem to be devoutly religious, the expressions *si Dios quiere*, 'God willing', and *gracias a Dios*, 'thanks to God', are used frequently in conversation.

Vocabulary

There are many differences in vocabulary between European and American Spanish, and among Spanish-speaking countries in the Americas. There are also considerable regional differences within these countries which are not attributable to accent alone; the locals have created a number of words which reflect features peculiar to their region. The Indian tongues have also influenced Spanish vocabulary, and some words from Indian languages are now included in the vocabulary of Venezuelan Spanish. Check the Glossary for some of these terms.

Venezuelans and other South Americans often refer to the Spanish language as *castellano* rather than *español*.

Note that 'ñ' is a separate letter and is listed after 'n' in dictionaries. Until recently, 'ch' and 'll' were also considered letters in their own right, and were listed after 'c' and 'l' respectively. This has been changed at a recent congress of the Spanish-language academies. Most Spanish dictionaries published in 1996-97 have already incorporated 'ch' into the letter 'c', and 'll' into 'l'.

Pronunciation

Once you know the basic rules, Spanish pronunciation should cause little difficulty.

Vowels Spanish vowels are consistent in their pronunciation and all have close English equivalents. For example, the Spanish 'a' has only one pronunciation, in contrast to the numerous possibilities we find in English, such as the 'a' in 'cake', 'art' or 'all'.

a	as in 'father'
e	as in 'met'
i	like the 'ee' in 'feet'
o	like the 'o' in 'for'
u	like the 'oo' in 'boot'
y	is a consonant except when it stands alone or appears at the end of a word, in which case it is pronounced as per the Spanish 'i'

Consonants Pronunciation of the letters 'b', 'f', 'k', 'l', 'n', 'p', 'q', 's' and 't' is virtually identical to English, as is 'y' when used as a consonant. The major differences include:

c	like the 's' in 'see' before 'e' and 'i', otherwise like English 'k'
ch	as in 'chair'
d	in initial position and after 'l' and 'n', as in 'dog'; elsewhere as 'th' in 'though'
g	similar to the 'h' in 'hell' before 'e' and 'i'; elsewhere as in 'go'
h	never pronounced
j	similar to the 'h' in 'hell'
ll	similar to 'y' in 'yellow'
ñ	similar to 'ni' in 'onion'
q	like 'k' in 'key'; 'q' is always followed by a silent 'u' and is only ever combined with 'e' as in *que* and 'i' as in *qui*
r	strongly rolled at the beginning of a word, or after 'n', 'l' and 's'; in other positions it is pronounced with one trill (a tap of the tongue)
v	like the 'b' in 'book'; the letters 'b' and 'v' represent the same sound in Spanish
x	like the 'x' in 'taxi'
z	like the 's' in 'sun'

Stress There are two general rules regarding stress. Words ending in a vowel, or the letters 'n' or 's', are stressed on the second-to-last syllable. For example, *amigo*, 'friend', is stressed on 'mi'. For words ending in a con-

sonant other than 'n' or 's' the stress is on the last syllable. For example, *amor*, 'love', is stressed on 'mor'.

Any deviation from these rules is indicated by a visible accent. For example, with *sótano*, 'basement', the stress is on the 'só'. Accents over capital letters are often not shown, but they still affect the pronunciation.

Basic Grammar

Nouns in Spanish are masculine or feminine. The definite article ('the' in English) agrees with the noun in gender and number; for example, the Spanish word for 'train' is masculine, so 'the train' is *el tren*, and the plural is *los trenes*. The word for 'house' is feminine, so 'the house' is *la casa*, and the plural is *las casas*.

The indefinite articles ('a', 'an' and 'some' in English) work in the same way; *un libro*, 'a book', is masculine singular, while *una carta*, 'a letter', is feminine singular. Their plurals are, respectively, *unos libros*, 'some books' and *unas cartas*, 'some letters'.

Most nouns ending in 'o' are masculine while those ending in 'a' are generally feminine. Normally, nouns ending in a vowel add 's' to form the plural, while those ending in a consonant add 'es'.

Adjectives usually come after the noun they describe, and agree with its gender and number. Possessive adjectives *mi*, 'my', *tu*, 'your', *su*, 'his/her', etc come before the noun and agree with the thing possessed, not the possessor. For example 'his suitcase' is *su maleta*, while 'his suitcases' are *sus maletas*. A simple way to indicate possession is to use the preposition *de*, 'of'. 'Juan's room', for instance, would be *la habitación de Juan* (literally 'the room of Juan').

A characteristic feature of Latin American Spanish is the extremely common use of diminutives. They either describe smallness or, more often, express affection. They are formed by adding suffixes *-ito/a*, *-cito/a*, *-illo/a* and *-cillo/a* to nouns and adjectives. For example, *cafecito* is the diminutive form of *café*, 'coffee', meaning 'small coffee', and *amorcito* is a tender version of *amor*, 'love'.

Greetings & Civilities

Hello.	*Hola.*
Good morning.	*Buenos días.*
Good afternoon.	*Buenas tardes.*
Good evening.	*Buenas noches.*
Good night.	*Buenas noches.*
Goodbye.	*Adiós/Chao.*
Please.	*Por favor.*
Thank you.	*Gracias.*
Excuse me.	*Disculpe.*
I'm sorry.	*Disculpe/Lo siento.*
You're welcome.	*De nada.*

Useful Words & Phrases

Yes.	*Sí.*
No.	*No.*
and	*y*
to/at	*a*
for	*por, para*
of/from	*de, desde*
in	*en*
with	*con*
without	*sin*
here/there	*aquí/allí*
Where?	*¿Dónde?*
Where is ...?	*¿Dónde está/ queda ...?*
When?	*¿Cuándo?*
How?	*¿Cómo?*
I'd like ...	*Me gustaría ...*
How much?	*¿Cuánto?*
How many?	*¿Cuántos?*

People & Personal Pronouns

Madam/Mrs	*Señora*
Sir/Mr	*Señor*
Miss	*Señorita*
man	*hombre*
woman	*mujer*
husband	*marido, esposo*
wife	*mujer, esposa*
boy	*chico, chamo*
girl	*chica, chama*
child	*niño/a*
father	*padre, papá*
mother	*madre, mamá*
son	*hijo*
daughter	*hija*
grandfather	*abuelo*
grandmother	*abuela*
family	*familia*
friend	*amigo/a*
I	*yo*
you (sing.)	*tú* (informal), *usted* (polite)
he	*él*
she	*ella*
you (pl)	*ustedes*
we	*nosotros/as*
they	*ellos/ellas*

Emergencies

accident	*accidente*
ambulance	*ambulancia*
clinic	*clínica*
dentist	*dentista*
doctor	*doctor, médico*
help	*auxilio, ayuda*
hospital	*hospital*
medicine	*medicina*
pharmacy	*farmacia*
police	*policía*
I feel bad.	*Me siento mal.*
I have a fever.	*Tengo fiebre/ temperatura.*
Please call a doctor/the police.	*Por favor llame a un doctor/la policía.*
Where is the nearest hospital?	*¿Dónde queda el hospital más cercano?*
Could you help me, please?	*¿Me podría ayudar, por favor?*
Could I use your telephone?	*¿Podría usar su teléfono?*
I want to call my embassy.	*Quiero llamar a mi embajada.*

Language Problems

Do you speak English?	*¿Habla inglés?*
Does anyone here speak English?	*¿Alguien habla inglés aquí?*
I don't speak Spanish.	*No hablo castellano/ español.*
I understand.	*Entiendo.*
I don't understand.	*No entiendo.*

Please speak more slowly.	*Por favor hable más despacio.*	castle	*castillo*
Could you repeat that, please?	*¿Puede repetirlo, por favor?*	cathedral	*catedral*
What does it mean?	*¿Qué significa?/ ¿Qué quiere decir?*	church	*iglesia*
		market	*mercado*
		monument	*monumento*
Please write it down.	*Por favor escríbalo.*	monastery	*monasterio*
		museum	*museo*
		palace	*palacio*
		park	*parque*
Getting Around		square	*plaza*
plane	*avión*	university	*universidad*
train	*tren*		
bus	*bus*	entrance	*entrada*
small bus	*por puesto, colectivo, micro, buseta, carrito*	exit	*salida*
		open	*abierto/a*
		closed	*cerrado/a*
ship	*barco, buque*		
boat	*bongo, lancha, bote*	ticket	*boleto, pasaje*
car	*auto, carro*	ticket office	*taquilla*
taxi	*libre, taxi*	first/last/next	*primero/último/ próximo*
truck	*camión*		
pickup truck	*camioneta*	1st/2nd class	*primera/segunda clase*
bicycle	*bicicleta*		
motorbike	*motocicleta*	one-way/return	*ida/ida y vuelta*
hitchhike	*pedir cola*	left luggage	*guardaequipaje*
airport	*aeropuerto*	Where is …?	*¿Dónde queda/ está …?*
train station	*estación del tren*		
bus terminal	*terminal de pasajeros*	How can I get to …?	*¿Cómo llegar a …?*
bus stop	*parada*	I'd like a ticket to …	*Quiero un boleto/ pasaje a …*
port	*puerto*		
wharf, pier	*muelle*	What's the fare to …?	*¿Cuánto cuesta a …?*
city	*ciudad*	When does the next bus leave for …?	*¿Cuándo sale el próximo bus para …?*
town	*pueblo*		
village	*pueblo, caserío*		
road	*carretera*		
freeway	*autopista*	**Geographical Terms**	
street	*calle*		
street corner	*esquina*		
bridge	*puente*		
downtown	*centro*		
tourist office	*oficina de turismo*	archipelago	*archipiélago*
petrol (gas) station	*bomba de gasolina*	bay	*bahía*
police station	*estación de policía*	beach	*playa*
embassy	*embajada*	cave	*cueva*
consulate	*consulado*	coast	*costa*
bank	*banco*	gulf	*golfo*
public toilet	*baño público*	hill	*cerro*

Geographical Terms

The expressions below are among the most common you will encounter in this book and in Spanish language maps and guides.

island	*isla*
lake	*lago*
lagoon	*laguna*
mountain	*montaña*
mountain range	*cordillera, serranía, sierra*
national park	*parque nacional*
pass	*paso*
peak	*pico*
peninsula	*península*
rapids	*raudales*
river	*río*
sea	*mar*
valley	*valle*
waterfall	*cascada, salto*

Accommodation

hotel	*hotel, pensión, residencia, posada*
room	*habitación*
single room	*habitación sencilla*
double room	*habitación doble*
toilet, bathroom	*baño*
shared bathroom	*baño compartido*
private bathroom	*baño privado*
shower	*ducha*
towel	*paño, toalla*
soap	*jabón*
toilet paper	*papel higiénico*
bed	*cama*
double bed	*cama matrimonial*
sheets	*sábanas*
pillow	*almohada*
blanket	*manta*
fan	*ventilador, abanico*
air-conditioning	*aire acondicionado*
key	*llave*
padlock	*candado*

cheap	*barato/a*
expensive	*caro/a*
clean	*limpio/a*
dirty	*sucio/a*
good	*bueno/a*
poor	*malo/a*
noisy	*ruidoso/a*
quiet	*tranquilo/a*
hot	*caliente*
cold	*frío/a*

Do you have rooms available?	*¿Hay habitaciones?*
May I see the room?	*¿Puedo ver la habitación?*
What does it cost?	*¿Cuánto cuesta?*
Does it include breakfast?	*¿Incluye el desayuno?*

Food

Only some basic words are given here. See the Food & Drink Glossary at the back of the book for more terms.

the bill, check	*la cuenta*
cup	*taza*
dish	*plato*
fork	*trinche, tenedor*
glass	*vaso*
knife	*cuchillo*
menu	*menú, carta*
plate	*plato*
spoon	*cuchara*
teaspoon	*cucharita*
bread	*pan*
butter	*mantequilla*
egg	*huevo*
fish	*pescado*
fruit	*fruta*
ham	*jamón*
meat	*carne*
milk	*leche*
pepper	*pimienta*
potatoes	*papas*
rice	*arroz*
salad	*ensalada*
salt	*sal*
sandwich	*sánduche*
sugar	*azúcar*
vegetables	*verduras*
water	*agua*

The following words will help you judge how food has been prepared:

baked	*al horno*
boiled	*cocido/a*
braised, stewed	*estofado/a*
fried	*frito/a*
grilled, broiled	*a la parrilla*
roasted	*asado/a*

smoked	*ahumado/a*	enough	*suficiente*
stewed	*guisado/a*	more	*más*
		less	*menos*
rare	*poco cocido/a*		
medium	*término medio*	How much is it?	*¿Cuánto cuesta/vale?*
medium well	*tres cuartos*	I (don't) like it.	*(No) me gusta.*
well-done	*bien cocido/a*	Do you have …?/	*¿Hay …?*
		Are there …?	

Post & Telecommunications

airmail	*correo aéreo*
letter	*carta*
letter box	*buzón*
parcel	*paquete*
post office	*correo*
postcard	*postal*
registered mail	*correo certificado*
stamps	*estampillas*
reverse-charges call	*cobro revertido*
international call	*llamada inter- nacional*
long-distance call	*llamada de larga distancia*
person to person	*persona a persona*
public telephone	*teléfono público*
telephone card	*tarjeta CANTV*

Shopping

banknote	*billete*
cash	*efectivo*
change	*vuelta*
cheque	*cheque*
coin	*moneda*
credit card	*tarjeta de crédito*
money	*dinero, plata*
price	*precio*
shop	*almacén, abasto, bodega*
shopping centre	*centro comercial*
supermarket	*supermercado*
cheap	*barato*
expensive	*caro*
big	*grande*
small	*pequeño*
many/much	*muchos/mucho*
few	*pocos*
a little	*un poco*
a pair	*un par*
a dozen	*una docena*

Time

time	*hora, tiempo*
today	*hoy*
tonight	*esta noche*
this week	*esta semana*
now	*ahora*
yesterday	*ayer*
day before yesterday	*anteayer, antier*
last week	*la semana pasada*
tomorrow	*mañana*
day after tomorrow	*pasado mañana*
next week	*la semana entrante*
early	*temprano*
late	*tarde*
often	*con frecuencia*
seldom	*de vez en cuando, pocas veces*
before	*antes*
after	*después*
soon	*pronto*
already	*ya*
right away	*en seguida*
sunrise	*amanecer*
morning	*mañana*
noon	*mediodía*
afternoon	*tarde*
sunset	*atardecer*
evening	*tarde*
night	*noche*
midnight	*medianoche*
second	*segundo*
minute	*minuto*
hour	*hora*
day	*día*
week	*semana*
month	*mes*
year	*año*
century	*siglo*

The Clock

Eight o'clock (8.00) is *las ocho*, while 8.30 is *las ocho y treinta* (lit: 'eight and thirty') or *las ocho y media* ('eight and a half'). Quarter to eight (7.45) can be *las ocho menos quince* (lit: 'eight minus fifteen'), *las ocho menos cuarto* ('eight minus one quarter'), *un cuarto para las ocho* ('one quarter to eight') or *quince para las ocho* ('fifteen to eight').

A 24-hour clock is often used for official purposes, especially with transportation schedules. In everyday conversations, however, people commonly use the 2 x 12 hour system and, if necessary, add *de la mañana* ('in the morning'), *de la tarde* ('in the afternoon') or *de la noche* ('at night').

What time is it?	*¿Qué horas son?/* *¿Qué hora es?*
It's 7 am.	*Son las siete de la mañana.*
It's 7.15.	*Son las siete y cuarto.*
It's late.	*Es tarde.*
It's early.	*Es temprano.*

Days of the Week

Monday	*lunes*
Tuesday	*martes*
Wednesday	*miércoles*
Thursday	*jueves*
Friday	*viernes*
Saturday	*sábado*
Sunday	*domingo*

Months

January	*enero*
February	*febrero*
March	*marzo*
April	*abril*
May	*mayo*
June	*junio*
July	*julio*
August	*agosto*
September	*septiembre*
October	*octubre*
November	*noviembre*
December	*diciembre*

Seasons

rainy season/winter	*invierno*
dry season/summer	*verano*
spring	*primavera*
autumn	*otoño*

Cardinal Numbers

0	*cero*
1	*uno*
2	*dos*
3	*tres*
4	*cuatro*
5	*cinco*
6	*seis*
7	*siete*
8	*ocho*
9	*nueve*
10	*diez*
11	*once*
12	*doce*
13	*trece*
14	*catorce*
15	*quince*
16	*dieciseis*
17	*diecisiete*
18	*dieciocho*
19	*diecinueve*
20	*veinte*
21	*veintiuno*
22	*veintidós*
30	*treinta*
31	*treinta y uno*
32	*treinta y dos*
40	*cuarenta*
50	*cincuenta*
60	*sesenta*
70	*setenta*
80	*ochenta*
90	*noventa*
100	*cien*
101	*ciento uno*
102	*ciento dos*
110	*ciento diez*
120	*ciento veinte*
130	*ciento treinta*
200	*doscientos*
300	*trescientos*
400	*cuatrocientos*
500	*quinientos*
600	*seiscientos*
700	*setecientos*
800	*ochocientos*

900	*novecientos*		3rd	*tercero/a*
1000	*mil*		4th	*cuarto/a*
1100	*mil cien*		5th	*quinto/a*
1200	*mil doscientos*		6th	*sexto/a*
2000	*dos mil*		7th	*séptimo/a*
5000	*cinco mil*		8th	*octavo/a*
10,000	*diez mil*		9th	*noveno/a*
50,000	*cincuenta mil*		10th	*décimo/a*
100,000	*cien mil*			
one million	*un millón*			
two million	*dos millones*			

Fractions

¼	*un cuarto*
⅓	*un tercio*
½	*medio/a*
¾	*tres cuartos*

Ordinal Numbers

1st	*primero/a*
2nd	*segundo/a*

Facts for the Visitor

PLANNING

When to Go

The tourist season in Venezuela runs year-round so, theoretically at least, any time you visit is OK. There are two factors, however, which you might like to consider before you finalise travel plans.

The first is the climate. Venezuela has one dry season (roughly November or December to April or May) and one wet season (the rest of the year). The dry season is certainly more pleasant for travelling. This is particularly true if you plan on hiking or some other outdoor activities. In the wet season, paths are muddy and views obscured, and it's not much fun trudging in rain all day anyway. If you plan on mountaineering high in the Andes, the rainy (or, more correctly, snowy) season is not only unpleasant but can be dangerous. Conventional sightseeing in the cities or towns won't be greatly disturbed by rain.

Keep in mind, too, that the weather pattern is not uniform throughout the country. Some regions (eg parts of Lara, Falcón, Anzoátegui and Sucre states as well as Isla de Margarita) are relatively dry for most of the year, so the season doesn't really matter much. On the other hand, the upper Amazonas is wet more or less year-round.

In some regions, the season doesn't determine which time is better for visiting. For example, wildlife trips to Los Llanos can be just as fascinating during the dry season as in the wet season, though you'll encounter completely different landscapes and animal life. Salto Angel (Angel Falls), a must for many tourists, is certainly more impressive in the wet season. Furthermore, boat trips to the waterfall (which arguably are a more attractive option of visiting the falls than flights) are only possible in the rainy season, when the river level is sufficiently high.

The second consideration when planning your trip are the periods when Venezuelans take their holidays. They are mad about travelling to visit friends and family over Christmas, Carnaval and Holy Week (Easter).

During these three periods, air and bus transport get pretty busy and hotels fill up quickly, so you'll have to plan ahead and do more legwork before you find a place to stay. On the other hand, these periods are colourful and alive, with a host of festivities. Schools break for annual vacations in August but this doesn't significantly affect public transport or accommodation.

Maps

You'll probably find it difficult to buy anything other than general maps of Venezuela outside the country itself. Check with good travel bookshops and map shops to see what is available. In the USA, Maplink (☎ (805) 965-4402), 25 E Mason St, Dept G, Santa Barbara, CA 93101, has an excellent supply of maps. A similarly extensive selection of maps is available in the UK from Stanfords (☎ (0171) 836-1321), 12-14 Long Acre, London WC2E 9LP.

Both these distributors, as well as many other map retailers in North America, Europe and Australia, should have the folded map of Venezuela (scale 1:1,750,000) published in 1994 by International Travel Maps (ITM; ☎ (604) 687-3320, fax 687-5925), 736A Granville St, Vancouver, BC, Canada V6Z 1G3. This is the best general map of the country so far published. It has excellent topographical detail and heaps of information, and it's better than any map produced in Venezuela. The map is also available from some bookshops and travel agencies in Venezuela, probably only in Caracas. When there, try IVI Tours (☎ 993 60 82, 993 87 38, 993 39 30; fax 92 96 26), Residencia La Hacienda, Piso Bajo, Local 1-4-T, Final Avenida Principal de las Mercedes; Marumen Store (☎ 261 81 34, 262 06 61), 3a Transversal, between Avenidas Luis Roche and San Juan Bosco, Altamira; and the Tecni-Ciencia Libros and Librería Alemana Oscar Todtmann (see Bookshops in the Caracas chapter). More places are likely to distribute this map by the time you arrive.

ITM has also published three sectional maps of South America (North West, North East and South), plus individual maps to several Latin American countries. All these maps are excellent.

Within Venezuela, folded road maps of the country are produced by Lagoven and Corpoven oil companies (available at their petrol stations, but almost out of print) and several other publishers (distributed through bookshops).

For large-scale regional maps, Caracas is your best bet. Go to the Dirección de Cartografía Nacional (☎ 408 16 15, 408 16 37), Calle Este 6, Colón a Dr Díaz, near Plaza Diego Ibarra (metro La Hoyada). The office (in room No 111 on the 1st floor) is open Monday to Friday from 8.30 am to noon and 2 to 4.30 pm. There are 1:100,000 and 1:25,000 maps available, but so far only the northern part of the country is well covered; there is only a handful of maps of Amazonas and Guayana. There also are some major city maps. Unfortunately, many of these maps are out of date.

If the Dirección de Cartografía Nacional runs out of colour originals (which is usually the case), it will make a black and white copy for you on the spot. Maps featuring border areas or strategic installations such as military zones, oil refineries etc require a special permit from military authorities, which takes several days to be issued if granted. Maps cost somewhere between US$2 and US$4 per sheet, depending on size.

What to Bring

The first and most important rule of travel is to bring with you the minimum possible – a large, heavy backpack soon becomes a nightmare. Almost everything you might need can easily be bought in Venezuela. Clothes, footwear, toiletries, stationery etc are readily available in Venezuelan shops, supermarkets and markets, and they are usually cheaper than their equivalents in other countries. There's absolutely no need to bring in large stocks of envelopes, spare batteries, or a bottle of shampoo big enough to last the whole trip. Instead, pay attention to the most important items such as a good backpack, comfortable shoes, a basic set of clothes and photographic gear.

The overwhelming majority of the country is lowland, so you don't need much in the way of warm clothing. If you stick to hotels, you don't need bedsheets or blankets, as even the most basic residencias provide them.

Some essentials which might be worth packing include: a travel alarm clock (for those early morning buses), a small torch (for dodgy electricity supplies), sunglasses and a hat, a Spanish/English dictionary, flip-flops or thongs (to protect feet against fungus infections in shabby hotel bathrooms), and a small pocketknife.

Make sure to bring with you any prescription medications you would normally take, and a spare pair of glasses or contact lenses if applicable. A small medical kit is recommended if you plan on leaving the beaten track – refer to the Health section for specifics.

Rain gear will come in handy if you're visiting the country during the wet season. A swimming suit is essential if you're heading to one or more of the hundreds of beaches on the coast. Bring a mask and snorkel (to save on rental fees), and old running shoes to protect your feet against the coral. Plastic bags will protect your gear from rain and dust. Consider a set of nice clothes for dining out in fancy restaurants and special occasions. Bookworms might want to bring along some paperbacks as the choice offered by local bookshops may not be extensive.

Think about bringing some small gifts, to give people for their hospitality or help. Foreign coins, stamps, postcards and small handicrafts from your country are just a few obvious suggestions.

If you plan on overnight hiking in the mountains or the jungle, ideally you should include in your luggage the necessary equipment such as a tent, sleeping bag, warm clothes, cooking stove etc. The Camping Gaz Bluet is the most common brand of cooking gear, and you can stock up on gas canisters in Caracas, Mérida and some other large cities.

Camping equipment is available in Venezuela, but it can be quite expensive and the choice is limited. It also can be rented in some cities (mostly in Caracas and Mérida), but if you need it for a longer period, it may be better to bring your own. The week-long Roraima trip alone probably justifies bringing your camping gear with you (see the Guayana chapter). You will also save quite a bit of money by camping at Canaima and Archipiélago Los Roques and you'll enjoy more flexibility in your itinerary while travelling around the country.

SUGGESTED ITINERARIES

Your itinerary will largely depend on your particular interests, your budget, your customary speed of travelling (mad dash versus staying longer in fewer places), the season (dry or wet), your companion etc. Some travellers will rush through half of the country in a week, while others will prefer to spend the same time on one beach. One person can be crazy about colonial architecture while another about bird-watching. Some visitors would like to see briefly most major attractions regardless of how distant they are from each other, whereas others are more interested in visiting some regions in-depth, bypassing the rest of the country.

Organised tours are an important variable in your itinerary. Some of the country's major attractions can only be reached by taking a tour (Salto Angel, Delta del Orinoco, Los Llanos, among others). If you can't afford tours, you unfortunately have to delete these places from your programme. On the other hand, if money is no problem, reputable tour operators will whisk you comfortably around important sights of their or your choice.

Finally, since Venezuela is the cheapest entry point to the continent from both the USA and Europe, many travellers treat the country as just a stopover on their South American trip, before heading further south to either Colombia or Brazil. Depending on the route, many of them will be inclined to concentrate on Venezuela's west or southeast.

To sum up, it's difficult to recommend any specific itineraries for a visitor. The following suggestions have been made assuming you arrive at Caracas and plan on visiting just Venezuela, but please consider them as rough guidelines only. For more suggestions, see the following Highlights section and the individual Highlights at the beginning of each regional chapter.

One week
   Spend one to three days exploring Caracas and its environs, possibly including snorkelling and a trip to Archipiélago Los Roques; go to Choroní and/or Rancho Grande in the Parque Nacional Henri Pittier, and take a tour to Canaima/Salto Angel.

Two weeks
   To the above, add one of the three following options: Mérida and the surrounding mountains; Ciudad Bolívar and La Gran Sabana; or a trip to the top of Roraima.

One month
   You'll be able to do all the options listed above, possibly even including a tour to Los Llanos from Mérida.

Two months
   To the above, add Coro with its environs and Parque Nacional Morrocoy in the west, and Parque Nacional Mochima, Cueva del Guácharo and Península de Paria in the east; if time allows and your wallet is still thick enough, you may consider adding a tour to Delta del Orinoco and/or Río Caura.

HIGHLIGHTS

As mentioned earlier, this is a subjective issue, depending on individual interest and preferences, but some of Venezuela's attractions are likely to appeal to most visitors.

Salto Angel is Venezuela's promotional landmark, and few tourists want to miss a view of this 1km-high waterfall. For more adventurous travellers, a trek to the top of Roraima is without doubt a fascinating and unforgettable experience. Other natural highlights include Andean peaks around Mérida, coral reefs along the coast and off-shore islands, the tepuis and waterfalls of La Gran Sabana, and the wildlife of Los Llanos, Delta del Orinoco and Cueva del Guácharo.

TOURIST OFFICES
Local Tourist Offices
Corporación de Turismo, or Corpoturismo, is the government agency promoting tourism and providing tourist information. Its head office is in Caracas (see that chapter for details). It publishes material on many of the country's attractions but it's not always available.

Outside Caracas, the provision of tourist information has been taken over by regional tourist bodies which have offices in state capitals and some other cities. Some are better than others but, on the whole, they lack city maps and brochures. The staff are usually friendly but don't always speak English. The practical information they provide sometimes leaves something to be desired, especially if you are a budget traveller. They seldom know which banks currently change money and which is the cheapest hotel in town.

Tourist Offices Abroad
Outside Venezuela there aren't many tourist information agencies focusing specifically on Venezuela. One of the few is the Venezuelan Tourist Association (VTA) (☎ (415) 331-0100 or toll-free 1-800 331 0100; fax (415) 332 2720), PO Box 3010, Sausalito, CA 94966, USA, which provides general information and maps. Some of the Venezuelan consulates and embassies can provide limited tourist information.

Other Sources of Information Abroad
One of the most useful resources for visitors to South America is the South American Explorers Club (☎ (607) 277-0488), 126 Indian Creek Rd, Ithaca, NY 14850, USA. The club provides services, information and support to travellers, researchers, mountaineers and explorers. It sells a wide range of books, guides and maps of South America, publish-es a quarterly journal and a mail order catalogue. The club maintains clubhouses in Quito, Ecuador and Lima, Peru. Membership is US$30 a year per individual, US$40 per couple.

The counterpart in Germany is the Lateinamerikanischer Freundeskreis e.V. (☎ (0421) 239245, fax 234267), Schwachhauser Heerstrasse 222, D-28213, Bremen.

A useful contact in the UK is the Latin American Bureau (☎ (0171) 278 2829, fax 278 0165), 1 Amwell St, London EC1R 1UL, which keeps up to date with all Latin American happenings, and publishes a list of titles dealing with politics, culture and travel throughout the region.

The Latin American Travel Consultants, PO Box 17-17-908, Quito, Ecuador (fax (02) 562566, email rku@pi.pro.ec) publishes a quarterly news bulletin, *The Latin American Travel Advisor*, which features news on travel, public safety, health, climate, costs and so on for travellers in the region. Books, maps and videos are available by mail order.

VISAS & DOCUMENTS
Passport
A valid passport is your essential document and it must be stamped with a visa if you need one. If your passport is due to expire within a year, get a new one before you leave on a South American circuit. Many countries won't issue a visa or admit you at the border if your passport has less than six months or even one year validity remaining. Even if expiry isn't a problem, make sure that your passport has a few blank pages for visas and entry and exit stamps.

Once in Venezuela, you must carry your passport with you at all times. Identity document checks are not uncommon on country roads and city streets. Your passport is the first document the police will ask for. Some police officers may be satisfied with a certified photocopy of your passport but most won't accept it as a valid document.

Visas & Tourist Cards
Since December 1992, nationals of the USA, Canada, Australia, New Zealand, South

Africa, Japan, the UK and most western and Scandinavian European countries don't need visas if they fly into Venezuela. A Tourist Card (Tarjeta de Ingreso, officially denominated DEX-2) is given to these visitors free of charge on board the airline they fly with. The tourist card is valid for 90 days and can be extended.

Until recently, all foreigners who entered Venezuela by land from any neighbouring country (Colombia, Brazil or Guyana) needed a visa, obtainable from Venezuelan consulates. However, few of the consulates in South American countries issued visas.

It seems that this strict rule is currently being liberalised. Overland visitors bearing passports of the countries listed above are now allowed to enter Venezuela with the tourist card. It can be obtained, in theory at least, from Venezuelan consulates and at border crossings, and it's free. In practice, though, border posts are a sort of lottery. You're strongly advised to get one from a consulate beforehand, yet again, not all consulates provide tourist cards. Some may still insist that you need a tourist visa, which they can issue for US$30 to US$40, others can only give you a 72-hour transit visa (these visas cannot be extended in Venezuela, whatever the consulate tells you!), while still others may offer you nothing at all. Plan ahead, enquire at the consulates you pass by on your route, and get the tourist card from the first consulate eager to give one to you. According to recent reports, Venezuelan consulates in Cartagena and Cúcuta (Colombia) and Manaus and Boa Vista (Brazil) were issuing tourist cards.

The tourist card is a small form with a yellow-coloured carbon copy. You must fill it in and present it, together with your passport, to immigration officials at the border. They will put an entry stamp in your passport and on the yellow copy, which will be given back to you (make sure that both documents are stamped). You then have to keep the yellow copy at all times while travelling in Venezuela (you may be asked for it by the police or Guardia Nacional during passport controls), and return it to

immigration officials when leaving the country (although not all are interested in collecting the cards).

If you plan on travelling overland, and want to play it completely safe, you can get a Venezuelan visa in your country of residence. Consulates in most major western countries, including the USA, the UK and Australia, issue multiple-entry tourist visas which are valid for one year from the date of issue. The official requirements are: your passport (valid for at least one year), a bank letter stating your funds, an employer's letter stating your wages, an onward ticket and one photo. The visa may take several days to be issued, and its cost varies depending on the country from which you apply (up to US$40).

Officially, every tourist entering Venezuela should have an onward ticket. You may be asked by immigration officials to present it, though it's no longer standard and varies from one border crossing to another and from one official to another.

Matters related to foreigners and immigration (border passport control, visas, visa extensions, work permits etc) are handled by a department of the Ministry of Interior Affairs, commonly known as DIEX (Dirección de Identificación y Extranjería) or DEX (Dirección de Extranjería). It has offices in Caracas, in state capitals and also at border crossings.

Visa & Tourist Card Extensions Extensions are handled by the Caracas office of DIEX. Visas and tourist cards can be extended for a maximum of one month, which costs US$24. Plan ahead and don't leave it to the last minute. See the Caracas chapter for further details.

Travel Insurance
Ideally, all travellers should have a travel insurance policy, which will provide some sense of security in the case of a medical emergency or the loss or theft of money or belongings. Even if you never use it, it will probably help you to sleep more peacefully during the trip. It may seem an expensive

luxury, but if you can't afford a travel health insurance policy, you probably can't afford medical emergency charges abroad either, if something goes wrong. See the Health section in this chapter for details.

If you do need to make a claim on your travel insurance, you must produce a police report detailing loss or theft (refer to the Dangers & Annoyances section later in this chapter). You also need proof of the value of any items lost or stolen. Receipts are the best bet, so if you buy a new camera for your trip, for example, hang onto the receipt.

Driving Licence
If you plan on driving in Venezuela, make sure you bring your driving licence. According to Venezuelan law, driving licences valid in other countries are also valid in Venezuela for a period of one year from the date of arrival, provided the licence is not used to drive vehicles for profit. Despite this, some police and rental company staff may be unfamiliar with foreign driving licences, so it's best to bring along an International Driving Permit as well. The minimum driving age in Venezuela is 18 years of age but in order to rent a car you must be at least 21 and have a credit card.

Student Card
A student card is of rather limited use in Venezuela. Some airlines (eg Avensa and Aeropostal) give a 15% discount on their domestic flights to full-time local students, but they may be reluctant to sell discounted tickets to foreign students identifying themselves with an International Student Identity Card (ISIC). There are no student reductions on other means of transport such as buses or ferries. A student card will save a few bolívares at museums, but most museums have free admission to all visitors anyway. For further information, contact IVI Tours (see Travel Agencies in the Caracas chapter).

Hostel Card
An International Youth Hostel card is useless as there are no youth hostels in Venezuela.

International Health Card
This card is not required for entry into Venezuela unless you're arriving from an area infected with yellow fever or cholera, but even in this case you'll rarely be asked for the card. Yet, it's a good idea to get inoculated against some diseases before you set off for the trip – see the Health section later in this chapter for full details.

Photocopies
Make copies of important documents such as your passport (data pages plus visas), credit cards, airline tickets, travel insurance policy and travellers cheque receipt slips. Take notes of the serial numbers of your cameras, lenses, camcorder, lap-top computer and any other pieces of high-tech stuff you'll be taking on the trip. Make a list of phone numbers of emergency assistance services (credit cards, insurance, your bank etc). Keep all that material separate from your passport, money and other valuables. It's a good idea to keep one copy with you, one copy inside your luggage and (if applicable) deposit another with a travelling companion. Also leave a copy of all these things with someone at home. Slip US$50 or US$100 into an unlikely place to use as an emergency stash.

EMBASSIES
Venezuelan Embassies & Consulates Abroad
Venezuelan embassies include:

Australia
    Tulgoa Circuit, Omalley, ACT 2606 (☎ (02) 6290 2900; fax 6290 2911)
Belgium
    10 Avenue Franklin Roosevelt, 1050 Brussels (☎ (2) 287 284; fax 292 370)
Canada
    32 Range Rd, Ottawa, Ontario K1N 8J4 (☎ (613) 235 5151, 235 5697; fax 235 3205)
France
    11 Rue Copernic, 75116 Paris (☎ (1) 45 53 29 98; fax 47 55 64 56)
Germany
    Im Rheingarten 7, D-53225 Bonn 3 (☎ (0228) 400 920; fax 400 922)

Italy
>Via Nicolo Tartaglia 11, 00197 Rome (☎ (06) 807 9797, 807 9464; fax 808 4410)
Japan
>38 Kowa Building, Room 703, 12-24 Nishi Azabu, 4 Chrome, Minato Ku, Tokyo 106 (☎ (3) 3409 1501; fax 3409 1505)
Netherlands
>Nassaulaan 2, 2514 JS The Hague (☎ (70) 352 3851, 352 4351; fax 365 6954)
Portugal
>Avda Duque de Loule 47-4, 1000 Lisbon (☎ (1) 357 3803, 357 3865; fax 352 7421)
Spain
>Calle Capitan Haya No 1, Edificio Eurocentro, Planta 13, Madrid (☎ (1) 555 8452, 555 8455; fax 597 1583)
Sweden
>Engelbrektsgatan 35-B, 11432 Stockholm (☎ (8) 411 0996; fax 213 100)
Switzerland
>Morillonstrasse 9, 3007 Bern (☎ (31) 371 3282; fax 371 0424)
UK
>1 Cromwell Rd, London SW7 2HW (☎ (0171) 581 2776, 584 4206; fax 589 8887)
USA
>1099 30th St, NW, Washington DC 20007 (☎ (202) 342 2214; fax 342 6820)

In the USA, Venezuela has consulates in Boston, Chicago, Houston, Miami, New Orleans, New York, San Francisco and Washington. In Canada, there are consulates in Montreal and Toronto. There's no Venezuelan embassy in New Zealand; that country is under the jurisdiction of the embassy in Australia.

In Colombia, there's a Venezuelan embassy and consulate in Bogotá, and consulates in Arauca, Barranquilla, Bucaramanga, Cartagena, Cúcuta, Medellín, Puerto Carreño, Puerto Inírida and Riohacha. In Brazil, Venezuela has its embassy and consulate in Brasilia, and consulates in Belém, Boa Vista, Manaus, Rio de Janeiro and São Paulo.

Other Venezuelan representatives in the region include embassies and consulates in Argentina (Buenos Aires), Barbados (Bridgetown), Bolivia (La Paz), Chile (Santiago), Costa Rica (San José), Cuba (Havana), Dominican Republic (Santo Domingo), Ecuador (Quito), El Salvador (San Salvador), Grenada (St Georges), Guatemala (Guatemala City), Guyana (Georgetown), Haiti (Port-au-Prince), Jamaica (Kingston), Mexico (Mexico City), Nicaragua (Managua), Panama (Panama City), Paraguay (Asunción), Peru (Lima), Puerto Rico (San Juan), St Lucia (Castries), St Vincent (Kingstown), Suriname (Paramaribo), Trinidad & Tobago (Port of Spain), Uruguay (Montevideo) and the Netherlands Antilles (Aruba, Bonaire and Curaçao).

Foreign Embassies & Consulates in Venezuela

All countries which maintain diplomatic relations with Venezuela have their embassies in Caracas. Some of them are listed below. If you can't find your home embassy, check the Caracas phone directory, which includes a full list. Consulates are at the same address as the embassies unless indicated otherwise. There are also some consulates in other large cities and border towns; these have been listed in the relevant sections throughout the book.

Australia
>Quinta Yolanda, Avenida Luis Roche entre 6a y 7a Transversal, Altamira (☎ 263 40 33)
Austria
>Torre Las Mercedes, Piso 4, Oficina 408, Avenida La Estancia, Chuao (☎ 91 38 63, 92 29 56)
Barbados
>Edificio Los Frailes, Piso 5, Oficina 501, Calle La Guairita con Avenida Principal de Chuao (☎ 91 67 21, 92 05 45)
Belgium
>Quinta La Azulita, 11a Avenida entre 6a y 7a Transversal, Altamira (☎ 261 93 97, 262 04 21)
Bolivia
>Quinta Embajada de Bolivia, Avenida Luis Roche con 6a Transversal, Altamira (☎ 261 45 63, 263 30 15)
Brazil
>Centro Gerencial Mohedano, Piso 6, Calle Los Chaguaramos con Avenida Mohedano, La Castellana (☎ 261 44 81, 261 75 53)
Canada
>Torre Europa, Piso 7, Avenida Francisco de Miranda, Campo Alegre (☎ 951 61 74, 951 63 06)

Colombia
  Embassy: Torre Credival, Piso 11, Segunda Avenida de Campo Alegre con Avenida Francisco de Miranda, Campo Alegre (☎ 261 65 92, 261 83 58)
  Consulate: Edificio Consulado de Colombia, Calle Guaicaipuro, El Rosal (☎ 951 36 31, 951 66 92)
Costa Rica
  Edificio For You, Pent House, Avenida San Juan Bosco entre 1a y 2a Transversal, Altamira (☎ 265 78 89, 267 11 04)
Denmark
  Torre Centuria, Piso 7, Avenida Venezuela con Calle Mohedano, El Rosal (☎ 951 46 18, 951 66 18)
Ecuador
  Centro Empresarial Andrés Bello, Torre Oeste, Piso 13, Avenida Andrés Bello, Maripérez (☎ 781 31 80, 781 37 35)
Finland
  Edificio Atrium, Piso 1, Calle Sorocaima entre Avenidas Tamanaco y Venezuela, El Rosal (☎ 952 41 11)
France
  Edificio Embajada de Francia, Calle Madrid con Avenida La Trinidad, Las Mercedes (☎ 993 66 66, 993 85 92)
Germany
  Edificio Panaven, Piso 12, Avenida San Juan Bosco con 3a Transversal, Altamira (☎ 261 01 81, 261 12 05)
Grenada
  Edificio Los Frailes, Piso 5, Calle La Guairita, Chuao (☎ 91 12 37, 91 93 59)
Guyana
  Quinta Roraima, Avenida El Paseo, Prados del Este (☎ 977 11 58, 978 27 81)
Israel
  Centro Empresarial Miranda, Piso 4, Oficina 4-D, Avenida Francisco de Miranda con Avenida Principal de Los Ruices, Los Ruices (☎ 239 45 11, 239 49 21)
Italy
  Embassy: Edificio Atrium, Pent House, Calle Sorocaima entre Avenidas Tamanaco y Venezuela, El Rosal (☎ 952 73 11, 952 89 39)
  Consulate: 6a Avenida entre 3a y 5a Transversales, Altamira (☎ 261 07 55, 261 28 03)
Japan
  Edificio Bancaracas, Piso 12, Plaza La Castellana (☎ 261 83 33)
Mexico
  Edificio Forum, Piso 5, Calle Guaicaipuro con Avenida Principal de Las Mercedes, El Rosal (☎ 952 44 57, 952 57 77)
Netherlands
  Edificio San Juan, Piso 9, 2a Transversal con Avenida San Juan Bosco, Altamira (☎ 263 30 76, 263 36 22)
Norway
  Centro Lido, Torre A, Piso 9, Avenida Francisco de Miranda (☎ 253 06 71, 253 19 73)
Panama
  Edificio Los Frailes, Piso 6, Calle La Guairita, Chuao (☎ 92 90 93, 92 91 82)
Peru
  Embassy: Edificio San Juan, Piso 5, 2a Transversal con Avenida San Juan Bosco, Altamira (☎ 264 14 20, 264 14 83)
  Consulate: Quinta Uno, 4a Avenida entre 3a y 4a Transversal, Altamira (☎ 261 93 89, 266 49 36)
Spain
  Embassy: Quinta Marmolejo, Avenida Mohedano entre 1a y 2a Transversal, La Castellana (☎ 263 28 55, 263 38 76)
  Consulate: Edificio Bancaracas, Piso 7, Plaza La Castellana (☎ 266 02 22)
Suriname
  Quinta Los Milagros, 4a Avenida entre 7a y 8a Transversal, Altamira (☎ 261 27 24, 263 15 54)
Sweden
  Torre Europa, Piso 8, Avenida Francisco de Miranda, Campo Alegre (☎ 952 20 58, 952 20 70, 952 21 11)
Switzerland
  Torre Europa, Piso 6, Avenida Francisco de Miranda, Campo Alegre (☎ 951 40 64, 951 41 66, 951 46 06)
Trinidad & Tobago
  Quinta Serrana, 4a Avenida entre 7a y 8a Transversal, Altamira (☎ 261 37 48, 261 47 72)
UK
  Torre Las Mercedes, Piso 3, Avenida La Estancia, Chuao (☎ 993 41 11)
USA
  Calle F con Calle Suapure, Colinas de Valle Arriba (☎ 977 20 11, 977 41 11)

CUSTOMS

Customs regulations don't differ much from those in other countries on the continent. You are allowed to bring in personal belongings and presents you intend to give to Venezuelan residents. The quantity, kind and value of these items shouldn't arouse suspicion that they may have been imported with a commercial purpose in mind. You can bring with you cameras (still, video and movie), a tape recorder, a radio, camping equipment, sports accessories, a lap-top computer and the like without any problems.

The entry of products derived from milk or pork is prohibited. It's also forbidden to introduce seeds, flowers, fruit or plants of any kind. According to Venezuelan law, the possession, trafficking or consumption of drugs is a serious offence and subject to heavy penalties. You would be crazy to try smuggling them across the border.

When leaving the country, you can take souvenirs and handicrafts with you, but not in quantities that could be suspected of being commercial.

Customs formalities are usually not much more than that, formalities. However, you may encounter a thorough check. If you're coming overland from Colombia your baggage is likely to be searched at the border and/or at *alcabalas* (police road checkpoints). This is because of the considerable drug traffic that passes this way.

MONEY
Costs
Venezuela is no longer one of the most expensive Latin American countries, as it was during the oil bonanza of the late 1970s and early 80s when the prices of goods and services soared almost to US levels. With the economic boom long over, and a recent dramatic devaluation of the local currency, Venezuela is now quite a cheap country for foreigners. By and large, it's more expensive than Ecuador and Bolivia, comparable to Peru, but probably cheaper than all the other countries on the continent.

How much you spend in Venezuela largely depends on what degree of comfort you require, what kind of food you eat, where you go, how fast you travel and the means of transport you use. If, for instance, you are used to rental cars and plush hotels, you will probably spend just as much as you would if you were travelling in North America or Europe. If you're a budget traveller, though, prepared for basic conditions and willing to endure some discomfort on the road, you should find that you get by on US$20 to US$25 per day. This would cover accommodation in budget hotels, food in low to middle-range restaurants, bus transport at a reasonable pace, and probably still leave a small margin for some beers, movies and

taxis. These averages don't obviously include rental cars, tours and flights.

If you economise, it's possible to cut the average daily cost down to US$15, but this may limit your experience of the country and can turn your trip into more of an endurance test rather than a holiday. After all, you don't set off on a trip to put yourself through hell.

Accommodation, food and transport are the three major expenses. If you are prepared for basic conditions, you shouldn't have to spend more than US$6 a night (on average) for a budget hotel. The cost will be lower (or the standard better) if you travel in a group or, better still, as a couple.

If budget dining is what you're used to, you shouldn't have to spend more than US$10 a day on food. Because Venezuela's average temperatures are fairly high, you'll drink a lot, but soft drinks and mineral water are inexpensive.

Buses are the main means of transport and they're pretty cheap, considerably cheaper than in neighbouring Colombia and Brazil. City buses cost next to nothing. Taxis aren't expensive either, particularly when you're in a group and split the cost. They are well worth considering for trips to or from the airport or bus terminal, when you're carrying all your gear.

Most museums don't charge an admission fee – a welcome custom – and those which do, usually keep the fee well under a dollar. Cultural events (cinema, theatre, music etc) are all fairly inexpensive. On the other hand, drinking sessions in some nightclubs can deplete your funds quickly, especially if you drink at the same rate as Venezuelans.

What can really eat into your budget, however, are organised tours. They cost roughly between US$40 and US$100 per day and rarely are just day trips. A tour to Salto Angel is a considerable expense.

On the whole, travel in the countryside is cheaper than in the cities. Caracas is the most expensive Venezuelan city. There will be a hell of a difference in cost between camping on the beach for a week, and exploring Caracas night spots for the same length of time.

Prices in this book are correct as we went to press, but keep in mind that economic instability may affect them considerably.

Carrying Money

Although Venezuela is not a particularly dangerous country to travel in, you should always keep money and documents as secure as possible. The most common protection used by travellers are money belts. They come in a variety of types and styles, of which the most popular are those that can be worn around the waist. Those made of leather or cotton are more comfortable than the synthetic variety. Money belts are only useful if worn under clothing – pouches worn outside clothes attract thieves' attention and are easy prey. In order to stash the emergency cash, some travellers sew cloth pouches into their trousers or other items of clothing.

While most of your money should be well hidden, give yourself easy access to enough cash to cover your expected daily expenditure. You can then pay expenses without extracting money from your belt or pouch and attracting attention. This money is also useful in case you are assailed – muggers can become annoyed if you don't have anything for them and they may react unpredictably. Leave your wallet at home as it's an easy mark for pickpockets. Don't carry money or documents in back pockets.

Currency

The unit of Venezuelan currency is – yes, you guessed it – the bolívar. In written listings, it's abbreviated to Bs, which usually stands before the figure it refers to. There are 5, 10, 20, 50, 100, 500, 1000, 2000 and 5000 bolívar notes in circulation. There are also ½, 1, 2 and 5 bolívar coins, but they have virtually disappeared from the market. They are almost worthless.

Currency Exchange

Following are approximate exchange rates at the time of going to press.

Australia	A$1	=	Bs 324
Canada	C$1	=	Bs 353
France	1FF	=	Bs 83
Germany	DM1	=	Bs 277
Japan	¥100	=	Bs 382
New Zealand	NZ$1	=	Bs 287
United Kingdom	UK£1	=	Bs 815
USA	US$1	=	Bs 505

Changing Money

An essential question for many travellers is what to bring: cash, travellers cheques or credit cards. In Venezuela, the easiest and fastest way of getting local currency is a credit card, and you are strongly recommended to bring one with you. The next best are travellers cheques, though there are fewer places to change them and it takes more time to do it. Then there's cash, the riskiest form of carrying money, but necessary in case you are stuck off the beaten track or for some such emergency. Read what follows and decide for yourself.

Changing Cash By far the most popular foreign currency in Venezuela is the US dollar, so stick strictly to the greenback. Bring a balanced variety of denominations, large and small, to be able to pay airport departure tax, for example, if you have run out of bolívares. Other worldwide known currencies such as the pound sterling or Deutschmark can occasionally be exchanged, but places which accept them are few and far between, and the rate will usually be poor. Don't bring anything too exotic for Venezuelans like Australian dollars or Japanese yen.

The usual place to change cash is a *casa de cambio*, an authorised money exchange office. There are many in Caracas, but in other large cities there may be just a couple. Elsewhere they are virtually nonexistent except for some border towns and popular tourist destinations.

Casas de cambio change cash at a slightly lower rate than you would get for travellers cheques in the banks, but you save a lot of time, as the whole operation takes just a minute or less. Casas de cambio also sell foreign currency, mostly, or exclusively, US dollars.

Banks, which previously happily changed foreign currencies at good rates, are now very reluctant to do so. This may change in the future, so check when you arrive. Other places which may change US dollars include top-end hotels and some travel agencies, but the rate they give will usually be poorer than that in casas de cambio.

US dollars are accepted by many tour operators as payment and are also useful for buying currencies of neighbouring countries from moneychangers at the borders.

Changing Travellers Cheques The only really useful brand of travellers cheques in Venezuela is American Express. It is accepted by most outlets of the Banco Consolidado, which has a pretty wide array around the country. The bank changes cheques at a good rate and normally doesn't charge commission. Some other major banks may also exchange Amex cheques, but there are not many of them and they will usually charge commission. Some banks may occasionally change other brands of cheques and (as mentioned above) cash, but you'll be lucky to find them.

The opening hours of banks are the same throughout the country: Monday to Friday from 8.30 to 11.30 am and 2 to 4.30 pm. Banks are closed on Saturday, Sunday and public holidays. Banks are also closed on the first Monday after 6 January (Epiphany), 19 March (St Joseph's Day), Ascension Day, 29 June (St Peter's & St Paul's Day), 15 August (Assumption), 1 November (All Soul's Day) and 8 December (Immaculate Conception).

However, banks usually handle foreign exchange operations within limited hours, which sometimes can mean during morning hours only. Each branch of every bank seems to have its own schedule, which moreover can change from day to day. Some banks set limits on the number of foreign exchange operations they do per day (or the total amount of money they can change daily) so if you arrive too late they may refuse to

change your money. The best time to try is somewhere between 9 and 10 am.

Major branches in big cities are usually more reliable (and handle foreign exchange for longer times) than minor outlets in smaller provincial localities. It's always wise to change enough money to last you through to the next large city.

Another frustrating feature of Venezuelan banks is that they are almost always crowded, inefficient and painfully slow. It can easily take an hour to change travellers cheques. Local branches have to call the main bank to ask for the day's exchange rates, and sometimes they can't get through for an hour or two, or not at all, in which case they don't change money.

If you are in a provincial bank ask more than one teller whether the bank changes money. Not all tellers are sure of what the bank can do, so they usually take the safest (and easiest) line and say that no exchange is possible. And there may still be more surprises with the banks, for example:

A couple went to the Banco Consolidado in central Maracaibo to exchange their Amex cheques. A charming young teller received the signed cheques and became engrossed in her computer while processing the transaction. However, after a short while she informed the travellers that her computer revealed their cheques had been reported as lost or stolen. She then kindly advised the couple to go to the Turisol (see below) and replace their cheques. The tourists rushed to the appropriate office at the other end of the city and, after lengthy paperwork which included some international calls, the cheques were reimbursed. By the same afternoon, the travellers were back in the same bank with their brand-new cheques in hand. The same enchanting teller executed some operations on her computer and, to the tourists' astonishment, informed them that their cheques were again reported as lost. Amid a mix of disbelief and annoyance, the couple requested to see the manager. It took quite a while before the matter was sorted and the cheques eventually exchanged. Apparently, the employee was not particularly adept at using a computer ...

Your passport is required in any bank transaction. When it comes to changing cheques, some banks may also require you to produce your purchase receipt (the form titled purchase record customer's copy, which you get when buying the cheques). Make sure to carry this copy with you.

Casas de cambio rarely exchange travellers cheques, except for a few in Caracas which do offer this service. On the other hand, some tour operators will accept travellers cheques as a means of payment.

The place to report the loss or theft of Amex cheques and apply for a replacement or refund is the Turisol. It has a head office in Caracas and branches in Barquisimeto, Maracay, Valencia, Maracaibo, Mérida, Puerto La Cruz and Porlamar. See the relevant sections for addresses and phone numbers. Keep in mind that you may be asked for details of where you bought the cheques and the date of purchase.

Credit Cards

Although the use of credit cards in Venezuela is still not as common as it is in western countries, they have become wildly popular over the past decade. They can be used for cash advances from banks and ATMs, and for purchases of goods and services in a variety of establishments.

The most useful card for cash advances is Visa, as it's accepted by the largest number of banks, including Banco Unión, Banco de Venezuela, Banco Mercantil and Banco Provincial. The second best is MasterCard, which is also honoured by a number of banks. It's much easier to find a bank which will service your Visa or MasterCard than it is to find a bank which will exchange US dollars or travellers cheques. Moreover, advance payments on cards take less time than changing cheques or cash.

Many of the major banks, including those listed above, have adjacent ATMs, and they usually work fine with cards issued outside Venezuela. Some ATMs even offer a choice of instructions displayed in Spanish or English. All in all, bringing Visa or MasterCard will save you a lot of time and hassle.

The two cards, and the American Express charge card, are most useful as a means of payment. They are accepted in most upmarket hotels and restaurants, airline offices and many stores. If you plan on renting a car,

they are essential. Curiously, many regional tour operators may refuse payment by credit card, or charge 10% to 15% more if you pay with plastic money. To avoid this surcharge, get a cash advance and pay in bolívares.

Make sure you know the number to call if you lose your credit card, and be quick to cancel it if it's lost or stolen.

Black Market

During the period of state-imposed fixed exchange rates of the bolívar against foreign currencies (June 1994 to April 1996), there was a thriving black market in Venezuela, and you could get up to 70% more bolívares for your dollars on the street than in the bank or casa de cambio. Since the bolívar was floated, it seems the situation has returned to normal. This means that there's no longer a black market and you will normally change money in the bank or other authorised money-exchange office. Given the precarious state of the economy, however, this situation may change.

Tipping

In virtually every dining or drinking establishment with table service, a 10% service charge will automatically be added to the bill, so further tipping is theoretically unnecessary. In practice, few people leave any tip in budget eateries, but in upmarket restaurants, a small tip is customary. One way to avoid a service charge is to eat and drink *en la barra* (at the bar), if the place provides such a facility. The barra is common in the *tascas* (Spanish-style bar-restaurants), taverns, pubs, and in some other types of eating outlets.

Tipping in hotels is essentially restricted to four and five-star establishments, which usually have decent room service and porters, and all expect to be tipped. Going down the star ladder, the service thins out, so tipping is uncommon, unless you want to reward someone for their particularly outstanding effort, help or dedication.

Taxi drivers are normally not tipped. After all, given the fact that drivers are reluctant to use meters, or don't have them at all, the fare is often just a verbal agreement between the driver and passenger, in which case no tip is expected.

Bargaining

As in most Latin American countries, bargaining in Venezuela is a part of everyday life. Obviously, not everything is a matter of negotiation; prices of things such as airfares, goods in supermarkets, food in restaurants and rates of finer hotels are fixed, and no-one will try to bargain over them. However, since a good part of the economy is informal, quasi-legal or uncontrolled, prices for some goods and services, including products purchased at the market, bus and taxi fares, and even less reputable hotel tariffs, are to some extent negotiable.

No matter how adept your bargaining skills, you won't probably get things as cheaply as the locals can, particularly if your Spanish is limited. Nonetheless, you shouldn't be intimidated about haggling over prices. You can easily save some bolívares while buying food and handicrafts at the markets or negotiating a taxi fare, and perhaps have an occasional success in beating down a hotel price. You also should try negotiating tour fares offered by regional operators and independent guides, particularly if you are travelling in a large party. Whenever and wherever you bargain, do it in a friendly and easy-going manner, with a smile and in a jocular fashion. Don't lose your temper or express anger, even if you know that you've been given a gringo price, considerably higher than the price for locals.

Taxes

Many goods and services in Venezuela (including luxury products, hotels, restaurants, car rentals and tours) are officially subject to a 16.5% sales tax levy, called IVA *(impuesto de valor agregado)*, or value-added tax (VAT). Like many financial aspects of the local economy, however, IVA seems to be a flexible concept, and it's not exactly clear if and when you'll pay it and when you won't. For example, many upmarket hotels charge the tax, but budget residencias and posadas

usually don't do it. Some retailers will sell you products at a tax-free price, but if you ask for a *factura* (receipt), they will add the tax.

Businesses which charge IVA usually state the total price to the customer, but some list net prices. In some finer hotels, for instance, you may find a displayed price list, with a discreet comment in small print below that says *no incluye IVA* (doesn't include VAT).

POST & COMMUNICATIONS
Post

The postal service is run by Ipostel which has post offices throughout the country. There are a score of Ipostel offices in Caracas, a few in each of the other big cities but only one post office in the smaller cities and towns. The Ipostel offices in the major cities are usually open during normal office hours (8 am to noon and 2 to 6 pm, Monday to Friday), but elsewhere they tend to open later and close earlier.

Postal Rates Airmailing a letter up to 20 grams costs US$0.60 to anywhere in the Americas, US$0.80 to Europe or Africa and US$1.20 elsewhere. Letters between 20 and 50 grams cost US$1.20/1.50/2.40, respectively.

A 1kg airmail parcel costs US$12 to the Americas, US$15 to Europe or Africa and US$23 elsewhere. A 10kg parcel will cost US$50/75/120 and a 20kg parcel (the maximum weight allowed) will cost US$95/140/200. Ipostel staff will assure you it only takes eight days for a parcel to reach its destination, but you shouldn't take this claim too seriously.

It is cheaper to send parcels by surface mail. A 1kg parcel costs US$23/27/30 and a 20kg parcel costs US$36/48/56. You will be told that it will take up to a month for delivery but this is Ipostel's rather wishful thinking.

Sending Mail Ipostel service is slow, inefficient and unreliable. Air mail to the USA or Europe can take up to a month to arrive, if it arrives at all. Aerogrammes are more likely to arrive safely, although, perhaps, no quicker than stamped letters. Internal mail is also painfully slow.

A more secure way of sending letters is by certified mail *(correo certificado)*, although its delivery rate is not perfect either. Bear this in mind before sending an important letter or a valuable parcel through Ipostel. Avoid problems by using telephones, faxes, or courier services. If you are on your way to Colombia or Brazil, wait and post items from there as both these countries have more reliable postal services.

As might be expected, Ipostel's inefficiency has spawned a rash of courier services, both national and international ones. DHL and other big companies are well established in Caracas and other big cities, and offer fast and secure service at their usual rates.

Receiving Mail Expect similar problems: letters and parcels sent to Venezuela from abroad take a long time to be delivered and sometimes simply never make it. The confusing and imprecise local system of addresses only exacerbates the problems. Mail sent to an *apartado* (PO box) has a better chance of arriving safely than that posted to a home or office address.

Poste restante is handled by Ipostel offices, but if you decide to use its services in the first place, stick to the main offices in a few major cities. If you can use somebody's PO box address, it will probably be more reliable for your mail than Ipostel's poste restante service. In any case, if there's anything to be sent to you that you can't risk losing, ask your senders to use courier services.

Telephone

Venezuela's telephone network is operated by CANTV (Compañía Anónima Nacional de Teléfonos de Venezuela). This once fully state-owned company was partially privatised in 1991 and the sale of the remaining 60% of shares was negotiated when this book was researched.

In addition to CANTV, there are two cellular providers, Movilnet and Telcel. Since its introduction in 1991, cellular telephony expanded dramatically to the point that today Venezuela has the highest cellular phone per capita ratio in Latin America. In absolute terms, it comes third after Brazil and Mexico, both of which have far larger populations. Cellular phones have become both a status symbol and a more reliable alternative to CANTV's jammed lines and often inoperable public phones.

The telephone system is largely automated for both domestic and international connections. Public telephones exist in cities and large towns but many are out of order. Those which do work often have lines of people waiting to place calls. Street phones are usually the most besieged, so look for public phones in more secluded locations such as hotel lobbies, shopping centres etc. As a rule, CANTV offices have some operable phones. Also keep in mind that every metro station in Caracas has a row of public phones.

Since coins disappeared from the market, so did coin phones, and now almost all public telephones only operate on phone cards *(tarjeta CANTV)*. It's worth buying a card as soon as you arrive, unless you don't plan on calling from public phones at all. Phone cards come in denominations of 2000 and 5000 bolívares, and they are useful for local and long-distance domestic and international calls. The cards can be bought from CANTV offices, various establishments such as stationers and pharmacies, and countless street vendors.

Most of the newly installed card phones are incorporated into the long distance direct dialling system, both domestic and international, so you can call anywhere without having to place your call through an operator at the CANTV office. You will probably be obliged to call direct anyway, as most CANTV offices eliminated the service of connecting long distance calls through the operator from their offices (though they do this for customers using private phones).

Domestic Calls You can call direct to virtually every city and town in Venezuela. A three-minute local call within a city costs about US$0.10. The cost of long-distance calls rises with distance, and reaches about US$0.40 a minute for connections between the most distant localities across the country. A reduced rate *(tarifa reducida)* is applied from 7 to 11 pm, and there's an even cheaper rate *(tarifa económica)* from 11 pm to 7 am.

The area codes of the places detailed in this book have been included in the relevant sections. They are listed just under the heading of the destination. Drop the initial 0 if you are calling from abroad.

Cellular phone numbers begin with the 014 (Telcel) or 016 (Movilnet) prefix, followed by the proper seven-digit number. You don't dial any area codes beforehand. Note that calling cellular numbers eats quickly into your phone card, even if your recipient is just a block away, so try to use the regular phone system as long as you can before appealing to the cellular network.

International Calls International connections are possible to just about any corner of the world, but not all countries can be called collect (reverse charge). Theoretically, you can call abroad in any of the following ways: direct from a public phone using the phone card, direct or through the CANTV international operator from a private/office telephone that you have access to, through the operator from the CANTV office (but, as mentioned above, not many are left), and reverse-charge through the operator in the country you are calling.

When dialling direct, either from a public phone booth or from a private telephone, the call will be charged according to the length of time you were talking. The sample daytime tariffs per minute are: US$2 to the USA and Canada, US$2.50 to France and Switzerland, US$4 to the UK and Germany, and US$4.50 to Australia and New Zealand. Night-time tariffs (different hours for different countries) are up to 30% cheaper. If you place the call through the international operator, either at a CANTV office or from a private phone, the minimum charge is the same as for a three-minute call.

As you can see, the Venezuelan international telephone service is expensive, so you may be interested in calling reverse-charge *(llamada de cobro revertido)*. Fortunately, reverse-charge phone calls are possible to a number of countries, and are easy to place (see boxed text entitled Reverse-Charge Calls).

If you can't call collect, call direct using the phone card. One card doesn't allow for long conversations, but you can use a few cards without breaking the connection. Put the card in, dial your number and the telephone display will tell you when the card is empty. You then press the # button, take the empty card out and put in the new one.

The country code for Venezuela is 58. To

Reverse-Charge Calls
Calling reverse-charge (collect) will usually be much cheaper than using the Venezuelan services. What follows are the international direct-dialing numbers of some selected countries:

Australia	☎ 800-11-61-0
Canada	☎ 800-11-10-0
France	☎ 800-11-33-0
Germany	☎ 800-11-49-0
Italy	☎ 800-11-39-0
Japan	☎ 800-11-81-0
Netherlands	☎ 800-11-31-0
UK	☎ 800-11-44-0
USA (AT&T)	☎ 800-11-1-21
(MCI)	☎ 800-11-1-41
(Sprint)	☎ 800-11-1-11
(IDB)	☎ 800-11-1-51

Dialing the chosen number will put you through (free of charge) to the operator of that country, from where you can make a reverse-charge or collect call (or use your credit card). To call countries other than those listed, just replace the country code (the double digit after '11') with the code of the country you want to call.

You can dial from anywhere in Venezuela, from any private or public telephone incorporated into the international direct dialing system, and you don't need to use phone card. Don't dial '00' (Venezuela's international access code) before the numbers listed.

call a number in Venezuela from abroad, dial the international access code of the country you're calling from, the country code (58), the area code (they are given in the relevant sections, but drop the initial 0) and the local phone number.

To call abroad from Venezuela, first dial 00, which is Venezuela's international access code. A click should follow the first 0 before the next one is dialled. Then dial the country code, area code and the local number.

Fax
Faxes can be sent from major branches of CANTV offices. There's also a growing number of private companies in large cities offering fax services. The best hotels, too, will send and receive faxes for you, but will charge heavily for this already expensive service.

Email
There's still no public service offering email facilities, though there may be some providers by the time you arrive. Meanwhile, a logical strategy might be to befriend somebody with their own email account or try some travel agencies, tour operators etc connected to the Web.

BOOKS
You will get far more out of your visit if you read about the country before you go. There are plenty of books in English which cover various aspects of Venezuela, some of which are recommended below. If you want to study a particular aspect of the country in detail, have a look at *Venezuela: World Bibliographic Series* by DAG Waddell (Clio Press, Oxford and Santa Barbara, California, 1990), which lists over 800 books concerning Venezuela.

If you read Spanish, you'll find invaluable sources of information in Venezuela itself. The country publishes many books and other publications, few of which have been translated into foreign languages.

Lonely Planet
If you're planning a wider journey than just

Venezuela, consider taking LP's *South America on a Shoestring*, which covers the whole continent. Also note that LP has individual guidebooks to most Latin American countries, including Venezuela's neighbours, Brazil and Colombia. For a complete rundown, see the back of this book.

Other Guidebooks
There are some English-language guides published in Venezuela. They are almost inaccessible outside the country but you can buy them in some local bookshops.

The 925-page *Guide to Venezuela* by Janice Bauman & Leni Young (Ernesto Armitano Editor, Caracas, 1987) is not a practical companion to take on your trip, but rather a comprehensive reference book.

Ecotourism Guide to Venezuela (Miro Popić Editor, Caracas, 1996) is a bilingual Spanish/English guidebook focusing on ecological tourism. Updated annually, the guidebook features brief descriptions of all the national parks and nature reserves, plus detailed information on nearly 300 lodging options located mostly in the countryside, including protected areas.

Even more detailed is the *Guide to Camps, Posadas and Cabins in Venezuela* by Elizabeth Kline (Caracas, 1996). Also a bilingual edition, the guide details several hundred mostly rural accommodation options. Both of these publications can be particularly useful for visitors planning outdoor activities.

History & Politics
A good overview of the period of Spanish colonisation is provided by John Hemming's *The Search for El Dorado*. The book is a fascinating insight into the conquest of Venezuela and Colombia.

Equally captivating is *The Explorers of South America* by Edward J Goodman (Collier MacMillan, London, 1972) which brings to life some of the more incredible explorations of the continent, from Columbus to Humboldt. You'll read more about explorers and their studies in the following Geography & Wildlife section.

In Focus: Venezuela – A Guide to the People, Politics and Culture by James Ferguson (Latin American Bureau, London, 1994) is a good introduction to the country, as well as its history and contemporary issues. *Venezuela: the Search for Order, the Dream of Progress* by John V Lombardi (Oxford University Press, New York, Oxford, 1982) provides general reading on history, politics, geography and people.

For a comprehensive 20th-century history, try *Venezuela, a Century of Change* by Judith Ewell (C Hurst & Co, London, 1984) or *Venezuela* by David Eugene Blank (Praeger Publishers, New York, 1984). *Paper Tigers and Minotaurs* by Moisés Naim (The Carnegie Endowment for International Peace, Washington, 1993) gives a good insight into recent economic policies.

Geography & Wildlife

Venezuela's unique geological phenomenon, tepuis, has captivated explorers, scientists and writers for ages. One of the first authors attracted by the tepuis was Sir Arthur Conan Doyle who – although he had never been to Venezuela – was inspired by fabulous stories of Colonel Fawcett's explorations of the plateaux. Conan Doyle gave play to his imagination in *The Lost World* (Buccaneer Books, 1977, originally published 1912), a rollicking science-fiction tale set in a pre-historic world.

For something less fanciful, read 'Venezuela's Islands in Time', an article by Uwe George, published in *National Geographic* (May 1989). It has good general information about the tepuis and how they emerged, and is illustrated with spectacular photos of these unique formations.

The Lost World of Venezuela and its Vegetation by Charles Brewer-Carías (Caracas, 1987) looks at the mysterious and endemic plant life of the tepuis. The study contains a photographic record of the plants and describes the research carried out by the author on the top of several tepuis. The book also has a Spanish edition, but neither is easy to find in local bookshops, let alone outside Venezuela.

Another explorer's account of the tepuis is *Churún Merú, the Tallest Angel* by Ruth Robertson (Whitmore Publishing, Pennsylvania, 1975), which is the report of the expedition to Auyantepui. It was on this expedition that the height of Salto Angel was measured for the first time, confirming its status as the world's highest waterfall.

The famous German geographer and botanist Alexander von Humboldt didn't make it to the tepuis, but explored and studied other regions of Venezuela (as well as parts in Colombia, Ecuador and Peru). He describes it all in amazing detail in his three-volume *Personal Narrative of Travels to the Equinoctial Regions of America, 1799-1801*. Volume No 2 covers the Venezuelan section of his journey.

Travellers with a serious interest in South American wildlife have quite a choice when it comes to background reading and practical guides. *A Neotropical Companion: An Introduction to the Animals, Plants, and Ecosystems of the New World Tropics* by John C Kricher (Princeton University Press, Princeton, New Jersey, USA, and Chichester, West Sussex, UK, 1989) is an excellent source of information and fascinating reading. *World of Wildlife – Animals of South America* by FR de la Fuente (Orbis Publishing, 1975) is a good basic reference work. *Neotropical Rainforest Mammals – A Field Guide* by Louise H Emmons (University of Chicago Press, Chicago, 1990) is a practical guide containing descriptions and illustrations of several hundred species, many of which can be found in Venezuela.

If birds are what interest you most, you could start with *A Guide to the Birds of South America* (Academy of Natural Science, Philadelphia). Alternatively, try the valuable reference work, *The Birds of South America* by RS Ridgley & G Tudor (University of Texas Press, 1989). It comes in several volumes, and amateurs may find it extremely detailed and technical. There's also helpful *Where to Watch Birds in South America* by Nigel Wheatley (Princeton University Press, Princeton, New Jersey, 1995).

For the trip itself, get a copy of *A Guide to*

the *Birds of Venezuela* by Rodolphe Meyer de Schauensee & William H Phelps (Princeton University Press, New Jersey, 1978) which is a good, illustrated field-guide. *South American Birds – A Photographic Aid to Identification* by John S Dunning (1987) might be another good companion on your trip. A number of the bird species featured in the book are found in Venezuela. You can also consider getting the useful *Birding in Venezuela* by Mary Lou Goodwin (Sociedad Conservacionista Audubon de Venezuela, Caracas, 1994), which advises the best areas for birding and lists the bird species which can be found there. The guide is available in Venezuela (see the Caracas chapter).

A recommended rainforest guide is *Rainforests – A Guide to Research and Tourist Facilities at Selected Tropical Forest Sites in Central and South America* by James L Castner (Feline Press, Florida, 1990). This book has useful background information and has descriptions of 40 rainforests in half a dozen countries.

Society & Culture
What is probably most intriguing for foreign travellers to Venezuela is the native Indian population. By far the most complete work on the subject is the three-volume *Los Aborígenes de Venezuela* (Fundación La Salle, Caracas). Volume No 1 (1980) refers to the Indian groups of the past, whereas volume Nos 2 and 3 (1983 and 1988, respectively) feature all the major communities (15 groups) currently living in Venezuela. The work was researched and written by an international group of anthropologists and ethnologists and gives a thorough insight into the social organisation, religion and culture of each group. It is well illustrated with maps and photos. There is only a Spanish edition and it's hard to get a hold of outside Venezuela; for those who read Spanish it's a treasure-trove of information.

Internationally, the most widely publicised Indian group is the Yanomami. The tribe was considered to have an essentially Stone Age culture when it was first discovered in modern times. Perhaps the best authority on the matter is Jacques Lizot, who published a score of research studies on the group, including *Le Cercle des Feux: Faits et Dits des Indiens Yanomami* (Recherches Anthropologiques, Editions du Seuil, Paris, 1976). The work has been translated into English.

Another noted investigator of Yanomami culture is Napoleon Chagnon, whose doctoral dissertation emphasised the Indians' warrior culture. He was later criticised for this. Read 'Yanomamo, the True People', his article in the *National Geographic* (August 1976). Also, have a look into *Aborigines of the Amazon Rain Forest: The Yanomami* by Robin Hanbury-Tenison (Time Life Books, 1982).

Useful Local Publications
Coffee-table books dealing with Venezuelan nature, architecture and art often have an English-language edition in addition to the Spanish one. Some of these books are really marvellous and make great souvenirs. They can also help you to decide where to go and what to see. For example, if you were mad about colonial churches, skimming through *Templos Coloniales de Venezuela* by Graziano Gasparini (Ernesto Armitano, Caracas), which features over a hundred photos of remarkable old churches, would ensure you included the best in your itinerary.

Corpoven and Lagoven, two major oil companies, publish a wealth of material, and it's not all necessarily about oil. Corpoven's *Tierra Mágica* covers a variety of local issues such as ethnography, architecture, popular feasts and religion. Lagoven's publications tend more towards geography and natural history. It has a series of brochures dealing with national parks and wildlife. These are not commercial publications and you won't find them in bookshops. If you're particularly interested, visit either company's Caracas or Maracaibo offices, and they may give you some of their currently published stuff.

Phrasebooks & Dictionaries
Lonely Planet's *Latin American Spanish*

Phrasebook is a worthwhile addition to your backpack.

Because Spanish is one of the world's major languages there are loads of Spanish-English dictionaries available all over the world. Just as an example, the *University of Chicago Spanish-English, English-Spanish Dictionary*, is small, lightweight and good for overseas travel.

For something more comprehensive, look for the *Pequeño Larousse Español-Inglés, English-Spanish* dictionary. This detailed yet compact reference is one of the most helpful dictionaries you'll ever come across. It's published as either a single volume or as two separate volumes but contains the same amount of information in each edition.

ONLINE SERVICES
Lonely Planet's home page (www.lonely planet.com/dest/sam/ven.htm) has an overview of Venezuelan culture, general information, travel suggestions and much more.

NEWSPAPERS & MAGAZINES
All the main cities have their own daily newspapers. The two leading Caracas papers, *El Universal* (www.el-universal.com) and *El Nacional* (www.el-nacional.com), have country-wide distribution. Both have good coverage of national and international affairs, sports, economics and culture. Both cost US$0.45 except on Sunday when they cost US$0.60. Caracas has several other newspapers and periodicals, including *Economía Hoy*, *El Mundo* and *El Globo*.

The major newspaper in Maracaibo is *Panorama*, in Valencia it's *El Carabobeño*, and in Barquisimeto they have *El Informador* and *El Impulso*.

The Daily Journal is the main English-language newspaper published in Venezuela. It will keep you up to date on national politics and economics, social and cultural events and sports. It's available at major newsstands and at selected bookshops in Caracas. Elsewhere, it can be more difficult to come by.

The Guardian Weekly (Latin American Edition), is a UK paper focusing on South American issues. It comes as a supplement to the Monday edition of *Economía Hoy* newspaper, which can be easily recognised by the cream-orange colour of the paper on which it's printed.

Major international dailies and periodicals, such as *The New York Times*, *The International Herald Tribune*, *Der Spiegel*, *Le Monde*, *Time*, *Newsweek* and *The Economist*, can be bought in Caracas and some large cities from selected newsstands and bookshops. The best place to look for them is at the newsstands in five-star hotels. The easiest to get is the international satellite edition of *The Miami Herald*. It is printed in Caracas and appears the same morning as in its home city, unlike imported papers which may come a day or two late.

RADIO
There are over a hundred radio stations in Venezuela broadcasting on either AM or FM. Every fair-sized town has its own local radio station. In Caracas, there are at least 15 stations broadcasting on FM stereo alone.

Most of the programming is dominated by imported pop, rock, disco and the like. Jazz and classical music are less popular but some stations do grant them air-time. Of these, Radio Nacional, which broadcasts on 630 kHz (AM), is one of the best examples. In Caracas, La Emisora Cultural broadcasts a balanced menu of classical music, jazz and spoken programmes on 91.1 and 97.7 MHz (FM).

Almost all programmes are transmitted in Spanish. If you need English-language news, tune into the BBC World Service which can be picked up on various short wave AM frequencies.

TV
One government and three private TV stations operate out of Caracas and reach most of the country. The government-owned Venezolana de Televisión broadcasts on Channel 8, while the three commercial networks, Radio Caracas La Televisión, Venevisión and Televén, broadcast on Channels 2, 4 and 10, respectively. All four have

morning and evening news programmes and some of them also offer midday news. They all offer the usual fare, ranging from music to feature films to sports to cultural programmes. Prime-time is dominated by *telenovelas*, or soap operas, Venezuelans' favourite TV entertainment. Almost all programming is in Spanish, including foreign films which are dubbed.

A second government-owned station, Televisora Nacional (Channel 5), closed down in 1993, but there are efforts to reopen it. It featured educational and cultural programmes, news and some of the more mentally stimulating films.

Apart from the above-mentioned stations, there are several pay-TV providers, including Omnivisión, Cablevisión, Supercable and DirecTV, which offer mixed Spanish/English packages of feature films, sports, music, soap operas and news.

Satellite TV has boomed in Caracas and, to a lesser extent, in the other major cities. The *parabólica* (satellite dish) has become the ultimate status-symbol, and a feature of the Caracas skyline. They are conspicuous in the wealthier suburbs and are spreading like wildfire in other districts.

Caracas' major papers list the programmes of all TV channels and a score of satellite stations which can be picked up in the city.

VIDEO SYSTEMS

If you want to record or buy video tapes to play them back home, you won't get a picture if the image registration system is different. Venezuela uses the NTSC system, the same as in North America and Japan, but incompatible with the French SECAM system, and PAL which is used in most of Europe and Australia.

PHOTOGRAPHY & VIDEO

Given the country's spectacular and varied geography, wildlife, colonial and modern architecture, and its ethnic mosaic, there's plenty to capture on film or video. How you go about it is up to you. Some travellers are happy with a small automatic camera, while others travel with backpacks almost brimful with photographic gear.

Except for restrictions on photographing military installations and some other strategic facilities (eg oil refineries) you can take pictures almost anywhere and of just about anything. Taking photos is permitted in virtually every church and in some museums (although few allow flash).

Photography Equipment

Bring all necessary equipment from home. Cameras and accessories can be bought in Venezuela but the choice is limited, unpredictable and prices hardly welcoming. It's difficult to get cameras repaired in Venezuela, so make sure your gear is reliable.

The first thing to consider before you leave home is what camera and accessories you will need. An automatic 35mm reflex with a zoom lens is universally considered appropriate for general purposes, including landscapes, portraits and architecture. The choice between a zoom and a set of straight lenses is a matter of individual preference.

Zooms are definitely more convenient, as you can frame your shot easily and work out the optimum composition. The problem is that they absorb a lot of light and require higher speed film for photographs taken in anything but bright daylight. A fixed focal length lens may yield better results and greater clarity than a zoom, but you then have to carry several different lenses and change them according to the particular shot.

Serious wildlife photography requires a long telephoto lens. A reasonable length would be somewhere between 200 and 300mm. Of course, a 500mm lens will bring the action even closer, but it is heavier, and requires faster films and/or a tripod. Long lenses are also useful for taking photos of people, but do it discreetly and be sensitive. If necessary, ask for permission to photograph and don't insist or take a picture if permission is denied.

A wide-angle lens can be useful, sometimes indispensable, for photographing architecture or tight interiors. The macro, which comes as a standard feature in most zooms, comes in handy for taking photos of small insects, tiny flowers and the like. A UV filter is important when photographing at high altitudes to minimise the effects of ultraviolet rays.

A tripod is an important but heavy and bulky piece of equipment. It is particularly useful in dim interiors (eg churches) and may also be necessary when using long lenses. If you decide to take one, don't forget to also take a cable release. Other useful accessories include a flash, a spare set of batteries for your camera, a lens cleaning kit and plenty of silica-gel packs and plastic bags to protect your gear from humidity, dust, sand and water.

Whatever combination of lenses and accessories you decide to bring, make sure they are carried in a sturdy bag which will protect them from the elements and the hard knocks they're sure to receive. It's much better if the bag looks scruffy because it's less likely to attract the attention of thieves. And make sure your equipment is insured.

Film

Film is easy to come by and there's quite a choice in Caracas and a few of the other big cities. Elsewhere, particularly in the outback, it may be difficult to get the film type and speed you require. The price of film is comparable to, or slightly higher than, what you would spend in the USA.

Kodak, Fuji and, to a lesser extent, Agfa are the most popular brands. Negative film is found almost everywhere. Slide film, especially the high-speed and professional type, is harder to find. Prints can be processed in any number of laboratories, often within an hour or two, and the quality is usually OK, but E6 slide processing is not common and the quality is not always good. See the Caracas chapter for some hints on where to buy and process film.

Don't be caught without a healthy supply of film. And bring a variety of film – rainforests are surprisingly dark and may require fast film (eg 400 ASA) whereas the snowy peaks of the Andes and the sunny white beaches along the coast usually don't need anything faster than 50 ASA.

Heat and humidity can ruin film, so remember to keep it in the coolest, driest place available, both before and after exposure. Film should be processed soon after exposure, but don't panic about it; you might get a better result by waiting for two months to have it developed in a professional laboratory at home rather than processing it immediately in an unknown local venue.

Video

Venezuela is sufficiently safe (except perhaps for Caracas) and attractive enough to justify carrying a video camera. If you decide to bring a camcorder, don't forget to bring along a conversion plug to fit electric sockets (US flat two-pin type) if you have a different system. Remember that Venezuela's electricity is 110 volts, 60 cycles.

VHS is the standard format for recording from TV and viewing rented videos at home. Betamax exists but it is less popular. Most amateurs shooting their own videos opt for a Video 8mm system. The equipment, cassettes and accessories for all systems are available, but the variety is limited and it's expensive.

TIME

All of Venezuela lies within the same time zone, four hours behind Greenwich Mean Time. There's no daylight saving (see boxed text entitled Times in Other Cities When it is Noon in Caracas on the following page).

ELECTRICITY

Electricity is 110 volts, 60 cycles AC throughout the country. US-type flat two-pin plugs are used.

WEIGHTS & MEASURES

Venezuela uses the metric system. There's a conversion chart on the inside back cover of this book.

LAUNDRY

There are dry cleaners in large cities and it usually takes a couple of days to get your

Times in Other Cities When it is Noon in Caracas

Auckland	4 am next day
Berlin	5 pm
Bogotá	11 am
Buenos Aires	1 pm
Frankfurt	5 pm
Hong Kong	midnight
Lima	11 am
London	4 pm
Los Angeles	8 am
Melbourne	2 am next day
Mexico	10 am
Montreal	11 am
New York	11 am
Paris	5 pm
Quito	11 am
Rio de Janeiro	1 pm
San Francisco	8 am
Sydney	2 am next day
Tokyo	1 am next day
Toronto	11 am
Vancouver	8 am

clothes cleaned. Top-class hotels offer laundry facilities for guests, but prices for this service are rather high. In budget hotels, you can usually make arrangements with the hotel staff, or relatives of the staff, to have clothes washed, usually by hand, at fair rates.

Self-service laundrettes are scarce but there are quite a lot which offer service washes. They exist in the cities and many larger towns, and are particularly numerous in major tourist destinations such as Mérida and Porlamar. They may be a bit hard to find without help, but ask the locals for the *lavandería*. They are usually equipped with modern machinery, do a good job and charge reasonable fees. Most offer the full service including washing, drying and ironing, if requested. It usually takes a few hours to wash and dry, and will cost around US$2.50 for a 5kg load, detergent included.

TOILETS
There are virtually no self-contained public toilets in Venezuela. If you are unexpectedly caught in need, use a toilet in a restaurant. Choose better-looking establishments because basic eateries either don't have toilets or, if they do, you're better off not witnessing them. If you feel uncomfortable about sneaking in just to use the toilet, order a soft drink, a coffee or whatever. Museums and large shopping centres usually have toilets, as do bus and airport terminals. Toilets are usually the sit-down style, but they often lack boards, so they effectively become the squat variety.

You will rarely find toilet paper in toilets, so make sure you carry some at all times. Some toilets charge fees (normally not exceeding US$0.10), but in return you can receive a short piece of single-ply toilet paper. If it seems to be too small for your needs, don't hesitate to ask for more.

Except for toilets in some upmarket establishments, the plumbing might not be of a standard you are accustomed to. The tubes are narrow and water pressure is weak, so toilets usually can't cope with toilet paper. A wastebasket is normally provided.

The most common word for toilet is *baño*. Men's toilets will usually bear a label saying *señores*, *hombres* or *caballeros*, while women's toilets will be marked *señoras*, *mujeres* or *damas*.

HEALTH
Venezuela has a fairly well-developed health service, with an array of well-stocked *farmacias* (pharmacies), private clinics and hospitals. Sanitary conditions are better than the South American average, though the current economic decline is putting this standard at risk.

Your health while travelling depends on your predeparture preparations, your day-to-day health care and how you handle medical problems or emergencies that develop. The list of potential dangers included in this section may seem frightening, but don't panic; with some basic precautions and adequate information, few travellers experience anything more than minor stomach upsets.

This section includes preventative

measures, descriptions of symptoms and suggestions about what to do if there is a problem.

It isn't meant to replace professional diagnosis or prescription, and visitors to South America should discuss with their physician the most up-to-date methods used to prevent and treat the health threats which may be encountered.

If a serious medical problem arises during the trip, seek qualified help wherever possible, as self-diagnosis and treatment can be risky.

Your embassy or consulate can usually recommend a good place to go for medical help. So can five-star hotels, although they often recommend doctors with five-star prices – this is when medical insurance really is useful.

Predeparture Preparations

Health Insurance A travel insurance policy to cover medical problems is highly recommended. However fit and healthy you are, do take out medical insurance. Even if you don't get sick, you might be involved in an accident.

There are a wide variety of policies and your travel agent can make recommendations. The international student travel policies handled by STA and other student travel organisations are usually good value. When buying a policy, it's important to check the small print:

- Some policies specifically exclude dangerous activities which can include scuba diving, motorcycling or even trekking. If these activities are on your agenda, such a policy would be of limited value.
- You may prefer a policy which pays doctors or hospitals directly rather than you having to pay them on the spot and claim later. If you have to claim later, make sure you keep all documentation. Some policies ask you to call back (reverse charges) to a centre in your home country where an immediate assessment of your problem is made.
- Check if the policy covers ambulances or an emergency flight home – someone has to pay if you have to stretch out across a few airline seats.

Travel Health Information In the USA, you can contact the Overseas Citizens Emergency Center and request a health and safety information bulletin on foreign countries by writing to the Bureau of Consular Affairs Office, State Department, Washington, DC 20520. There's also a special telephone line (☎ (202) 632-5525) for emergencies while abroad.

The Center for Disease Control's (CDC) *Health Information for International Travel* and the World Health Organisation's (WHO) *Vaccination Certificate Requirements for International Travel & Health Advice to Travellers* are useful references. CDC has a free fax-back service in the USA (fax (404) 332-4565).

The International Association for Medical Assistance to Travelers (IAMAT) (email iamat@sentex.net) at 417 Center St, Lewiston, New York, NY 14092, can provide travellers with a list of English-speaking physicians in South America. In Canada, its address is 40 Regal Rd, Guelph, Ontario N1K 1B5. The European office is at Voirets 57, 1212 Grand Lancy, Geneva, Switzerland.

In the UK, contact the Medical Advisory Services for Travellers Abroad (MASTA) (☎ (0171) 631-4408), Keppel St, London WC1E 7HT. MASTA provides a variety of services, including health briefs and a range of medical supplies. Another source of medical information and supplies is the British Airways Travel Clinic (☎ (0171) 831-5333). The Department of Health publishes leaflets detailing travellers' health requirements, and operates a Freephone service (☎ 0800-555777).

In Australia, contact the Traveller's Medical and Vaccination Centre in Sydney (☎ (02) 9221-7133) or Melbourne (☎ (03) 9602-5788) for general health information pertaining to Venezuela and the requisite vaccinations for travel in South America. MASTA (toll-free ☎ 1800-269917) will provide an up-to-date country-specific health brief for about A$10.

There are a number of books on travel health. *Staying Healthy in Asia, Africa & Latin America* by Dirk Schroeder (Moon

Publications, 1995) is probably the best all-round guide to carry as it's detailed and well organised. *Travellers' Health* by Richard Dawood (Oxford University Press, 1995) is comprehensive, easy to read and authoritative, although it's rather large to lug around.

There are also a number of excellent travel health sites located on the Internet. From the Lonely Planet home page there are links at www.lonelyplanet.com/weblinks/wlprep.htm to the World Health Organisation and the US Center for Diseases Control & Prevention.

Medical Kit Give some thought to a medical kit for your trip. The size and contents of your first-aid kit will depend on your knowledge of first-aid procedures, where and how far off the beaten track you are going, how long you will need the kit for, and how many people will be sharing it.

It's not necessary to take every remedy for every illness you might contract during your trip. Venezuelan pharmacies stock all kinds of drugs, and medication is cheaper than in many other countries. There are few restricted drugs; almost everything is sold over the counter. Many drugs are manufactured locally under foreign licence. Be sure to check expiry dates.

Travellers should be aware of any drug allergies they may have, and avoid using such drugs or their derivatives. Since common names of prescription medicines in South America may be different from the ones you're used to, ask a pharmacist before taking anything you're not sure about.

A possible kit may include:

- Any prescription medications you normally take
- Aspirin or Panadol – for pain or fever
- Antihistamine (such as Benadryl) – useful as a decongestant for colds and allergies, to ease itching from insect bites, or to help prevent motion sickness
- Antibiotics – useful if you're travelling well off the beaten track
- Loperamide (eg Imodium) or Lomotil for diarrhoea; prochlorperazine (eg Stemetil) or metaclopramide (eg Maxalon) for nausea and vomiting.
- Rehydration mixture – for treatment of severe diarrhoea; this is particularly important if travelling with children
- Antiseptic liquid or cream and antibiotic powder – for cuts and grazes
- Calamine lotion – to ease irritation from bites or stings
- Ear and eye drops
- Foot and groin (antifungal) powder
- Bandages and band-aids
- Scissors, tweezers and a thermometer (note that mercury thermometers are prohibited by airlines)
- Insect repellent, sunscreen, chap stick and water purification tablets
- Plastic container with a sealable lid, to pack your medical kit in

Ideally, antibiotics should be administered only under medical supervision and should never be taken indiscriminately. Overuse of antibiotics can weaken your body's ability to deal with infections naturally, and can reduce the drug's efficacy in future. Take only the recommended dose at the prescribed intervals and continue using the antibiotic for the prescribed period, even if the illness seems to have been cured.

Remember that antibiotics are quite specific to the infections they treat, so if there are any serious unexpected reactions, discontinue use immediately. If you are not sure whether you have the correct antibiotic, don't use it at all.

Health Preparations Make sure you're healthy before you start travelling. Have your teeth checked and make sure they are OK.

If you wear glasses or contact lenses, bring a spare pair and your optical prescription. Losing your glasses can be a real problem, although in many Venezuelan cities you can get new spectacles made up quickly, cheaply and competently.

At least one pair of good-quality sunglasses is essential because there is strong glare, and dust and sand can get into the corners of your eyes. A hat, sunscreen lotion and lip protection are also important.

If you require a particular medication take an adequate supply with you, as it may not be available locally. Take the original prescription specifying the generic rather than the brand name; it will make getting replacements easier. It's also wise to have the prescription with you to prove you're using the medication legally. Customs and immigration officers may get excited at the sight of syringes or mysterious powdery preparations. The organisations listed under Travel Health Information can provide medical supplies and multilingual customs documentation.

Immunisations No immunisations are necessary for Venezuela, unless you are coming from an area infected with cholera or yellow fever. However, the further off the beaten track you go, the more necessary it is to take precautions. All vaccinations should be recorded on an International Health Certificate, which is available from your physician or government health department.

Plan your vaccinations ahead of time; some of them require an initial shot followed by a booster, and some vaccinations should not be administered at the same time. Most travellers from western countries will have been immunised against various diseases during childhood, but your doctor may still recommend booster shots. The period of protection offered by vaccinations differs widely. Note that some are not advisable for pregnant women.

The list of possible vaccinations includes:

Cholera Venezuelan authorities may require that you have a cholera vaccination if you are coming from an infected area, particularly from Colombia where there were outbreaks in recent years. In Venezuela itself there has been an outbreak recently. However, the World Health Organisation no longer recommends cholera vaccination as the vaccine offers incomplete and unreliable protection.

Hepatitis The most common travel-acquired illness after diarrhoea which can put you out of action for weeks. Havrix 1440 is a vaccination which provides long term immunity (possibly more than 10 years) after an initial injection and a booster at six to 12 months. Gamma globulin is not a vaccination but a ready-made antibody collected from blood donations. It should be given close to departure because, depending on the dose, it only protects for two to six months. Combined hepatitis A and hepatitis B vaccina-

tions, Twinrix and Vaqta, are also available. These combined vaccinations are recommended for people wanting protection against both types of viral hepatitis. Three injections over a six month period are required.

Polio This has been wiped out in Venezuela, but is endemic in Brazil, where outbreaks have been reported in the southern states. Westerners will usually have had an oral polio vaccine while at school, but you should undertake a booster course if more than 10 years have elapsed since your last vaccination.

Tetanus Most people in developed countries have been vaccinated against this disease at school age. Boosters are necessary every 10 years and are recommended as a matter of course.

Typhoid Protection lasts for three years and is useful if you are travelling for longer periods in rural tropical areas. The vaccination consists of two injections, taken four weeks apart, so you have to think well ahead, especially if you plan on having other vaccines. You may get some side effects, such as pain at the injection site, fever, headache and a general feeling of being unwell.

Yellow Fever Protection lasts 10 years and is recommended for all travel in South America. You usually have to go to a special yellow fever vaccination centre. Vaccination isn't recommended during pregnancy, but if you must travel to a high-risk area, it is probably better to take the vaccine.

Basic Rules

Paying attention to what you eat and drink is the most important health rule. Stomach upsets are the most common travel health problem, but most of these upsets will be relatively minor. Don't be paranoid about trying local food – it's part of the travel experience and you wouldn't want to miss it.

Water & Drinks The tap water in Caracas and several other large cities is considered safe to drink, but it's better to avoid it, and that's pretty easy; bottled water and soft drinks are readily available in shops, supermarkets, restaurants, bakeries etc. Outside the big cities, tap water should never be drunk. Generally speaking, if you don't know for certain whether or not the water is safe, don't drink it. This goes for ice as well.

In rural areas, take care with fruit juice, particularly if water may have been added. Milk should be treated with suspicion because it is often unpasteurised. Boiled milk is fine if it is kept hygienically, and yoghurt is always good. Hot tea or coffee should also be OK, since the water will probably have been boiled. Even in the most remote villages bottled drinks are almost always available.

Problems begin when you venture into wilderness areas, where there are no Coca Cola stands. One solution is to bring drinkable water with you, the other is to purify local water. The simplest way of purifying water is to boil it thoroughly; technically this means boiling it for 10 minutes. Remember that at higher altitudes, water boils at lower temperatures, so germs are less likely to be killed.

Simple filtering will not remove all dangerous organisms, so if you cannot boil suspect water, it should be treated chemically. Chlorine tablets (Puritabs, Steritabs or other brand names) will kill many but not all pathogens. Iodine is an effective water purifier and is available in tablet form (such as Potable Aqua), but follow the directions carefully and remember that too much iodine is harmful. If you can't find tablets, tincture of iodine (2%) or iodine crystals can be used.

Food Salads and fruit should, theoretically at least, be washed with purified water, or peeled whenever possible. Ice cream is usually OK, but beware of street vendors selling ice cream that has melted and been refrozen. Thoroughly cooked food is safe but not if it has been left to cool or if it has been reheated. Take great care with shellfish or fish, and avoid undercooked meat. If a place looks clean and well run and if the vendor also looks clean and healthy, then the food is probably all right. In general, places that are packed with locals will be fine, while empty restaurants are questionable.

Nutrition If your diet is poor or you're travelling hard and fast and missing meals, you can soon start to lose weight and place your health at risk.

It's important to make sure that your diet is well balanced. Eggs, beans, lentils and nuts are all safe sources of protein. Fruit you can peel (bananas, oranges or mandarins, for example) is always safe and a good source of vitamins. Eat sufficient rice and bread. Remember that although food is generally safer if it is cooked well, overcooked food loses much of its nutritional value. If your diet isn't well balanced or if your food intake is insufficient, it's a good idea to take vitamin and iron pills.

Most of Venezuela is hot lowland terrain, so make sure you drink enough – don't rely on thirst alone to tell you when to drink. Not needing to urinate or dark-yellow urine are signs of dehydration. Always carry a water bottle with you on trips off the beaten path. On the other hand, excessive drinking can cause excessive sweating. This can lead to a loss of salt resulting in muscle cramps. If you find that your sweat is not salty, add more salt than usual to your food.

Everyday Health Normal body temperature is 37°C (98.6°F); more than 2°C higher is a high fever. A normal adult pulse rate is 60 to 80 beats per minute (children 80 to 100, babies 100 to 140). You should know how to take a temperature and a pulse rate. As a general rule, the pulse increases about 20 beats per minute for each °C rise in fever.

Respiration rate can also be an indicator of health or illness. Count the number of breaths per minute; between 12 and 20 is normal for adults and older children (up to 30 for younger children, 40 for babies). People who have a high fever or serious respiratory illness (like pneumonia) breathe more quickly than normal. More than 40 shallow breaths a minute usually means pneumonia.

Many health problems can be avoided by taking care of yourself. Wash your hands frequently – it's quite easy to contaminate your own food. Clean your teeth with purified water rather than water which has come straight from the river. Avoid extremes of temperature – keep out of the sun when it's hot, dress warmly when it's cold.

Some diseases can be avoided by dressing sensibly. Worm infections can be caught by walking barefoot, and dangerous cuts are likely if you walk over coral without shoes. Avoid insect bites by covering bare skin and using insect repellents or a mosquito net at night. Seek local advice – if you're told water is unsafe due to crocodiles or piranhas, obviously don't go in.

Environmental Hazards

Altitude Sickness Popularly referred to as *soroche*, altitude sickness, and its more serious form known as acute mountain sickness (AMS), occur at high altitudes and in extreme cases can be fatal. They are caused by ascending to high altitudes so quickly that the body does not have time to adapt to the lower oxygen concentration in the atmosphere. Light symptoms can appear at altitudes as low as 2500m, and they become increasingly severe the higher you go. Most people are affected to some extent at altitudes between 3500 and 4500m. You may reach these altitudes if trekking in the Andes around Mérida.

The best way to minimise the risk of altitude sickness is to ascend slowly, to increase liquid intake and to eat meals containing energy-rich carbohydrates. Even with acclimatisation, however, you may still have trouble if you visit high-altitude areas. Headaches, nausea, dizziness, a dry cough, breathlessness and loss of appetite are the most frequent symptoms. As long as they remain mild, there's no reason to panic, but the ascent should be halted and the sufferer watched closely and given plenty of fluids and rest. If the symptoms become more pronounced or there is no improvement after a few hours, descend to a lower altitude.

Often a descent of a few hundred metres is enough to provide considerable relief. Descend further and rest for a day or two. Don't take risks with altitude sickness; many people have died because they have ignored the early symptoms and pressed on to higher altitudes.

Altitude sickness is completely unpredictable – youth, fitness or experience at high altitudes are no protection. Even people who have had no problems at high altitudes before may suddenly suffer altitude sickness at relatively low altitudes.

Diarrhoea Simple things like a change of water, food or climate can all cause a mild bout of diarrhoea, but a few rushed toilet trips with no other symptoms is not indicative of a major problem.

Dehydration is the main danger with any diarrhoea, particularly in children or the elderly as dehydration can occur quite quickly. Under all circumstances *fluid replacement* (at least equal to the volume being lost) is the most important thing to remember. Weak black tea with a little sugar, soda water, or soft drinks allowed to go flat and diluted 50% with clean water are all good. With severe diarrhoea a rehydrating solution is preferable to replace minerals and salts lost. Commercially available oral rehydration salts (ORS) are very useful; add them to boiled or bottled water. In an emergency you can make up a solution of six teaspoons of sugar and a half teaspoon of salt to a litre of boiled or bottled water. You need to drink at least the same volume of fluid that you are losing in bowel movements and vomiting. Urine is the best guide to the adequacy of replacement – if you have small amounts of concentrated urine, you need to drink more. Keep drinking small amounts often. Stick to a bland diet as you recover.

Lomotil or Imodium can be used to bring relief from the symptoms, although they do not actually cure the problem. Only use these drugs if you do not have access to toilets eg if you *must* travel. For children under 12 years Lomotil and Imodium are not recommended. Do not use these drugs if the person has a high fever or is severely dehydrated.

In certain situations antibiotics may be required: diarrhoea with blood or mucous (dysentery), any fever, watery diarrhoea with fever and lethargy, persistent diarrhoea not improving after 48 hours and severe diarrhoea. In these situations gut-paralysing drugs like Imodium or Lomotil should be avoided.

A stool test is necessary to diagnose which kind of dysentery you have, so you should seek medical help urgently. Where this is not possible the recommended drugs for dysentery are norfloxacin 400mg twice daily for three days or ciprofloxacin 500mg twice daily for five days. These are not recommended for children or pregnant women. The drug of choice for children would be co-trimoxazole (Bactrim, Septrin, Resprim) with dosage dependent on weight. A five-day course is given. Ampicillin or amoxycillin may be given in pregnancy, but medical care is necessary.

Amoebic dysentery is more gradual in the onset of symptoms, with cramping abdominal pain and vomiting less likely; fever may not be present. It will persist until treated and can recur and cause other health problems.

Giardiasis is another type of diarrhoea. The parasite causing this intestinal disorder is present in contaminated water. The symptoms are stomach cramps, nausea, a bloated stomach, watery, foul-smelling diarrhoea and frequent gas. Giardiasis can appear several weeks after you have been exposed to the parasite. The symptoms may disappear for a few days and then return; this can go on for several weeks. Tinidazole, known as Fasigyn, or metronidazole (Flagyl) are the recommended drugs. Treatment is a 2gm single dose of Fasigyn or 250mg of Flagyl three times daily for five to 10 days.

Fungal Infections Hot-weather fungal infections are most likely to occur between the toes or fingers or around the groin. The infection is spread by infected animals or humans; you may contract it by walking barefoot in damp areas, for example.

To prevent fungal infections wear loose, comfortable clothes, avoid artificial fibres, wash frequently and dry thoroughly. Use thongs (flip-flops) while taking a shower in bathrooms of cheap hotels.

If you become infected, wash the infected area daily with a disinfectant or medicated soap, and rinse and dry well. Apply an antifungal powder, expose the infected area to air or sunlight as much as possible, and wash all towels and underwear and change them often.

Heat Exhaustion Serious dehydration or salt deficiency can lead to heat exhaustion. Salt deficiency, which can be brought on by diarrhoea or vomiting, is characterised by fatigue, lethargy, headaches, giddiness and muscle cramps. Salt tablets may help. The best way to avoid heat exhaustion is by drinking lots of liquids and eating salty foods.

Heatstroke This very serious and sometimes fatal, condition can occur if the body's heat-regulating mechanism breaks down and the body temperature rises to dangerous levels. Long, continuous periods of exposure to high temperatures can leave you vulnerable to heatstroke. Alcohol intake and strenuous activity can increase chances of heatstroke, especially among new arrivals to a hot climate.

Symptoms include minimal sweating, a high body temperature (39°C to 40°C), and a general feeling of being unwell. The skin may become flushed and red. Severe throbbing headaches, decreased coordination, and aggressive or confused behaviour may be signs of heatstroke. Eventually, the victim may become delirious and go into convulsions. Get the victim out of the sun, if possible, remove clothing, cover with a wet towel and fan continually. Seek medical help as soon as possible.

Hypothermia Too much cold is just as dangerous as too much heat, and may lead to hypothermia. There are not many really cold areas in Venezuela, but nonetheless hypothermia can be a threat in the highest reaches of the Andes and, occasionally, on the top of Roraima.

Hypothermia occurs when the body loses heat faster than it can produce it. It is caused by exhaustion and exposure to cold, wet or windy weather. It is surprisingly easy to progress from being very cold to dangerously cold due to a combination of wind, wet clothing, fatigue and hunger, even if the air temperature is well above freezing.

It is best to dress in layers; silk, wool and some of the new artificial fibres are all good insulating materials. A hat is important because a lot of heat is lost through the head. A strong, waterproof outer layer is essential, and keeping dry is vital. Carry food containing simple sugars to generate heat quickly, and lots of fluid to drink.

Symptoms of hypothermia include exhaustion, numb skin (particularly toes and fingers), shivering, slurred speech, irrational or violent behaviour, lethargy, stumbling, dizzy spells, muscle cramps and violent bursts of energy.

To treat hypothermia, get sufferers out of the wind or rain, remove their clothing if it's wet and replace it with dry, warm garments. Give them hot liquids – not alcohol – and easily digestible food. This should be enough for the early stages of hypothermia, but if it has gone further, it may be necessary to place sufferers in a sleeping bag and get in with them in order to provide as much warmth as possible.

If no improvement is noticed within a few minutes, seek help, but don't leave the victim alone while doing so. The body heat of another person is more important in the short term than medical attention.

Motion Sickness If you are prone to motion sickness, try to choose a place that minimises disturbance – near the wing on an aircraft, midship on a boat or between the front and the middle of a bus. Eating lightly before and during a trip will reduce the chances of motion sickness. Fresh air almost always helps, while reading or cigarette smoking make matters worse.

Commercial motion-sickness preparations, which can cause drowsiness, have to be taken before the trip; if you're already feeling sick, it's too late. Dramamine tablets, one of the most popular medications, should be taken three hours before departure. Ginger can be used as a natural preventative and is available in capsule form.

Prickly Heat This is an itchy rash caused by excessive perspiration trapped under the skin. It usually strikes people who have just arrived in a hot climate and whose pores have not yet opened sufficiently to cope with increased sweating. Frequent baths and application of talcum powder will help relieve the itchiness.

Sunburn The sun's rays in tropical zones are more direct and concentrated than in temperate zones. In highland areas, such as the Andean region, you will be additionally exposed to hazardous UV rays and can become sunburnt surprisingly quickly, even through cloud. Use a sunscreen and take extra care to cover areas which are not normally exposed to sunlight – for example, your feet. A hat provides added protection, and sunglasses will prevent eye irritation (especially if you wear contact lenses).

Infectious Diseases
Cholera This disease is transmitted orally by the ingestion of contaminated food or water. The symptoms, which appear one to three days after infection, consist of a sudden onset of acute diarrhoea with rice water stools, vomiting, muscular cramps, and extreme weakness. You need medical attention but your first concern should be rehydration. Drink as much water as you can – if it refuses to stay down, keep drinking anyway. If there is likely to be a considerable delay in getting medical treatment, begin a course of Tetracycline, but it should not be administered to children or pregnant women.

Hepatitis Hepatitis is a general term for inflammation of the liver. It is a common disease worldwide. The symptoms are fever, chills, headache, fatigue, feelings of weakness and aches and pains, followed by loss of appetite, nausea, vomiting, abdominal pain, dark urine, light-coloured faeces, jaundiced (yellow) skin and the whites of the eyes may turn yellow. **Hepatitis A** is transmitted by contaminated food and drinking water. The disease poses a real threat to the western traveller. You should seek medical advice, but there is not much you can do apart from resting, drinking lots of fluids, eating lightly and avoiding fatty foods. People who have had hepatitis should avoid alcohol for some time after the illness, as the liver needs time to recover.

Hepatitis E is transmitted in the same way and can be extremely serious in pregnant women.

There are almost 300 million chronic carriers of **Hepatitis B** in the world. It is spread through contact with infected blood, blood products or body fluids, for example through sexual contact, unsterilised needles and blood transfusions, or contact with blood via small breaks in the skin. Other risk situations include having a shave, tattoo, or having your body pierced with contaminated equipment. The symptoms of type B may be more severe and may lead to long term problems. **Hepatitis D** is spread in the same way, but the risk is mainly in shared needles.

Hepatitis C can lead to chronic liver disease. The virus is spread by contact with blood – usually via contaminated transfusions or shared needles. Avoiding these is the only means of prevention.

HIV & AIDS Like almost everywhere else, these diseases have become a concern in Venezuela. Although there are no credible statistics, it's estimated that at least 100,000 Venezuelans are HIV-positive. HIV (Human Immunodeficiency Virus), is likely to develop into AIDS (Acquired Immune Deficiency Syndrome). It is impossible to detect the HIV-positive status of an otherwise healthy-looking person without a blood test. In South America HIV/AIDS is transmitted primarily through sexual contact between heterosexuals.

HIV/AIDS can also be contracted through infected blood transfusions; and you should be aware that most developing countries cannot afford to screen blood for transfusions. The virus may also be picked up through injection with an unsterilised needle. Acupuncture, tattooing and ear or nose piercing are other potential dangers. There is currently no cure for AIDS.

Schistosomiasis Also known as bilharzia, this disease is carried in water by minute worms. The disease is found in rivers and streams in north-central Venezuela.

The worm enters through the skin and attaches itself to your intestines or bladder. The first symptom may be a tingling and sometimes a light rash around the area where it entered. Weeks later a high fever may develop. A general feeling of being unwell may be the first symptom, or there may be no symptoms. Once the disease is established abdominal pain and blood in the urine are other signs. The infection often causes no symptoms until the disease is well established (several months to years after exposure) and damage to internal organs irreversible.

Avoiding swimming or bathing in fresh water where bilharzia is present is the main method of preventing the disease. Even deep water can be infected. If you do get wet, dry off quickly and dry your clothes as well.

A blood test is the most reliable test, but it will not show positive in results for a number of weeks.

Sexually Transmitted Diseases Sexual contact with an infected partner can result in you contracting a number of diseases. While abstinence is 100% effective, the use of a condom lessens the risk of infection considerably.

The most common sexually transmitted diseases are gonorrhoea and syphilis, which in men first appear as sores, blisters or rashes around the genitals and a discharge or pain when urinating. Symptoms may be less marked or not present at all in women. Syphilis' symptoms eventually disappear but the disease continues and may cause severe problems in later years. Gonorrhoea and syphilis are treatable with antibiotics.

Typhoid This is gut infection which travels via contaminated water and food. Vaccination against typhoid is not 100% effective and, since it is one of the most dangerous infections, medical attention is necessary if you are infected. Early symptoms are similar to those of many other travellers' illnesses – you may feel as though you have a bad cold or the flu combined with a headache, a sore throat and a fever. The fever rises a little each day until it exceeds 40°C, while the pulse rate slows – unlike a normal fever where the pulse increases. These symptoms may be accompanied by vomiting, diarrhoea or constipation.

In the second week, the high fever and slow pulse continue and a few pink spots may start to appear on the body. Trembling, delirium, weakness, weight loss and dehydration set in. If there are no further complications, the fever and other symptoms will slowly fade during the third week. Medical attention is essential, however, since typhoid is extremely infectious and possible complications include pneumonia or peritonitis (burst appendix).

When feverish, the patient should be kept cool and watch for dehydration. The recommended antibiotic is Chloramphenicol.

Worms These parasites are common in most humid, tropical areas. They can be present on unwashed vegetables or in undercooked meat, or you can pick them up through your skin by walking barefoot. Infestations may not show up for some time and although they are generally not serious, they can cause further health problems if left untreated. A stool test on your return home is not a bad idea if you think you may have contracted them. Once the test pinpoints the problem, medication is usually available over the counter and treatment is easy and short.

The most common form you're likely to contract are hookworms. They are usually caught by walking barefoot on infected soil. The worms bore through the skin, attach themselves to the inner wall of the intestine and proceed to suck your blood, resulting in abdominal pain and sometimes anaemia.

Insect-Borne Diseases
Malaria This serious and potentially fatal disease is spread by mosquito bites. If you are travelling in endemic areas it is extremely important to avoid mosquito bites and to take

tablets to prevent this disease. Symptoms range from fever, chills and sweating, headache, diarrhoea and abdominal pains to a vague feeling of ill-health. Seek medical help immediately if malaria is suspected. Without treatment malaria can rapidly become more serious and can be fatal.

If medical care is not available, malaria tablets can be used for treatment. You need to use a malaria tablet which is different to the one you were taking when you contracted malaria. The treatment dosages are mefloquine (two 250mg tablets and a further two six hours later), or fansidar (single dose of three tablets). If you were previously taking mefloquine then alternatives are halofantrine (three doses of two 250mg tablets every six hours) or quinine sulphate (600mg every six hours). There is a greater risk of side effects with these dosages than in normal use.

A vaccine against malaria has recently been invented by a Colombian scientist, Manuel Elkin Patarroyo. It's still in the experimental stage and, so far, hasn't been introduced on the market, but commercialisation is expected soon. Check with the World Health Organisation (WHO) because Patarroyo granted it exclusive rights for the production and distribution of the vaccine.

You can get antimalarial tablets in pharmacies in Venezuela, but primary prevention should always be to avoid mosquitoes. The mosquitoes that transmit malaria bite from dusk to dawn and during this period travellers are advised to:

- Wear light coloured clothing
- Wear long trousers and long-sleeved shirts
- Use mosquito repellents containing the compound DEET on exposed areas
- Avoid highly scented perfumes or aftershaves
- Use a mosquito net – it may be worth bringing your own.

Mosquitoes are prevalent throughout Venezuela and can live up to about 3000m. However, the anopheles, ie those which can transmit the disease, are mostly confined to lowland areas. The risk of infection is higher during the wet season. The areas of greatest risk include the Amazonas, Los Llanos and the Orinoco Delta.

The symptoms of malaria only appear several weeks after contraction, which may lead to confusion in diagnosis. By the time symptoms appear, you may be home and local doctors will not be looking for such an exotic disease. Make sure you give your doctor details of your trip.

Yellow Fever This is found in most of South America, except for the Andean highlands and the southern part of the continent. This viral disease, which is transmitted by mosquitoes, first manifests itself as fever, headaches, abdominal pain and vomiting. There may appear to be a brief recovery before it progresses into its more severe stages, including possible liver failure. There is no treatment apart from keeping the fever as low as possible and avoiding dehydration. The yellow fever vaccination gives good protection for 10 years, and is highly recommended for every person travelling on the continent.

Cuts, Bites & Stings
Cuts & Scratches In warm, moist, tropical lowlands, skin punctures can easily become infected and may have difficulty healing. Even a small cut or scratch can become infected and this can lead to serious problems.

The best treatment for cuts is to cleanse the affected area frequently with soap and water and to apply an antiseptic cream. Whenever possible, avoid using bandages, which keep wounds moist and encourage the growth of bacteria. If the wound becomes tender and inflamed, use a mild, broad-spectrum antibiotic. Remember that bacterial immunity to certain antibiotics may build up, so it's not wise to take these medicines indiscriminately or as a preventative measure.

Coral cuts are notoriously slow to heal because coral injects a weak venom into the wound. Avoid coral cuts by wearing shoes when walking on reefs.

Bites & Stings The plethora of ants, gnats, mosquitoes, bees, spiders, flies and other exotic creatures living in Venezuela means that you may experience a variety of bites and stings. Some are more dangerous or annoying than others, but it's best to protect yourself from bites altogether. Cover your skin, especially from dusk to dawn when many insects, such as malaria-transmitting mosquitoes, feed. The problem is more serious in rural areas than in cities, and dense rainforests are probably the worst.

Wear long-sleeved shirts and long trousers, instead of T-shirts and shorts, and wear shoes instead of sandals or thongs. Use insect repellent on exposed skin and, if necessary, spray it over your clothes. Sleep under a mosquito net if you are outdoors or if your hotel room does not have a sufficiently strong fan. Burning incense also lowers the risk. Good repellents, mosquito nets and incense are available in Venezuela.

If you are bitten, avoid scratching, as this easily opens bites and may cause them to become infected. Use creams and lotions which alleviate itching and deal with infection. They are sold in local pharmacies.

Bee and wasp stings are usually more painful than dangerous. Calamine lotion will give some relief and ice packs will reduce the pain and swelling.

Body lice and scabies mites are common, but shampoos and creams are available to eliminate them. In addition to hair and skin, clothing and bedding should be washed thoroughly to prevent further infestation.

Bedbugs love to live in the dirty mattresses and bedding of seedy hotels. If you see spots of blood on bedclothes, look for another hotel. Bedbugs leave itchy bites; calamine lotion may help alleviate them.

Leeches may be present in damp rainforests. They attach themselves to your skin and suck your blood. Trekkers may get them on their legs or in their boots. Salt or a lighted cigarette end will make them fall off. Do not pull them off because the bite is more likely to become infected and the head of the leech can remain in your body. An insect repellent may keep them away.

Vaseline, alcohol or oil will persuade a tick to let go. You should always check your body if you have been walking through a tick-infested area because ticks can spread typhus. They like the warmest parts of the body and often go to the genital area or the armpits, so be sure to inspect all of these areas.

It's rather unlikely that you'll get stung by a scorpion or a spider, but if you do, it may be severely painful (though rarely more than that). They tend to shelter in shoes and clothing, so check them before putting them on. Also, check your bedding or sleeping bag before going to sleep.

Snakebite There's only a small chance of being bitten by a snake in Venezuela, but you should take precautions. To minimise the chances of being bitten, wear boots, socks and long trousers when walking through undergrowth. A good pair of canvas gaiters will further protect your legs. Don't put your hands into holes and crevices, and be careful when collecting firewood. Check shoes, clothing and sleeping bags before use.

Snakebites do not cause instantaneous death and antivenenes are available. If someone is bitten, it's vital that you identify the snake immediately, or at the very least, are able to describe it. Keep the victim calm and still, wrap the bitten limb tightly, as you would a sprain, then attach a splint to immobilise it. Seek medical help immediately and, if possible, bring the dead snake along for identification.

Don't attempt to catch the snake if there is a chance of being bitten again. Tourniquets and sucking out the poison are now comprehensively discredited.

If you plan on a serious expedition into the wilderness, antivenenes for some local snakes (but not all) can be bought at the Universidad Central de Venezuela (UCV) in Caracas. Antivenenes must be kept at a low temperature, otherwise their efficiency quickly decreases. It's a good idea to carry a field guide with photographs and detailed descriptions of snakes.

Women's Health
Gynaecological Problems Sexually transmitted diseases are a major cause of vaginal problems. Symptoms include a smelly discharge, painful intercourse and sometimes a burning sensation when urinating. Male sexual partners must also be treated. Medical attention should be sought and remember in addition to these diseases HIV or hepatitis B may also be acquired during exposure. Besides abstinence, the best thing is to practise safe sex using condoms.

Antibiotic use, synthetic underwear, sweating and contraceptive pills can lead to fungal vaginal infections when travelling in hot climates. Maintaining good personal hygiene, and loose-fitting clothes and cotton underwear will help to prevent these infections.

Fungal infections, characterised by a rash, itch and discharge, can be treated with a vinegar or lemon-juice douche, or with yoghurt. Nystatin, miconazole or clotrimazole pessaries or vaginal cream are the usual treatment.

Pregnancy Most miscarriages occur during the first three months of pregnancy, so this is the most risky time to travel. The last three months should also be spent within reasonable reach of good medical care because serious problems can develop at this stage. Pregnant women should avoid all unnecessary medication, but vaccinations and malarial prophylactics should still be taken when possible. Additional care should be taken to prevent illness and particular attention should be paid to diet and nutrition.

Less Common Diseases
Rabies Rabies is present in most of South America. It is caused by a bite or scratch by an infected animal. Bats and dogs are the most notorious carriers. Any bite, scratch or lick from a mammal should be cleaned immediately and thoroughly. Scrub the site with soap and running water and then clean it with an alcohol solution. If there is any possibility that the animal is infected, medical help should be sought. Even if the animal

is not rabid, all bites should be treated carefully because they can become infected or result in tetanus. Avoid any animal that appears to be foaming at the mouth or acting strangely. If bitten, try to capture the offending animal for testing. If that's impossible, you must assume the animal is rabid. Rabies is fatal if untreated, so don't take the risk. Medical attention should not be delayed.

Treatment consists of a series of injections (usually seven) around the navel over consecutive days. A rabies vaccination is now available and should be considered if you intend to spend a lot of time around animals.

Tetanus This potentially fatal disease is difficult to treat but is easily prevented by immunisation. Tetanus occurs when a wound becomes infected by a germ which lives in human and animal faeces. Clean all cuts, punctures and animal bites.

Tetanus is also known as lockjaw because the first symptom may be a stiffening of the jaw and neck or difficulty swallowing; this can be followed by painful convulsions of the jaw and body.

Typhus This is spread by ticks, mites and lice. It begins as a severe cold followed by a fever, chills, headaches, muscle pains and a body rash. There is often a large and painful sore at the site of the bite, and nearby lymph nodes become swollen and painful.

Trekkers may be at risk from cattle or wild

Health Glossary

This basic glossary of illnesses and other health-related terms may be useful. See the Language section in the Facts about the Country chapter for emergency terms and phrases.

abortion – *aborto*
AIDS – *SIDA (síndrome de inmunodeficiencia adquirida)*
allergy – *alergia*
antibiotic – *antibiótico*
bite – *picadura* (insect, snake) *mordedura* (dog)
blood – *sangre*
blood test – *examen de sangre*
cold or flu – *gripe*
cholera – *cólera*
condom – *condón*
cough – *tos*
cramp (menstrual) – *cólico*
cramp (muscular) – *calambre*
cut – *cortadura, cortada*
diarrhoea – *diarrea*
disease – *enfermedad*
dizziness – *mareo*
dysentery – *disentería*
earache – *otitis, dolor de oído*
fatigue – *fatiga, cansancio*
fever – *fiebre*
headache – *dolor de cabeza*
heart attack – *ataque cardíaco, infarto*
hepatitis – *hepatitis*
health – *salud*
heatstroke – *insolación*
HIV – *VIH (virus de inmunodeficiencia humana)*
injection – *inyección*

insurance – *seguro*
itching – *ardor*
malaria – *malaria*
medication – *droga, medicamento, remedio*
miscarriage – *aborto*
nausea – *náusea*
pain – *dolor*
penicillin – *penicilina*
contraceptive pills – *pastillas anticonceptivas*
pneumomia – *pulmonía*
polio – *polio*
pregnancy – *embarazo*
prescription – *receta, fórmula*
rabies – *rabia*
rash – *escozor, rasquiña*
stomach – *estómago*
symptom – *síntoma*
syringe – *jeringa*
sore throat – *dolor de garganta*
sunburn – *quemadura de sol*
tablets – *pastillas*
tetanum – *tétano*
toothache – *dolor de muelas*
typhoid – *fiebre tifoidea*
vaccination – *vacuna*
vomiting – *vómito*
weakness – *debilidad*
wound – *herida*
yellow fever – *fiebre amarilla*

game ticks. Seek local advice about whether or not ticks are present in the area and check yourself carefully after walking in suspect areas. A strong insect repellent can help.

Back Home
Be aware of illnesses after you return home; take note of odd or persistent symptoms of any kind, get a check-up and remember to give your physician a complete travel history. Most doctors in temperate climates will not be looking for unusual tropical diseases. If you have been travelling in malarial areas, have yourself tested for the disease.

WOMEN TRAVELLERS
Like most of Latin America, Venezuela is very much a man's country. Machismo and sexism are palpable throughout society, so it's not difficult to imagine how a gringa travelling by herself is regarded.

Women travellers will attract more curiosity, attention and advances from local men than they would from men in the west. Many Venezuelan men will stare at women, use endearing terms, make comments on their physical appearance and, in some cases, try to make physical contact. It is just the Latin-American way of life, and local males would not understand if someone told them that their behaviour constituted sexual harassment. On the contrary, they would argue that they are just paying the woman a flattering compliment.

Gringas are often seen as exotic and challenging conquests. Local males will quickly pick them out in a crowd and use a combination of body language and flirtatiousness to capture their attention. These advances may often be light-hearted, but can sometimes be more direct and rude.

Men in large cities, especially when they are in male-only groups, and particularly when they are drunk, will generally display more bravado and be more insistent than those in small villages. To balance things a little, some male travellers have reported that they themselves felt hassled by Venezuelan women, who are seen as being rather sexually aggressive.

The best way to deal with unwanted attention is usually to ignore it. Maintain your self-confidence and assertiveness and don't let macho behaviour disrupt your holiday. Dressing modestly may lessen the chances of you being the object of macho interest, or at least make you less conspicuous to the local peacocks. Wearing a wedding band and carrying a photo of a make-believe spouse may minimise harassment.

Don't follow local fashions in dressing. Most Venezuelan women are dressed up and beautifully turned out – whether it is on the beach or the bus. You can guarantee they will wear lots of make-up, high heels and plenty of gold, silver and bright colours on usually skintight clothes.

Harassment aside, women travelling alone face more risks than men. Rape is a potential danger. Women are often targets for bag-snatchers and assault, but female travellers need not walk around Venezuela in a constant state of fear. Just be conscious of your surroundings and aware of situations that could be dangerous. Shabby barrios, solitary streets and beaches, and all places considered male territory, such as bars, sports matches, mines and construction sites should be considered risky. Do not hitchhike alone.

There isn't much in the way of women's support services in Venezuela, let alone resources specifically for women travellers. Books which might be worth looking at before the trip include *Handbook for Women Travelers* by Maggie & Jemma Moss (Piatkus Publishers) and *Women Travel – Adventures, Advice & Experience* by Natania Jansz & Miranda Davies (Prentice Hall).

GAY & LESBIAN TRAVELLERS
Homosexuality isn't illegal in Venezuela, but the overwhelmingly Catholic society tends to both deny and suppress it.

The gay and lesbian movement is still very underdeveloped. Caracas has the largest gay and lesbian community and the most open gay life, and therefore is the best place to make contacts and get to know what's going on. Get as much information there as you can, because elsewhere in Venezuela it can be difficult to contact the community.

Gay bars, discos and other venues are limited to the larger cities, but because of social pressures they come and go frequently. Again, Caracas offers the largest choice.

DISABLED TRAVELLERS

Venezuela offers very little to people with disabilities. Wheelchair ramps are available only at a few upmarket hotels and restaurants, and public transport will be a challenge for any person with mobility problems. Hardly any office, museum or bank provides special facilities for disabled travellers, and wheelchair-accessible toilets are virtually non-existent.

Much to blame for the lack of any infrastructure is the general perception of handicapped people. The relatively enlightened attitudes towards disability that prevail in many countries haven't yet taken hold in Venezuela. Here, as in much of the developing world, people with visible disabilities are expected to beg, sell lottery tickets on the street, or stay at home. They are generally not perceived as capable of living a normal active life, let alone handle the rigours of travelling.

Organisations

Disabled travellers in the USA might like to contact the Society for the Advancement of Travel for the Handicapped (☎ (212) 447-SATH; fax (212) 725-8253), 347 Fifth Ave, Suite 610, New York, NY 10016. In the UK, a useful contact is the Royal Association for Disability & Rehabilitation (☎ (0171) 242-3882), 25 Mortimer St, London W1N 8AB. You may also be interested in picking up *Nothing Ventured: Disabled People Travel the World* (Rough Guides), which provides helpful general advice.

SENIOR TRAVELLERS

By and large, senior travellers may often expect more respect and help from locals than young visitors. This attitude doesn't necessarily prevail with some attendants in shops, bank tellers and employees of public institutions. The difference in attitudes towards the youth and elderly is likely to be more pronounced among rural communities.

As far as discounts go, senior travellers get airfare reductions on Avensa (30%) and Aeropostal (50%) flights, and on airfares of some other carriers. So far, there are no discounts for senior citizens on bus fares, accommodation rates, cinema and theatre tickets etc.

TRAVEL WITH CHILDREN

As with most Latin Americans, Venezuelans adore children. Due to a high rate of population growth, children are a significant proportion of the population, and they are omnipresent. Few foreigners travel with children in Venezuela, but if you do plan on taking along your offspring, he or she will easily find plenty of local companions.

Children enjoy numerous privileges on local transport and in accommodation and entertainment. Age limits entitled to particular freebies or discounts vary from place to place, but are rarely rigidly enforced. Free rides on buses and the Caracas metro formally mean that the child doesn't occupy a separate seat, but this is not always the case.

Basic supplies are usually no problem in the cities. There are quite a few shops devoted to kids' clothes, shoes and toys, and you can buy disposable nappies and baby food in supermarkets and pharmacies. Health is a bit more of a problem, given numerous potential hazards (refer to the Health section earlier in this chapter). For general suggestions on how to make a trip with kids easier, pick up the current edition of Lonely Planet's *Travel with Children*.

DANGERS & ANNOYANCES

Venezuela is a relatively safe country to travel in, though robbery is becoming more common, and violent crime is on the increase in large cities. Caracas is the most dangerous place in the country and you should take care while strolling about the streets, particularly at night. Elsewhere, you can travel more peacefully, but you should nonetheless always observe basic precautions and use common sense.

This section covers a variety of potential dangers and may look alarming, but don't panic; the intention is not to frighten you by listing how many bad things can happen to you, but to demonstrate how many things you can do to prevent mishap.

Predeparture Precautions

When choosing things for your trip, try to take only those items which you are prepared to lose, such as used clothes, a cheap watch or an ordinary rain jacket. Take as little as possible as the less you carry with you, the less you have to lose. Don't bring jewellery, chains or anything flashy – this will only increase the chances of robbery. Don't bring anything of such sentimental value that its loss would cause significant grief. If you have to take an expensive item (such as a camera), try to make sure it's a standard model which is easy to replace.

The only guarantee of replacement is to have travel insurance. A good policy is essential for two reasons – it gives you peace of mind while travelling (because you know that a loss won't ruin you or the trip), and it gives you the actual security of replacement if something is lost (touch wood). Loss through violence or petty theft is always a stressful experience, but an insurance policy can relieve some of the pain.

If you are careful about choosing what you take, you'll find there is only a handful of items which you really wouldn't like to lose, including money, documents, your passport and air-tickets. Keep these items as secure as possible (see Carrying Money in the Money section earlier in this chapter). Take photocopies of your documents (see Photocopies in the Visas & Documents section, also in this chapter).

It's best if your backpack is fitted with double zippers, which can be secured with small combination locks. Padlocks are also good, but are easier to pick. A thick backpack cover or modified canvas sack improves protection against pilfering, the planting of drugs, and general wear and tear. A spare combination lock or padlock is useful for replacing the padlocks on your hotel door.

A swanky camera bag is not a good idea; take something less conspicuous. Many travellers carry their photographic equipment in day packs. If you have a choice, bring a plain day pack rather than one which is a fluorescent orange or purple. If you wear glasses, secure them with an elastic strap to prevent them falling off and breaking, and to deter petty theft.

Travelling with a friend or two is theoretically always safer than travelling on one's own. An extra pair of eyes makes a lot of difference.

Precautions on the Road

Firstly, don't put all your eggs in one basket; distribute your valuables about your person and luggage to avoid the risk of losing everything in one fell swoop. It's a good idea to carry a small emergency packet containing important records of your passport, cheques, credit cards, tickets etc plus a few US$20 bills. While keeping the packet separately in a safe place, for example sewn inside your trousers, always keep in mind that good-looking, expensive clothes are also appreciated by robbers.

Try not to attract the attention of thieves and robbers. Your dress is an important piece of information for them. One rule that works quite well in risky areas is the shabbier you look, the better, but use common sense and wear more decent clothes in less dangerous places. Your dress should be casual and inexpensive.

If you carry a day pack, it's safer to wear it strapped to your front rather than on the back, so you can keep a constant eye on it. Many local youths now carry their packs that way, particularly in Caracas, so you won't stand out in a crowd. If you carry a handbag, keep it in the hand away from the street – there have been some reports about purse-snatchers in Caracas, operating from motor-bikes.

If you're in a bus terminal, restaurant, shop or any other public place and have to put your day pack down, put your foot through the strap. If you have a camera, don't wander around with it dangling over your shoulder or around your neck – keep it out of sight as much as possible. In genuinely risky areas, you shouldn't carry your camera at all. If you have to, for whatever reason, camouflage it the best you can – an ordinary plastic bag from a local supermarket is one possible way to disguise it.

Behave confidently when you're on the street; don't look lost or stand with a blank expression in the middle of the street or in front of the bus terminal. Helpless-looking tourists are favourite targets of thieves and robbers.

Before arriving in a new place, make sure you have a map or at least a rough idea about orientation. Try to plan your schedule so you don't arrive at night, and use a taxi if this seems the appropriate way to avoid walking through risky areas. Be vigilant and learn to move like a street-smart local.

Keep your eyes open while you're leaving your hotel, bank, casa de cambio etc. Look around to see whether there is anyone watching you, and if you notice you're being followed or closely observed, let them understand that you are aware and alert.

If you happen to be in a crowded place (urban bus, market, bus terminal, busy street etc) keep a close eye on your pockets and day pack. Even if you have a cheap watch, it's better to keep it in your pocket rather than on your wrist – it attracts attention.

On intercity bus journeys, put your backpack in the luggage compartment, where it will be relatively safe. Don't put your day pack or handbag on the floor or on the luggage rack – keep it under your arm next to you or, if you are with a companion, wedge it between the two of you. On long night bus rides, it is better if one of your party is awake.

Theft & Scams

Theft is the most common travellers' danger. Generally speaking, the problem is more serious in the largest cities, with Caracas being the worst. The more rural the area, the quieter and safer it is. Favourite settings for thieves are crowded places such as markets, festivals and fiestas, bus terminals and buses (both long-distance and urban).

The most common methods of theft are snatching your day pack, camera or watch, pickpocketing, or taking advantage of a moment's inattention to pick up your gear and run away. Distraction is often part of the thieves' strategy.

Thieves often work in pairs or groups; one or more will distract you, while an accomplice does the deed. There are hundreds, if not thousands, of possible ways to distract you, and new scams are dreamt up every day. Here are some common ones: someone 'accidentally' bumps into you (sometimes throwing you off balance); a group of strangers appear in front of you and greet you jovially as if you were lifelong friends; a woman drops her shopping bag right at your feet; a character spills something on your clothes or your day pack; several kids start a fight around you. Try not to get distracted – of course, it's easier said than done.

Some thieves are even more innovative and will set up an opportune situation to separate you from your belongings. They may begin by making friends with you, or pretend to be the police and demand to check your belongings. Their imagination is infinite in this respect, so keep your wits about you. Stay aware of changes and innovations by talking to other travellers on the road.

Mugging

Mugging is far more dangerous than theft. Armed hold-ups are rare in Venezuela except in Caracas, where they have become more common over the last few years. The favourite places for robbery are slum areas, but some Caracas gangs have been known to work the central districts during daylight hours. The usual weapon is a knife, but guns are not unheard of.

The assault usually goes something like this: you are stopped on the street by a man or, more often, a group of men; they show you a knife to be better understood and either ask for your money and valuables, or set about searching for themselves. Even if they don't show you a knife, you can take it for granted that they have one. They will usually be satisfied with your day pack, watch and a bundle of notes you keep in your pocket for daily expenditure, but some more determined criminals may keep searching trying to get to your money belt. If this is the case, it's best to give them whatever they are after. Don't try to escape or struggle – your chances are slim. Don't count on any help from passers-by.

Police

Cases of police corruption, abuse of power and use of undue authority have been known, so it's probably best to stay a safe distance from them if you don't need them, just in case. This, of course, doesn't mean that they will stay away from you.

In the cities, ID checks by the police are not common but they do occur, so always have your passport with you. If you don't you may end up at the police station. By law, you must carry your passport with you at all times. A certified photocopy of the passport is not a legal identity document, although some police officers may be satisfied with it.

While travelling in the countryside, you'll experience plenty of stops at alcabalas (road checkpoints operated by the police or, more often, by the Guardia Nacional). They stop and control traffic, including cars, trucks and public buses. They check the identity documents of the driver and passengers and, sometimes, search their luggage.

If you do get your passport, valuables and/or other belongings stolen or robbed, go to the nearest PTJ (Policía Técnica Judicial) office to make a *denuncia*, a report. The officer on duty will write a statement according to what you tell them. It should include the description of the events and the list of stolen articles. Pay attention to the wording you use, make sure you include every stolen item and document, and carefully check the statement before signing it to ensure it contains exactly what you've said. They will give you a copy of the statement, which serves as a temporary identity document, and you will need to present it to your insurer in order to make a claim. Don't expect your

things to be found, as the police are unlikely to even try to do anything about it. Stolen cars and motorcycles should also be reported at the PTJ.

If you happen to get involved with the police, keep calm and be polite, but not overly friendly. Don't get angry or hostile – it only works against you.

Be wary of criminals masquerading as plain-clothes police. They may stop you on the street, identify themselves with a fake ID, then request to inspect your passport and money. If you follow suit, forget about your stuff. If you hesitate, the 'officers' may try to persuade you to go with them to the 'police station' in their car or in a taxi (which are, of course, as genuine as the officers themselves), and probably will clean you out in the vehicle. Under no circumstances should you agree to a search or a lift. Call a uniformed police officer, if there happens to be one around, or decent-looking passers-by to witness the incident, and insist on phoning a bona fide police station. By that time, the 'officers' will probably walk discreetly away.

This scam is still rare in Venezuela, but it's well known in other South American countries including Colombia, and this sort of disease spreads quickly over the borders.

Drugs

The presence of Colombian cocaine in Venezuela is on the rise. Drugs pass through Venezuela en route to US and European destinations. The number of locals involved in drug trafficking is increasing and so is corruption and other crimes that accompany this illicit business. Fortunately, planting drugs on tourists in order to extort bribes hasn't, as yet, been reported.

Keep well away from drugs, don't carry even the smallest quantity, and watch carefully while police officers search your luggage. Always refuse if a stranger at an airport asks you to take their luggage on board as part of your luggage allowance. Needless to say, smuggling dope across borders is a crazy idea. Have you ever seen the inside of a Venezuelan prison?

Some isolated cases of drugging tourists with *burundanga* have recently been reported. Burundanga – which also comes from Colombia, where it is widespread – is a drug used by thieves to eliminate the victim's ability to respond, and thus clean them out without resistance. The drug can be added to virtually any substance – sweets, cigarettes, chewing gum, spirits, beer – and it has no noticeable taste or smell. It is then offered to the potential victim. If circumstances appear suspicious, think twice before accepting a cigarette from a stranger or a drink from a new friend.

LEGAL MATTERS

Foreigners here, as elsewhere, are subject to the laws of the host country. Penalties for trafficking, possessing and using illegal drugs are stiff in Venezuela, and sentences usually end up with long jail terms.

While your embassy or consulate is the best stop in any emergency, bear in mind that there are some things it cannot do for you. These include getting local laws or regulations waived because you're a foreigner, investigating a crime, providing legal advice or representation in civil or criminal cases, getting you out of jail, and lending you money. A consul can, however, issue emergency passports, contact relatives and friends, advise on how to transfer funds, provide lists of reliable local doctors, lawyers and interpreters, and visit you if you've been arrested or jailed.

BUSINESS HOURS

The office working day is theoretically eight hours long, usually from 8 am to noon and 2 to 6 pm, Monday to Friday. In practice, offices tend to open later and close earlier, and the opening hours for the public may be only until 4 pm. Some offices in Caracas are adopting the so-called *horario corrido*, a working day without a lunch break, which finishes two hours earlier. However, it's nearly impossible to arrange anything between noon and 2 pm, as most of the staff are at lunch anyway.

All banks in Venezuela have the same business hours and keep pretty close to them (see the Money section). Most tourist offices are closed on Saturday and Sunday, and travel agencies usually only work on Saturday until noon.

As a rough guide only, the usual shopping hours are from 9 am to 6 or 7 pm, Monday to Saturday. Many shops close for lunch but some work without a lunch break. Large stores and supermarkets in the cities usually stay open until 8, 9 or sometimes even 10 pm, and some also open on Sunday. Shopping hours vary considerably from shop to shop and from city to countryside. In remote places, opening hours are shorter and are often taken less seriously.

Pharmacies alternate Sunday and all-night opening. Check local newspapers for the list of pharmacies on 24-hour duty. You can recognise them by a board or a neon sign saying TURNO (on duty).

Most of the better restaurants in the larger cities, particularly in Caracas, tend to stay open until 11 pm or midnight (some stay open even longer), whereas restaurants in smaller towns often close by 9 pm or earlier. Many restaurants simply don't open at all on Sunday.

The opening hours of museums and other tourist sights vary greatly. Most museums are closed on Monday but are open on Sunday. The opening hours of churches are even more difficult to pin down. Some are open all day, others for only certain hours, while the rest remain locked except during mass, which in some villages may be only on Sunday morning.

PUBLIC HOLIDAYS

Official public holidays include 1 January (New Year's Day), Monday and Tuesday before Ash Wednesday (Carnival), Maundy Thursday and Good Friday (Easter), 19 April (Declaration of Independence), 1 May (Labour Day), 24 June (Battle of Carabobo), 5 July (Independence Day), 24 July (Bolívar's Birthday), 12 October (Discovery of America) and 25 December (Christmas Day).

SPECIAL EVENTS

Given the strong Catholic character of Venezuela, many feasts and celebrations follow the Church calendar. Accordingly, Christmas, Easter, Corpus Christi and the like are celebrated all over the country. The religious calendar is dotted with saints' days, and every village and town has its own patron saint – you can take it for granted the locals will be holding a celebratory feast on that day. In many cases, solemn church ceremonies are accompanied by popular feasts that may include beauty pageants and bullfights. Some events are celebrated throughout the country, but most are local, confined to a particular region or town.

One of the biggest nationwide events is Carnaval, which takes place on the Monday and Tuesday prior to Ash Wednesday. Feasting usually breaks out by the end of the preceding week. The festival is characterised by plenty of music and dancing, parades and masquerades, bullfighting and *toros coleados* (local sort of rodeo), lots of food and, particularly, beer and spirits. Carnaval varies from region to region in terms of its length, intensity and character. In Santa Elena de Uairén, for example, it has a distinct Brazilian feel, a reflection of the town's proximity to that border. Carúpano is known nationwide for its elaborate Carnaval, as is, to a lesser extent, El Callao.

One of the most colourful regional events is the Diablos Danzantes, or the Dancing Devils. It's held on Corpus Christi in San Francisco de Yare and several other villages in Venezuela's central north. The ceremony consists of a parade and the ritual dance of devils, performed by dancers disguised in elaborate, if grotesque, masks and costumes.

Cultural events such as festivals of theatre, film or classical music, are almost exclusively confined to Caracas.

Venezuela's main religious and cultural events include:

Paradura del Niño – Mérida state; January.
La Divina Pastora – Barquisimeto; 14 January.
Feria de San Sebastián – San Cristóbal; second half of January.

Carnaval – throughout the country; February or March.
Semana Santa – processions on Maundy Thursday and Good Friday in many towns; March or April.
Festival Internacional de Teatro – Caracas; April of even years.
Velorio de la Cruz de Mayo – throughout the country; May.
Diablos Danzantes – San Francisco de Yare, Chuao, Naiguatá and some other villages in the region; Corpus Christi, May or June.
Fiesta de San Juan – Curiepe, Higuerote, Chuao, Cuyagua and many other towns of the central coastal region; dances to drum music, with an African flavour (the region is the centre of black culture); 23 & 24 June, but usually extending till 28 June.
Fiesta de la Virgen María – La Asunción (Isla de Margarita); 15 August.
Fiesta de la Virgen de Coromoto – Guanare; 8 September.
Fiesta de Nuestra Señora del Valle – Valle del Espíritu Santo (Isla de Margarita); 8-15 September.
Feria de la Chinita – Maracaibo; 18 November.

ACTIVITIES

Venezuela has much to offer those who love the great outdoors. Its 40-odd national parks provide a good choice of walks ranging from easy, well-signposted trails to jungle paths where a machete might be a useful tool. If you arrive in Venezuela at Caracas, try Parque Nacional El Ávila first before heading for less developed trails in Guatopo, Henri Pittier, San Esteban and Canaima national parks.

Sierra Nevada de Mérida is the best region in Venezuela for high-mountain trekking and, if you're up to it, you can try mountaineering and rock climbing there; guides and equipment are available in Mérida. Incidentally, Mérida state is also the best area for mountain bike riding, which has become quite popular; bikes and guides can be hired in the city.

Mérida is also the best place to go paragliding. It's a relatively new activity but is becoming widespread in Caracas and Mérida. Double gliders are available, so even greenhorns can try this breathtaking experience.

Rafting is also gaining in popularity. So far, organised rafting trips are run on some

Andean rivers (arranged in, again, Mérida) and over Orinoco rapids (arranged in Puerto Ayacucho).

Some national parks, including Morrocoy, Henri Pittier and Yacambú, are good for wildlife watchers, and particularly for bird-watchers. You can go on your own, combining hiking and bird-watching, or if you'd prefer a more comfortable way to observe wildlife, go to one of the hatos in Los Llanos, where a boat or a jeep will take you on a guided safari through the animal world.

With 3000km of coastline, beach enthusiasts can sunbathe to their hearts' content. Snorkelling and scuba diving is good in some areas, including the Archipiélago Los Roques and Mochima national park, and in both these places local operators offer courses and diving trips, and rent relevant equipment. Sailing is another attractive option, but unless you come with your own yacht you'll need a fat wallet to hire one.

Fishing enthusiasts can try their luck on the coast or they can go fishing in rivers; the Orinoco and some of its tributaries are good places for this. Before you go fishing, enquire about seasonal permits at the Inparques offices if you plan on fishing in national parks; and the Ministerio de Agricultura y Cría in Caracas for fishing in rivers and lakes outside the parks.

Speleologists can explore some of Venezuela's several hundred caves. The longest and possibly the most spectacular is the Cueva del Guácharo. If you want to visit its galleries which are closed to the general public, you need a special permit from Caracas. Enquire at the Inparques office.

COURSES

Spanish language courses are available in some large cities, of which Caracas and Mérida offer the widest choice (see the relevant chapters for details).

WORK

Travellers looking for paid work on the spot in Venezuela will probably be disappointed. First of all, to work legally, you need a work visa, and getting one is a journey through hell. It's a complex and lengthy paperwork procedure, and it's practically impossible to start the process unless you already have a job lined up. Secondly, wages are low in Venezuela, unless you are a highly qualified specialist. Lastly, forget about unskilled casual jobs (such as picking grapes or playing waiter, which you might remember fondly from your trips to more developed countries), as there will always be plenty of competing Venezuelans eager to work for much less than you would ever expect to be paid.

Qualified English teachers have perhaps the best chance of getting a job, yet it's not that easy. Try English-teaching institutions, such as Centro Venezolano Americano, the British Council, linguistic departments at universities and private language schools. If you don't have bona fide teaching credentials, you may still try to organise some informal arrangements, eg giving private language lessons.

If you are interested in voluntary work with an emphasis on environmental protection, contact environmental organisations (see the Ecology & Environment section in the Facts about the Country chapter), which may sponsor some projects in Venezuela. Enquire well in advance of your trip.

ACCOMMODATION

Accommodation listed in Places to Stay sections of this book is ordered according to price, from the bottom to the top. Where sections are broken down into price categories the bottom-end accommodation includes anything costing less than about US$15 for a double room, the middle bracket covers hotels rated from approximately US$15 to US$30 per double, and the top end is anything over US$30 a double. Caracas has slightly higher price brackets – see that chapter for details.

Venezuela doesn't belong to Hostelling International and has no youth hostels. In some resorts, mostly on the coast, locals rent out rooms in their homes to provide additional accommodation for beachgoers, who arrive en masse on weekends and holidays.

Camping

Purpose-built campgrounds – fenced-off compounds for camping equipped with electricity, running water, showers, a cooking area and caravan facilities – are virtually non-existent in Venezuela. What you can find here are bivouac sites, or just open grounds for camping with scarce or, more often, no facilities, but even these places are few and far between.

Locals who go for their holidays with camping in mind, pitch their tents wherever they feel like doing so, practically anywhere outside urban centres. Accordingly, if you plan on camping, follow the local style. Camping on the beach is particularly popular (that's where most local holidaymakers go), but be careful and don't leave your tent unattended.

If you camp in wilderness or other fragile areas, try to minimise your impact on the environment. Ideally, all the food residue, cigarette butts and other rubbish should be removed.

If there are no toilet facilities, select a site at least 50m from water sources, and bury waste. If possible, burn used toilet paper or bury it well. And use biodegradable soap products. Wash dishes and brush your teeth well away from watercourses. Make sure you have a sufficient stock of sturdy bags to take your garbage out of the area.

Hotels

There are heaps of hotels for every budget and it's usually easy enough to find a room, except perhaps on major feast days. The cheapies tend to be grouped together in certain areas, such as around the market, bus terminal and in the back streets of the city centre.

Top-class hotels, on the other hand, are usually scattered around the wealthier districts, which aren't necessarily close to the centre. You can expect to find at least one mid-priced hotel on the Plaza Bolívar or in its immediate vicinity.

Bottom End Budget places to stay appear under a variety of names such as *hotel*, *residencia, hospedaje, posada* and *pensión*. The last two are meant to be small, family-run guesthouses. Posadas, which have mushroomed recently in both the cities and countryside, often have more character and offer more personalised attention than the rest, but not always. Don't jump to conclusions by just seeing the label on the door; check inside.

Most of the cheapies have a private bathroom (in this book simply called bath), which includes a toilet and shower. The bathroom is sometimes separated from the room by only a partial partition (eg a section of wall which doesn't even reach the ceiling), and there is hardly ever a door between the two areas. Note that cheap hotel plumbing can't cope with toilet paper, so throw it in the wastebasket which is normally provided.

As most of the country lies in the lowland tropics, a fan or air-conditioning is a staple in cheap hotel rooms, but hot water in the shower is rare. Air-conditioning may not always be advantageous. The equipment often dates from oil-rich years and, after a decade or more of use, it may be in a desperate state of disrepair and as noisy as a tank. There's usually only the on/off alternative, and it's not always clear which is better. Sometimes they're *very* efficient and turn the room into a freezer; at other times they don't cool the room at all.

Always have a look at the room before booking in and paying. When inspecting the room, make sure the toilet flushes and the water runs in the shower. Check that the fan (or air-conditioning) works and that the lock on the door is sufficiently secure. If you're not satisfied with the room you're shown, ask to see another. After checking in, you'll usually get a towel, a small piece of soap and a roll of toilet paper.

One more factor to consider before deciding which room to take is TV noise. Venezuelans enjoy TV, so many budget hotels provide a set in the reception area for their clients, and it is usually kept at top volume until late at night. Since the insulation between the rooms and corridors is often very flimsy, TV noise can be a nightmare. Look around to see where the noise-making box stands and try to take a room as far from it as possible. Check also that there isn't a bar or taberna downstairs or next door, especially on a Friday or Saturday night.

Love hotels, or places which rent rooms by the hour (informally known as *tiraderos*), are common in Venezuela. Many cheap hotels double as love hotels, and it's often impossible to recognise them and to avoid staying in one from time to time. They are probably as safe as other places (the guests have more interesting things on their minds than stealing your belongings), and the staff normally keep the sex section separate from other hotel rooms.

The price of cheap hotels is roughly similar throughout the country (except in Caracas, where it's higher) and doesn't seem to depend much on whether you're in a big city or a small town, or whether the place is touristy or not. Count on roughly US$5 to US$7 for a single room *(habitación sencilla)* and US$6 to US$10 for a double *(habitación doble)*. In this book, a double denotes a room with two beds. Many hotels don't have singles and the cheapest is the so-called *habitación matrimonial*. This is a room with one wide double bed intended for couples. It often costs the same for one as for two, so travelling as a couple considerably reduces the cost of accommodation. Payment is almost exclusively upfront and by cash.

By and large, hotels are safe places, but certain precautions and common sense are always advisable. Most budget places lock their doors at night, and some even keep them locked during the day, opening them only for guests. The biggest danger of being ripped-off is most likely to come from other guests. The thieves' task is made easier by partial hardboard partitions between rooms and flimsy catches and easily-picked padlocks on doors. Hotels provide padlocks, but it's recommended that you use your own combination lock (or padlock) instead. As a rule, bigger hotels are less safe than smaller ones because the atmosphere is more impersonal and a thief won't stand out in a crowd.

Some budget hotels offer a deposit facility which practically means that the management will guard your gear in their own room as there are no other safe places. This reduces the risk but doesn't eliminate it completely. In most cheapies, the staff won't want to give you any receipt for receiving your valuables, and if you insist on one, they may simply refuse to guard them. Decide for yourself if it's safe.

Middle & Top End Mid-range hotels provide more facilities although they often lack character. They will almost always have private baths, but air-conditioning may be equally noisy as in the cheapies. Some of these hotels are very reasonably priced for what they offer, and you may sometimes find an excellent place for, say, US$20 per double room. Others are outrageously overpriced. It's a good idea to inspect the room in these hotels before you commit yourself.

In top-end hotels, you can be more sure about standards, including silent central air-conditioning and a reception desk open round the clock with proper facilities to safeguard guests' valuables. However, prices vary greatly and don't always reflect quality. Except for Caracas, where prices seem to be inflated, you can normally grab a quite posh double with all facilities for somewhere between US$50 and US$80.

Only Caracas and Isla de Margarita, and to a lesser extent Puerto La Cruz and Maracaibo, have a reasonable choice of five-star hotels. Be prepared to pay about US$100 upwards for a single and US$120 upwards for a double.

Hotels charge foreigners a 10% tax on top of the room price, though few budget places do it. The prices listed in this book have included this tax already. Most top-end hotels will accept payment by credit card, but some may charge you more if you pay with a card. Make it clear before checking in and, if necessary, get an advance on your card from a bank or ATM and pay in cash.

Campamentos

The *campamento* (literally camp) is a place

to stay in the countryside, which often also provides food and tours (which can be optional or compulsory). The campamento can be anything from a rustic shelter with a few hammocks to a posh country lodge with a swimming pool and its own airstrip. Most commonly, however, it will be a collection of *cabañas* (cabins) plus a restaurant. Until recently quite scarce, today camps spring up like mushrooms in the most remote areas.

Campamento is rarely a place for just an overnight stop on the road, but rather a destination in itself and a base for tours organised from there. Most camps are off the beaten track anyway, and some are sheltered deep in the wilderness and accessible by a jeep track or sometimes only by air.

Some more upmarket camps require you to buy an all-inclusive package which covers lodging, full board and tours. This usually has to be done in advance at a designated travel agency or from the camp's representative. The cost of such packages can easily reach hundreds of dollars. Tours offered in the package depend on the region's characteristics and may include anything from walks in the environs to wildlife safaris by jeep or boat, bird-watching, fishing or even helicopter flights.

FOOD

Venezuelans eat well and restaurants are abundant. On the whole, food is good and relatively inexpensive, although this can depend on where and what you eat. Apart from a variety of typical local dishes, there are plenty of western cuisines available. Gourmets will enjoy their stay in Caracas which offers the widest range of eating establishments and international cuisines.

Since Venezuela is one of the most Americanised countries on the continent, there's a dense array of gringo fast-food outlets including McDonald's and Pizza Hut. Spanish and Italian restaurants are well represented thanks to the sizeable migration from these two countries. There are also some good Chinese and Middle Eastern restaurants, mostly in the main cities. For self-caterers, there's a satisfactory choice of supermarkets and shops.

Budget travellers should look for restaurants which serve the so-called *menú del día* or *menu ejecutivo*, a set lunch consisting of soup and a main course, which is cheaper than any à la carte dish. Depending on the establishment, the set lunch will cost between US$2 and US$4.

A cheap alternative might be spit-roasted chicken, served at a variety of restaurants, including specialist chicken eateries called *pollo en brasas*. Half a chicken with arepa, potatoes, yucca or another side dish shouldn't cost more than US$4. Another budget option is the *arepa*, a wonderful Venezuelan snack (see the Food & Drink Glossary) for about US$1 to US$1.50, served in places called *areperas*, which are everywhere.

For breakfast, go to any of the ubiquitous *panaderías* (bakeries), which serve sandwiches, pastries and a variety of typical snacks, plus invariably delicious espresso. The market is, as in most of South America, a good cheap option, offering food which is usually tasty and fresh.

Etiquette and table manners are more or less the same as in the west and there are no particular oddities to observe. When beginning a meal, it's good manners to wish your fellow diners *buen provecho*, which means bon appetit. When drinking a toast, the Spanish equivalent of cheers is *salud*.

Venezuelan Cuisine

Venezuelan cuisine is varied and regional. The most typical snacks and dishes, collectively referred to as *comida criolla*, include *arepa*, *cachapa*, *hallaca*, *hervido*, *lechón*, *mondongo*, *muchacho*, *pabellón criollo* and *sancocho*. See the Food & Drink glossary at the back of the book for details.

DRINK

Nonalcoholic Drinks Espresso coffee is strong and excellent in Venezuela. It's served in panaderías and a variety of other establishments. Ask for *café negro* if you want it black; for *café marrón* if you prefer half coffee half milk; or *café con leche* if you like very milky coffee.

Fruit juices are popular and readily available in restaurants, *fuentes de soda, fruterías, refresquerías* and other eating outlets. Given the variety of fruit in the country, you have quite a choice. Juices come either pure or watered-down *(batidos)*, or as milk shakes *(merengadas)*.

Bottled and canned soft drinks *(refrescos)* can be bought everywhere (accordingly, you can find empty bottles and cans everywhere).

Alcoholic Drinks The favourite alcoholic drink is beer, particularly Polar beer which is the dominant brand. It is sold everywhere in either cans (0.3 litre) or bottles (0.22 litre) and costs about US$0.30 in shops and US$0.40 in the cheapest bars and eateries. The Brazilian Brahma beer is now making inroads into the local market.

The local production of wine is small and the quality poor, except for the acceptable Altagracia wines. There are plenty of imported wines available from other South American countries, Europe and the USA. Chilean and Argentine wines are fine and come at affordable prices, but European wines are expensive, especially so in restaurants.

Among spirits, *ron* (rum) heads the list and comes in numerous varieties and different quality. The Ron Añejo Aniversario Pampero is the best dark rum Venezuela produces. The 0.75-litre bottle, elegantly packed in a leather pouch, will cost about US$8 in a liquor store. If you want to take one home, buy it in the city; it's rarely available in the airport duty-free shops.

ENTERTAINMENT
Cinemas
Movies are popular and there are cinemas in almost every town. In Caracas alone, there are more than 40 cinemas. Most movies are the regular US commercial fare. If you need something more mentally stimulating, try the *cinematecas* (art cinemas) in Caracas.

Most movies are screened in their original language with Spanish subtitles. A cinema ticket costs between US$2 and US$4. Cinemas in the lowlands are air-conditioned and may sometimes be cool; come prepared. In some towns men in T-shirts or shorts will not be let in.

Theatre & Classical Music
Most theatre activity is confined to Caracas, where there are a dozen theatres. Other large cities have their theatres but the choice, and usually the quality of productions, doesn't match that of Caracas. Much the same can be said about other areas of artistic expression such as ballet, opera and classical music. Refer to the Entertainment section in the Caracas chapter for further information.

Discos
Venezuelans love to dance and are good dancers. By far, the largest choice of discos is in Caracas, followed by Porlamar and Puerto La Cruz. The usual fare is a mix of western rock, reggae, salsa and merengue, but some discos in Caracas focus mainly on Cuban/Caribbean rhythms. There may be live music on weekends in some places.

Some discos operate nightly (sometimes except Monday which is the slowest day), but many open from Thursday to Saturday only. Discos open their doors around 9 pm, but the action doesn't usually begin before 11 pm, when most of the patrons turn up. There may be an entry fee on weekends, but rarely on other days of the week.

Discos don't usually serve food but offer plenty of drinks, which can be cheap or expensive, depending on the particular establishment. Most Caracas discos won't let you enter in a T-shirt and sneakers, but provincial venues tend to be more tolerant. Some discos are of suspicious reputation, stocked with prostitutes and with drugs sold openly – be careful.

Bars & Pubs
Don't worry about them – there are plenty of watering holes open late into the night, although they don't necessarily remind you of classic English or Irish pubs. Bottles are emptied quickly, so if you keep up with your

Venezuelan friends, you may have some problems returning safely to your hotel.

SPECTATOR SPORTS

Baseball *(béisbol)* is the most popular sport, attracting large crowds. The professional league is composed of eight teams (based in Caracas, La Guaira, Maracaibo, Valencia, Barquisimeto, Maracay, Puerto La Cruz and Cabimas), which often feature US players. The season goes from October to February.

The second most popular sport is probably basketball, with a professional league also comprising eight teams and the season running from March to July.

Horse races have been run in Los Llanos for centuries, but they are now run on racetracks built according to international rules, betting included. La Rinconada in Caracas is the best racetrack in the country, but other large cities such as Maracaibo and Valencia have their own tracks.

Unlike in most other South American countries, soccer *(fútbol)* has found few fans in Venezuela, though it does exist and there's even a professional league which plays from August till May.

The *corrida* or bullfighting was imported from Spain and found fertile soil in Venezuela, and now most major cities have their own *plaza de toros* (bullring). The bullring in Valencia, capable of seating 27,000 people, is the largest in the country, followed by the one in San Cristóbal with 22,000 seats. The Plaza de Toros Maestranza in Maracay is among the country's most stylish bullrings. The bullfighting season peaks during the Carnaval, when top-ranking matadors are invited from Spain and Latin America (especially Mexico and Colombia).

Another cruel and breathtaking spectator sport is cockfighting. As in most countries on the continent, it's popular in Venezuela and *galleras*, or cockfight rings, can be found in most cities.

Also thrilling but bloodless is the *coleo* or *toros coleados*, a sort of rodeo popular in Los Llanos, in which four riders compete to bring down a bull. The aim is to ground the bull after grabbing it by the tail from a galloping horse.

Another popular game, and an easier one to participate in, is *bolas criollas*, the Venezuelan variety of bowls. Two teams, each consisting of two players, throw eight wooden balls, aiming to place them as close as possible to the smaller ball known as *mingo*.

Chess and dominoes have plenty of addicts throughout the country and they are played as much in the villages as they are in Caracas.

THINGS TO BUY

Given a number of Indian communities living in the country, there is a variety of crafts to buy. Some of the most interesting are the crafts of the Guajiro, Warao and the groups of Amazonas. For example, a *chinchorro* (hammock) of the Warao, a *manta* (colourful, long loose-flowing dress) of the Guajiro, or some fine baskets of the Yanomami, make excellent collector's items, and are as decorative as they are useful.

Although there are plenty of handicraft shops in Caracas and most major cities, you should always try to buy crafts in their region of origin, ideally from the artisans themselves; not only are the crafts more authentic, but they are also much cheaper. If you can't get to the Indian communities, shop in the markets in nearby towns.

If you are interested in local music, comb Caracas's music shops which have the best selection. Most of the music is now recorded on CDs. The price of a CD ranges from about US$10 to US$20.

Venezuela is noted for gold and diamonds, but don't expect to find great bargains everywhere. Possibly the best place to buy gold jewellery is El Callao.

Leather footware is a good buy in Venezuela, and shops selling shoes are plentiful. It appears that every third shop is a *zapatería*, as if Venezuelans are shoe-crazy.

Getting There & Away

AIR

Sitting at the northern edge of South America, Venezuela has the cheapest air links with both Europe and North America, and is therefore the most convenient northern gateway to the continent.

Airports & Airlines

The country is serviced by a number of major intercontinental airlines, including British Airways, Air France, KLM, American Airlines and United Airlines. Venezuelan carriers do not fly on any routes outside the Americas.

Viasa, until recently the country's flagship, which had flights to Europe and much of the Americas, was grounded in January 1997 and liquidated soon after. In its absence, Avensa/Servivensa is today Venezuela's main international carrier. It now only flies within the Americas, as far as New York, Miami and Mexico City in the north and Quito and Lima in the south, but is planning to take over Viasa's flights to Europe. Aeropostal operates several international routes in the Caribbean.

Most travellers arrive at Caracas, which is Venezuela's major international airport. Charter flights bringing package tourists also fly into Porlamar (Isla de Margarita).

Buying Tickets

Your plane ticket will probably be the single most expensive item in your budget, and buying it can be an intimidating business. It's worth remembering that return fares are almost always cheaper than two one-way tickets.

Similarly, a single air ticket which includes a number of stopovers will be cheaper than a number of separate tickets for the same route. Note also, that the straight return ticket may not necessarily be the cheapest option for flying to Venezuela.

Other types of discount airfares, such as round-the-world (RTW) or open jaw tickets (see boxed text entitled Air Travel Glossary) may work out cheaper. They can also be more attractive because they allow you to visit other countries.

Air tickets bought from travel agents are generally cheaper than those bought directly from an airline, even if they cover the same route and have similar conditions or restrictions. How much you save largely depends on where you buy.

In some countries or cities there is a big trade in budget tickets; in others, the discount ticket market is limited, and the prices are unattractive.

It is always worth putting aside a few hours to research the current state of the market. It's advisable to start early as some of the cheapest tickets have to be bought well in advance, and some popular flights sell out quickly.

Make a point of talking to other recent travellers – they may be able to stop you making some of the same old mistakes. Look at advertisments in newspapers and magazines (including the Latin American press published in your country), consult reference books and keep an eye out for special offers. Read our Air Travel Glossary to get familiar with basic terms. Then phone travel agents for bargains.

If you are travelling from the UK or the USA, you will most likely find that the cheapest flights are advertised by obscure bucket shops (known as consolidators in the USA) whose names haven't yet reached the telephone directory.

Many such firms are honest and solvent, but there are a few rogues who will take your money, disappear, and reopen somewhere else a month or two later under a new name. If you feel suspicious about a firm, go somewhere else.

You may decide to pay a bit more than the rock-bottom fare by opting for the safety of a better-known travel agent.

Firms such as STA Travel, which has offices worldwide, Council Travel in the USA or Travel CUTS in Canada offer good prices to most destinations and are not going to disappear overnight, leaving you clutching a receipt for a non-existent ticket.

Once you have your ticket, write its number down, together with your flight number and other details (or make a photocopy of it), and keep the copy separate from the original. This will help you get a replacement if the ticket is lost or stolen.

It's sensible to buy travel insurance as early as possible. If you purchase it the week before you fly, you may find, for example, that you're not covered for delays to your flight caused by industrial action.

Use fares quoted in this book as a guide only. They are approximate and based on rates advertised by travel agents as we went to press. Remember that quoted airfares do not necessarily constitute a recommendation for that carrier.

If you plan on travelling by air within Venezuela, note that Avensa, one of the local carriers, offers a domestic air pass (see the Air section in the Getting Around chapter).

Onward Ticket Requirements

Venezuela requires, technically at least, that visitors have an onward ticket before they're allowed into the country. This is quite strictly enforced by airlines and travel agents, and probably none of them will sell you a one-way ticket unless you already have an onward ticket.

Upon arrival in Venezuela, however, hardly any immigration official will ask you to present your onward ticket. Yet, the ticket will be necessary if you want to extend your visa.

If you come without a return ticket and want to go home, you may be disappointed; Venezuela is not a good place to buy international air tickets.

Airfares to Europe and Australia are high and there are virtually no discounted tickets available. Only flights to Florida are cheap, simply because it's close. It's always better to have the whole route covered by a ticket bought at home.

Air Travellers with Special Needs

If you have special needs of any sort – you've broken a leg, you're vegetarian, travelling in a wheelchair, taking a baby or terrified of flying – you should let the airline know as soon as possible so that it can make appropriate arrangements.

You should remind it of your needs when you reconfirm your booking and again when you check in at the airport. It may be worth ringing around the airlines before you make your booking to find out how they can handle your particular requirements.

Airports and airlines can be surprisingly helpful, but they do need advance warning. Most international airports will provide escorts from the check-in desk to the plane when needed, and there should be ramps, lifts, and accessible toilets and phones. Aircraft toilets, on the other hand, are likely to present a problem; travellers should discuss this with the airline at an early stage and, if necessary, with their doctor.

Guide dogs for the blind will often have to travel separately from their owners in a specially pressurised baggage compartment with other animals, though smaller guide dogs may be admitted to the cabin.

All guide dogs are subject to the same quarantine laws (six months in isolation etc) as other domestic animals when entering or returning to countries currently free of rabies, such as the UK or Australia. Deaf travellers can ask for airport and in-flight announcements to be written down for them.

Children under two years of age travel for 10% of the standard fare (or free on some airlines), as long as they don't occupy a seat. They don't get a baggage allowance either. Skycots should be provided by the airline if requested in advance; these are capable of carrying a child weighing up to about 10kg.

Children between two and 12 years of age can usually occupy a seat for half to two-thirds of the full fare, and do get a baggage allowance. Pushchairs (pushers) can often be taken aboard as hand luggage.

Air Travel Glossary

Apex Tickets Apex stands for Advance Purchase Excursion fare. These tickets are usually between 30 and 40% cheaper than the full economy fare, but there are restrictions. You must purchase the ticket at least 21 days in advance (sometimes more) and must be away for a minimum period (normally 14 days) and return within a maximum period (90 or 180 days). Stopovers are not allowed, and if you have to change your dates of travel or destination, there will be extra charges to pay. These tickets are not fully refundable – if you have to cancel your trip, the refund is often considerably less than what you paid for the ticket. Take out travel insurance to cover yourself in case you have to cancel your trip unexpectedly – for example, due to illness.

Baggage Allowance This will be written on your ticket; you are usually allowed one 20-kg item to go in the hold, plus one item of hand luggage. Some airlines which fly transpacific and transatlantic routes allow for two pieces of luggage (there are limits on their dimensions and weight).

Bucket Shops At certain times of the year and/or on certain routes, many airlines fly with empty seats. This isn't profitable and it's more cost-effective for them to fly full, even if that means having to sell a certain number of drastically discounted tickets. They do this by off-loading them onto bucket shops (UK) or consolidators (USA), travel agents who specialise in discounted fares. The agents, in turn, sell them to the public at reduced prices. These tickets are often the cheapest you'll find, but you can't purchase them directly from the airlines. Availability varies widely, so you'll not only have to be flexible in your travel plans, you'll also have to be quick off the mark as soon as an ad appears in the press. Bucket-shop agents advertise in newspapers and magazines and there's a lot of competition, so it's a good idea to telephone first to ascertain availability before rushing from shop to shop. Naturally, they'll advertise the cheapest available tickets, but by the time you get there, these may be sold out and you may be looking at something slightly more expensive.

Bumped Just because you have a confirmed seat doesn't mean you're going to get on the plane – see Overbooking.

Cancellation Penalties If you have to cancel or change an Apex or other discount ticket, there may be heavy penalties involved; insurance can sometimes be taken out against these penalties. Some airlines impose penalties on regular tickets as well, particularly against 'no show' passengers.

Check In Airlines ask you to check in a certain time ahead of the flight departure (usually two hours on international flights). If you fail to check in on time and the flight is overbooked, the airline can cancel your booking and give your seat to somebody else.

Confirmation Having a ticket written out with the flight and date on it doesn't mean you have a seat until the agent has confirmed with the airline that your status is 'OK'. Prior to this confirmation, your status is 'on request'.

Courier Flights Businesses often need to send their urgent documents or freight securely and quickly. They do it through courier companies. These companies hire people to accompany the package through customs and, in return, offer a discount ticket which is sometimes a phenomenal bargain. In effect, what the courier companies do is ship their freight as your luggage on the regular commercial flights. This is a legitimate operation – all freight is completely legal. There are two shortcomings, however: the short turnaround time of the ticket, usually not longer than a month; and the limitation on your luggage allowance. You may be required to surrender all your baggage allowance for the use of the courier company, and be only allowed to take carry-on luggage.

Discounted Tickets There are two types of discounted fares – officially discounted (such as Apex – see Promotional Fares) and unofficially discounted (see Bucket Shops). Unofficially discounted fares can save you more than money – you may be able to pay Apex prices without the associated Apex advance booking and other requirements. The lowest prices often impose drawbacks, such as flying with unpopular airlines, inconvenient schedules, or unpleasant routes and connections.

Economy-Class Tickets Economy-class tickets are usually not the cheapest way to go, though they do give you maximum flexibility and they are valid for 12 months. If you don't use them, most are fully refundable, as are unused sectors of a multiple ticket.

Full Fares Airlines traditionally offer first-class (coded F), business-class (coded J) and economy-class (coded Y) tickets. These days there are so many promotional and discounted fares available that few passengers pay full fare.

Lost Tickets If you lose your airline ticket, an airline will usually treat it like a travellers' cheque and, after inquiries, issue you with a replacement. Legally, however, an airline is entitled to treat it like cash, so if you lose a ticket, it could be forever. Take good care of your tickets.

MCO An MCO (Miscellaneous Charges Order) is a voucher for a value of a given amount, which resembles an airline ticket and can be used to pay for a specific flight with any IATA (International Air Transport Association) airline. MCOs, which are more flexible than a regular ticket, may satisfy the irritating onward ticket requirement, but some countries are now reluctant to accept them. MCOs are fully refundable if unused.

No Shows No shows are passengers who fail to show up for their flight for whatever reason. Full-fare no shows are sometimes entitled to travel on a later flight. The rest of us are penalised (see Cancellation Penalties).

Open Jaw Tickets These are return tickets which allow you to fly to one place but return from another, and travel between the two 'jaws' by any means of transport at your own expense. If available, this can save you backtracking to your arrival point.

Overbooking Airlines hate to fly with empty seats, and since every flight has some passengers who fail to show up (see No Shows), they often book more passengers than they have seats available. Usually the excess passengers balance those who fail to show up, but occasionally somebody gets bumped. If this happens, guess who it is most likely to be? The passengers who check in late.

Promotional Fares These are officially discounted fares, such as Apex fares, which are available from travel agents or direct from the airline.

Reconfirmation You must contact the airline at least 72 hours prior to departure to 'reconfirm' that you intend to be on the flight. If you don't do this, the airline can delete your name from the passenger list and you could lose your seat.

Restrictions Discounted tickets often have various restrictions on them, such as necessity of advance purchase, limitations on the minimum and maximum period you must be away, restrictions on breaking the journey or changing the booking or route etc.

Round-the-World Tickets These tickets have become very popular in the last few years; basically, there are two types – airline tickets and agent tickets. An airline RTW ticket is issued by two or more airlines that have joined together to market a ticket which takes you around the world on their combined routes. It permits you to fly pretty well anywhere you choose using their combined routes as long as you don't backtrack, ie keep moving in approximately the same direction east or west. Other restrictions are that you (usually) must book the first sector in advance and cancellation penalties then apply. There may be restrictions on how many stopovers you are permitted. The RTW tickets are usually valid for 90 days up to a year.The other type of RTW ticket, the agent ticket, is a combination of cheap fares strung together by an enterprising travel agent. These may be cheaper than airline RTW tickets, but the choice of routes will be limited.

Standby This is a discounted ticket where you only fly if there is a seat free at the last moment. Standby fares are usually only available directly at the airport, but sometimes may also be handled by an airline's city office. To give yourself the best possible chance of getting on the flight you want, get there early and have your name placed on the waiting list. It's first come, first served.

Student Discounts Some airlines offer student-card holders 15% to 25% discounts on their tickets. The same often applies to anyone under the age of 26. These discounts are generally only available on ordinary economy-class fares. You wouldn't get one, for instance, on an Apex or an RTW ticket, since these are already discounted.

Tickets Out An entry requirement for many countries is that you have an onward or return ticket, in other words, a ticket out of the country. If you're not sure what you intend to do next, the easiest solution is to buy the cheapest onward ticket to a neighbouring country or a ticket from a reliable airline which can later be refunded if you do not use it.

Transferred Tickets Airline tickets cannot be transferred from one person to another. Travellers sometimes try to sell the return half of their ticket, but officials can ask you to prove that you are the person named on the ticket. This may not be checked on domestic flights, but on international flights, tickets are usually compared with passports.

Travel Periods Some officially discounted fares, Apex fares in particular, vary with the time of year. There is often a low (off-peak) season and a high (peak) season. Sometimes there's an intermediate or shoulder season as well. At peak times, when everyone wants to fly, both officially and unofficially discounted fares will be higher, or there may simply be no discounted tickets available. Usually the fare depends on your outward flight – if you depart in the high season and return in the low season, you pay the high-season fare. ■

The USA

Two of the most reputable discount travel agencies in the USA are STA Travel and Council Travel Services. Although they both specialise in student travel, they may offer discount tickets to nonstudents of all ages. Their national head offices are:

STA Travel
5900 Wiltshire Boulevard, Los Angeles, CA 90036 (☎ 1-800 777 0112, (213) 937 8722; (213) fax 937 2739)
Council Travel Services
205 East 42nd St, New York, NY 10017 (☎ 1-800 223 7402, (212) 661 1414; fax (212) 972 3231)

STA Travel has offices in Los Angeles, San Diego, San Francisco, Berkeley, Boston, Cambridge and New York. Council Travel has offices in all these cities and in 20 others around the country.

For more discount travel agencies, check the Sunday travel sections in major newspapers, such as the *Los Angeles Times*, the *San Francisco Examiner* and the *Chronicle* on the west coast and *The New York Times* on the east coast.

Another useful resource is the monthly newsletter *Travel Unlimited* (PO Box 1058, Allston, MA 02134) which gives details of cheap airfares and courier flights (see Air Travel Glossary) for destinations all over the world from the USA. Send US$5 for the latest edition, or buy a one-year subscription for US$25.

New York and Miami are the only places to look for courier flights to South America. For the widest selection of destinations, try Now Voyager (☎ (212) 431-1616), Air Facility (☎ (718) 712-0630) or Travel Courier (☎ (718) 738-9000) in New York, and Linehaul Services (☎ (305) 477-0651) or Discount Travel International (☎ (305) 538-1616) in Miami. As an example only, a courier fare on the Miami-Caracas-Miami route shouldn't cost more than around US$200, while the New York-Caracas-New York fare will go for around US$400.

The major US gateway for Venezuela is Miami, from where several carriers fly to Caracas, including American Airlines, Unit-ed Airlines and Servivensa. A 30 day Apex return ticket normally costs about US$500, but at the time of writing, Servivensa (Venezuelan carrier) offered a cut-down airfare of US$131 one way. The offer was valid from either end and tickets were available directly from the airline offices. Contact the Miami office (☎ (305) 381 8001 or toll-free 1-800 428 3672; fax (305) 381 6079), 800 Brickell Ave, Suite 1109, Miami, Florida 33131.

Another important gateway to Venezuela is New York. Again, American Airlines, United Airlines and Servivensa have flights between New York and Caracas, direct or with a stopover in Miami. A one way full economy fare to Caracas is likely to be around US$490, and the 30 day Apex ticket will cost around US$560. As we went to press, Servivensa offered one-way fares for US$275. Call its New York office at ☎ (718) 244 6857, 244 6859.

On the west coast, the major departure point is Los Angeles, but flights to Caracas are expensive. The cheapest return ticket (off-peak, for a stay of up to 21 days) will cost around US$700, whereas a 60 day peak round-trip fare will be around US$1100. Contact American Airlines (☎ 1-800 624-6262) and United Airlines (☎ 1-800 538-2929). It will probably work out cheaper to go on a cheap domestic flight to Miami and fly to Caracas from there, but check beforehand to see what discount fares are available from Miami.

Canada

American Airlines and United Airlines have connections from Calgary, Montreal, Toronto and Vancouver to Miami, and on to Caracas. Prices vary according to the length of your stay. For example, a return ticket from Toronto will cost about C$1000 if you stay less than 60 days and C$1300 if you want to stay longer.

To start with, check the fares offered by Travel Cuts, Canada's national student travel agency (you don't have to be a student to use its services). Its head office is in Toronto (☎ (416) 977-3703, 979-2406; fax (416)

977-4796), 171 College St, Toronto, Ontario M5T 1P7, and it has branch offices in Edmonton, Halifax, Montreal, Ottawa, Saskatoon, Vancouver and Victoria.

It's also worth contacting Andes Travel, one of the travel agents specialising in flights to South America. Call its office in Toronto on ☎ (416) 537 3447, or in Montreal on ☎ (514) 274 5565. Adventure Centre, which has offices in Calgary, Edmonton, Toronto and Vancouver, can also be useful. You'll find ads for other travel agencies in the travel sections of weekend editions of *The Toronto Star* and *The Montreal Gazette*.

Europe

A number of airlines, including Viasa, British Airways, Air France, KLM, Lufthansa, Alitalia, Iberia and Air Portugal, link Caracas with European cities. Venezuela is usually the cheapest South American destination to reach from Europe, and most travel agents will offer flights to Caracas.

London, where bucket shops are by the dozen, usually has the cheapest fares to Caracas. Other cities with long-standing traditions in ticket discounting include Amster- dam, Brussels, Frankfurt and Paris. Elsewhere, special deals come and go, but there are usually less to choose from and airfares are generally higher. This is particularly true in Scandinavia where budget tickets are difficult to find.

For this reason, many European budget travellers buy their tickets from London's bucket shops. In any case, it's worthwhile checking the London market before buying an expensive ticket from a local agent. Some London travel agents will make arrangements over the phone or by fax, so you don't actually have to go to London to shop around. However, you may be obliged to go to London to pick up your ticket in person, as not many British agencies will want to send the ticket outside the UK.

The UK London is Britain's major hub for discounted tickets. You'll find plenty of deals listed in the travel sections of weekend editions of London newspapers. A good source of information about cheap fares around the world is the weekly entertainment guide *Time Out*, available from newsstands in London, as is *TNT Magazine* which can be picked up free at underground stations. The Globetrotters Club, BCM Roving, London WC1N 3XX, publishes a newsletter called *Globe* which covers obscure destinations and can help in finding travelling companions.

A word of warning, however – don't take advertised fares as gospel. To comply with advertising laws in the UK, companies must be able to offer some tickets at their cheapest quoted price, but they may have only one or two of them per week. If you're not one of the lucky ones, you'll be looking at higher priced tickets. It's best to begin looking for deals well in advance of your intended departure, so you can get a fair idea of what's available.

Following is a list of recommended agencies selling discounted tickets:

Journey Latin America (JLA)
    14-16 Devonshire Rd, Chiswick, London W4 2HD (☎ (0181) 747 3108, 747 8315; fax (0181) 742 1312)
Passage to South America
    113 Shepherds Bush Rd, London W6 7LP (☎ (0171) 602 9889; fax (0171) 602 4251)
South American Experience
    47 Causton St, Pimlico, London SW1P 4AT (☎ (0171) 976 5511; fax (0171) 976 6908)
STA Travel
    74 Old Brompton Rd, London, SW7 3LQ (☎ (0171) 937 9962)
    117 Euston Rd, London NW1 2SX (☎ (0171) 465 0486)
    Priory House, 6 Wrights Lane, London W8 6TA (☎ (0171) 938 4711)
Trailfinders
    42-48 Earls Court Rd, London W8 6EJ (☎ (0171) 938 3366)
    194 Kensington High St, London W8 7RG (☎ 0171) 938 3939)
Travel Bug
    125A Gloucester Rd, London SW7 4SF (☎ (0171) 835 2000)

Apart from selling tickets, some of these travel agencies offer a variety of other services. JTA, consistently recommended by travellers, will arrange itineraries for both independent and escorted travel. It will make arrangements for you over the phone or by fax. Ask for its helpful free magazine *Papagaio*. The equally reputable Trailfinders publishes a free quarterly magazine, *Trailfinder*, packed with useful information on tickets, vaccinations, visas etc. The company has regional branches in Bristol, Glasgow and Manchester. STA Travel has regional offices in Bristol, Cambridge, Leeds, Oxford and Manchester.

Direct flights between London and Caracas are operated twice weekly by British Airways, but agents often use services of other carriers flying indirect routes via one of the mainland European cities, and they can work out cheaper.

Prices for discounted flights from London to Caracas start at around UK£220 one way and UK£400 return. Bargain hunters should have little trouble finding even lower prices, but make sure you use a travel agent affiliated with the ABTA (Association of British Travel Agents). If you have bought your ticket from an ABTA-registered agent who then goes out of business, ABTA will guarantee a refund or an alternative. Unregistered bucket shops are sometimes cheaper, but can be riskier.

France The Paris-Caracas route is serviced directly three times a week by Air France, but – as in London – travel agents may offer you cheaper indirect routes on board other carriers, eg via Lisbon with TAP Air Portugal, which is one of the cheapest airlines. Following is a list of selected travel agencies selling discounted tickets in Paris. Many have branch offices in other major French cities.

Forum Voyages
    67 Ave Raymond Poincaré, 75016 Paris (☎ 47 27 89 89)
Fuaj (Fédération Unies des Auberges de Jeunesse)
    9 Rue Brantôme, 75003 Paris (☎ 48 04 70 40)
Nouveau Monde
    8 Rue Mabillon, 75006 Paris (☎ 53 73 78 80)
OTU (Organisation du Tourisme Universitaire)
    39 Ave Georges Bernanos, 75005 Paris (☎ 44 41 38 50)

Usit Voyages
    12 Rue Vivienne, 75002 Paris (☎ 42 44 14 00)
Voyageurs en Amérique du Sud
    55 Rue Sainte-Anne, 75002 Paris (☎ 42 86 17 70)

The cheapest Paris-Caracas return tickets can be bought for about 3500FF in the low season and around 5000FF in the high season. Some agencies offer cheaper fares for students. Most discounted return tickets have a maximum stay period of two or three months, but sometimes they may allow for a stay of up to six months.

Australia & New Zealand

To start with, travel between Australasia and Venezuela is arduously long – possibly at least 20 hours in the air alone. Add to it several stopovers, as there are no direct flights. Secondly, there are a number of alternative routes, none of which is clearly better or cheaper than the others. Lastly, fares are high and there is not much in the way of budget tickets to be found in Australia or New Zealand.

In theory, there are four air routes to Venezuela. Many travellers first think about the route through Los Angeles as the seemingly best option, but note that getting from there to Venezuela is expensive (see The USA). Moreover, even a couple of days in the USA would eat up all the savings in airfares, so it's only good value if you want to visit the USA anyway or if you go through without stopping. Arrange the ticket for the whole route at home. A return ticket is likely to cost somewhere between A$2300 and A$2800, depending on the season, length of stay etc.

The route through Europe is the longest but not as absurd as it may sound. Given the discounted airfares to London, and interesting fares from London to Caracas, the total fare may be comparable or even lower than travelling via Los Angeles.

It's best to arrange the ticket for the whole route in Australia or have the London-Caracas leg prepared for you by a London agent.

The shortest route between Australasia

and South America goes over the South Pole. Aerolíneas Argentinas flies three times a week between Auckland and Buenos Aires, and has arrangements with other carriers which cover the Auckland-Australia leg. It may be an interesting proposition if you plan on beginning your overland trip from Argentina, but note that Venezuela is at the opposite end of the continent. Aerolíneas Argentinas can fly you to Caracas, but the total fare will be pretty high; expect to pay between A$2400 and A$3000 for the Sydney-Caracas return flight, depending on the length of stay and the season. The Auckland-Caracas fare will be only marginally lower.

Finally, you can fly right across the southern Pacific to Santiago de Chile. Lan Chile flies from Papeete (Tahiti) via Easter Island to Santiago, and also has flights on to Caracas. Associated carriers take passengers from Australia and New Zealand to Papeete. The Sydney-Caracas return fares of Lan Chile are slightly more expensive than those of Aerolíneas Argentinas.

Unless you are particularly interested in any of the four above-mentioned routes, it's worth thinking about a RTW ticket. RTW tickets with various stopovers can still be found for as little as A$2100, but these tend to include only northern hemisphere stopovers; RTWs which include Latin America or the South Pacific will automatically cost at least A$1000 more.

Of these, one of the more interesting options may be a one-year RTW ticket with Aerolíneas Argentinas and KLM on their Sydney-Auckland-Buenos Aires-Caracas-Amsterdam-Singapore-Sydney route. It's possible to include a couple of other South American destinations, such as Santiago, Lima or Rio de Janeiro.

Alternatively, look for a cheap northern hemisphere RTW which includes Miami, from where you can make a side trip to Venezuela for a few hundred US dollars (see The USA).

The Saturday editions of major newspapers, *The Sydney Morning Herald* and *The Age*, carry travel sections which have discount airfare ads, but very few of them include South American destinations. It may be worth getting a copy of some of the Spanish-language newspapers published in Australia such as *El Español* or *Extra Informativo*, which list travel agents specialising in South America.

STA Travel has Australian offices in Adelaide, Brisbane, Cairns, Canberra, Darwin, Melbourne, Perth, Sydney and Townsville. In New Zealand, it has offices in Auckland, Christchurch, Dunedin and Wellington. Flight Centres International, which has offices in most major cities in Australia and New Zealand, may also have good deals.

Central America

Lacsa (Costa Rican carrier) can take you to Caracas from all Central American capitals, including Guatemala (US$453 one way), Tegucigalpa (US$445), San Salvador (US$433), Managua (US$461), San José (US$315) and Panama (US$317). Except for Panama, you must first fly to San José, from where Lacsa has daily flights to Caracas via Panama. From Panama, you can also fly to Caracas with Servivensa.

You can also go from Central America to Venezuela via Colombia, using San Andrés Island (a Colombian sovereignty) as a bridge. The cheapest options are to fly to San Andrés from either Guatemala (US$125) or Tegucigalpa (US$117), and continue on to Cartagena on the Colombian mainland on a domestic flight (US$120).

Colombia

Several carriers, including Avianca, Servivensa and Saeta, operate flights between Bogotá and Caracas. The one-way fare offered by the airlines is US$218, a 30 day return ticket costs US$251, and a 60 day return goes for US$281. Lacsa flies three times a week from Barranquilla to Caracas (US$177 one way, US$193 for a 30 day return). At the time of writing, Aeropostal planned to introduce the Cartagena-Caracas flight.

There are daily flights with Servivensa between Bogotá and San Antonio del Táchira (US$50 one way, US$100 one-year return), and between Medellín and San Antonio del Táchira (US$45 one way, US$90 one-year return). These flights are the cheapest options of getting from Colombia to Venezuela (almost as cheap as it would be by bus) and avoiding visa problems. On the other hand, these are the cheapest onward tickets out of Venezuela.

Note that all international tickets bought in Colombia are subject to a 16% tax (8% on return flights) on top of the listed fares.

Brazil

Flying between Brazil and Venezuela is painfully expensive. The flight from Sao Paulo or Rio de Janeiro to Caracas will cost around US$780 (US$885 two-month return). The cheapest air connection between these two countries is the Manaus-Caracas flight which costs about US$460 (US$590 one-month return). There are no flights between Boa Vista and Santa Elena de Uairén.

Guyana

There are no direct flights between Venezuela and Guyana. You have to fly via Port of Spain (Trinidad) with BWIA (US$222), or Curaçao (Netherlands Antilles) with ALM (US$288).

Trinidad

Aeropostal has twice weekly flights from Port of Spain to Caracas (US$114) via Porlamar (US$90). BWIA flies four times a week direct from Port of Spain to Caracas (US$114). Rutaca operates flights between Port of Spain and Maturín (US$60, US$105 return).

Netherlands Antilles

Servivensa flies between Caracas and Aruba (US$115), Curaçao (US$91) and Bonaire (US$97). Aeropostal services Aruba and Curaçao. There are also regular scheduled flights from Aruba and Curaçao to Las Piedras, and charter flights on light planes from Aruba, Curaçao and Bonaire to Coro (see the Coro section in The North-West chapter for details).

LAND

Venezuela has road connections with Colombia and Brazil only. There is no road link with Guyana; you must go via Brazil.

Colombia

You can enter Venezuela from Colombia at four border crossings. Going from north to south, there's a coastal smuggling route between Maicao and Maracaibo (see the Maracaibo section in The North-West chapter for details). Further south is the most popular border crossing, between Cúcuta and San Antonio del Táchira (see the San Antonio del Táchira section in The Andes chapter for information). Next comes an unpopular, dangerous (because of Colombian guerrilla activity) and inconvenient crossing from Arauca to El Amparo de Apure. Finally, there's an unusual but interesting outback route from Puerto Carreño in Colombia to either Puerto Páez or Puerto Ayacucho in Venezuela (the Puerto Ayacucho section in the Guayana chapter will give you details).

Brazil

There's only one road connecting Brazil and Venezuela. It leads from Manaus to Boa Vista (Brazil) to Santa Elena de Uairén (Venezuela) and then continues on to Ciudad Guayana. See the Santa Elena de Uairén section in the Guayana chapter for details.

You may also enter Venezuela through the Amazon at San Simón de Cocuy. This is an adventurous river/road route seldom used by travellers. See the Puerto Ayacucho section for information.

SEA
Lesser Antilles

There's a ferry service between the Lesser Antilles (St Lucia, Barbados, St Vincent and Trinidad) and Pampatar (Isla de Margarita) and Güiria in Venezuela. Refer to the Güiria section in The North-East chapter for details.

Netherlands Antilles

Ferry services between Curaçao and La Vela de Coro (the port of Coro) and between Aruba and Punto Fijo on the Paraguaná

Peninsula were closed in 1992. As we went to press, both these services were due to reopen and may be in operation by the time you arrive.

DEPARTURE TAXES

On leaving Venezuela by air from Caracas and Porlamar, the airport tax is US$21, payable in either dollars or bolívares at the current exchange rate. There may be lower taxes at San Antonio del Táchira airport, from where Servivensa flies to Colombia.

There's also a departure tax for anyone going overland from Venezuela to Colombia via San Antonio del Táchira. This tax is changed frequently; expect anything between US$3 and US$10. There are no exit taxes on other border crossings, but don't be surprised if there are some when you arrive.

ORGANISED TOURS

Tours to South America have become popular, and there are hundreds of tour companies in the USA, the UK and elsewhere providing organised trips. They range from easy-going hotel-based sightseeing excursions, designed mainly for first-time tourists, to expeditions tailored to the particular interests of experienced independent travellers. The latter tours feature activities rather than sightseeing, and may include anything from trekking and bird-watching to mountain biking and rock climbing. An increasing number of tours are designed with some sort of ecotourism angle in mind. You'll find ads for these tours in hiking, mountaineering and wildlife magazines.

If you plan on taking an organised tour, start shopping early enough to make sure you get what you want. Some operators may offer slow-selling tours at considerably lower prices close to their scheduled departure. However, on the whole, tours to South America bought outside the continent tend to be an expensive way to travel.

Many overseas companies contract the services of local operators, obviously charging you more than you'd pay directly to that operator. Accordingly, you can save quite a bit by setting off on your own and arranging

the tour in the country you go to. Fortunately, Venezuela has quite a developed tour business with lots of tour operators (see the Organised Tours section in the Getting Around chapter). Naturally, flexibility is essential as tours may take a while to be put together, unless you arrange the tour in advance from home.

USA Given the proximity to South America and numerous flight connections, the USA has probably more tour companies specialising in the neighbouring continent than the rest of the world combined. They are advertised in travel and outdoor magazines such as *Outside*, *Escape* and *Ecotraveler*, as well as magazines of a more general nature, including *Natural History* and *Audubon*. Here is a list of some reputable operators:

Eco Voyager
6915 Red Rd, Suite 203, Coral Gables, FL 33143 (☎ (305) 665 9050 or toll-free 1-800 326 7088; fax (305) 665 1890 or toll-free 1-800 326 6276; email ecotour@ecovoyager.com; website www.ecovoyager.com)
Focus Tours
14821 Hillside Lane, Burnsville, MN 55306 (☎ (612) 892 7830; fax (612) 892 0900)
International Expeditions
One Environs Park, Helena, AL 35080 (☎ (205) 428 1700 or toll-free 1-800 633 4734; fax (205) 428 1714; email ietravel@aol.com)
Lost World Adventures
1189 Autumn Ridge Drive, Marietta, GA 30066 (☎ (404) 971 8586 or toll-free 1-800 999 0558; fax (404) 977 3095)
Mountain Travel Sobek
6420 Fairmount Ave, El Cerrito, CA 94530 (☎ (510) 527 8100 or toll-free 1-800 227 2384 or 1-888 687 6235; fax (510) 525 7710; website www.mtsobek.com)
Venezuela Ventures
156 Bedford Rd, Armonk, NY 10504 (☎ (914) 273 6411 or toll-free 1-800 810 5021; fax (914) 273 6370; email info@venez.com; website www.venez.com)
Wilderness Travel
801 Allston Way, Berkeley, CA 94710 (☎ (510) 548 0420 or toll-free 1-800 247 6700; fax (510) 548 0347; email info@wildernesstravel.com)
Wildland Adventures
3516 NE 155th, Seattle, WA 98155, USA (☎ (206) 365 0686 or toll-free 1-800 345 4453; fax (206) 363 6615; email wildadve@aol.com)

All the listed companies put an emphasis on responsible tourism. Further information about responsible travelling can be obtained from the following organisations: Center for Responsible Tourism (☎ (415) 843 5506), 2 Kensington Rd, San Anselmo, CA 94960; The Ecotourism Society (☎ (802) 447 2121; fax (802) 447 2122; ecotsocy@igc.apc.org), PO Box 755, North Bennington, VT 05257; and The Earth Preservation Fund, c/o Wildland Adventures (see the previous list).

Earthwatch organises trips for volunteers to work overseas on scientific and cultural projects with an emphasis on protection and preservation of ecology and environment. Other organisations which handle voluntary work include Conservation International and The Nature Conservancy. For the addresses of these and other environmental organisations, see the Ecology & Environment section in the Facts about the Country chapter.

UK Following is a list of some overland operators offering tours in South America:

Dragoman
Camp Green, Kenton Rd, Debenham, Suffolk IP14 6LA (☎ (01728) 861 133; fax (01728) 861 127)
Encounter Overland
267 Old Brompton Rd, London SW5 9JA (☎ (0171) 370 6845; fax (0171) 244 9737)
Exodus Expeditions
9 Weir Rd, London SW12 0LT (☎ (0181) 673 0859; fax (0181) 673 0779)
Geodyssey
29 Harberton Rd, London N19 3JS (☎ (0171) 281 7788; fax (0171) 281 7878)
Guerba Expeditions
Wessex House, 40 Station Rd, Westbury, Wiltshire BA13 3JN (☎ (01373) 826 611; fax (01373) 858 351)
Kamuka
40 Earls Court Rd, London W6 8EJ (☎ (0171) 937 88 55; fax (0171) 937 6664)
Last Frontiers
20 High St, Long Crendon, Bucks HP18 9AF (☎ (01844) 208 405; fax (01844) 201 400; website www.lastfrontiers.co.uk)
Top Deck
Top Deck House, 131/135 Earls Court Rd, London SW5 9RH (☎ (0171) 244 8641; fax (0171) 373 6201)

Geodyssey and Last Frontiers specialise in Venezuela and offer a variety of tours to almost every corner of the country. Also see the travel agencies listed in the Air section earlier in this chapter; some of these, including JLA, South American Experience and Passage to South America, offer tours to South America and may have Venezuela in their programmes.

As with US operators, many UK tour companies are environmentally aware. Should you need more information on responsible travelling, contact the Centre for the Advancement of Responsible Travel (☎ (01732) 352 757), Tourism Concern (☎ (0171) 753 3330) and Green Flag International (☎ (01223) 890 250).

Australia Few tour companies in Australia specialise in South America, and even fewer operators have Venezuela on their list. What is easiest to find in Australia, are general trips covering several South American countries, mostly Argentina, Chile, Peru and Bolivia. Venezuela appears on some of these routes, and occasionally it is a destination in its own right.

Following is a list of Australian travel agencies offering tours to South American countries including Venezuela. Some may offer programmes tailor-made for you.

Contours Travel
466 Victoria St, North Melbourne, VIC 3051 (☎ (03) 9329 5211; fax (03) 9329 6314; email contours@compuserve.com)
Destination Holidays
34A Main St, Croydon, VIC 3136 (☎ (03) 9725 4655; fax (03) 9723 9211; email desthols@acepia.net.au)
Encounter Overland
600 Lonsdale St, Melbourne, VIC 3000 (☎ (03) 9670 1123 or toll-free 1800 654 152; fax (03) 9642 5838)
Inca Tours
5 Alison Rd, Wyong, NSW 2259 (☎ (043) 512 133 or toll-free 1800 024 955; fax (043) 512 526; email inca@southamerica.com.au)
Peregrine Adventures
38 York St, Sydney, NSW 2000 (☎ (02) 9290 2770; fax (02) 9290 2155)
258 Lonsdale St, Melbourne, VIC 3000 (☎ (03) 9662 2700; fax (03) 9662 2422)

South America Travel Centre
    104 Hardware St, Melbourne, VIC 3000 (☎ (03)
    9642 5353 or toll-free 1800 655 051; fax (03)
    9642 5454)

WARNING

Information in this chapter is particularly vulnerable to change as prices for international travel are volatile, routes are introduced and cancelled, schedules are changed, special deals come and go, and rules and visa requirements are amended. Airlines and governments seem to take pleasure in making price structures and regulations as complicated as possible. You should check directly with the airline or a travel agent to make sure you understand how a fare (and ticket you may buy) works.

The travel industry is highly competitive, so you should get opinions, quotes and advice from as many airlines and travel agents as possible before you part with your hard-earned cash. The details given in this chapter should be regarded as pointers and are not a substitute for your own careful, up-to-date research.

Getting Around

AIR

Venezuela has a number of airlines and an extensive network of air routes. Caracas (or Maiquetía, where Caracas' airport is located) is the country's major aviation hub. It handles daily departures to most major cities around the country and flights to minor destinations. Cities most frequently serviced from Caracas include Porlamar, Maracaibo and Puerto Ordaz (Ciudad Guayana).

Domestic Air Services

Avensa and Servivensa are Venezuela's main domestic airlines. It's actually one company, although the planes are labelled with their own, distinctive logos. Servivensa was created by Avensa in 1978 as its subsidiary. Avensa itself has flown Venezuelan skies since 1943. The company has the widest network of internal routes, covering two dozen Venezuelan cities (see the Avensa/

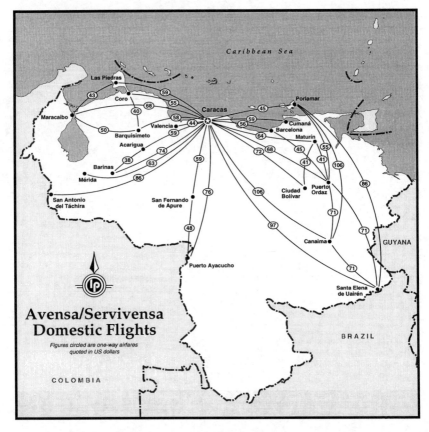

Avensa/Servivensa
Domestic Flights

Figures circled are one-way airfares
quoted in US dollars

Servivensa Domestic Flights map), and controls more than half of the domestic market.

Another Venezuelan carrier with a long tradition is Aeropostal. Founded in 1929, it had up to 40% of the domestic market in its heyday, but ceased operations after a strike in 1994. Following the government's unsuccessful attempts to sell it, Aeropostal eventually found a private buyer and returned to the air in early 1997. So far, it services half a dozen domestic destinations (against 22 it operated before its closure), but plans to re-open other routes – both domestic and international – in the hope of regaining its previous position.

This won't be easy, however. In recent years several new airlines, including Aserca, Air Venezuela and Laser, have appeared on the market. They successfully made their way into some of the most popular and lucrative routes, as well as opening others not previously serviced by air.

There's also Zuliana de Aviación, the Maracaibo-based carrier which services several major domestic destinations. It also operated some international routes, including Miami and Bogotá, but these flights have been suspended.

To complete the picture, there are perhaps a dozen minor provincial carriers which cover regional and remote routes on a regular or charter basis. They fly light planes, so they can reach even the most obscure destination. This group is also expanding. Further applications to open new airlines are currently being processed by the Ministry of Transport and Communications, so expect more competition.

Airfares

Domestic air travel in Venezuela is still relatively cheap when compared to neighbouring Colombia or Brazil, but no longer the bargain it used to be a decade ago. Airfares have doubled or even tripled over the past few years. Fortunately, they seem to have stabilised recently, mostly because of fierce competition between airlines.

Fares vary between carriers, so if the route you're flying is serviced by several airlines,

check their fares before buying your ticket. As a rough guide of what the fares might be, see the Avensa/Servivensa Domestic Flights map.

Some airlines, including Avensa/Servivensa and Aeropostal, may offer discount fares for students and senior travellers. Normally, the 15% student discount only applies to Venezuelan students, but some offices have been known to sell discounted tickets to foreign students with an international student card. The senior citizen discount (for passengers 60 years of age and over) generally applies to both nationals and foreigners.

Make sure to reconfirm your flight at least 72 hours before departure (preferably in person rather than by phone). Remember, not all flights depart on time, so be patient and have a flexible itinerary, particularly if you have transport connections. There's an airport tax of around US$0.50 on all domestic flights.

Air Passes

Avensa offers an air pass which allows you to fly within 45 days with Avensa and Servivensa on all the routes they service in the Americas, both domestic and international. Travel can begin and end in any city on the network. One-way, circle and open-jaw trips are permitted, but you cannot fly more than once on the same route.

The pass includes a number of flight coupons (minimum of four, maximum unlimited) of your choice, each of which has a determined price. Coupons for any of the domestic routes cost US$45 each; those for international routes range from US$55 to US$200. For example, the Mexico City-Caracas coupon costs US$200, the Lima-Caracas coupon is US$180, while Miami-Caracas, Quito-Bogotá and Bogotá-Caracas coupons are US$80 each.

The air pass can be bought both outside and inside Venezuela, but it's not sold to residents of any Latin American country. Information and sales are handled by Avensa's representatives in the Americas and Europe (there's none in Australia), including the USA (☎ toll-free 1-800 428 3672), the UK (☎ (0171) 610 4131), France

(☎ (01) 39 21 12 13), the Netherlands (☎ (23) 529 3972) and Germany (☎ (6852) 900 511), and Avensa offices in Venezuela.

If you plan on travelling on to Colombia, you may be interested in the Colombian domestic air pass offered by Avianca. Unlike the Avensa pass, the Avianca pass can only be bought outside Colombia, so Venezuela will actually be your last place to decide. The pass allows for five stopovers of your choice serviced by Avianca and Sam (two major Colombian carriers), but you cannot visit the same place twice.

If you fly into Colombia with Avianca, the pass costs US$260 (including San Andrés and Leticia as two of the five stopovers) or US$180 (excluding these two destinations), and is valid for 30 days from the date of the first flight. This is excellent value, when compared with regular airfares. If you fly into Colombia with any other carrier, the pass costs US$509 or US$399, respectively, and is valid for 21 days. All these prices are US$30 higher in the high season (June to August and December). Up to three additional stopovers can be purchased at US$40 each. For further information, contact Avianca offices in the USA, Europe or Latin America. In Venezuela, there's an Avianca office in Caracas.

BUS

As there's no passenger train service in Venezuela, most travelling is done by bus. Buses are generally OK, especially on main roads which are all surfaced, and run regularly day and night between major population centres. Bus transport is cheap in Venezuela; you probably won't go wrong if you allow for US$1.25 for one hour of an ordinary bus ride.

There are dozens of bus companies, each owning a plethora of buses ranging from archaic pieces of junk to the most recent models. The antiques usually ply the regional secondary roads, while the modern technology is put to service on major long-distance routes. If various companies operate the same route, fares are much the same with them all. The standard of service,

though, may differ from one company to another, and you'll soon become familiar with the better ones.

No matter how low or how high the standard, however, you can be pretty sure of having a lot of music on the bus ride – anything from joropo to salsa – according to the driver's taste. The volume is also at the whim of the driver, and you may experience a whole night of blasting merengue or rap – not necessarily great fun.

Another feature of local buses is the shading of windows with a dirty-purple tinted sticker. It's meant to be a protector against strong sun, but it ruins the view, unless you get access to an open window.

Many major companies have introduced the so-called *servicio ejecutivo* in modern air-conditioned buses, which provide better standards and shorter travelling time, and cost about 20% to 30% more than the ordinary service *(servicio normal)*. These buses have their windows shut, tinted and usually have curtains, and the air-conditioning can be *very* efficient, so have plenty of warm clothing at hand to avoid being frozen solid. These buses usually feature video entertainment, yet bloody US action movies played most of the night and often at full volume – not to mention the usually disastrous technical quality of the image and sound – can be real torture.

All intercity buses depart from and arrive at a *terminal de pasajeros* or bus terminal. Every city has such a terminal, usually outside the city centre but always linked to it by local transport. Caracas is the most important transport hub, handling buses to just about every corner of the country. Many terminals charge the *tasa de salida* (departure tax). It will probably be never more than US$0.10, but you have to pay it in a separate booth (not in the company's desk where you buy your bus ticket). The receipt you get will be collected by an attendant just before the bus leaves.

In general, there's no need to buy tickets in advance for major routes. You usually just go to the terminal, find which company has the next bus due to depart, buy your ticket and board the bus. On some minor routes, where there are only a few departures a day, it's worth considering buying your ticket several hours before the scheduled departure. The only times you really need to book well in advance are during and around Christmas, Carnaval and Easter, when Venezuelans rush to travel.

Many short-distance regional routes are serviced by the so-called *por puesto* (literally by the seat). It's a cross between a bus and a taxi – a similar kind of service as a *colectivo* in Colombia or Peru.

Por puestos are usually US-made large cars of the 60s and 70s vintage (less often, vans or minibuses), which ply fixed routes and depart when all seats are filled. They cost somewhere between 50% and 100% more than ordinary buses, but are faster and may be more comfortable. On some routes, they are the dominant or even the exclusive means of transport. Depending on the region and kind of vehicle, por puesto is also called a *carro* or *carrito*.

TRAIN

Venezuela had a railway network, but when the oil boom hit the nation, it was largely discarded in favour of road transport. The last railway that carried passengers, the 173km Barquisimeto-Puerto Cabello line, ceased this service a few years ago and now only carries freight.

CAR & MOTORCYCLE

Travelling by an independent means of transport – be it a car or motorcycle, owned or rented – is a comfortable and attractive way of getting around the country. Some advantages are schedule flexibility, access to remote areas, and the ability to seize fleeting photographic opportunities.

Venezuela is relatively safe, the road network is extensive and usually in acceptable repair, petrol stations are everywhere and petrol costs next to nothing – US$0.15 to US$0.20 per litre, depending on the octane level. It's among the cheapest petrol in the world, despite the fact that prices jumped by 500% in April 1996. There was another rise

(by 25%) in July 1997, and the government plans further increases on a regular basis, but petrol is likely to remain a bargain.

This rosy picture appears to be slightly obscured by Venezuelan traffic and local driving manners. Traffic in Venezuela, especially in Caracas, is not exactly what you're used to at home. It's wild, chaotic, noisy, polluting and anarchic.

You may still find some similarities if you're coming from, say, Italy or Spain, but if you're a novice traveller from Australia, Germany or Canada you're in for a shock. It's not that road rules don't exist; it's just that nobody respects them and they're not enforced.

Road Rules

Watching crazy traffic, reminiscent of Formula One racing, you'd never suspect that there are speed limits, but they do legally exist. Unless traffic signs say otherwise, the maximum speed limit in urban areas is 40km/h and outside built-up areas it's 80km/h.

Officially, traffic coming from the right has priority, unless indicated otherwise by signposts. In practice, however, it seems that right of way depends on the size of vehicle rather than the regulations. Accordingly, trucks generally take priority over cars, cars over motorcycles, and motorcycles over pedestrians.

Cars must be equipped with seat belts for front seats (which have to be used while driving both inside and outside urban areas), and they must have a spare tyre, wheel block, jack and a special reflector triangle which, in case of accident or breakdown, has to be placed 50m behind the car. Motorcyclists have to wear a crash helmet and motorcycles cannot be ridden at night. However, once again, all this is theoretical.

The minimum driving age in Venezuela is 18. Although there are limits on your blood alcohol level, driving drunk is not unusual and rules relating to this are seldom enforced. See the Facts for the Visitor chapter for information about driving licences.

Car Rental

There are several international car rental companies, including Hertz, Avis and Budget, and a number of local operators. They have offices at most major airports and in city centres, usually in top-end hotels. Any top-class hotel, tourist office or travel agency will provide you with detailed information about where to look for them. Many travel agents are only too willing to arrange car rental for you.

Car rental is not cheap in Venezuela – prices are higher than in the USA – and there are seldom any discounts. Local companies may be cheaper than international operators, but their cars and rental conditions can leave something to be desired.

When you get rental quotes, make sure they include insurance. Otherwise, you'll have to pay for it on top of the quoted price as it's compulsory. Some companies allow a set number of free kilometres per day or week, but others don't, and will apply a per kilometre rate from the moment you take the car.

As a rough guide only, a small car will cost around US$50 to US$60 per day (including insurance), while the discount rate for a full week will be about US$300 to US$350. A 4WD vehicle is usually considerably more expensive and harder to obtain; look for companies which have Lada Niva, which is by far the cheapest 4WD.

Rental agencies will require you to produce your driver's licence and a credit card (Visa, MasterCard and American Express are the most common). You need to be at least 21 years of age to rent a car, although renting some cars (particularly luxury models and 4WDs) may require you to be at least 23 or 25. Some companies also have an age ceiling of, usually, 65.

Read the rental contract carefully before signing (most contracts are in Spanish only). Pay close attention to any theft clause, as it will probably load any loss onto the hirer. Look at the car carefully and insist on listing any defects (including scratches) on the rental form. Check the spare tyre and take note of whether there is a jack.

Bringing your own Vehicle

Bringing a car into South America is expensive. Since there is no road through the Darien Gap it's impossible to drive all the way from North to South America. You can continue by road as far as Panama, from where the only way to move your vehicle further south is by sea or air.

The cheapest way will probably be by boat from Colón (Panama) to Barranquilla (Colombia). To find a cargo boat heading this way, go to the docks in Colón and ask what ships are sailing. Smaller cargo boats depart from Coco Solo pier in Colón. They may offer you a low price, but may not be able to help you with the paperwork you need to enter Colombia. These smaller vessels are sometimes contraband boats, and their service may be risky.

Prices are extremely variable and negotiable; you may end up paying anything between US$250 and US$600 for shipping your car, and US$100 to US$200 for a motorcycle. Prices apart, the procedure is time-consuming, as there's a lot of paperwork involved at both ends. The security of shipping is minimal, so take every possible precaution and the best insurance you can.

Motorcyclists may consider the air option, which is safer, easier and faster than boat, but more expensive. Start by asking the cargo departments of the airlines that fly to Colombia, or at the cargo terminal at Tocumen international airport in Panama City. Travel agents can sometimes help.

Another possibility is to ship your vehicle directly from the USA to Venezuela, in which case you are most likely to arrive in La Guaira, Puerto Cabello or Maracaibo. The cheapest point of departure from the USA will probably be Miami; look in the Yellow Pages under automobile transporters for toll-free 1-800 and 1-888 numbers. You usually need to give the shipping company one or two weeks notice, and expect it to take a month or more from the date of sailing. Prices are variable, so call several companies before committing yourself; the cost of shipping a car can be anywhere between US$500 and US$1500.

Drivers and motorcyclists will need their vehicle's registration papers, liability insurance and a Carnet de Passage en Douane, known in Spanish as Libreta de Pasos por Aduana. Contact your local automobile association and Venezuelan consulate for details about all documentation. Touring y Automóvil Club de Venezuela (see Automobile Club below) can be useful, and the South American Explorers Club in the USA (see the Tourist Offices section in the Facts for the Visitor chapter) may also have some helpful advice.

If planning to take your own vehicle with you, check in advance to see what spares and petrol are likely to be available. In Venezuela, you can readily get diesel and leaded petrol in three octane grades (87, 91 and 95 octanes), but there is no lead-free petrol. Venezuela has quite a developed automobile industry. Various foreign makes, including Chrysler, Fiat, Ford, General Motors, Mitsubishi, Renault and Toyota, are assembled locally, and most spare parts for these cars are easily available. Popular imported makes include Honda, Mazda, BMW, Hyundai, Peugeot and Volkswagen, so you can also expect a reasonable supply of their spare parts. However, spare parts for unpopular cars can be hard to get, so bring along a good supply if you bring your Jaguar.

Driving in Venezuela

Whether you bring your own vehicle or hire one, drive carefully and defensively. Don't expect local drivers to obey the rules. Don't assume, for example, that a vehicle will stop at a red light or stop sign. Using indicators before making a turn is rare, while driving the wrong way on one-way streets is not unusual. Pedestrians leap into traffic and often walk across highways, and sometimes freeways.

Although many roads look to be in good shape, you should always be prepared for unexpected potholes and occasional missing manhole covers. Some roads, including the notorious Caracas-La Guaira highway, have poor quality surfacing material and can be slippery, particularly when wet.

Road signposting is poor, and it's often difficult to find the right way without stopping and asking locals for directions. Signs are frequently vandalised or destroyed, and nobody seems to care much about replacing them.

When you drive in Caracas and other big cities, it's best to have the doors locked and windows rolled up (or almost rolled up), to prevent unexpected theft at red lights or in traffic jams. If you can't stand windows closed, don't have handbags and packets lying around on the seats, and wear your watch on the hand away from the window.

When driving on country highways, you'll be frequently stopped at the *alcabalas* (road check posts operated by the Guardia Nacional), where the guards will examine your passport and often car papers and driving licence as well, and sometimes will search the vehicle and your luggage.

Car security is a problem, so never leave valuables in the vehicle and lock it securely. If possible, always leave the vehicle in a guarded car park *(estacionamiento vigilado)*. If your car is stolen, report the theft immediately to the police, where a written report (known as a *denuncia*) will be produced. It is absolutely essential for claiming on your insurance or to give to your car rental company.

If you are involved in a road accident, don't move your car – regardless of how badly traffic is blocked – until the transit police arrive. They should be called as soon as possible on ☎ 167. If you move your vehicle before the transit police make a report, you can't claim on insurance. If you have an accident resulting in injuries or death, you'll be routinely detained and your vehicle impounded temporarily, even if you're not at fault.

Automobile Club

Touring y Automóvil Club de Venezuela (☎ (02) 781 4849, 781 9743, 782 1577), Torre Phelps (the board on the top of the building says Philips), Piso 15, Plaza Venezuela, Caracas, is a useful organisation for travellers with their own vehicles. The club provides general driving information and publishes a manual of traffic laws and regulations. It also offers a range of services such as towing, car maintenance, documentation, legal assistance in accident cases etc, which are usually discounted for members. The club can provide information and aid on importing and exporting vehicles into and out of Venezuela.

BICYCLE

Cycling is a cheap, convenient, healthy, environmentally sound and above all fun way of travelling. All this sounds terrific, but Venezuela is not the best place for cyclists. There are almost no bike tracks, bike rentals or any other facilities. Drivers don't show much courtesy to cyclists either. Cycling is not popular among locals, and foreign travellers with their own bikes are a rarity. Mérida is so far one of the few places where mountain bike riding has started to become popular and bikes can be hired.

This doesn't mean that cycling is impossible or not worth the bother. Roads are usually in good shape and most of the country is flat. Except for cities (particularly Caracas) where cycling can be annoying and dangerous, there are no major problems for independent cyclists. Cycling will let you cover a fair amount of ground without going too fast to enjoy the scenery. Locals will certainly be curious if you are travelling by bike and it's a good way to get talking.

Before you leave home, go over your bike with a fine-tooth comb and fill your repair kit with every imaginable spare. As with cars and motorcycles, you won't necessarily be able to buy that crucial gizmo for your machine when it breaks down somewhere in the back of beyond just as the sun sets. Bring along a solid lock to protect your bike.

Bicycles can be taken with you on the plane. You can dismantle them and put them in a bike bag or box, but it's much easier to simply wheel your bike up to the check-in desk, where it should be treated as a piece of baggage. You may have to remove pedals and handlebars so that it takes up less space in the aircraft's hold; check all this with the

airline well in advance, preferably before you pay for your ticket.

HITCHING

Hitching is never entirely safe in any country in the world, and Venezuela is no exception. Safety apart, the country is not that good for hitching. Although many people have cars, they are reluctant to stop to pick up strangers. If you decide to hitch, be prepared for long waits and even then don't count on reaching your destination. As bus transport is fast, efficient and relatively cheap, it's probably not worth wasting time hitching. Women travelling on their own shouldn't hitch at all, for they are taking a small but potentially serious risk.

BOAT

Venezuela has a number of islands off its Caribbean coast, the main one being Isla de Margarita. See the sections on Puerto La Cruz, Cumaná and Isla de Margarita for details about boats and ferries going to and from the island. There are no regular boat services to Venezuela's other islands.

The Río Orinoco is the country's major waterway, and is navigable from its mouth up to Puerto Ayacucho. However, there's no passenger service operating along the river.

LOCAL TRANSPORT
Bus

All cities and many major towns have their own urban transport, which in most places is serviced by a small bus or minibus. It is called, depending on the region, *buseta*, *carro*, *carrito*, *micro*, *camioneta* or *camionetica*. The standard, speed and efficiency varies from place to place, but on the whole city transport is slow and crowded.

Local bus transport costs next to nothing; the fare doesn't normally exceed US$0.20 and in most cities is a flat rate, so you pay the same to go one block as to go right across the city. Luggage is free, and drivers usually don't hassle you getting on with a large backpack, even into a crowded bus.

You get on and off by the front door and pay directly to the driver or his assistant, on entering or, more often, when you get off. You never get a ticket. To let the driver know that you intend to get off, simply shout *'parada'* (bus stop) or clap your hands twice, and he will stop at the nearest bus stop.

In many larger cities, bus transport is supplemented by por puestos, which are faster and more comfortable. The fare is somewhere between 20% and 80% higher than on buses, which is still a bargain. An urban por puesto has no designated stops; you just wave it down anywhere you happen to be on its route, and it will stop if it has a free seat. A por puesto also comes under a variety of names, of which a carro or carrito are the most popular.

Metro

Caracas is the only Venezuelan city that has the metro, an underground railway system. See the Caracas chapter for details.

Taxi

Taxis are a fairly inexpensive and convenient means of getting around, especially if you are travelling with a few companions. The fare will usually be the same regardless of the number of passengers, though some drivers may demand more if you have a lot of luggage.

Taxis are particularly useful when you arrive in an unfamiliar city and want to get from the bus terminal or the airport to the city centre to look for a hotel. A taxi may also be chartered for longer distances. This is convenient if you want to visit places near major cities, which are serviced by local transport infrequently or not at all.

Taxis are identifiable by a sign reading Taxi or Libre. In major cities some of them may have meters, but even so, drivers are rarely eager to switch them on, preferring to charge the fare agreed to with the passenger. Taxi drivers in touristy areas often try to charge foreign visitors a gringo fare, obviously much higher than it would be according to the meter. It's advisable to find out the correct fare beforehand from an independent source, eg from terminal officials or a hotel reception desk. Always fix the fare

with the driver *before* boarding the cab. If you can't agree on a price with the first driver, try another taxi.

ORGANISED TOURS

Tours are a popular way to visit some parts of Venezuela, largely because vast areas of the country are virtually inaccessible by public transport (eg the Orinoco Delta or Amazonas) or because a visit on one's own to scattered sights over a large territory (as in La Gran Sabana) may be considerably more time-consuming and, eventually, more expensive than a tour.

Although many companies in Caracas can send you on a tour to just about every corner of the country, it's cheaper and usually better to arrange the tour from the regional centre closest to the area you are going to visit. Accordingly, for hikes in the Andes, the place to look for a guide is Mérida; for excursions around La Gran Sabana, the cheapest organised trips are to be found in Santa Elena de Uairén; for Amazonas, the obvious point for talking to agents is Puerto Ayacucho; for the Orinoco Delta, Tucupita is the right address; and for tours to Salto Angel (Angel Falls), Ciudad Bolívar is the place to shop around. Note that not many regional tour agents accept credit cards or will charge you at least 10% more if you pay with one.

Many local tour companies receive mixed reports, sometimes totally contradictory. As a matter of fact, tours are probably some of the most difficult aspects of travel to be judged objectively. Travellers' taste is subjective and what some people consider great others can hardly stand. Furthermore, many variables, such as a particular guide you go with, weather or even the company of other travellers in your tour, may affect your general impression. It also seems that once a company is mentioned in a guidebook, it may get lazy and deliver a poor product, or an overly expensive one. To sum up, you shouldn't always jump to the first operator listed in this book, but shop around and check various options, getting a rundown on a variety of companies, prices, records, references etc.

Caracas

- *pop around 5 million*
- *area code ☎ (02)*

With 430 years of history under its belt, Caracas today is a sprawling metropolis and, like most of the large cities on the continent, it's a striking mixture of all things Latin American with its own distinctive traits. What is perhaps most characteristic of the city is its spectacular setting, pleasant climate and modern architecture. Very Yankeefied and almost denuded of its colonial character, Caracas is a vibrant, fast, progressive and cosmopolitan city – attractive, impressive and captivating in many aspects, though also depressing and disappointing in others. It's a huge Latin American city with every modern convenience and every third-world problem. You just have to go there and see for yourself.

It cannot be denied that Caracas today has some of the best modern architecture on the continent. And there are numerous sculptures, bas reliefs, mosaics and murals gracing streets, metro stations and the foyers of public buildings. However, unbalanced city growth has produced vast expanses of shantytowns that creep up hillsides all around the central districts. Caracas' setting in a valley amid rolling hills only highlights the contrast between wealth and poverty.

Caracas also has a web of motorways unseen in other South American capitals. However, the vast amount of motor vehicles in the city causes a kind of traffic frenzy, not to mention serious environmental problems. Traffic jams are a way of life, probably more so than in most large cities on the continent.

Its size and status as the capital city makes Caracas the unquestioned centre of Venezuela's political, scientific, cultural, intellectual and educational life. Whether you're interested in good food, plush hotels, theatre, museums, nightlife or shopping, nowhere else in the country will you find as much to choose from.

Set at an altitude of about 900m, Caracas

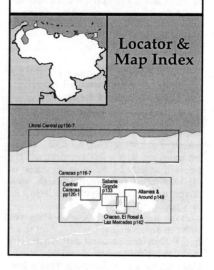

HIGHLIGHTS

- Visit the Museum of Contemporary Art
- Tour the Museum of Colonial Art
- Hike the mountains of El Ávila national park
- Explore the nightspots of Las Mercedes
- Take a weekend trip to El Hatillo

Locator & Map Index

Litoral Central pp156-7

Caracas p116-7

Central Caracas pp120-1

Sabana Grande p133

Altamira & Around p148

Chacao, El Rosal & Las Mercedes p142

enjoys an agreeable, relatively dry and sunny climate with a mean temperature of about 22°C. The rainy season lasts from June to October.

On a less enticing note, Caracas is the least secure of all Venezuelan cities. Petty crime in general, and robbery and armed assaults in particular, are increasing.

HISTORY

Caracas had a precarious beginning in 1560. It was then that Francisco Fajardo of Isla de Margarita discovered the verdant valley (today entirely taken up by the city) inhabited by Toromaima Indians. He founded a settlement named San Francisco, but was soon driven out by the natives. A year later, Juan Rodríguez Suárez, the founder of Mérida, arrived and resurrected San Francisco, which by then had been razed by the Indians. Years of struggle followed as the village tried to survive repeated Indian attacks in which many of the small population were killed, including Rodríguez.

In 1567, a complete conquest of the valley was ordered by the governor of the province, Pedro Ponce de León. An expedition of 136 men under the command of Captain Diego de Losada was sent from El Tocuyo. They defeated a brave Indian resistance before re-establishing the settlement yet again on 25 July 1567. The new township was named Santiago de León de Caracas; Santiago after the patron saint of Spain, León after the governor, and Caracas after the Indian group which inhabited the coastal cordillera and which was apparently less troublesome and hostile than other tribes in the region. The date is considered Caracas' formal birthday and Diego de Losada its official founder.

In 1577, Juan de Pimentel, the governor of the day, elected the young town as the administrative seat of the Province of Venezuela. Thus Caracas became the third and final capital of the province (Coro was the first, in 1527-46, followed by El Tocuyo in 1547-77).

The earliest map of Caracas, drawn in 1578, clearly shows the extension of the 'city'. It stretched two blocks each way from the Plaza Mayor, and consisted altogether of 25 blocks. Caracas at that time was inhabited by 60 families.

From the beginning, the town's development was hindered by constant setbacks, including pirate raids, plagues and natural disasters. The first pirate attack came in 1595, leaving the town sacked and burnt to the ground. Reconstructed and revived, Caracas went on to be destroyed by a violent earthquake in 1641, only four years after the bishops had moved the archdiocese here from Coro. Some 500 inhabitants died in the ruins.

The 18th century proved to be more for-

The centuries-old Caracas coat-of-arms

tunate. In 1725, the Universidad Real y Pontificia de Caracas (the present-day Universidad Central de Venezuela) became the province's first university. Three years later, the Real Compañía Guipuzcoana was created. This trading company, comprised of 700 captains and merchants from the Basque province, was given a monopoly over trade between Spain and the colony. In Venezuela, the company had its headquarters in the port of La Guaira and a branch in Puerto Cabello.

Guipuzcoana contributed greatly to Caracas' progress, though later on its aggressive practices and corruption aroused widespread discontent among the colonists. In 1749, Juan Francisco de León marched on Caracas with 800 men to protest against the company's oppressive tactics. In the opinion of many historians, this riot was the first open protest of importance, which sowed the seeds of what became the independence movement. The company was eventually dissolved in 1785.

On 28 March 1750 Caracas became the place of birth of Francisco Miranda and on 24 July 1783 that of Simón Bolívar; the former was to pave the way to independence, the latter was to realise that aim.

On 19 April 1810, a group of councillors, supported by some notable caraqueños, denounced the authority of the Spanish governor and formed a Supreme Junta to replace the government. The political struggle continued for over a year until 5 July 1811, when the congress convened in Caracas and solemnly declared the independence of Venezuela. The document was signed by all but one delegate.

On Maundy Thursday of 1812, an earthquake wrecked the town and killed some 10,000 people. The conservative clergy swiftly seized the opportunity to declare that it was a punishment from heaven for the rebellion against the Spanish Crown. Independence, however, was only nine years away, and was eventually sealed by Bolívar's victory at the Battle of Carabobo on 24 June 1821. Spain did not recognise the sovereignty of Venezuela until 1845.

Despite its political merits, Caracas continued to grow at a very modest pace. It wasn't until the 1870s that an extensive modernisation programme was launched by General Guzmán Blanco, the ruler of the day, known as El Modernizador. A number of monumental buildings, among them the National Capitol, were erected over the following decades, considerably changing the face of the city centre. Unfortunately, in 1900, yet another serious earthquake ruined much of the urban fabric and reconstruction had to begin all over again.

Then came the oil boom and things began to change at breakneck speed. Oil money was pumped into modernisation, successfully transforming the somewhat bucolic colonial town into a vast concrete sprawl. In the name of progress, most colonial buildings were demolished and their place taken by spanking commercial centres and steel-and-glass towers. Some ambitious projects, including the freeways to Maiquetía and

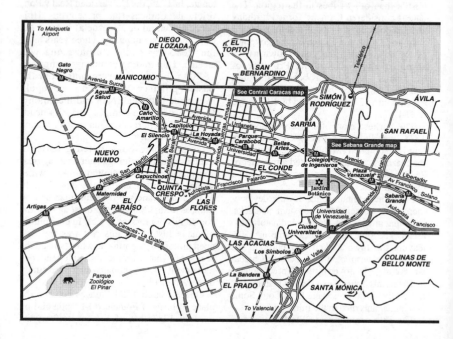

Valencia, the UCV university campus, La Rinconada horse-racing track and the cable car up to Mt El Ávila, were carried out in the 1950s, and rapid urban development continued into the 1980s, when the metro was opened. Growth has slowed considerably over the past decade as a result of the country's economic crisis.

Spurred on by the illusory dream of wealth, thousands of rural dwellers rushed into Caracas, but most never managed to get their share of the city's prosperity and now lead a hand-to-mouth existence in *ranchos* (ramshackle huts) covering the hills around the central districts. Over the last 50 years, the city's population has expanded from some 400,000 to nearly five million. Some unofficial estimates put the current population within the metropolitan boundaries at as high as six million. Expansion was so dramatic that the city spilled over well into the neighbouring state of Miranda.

ORIENTATION

Nestled in a long and narrow valley, the city spreads for at least 20km from west to east. To the north looms the steep, verdant wall of Parque Nacional El Ávila, refreshingly free of human dwellings. To the south, by contrast, the city is expanding up the hillsides, with modern *urbanizaciones* and derelict *barrios* invading and occupying every acceptably flat piece of land.

The valley itself is a dense urban fabric, with forests of skyscrapers sticking out of a mass of low-rise buildings. The area from El Silencio to Chacao can be considered the greater centre, packed with commercial centres, banks, offices, shops, hotels, eating establishments and public buildings. The main line of the metro (No 1) goes right along this axis.

The historic quarter (called the centre in this chapter) is at the west end of the greater centre, and is clearly recognisable on the map by the original chessboard layout of the

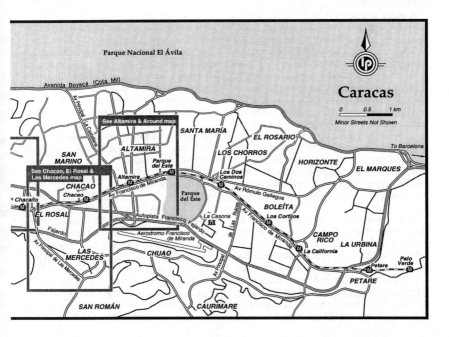

streets. About 1.5km to the east is the Parque Central area, noted for good museums, theatres and cinemas. Another 2km east is Sabana Grande, centred on an attractive pedestrian mall lined with shops and restaurants. Continuing east, you come to Chacao, a commercial district of rather low priority for tourists, and then to the trendy Altamira, which boasts a number of up-market restaurants and night spots. El Rosal and Las Mercedes, to the south of Chacao, are two other districts catering for gourmets and night trippers.

Although Caracas' attractions are scattered throughout the city, many of them are easily accessible by metro. In the addresses listed in this chapter, the nearest metro station is usually included if the place is within walking distance of the station.

A curiosity of Caracas is the street address system in the historic quarter, which might be difficult for newcomers to follow. It's actually not the streets which bear names but the street corners, or *esquinas*.

A place is identified by the street corners on either side, and its address is given corner to corner. If, for instance, the address is Piñango a Conde, you know that the place is between these two street corners. If the place is right on the corner, its address would be Esquina Conde. In modern times, authorities have given numbers and cardinal point designations to the streets (Este, Oeste, Norte and Sur), but locals continue to stick to the esquinas. Other than in the old town, a conventional system is used in which the streets, and not the corners, indicate where the place is located. Major streets are commonly named Avenidas. Street numbers are seldom used, and you'll rarely find one on façades or entrance doors.

The Venezuelan system of designating floors is the same as that used in the UK. The ground floor is the *piso bajo*, the 1st floor is the *primer piso*, then comes the *segundo piso* (2nd floor) etc. In addresses, floors are usually written in the form Piso 1, Piso 2 etc. In lifts (elevators), abbreviations used on the buttons include PB (ground floor), M (mezzanine), S (basement level) and PH (penthouse).

INFORMATION
Tourist Offices
The Corpoturismo tourist office (☎ 507 86 07; fax 573 89 83) is on the 35th floor of the Torre Oeste (West Tower), Parque Central (metro Bellas Artes). When you enter the tower, take the lift from Sótano Uno level (lifts from other levels don't go to this floor). The office is open Monday to Friday from 8.30 am to 12.30 pm and 2 to 5 pm. There's also a Corpoturismo outlet (☎ (031) 55 10 60) at the international terminal of Maiquetía airport (open daily from 7 am to 9 pm).

The Hotel Caracas Hilton (☎ 503 50 00) has an information desk (open daily) in the main lobby. It's officially a service for hotel guests only, but the friendly and knowledgeable English-speaking staff are likely to attend to you if they are not too busy.

Inparques
The Instituto Nacional de Parques Nacionales, commonly known as Inparques (☎ 285 41 06, 285 42 59, 285 50 56; fax 285 30 70), has its office just east of the Parque del Este metro station. It is open Monday to Friday from 8.30 am to 12.30 pm and 1.30 to 5 pm. The office may provide general information about the parks but has few maps or brochures. You can use its library, though it doesn't have many publications. You don't have to come here for permits to the parks, as they are no longer necessary.

Foreign Embassies & Consulates
These are listed under Embassies in the Facts for the Visitor chapter.

Visa Extensions
Visa and tourist card extensions are handled by the DIEX office (2nd floor) on Avenida Baralt, facing Plaza Miranda (metro Capitolio). The office is a classic example of Venezuelan bureaucracy and chaos; it's crowded, confusing and officials are not particularly friendly or helpful.

You are allowed to stay in Venezuela for up to four months, ie you can get an extension of a month on top of your three-month visa or tourist card. The extension costs

US$24. Your passport, one photo, a photocopy of your onward ticket and a letter explaining the purpose of the extension, written on a *papel sellado*, are required, plus the form which they'll give you to fill in. All that has to be delivered between 8 am and 11 am, Monday to Friday, and processing can take up to eight working days.

Money

There's a constellation of banks in Caracas, but almost none of them handle cash exchange transactions. One of the few exceptions is Banco do Brasil, Centro Lido, Avenida Francisco de Miranda (metro Chacaíto or Chacao), which often changes cash and, when it does, gives just about the best rate in town.

The usual place to change cash is the *casa de cambio*, and there are quite a lot of them. One with a good reputation is Italcambio, which has outlets in the historic centre, Sabana Grande and Altamira (see the maps for locations). They are all open Monday to Friday from 8 am to 12.30 pm and 1.30 to 5 pm, Saturday from 8.30 am until noon. There's also an Italcambio exchange desk at the international terminal of Maiquetía airport (see Getting There & Away later in this chapter for more information on changing money at the airport).

All Italcambio offices also sell foreign currency and change travellers cheques. However, Amex cheques can be exchanged at a better rate at Banco Consolidado (though the transaction will take longer), which has plenty of branches around the city.

The refund assistance point for holders of Amex travellers cheques is Turisol (☎ 959 60 91, 959 81 47, 959 94 17), in Centro Ciudad Comercial Tamanaco (CCCT), Nivel PB (see Metro under Getting Around later in this chapter for information on getting to CCCT). Amex has a 24-hour service on ☎ 206 03 33.

Cash advances on Visa and MasterCard can be easily obtained at most branches of Banco de Venezuela, Banco Unión, Banco Mercantil, Banco Provincial and some other banks. Many of them have ATMs.

Post & Communications

Post The main Ipostel post office, Avenida Urdaneta, Esquina Carmelitas, close to Plaza Bolívar, has a poste restante service. Letters sent here to you should be addressed with your name, Lista de Correos, IPOSTEL, Carmelitas, Caracas 1010.

Another convenient central post office is on Plaza La Candelaria, next to the church. Post offices are scattered throughout the city, including one in Sabana Grande (in the Centro Comercial Arta on Plaza Chacaíto), in Chacao (Avenida Francisco de Miranda) and in Altamira (Plaza Sur Altamira).

There are a number of international and local courier companies, including DHL (☎ 235 90 80, 235 20 49), UPS (☎ 41 64 54) and Fedex (☎ 273 30 00). Shop around as rates vary considerably.

Telephone Caracas' only CANTV office which offers an international call service through the operator is in Centro Plaza, Avenida Francisco de Miranda, Los Palos Grandes (metro Altamira). Many top-end hotels will place your call through the CANTV operator, but will add a hefty charge on top of this already expensive service.

It's best to call from public phones, either using a phone card or making a reverse-charge call. There are public phones everywhere, but many are out of order and those that work may be besieged by people.

Emergency
All the services listed below operate 24 hours a day. Don't expect the attendants to speak English, so if your Spanish is not up to scratch, try to get a local to call on your behalf.

Police	☎ 169
Traffic Police	☎ 167
Fire	☎ 166
Ambulance	
(central suburbs)	☎ 545 4545, 545 2111
(eastern suburbs)	☎ 265 0251, 261 7871
Medical Emergency	☎ 483 7021, 483 6092

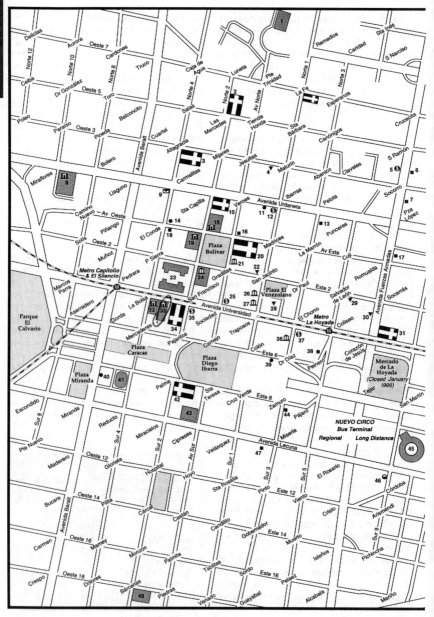

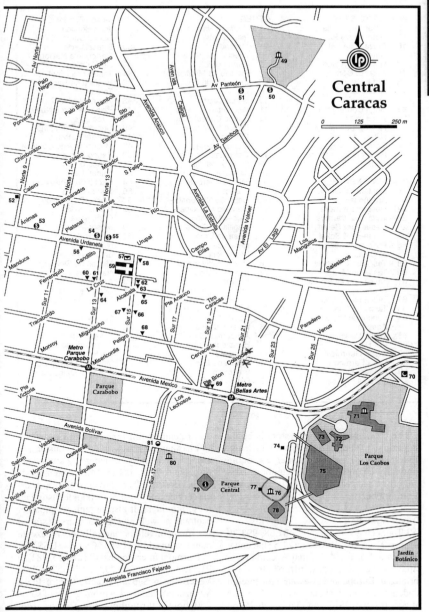

Central Caracas

0   125   250 m

PLACES TO STAY
6   Hotel Terepaima
7   Hotel Metropol
16 Plaza Catedral
    Hotel
17 Hotel Hollywood
18 Hotel El Conde
38 Hotel Caracol
44 Hotel Río
    Guarapiche
47 Hotel Center Park
52 Hotel Inter
74 Hotel Caracas
    Hilton
77 Caracas
    Residencias Anauco
    Hilton

PLACES TO EAT
4   Restaurant Dama
    Antañona
22 Restaurant Kafta
28 Tasca La Atarraya
29 Restaurant Beirut
30 Restaurant Sokol
56 Pollo en Brasas
    El Coyuco
58 Tasca La Carabela
60 Tasca de Manolo
61 Tasca La Mansión de
    Altamira
62 Tasca La Tertulia
63 Tasca La Cita
64 Lunchería Doña
    Agapita
65 Tasca Mallorca
66 Bar Basque
67 Tasca Guernica
68 Casa Farruco
69 Arepera Doña
    Arepota

OTHER
1   Panteón Nacional
2   Iglesia Las
    Mercedes
3   Iglesia Altagracia
5   Banco Unión
8   Palacio de Miraflores
9   Ipostel Main Post
    Office
10 Santa Capilla
11 Italcambio
12 Banco Consolidado
13 Banco Provincial
14 Biblioteca
    Metropolitana
15 Gobernación
19 Casa Amarilla
20 Catedral
21 Museo Sacro de
    Caracas
23 Capitolio Nacional
24 Consejo Municipal,
    Museo Criollo &
    Capilla de Santa
    Rosa de Lima
25 Banco de
    Venezuela
26 Museo Bolivariano
27 Casa Natal de
    Bolívar
31 Iglesia Sagrado
    Corazón de Jesús
32 Former Supreme
    Court
33 Palacio de las
    Academias &
    Biblioteca
    Nacional
34 Iglesia de San
    Francisco
35 Banco Mercantil

36 Museo Fundación
    John Boulton
37 Banco Unión
39 Dirección de
    Cartografía Nacional
40 DIEX Office
41 Teatro Municipal
42 Basílica de Santa
    Teresa
43 Teatro Nacional
45 Plaza de Toros Nuevo
    Circo
46 Carritos to Junquito
48 Cuadra Bolívar
49 Museo de Arte Colonial
50 Banco Consolidado
51 Banco Unión
53 Italcambio
54 Banco de Venezuela
55 Banco Unión
57 Ipostel Post Office
59 Iglesia de la
    Candelaria
70 Mosque
71 Galería de Arte
    Nacional & Museo
    de Bellas Artes
72 Museo de Ciencias
    Naturales
73 Ateneo de Caracas
75 Complejo Cultural
    Teresa Carreño
76 Museo de Arte
    Contemporáneo
78 Torre Este
79 Torre Oeste &
    Corpoturismo Tourist
    Office
80 Museo de los Niños
81 Buses to Maiquetía
    Airport

The Caracas telephone system is being modernised. There are both six and seven digit numbers, but the former are being gradually changed. The 02 telephone area code for Caracas is for both six and seven digit numbers.

Travel Agencies
IVI Tours (☎ 993 60 82, 993 87 38, 993 39 30; fax 92 96 26), Residencia La Hacienda, Piso Bajo, Local 1-4-T, Final Avenida Principal de las Mercedes, offers attractive airfares to Europe and elsewhere for foreign students, teachers and people under 26 years of age. It issues ISIC and ITIC cards if you are a genuine full-time student or teacher. IVI has agreements with various businesses around the country, which give cardholders discounts (about 10% to 20%) on their goods or services (hotels, restaurants, shops, medical services etc) – ask for a booklet listing all these providers. It also organises upmarket ecotours as well as cheaper tours designed for young travellers, and sells the Venezuela map produced by ITM of Canada (US$10).

Fairmont Internacional (782 84 33, 781 70 91, 782 08 51; fax 793 38 79), at Plaza Venezuela in Sabana Grande (metro Plaza Venezuela), can book a room in any of some 250 hotels throughout the country (not budget ones), charging US$4 for the service. It also sells air tickets and can arrange car rental.

Bookshops
The best bookshops specialising in English-language publications include The American Book Shop (☎ 263 54 55, 267 41 34), Edificio Belveder, Avenida San Juan Bosco, near the corner of 1a Transversal (metro Altamira), and The English Book Shop (☎ 979 13 08, 979 40 98), Centro Comercial Concresa, Prados del Este.

The Librería La France (☎ 952 08 18), in the Centro Comercial Chacaíto (basement level), Plaza Brión (commonly called Plaza Chacaíto), has the best selection of books in French, while the Librería Alemana Oscar Todtmann (☎ 71 08 81), in the Centro Comercial El Bosque, Avenida Libertador (metro Chacaíto), offers the most extensive choice of German-language publications.

For books in Italian, try the Librería Italiana (☎ 71 19 64), Avenida Francisco Solano, Sabana Grande, or the Librería Rizzoli (☎ 286 24 42), Centro Plaza, 1a Transversal between 1a Avenida and Avenida Andrés Bello, Los Palos Grandes (metro Altamira).

So far, Lonely Planet guidebooks can only be bought in the Tecni-Ciencia Libros (☎ 959 55 47, 959 50 35), in the Centro Ciudad Comercial Tamanaco (CCCT), Nivel C-2, Chuao. This amazing bookshop has heaps of publications, including dictionaries, specialist fare and coffee-table books. Its well-stocked travel section (undoubtedly the best in town) boasts more than 50 LP titles. As we went to press, The American Book Shop planned to sell LP guidebooks.

Nature lovers may want to check the small bookshop of the Sociedad Conservacionista Audubon de Venezuela (☎ 993 25 25), in the Centro Comercial Paseo Las Mercedes (next to the public toilets on the ground floor), and the Librería Ecológica (☎ 408 10 16), the bookshop of the Environment Ministry.

Specialist bookshops apart, Caracas has plenty of general-interest bookshops, which mostly deal in locally published Spanish-language books. If you've already mastered the language, you'll find a wide choice of tomes on Venezuelan history, politics, ethnology, ethnography, nature and the like, not to mention Latin American literature. You'll also find a large variety of lavishly illustrated coffee-table books on Venezuela's art, architecture and nature – a tempting buy to take back home. They also often stock dictionaries, maps and some locally produced guidebooks.

Books are not cheap in Venezuela. If you want to save some bolívares, first check the second-hand bookshops and markets. The cheapest place to buy books is the street market on Avenida Fuerzas Armadas, Romualda a Plaza López (metro La Hoyada). The bookstalls there have a haphazard range of new and second-hand books, including some rare old editions which are virtually unobtainable elsewhere. A similar street market, but smaller and not so cheap, is on Paseo Anauco just off Avenida México (metro Bellas Artes). There are also a dozen or so bookstalls in the grounds of Universidad Central de Venezuela. They sell new books below normal bookshop prices. All these markets deal almost exclusively in Spanish-language books. For second-hand books in English, try The American Book Shop listed above.

Libraries
Caracas has a number of libraries, the major one being the Biblioteca Nacional, Avenida Universidad, across the street from the Capitolio Nacional.

If you're interested in English-language publications, the widest selection is in the library of the British Council (☎ 91 52 22), Torre La Noria, Las Mercedes. Alternatively, try the library of the Centro Venezolano Americano, or CVA (☎ 993 79 11), Edificio CVA, Avenida Principal de las Mercedes.

The Asociación Cultural Humboldt (☎ 52 64 45, 52 76 34), Avenida Jorge Washington con Avenida Juan Germán Roscio, San Bernardino, has a library featuring German-language books, papers and periodicals. The library of the Alianza Francesa (☎ 267 64 58, 267 31 56), Quinta Wilmaru, Avenida Mohedano entre 1a y 2a Transversal, La Castellana, has publications in French.

Guidebooks

There are several locally published guidebooks concerning a number of aspects of Caracas, and some of them may be useful for visitors. The bilingual Spanish/English *Caracas Gastronomic Guide*, published by Miro Popic and updated annually, is an excellent insight into the local eating scene. The US$8 guide covers more than 600 restaurants, plus dozens of cafés, delicatessens, bars, pubs and discotheques.

The same publisher produces the bilingual *Ecotourism Guide to Venezuela* (see the Book section in the Facts for the Visitor chapter) and the Spanish-only *Guía Vial de Venezuela*. All three guidebooks are available in many of Caracas' larger bookshops.

Living in Venezuela, published by the Venezuelan-American Chamber of Commerce and Industry, may be useful for people staying in Caracas for a longer time. It's theoretically a guide to the whole country but most of it is dedicated to the capital. It's updated every two years and can be bought (for a hefty US$45) in the Chamber of Commerce office (☎ 263 08 33), Torre Credival, Segunda Avenida de Campo Alegre, near the corner of Avenida Francisco de Miranda, Campo Alegre (metro Chacaíto or Chacao).

Maps

Some of the better bookshops (see Bookshops earlier) sell folded Caracas city maps which have a map of Venezuela on the reverse. Perhaps the best Caracas/country map has been published by Lagoven oil company, but it's not distributed through bookshops. It may still be available at some Lagoven petrol stations but stocks seem to be running out.

If you can't get any of these, there's a reasonable Caracas city map at the back of the local phone directory. It's also worth remembering that every metro station has a Caracas map posted somewhere near the ticket booth, and usually another copy on the train platform.

For information on where to buy maps for the rest of Venezuela, see Maps in the Facts for the Visitor chapter.

Newspapers

El Nacional and *El Universal* are the two leading Caracas papers and both give a good rundown of local and international politics, economy, culture and sport. Another interesting local paper is the liberal *El Globo*, noted for its in-depth articles. In addition, there are several tabloids, including *El Mundo*, *El Nuevo País*, *Últimas Noticias* and *Reporte*.

Economía Hoy is a business newspaper, printed on cream-orange paper and published daily, except on weekends. The Monday edition carries a 20-page English-language *Guardian Weekly* supplement, which features international politics and culture, though rarely anything about Venezuela.

If you want to keep track of Venezuelan issues, buy *The Daily Journal*, a popular general-interest daily published in Caracas. Covering local and international news, culture, sport and entertainment, it's possibly the best source of information about local affairs for English-speaking readers.

The most recent English-language competitor on the local scene, introduced in 1997, is *The Miami Herald* (international edition), transmitted by satellite and printed and distributed every morning by *El Universal*. All the above-mentioned papers are available from newsstands throughout Caracas.

Major foreign papers such as *The New York Times*, *The International Herald Tribune*, *The Times*, *Le Monde*, *Der Spiegel* etc are sold by some of the better central newsstands, specialist bookshops and top-class hotels. *Time*, *Newsweek* and *The Economist* are the most widely distributed foreign weekly magazines.

Film & Photography Equipment

Kodak and Fuji print film is easily available from a variety of establishments, including photo shops, pharmacies, souvenir shops etc. Slide film is a bit harder to come by, especially if you're after professional products like Fujichrome's Velvia or Provia. Following is a list of some of the cheaper Fuji and/or Kodak slide film distributors:

Casa Hellmund
    Oficentro Los Ruíces, Piso 3, Avenida Diego Cisneros, Los Ruíces (metro Los Cortijos) (☎ 238 27 11)
Elinchrom Venezolana
    Villa Arenas, No 24, 4a Avenida de Campo Alegre (metro Chacao) (☎ 266 19 12, 266 24 01)
Foto Print
    Centro Comercial Chacaíto, Local 137 (metro Chacaíto) (☎ 952 08 29, 952 54 18)
Foto Profesional
    Edificio Mimi, Boulevard de Sabana Grande (metro Plaza Venezuela) (☎ 762 19 64, 762 57 43)

As a rough guide only, a Provia roll of 36 exposures will cost around US$10, and Velvia about US$12.

It's easy to have prints done at numerous minilabs, and the quality is usually acceptable, but you should be more careful with processing slides. Though a number of places offer this service, the quality is not always satisfactory. Below are some of the best slide processors in Caracas:

Tono Continuo
    Edificio Cosmos, Piso 9, Oficina 9-C, Calle La Joya, Chacao (metro Chacao) (☎ 261 84 89)
Foto Print
    see above for address
Cámara Grafic
    Edificio Feltre, Penthouse, Calle Capitolio, Boleíta Sur (metro La California) (☎ 239 12 73)

Slide processing costs about US$4 per roll. Foto Print does the best slide duplicates in town. Cámara Grafic is the only place which offers the Cibachrome process. The Foto Laboratorio G y P (☎ 263 85 31, 267 40 86), Edificio Centro Altamira, Mezzanina, Local 16, Avenida San Juan Bosco, Altamira, does some of the best large-format prints, from both slides and negative film.

Photo equipment is expensive and the choice limited, so be sure to bring reliable gear. If something goes wrong with your camera, try the Micromecánica Osmar (☎ 484 80 02, 481 17 83), Edificio Disconti, Mezzanina, Oficina 2, Padre Sierra a Muñoz (metro Capitolio).

Camping & Trekking Equipment

Imported camping and trekking gear is increasingly available but expensive. Locally produced gear is cheaper and often of satisfactory quality. Gas canisters for common camping stoves (such as Gas Bluet) can be bought without major problems.

Corporación Verotex (☎ 951 36 70, 977 45 03), Centro Comercial Arta, Piso 2, Oficina 2-6, Plaza Chacaíto, has a reasonable choice of camping, trekking and mountaineering equipment and is one of the cheapest retailers around. It's also one of the very few rental outlets. Sample rental prices per day are US$3.50 for a backpack or sleeping bag and US$6/8 for a two/three-person tent. You need to leave an imprint of your Visa or MasterCard when renting the equipment.

It may be even cheaper at Natura Aventura (☎ 21 48 79), Calle Principal de Campo Rico, Local 12 (metro La California). It makes backpacks, sleeping bags and high-mountain clothing, and imports other camping and mountaineering items, and may have some gear for rent. It plans to offer adventure tours.

More upmarket is the well-stocked Marumen Store (☎ 261 81 34, 262 06 61), 3a Transversal, between Avenidas Luis Roche and San Juan Bosco, Altamira, which also has some fishing gear, maps, hiking guides and camping accessories, but it doesn't offer rental.

Medical Services

Many minor health problems, such as mild diarrhoea, cold, cough, pain, small cuts and wounds etc, can be solved by just applying a proper remedy which you can buy in a pharmacy (farmacia). Caracas has a wide array of pharmacies, and there's always one in every suburb of the city that takes its turn and stays open the whole night. They are listed in the local press and you'll recognise them by a lit board or neon reading 'turno'. Some drugs, which can only be bought with a prescription in western countries (eg antibiotics), are readily available over the counter in local pharmacies. Always make sure you buy the proper drug (it may appear under a different name than in other countries) and check the expiry date.

If you happen to get really sick, seek qualified medical help promptly. Your embassy or consulate may recommend doctors or clinics, but if you can't get that advice, act on your own without delay. Fortunately, Caracas has a number of public hospitals, private clinics, specialist medical centres and dental surgeries.

If you're insured, it's preferable to use private clinics rather than government-owned institutions which are cheaper but may not be as well equipped. Most private clinics offer in-patient and out-patient services, carry out laboratory tests and have specialist doctors, some of whom speak English. Reputable medical facilities include:

Clínica El Ávila
    Avenida San Juan Bosco con 6a Transversal, Altamira (☎ 208 10 01, 208 11 11)
Clínica Instituto Médico La Floresta
    Avenida Principal de la Floresta con Calle Santa Ana (☎ 285 21 11, 285 32 22)
Policlínica Metropolitana
    Calle A con Avenida Principal de Caurimare (☎ 908 01 00, 908 01 40)
Centro Médico de Caracas
    Final de Avenida Eraso, San Bernardino (☎ 52 22 22, 509 91 11)

Most private clinics also offer vaccinations, but you can get them for free in public health centres called *unidades sanitarias*. They are in most suburbs, including a conveniently located one at Avenida Libertador in Las Delicias (☎ 71 92 81). They can inoculate you against yellow fever, and will also administer a series of injections against rabies if you've been bitten by a suspect animal.

The Escuela de Farmacia (☎ 605 26 86, 662 68 78) at the Universidad Central de Venezuela has antivenins for some snake species.

Caracas tap water is heavily chlorinated and is said to be safe to drink, but it's better to avoid it. Bottled water is readily available from most food shops, supermarkets, cafés, restaurants etc.

Dangers & Annoyances

Since the late 1980s, Caracas has become increasingly unsafe, more so than any other city in the country. One obvious reason for this is the city's large and rapidly growing population, many of whom live in ranchos far below the poverty level. Another cause is a declining standard of living, the result of a precarious economy and political instability. Predictably, poor barrios are where the majority of violent crimes are reported but, unfortunately, criminals of the slums are venturing into more affluent districts.

So be on your guard. See Dangers & Annoyances in the Facts for the Visitor chapter for general tips. Don't venture into shantytowns at any time of the day, let alone at night. Central districts are OK during the day, though armed robberies occasionally occur. Expensive jewellery, watches and cameras will definitely multiply your chances of being mugged.

The area around the Nuevo Circo bus terminal can be unsafe even during daytime. The historic centre is reasonably safe for daytime strolls, but may be risky after dark. The Sabana Grande is heading the same way, though so far it's quite secure until 8 to 9 pm, the time when crowds rapidly dwindle. Altamira, La Castellana, Los Palos Grandes and Las Mercedes have a reputation of being relatively safe at night.

The hillside Parque El Calvario, just west of the historic centre, appears in some guidebooks (not this one). Note that travellers have repeatedly been robbed at knife point in the park by what seem to be professional youth gangs. See The Airport and Metro towards the end of this chapter for other possible dangers.

Caracas' traffic is heavy, fast and wild – be careful! Drivers don't obey traffic rules and they may run red lights or crawl against the flow up a one way street if that's what they feel like doing. Crossing the street may involve some risk; take it for granted that no driver will stop to give you right of way.

Air pollution is largely a by-product of heavy traffic and the poor mechanical condition of many vehicles, which often spew out clouds of fumes. Pollution may appal visitors from cleaner countries, especially when there is no wind to disperse it.

Non-smokers may have a hard time. Venezuela is a smoking nation and it's permitted nearly everywhere: in just about all the restaurants, in offices, at the bus and airport terminals etc. Public transport is no-smoking territory, and the metro is probably the ultimate example of that, but in taxis much depends on the driver's habits.

THE CENTRE & AROUND

The historic sector, where the city was born, has lost much of its original identity. In a rush toward modernisation, many colonial houses were replaced with modern buildings, which range from nondescript plain edifices to futuristic tinted-glass towers. Architectural ragbag that it is, the centre is colourful and alive, and boasts some important sights, many of which are related to Bolívar. All are within easy walking distance of each other.

Plaza Bolívar

This is the nucleus of the old town, with the inevitable monument to Bolívar in the middle. The equestrian statue was cast in Europe, shipped in pieces, assembled and unveiled in 1874, later than planned because the ship carrying it had foundered on the Archipiélago de Los Roques. The plaza is a favourite playground for all sorts of political visionaries and religious messiahs, who deliver their passionate speeches to a casual audience, mostly at lunchtime. The leafy square is lined on all sides by a collection of buildings from different epochs, some of which are detailed in the following sections.

Catedral

Set on the eastern side of the plaza, the cathedral was built in 1665-1713 after the 1641 earthquake had destroyed the previous church. A wide five-nave interior supported on 32 columns was largely remodelled in the late 19th century. The Bolívar family chapel is in the middle of the right-hand aisle and can be easily recognised by a modern sculpture of El Libertador mourning his parents and wife.

Museo Sacro de Caracas

Accommodated in a meticulously restored colonial house next to the cathedral, the museum displays a modest but carefully selected collection of religious art. It also has an interesting cultural programme featuring theatre, poetry, musical recitals and concerts, which are staged on the premises, plus a pleasant café (see Places to Eat). The museum is open daily, except Monday, from 10 am to 5 pm.

Concejo Municipal

Occupying half of the southern side of the square, the building was erected by the Caracas bishops in 1641-96 to house the Colegio Seminario de Santa Rosa de Lima. In 1725, the Universidad de Caracas, the province's first university, was established here. Today, part of the building is open to the public (Tuesday to Friday from 9 to noon and 2.30 to 4.30 pm, Saturday and Sunday from 10 am to 4 pm) and is worth visiting.

The **Museo Criollo**, on the ground floor, features a collection of dioramas depicting the life of the turn-of-the-century Caracas. They were created by a local artist, Raúl Santana. Also on display are items related to the town's history. Don't miss the elaborate models of central Caracas as it looked in the 1810s and 1930s, if only to realise how drastically the city has changed.

On the 1st floor is a collection of 80 paintings by Emilio Boggio (1857-1920), a Venezuelan artist who lived in Paris. It's normally closed to the public, but the attendants by the main entrance may occasionally show you around.

The western side of the building houses the **Capilla de Santa Rosa de Lima**, where on 5 July 1811 the congress declared Venezuela's independence, though it was another 10 years before this became a reality. The chapel has been restored with the decoration and furniture of the time.

While strolling around the spacious courtyard with a fountain in the middle, look for the famous Caracas map of 1578; its enlarged reproduction is displayed in the courtyard's cloister.

Casa Amarilla

The 17th-century balconied mansion called the Yellow House, on the western side of the plaza, was originally the infamous royal prison. Wholly revamped and painted yellow (hence its name) after independence, the building was converted into a presidential residence. Today it's the seat of the Ministry of Foreign Affairs and can't be visited, but have a look at the well preserved colonial appearance of its exterior. The neighbouring building of the Gobernación stages temporary exhibitions in its ground-floor hall.

Santa Capilla

The Holy Chapel, one block north of Plaza Bolívar, is a neo-Gothic church modelled on the Sainte Chapelle of Paris and looking a bit like a wedding cake. It was ordered by Guzmán Blanco in 1883 and built on the site of the rustic San Mauricio chapel where the first mass was allegedly celebrated after the foundation of the town. Illuminated by the warm light passing through colourful stained-glass windows, the decorative interior boasts the painting *Multiplication of the Bread* by Arturo Michelena (in the right-hand aisle).

Capitolio Nacional

The neoclassical National Capitol, the seat of the congress, occupies the entire block just south-west of Plaza Bolívar. It's a complex of two buildings, commissioned in the 1870s by Guzmán Blanco and erected on the site of a convent, whose occupants had been expelled by the dictator and the old building razed.

In the central part of the northern building is the famous **Salón Elíptico**, the oval hall with a large mural on its domed ceiling. The painting, depicting the Battle of Carabobo, was done in 1888 by perhaps the most notable Venezuelan artist of the day, Martín Tovar y Tovar. The southern wall of the hall is crammed with portraits of distinguished leaders of the independence wars. In front of this wall is Bolívar's bust on top of a marble pedestal; the original Act of Independence of 1811 is kept in the chest inside the pedestal. It's put on public view on 5 July, which is Independence Day.

Tovar y Tovar has left behind more military works of art in two adjoining halls: the Salón Amarillo has on its ceiling a depiction of the Battle of Junín, while the Salón Rojo has been embellished with a scene from the Battle of Boyacá. The Capitolio is open for visits daily from 9 am to 12.30 pm and 3 to 5 pm.

Iglesia de San Francisco

Just south of the Capitolio, the San Francisco church was built in the 1570s but was remodelled on several occasions during the 17th and 18th centuries. Guzmán Blanco couldn't resist his passion for modernising and placed a new neoclassical façade on the church, to match the just completed Capitol building. Fortunately, the interior of the church didn't undergo such an extensive alteration and has preserved its colonial character and much of its old decoration. Have a look at the richly gilded baroque altarpieces distributed along both side walls, and stop at San Onofre, in the right-hand aisle. He is the most venerated saint in the church due to his miraculous powers of bringing health, happiness and a good job.

It was in this church in 1813 that Bolívar was proclaimed El Libertador, and also here that his much-celebrated funeral was held in 1842, after his remains had been brought from Santa Marta in Colombia, 12 years after his death.

Impressions of Caracas

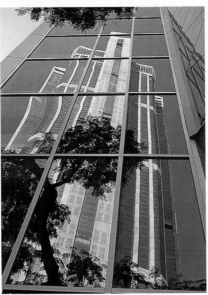

Top: Kinetic work by Jesús Soto, Cubo Negro, Caracas
Bottom: Modern face of Caracas

Guzmán Blanco

Casa Natal de Bolívar

Bolívar's funeral took place just two blocks from the house where, on 24 July 1783, he was born. The house's reconstructed interior (which has lost almost all its colonial features) has been decorated with a score of large paintings by Tito Salas, depicting Bolívar's heroic battles and scenes from his life. The house is open Monday to Friday from 9 am to noon and 2 to 5 pm, and on Saturday and Sunday from 10 am to 1 pm and 2 to 5 pm.

Museo Bolivariano

The museum, a few paces north from the Casa Natal, is also in a colonial house (which has preserved a bit more of its original style). It displays a variety of independence memorabilia, documents, period weapons and banners, plus a number of Bolívar's portraits. Among the exhibits is the coffin in which the remains of Bolívar were brought from Santa Marta. The ashes were then kept in the cathedral, from where they were moved in 1876 in the *arca cineraria* (a funeral ark, also exhibited in the museum) to their eventual resting place, the National Pantheon. The opening hours are the same as for Casa Natal.

Museo Fundación John Boulton

The museum features a collection of historic and artistic objects that have been accumulated over generations by the family of British merchant John Boulton (1805-75). Among the exhibits are paintings by Arturo Michelena, colonial furniture, Bolívar's memorabilia and an extensive collection of ceramics from all over the world. The museum is in the Torre El Chorro, Piso 11, Esquina El Chorro, and is open Monday to Friday from 9 am to noon and 2 to 5 pm.

Cuadra Bolívar

Located at the far southern edge of the historic centre, this is the Bolívar family summer house where Simón spent much of his childhood and youth. Restored to its original appearance and stuffed with period furniture, the house is today a museum, open Monday to Friday from 9 am to noon and 2 to 5 pm, Saturday and Sunday from 10 am to 1 pm and 2 to 4 pm.

Panteón Nacional

The National Pantheon is at the opposite, northern edge of the old town, five blocks due north of Plaza Bolívar. There was once a church on the site but it was destroyed in the 1812 earthquake. It was reconstructed and continued as a place of worship until 1874, when, by decree, Guzmán Blanco turned it into the pantheon. Since then it has been the last resting place for eminent Venezuelans.

The entire central nave is dedicated to Bolívar – his bronze sarcophagus placed in the chancel instead of the high altar – while 163 tombs of other revered personages (including only three women) were pushed out to the aisles. Two tombs are empty, awaiting the remains of Francisco de Miranda, who died in a Spanish jail in 1816 and who was buried in a mass grave, and Antonio José de Sucre, assassinated in Colombia and whose ashes are in the Quito Cathedral, as he is considered by Ecuadorians as the liberator of their country.

The vault of the pantheon is covered by paintings depicting scenes from Bolívar's life, all done by Tito Salas in the 1930s. Note the huge crystal chandelier made and hung in 1883 on the centenary of Bolívar's birth. It consists of 4000 pieces and 230 lights. The pantheon is open Monday to Friday from 9 am to noon and 2.30 to 5 pm, Saturday and Sunday from 10 am to noon and 3 to 5 pm.

Iglesia de la Candelaria

This church, seven blocks east of Plaza Bolívar, stands amid an area tingling with a Spanish flavour, thanks to Iberian migrants who settled here and opened up *tascas* (Spanish-style bar-restaurants). The church itself is noted for the richly gilded monumental retables which cover the chancel's walls. The central retable dates from about 1760 while the lateral ones are modern replicas.

For the majority of the faithful, however, the holiest place in the church is the tomb of José Gregorio Hernández, in the first chapel off the right-hand aisle. Though not canonised, José Gregorio is considered one of the most important saints by many Venezuelans, more so than many genuine saints whose images adorn the altars of this and other churches (see boxed text entitled José Gregorio Hernández).

Museo de Arte Colonial

The museum is housed in a beautiful colonial country mansion known as Quinta de Anauco, laid out around a charming patio and surrounded by gardens. When built in 1797, the quinta was well outside the historic town; today it's just a green oasis in the inner suburb of San Bernardino, a 10-minute walk north-east of La Candelaria.

If you make the effort to go there, you'll be rewarded with a guided tour around meticulously restored interiors filled with carefully selected works of art, furniture and household implements. The museum is open Tuesday to Friday from 9 to 11.30 am and 2 to 4.30 pm, Saturday and Sunday from 10 am to 5 pm. Entry costs US$0.50 and covers the

guide service. English-language guides are sometimes available at no additional cost. Chamber music concerts are held in the adjacent former stables, usually on Sunday at 11 am.

PARQUE CENTRAL & AROUND

Parque Central is a good place to go for a taste of modern Caracas. It's 1.5km southeast of Plaza Bolívar, but if it's too far for you to walk, take the metro to Bellas Artes station.

The parque is not, as you might expect, a green area, but a concrete complex consisting of several high-rise residential slabs of rather apocalyptic appearance, crowned by two 53-storey octagonal towers, the tallest in the country. Even if you are not impressed by the architecture, don't retreat, for there are some important sights around, especially if you are after cultural fare.

Actually, the Parque Central area is Caracas' art and culture hub, boasting half a dozen museums, the major performing-arts centre, two art cinemas and arguably the best theatre in town. Also here is the tourist office which, apart from information, provides a splendid bird's-eye view from the 35th floor.

Museo de Arte Contemporáneo

Occupying the eastern end of the complex, this is by far the best contemporary art museum in the country, if not the continent. In 16 halls on five levels you'll find works by many prominent Venezuelan artists, including Jesús Soto, noted for his kinetic pieces.

There are also some remarkable paintings by international giants such as Picasso, Chagall, Leger and Miró, and – the pride of the museum – a collection of a hundred or so engravings by Picasso, created by the artist from 1931-34. Part of the exhibition space is given to changing displays; since its opening in 1974 the museum has presented over 300 temporary exhibitions dedicated to both locally and internationally renowned artists. The museum is open Tuesday to Sunday from 10 am to 6 pm.

José Gregorio Hernández

Ask Venezuelans who is their most important saint and most will give you the same answer – José Gregorio, as people familiarly refer to Hernández. Indeed, his image is omnipresent in private homes and stalls of religious paraphernalia, where you can buy a range of his pictures or plaster statues. At first sight, you might be confused by his appearance – he is always portrayed in a well tailored suit with a white shirt and tie, usually with a black trilby on his head, which you'd hardly associate with a saint – but don't worry, it's him. A more serious problem is his fragile holy credentials; in fact, Hernández doesn't appear on the Vatican's list of saints. So far, the church has elevated him to venerable status, but further steps along the way to sainthood – beatification and canonisation – seem to be still a way off.

Candle-wrapper featuring José Gregorio Hernández

Hernández was born in 1864 in the obscure Andean village of Isnotú near Valera, in Trujillo state. He was the eldest of seven kids of the humble campesino family which fled up the mountains seeking refuge from the federation wars which plagued their native Los Llanos. After his mother died when he was nine, young José Gregorio helped his father to take care of the youngsters, before he went to Caracas to study.

Reputedly extraordinarily gifted and a hard-working student, Hernández graduated in medical sciences from the Universidad Central de Venezuela (UCV) in 1888. The following year, he went to Paris to specialise in histology, physiology and bacteriology in some of the best laboratories led by world-class medical eminences. Back home in 1891, he was appointed to the UCV to conduct the newly created subjects he had mastered in Europe.

Hernández has been commonly considered the founder of experimental medicine in Venezuela. He was also a creator of the so-called Commission of the Public Health, the embryo of the present day Health Ministry. He began his brilliant career as a university professor at the age of 27, and was the personal doctor of the president. He also left behind some literary work (including a philosophical treatise) and was allegedly a skilled pianist.

José Gregorio also was a devotedly religious person, following God's gospel to the word. He distinguished himself by treating the poor without charging a fee, and even bought medicine for his patients. He intended to dedicate himself completely to a monastic life on various occasions. In his most decisive attempt, in 1913, he went to Rome to study theology and Latin, but his developing tuberculosis forced him to resign and search for more favourable climatic conditions. He returned to Caracas and gave his energy and time to treating the poor.

Hernández died in a car accident in Caracas in 1919. Soon after his tragic death, a cult emerged around him and has spread throughout the country and beyond. Countless miracles are attributed to him, including numerous healings. Interestingly, Hernández was adopted as one of the principal deities of the mysterious María Lionza cult. Some consider him to be the second holiest figure in the cult's pantheon after María Lionza herself. ∎

Museo de los Niños The Children's Museum is at the opposite, western end of the complex, and is open Wednesday to Sunday from 9 am to noon and 2 to 5 pm.

It stops selling tickets one hour before closing, but it's best to allow at least two hours anyway. It's an excellent hands-on museum where adults have as much (or perhaps more) fun as the kids. Avoid weekends, when the museum is literally besieged by families.

Museo de Instrumentos de Teclado This keyboard-instruments museum has a collection of historic musical instruments. It's in Parque Central, next to the Museo de los Niños, and is open Tuesday to Sunday from 9 to 11 am and 2 to 4 pm.

Complejo Cultural Teresa Carreño Looking like a gigantic concrete sculpture, just to the east across the street from Parque Central (and linked to it by a foot bridge), the Complejo Cultural is a modern performing-arts centre. Opened in 1983, it has a spacious main auditorium capable of seating 2500 patrons, and a 400-seat side hall. The centre hosts concerts, ballet, plays, recitals etc by both local and visiting performers. Hourlong guided tours around the complex are conducted several times a day. At the back of the building is a small museum dedicated to Teresa Carreño (1853-1917), the best pianist Venezuela has ever produced.

Ateneo de Caracas Next to the Complejo Cultural, the Ateneo is another cultural centre, complete with a concert hall, theatre, cinema, art gallery, bookshop and café. The Ateneo is home to the *Rajatabla*, probably the best known (both in and outside the country) local theatre company.

Museo de Ciencias Naturales
The Natural Sciences Museum, behind the Ateneo, tracks the history of evolution, displaying minerals, fossils, stuffed animals and artefacts of pre-Hispanic communities from Venezuela and beyond. The museum is open Tuesday to Friday from 9 am to 5 pm, Saturday and Sunday from 10 am to 5 pm.

Galería de Arte Nacional
Opposite the Museo de Ciencias, the National Art Gallery has a permanent collection of some 4000 works of art embracing four centuries of Venezuela's artistic expression, plus some pre-Hispanic art. The building, which owes much to the neoclassical style, was designed in 1935 by a noted Venezuelan architect, Carlos Raúl Villanueva. Don't miss the three bas-reliefs by Francisco Narváez, Venezuela's first modern sculptor, placed over the doors at the entrance to the building. The gallery is open Tuesday to Friday from 9 am to 5 pm, Saturday and Sunday from 10 am to 5 pm. The gallery houses Caracas' leading art cinema.

Museo de Bellas Artes
Adjoining the gallery, the Museum of Fine Arts, in the modern six-storey building also designed by Villanueva, features mainly temporary exhibitions. Go to the rooftop terrace for fine views over the city and the spanking brand-new mosque (the largest in South America) just to the north. The museum, open the same hours as the gallery, has a shop which sells contemporary art.

SABANA GRANDE & AROUND
Sabana Grande, 2km east of the Parque Central, is a thrilling district packed with hotels, restaurants and shops. There are no particular tourist sights here, but the place is enjoyable and popular with both locals and visitors, who come en masse and stroll along its trendy, vibrant mall, the **Boulevard de Sabana Grande**. The mall stretches between the metro stations of Plaza Venezuela and Chacaíto. It is pretty wide at its western end, with room for several open-air street cafés – a good place to sit over a usually delicious espresso and watch the world go by.

Jardín Botánico
If Sabana Grande is too busy or crowded for you, relax in the botanical gardens, a 10-minute walk from the western end of the mall. The gardens, open daily from 8 am to 5 pm, are extensive, but only part of them are open to the public. They are well maintained and boast a good variety of local flora, yet their northern fringe, along the Autopista Francisco Fajardo, badly suffers from traffic noise. Occasional exhibitions are held in the Instituto Botánico building in the grounds. The only entrance to the gardens is from Avenida Interna UCV, a short walk south of Plaza Venezuela (there's no access from Parque Central or Parque Los Caobos).

Universidad Central de Venezuela
Commonly referred to as UCV, this is Caracas' largest university (about 70,000 students) and a nest of frequent student protests. The vast university campus was designed by Carlos Raúl Villanueva and is considered to be one of the milestones of his

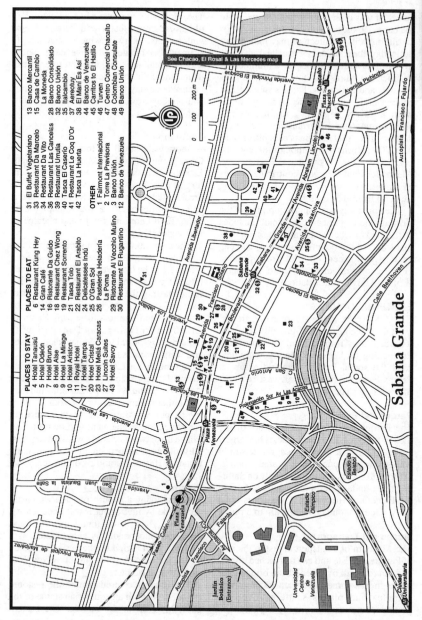

PLACES TO STAY
4 Hotel Tanausú
5 Hotel Odeón
7 Hotel Bruno
8 Hotel Alse
9 Hotel La Mirage
10 Hotel Ariston
11 Royal Hotel
17 Hotel Tampa
20 Hotel Cristal
23 Hotel Meliá Caracas
27 Lincoln Suites
43 Hotel Savoy

PLACES TO EAT
6 Restaurant Kung Hey
14 Gran Café
16 Ristorante Da Guido
18 Restaurant Chez Wong
19 Restaurant Sorrento
21 Tasca Tolo
22 Restaurant El Arabito
24 Delicatesses Indú
25 O'Gran Sol
26 Pastelería Heladería La Poma
29 Ristorante Al Vecchio Mulino
30 Restaurant El Rugantino
31 El Buffet Vegetariano
33 Restaurant Da Marcelo
34 Restaurant Da Vito
36 Restaurant Las Cancelas
39 Restaurant Urrutia
40 Tasca El Caserío
41 Restaurant Le Coq D'Or
42 Tasca La Huerta

OTHER
1 Fairmont Internacional
2 Torre La Previsora
3 Banco Unión
12 Banco de Venezuela
13 Banco Mercantil
15 Casa de Cambio La Moneda
28 Banco Consolidado
32 Banco Unión
35 Italcambio
37 Aereotuy
38 El Maní Es Así
44 Banco de Venezuela
45 Carritos to El Hatillo
46 Turven
47 Centro Comercial Chacaíto
48 Colombian Consulate
49 Banco Unión

Sabana Grande

career. It was built from scratch in one go in the early 1950s.

Although its architecture may look pretty dull today, the campus is still a pleasant place to stroll around, thanks to a number of abstract sculptures and murals adorning its grounds and buildings. There's an excellent concert hall, Aula Magna, on the grounds, with a fairly regular and interesting programme (see Entertainment for more details). The Aula Magna is capable of seating 2700 patrons and is thought to have the best acoustics in the country. A US designer, Alexander Calder, largely contributed to this by hanging a set of *platillos volantes* (flying saucers) from the ceiling.

The university has a sports complex, at the eastern side of the campus, which includes soccer and baseball stadiums. The campus is just south of the botanical gardens, and can be easily reached on foot from Sabana Grande, or you can get there by metro (Ciudad Universitaria station).

EASTERN SUBURBS

East of Sabana Grande are some of Caracas' most fashionable suburbs, possibly reaching its peak at Altamira and its environs. Proceeding further east, you gradually descend the social ladder, reaching a low at Petare. Eastward from here are vast expanses of appalling shantytowns.

Parque del Este

The Parque del Este, directly south of the metro station of the same name, is the largest city park. It's a good place for leisurely walks, and you can visit the snake house, aviary and cactus garden, and (only on Saturday and Sunday afternoons) enjoy a show in the Planetario Humboldt. The park is open daily, except Monday, from 5 am to 5 pm.

Museo del Transporte

The Museum of Transport is just to the east of Parque del Este and can be reached directly from the park by a pedestrian bridge. The museum has some old steam locomotives, vehicles and planes scattered over the grounds, but most exhibits are kept indoors.

The highlights are extensive collections of old horse-drawn carts and carriages, and vintage cars, many of which are related to eminent personages of Venezuelan social and political life, including former presidents and military rulers. The museum is open Wednesday from 8.30 am to 12.30 pm, and Sunday from 9 am to 4.30 pm. Admission is US$0.50.

La Casona

A short walk south of the museum is La Casona, the home of Venezuela's presidents. Established at the beginning of the 18th century as a cacao hacienda, it was decreed the presidential residence by Rómulo Gallegos, and after remodelling was completed in 1966, Raúl Leoni moved in and became its first resident.

The complex consists of several buildings – some dating from the colonial period, others from the late 19th century – and seven internal patios and gardens. A part of the hacienda (not the area where the president lives, of course) can be visited. You'll be guided around interiors fitted with Spanish-Criollo furnishings and graced with paintings by prominent Venezuelan artists, and walk around some of the gardens.

A visit to La Casona is not a straightforward proposition. You must first call ☎ 284 63 22 and ask for permission, and they will either organise a tour for your party or try to put you into one of their already scheduled tours. The waiting time for a visit can be up to two weeks. As we went to press, all visits were suspended and it was unclear when, or if, tours would recommence.

Petare

Petare is today a suburb of Caracas, easily accessible by metro, but it was once a town in its own right. It was founded in 1621 and developed independently side by side with Caracas. Although it has been swallowed up by the metropolis, it has preserved much of its historic character.

The town is centred around the restored Plaza Sucre, with an equestrian statue of the Gran Mariscal in the middle. The eastern side of the square is occupied by the large mid-18th century **Iglesia del Dulce Nombre de Jesús**, which still boasts some of the original retables dating from the time of the church's construction.

Two blocks south of the plaza, on the corner of Calle Guanche and Calle Lino de Clemente, is the **Museo de Arte Popular de Petare** in a beautiful colonial house. The museum presents daily temporary exhibitions of naive art, except Monday, from 10 am to 5 pm.

Stroll around the town's central streets, and have a look at the old houses, some of which have been adorned with paintings by local artists. Take precautions though; the town doesn't seem to be absolutely secure.

SOUTHERN SUBURBS

The southern part of Caracas, set on the rolling hills, is the most heterogeneous. Here are some of Caracas' wealthiest suburbs and also numerous pockets of ramshackle barrios, sometimes neighbouring each other.

Parque Zoológico de Caricuao

This is Caracas' main zoo, located in the far south-western suburb of Caricuao, about 10km from the centre, but easily accessible by metro. Get off at Zoológico station (terminus of the line), from where it's a seven-minute walk to the zoo's entrance.

The zoo has a selection of native birds, reptiles and mammals, plus some imported large cats and elephants. Most animals seem to enjoy a fair degree of freedom in their enclosures, and some, including monkeys, peacocks, ibis, flamingos and macaws, are virtually free. The zoo is open Tuesday to Sunday from 9 am to 4 pm.

There's also the small Parque Zoológico El Pinar, 4km south-west of the centre, but it's poorer and not as convenient to get to.

Fundación de Etnomusicología y Folklore

Commonly referred to as FUNDEF, the foundation aims at preserving traditional popular Latin American culture, carrying out research programmes and collecting artefacts. The museum on the premises features a collection of popular musical instruments and a variety of crafts, including pottery, basketry, woodcarving and textile. It's open Monday to Friday from 8.30 am to noon and 2 to 4.30 pm. The foundation (☎ 62 70 27) is in a fine old house known as Mansión Zuloaga, Quinta Micomicona, Avenida Zuloaga, Los Rosales. It's two blocks east from La Bandera metro station.

El Hatillo

A small old town, 15km south-east of the city centre, El Hatillo is today a distant suburb of Caracas. Like Petare, it lived its own life for centuries, until becoming a part of Caracas' metropolitan area. Centred around the Plaza Bolívar, the town still retains some of its colonial architecture. The parish church on the plaza has preserved its exterior pretty well, but its interior was radically (and rather controversially) modernised. Many central houses have been restored and painted in bright colours, which gives the town an attractive and lively look.

El Hatillo has become a trendy weekend getaway for caraqueños and is packed with cars and people on Saturday and Sunday. Every house is either a restaurant, café, boutique, art gallery or handicraft shop. The biggest craft shop, the Hannsi, is half a block north of the church. The recent explosion of eating outlets has been extraordinary, and today you can find most major foreign cuisines represented, from French and Italian to Japanese and Thai.

Frequent carritos run to El Hatillo from Avenida Humboldt, which is just off Boulevard de Sabana Grande, near the Chacaíto metro station.

ACTIVITIES

The best place for **hiking** near Caracas is the Parque Nacional El Ávila – see Around Caracas. If you're looking for organised hiking trips, contact one of the Centros Excursionistas – see Excursion Centres under Organised Tours.

The favourite **rock climbing** spot within the city is the Parque de Recreación Cuevas del Indio, Avenida Principal de la Guairita (southern continuation of Avenida Principal del Cafetal). Local climbers flock here at weekends.

There are few public **tennis** courts in the city, but some private clubs hire out their courts to non-members. Contact the Federación Venezolana de Tenis (☎ 979 74 62, 979 70 95). Public **golf** courses are nonexistent, but some clubs offer their facilities to the general public for a fee. Information can be got from the Federación Venezolana de Golf (☎ 731 05 53).

LANGUAGE COURSES
Caracas has quite a choice of institutions offering Spanish-language courses, and most can also provide teachers for individual classes. The places to check include:

Centro de Idiomas Berlitz
 Quinta Manuela, Calle Madrid, Las Mercedes (☎ 993 55 74, 993 68 51)
Centro Venezolano Americano (CVA)
 Avenida Principal de las Mercedes (☎ 993 84 22, 993 79 11; fax 993 68 12)
Centro Venezolano de Español
 Torre Phelps, Piso 19, Plaza Venezuela (☎ 781 20 20, 794 06 41; fax 781 34 17)

ORGANISED TOURS
Caracas tour companies can send you to virtually any corner of the country, but these trips will rarely be cheap. It will always be cheaper to get to the region on your own and contract a local operator (see Organised Tours in the Getting Around chapter). However, some tours organised from Caracas may not be available in the region concerned. Furthermore, Caracas companies may conveniently link various regional tours into one chain, so you save time on transferring. All in all, if you plan on taking tours, carefully read the information on regional operators in this book before leaving Caracas.

Tour Companies
There are over 600 travel agencies in Caracas and most offer tours. Some of them (the so-called *mayoristas*, or wholesalers) simply sell tours organised by other companies. Of the latter kind, many agencies use some of the services of selected regional operators, adding their own guides and transfers, and sometimes altering routes and upgrading lodging facilities. Some Caracas operators, though, organise the entire trip themselves, using their own camps and means of transport. Some companies can prepare tailor-made trips, which will usually take a while and cost considerably more than standard tours.

Following are some reputable tour companies, complete with brief descriptions of their services. Listed prices (per person) are approximate; they don't include transport to/from the tour's area, and may vary depending on the number of people in the tour.

All the listed companies focus heavily on responsible tourism and have English and German-speaking guides. For more information on responsible travelling, contact the Sociedad Conservacionista Audubon de Venezuela (☎ 92 28 12, 92 32 68; fax 91 07 16), Edificio Matisco, Piso 1, Oficina 5, Calle Veracruz, Las Mercedes. This leading environmental society doesn't organise tours, but provides information on ecological issues and can recommend tour companies.

Akanan Travel & Tours
 Edificio Claret, Mezzanina, Avenida Sanz con Calle La Laguna, El Marqués (☎ 238 14 57, 238 17 24; fax 234 4789; email akanan@sa.omnes. net). Specialist in adventure trips not often offered by mainstream operators, including treks to the top of Auyantepui (eight days, US$700) and Roraima (eight days, US$500), a boat trip following the Humboldt route in Amazonas (eight days, US$900) and La Paragua to Canaima by bicycle (six days, US$450).
Cacao Expediciones
 Torre Humboldt, Piso 22, Oficina 22-03, Avenida Caura, Prados del Este (☎ 977 12 34, 977 27 98; fax 977 01 10). Expert in Caura River tours (six days, US$360), where it has its own lodge. It also has a lodge in the Amazonas, serving as a base for boat trips in the region.
Cóndor Verde
 Torre Humboldt, Mezzanina 03, Avenida Caura, Prados del Este (☎ 975 43 06, 975 36 60; fax 975 23 85; email condor@etheron.net). German-run

agency offering one of the widest spectrums of tours, ranging from leisurely beach holidays on Margarita Island to adventurous boat trips in the Amazonas, plus special interest packages such as fishing, diving, golf and even air safaris. Its tours include Orinoco Delta (four days, US$360), Gran Sabana (three days, US$190), Roraima (seven days, US$600) and Caura River (six days, US$350).

Orinoco Tours
Edificio Galerías Bolívar, Piso 7, Oficina '5-A, Boulevard de Sabana Grande (metro Plaza Venezuela) (☎ 761 77 12, 761 40 30; fax 761 68 01; email orinoco@sa.omnes.net; website www.he.net/ven/orinoco). German-run agency offering soft to hard adventure tours. Programmes include Gran Sabana (five days, US$480), Roraima (nine days, US$800) and Los Llanos (two days, US$170). Truly adventurous tours, such as a trek to the top of Auyantepui or week-long Kavanayén to Kamarata jungle hike, prepared on request. Scuba diving, kayaking and mountain biking also feature.

Turven
Edificio Unión, Piso 1, Local 13, Boulevard de Sabana Grande (metro Chacaíto) (☎ 951 10 32, 951 17 87, 952 69 61; fax 951 11 76; email turven@euribia.it; website www.euribia.it/host/turven). One of Caracas major wholesalers, with wide offer of mainstream and soft-adventure tours to most regions. Represented in the USA by Venezuela Ventures (see Organised Tours in the Getting There & Away chapter).

Salto Angel Tour Operators Traditionally, the major operator of tours to the falls has been Hoturvensa, an offspring of Avensa airlines and owner of the Canaima camp. It offers two packages (two days for US$374, and three days for US$724), which include accommodation and board at the Canaima camp plus the flight over the falls (Caracas-Canaima flight extra). This is probably the most expensive offer you can find on the market. You can buy these packages at any Avensa office and most travel agencies throughout the country.

Since Salto Angel is arguably Venezuela's No 1 tourist attraction, many Caracas tour companies (including Akanan, Cóndor Verde and Orinoco, listed above) have the falls in their programmes, and they may have more innovative (and cheaper) tours than Hoturvensa. However, the cheapest tours will possibly be offered by the small

Canaima-based tour operators, some of which have desks at the domestic terminal of Maiquetía airport. They include Tiuna Tours (☎ 014 939 52 07) and Canaima Tours (☎ 014 986 05 86). If you decide to go to the airport to shop around, be there in the morning (preferably before 10 am) because they tend to close their desks early. See Salto Angel in the Guayana chapter for further information, and Ciudad Bolívar in the same chapter for more tour options.

Los Roques Tour Operators The Archipiélago Los Roques is a popular tourist destination, and the trip to the islands is usually done as a tour. These tours appear on some companies' lists, but the major operators are small airlines which provide flights to the archipelago. They all offer a flight-only option, and some also offer tours.

All these airlines, including Rutaca (☎ (031) 52 44 12, (031) 52 47 65), Aero-Ejecutivos (☎ 014 930 01 22, 014 913 15 91), Chapi Air (☎ (031) 52 45 60, (031) 52 28 67, 014 923 24 57), Viprovías (☎ (031) 52 32 32, (031) 52 27 54, 014 922 69 38) and Línea Turística Aereotuy (LTA), have their desks at the domestic terminal of Maiquetía airport. LTA is the major (and possibly the best) operator, and has its main office in Caracas (☎ 71 73 75, 71 50 72, 761 97 82; fax 762 52 54), Edificio Gran Sabana, Piso 5, Boulevard de Sabana Grande (metro Sabana Grande). See Archipiélago Los Roques in The Central North chapter for further information.

Los Llanos Representatives If you plan on tours to the hatos in Los Llanos (see the Hatos section in the Los Llanos chapter for full details), note that some hatos may require you to book and pay beforehand through a Caracas agent. They include:

Hato El Cedral
Turven (listed above)
Hato Piñero
Biotur Hato Piñero, Edificio General de Seguros, Piso 6, Oficina 6-B, Avenida La Estancia, Chuao (☎ 91 11 35, 92 44 13; fax 91 66 68)

Hato San Leonardo
Escritorio Jurídico, Edificio Helena, Piso 9,
Oficina 91, Avenida Luis Roche, Altamira
(☎ 285 51 82, 285 71 29; fax 284 39 39; website
www.vzla.com/aventura)

Excursion Centres

Not precisely tour companies, the *centros excursionistas* are associations of outdoor-minded people who organise excursions for themselves. These are essentially one or two-day weekend trips around Caracas and the central states, but longer journeys to other regions are often scheduled for long weekends and holiday periods. The trips include walking in the countryside, and though the focus is usually on nature, cultural sights are often part of the programme. Each trip is prepared by a member of the group who then serves as a guide. The excursionists use public transport and take their own food and camping gear if necessary. Foreign travellers are welcome to take part, and you can usually find a companion for conversation in English, German etc.

Founded in 1929, the Centro Excursionista Caracas (CEC) is the oldest and best known club of this kind. It affiliates people of all ages and has regular weekend trips, which are detailed in a CEC monthly bulletin. Club meetings are on Saturday (if there is no excursion that day), between 2.30 and 5 pm, in a house in the Zona Verde (green area) of Urbanización San Román, Calle Chivacoa con Calle Yare.

It's best to call a club member beforehand, to ask about forthcoming trips and check the meeting's details. Contact persons include: Lucy Alió (speaks English and French) ☎ 782 41 82 (home); Samuel Bendayán (English) ☎ 963 17 12 (home); Fritz Werner (German) ☎ 93 01 46 (home), ☎ 943 14 65 (work); and Andrea Würz (English and German) ☎ 21 82 72 (home), 267 14 11 (work).

Younger travellers may be interested in the Centro Excursionista Universitario (CEU), which bands together mostly university students. They walk faster and may have some more adventurous trips. They meet on Tuesdays between 6 and 8 pm in the base-ment *(sótano)* under the swimming pool *(piscina)* of the sports compound at the Universidad Central de Venezuela (metro Ciudad Universitaria).

The CEU contacts include: Virginia Alió (English) ☎ 781 38 73 (home); María Grazzia Cattinari (English and Italian) ☎ 573 44 70, 014 931 81 92; Angela Ruggiero (Italian) ☎ 862 18 59 (work); and Henry Guerra ☎ 562 42 49 (home). You could also try María Eugenia Alvarez. Her email address is jralvarez@etheron.net.

Guides

The Asociación Venezolana de Instructores y Guías de Montaña is a young association of over 30 guides, some of whom are very experienced. They can provide mountain guide services (mountaineering, rock climbing, mountain trekking etc), and may find guides for other activities such as paragliding or bird-watching. They still don't have an office, but you can call them at home. Contact members include Alfredo Autiero (speaking English and Italian) ☎ 443 05 97; Marco Cayuso (English) ☎ 986 09 26; Luis Martínez ☎ 661 99 94; and Marcus Tobía (German and English) ☎ 987 39 26.

SPECIAL EVENTS

Caracas is not particularly renowned for its religious or popular festivities, though Christmas, Carnaval and Easter are celebrated with due fervour. During these times, all offices close, as do most shops, and intercity bus transport is frantic. Flights are fully booked for a week or two beforehand.

Possibly the biggest religious feast in Caracas is the Easter celebration in Chacao, which begins with the Bajada de Palmeras on Friday before Palm Sunday, and goes on for over a week, culminating with solemn processions on Maundy Thursday and Good Friday, and concluding with the Quema de Judas on Easter Sunday.

Traditional suburbs are likely to celebrate holy days with more vigour than central districts. El Hatillo boasts local feasts on several occasions during the year (including 3 May, 16 July and 4 September), as does

Petare (30/31 January and the last Sunday of September).

More characteristic of Caracas are cultural events, of which the *Festival Internacional de Teatro* (International Theatre Festival) is the city's highlight. Initiated in 1976, it has been held in April of every even-numbered year, but it seems that organisers are going to shift it to another as yet undisclosed month. El Hatillo is home to the International Music Festival, which covers everything from jazz to ethnic to classical to contemporary music and takes place every year in late October or early November. The new August International Festival focusses on guitar music. The planned Dance Festival may add even more to Caracas' cultural profile.

The week around 25 July usually witnesses an increase of cultural activities such as concerts, exhibitions and theatre performances, organised to celebrate the anniversary of Caracas' foundation on that date in 1567.

PLACES TO STAY

There are loads of hotels scattered throughout the city, but most are located in the central districts, particularly in the centre and Sabana Grande. Note that staying in a distant district of the city is not a problem, as long as you are close to the metro.

Accommodation in Caracas is more expensive than elsewhere in the country. A simple budget hotel which costs, say, US$12 per double in a provincial city, won't go for less than US$15 in Caracas. Therefore, the price brackets in the following sections have been pushed a bit upwards compared to those in the rest of the book. The bottom-end section has been extended to cover anything up to about US$18 a double, and the middle bracket up to roughly US$36 a double. Otherwise, you would have very few places in the bottom-end category.

All hotels listed in the following sections have rooms with private baths and either fan or air-conditioning (as indicated), and most have hot water. Many bottom-end estab-

lishments, as well as almost all middle and top-end places, offer carpark facilities.

Places to Stay – bottom end

On the whole, Caracas' low-budget accommodation is poor and styleless, and is usually located in unimpressive, sometimes unsafe areas. Many bottom-end hotels double as love hotels, and some as brothels; business is particularly brisk on Friday and Saturday. Consequently, some hotels may turn you down on weekends. If your itinerary is flexible, try to avoid arriving in Caracas on these days, or at least come reasonably early so as to allow some time for possible hotel hunting.

The Centre This area roughly corresponds with what is covered by the left page of the Central Caracas map. The cheapest accommodation in this sector is to be found south of Avenida Bolívar. There are perhaps at least 50 basic hotels there, most of which are concentrated in two areas: immediately south of Nuevo Circo bus terminal and between Teatro Nacional and Cuadra Bolívar.

However, this entire area is unattractive and is not safe at night, and even during the daytime you should be on your guard. The advantage of being close to the Nuevo Circo bus terminal (if you plan on leaving Caracas by bus from here) is probably not sufficient to justify staying there. Furthermore, most of the hotels are scruffy shelters and more often than not rent rooms by the hour.

One of the few acceptable places in the area is the *Hotel Center Park* (☎ 541 86 19), Avenida Lecuna, Velásquez a Miseria, a block west of the bus terminal. It's clean and is sometimes used by travellers. It offers relatively small singles/matrimoniales/doubles with fan for US$8/10/12. Alternatively, try the nearby family-run *Hotel Río Guarapiche* (☎ 545 30 73), Calle Este 8, Zamuro a Pájaro, which has spacious air-conditioned matrimoniales/triples/quads with TV for US$14/20/26.

It's more convenient for sightseeing, and probably safer, to stay north of Avenida Bolívar. The *Hotel Caracol* (☎ 545 12 28,

545 53 79), Esquina Peinero, just a few steps south from La Hoyada metro station, has reasonable air-conditioned matrimoniales for around US$12. Ask for a room facing east on one of the top floors, and you'll have a superb view over some of the busiest and shabbiest parts of the centre, including a ramshackle slum-looking Mercado de la Hoyada and the Nuevo Circo bus terminal.

One of the cheapest options in the centre is the *Hotel Hollywood* (☎ 561 49 89), Avenida Fuerzas Armadas, Esquina Romualda, which charges US$12 for air-conditioned matrimoniales or doubles. However, the music played till late in the hotel's bar may be disturbing for light sleepers.

Two blocks north along the same road you have the *Hotel Metropol* (☎ 562 86 66), Plaza López a Socorro, and the *Hotel Terepaima* (☎ 562 51 84), Socorro a San Ramón. Both have air-conditioned rooms and are OK if a bit noisy due to heavy traffic. The Metropol costs US$14/18/24 for singles/doubles/triples with TV; the Terepaima is marginally worse but slightly cheaper at US$13/16/22.

One block east, on Esquina Calero, is the *Hotel Inter* (☎ 564 02 51, 564 70 31). It costs much the same as the Metropol but is quieter and perhaps better kept. It's popular with business people and is often full. No wonder, as this is one of the best options in the centre in this price bracket.

Sabana Grande Sabana Grande is a popular area to stay among travellers. It has plenty of hotels and feels safer than the centre, and it sits on the metro line, so you can easily get around to other districts.

Most of the budget hotels are concentrated in the western end of the district, on Prolongación Sur Avenida Las Acacias and neighbouring streets. There are perhaps more than 30 hotels here, packed in a small area just a few minutes walk south of Plaza Venezuela metro station.

One of the cheapest is the *Hotel Tanausú* (☎ 793 19 22, 793 76 91), charging US$11/13 a double/triple, yet it's basic and rents out

rooms by the hour. Just across the street is the better *Hotel Odeón* (☎ 793 13 45, 793 13 22), which has air-conditioned matrimoniales/doubles/triples with TV for US$14/16/18.

Walking southwards along Prolongación Sur Avenida Las Acacias, you'll find perhaps a dozen budget hotels (including some love hotels) within a distance of 200m. The more orthodox options on this street include (from north to south) the high-rise *Hotel Bruno* (☎ 781 83 24, 781 84 44) (US$14/15/16 a single/double/triple with fan); the *Hotel La Mirage* (☎ 793 27 33) (US$16/18 a matrimonial/double with air-conditioning and TV); and the *Hotel Ariston* (☎ 782 77 23) (US$14 a matrimonial which includes air-conditioning and TV). You could also check the cheaper *Hotel Alse* (☎ 781 63 90, 782 55 10), which has dim air-conditioned singles/ doubles for US$13/13.

There are more cheapies on Calle San Antonio and Calle El Colegio, two parallel streets to the east, but again, note that many of these hotels cater not only to tourists but also to couples wanting to have sex.

If you need somewhere more central, try the *Hotel Cristal* (☎ 761 91 31), perfectly located on Boulevard de Sabana Grande (corner of Pasaje Asunción). It's not the classiest place around, but it has reasonable matrimoniales/doubles which includes air-conditioning and TV for US$16/19. It also has large rooms equipped with two double beds (which may suit two couples) for US$25. Ask for a room with a balcony overlooking the mall.

Places to Stay – middle
Middle-priced hotels have private baths with hot water and air-conditioning as standard facilities. They sometimes don't offer much more luxuries than some of the budget places, but at least you can be almost sure that they don't double as love hotels (though some do). The following list is of 'clean' establishments:

The Centre There are few middle-priced hotels in the old town, but one stands out, the

Plaza Catedral Hotel (☎ 564 21 11, 563 33 94; fax 564 17 97), overlooking Plaza Bolívar from Esquina La Torre. It is the best-located mid-priced hotel in the area and well worth US$26/32/36 for comfortable singles/doubles/triples. A bonus is the hotel's own restaurant on the top floor – a handy facility if you don't feel like strolling the streets after dark.

Sabana Grande The district has a choice of hotels in this price bracket, though few are really good value. The tranquil *Royal Hotel* (☎ 762 54 94, 762 29 43; fax 762 64 59), is conveniently sited on Calle San Antonio just off Boulevard de Sabana Grande. It offers decent singles/doubles/triples for US$20/24/27.

Altamira Altamira is worth considering, for it's a pleasant and safe area dotted with a number of good restaurants and nightspots, and you are just a 15-minute trip by metro from the centre (or seven minutes from Sabana Grande). It's essentially an upmarket suburb, but has affordable accommodation.

The *Hotel Residencia Montserrat* (☎ 263 35 33; fax 261 13 94), Avenida Ávila, Sur Plaza Altamira, just a few steps from the metro station, is the best value for money (US$28/32/36/40 a single/double/triple/quad) therefore it's often full.

If you are unsuccessful here, check the *Hotel La Floresta* (☎ 263 19 55; fax 262 12 43), next door. At US$30/36/45 a single/double/triple, it's slightly more expensive, but still well worth it. Generally speaking, it's easier to get a room in these hotels at weekends.

Places to Stay – top end
The city has quite a number of four and five-star hotels, though their standards don't always match their hefty rates. It's often better to stay in a decent three-star establishment for a fraction of the price, spending the money you've saved (if you have to do it) on great dining, tours etc. Possibly the biggest single advantage of upmarket hotels is noiseless central air-conditioning, instead of noisy room conditioners commonly used in bottom-end and most middle-priced hotels. Some top-end hotels offer lower rates at weekends.

The Centre The top end in the centre is represented by the three-star *Hotel El Conde* (☎ 81 11 71; fax 862 09 28), Esquina El Conde, one block west of Plaza Bolívar. It's not one of the city's best hotels, but it's not particularly expensive at US$40/48/60 a single/double/triple.

Parque Central The five-star *Hotel Caracas Hilton* (☎ 503 50 00; fax 503 50 03), facing Parque Central, is one of the most respected upmarket hotels in town. Its trump cards are good location, splendid views from the top floors, an excellent tourist information desk, swimming pool, tennis courts, gym and two of the city's best eateries – La Rotisserie (French cuisine) and the Sushi Bar. Yet, the hotel is not that cheap at US$245 a double, though US$128 weekend rates may be more tempting.

Cheaper is the four-star *Caracas Residencias Anauco Hilton* (☎ 573 41 11; fax 573 77 24), in one of the apartment buildings within the complex of Parque Central. Suites range from studios to three bedrooms, kitchen included, and may be particularly suitable for larger parties. Reservations for both hotels can be made through any Hilton worldwide.

Sabana Grande There's a reasonable choice of affordable three-star options (costing somewhere between US$40 and US$60 a double) scattered throughout the area. They include the *Hotel Tampa* (☎ 762 37 71; fax 762 01 12), Avenida Francisco Solano near the corner of Avenida Los Jabillos (metro Plaza Venezuela), and the *Hotel Savoy* (☎ 762 19 71; fax 762 27 92), Avenida Francisco Solano con 2a Avenida Las Acacias (metro Sabana Grande or Chacaíto).

However, the best value is probably the *Lincoln Suites* (☎ 761 27 27, 762 85 75; fax 762 55 03), Avenida Francisco Solano between Avenida Los Jabillos and Calle San Jerónimo (also accessible directly from

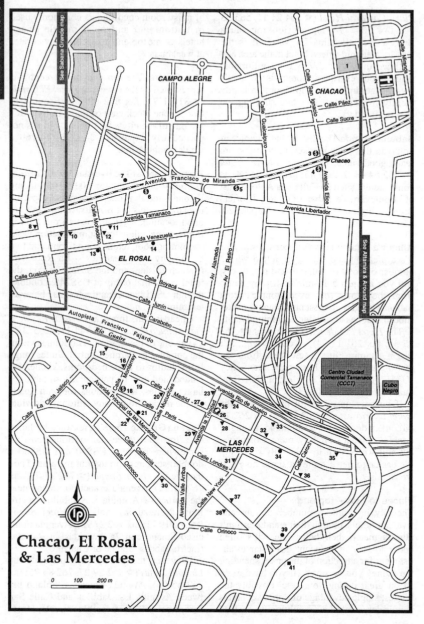

CAMPO ALEGRE

CHACAO

Calle Páez

Calle Sucre

1

2

3

Chacao

4

7

Avenida Francisco de Miranda

6

5

Avenida Libertador

Avenida Tamanaco

8

11

9 10

12

Avenida Venezuela

14

13

EL ROSAL

Calle Guaicaipuro

Calle Boyacá

Calle Junín

Calle Carabobo

Autopista Francisco Fajardo

Río Guaire

15

16

17

18

19

20

21

22

23 27

24

25

26

28

29

LAS MERCEDES

30

31

32

33

34

35

36

37

38

39

40

41

Centro Ciudad Comercial Tamanaco (CCCT)

Cubo Negro

Chacao, El Rosal & Las Mercedes

0   100   200 m

PLACES TO STAY		17	Arepera Doña	38	Le Petit Bistrot de
40	Hotel Paseo Las Mercedes		Caraotica		Jacques
41	Hotel Tamanaco Inter-Continental	19	Restaurant Aranjuez	**OTHER**	
		20	Kibbe Steak	1	Mercado Chacao
		22	Restaurant Crabs	2	Iglesia San José de Chacao
PLACES TO EAT		23	Ristorante Il Cielo	3	Banco de Venezuela
8	Arepera Misiá Jacinta	24	Maute Grill	4	Banco Unión
9	Restaurant Barba Roja	25	Restaurant Taiko	5	Banco Consolidado
10	Restaurant El Chocolate	28	Jardín des Crêpes	6	Banco do Brasil
11	Restaurant La Mansión	29	Restaurant La Castañuela	7	Avianca
12	Restaurant El Mar	30	Terraza Ibiza	13	Juan Sebastián Bar
15	Restaurant Real Past	31	La Romanissima	14	República Rockatanga
16	Restaurant Casa Urrutia	32	Hereford Grill	18	Banco Unión
		33	El Granjero del Este	21	Discoteca Boomker
		35	Zoe Caffe	26	French Embassy
		36	Pollo en Brasas Los Rivera	27	Discoteca Ozono
		37	Las Tapas de Madrid	34	Magic Discotheque
				39	IVI Tours

Boulevard de Sabana Grande). Comfortable double suites with full amenities cost around US$90.

The five-star *Hotel Meliá Caracas*, Avenida Casanova, has been under construction for over a decade and will be the poshest (and certainly the most expensive) option in Sabana Grande.

Las Mercedes Should you want to stay close to Caracas' major nightlife hub, the four-star *Hotel Paseo Las Mercedes* (☎ 91 00 33; fax 993 03 41), in the shopping centre of the same name, Avenida Principal de Las Mercedes, is handy. It offers decent standards and service for US$100 a double. Across the road is the twice as costly five-star *Hotel Tamanaco Inter-Continental* (☎ 909 71 11; fax 909 89 50). The nearby *Hotel Eurobuilding Caracas* (☎ 902 11 11, 959 11 33; fax 907 21 89) costs much the same as the Tamanaco.

Altamira The alternative centre of night entertainment, Altamira can accommodate you in its modern, high-rise, three-star *Hotel Continental Altamira* (☎ 261 60 19; fax 261 01 31) on Avenida San Juan Bosco, a five-minute walk north of the Altamira metro station.

PLACES TO EAT

Caracas has an enormous choice of places to eat, and you could easily stay in town a full year and eat out three times a day without visiting the same restaurant twice. This unfortunately makes any objective and comprehensive selection difficult. However, the food is generally good, even in cheap eateries, so you can safely explore the culinary market by yourself. Many restaurants place their menus outside, so you can get an idea of what's on offer and how much it costs. The *Caracas Gastronomic Guide* (listed in the Guidebooks section earlier in this chapter) is a great help in discovering the local cooking scene.

At the bottom end, there's a range of budget eateries city-wide, which have menú del día for about US$2 to US$4. An alternative can be chicken, and the places which serve it, usually called *pollo en brasas*, are also in good supply. Don't forget arepas – a perfect snack or even a meal – sold in numerous areperas.

For breakfast, go to any of the ubiquitous panaderías, which will invariably have a choice of croissants, pasteles and cachitos, and fresh bread. Sandwiches are rarely pre-made and on display, but can be prepared in a minute on request. Wash it all down with a batido or coffee. In the evening, countless

Spanish tascas (bar-cum-restaurants) dot many streets of inner suburbs, particularly in La Candelaria and Sabana Grande. If you can't live without your burgers and pizzas, numerous outlets of McDonald's, Burger King, Pizza Hut and other big chains will keep you alive.

Going more upmarket, suburbs such as Las Mercedes, Altamira and La Castellana boast dozens of well-appointed restaurants which will serve you a worldwide range of delicacies without eating too much into your pocket. A great dinner can be had for below US$20 per head, drinks apart.

Many restaurants, particularly cheaper ones, don't open on Sunday, but fast-food outlets operate seven days a week. Some areperas keep going 24 hours a day. Most upmarket restaurants are open until at least 10 pm.

A phone number after the restaurant's name in the following text suggests that it's an upper-middle to top-end establishment, and you might want to book a table. This may be a good idea if you plan to dine in some trendy restaurants at the weekend.

The Centre
The centre doesn't abound in chic restaurants, but has a great variety of low to middle-priced eateries, many of which serve local fare known as comida criolla (creole cuisine). One of the best central places for this cuisine is the *Restaurant Dama Antañona*, Jesuitas a Maturín. It offers traditional cooking at reasonable prices in appropriately craft-decorated surroundings.

The *Café Sacro*, in the Museo Sacro de Caracas at Plaza Bolívar, is an ideal place to escape from the city rush and enjoy some of its delicious (if not that cheap) fresh salads and sandwiches, plus a great espresso (open Tuesday to Saturday from noon to 4 pm). Another pleasant place on the plaza, though of completely different character, is the top-floor *Restaurant Les Grisons* in the Plaza Catedral Hotel. It does local and international dishes, including some Swiss specialities, and you have the whole plaza at your feet.

For an inexpensive set lunch that tastes as if it was cooked by your mum, few places can beat the rather plain-looking but clean and patron-attentive *Restaurant Sokol* on Avenida Fuerzas Armadas, Socarrás a Corazón de Jesús (closed Saturday and Sunday). For cheap felafels and other popular Middle Eastern fast food, try the basic *Restaurant Kafta*, Esquina San Jacinto, or the slightly better *Restaurant Beirut*, Salvador de León a Socarrás (both closed on Sunday).

The area east of Avenida Fuerzas Armadas, known as La Candelaria, is literally swamped with tascas, where you can try some traditional Spanish cooking, including a variety of tapas (hearty snacks), or dedicate yourself to drinks, and there's always a good choice of them. Many tascas are on or just off Calle Sur 15, between the Iglesia de la Candelaria and Parque Carabobo. Here are a few: *La Carabela*, *La Tertulia*, *La Cita*, *Guernica* and *Bar Basque*. You'll find the location of these and other good tascas on the Central Caracas map.

La Candelaria also has some good eateries serving local food. The *Pollo en Brasas El Coyuco*, Avenida Urdaneta, Platanal a Candilito, is one of the better budget places for chicken and parrillas. It's popular with locals and often crowded at meal times despite its enormous size. Some of the best and cheapest cachapas (corncakes) with ham and/or cheese can be had at the tiny *Lunchería Doña Agapita*, off Plaza La Candelaria. Don't miss trying one.

Sabana Grande
Sabana Grande boasts enough restaurants, cafés and snack bars to suit any budget and taste. Avenida Francisco Solano (not Boulevard de Sabana Grande) is the area's main culinary artery. Here you'll find a number of Italian restaurants such as *Da Guido*, *El Rugantino* and *Al Vecchio Mulino*, and several Spanish tascas including *El Caserío* and *La Huerta*. Here also is the upmarket *Urrutia* (☎ 71 04 48), considered to be one of the best Basque restaurants in town, and the respectable but pricey *Chez Wong* (☎ 761 41 94), which serves excellent Sichuan and Hunan food. Also recommended for Sichuan

specialities is the *Kung Hey* (☎ 782 56 10), Prolongación Sur Avenida de las Acacias.

For somewhere more affordable, check the *Sorrento*, next door to Chez Wong, and *Da Vito*, on Avenida Casanova. Both offer straightforward tasty home cooking at low prices; the former does local food, the latter specialises in pasta dishes. *Da Marcelo*, Calle Coromoto, is another good example of an unpretentious budget eatery.

For cheap Middle Eastern fast food, including tabule, felafel and the like, go to *O'Gran Sol*, Calle Villaflor, or, better, to *El Arabito*, half a block away, on Avenida Casanova. *Las Cancelas* has some of the best paellas in town (US$12 for two people). *Le Coq D'Or*, Calle Los Mangos, offers classic French cooking at prices that are lower than those of trendy French restaurants in the eastern suburbs.

Vegetarians can get cheap set meals (US$2.50) at the *Tasca Tolo*, Pasaje Asunción, just south of the Boulevard (Monday to Friday from noon to 4 pm). However, probably the best place for a vegetarian lunch (all you can eat for US$4) is *El Buffet Vegetariano*, Avenida Los Jardines, La Florida, one block north of Avenida Libertador (Monday to Friday from 11.30 am to 2.30 pm). You can have appetising Indian vegie dishes (including a set lunch for US$4) until 8.30 pm at the *Delicatesses Indú*, Calle Villaflor (closed on Sunday).

The western end of the Boulevard de Sabana Grande is filled with a number of open-air cafés, which are popular with both locals and visitors. Among them is the *Gran Café*, which is reputed to make one of the best cappuccinos in town. *Pastelería Heladería La Poma*, a short walk eastwards, has some of the best ice cream and also offers a large selection of creative high-calorie cakes and pastries.

Las Mercedes

Las Mercedes has a long-standing reputation as a fashionable dining district. There are perhaps a hundred restaurants, bars, cafés etc here, and they become particularly lively in the evening. It's a pleasant area to stroll

around and explore its gastronomic diversity and you'll discover many more attractive eating venues than just those included in this text.

Most restaurants cater for a more affluent clientele, but there are also some which do serve cheap food. A good example of these is the *Real Past*, Avenida Río de Janeiro, which is the cheapest pasta house in the area. None of its appetising plates costs more than US$2. *Los Riviera*, Calle París, is another inexpensive place, specialising in spit-roasted chicken and parrillas. Marginally more expensive is the deservedly popular *El Granjero del Este*, Avenida Río de Janeiro, which is open round the clock. This full-service arepera offers hearty comida criolla, including a variety of arepas, cachapas, soups, chicken and parrillas, in informal cheerful surroundings. Similar in menu and price is *Doña Caraotica*, another 24-hour arepera, situated on Avenida Principal de Las Mercedes.

There's a choice of restaurants offering international and local cuisines at reasonable (though not rock-bottom) prices. The *Jardín des Crêpes*, Calle Madrid, is an enjoyable place that does a variety of French-inspired crêpes (both sweet and non-sweet versions) as well as some fish and meat dishes. *La Romanissima*, Calle New York, cooks good home-style pastas. The *Terraza Ibiza*, Calle California, has a menu rich in eclectic proposals with some Mediterranean flavour. Each of the above will have something for vegetarians, but perhaps the best place for a natural and healthy vegie meal is the *Zoe Caffe*, Avenida Río de Janeiro.

Las Mercedes is particularly known for its upmarket establishments, which are by the dozen and offer a variety of delicacies from most of the world. Following are just a few highlights; you'll find other reputable places marked on the El Rosal & Las Mercedes map.

Le Petit Bistrot de Jacques (☎ 993 40 93), Avenida Principal de Las Mercedes, has a reputation as the most authentic French bistro outside France, but if you need somewhere more formal (and expensive), *Le*

Gourmet (☎ 208 72 42), in the nearby Hotel Tamanaco, will do the honours. *Il Cielo* (☎ 993 40 62), Avenida La Trinidad, is arguably the best Italian restaurant in the area, and there's probably nothing better for Japanese specialities than *Taiko* (☎ 993 56 47), Avenida La Trinidad.

Las Tapas de Madrid (☎ 91 78 94), Avenida Principal de Las Mercedes, is a new but already popular tasca which offers a large variety of typical Spanish tapas, tapitas and more elaborate dishes. For grilled beef, choose between *Hereford Grill* (☎ 993 96 10), Calle Madrid, *Maute Grill* (☎ 993 38 46), Avenida Río de Janeiro, and *Aranjuez* (☎ 993 13 26), Calle Madrid. If you are specifically after crabs, go to (yes, you've guessed it) the *Crabs* (☎ 993 53 48), Avenida Principal de Las Mercedes, which has nothing but crabs.

Altamira & Around

Altamira and its neighbouring suburbs of La Castellana and Los Palos Grandes is another trendy area dotted with posh restaurants, smart cafés, discos and bars. Like Las Mercedes, it's essentially an upmarket zone, catering for Caracas' young and wealthy, yet budget travellers will find something too.

Beginning from the bottom end, the *Pollo en Brasas El Coyuco*, 3a Transversal con 4a Avenida, Los Palos Grandes, will fill you up nicely for under US$5. One block north is another smoky grill, the *Carbón y Leña*, which serves a similar fare of chicken and parrillas for much the same. South of El Coyuco, the simple, plain *El Presidente* provides home-style meals at lunchtime.

La Castellana also has some down-to-earth options, including the good chicken outfit, *El Mundo del Pollo*, and the round-the-clock *Arepera La Sifrina*. In the same area is the inexpensive *Pizzería La Romanina*, but probably better pizzas for the same money are to be found in *Peppe's Pizza*, next to Altamira metro station.

Going a step up the price ladder, the *Café L'Attico* (261 28 19), Avenida Luis Roche, is an attractive, charmingly informal bar-cum-restaurant, and one of the trendiest places in

town. It has good food (including some North American offerings) at affordable prices, lively bar, videos and music, and usually great atmosphere. It's hard to get a table on weekday evenings, let alone on weekends, when it's packed completely with joyful folks.

The open-air *Art Café*, Avenida Andrés Bello con 4a Transversal, serves exquisite sandwiches with chips and salad – a filling meal in itself for US$5. *Fritz & Franz*, Avenida San Juan Bosco con 3a Transversal, offers reasonably priced German fare, including grilled sausages, potato salads, sauerkraut and apple strudel. *Il Ritrovo*, Avenida Francisco de Miranda, is one of the better-value eateries among numerous Italian ones in the area; it has unpretentious but well-prepared food at good prices. The nearby *Portofino* is more informal and a bit cheaper. Alternatively, try the tiny *Mediterráneo*, 1a Avenida entre 1a y 2a Transversal. *Le Bistró de la Torre*, Torre Británica, Avenida José Félix Sosa, is an option for a reasonable French lunch, though at dinner time they put on more elaborate and expensive productions.

Turning to the upper price bracket, *El Hostal de la Castellana* (☎ 266 42 60), at Plaza La Castellana, is a classy Spanish restaurant with three separate dining rooms, each with its own ambience. One block south, *La Estancia* (☎ 261 18 74) is well known for its grilled meats in every cut and style, as is *El Gran Charolais* (☎ 263 55 02), Avenida Principal de La Castellana. The *Via Appia* (☎ 266 79 10), Avenida San Felipe, probably heads the league of Italian restaurants in the area, for its delicious home-made pasta in various creative forms. The small *Muñeiras* (☎ 261 44 61), 4a Avenida con Avenida El Bosque, doesn't look particularly attractive, but has excellent Spanish cooking and good service. Despite its high prices, it's often full.

Other commendable upmarket restaurants in the area include *El Barquero* (☎ 261 25 97), Avenida Luis Roche (Spanish cooking with emphasis on fish and seafood); *Altamar* (☎ 262 18 13), 3a Transversal (cuisine as above); *Casa Juancho* (☎ 263 55 26), Avenida San Juan Bosco (cuisine as above); *Hatsuhana* (☎ 264 18 19), Avenida San Juan Bosco (Japanese fare); *Lasserre* (☎ 283 45 58), 4a Avenida con 3a Transversal (French cuisine); and *El Alazán de Altamira* (☎ 285 02 08), Avenida Luis Roche (steaks).

ENTERTAINMENT

The Friday edition of *El Universal* carries a what's-on section called *La Brújula*, which covers museums, art galleries, music, theatre, cinemas and other cultural events. The *Urbe*, a magazine published every Wednesday, covers mostly lighter entertainment, including commercial cinema, live music, night spots etc.

Cinema

Caracas has about 40 cinemas screening the usual commercial fare, peppered with big-budget US blockbusters which come here soon after their release at home. For something more intellectually demanding, check the programme of the Cinemateca Nacional (☎ 571 14 91; website www.cinemateca. org), the leading art cinema, in the Galería de Arte Nacional. The Cine La Provisora (☎ 709 18 41) in the Torre La Provisora also focuses on quality arthouse films, as does the cinema in the Ateneo de Caracas (☎ 571 42 19, 571 38 32).

There are usually three afternoon shows. Films are shown with the original soundtrack and Spanish subtitles. A cinema ticket costs US$3 to US$4, but can be less in art cinemas. Programmes of both commercial and art cinemas are listed in the local daily press (including *The Daily Journal*).

Theatre

There are a dozen regular theatres in the city. They are usually open from Wednesday to Sunday but some only have performances at weekends. Tickets cost between US$2 and US$5, and there are student discounts in some theatres. Midweek sessions (usually on Wednesday) may be cheaper than weekend performances. The Ateneo de Caracas often has something interesting in its theatre, and

you can see here the productions of Rajatabla, Venezuela's best known theatre company. It may be also worth checking the programmes of La Compañía Nacional de Teatro, presenting their plays in the *Teatro Nacional* (☎ 484 59 56), and the Teatro Profesional de Venezuela, based at the *Teatro El Paraíso* (☎ 462 44 61, 462 67 44).

If you are lucky enough to arrive during the Caracas International Theatre Festival, you'll have a chance to see some of the best theatre from Latin America and beyond. Festival performances are staged at theatres around the city.

Classical Music & Ballet

The city's major stage for concerts and ballet, by both local and invited foreign performers, is the *Complejo Cultural Teresa Carreño* (☎ 574 91 22, 574 93 33). Also check the programme of the *Aula Magna* (☎ 61 98 11) in the Universidad Central de Venezuela, which hosts performances by the symphony orchestra, usually on Sunday morning, among other spectacles. Tickets for Sunday concerts (US$1, half price for students) can be bought from the Aula's ticket office, Thursday to Saturday from 2 to 5 pm, and directly before the concerts.

Other places which stage concerts include the Ateneo de Caracas, Museo Sacro de Caracas, Quinta Anauco, Centro Cultural Consolidado, Centro Venezolano Americano and Asociación Cultural Humboldt.

Nightlife

The scene of night-time entertainment is centred around Las Mercedes, El Rosal, Altamira and La Castellana, where most discos, bars and other night spots are located. Incidentally, these are relatively safe areas for night strolls.

Bar & Pubs The *Gran Pizzería El León*, at Plaza La Castellana (metro Altamira), is possibly the largest night-time drinking hole, with dozens of tables placed outdoor on a vast terrace in front of the pizzería. If you turn up on a weekend night, you'll find a large college crowd, jovially debating over

CARACAS

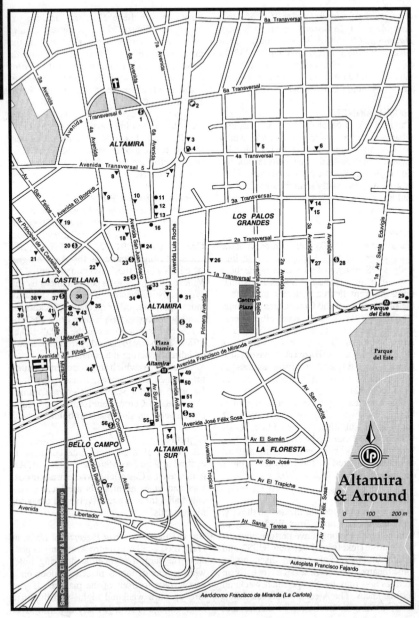

PLACES TO STAY		22	Restaurant Via Appia	2	Bolivian Embassy & Consulate

PLACES TO STAY
24 Hotel Continental Altamira
50 Hotel Residencia Montserrat
51 Hotel La Floresta

PLACES TO EAT
3 El Alazán de Altamira
5 Art Café
6 Restaurant Criollo Carbón y Leña
7 Restaurant El Barquero
8 Restaurant Japonés Hatsuhana
9 Restaurant Muñeiras
10 El Palacio del Mar
13 Restaurant Altamar
14 Pollo en Brasas El Coyuco
15 Restaurant Lasserre
17 Fritz & Franz
18 Casa Juancho
19 Steak House de Lee Hamilton
21 Restaurant El Gran Charolais

22 Restaurant Via Appia
26 Restaurant Mediterráneo
27 Restaurant El Presidente
32 Café L'Attico
38 Arepera La Sifrina
39 El Mundo del Pollo
40 Pizzería La Romanina
41 Restaurant El Solar del Vino
43 El Hostal de la Castellana
44 Restaurant Brava Mar
45 Restaurant La Estancia
46 Restaurant La Trainera
47 Restaurant Il Ritrovo
48 Peppe's Pizza
49 Restaurant Portofino
52 Pastelería Flor de Castilla
54 Le Bistró de la Torre

OTHER
1 Banco Unión

2 Bolivian Embassy & Consulate
4 Petrol Station
11 Little Rock Café
12 Discoteca Khrôma
16 Marumen Store
20 Banco Consolidado
23 Banco Provincial
25 Banco de Venezuela
28 Banco Consolidado
29 Inparques Office
30 Banco Unión
31 Jazz & Restaurant Stage
33 Weekends
34 The American Book Shop
35 Gran Pizzería El León
36 Plaza La Castellana
37 Banco Consolidado & Centro Cultural Consolidado
42 Discoteca Xanadú
53 Italcambio
55 Greenwich Pub
56 Banco Consolidado
57 Aeroexpresos Ejecutivos Bus Terminal

bottles of beer which completely cover the tables. And yes, you can also have your pizza, though this is not what attracts people to the premises.

Completely different is the *Greenwich Pub*, Avenida Sur Altamira (metro Altamira), an intimate indoor place with taped (at times live) music, often at high volume, and a variety of beer and pasapalos (finger food). The place is trendy, but is so small that getting a table here at night is a challenge.

Don't forget *Café L'Attico* (listed in Places to Eat), which is as much a place to eat as to drink.

The *Weekends*, Avenida San Juan Bosco, one long block north of the Altamira metro station, is a North American-style short-order restaurant open till late, with pool tables, electronic games, darts, karaoke, music, video and the like.

Discos Caracas has quite a number of discos scattered throughout the city, with Las Mer-

cedes possibly heading the league. Most discos are open nightly except Monday and sometimes also Sunday, which are the slowest days, but some only open Thursday to Saturday. The music is usually a ragbag of western and Caribbean rhythms, though some discos focus on specific genre, such as salsa or western oldies, which may be their general musical theme or the theme of a particular day of the week.

Thursday, Friday and Saturday, especially after midnight, are when things are hottest. On these days, there may be live music in some places. There's usually no entrance fee on weekdays but there may be on the weekend. This may include a voucher to the value of a few beers. Discos don't usually serve snacks or meals (so come after your dinner) but have plenty of drinks. Most Caracas discos won't let you in if you wear sneakers or a T-shirt, and some don't even accept jeans. Don't take handbags or cameras, as you will have to keep a constant eye on them; these places are often crowded and thieves never sleep.

The *Boomker*, Avenida Principal de Las Mercedes, is one of the largest discos, with different levels, a well-stocked bar, pool tables and lots of bells and whistles. The *Magic Discotheque*, Calle Madrid, is quieter and more formal, though not more expensive, and its musical programme includes a good deal of classics and oldies. It attracts a more mature clientele than most other discos. The *Caramba*, Calle París, is in turn often full of youngsters. It serves snacks and has pool tables. Other discos in Las Mercedes include the *Ozono*, Calle Madrid, and the small *Ku*, Avenida Principal.

In the eastern suburbs, try the *Khrôma*, 6a Avenida entre 3a y 5a Transversal in Altamira, or the *Xanadú* at Plaza La Castellana. One block south is the *Espacio*, an informal disco popular with young folk.

Live Music The *Juan Sebastián Bar*, Avenida Venezuela in El Rosal (metro Chacaíto), is a bar-cum-restaurant, and one of the few real jazz spots in the city. Live jazz, performed by various groups, goes from the afternoon till 2 am. There's no cover charge. The newly opened *Stage*, Avenida Luis Roche in Altamira, may bring some more vigour to Caracas' jazz scene.

El Maní es Así, Avenida El Cristo, Sabana Grande, has a long-standing reputation as a hot live salsa spot. Another place in Sabana Grande which hosts salsa bands (Tuesday to Saturday) is *O'Gran Sol*, a two-level restaurant next door to a Middle Eastern food outlet of the same name. The music is staged on the upper floor.

In La Castellana, *El Solar del Vino* is similar to O'Gran Sol; it's a Spanish restaurant which has live music (usually salsa, antillana and other Caribbean rhythms) on Wednesday to Saturday nights.

The *República Rockatanga*, Avenida Venezuela in El Rosal, features rock bands, as does the brand-new, castle-style *Little Rock Café*, 6a Avenida entre 3a y 5a Transversal in Altamira.

SPECTATOR SPORT
Professional baseball league games are played from October to February at the baseball stadium in the grounds of the Universidad Central de Venezuela (metro Ciudad Universitaria). Tickets should be bought early in the morning, particularly for games featuring local team Leones de Caracas.

The neighbouring soccer stadium hosts major soccer matches, though Venezuelans don't seem to be as crazy about this sport as are the Brazilians and Colombians. Most matches take place between December and March, with the major events usually scheduled on Saturday evening.

Caracas' excellent horse-racing track, the Hipódromo La Rinconada, has racing on Saturday and Sunday afternoons from 1 pm on. The track is 6km south-west of the centre, off the Caracas-Valencia freeway.

GETTING THERE & AWAY
Air
The Simón Bolívar airport is in Maiquetía near the port of La Guaira on the Caribbean coast, 26km from central Caracas. It's linked to the city by a freeway (built in 1950-53) which cuts through the coastal mountain range with three tunnels, the main being 2km long.

The airport has two separate terminals, one for international and another for domestic flights, located 400m from each other. There's a free shuttle bus service between the terminals.

The international terminal has a range of facilities, including a tourist office, car rental desks, three or four casas de cambio, a bank, post and telephone offices, a restaurant, several cafés and snack bars, and a bunch of travel agencies. It even has a chapel but no left-luggage office. Note that arriving passengers are not allowed to take luggage trolleys beyond the customs area. The domestic terminal doesn't have money changing facilities, but has a dozen desks of car rental companies, domestic airlines and tour operators, plus a collection of fast-food outlets.

If you fly into Venezuela via Maiquetía airport, change your money upon arrival. There are several casas de cambio in the main hall on the ground floor, including Italcambio which changes cash and travellers cheques and usually offers the best rates. It's open daily until the last flight. There are also money changing facilities before the customs, and it may be worth changing money here if you don't want to queue at the casas de cambio in the concourse. Advances on Visa and MasterCard can be obtained in the Banco de Venezuela on the upper level, but only during normal opening hours (Monday to Friday from 8.30 to 11.30 am and 2 to 4.30 pm). The bank has an ATM, but it's often out of service.

Ignore any individuals who approach you claiming that they are from the tourist office (they're not) and offering help and information; they'll demand a hefty fee for anything they do. The genuine Corpoturismo tourist office (open daily from 7 am to 9 pm) is on the ground floor, and may have some brochures on Caracas. If you plan on phoning from the terminal, buy a phone card in CANTV or the newsagency (both on the upper level). When calling Caracas, remember to add the 02 area code before the local Caracas number.

There are plenty of international and domestic flights. For international connections see the Getting There & Away chapter. For domestic flights, refer to the Getting Around chapter. More specific information about internal flights is included in the relevant sections of this book. For example, if you need details of flights to Maracaibo, see that destination in The North-West chapter and assume that there's the same number of flights in each direction.

Airline Offices There's no need to go to a particular airline office to buy tickets for its flights. Just about every travel agency – and there are about 600 of them in the city – will sell you tickets for flights by most airlines and, consequently, will know which is the cheapest carrier on a particular route and

which are the best connections. This essentially refers to domestic routes and popular international flights such as Caracas to Miami. When it comes to more complex intercontinental connections, not all agencies are experts, so you should shop around.

If you are looking for a flight to Europe, some of the cheapest airfares are offered by TAP Air Portugal (☎ 951 05 11, 951 55 08, 951 64 03), Edificio Canaima, Avenida Francisco de Miranda (metro Chacaíto). However, it will be cheaper to fly with Avensa to Miami and take one of the relatively cheap transatlantic flights (eg with United Airlines).

Some Caracas travel agencies will sell combined tickets for the whole route. Students and teachers will find best deals at IVI tours (see Travel Agencies earlier in this chapter).

If you plan on travelling to Colombia and flying within the country, enquire about the domestic air pass offered by Avianca (☎ 953 72 54, 953 57 32), Edificio Roraima, Avenida Francisco de Miranda, Chacao (metro Chacaíto). See Air Passes under Air in the Getting Around chapter.

Bus

Caracas has two bus terminals. The old Nuevo Circo terminal, until recently the only one, occupies two large blocks in the city centre. Its eastern half handles long-distance intercity buses to anywhere in the west and south-west of the country; the western half services regional routes. The terminal is anarchic, chaotic, confusing, noisy, dirty and unsafe, to name just a few of its characteristics. It is going to be replaced by the Terminal de Occidente, to be built at what is now Mercado de Coche, just off the freeway to Valencia, near La Rinconada horse-racing track, and completed by the year 2000, si Dios quiere.

All buses coming to Caracas from the west and south-west via the Valencia freeway, pass by La Bandera metro station before arriving at Nuevo Circo terminal. Get off here and continue by metro, unless you plan on staying around the terminal (or have bulky bags – see Metro below).

The city's other bus terminal, the new Terminal de Oriente, is on the eastern outskirts of Caracas, on the highway to Barcelona, 5km beyond the suburb of Petare. It's accessible by local carritos from both Nuevo Circo and Petare. The terminal is modern and functional, and has computerised ticket booths. It handles all traffic to the east and south-east.

Approximate fares and travelling times to major destinations around the country from both terminals are listed in the boxed text entitled Major Bus Routes from Caracas. Also see the chapters covering your destinations, which contain more specific information and comments. There may be direct buses to Santa Elena de Uairén, but they hardly ever reach their final destination. It's better to go to Ciudad Bolívar and change.

The Aeroexpresos Ejecutivos bus company (☎ 266 36 01, 266 23 21, 266 12 95) services several major cities, including Valencia, Barquisimeto and Puerto La Cruz,

in modern, comfortable air-conditioned buses with TV and toilet. It's more expensive than other companies but, as some travellers report, it's worth it. The company has its own bus terminal on Avenida Bello Campo (metro Altamira).

Car & Motorcycle

Driving into/out of Caracas is pretty straightforward. The major western access is by the Valencia-Caracas freeway, which enters the city from the south and joins Autopista Francisco Fajardo, the main west-east city artery, next to the Universidad Central de Venezuela. From anywhere in the east, access is by the Barcelona-Caracas freeway which will take you directly into Avenida Francisco Fajardo.

If you need a car in Venezuela, try to make an arrangement at home with one of the international car-rental companies such as Avis, Hertz, Budget or Dollar, all of which operate here. That way you can have a car waiting for you upon arrival.

Major Bus Routes from Caracas				
Destination	Distance (km)	Ordinary Fare (US$)	Deluxe Fare (US$)	Time (hours)
Barcelona	310	6.25	7.75	4½
Barinas	515	8.00	10.00	8½
Barquisimeto	341	5.50	6.75	6.0
Carúpano	521	9.75	12.00	8½
Ciudad Bolívar	591	10.50	13.25	9.0
Ciudad Guayana	698	12.00	15.00	10½
Coro	453	7.00	8.75	7.0
Cumaná	402	7.25	9.00	6½
Guanare	427	6.50	8.25	7.0
Güiria	663	12.50	15.50	11.0
Maracaibo	706	10.75	13.50	11.0
Maracay	109	2.50	3.00	2.0
Maturín	518	9.25	11.50	8½
Mérida	682	12.00	15.50	12.0
Puerto Ayacucho	841	14.50	18.00	16.0
Puerto La Cruz	320	6.25	7.75	5.0
San Antonio del Táchira	877	13.25	16.75	14.0
San Cristóbal	841	12.50	15.75	13.0
San Fernando de Apure	404	6.75	8.50	8.0
Tucupita	730	11.25	14.00	11.0
Valencia	158	3.00	3.75	3.0
Valera	602	8.75	11.00	9½

If you fly into Caracas without any previous arrangements, contact car-rental companies at Maiquetía airport. There are half a dozen operators in the international terminal, including Avis, Hertz and Dollar, but they can't always provide a car at call. You'll find desks of another dozen or so (mostly local) companies in the domestic terminal, and these may have something on the spot. Major rental companies also have offices in Caracas and desks in the lobbies of top-end hotels, including the Caracas Hilton, Tamanaco and Eurobuilding. Cars can also be hired through Fairmont Internacional and many other travel agencies.

For more information about rental conditions, prices and driving in general, see Car & Motorcycle in the Getting Around chapter.

Boat

La Guaira, the port of Caracas, is one of the busiest freight terminals in the country, but there's no passenger service to any of Venezuela's offshore possessions. The boat to Los Roques is no longer operating.

GETTING AROUND
The Airport

There's a bus service between Maiquetía airport and Caracas, daily from 5.30 am till the evening. Buses are supposed to depart every half an hour but in practice they usually don't leave until full. In the city, the buses depart until 7 pm from Calle Sur 17, directly underneath Avenida Bolívar, next to Parque Central. There are no stairs connecting the two levels; get down to the buses by Calle Sur 17 from Avenida Mexico (or Avenida Lecuna). At the airport, buses leave from the front of both the domestic and international terminals. The final bus is supposed to service the last flight.

The trip either way costs US$2 and normally takes about 40 minutes, but traffic jams, particularly on weekends and holidays, can double that time. If you are going from the airport to the city, it's faster and more convenient to get off at Gato Negro metro

station and continue by metro to your final destination.

A taxi fare from the airport to Caracas depends on which suburb you go to. Sample daylight tariffs are: to the centre US$18, Sabana Grande US$20, and Altamira US$22. Night-time fares (from 6 pm to 6 am on weekdays, and the whole day Saturday, Sunday and holidays) are about 10% higher. Air-conditioned taxis charge 25% more. A taxi takes up to four passengers. Before boarding a taxi, check the official tariffs in order to avoid overcharging. They are posted on the external wall of the airport terminal next to the taxi stand.

You may be approached by 'taxi drivers' inside the international terminal, who will offer you a ride to Caracas for less than the official tariff, but this should be viewed with suspicion. Their taxis are usually not in the regular taxi line but parked elsewhere. Some of these drivers are honest, but there may be some who mug you in the middle of nowhere.

If you have just an overnight stop in Maiquetía, there's probably no point in going to Caracas. Instead, you can stay the night on the coast, eg in Macuto (see Litoral Central in the Around Caracas section). To get to Macuto, leave the terminal through a passageway leading from the building's upper level to the car park, get to the main road, cross that road and wave down the eastbound Macuto/Caraballeda carrito which will cost about US$0.50. Don't do it after dark. A taxi to Macuto shouldn't cost any more than US$7.

If you're arriving late at Maiquetía, don't venture outside the terminal further than the bus stop and taxi stand (both of which are just at the building's doors).

Metro

This is the major means of getting around Caracas. It's fast, well organised, easy to use, clean and cheap, and provides access to most major city attractions and tourist facilities.

The French-made metro system has three lines, with a total length of 44km and 39 stations. The longest line, No 1, goes east-west all the way along the city axis, and you will use it most frequently. Line No 2 leads from the centre south-west to the distant suburb of Caricuao and the zoo. The newest and shortest line, No 3, runs from Plaza Venezuela south-west to El Valle. Further lines are planned, but it will take a while before they open.

The system also includes a number of bus routes, called metrobus, which link some of the suburbs to metro stations. You can thus easily reach San Bernardino, El Cafetal, Prados del Este, La Trinidad and other suburbs (plus intermediate points) which are not reached directly by metro. For example, the Centro Ciudad Comercial Tamanaco (CCCT) is accessible by Metrobus No 211 (La Trinidad) from Chacao station and No 201 (El Cafetal) from Altamira station (ask the driver to indicate where to get off – it's not immediately obvious). The metro lines and metrobus routes are marked on Caracas map posted in every metro station.

The metro operates daily from 5.30 am to 11 pm. The air-conditioned trains run every few minutes, but less frequently early in the morning and late in the evening. Yellow tickets cost US$0.23 for a ride up to three stations, US$0.25 for four to seven stations, and US$0.28 for any longer route. The transfer ticket *(boleto integrado)* for the combined metro-plus-bus route costs US$0.30. Consider buying the *multiabono*, a multiple orange ticket costing US$2.30, which is valid for 10 metro rides of any distance. Not only do you save money, but you also avoid queuing each time at the ticket counters – there are always lines at the counters. Some newspaper kiosks near the stations also sell metro tickets.

To get to the train platform, you put your ticket into the slot on the turnstile, which opens and flips your ticket back out to you. Preserve it, because you have to use it again to open a similar turnstile at your destination. This time your ticket won't be flipped back, unless it's a multiabono. Bulky packages which might obstruct other passengers – as the regulations say – are not allowed in the metro. Backpacks are usually no problem, but use common sense and don't carry large bags during rush hours, when trains are really crowded.

The metro is generally safe, though there have been some comments about pick-

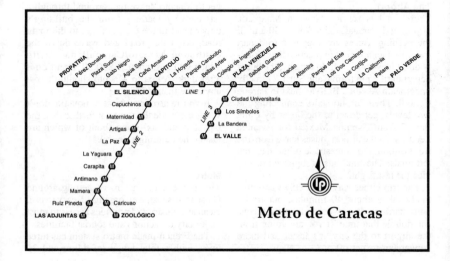

Metro de Caracas

pockets operating in groups on the escalators of the busy stations, eg La Hoyada, Bellas Artes and Plaza Venezuela. The man in front of you drops something and bends down to retrieve it. His accomplices at the back push you, while the one directly behind you tries to pick your pockets.

Bus

The bus network is extensive and covers all suburbs within the metropolitan area as well as all the major neighbouring localities. The main type of vehicle operating city routes is a small bus, commonly called carrito. They run frequently but move only as fast as the traffic allows, and may often be trapped in traffic jams. Use carritos only if you are going to destinations which are inaccessible by metro. It's probably worth taking a carrito ride anyway, just to get a taste of local culture; the radio will be blasting and the driver undertaking breathtaking manoeuvres – definitely a different kind of trip to the smooth and silent metro ride.

Taxi

Taxis, identifiable by either the Taxi or Libre sign, are a fairly inexpensive means of transport and useful to get to places not reached by the metro. Not many of them have meters, so always fix the fare before boarding the taxi. It may be difficult to wave a taxi down on the street, so either look for them at a taxi stand (there are plenty of them) or request one by phone by calling any of the numerous companies that provide a radio service. Several companies such as Teletaxi (☎ 752 91 22, 752 41 55) or Móvil-Enlace (☎ 577 09 22, 577 33 44) service the entire Caracas area 24 hours a day.

Around Caracas

This section includes only places in the close vicinity of the capital, in the Distrito Federal. You will find other one day destinations out of Caracas in The Central North chapter.

PARQUE NACIONAL EL ÁVILA

El Ávila national park is a steep, verdant mountain which looms just to the north of Caracas. The park encompasses about 90km of the range running east-west along the coast and separating the city from the sea. The highest peak is Pico Naiguatá (2765m).

The southern slope, overlooking Caracas, is virtually uninhabited, but is crisscrossed with dozens of walking trails. The northern face, running down to the sea, is dotted with hamlets and haciendas, yet few tourist trails are on this side. The park is crossed north to south by a few 4WD tracks and the inoperable *teleférico* (cable car).

Teleférico

The cable car was built by a German company in 1956-57, during the dictatorship of Marcos Pérez Jiménez. It consists of two lines: the one-stage, 4km run from Caracas up to El Ávila peak, and the three-stage, 7.5km run from El Ávila down to Macuto on the coast. Both lines have been closed since 1988. There have been murmurs about privatising the facility, which might speed up its reopening, but so far its future is unclear. Pérez Jiménez also commissioned the teleférico in Mérida.

The teleférico used to go from the Maripérez station (980m), next to Avenida Boyacá in Caracas, up to El Ávila station (2150m), close to Pico El Ávila (2175m), crowned by the sparkling, circular 14-storey Hotel Humboldt built in 1956. The hotel was closed soon after the cable car stopped running. Today it's just a fantastic landmark overlooking Caracas, visible from just about every point of the city.

The area around the upper station offers breathtaking views of Caracas and the Valle del Tuy beyond, and, towards the north, a beautiful panorama of the coast with the Caribbean Sea stretching to the horizon.

Walks

El Ávila provides the best infrastructure for walkers of any of Venezuela's parks. There are about 200km of walking trails, most of them well signposted. Half a dozen camping grounds distributed around the park are equipped with sanitary facilities and there are many more places designated for camping, though without facilities.

There are a dozen entrances which lead into the park from Caracas; all originate from Avenida Boyacá, commonly known as Cota Mil, as it runs at an altitude of 1000m. Whichever route you choose, you'll have a short ascent before you get to a guard post where you pay a nominal park entrance fee. The rangers *(guardaparques)* may provide information about routes, and suggest one if you haven't yet decided. Before you come, however, buy the recently published, useful *Mapa para el Excursionista – Parque Nacional El Ávila* (scale 1:40,000), which has marked trails and camping facilities.

You have plenty of options for a half or full-day hike. You can, for example, go up to Pico El Ávila; there are at least four routes leading there. Start early as it gets pretty hot by mid-morning. If you are prepared to camp, probably the most scenic route is the two day hike to Pico Naiguatá. Take rain gear and warm clothes. Water is scarce, so bring some along. Don't forget plastic bags to bring all your rubbish back down. The dry season is from December to April, but even then there may be rain in the upper reaches.

LITORAL CENTRAL
• *pop 400,000*
• *area code* ☎ (031)
The northern face of El Ávila park slopes steeply down almost right into the sea, leaving only a narrow flat strip of land between the foothills and the shore, referred to as Litoral Central. Still, the area is quite well urbanised and densely populated, with a chain of towns lining the waterfront. From west to east, the most populous urban centres are Catia La Mar, Maiquetía, La Guaira, Macuto, Caraballeda and Naiguatá. The first two towns sit at opposite ends of the airport and have little charm. La Guaira is an important and busy Caracas port, while the three remaining places have developed into popular seaside resorts for caraqueños, who come here en masse on weekends to enjoy the sea air. Further east, the holiday centres thin out, though the paved road continues for another 20km to Los Caracas.

This part of the coast is dramatic and spectacular (especially the stretch from Naiguatá to Los Caracas) but not particularly good for bathing. The shore is mostly rocky all the way from Catia La Mar to Los Caracas, and there are only short stretches of beach (good wild beaches begin east of Los Caracas). The straight coastline is exposed to open-sea surf, and strong currents can make swimming dangerous. Most of the holidaying activity is confined to *balnearios*, small sections of beach with facilities, and to private beach clubs. Macuto, Caraballeda and Naiguatá all have balnearios, and there are a few more, such as Camurí Chico, between Macuto and Caraballeda. An array of hotels and restaurants has sprung up along the waterfront, providing an adequate choice of comfortable beds and good fried fish.

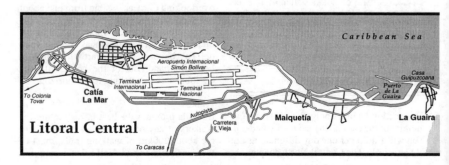

All in all, if you like the seaside ambience and want to escape from Caracas' rush, this might be an easy option, though there are many nicer coastal towns and better beaches elsewhere on Venezuela's coast. If you fly through Maiquetía and have an overnight stop between your flights, it's probably better to stay on the coast than to go to Caracas just for the night. Macuto is possibly the most enjoyable town in the area.

Things to See
The sea apart, you have some cultural attractions on the central coast. La Guaira has a partly preserved and restored old town, noted for its narrow streets lined by houses with grilled windows. The largest and most imposing building in town is the **Casa Guipuzcoana**, the customs house built on the waterfront in 1734 by the infamous trade company of the same name. Enveloped by shantytowns, La Guaira doesn't seem to be the safest place on earth, so be on your guard while visiting.

Macuto feels much safer, and here you can visit the **Museo Reverón**, established in the grounds where a renowned painter, Armando Reverón (1889-1954), lived and worked. The place, named El Castillete by the artist, is a walled-in garden featuring several original rustic structures, including a studio, dormitory, kitchen and chapel, all built by the painter, plus a modern exhibition hall added at the back. It's in the eastern part of the town, 100m from the waterfront, sheltered amid modern residential blocks. It's

open Tuesday to Friday from 9 am to 5 pm, Saturday and Sunday from 10 am to 6 pm.

Places to Stay & Eat
There are few hotels in Maiquetía and La Guaira, but Catia La Mar, Macuto and Caraballeda have a good supply of accommodation. Of all these towns, Macuto has the largest choice of places to stay, including a number of budget hotels.

Catia La Mar This is a large and uninspiring town, except, perhaps, for the seaside strip east of town where a collection of modern residential towers has sprung up. Some of the cheaper hotels, including *Hotel de París* (☎ 51 12 48), *Hostal Tanausú* and *Hotel Scorpio*, are in the seaside suburb of Atlántida in the northwestern part of town. Half a km east from the Scorpio is the upmarket *Hotel Puerto Viejo* (☎ 51 14 01, 52 40 44).

Macuto The town has plenty of hotels, a dozen of which are located on or just off Paseo La Playa, a 600m-long waterfront promenade. The better budget places in this area include the *Hotel Diana* (☎ 46 14 53), *Hotel Colonial* (☎ 46 14 62), *Hotel Darimar* and *Hotel Plazamar*. Prices tend to fluctuate, rising at weekends, but you shouldn't pay more than US$15 for a double in any of these hotels. There are some cheaper but basic places around. The promenade is also swamped with restaurants and snack bars.

There are more hotels and restaurants towards the west, including the pleasant

budget *Hotel Isaibel* and the more expensive *Hotel Macuto* (☎ 46 13 10), which has a swimming pool. In the same area are two attractive open-air restaurants, *El Coral* and *La Choza del Santiago*, next to each other right on the waterfront.

Caraballeda Just 5km east of Macuto, Caraballeda is larger and more modern. It has fewer accommodation options, particularly at the bottom end. It's hard to find anything cheaper than US$20 to US$25 for a double room. In this price range check the *Hotel Costa Azul* (☎ 94 01 74), *Hotel Royal Atlantic* (☎ 94 13 50) or *Hotel Fioremar*

(☎ 94 17 43), all three on Avenida Principal (the main road) close to *McDonald's*.

If you need somewhere upmarket you are in the right place as Caraballeda hosts the two best hotels on the central coast, the *Macuto Sheraton* (☎ 94 43 00; fax 94 43 18) and *Meliá Caribe* (☎ 94 55 55; fax 94 15 09).

Getting There & Away
There are regular frequent services from Nuevo Circo bus terminal in Caracas to Catia La Mar and Macuto, and many go all the way up to Caraballeda. The fare is around US$1 to any of these towns.

The Central North

Commonly referred to as El Centro, the central north encompasses the states of Carabobo, Aragua, Miranda and Distrito Federal. This is Venezuela's most developed region, both industrially and agriculturally. It is also the most densely populated: occupying less than 2.5% of the national territory, these four states are home to around 45% of Venezuela's population. Half live in Caracas, while the other half is distributed throughout a dozen fair-sized towns and the two large cities of Valencia and Maracay.

Despite its development, though, El Centro boasts extensive areas of woodland, some of which have been decreed national parks. There are six mainland parks in the region (the most popular of them, El Ávila, has been included in the Around Caracas section of the previous chapter) plus the marine park of Los Roques off the coast. The central north also has a number of other attractions, including the mountain town of Colonia Tovar and Venezuela's best hot spring complex at Las Trincheras.

Some of the places included in this chapter, such as Colonia Tovar, San Francisco de Yare and Parque Nacional Guatopo, can be visited as one day trips out of Caracas. Caracas is also the departure point for the Archipiélago Los Roques.

Archipiélago Los Roques

Los Roques is a beautiful archipelago of small coral islands about 150km due north off the central coast. Stretching 36km east to west and 25km north to south, it consists of some 40 islands big enough to name and perhaps 250 other islets, sandbars and cays. The whole archipelago, complete with the surrounding waters (2211 sq km), was made

HIGHLIGHTS

- Enjoy bird-watching in Henri Pittier and Guatopo national parks
- Marvel at the Dancing Devils of San Francisco de Yare and Chuao
- Try snorkelling at Los Roques
- Sunbathe on solitary beaches at the foot of Henri Pittier park
- Visit the tiny colonial town of Choroní
- Dance to night-time drumbeats in Puerto Colombia and Chuao
- Explore the German town of Colonia Tovar
- Soak in the thermal baths at Las Trincheras
- Stroll about the colonial core of Puerto Cabello

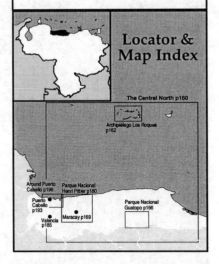

a national park in 1972. Administratively, it's a dependency of the Distrito Federal.

The archipelago was originally inhabited by a group of Indians who arrived from the mainland about a thousand years ago. Some pirates and explorers occasionally visited the

THE CENTRAL NORTH

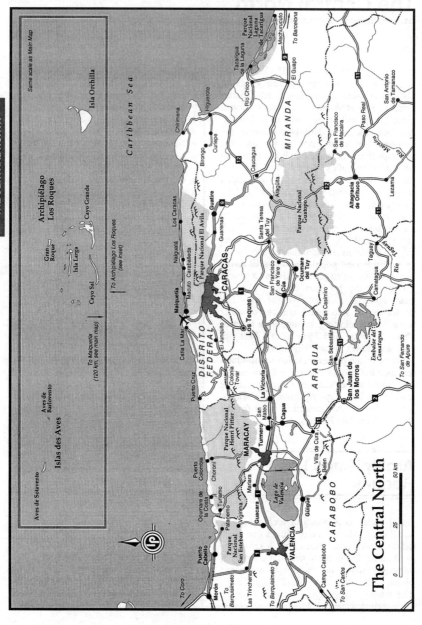

The Central North

Same scale as Main Map

Isla Orchilla

Caribbean Sea

Archipiélago
Los Roques

Gran
Roque

Isla Larga

Cayo Grande

Cayo Sal

To Archipiélago Los Roques
(see inset)

To Maiquetía
(120 km, see main map)

Aves de Sotavento

Aves de
Barlovento

Islas des Aves

0   25   50 km

Top Left: Devil dancer's mask & baskets
Top Right: Preparations for beauty contest
Bottom Left: Powerful sound system – the most important feature of a Venezuelan bus
Bottom Right: Tyres, in contrast, are of little priority

Top: Bird's-eye view of Archipiélago Los Roques
Left: Local church, Choroní
Right: Old town's street, Puerto Cabello

islands during colonial times, but none of them seemed to be interested in settling there for good. In the late 19th century, fishermen from Isla de Margarita were attracted by the abundance of fish, and gradually settled the archipelago's main island, Gran Roque. Known as the *roqueños*, they now make up the majority of the local population.

The islands' vegetation consists mainly of grasses, cacti, low bushes and mangroves. Local fauna is best represented by birds – about 80 species have been recorded as either living permanently or seasonally on the archipelago. There are no native mammals on the islands, but there are reptiles, including four species of turtle and some small lizards, salamanders and iguanas. The waters abound in fish and lobster, though the latter has been overfished over the past decade.

Los Roques is swiftly becoming a popular tourist destination. What draws people in here are soft white sandy beaches and extensive coral reefs – a paradise for snorkelling and scuba diving. The tourist infrastructure has expanded over recent years, as did flight services providing access to the archipelago. All visitors to Los Roques pay the US$12 national park entry fee upon arrival.

Gran Roque

Gran Roque, on the northern edge of the archipelago, is the main island. On its southern side is a fishing village of the same name with a population of 1200. It has a Plaza Bolívar, an Inparques office, a Guardia Nacional post, 40-odd posadas, a few shops and three public phones. The sandy streets are lined with brightly painted houses, and there are no traffic problems as the only vehicle is a garbage truck. The village has desalinisation and electricity plants, neither of which is very reliable.

Gran Roque is the transport hub of the archipelago. It has an airstrip, just to the east of the village, which handles all flights. The village's waterfront is packed with fishing boats, tour operators' vessels, visiting yachts and pelicans.

Gran Roque is the only island of volcanic origin. Unlike the other islands, which are all sandy and completely flat, Gran Roque has two massive rocky humps at its western end – the tallest is 110m – and cliffs which drop almost vertically into the sea. Climb the rocks for sweeping views over the village, the neighbouring islands, their coral reefs and the surrounding crystal clear turquoise sea.

Other Islands

The nearest island to Gran Roque is Madrizquí, about 1km to the south-east. It was the favourite island among affluent caraqueños who discovered Los Roques several decades ago and built their summer beach houses here before the archipelago was made a national park. Other nearby islands with dwellings are Cayo Pirata and Crasquí, which have fishing shelters known as *rancherías*, and Francisquises, which has a *campamento*.

The island of Dos Mosquises Sur, at the far south-western edge of the archipelago, has the Marine Biological Station run by the Fundación Científica Los Roques which can be visited.

The station has breeding tanks where turtles and other endangered species are raised before being released around the archipelago; more than 5000 turtles have already been reared.

In order to protect the habitat and control the tourist traffic, the so-called Zona de Recreación was created, comprising Gran Roque and the nearby islands. Tourists can visit the recreation zone but the remaining part of the archipelago (except for the biological station) has a restricted access requiring special permits.

You will probably wonder about the islands' strange names. Many of the islands were first named by English explorers. The fishermen from Margarita preserved most of the original names but wrote them down phonetically. Then apparently along came the linguistically-correct cartographers who changed the spelling according to the standard Spanish grammar. This is how the original Northeast Key in English was recorded as Nordisky, to eventually become

THE CENTRAL NORTH

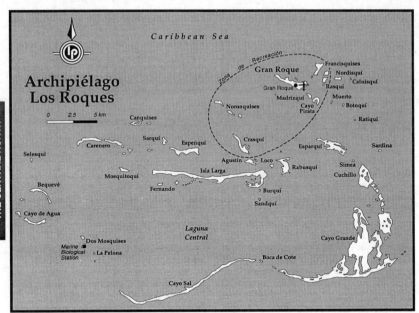

Nordisquí. Similarly, the Sails Key went through Selesky to Selesquí, and St Luis Key has become Celuisquí. You may find different spellings on other maps.

Organised Tours

The usual way of visiting the archipelago is on a one or two day tour. Tours are run by most of the small airlines with flights to Los Roques, and they all have their desks at the domestic terminal of the Maiquetía airport (see Organised Tours in the Caracas chapter for airlines and phone numbers). The prices and services may vary between operators. Línea Turística Aereotuy (LTA) is the main operator and possibly the most reliable.

The all-inclusive one day tour from Maiquetía normally costs about US$140 to US$150 and includes the return flight, a boat excursion from Gran Roque to one or two of the nearby islands, lunch, soft drinks, one hour of snorkelling (equipment provided) and free time on the beach. The tour programme is pretty similar among all the operators, though they go to different islands and have their own preferred snorkelling areas. LTA is the only company which runs trips in large catamarans (others have boats only).

The two day tour includes accommodation in Gran Roque and all meals, and costs around US$250 to US$350, depending on the season, lodging standards and the occupancy of the room. Additional days cost US$100 to US$150. Note that tour prices don't include the US$12 entry fee to the archipelago.

Some operators, including LTA, also run tours from Isla de Margarita (US$200 for one day tour, US$300 to US$450 for two day tour). LTA also offers fishing programmes and can include scuba diving for US$70 extra per day. Diving is operated by Gran Roque-based Sesto Continente dive centre, which can be contacted in Caracas on ☎ (02) 74 90 80; ☎ & fax 74 38 73.

A day tour is an enjoyable escape from Caracas, but gives just a brief taste of what the archipelago has to offer. If this is all you want, the package is good value, as it's not much more expensive than the airfare. Two day tours give a better insight, but are far more expensive, largely because the tour companies use rather upmarket accommodation. Some travellers consider them poor value. If you plan on staying two or more days it's worth considering going on your own, which is pretty straightforward and far cheaper than taking a tour.

Places to Stay & Eat
Responding to tourism, locals have moved swiftly to transform their homes into guest houses, and the result is truly impressive. There are already more than 40 posadas in the tiny village of Gran Roque, providing about 300 beds in all. Most of them are small and simple places which offer both lodging and dining. Food is expensive and limited, because everything, except fish, has to be shipped in from the mainland. The cheapest you'll pay is about US$20 to US$25 for a bed in a room with shared facilities, plus breakfast and dinner. Prices seem to vary from weekdays to weekends and depend on demand. Many posadas have boats and may provide trips to other islands at discounted prices for guests.

Among the cheapest places are *Posada Doña Carmen* and *Posada Doña Magalys*, both on Plaza Bolívar; *Posada Roquelusa* on Calle Principal near Inparques office; and *Posada La Lagunita* on Calle La Laguna.

The cheapest option is to camp. Camping is allowed on all the islands within the recreation zone, including Gran Roque, and is free. After arrival, go to the Inparques office in the village (open daily from 8 am to noon and 2 to 6 pm) for a free camping permit. The friendly staff will tell you which islands are good for camping and snorkelling, and can give you other practical tips.

Fishermen in the village can take you to the island of your choice and pick you up at a pre-arranged time in the afternoon of the same day or on a later date. Fares are nego-

tiable, depending mostly on your party's size. Use the following figures (return fares per person) as a rough guide only: Madrizquí (US$5), Francisquises (US$9), Crasquí (US$16) and Noronquises (US$18).

If you plan on camping on any island other than Gran Roque, then you should be self-sufficient with camping gear, food and water. Bring along snorkelling gear and good sun protection – there's almost no shade on the islands.

Getting There & Away
Air Most of the airlines that fly to Los Roques have pretty similar airfares. The Maiquetía-Los Roques one-way fare is about US$75, and the return fare is US$110. The flight takes about 40 minutes.

LTA offers budget one-way fares of US$35 on their afternoon flights to Los Roques, and on the morning flights back to Maiquetía. In effect, you can have a return for US$70. This may be a great saving if you plan on camping but less so if you'll stay in a posada. LTA also flies to Los Roques from Isla de Margarita, offering a similar budget option (US$90 normal one way, US$65 discounted one way).

Normally, only 10kg free luggage is permitted on flights to Los Roques, and you pay US$0.50 for every additional kg. Some airlines may be more tolerant about excess luggage.

Boat There's no passenger boat service to Los Roques. You can try the fishermen in La Guaira port, or ask around the marinas in Caraballeda and Naiguatá for boats going there.

Miranda State

San Francisco de Yare
* pop 17,000
* area code ☎ (039)

San Francisco de Yare is a small, quiet town, about 70km by road south-east of Caracas. The town was founded in 1718 and boasts a fine mid-18th century church, Iglesia de

San Francisco, and some preserved colonial architecture. However, what has really made the place famous are the colourful celebrations of Diablos Danzantes (see boxed text), when up to 1000 devils take to the streets to perform their ritual dance to the rhythm of drums. The feast has been celebrated here annually on Corpus Christi since 1742.

Festival de Diablos Danzantes
The celebrations begin at noon on Wednesday, which is the day prior to Corpus Christi, when crowds of devil dancers wearing their colourful masks depart from the Casa de los Diablos Danzantes and take up the central streets for the whole afternoon. In the evening, they go to El Calvario for the lengthy

Diablos Danzantes
The Dancing Devils is one of Venezuela's most colourful events. Its central feature are the devils, portrayed by dancers wearing monstrous masks. The dance can be anything from ceremonial march-like movements in double files to spasmodic squirms to the beat of drums. Paradoxically, the devil dancers take to the streets on Corpus Christi, one of the holiest days on the Roman Catholic calendar, held in honour of the Eucharist.

Devil dancer's mask

The ceremony is thought to manifest the struggle between Evil and Good, and the eventual triumph of the latter. Effectively, no matter how profane the devil dances may look, the devils come at some stage to the steps of the church to submit themselves to the Eucharist. In turn, they get the priest's blessing and can then return to their whirling dances.

The event has a magical-religious appearance and meaning. Locals believe that the dance ritual will ensure abundant crops, welfare, prosperity and protection against misfortune and natural disasters. For the devils, the dance is their religion.

Broadly speaking, Diablos Danzantes is the product of the blend of Spanish and African traditions. The event has its roots in Spain, where the devils' images and masks featured in Corpus Christi feasts in medieval Andalusia. When the festival was brought to the New World by the Spanish missionaries in colonial times, it found a fertile soil among the black slaves, who re-interpreted the Catholic devotion in their own way. They happily put on traditional masks from their homeland, and danced to the rhythm of familiar drumbeats. Some academics consider this an act of protest by the black community against the white god, a symbol of Spanish oppression and cruelty. Whatever the reason, the profane and the divine gradually merged, producing a striking cross-cultural ritual.

The African origins are palpable, even though the dances today are not performed exclusively by blacks. Devil dances have been preserved only in areas which have traditionally had a significant black population. Some of the modern masks are similar to those of West African countries such as Congo, Benin and Nigeria. The usual accompanying instrument is the drum, though maracas and *cuatro* (a small guitar) are also used in some areas.

The towns and villages which boast devil dances today include Naiguatá (Distrito Federal); Cata, Chuao, Cuyagua, Ocumare de la Costa and Turiamo (Aragua); Canoabo, Guacara, Los Caneyes, Patanemo and Tocuyito (Carabobo); Tinaquillo (Cojedes); and San Francisco de Yare (Miranda). All these localities are in the area which witnessed the heaviest import of black slaves. The celebrations in Chuao and San Francisco de Yare are best known throughout the country, as are their masks.

Dances, costumes and masks of each community have developed their own forms and features. Although masks today are commonly made of papier-mâché, they differ notably from town to town. Those from San Francisco de Yare, for example, are large, elaborate and brightly painted in just about every colour of the rainbow. They depict horned demons, monsters, fantastic animals and the like. The masks from Chuao are smaller and more modest. They are essentially painted with three colours – white, black and red – and have clear characteristics of those from Congo. ■

Velorio (vigil), which can take most of the night.

On Corpus Christi the devils gather early in the morning at the Casa de los Diablos Danzantes, before heading for the local cemetery to pay honour to their predecessors. They then group at the door of the parish church (but don't enter it), while the morning mass is celebrated inside. When the mass is over, the ceremony of the Juramentación is performed in front of the church, in which young apprentices for devil dancers take a symbolic oath. The priest gives his blessing to the devils and they all set off for the procession carrying the image of the Holy Sacrament.

The procession heads along Calle Bolívar to the Monumento de los Diablos Danzantes, and returns to the church along the parallel Calle Rivas. It's just 10 blocks in all but it can take a couple of hours to complete the loop, stopping at the makeshift altars en route. The devils continue their street dancing programme throughout the afternoon, before returning to the church at about 6 pm for another procession, this time to El Calvario where the celebrations conclude.

Other Attractions

Obviously, Corpus Christi is the best day to visit the town, but it's still worth coming at other times. The ambience of Diablos Danzantes is omnipresent anytime, particularly in the weeks prior to the festival.

The Casa de los Diablos Danzantes (where the Corpus Christi celebrations begin), on Calle Rivas, next door to the police station, is a museum which has a collection of devil masks and photos from previous festivals. It's open Tuesday and Thursday from 7 to 11 am and 2 to 4 pm, and Sunday from 7 to 11 am. The family living in the house next door to the museum has the keys and may open it for you at other times.

There are several workshops manufacturing devil masks, where you can see the production process and buy masks (at much more reasonable prices than anywhere else). Reputedly the best is the Artesanía El Mocho, led by Manuel Sanoja. It's on Calle

Rivas, opposite the Monumento de los Diablos Danzantes, above the Bodega San Antonio – enquire in this shop. The Artesanía Morgado, one block away on the same street, is run by another noted local artisan, Juan Morgado. One of his relatives living in the adjacent house makes amazing ceramic miniatures of the masks.

Places to Stay & Eat

There are no regular hotels in town, but some locals provide informal accommodation in their homes. There are several basic places to eat, including the *Bar Restaurant El Deporte* on Plaza Bolívar, and the *Lunchería La Flor de Yare*, just off the plaza.

The nearest reliable accommodation is in Santa Teresa del Tuy and Ocumare del Tuy.

Getting There & Away

There's no direct transport from Caracas to San Francisco de Yare, but you can get there easily with one connection. Take one of the frequent buses to Ocumare del Tuy (US$0.75, 1¼ hours) or Santa Teresa del Tuy (US$0.75, 1¼ hours) from the Nuevo Circo bus terminal (regional sector), and change at your destination. Buses shuttle between Ocumare and Santa Teresa every 15 minutes or so, and pass through San Francisco de Yare, providing convenient access.

PARQUE NACIONAL GUATOPO

Established in 1958, Guatopo is Venezuela's third oldest national park. About 100km by road (60km as the crow flies) south-east of Caracas, it encompasses 1225 sq km of the rugged Serranía del Interior, a mountain range which splits off the Cordillera de la Costa and winds inland. The altitude in the park ranges between 200 and 1430m above sea level.

Most of the park is covered by lush rainforest, which makes it an important biological enclave in the otherwise heavily developed and populated hinterland of Caracas. Guatopo is also an important water supplier for the region, since several dams have been built in or just off the park, creating water reservoirs *(embalses)*.

The climate is wet and warm. The average annual rainfall ranges from about 1500mm in low-lying areas to nearly 3000mm in the upper reaches. The rainiest months are October to December, while the driest ones are March and April, but even then rains are not uncommon. Reliable rain gear is recommended for travel any time of the year. The temperatures in the lower parts of the park range between 25°C and 30°C, and drop to about 15°C on the highest tops.

Thanks to the wide range of elevations and high rainfall, the park's vegetation is varied and exuberant, with numerous species of trees (some up to 40m high), palms, ferns and orchids. The rich mammal world includes jaguar, puma, tapir, peccary, armadillo, margay and sloth, to name just a few. Guatopo is also good for bird-watching. Birds such as macaws, parakeets, woodpeckers, hummingbirds, honeycreepers, tanagers, trogons, grosbeaks and dozens of others, can be observed quite easily. There are also some poisonous snakes,

including the coral snake, tigra mariposa, rattlesnake and, the most common and dangerous, macagua *(Bothrops colombiensis)* – watch out when you walk. Insects are plentiful, so it's worth bringing along an effective insect repellent.

Orientation

The sealed road between Santa Teresa del Tuy and Altagracia de Orituco runs through the middle of the park, providing access to all recreational areas and starting points for walks. Public transport from Caracas travels along this road, but it's infrequent and dies in the afternoon. Given this, a one day trip to the park from Caracas gives you a pretty limited time in the park. If you decide to do this, make an early start and go to Agua Blanca, which is a good starting point for walking. If you have your own transport, you can easily visit several areas in the park, and still have reasonable time for walking.

The park offers some basic lodging and

camping facilities, which allow for longer stays in the heart of the rainforest. The following sections detail the major stopovers on the route, from north to south, along with their tourist facilities.

Los Alpes del Tuy

About 30km from Santa Teresa, Los Alpes is just a roadside cafeteria, *Parador Turístico Los Alpes*, sitting on a Y junction and serving hot snacks and drinks. The road branching to the south will take you to a viewpoint (3.5km from Los Alpes), then to another viewpoint (1km beyond), and 5km further on you reach La Macanilla.

La Macanilla

The Inparques visitors' centre here has a small exhibition on the park's flora, fauna and geology. The *guardaparque* (park's ranger) can give you information about the park. La Macanilla is the starting point for a beautiful 9km trail, which winds through thick forest up to the mountain ridge, continues along it and comes down back to the road 4km from La Macanilla. However, the trail hasn't been maintained and became overgrown several years ago. It was impassable at the time of writing. There's no accommodation or food in La Macanilla, and camping is not allowed.

Agua Blanca

Agua Blanca, 13km by road from La Macanilla, is the park's major recreational area. It can be swamped with day-trippers on weekends, but is usually quiet on weekdays. You can visit a reconstructed *trapiche* (traditional sugarcane mill), and have a bath in the *pozo* (pond) on the opposite side of the road, though the water is not crystal clean.

From the pond, an interesting 3km walking trail goes to Santa Crucita. This trail is steep in parts and often muddy; allow up to 1½ hours to walk it at a leisurely pace. There's another, shorter trail between Agua Blanca and Santa Crucita (1650m, 45 minutes), running on the opposite, eastern side of the road, which allows for a round trip without returning the same way. See the

following Santa Crucita section for more walks.

Agua Blanca has a picnic area, toilets, car park (guarded on weekends), snack kiosk (open on weekends) and some accommodation options. The *Campamento Los Monos* is a 30-bed dormitory which is rented as a whole (US$25) through Caracas' Inparques office. Bring your own sheets and blankets. There are also five *cabañas*, rustic timber structures on stilts, scattered around the forest. You actually get just a bare wooden floor under the roof, but it's a pleasant shelter and doesn't cost much: US$1.50 for the whole cabaña (four persons will fit). Bring your mats, sheets, blankets or a sleeping bag. There's also a *camping area*. Bring your food if you come on weekdays.

Santa Crucita

Santa Crucita is 1.5km by road from Agua Blanca. There is a small lagoon here, and you can pitch your tent on the grassy *camping ground*. Apart from the two trails coming here from Agua Blanca (see earlier), there are two short local walking loops, one skirting around the lagoon (700m) and another one going through the nearby forest (800m).

El Lucero

El Lucero, 5.5km down the road from Santa Crucita, is the administrative centre of the park. There's a *camp site* here and the *Casa de Huéspedes*, a house with half a dozen beds, which has to be hired through Caracas Inparques office (US$12 the house, no per bed price). No food is available in El Lucero.

Quebrada de Guatopo

Quebrada de Guatopo, 2km beyond El Lucero, has a picnic area, a creek and yet another *camping ground* where you stay overnight in your tent. Again, bring your own food.

Altagracia de Orituco

Altagracia de Orituco is beyond the national park's boundaries, 24km south of Quebrada de Guatopo. It's quite an ordinary town, but it's big enough to be a terminus for buses from Caracas, and to have a collection of hotels and restaurants.

Buses to Caracas depart from the junction where the petrol stations are located, 1km from Plaza Bolívar. Here you'll also find several hotels, including the *Hotel La Avenida* and the more decent *Hotel Amazor*, which has a good restaurant. Halfway between the Plaza Bolívar and the bus terminus is the *Pensión Los Angeles*.

Hacienda La Elvira
This old coffee hacienda is 26km north-east of Altagracia. The central feature is the 19th century country mansion, which is open to visitors. There's no accommodation, but camping is permitted.

To get there from Altagracia, you have to drive 8km east on the road to Paso Real and take the left turn-off north to San Francisco de Macaira. Follow this sealed but pothole-ridden road for 14km, and take the jeep track branching off to the north-west and leading to La Elvira (4km). Getting anywhere nearby by public transport is difficult.

Getting There & Away
The usual starting point for Guatopo is Caracas. There are hourly buses from Nuevo Circo terminal (regional sector) to Altagracia de Orituco (US$2.75, four hours), but they go by the road via Cúa and San Casimiro, and don't pass through the park. There are also minibuses operating as por puestos (locals call them *camionetecas)* to Altagracia. They run from about 5 am to 2 pm, depart when full and are faster than buses. They go via Santa Teresa and the park, and can let you off at any point on the road, eg Agua Blanca (US$3, two hours).

Aragua State

MARACAY
* *pop 510,000*
* *area code* ☎ (043)

The capital of Aragua state, Maracay is the centre of an important agricultural area. It's

also quite developed industrially, though most factories are outside the city limits. There's almost nothing left of the colonial legacy in this 300-year-old city, and modern architecture is not Maracay's strong point either. What the city does possess are plenty of parks and leafy plazas, including the largest Plaza Bolívar in the country. Justifiably, Maracay's called the Ciudad Jardín, or the Garden City.

At an altitude of about 450m, Maracay has a pretty hot yet tolerable climate (warmer than Caracas, but more pleasant than Maracaibo), with an average temperature of 25°C and most of the rain falling between April and October.

History
At the time of the Spanish conquest, the valley in which Maracay is set was inhabited by the Aragua Indian group, led by Cacique Maracay; this is where the name of the city and the state comes from.

A Spanish settlement was established somewhere around the mid-16th century, but it was not until 1701 that a formal act of foundation was signed, and ever since this has been considered the official birth of Maracay. At that time the town numbered about 750 inhabitants.

Thanks to the valley's fertile soil, agriculture became the basis of the region's development – cacao, indigo, coffee, sugar-cane, cotton and tobacco were the major crops. Yet the town's growth was pretty slow; by 1900 the population had reached a mere 7000.

Maracay would have probably continued at this unhurried rate if it hadn't been for Juan Vicente Gómez, the most enduring and probably the most ruthless of Venezuela's *caudillos*. He first came here in 1899 and fell in love with the town. After he seized power in 1908, he settled for good in Maracay in 1912 and five years later moved the Aragua state capital from La Victoria to Maracay which became not only the state capital but virtually the national capital. From here Gómez ruled the country until his death in 1935.

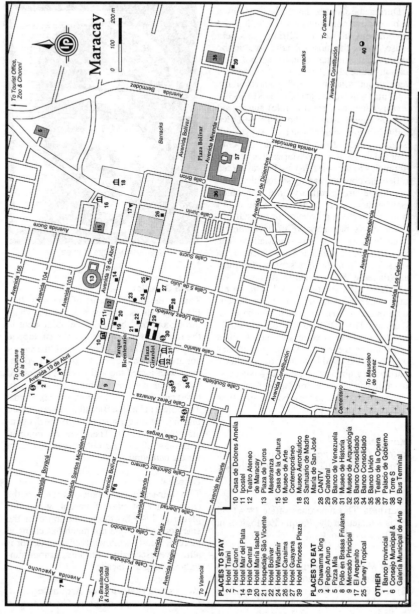

Maracay

0   100   200 m

To Tourist Office,
Zoo & Choroní

To Ocumare
de la Costa

To Brasilandia
& Hotel Cristal

To Valencia

To Ayacucho

To Caracas

To Mausoleo
de Gómez

Barracks

Barracks

Plaza Bolívar

Parque
Bicentenario

Plaza
Girardot

Cementerio

PLACES TO STAY
2   Hotel Traini
7   Hotel Caroní
14 Hotel Mar del Plata
19 Hotel Central
20 Hotel María Isabel
21 Hospedaje São Vicente
22 Hotel Bolívar
24 Hotel Wladimir
26 Hotel Canaima
27 Hotel Guayana
39 Hotel Princesa Plaza

PLACES TO EAT
3   Chawama King
4   Pepito Arturo
5   Pizza Mía
8   Pollo en Brasas Fruilana
9   Mercado Principal
17 El Arepanito
25 Caney Tropical

10 Casa de Dolores Amelia
11 Ipostel
12 Teatro Ateneo
    de Maracay
13 Plaza de Toros
    Maestranza
15 Casa de la Cultura
16 Museo de Arte
    Contemporáneo
18 Museo Aeronáutico
23 Santuario de Madre
    María de San José
28 CANTV
29 Catedral
30 Banco de Venezuela
31 Museo de Historia
32 Museo de Arqueología
33 Banco Consolidado
34 Banco Consolidado
35 Banco Unión
36 Teatro de la Opera
37 Palacio de Gobierno
38 Torre S
40 Bus Terminal

OTHER
1   Banco Provincial
6   Consejo Municipal &
    Galería Municipal de Arte

During the Gómez days, Maracay saw a rash of new constructions, including the government house, a bullring, an opera house, a zoo, the most splendid hotel in the country and a military aviation school. This school, founded in 1920, was the cradle of Venezuelan aviation, both civil and military.

Gómez was well aware of threats to his life (a consequence of his iron rule) and is said to have never slept in the same bed two nights in a row, and to have built a system of escape tunnels from his office. He constructed a road from Maracay over the mountains to the coast, in case he was forced to flee the country, and he surrounded himself with a strong military force, for which vast barracks were built. Lastly, he didn't forget to erect a mausoleum for himself.

The city's second wave of development came with postwar industrialisation. The freeway linking Caracas with Valencia via Maracay, built in the 1950s by another ruthless dictator, Marcos Pérez Jiménez, also contributed to the city's growth. During his rule, Venezuela had the most powerful airforce in Latin America, much of it based in Maracay. The 1950 population of 65,000 doubled over the next decade, and doubled again during the 1960s. Maracay continues to grow quickly and is an important military (particularly airforce) base. The unsuccessful military takeover in November 1992 began in Maracay and the rebels' planes flew to Caracas from here.

Information

Tourist Office The tourist office is in Edificio Fundaragua, in La Soledad district, north of the city centre.

Inparques The Inparques office (☎ 41 39 33) is situated in the Parque Zoológico, in Las Delicias district.

Money Most of the useful banks are within a few blocks of Plaza Girardot. Turisol (☎ 41 10 58) is in Centro Comercial y Residencial La Floresta, Avenida Las Delicias, La Floresta.

Juan Vicente Gómez

Plaza Girardot

This is the historic heart of Maracay (not Plaza Bolívar as is the rule almost anywhere throughout the country). The monument in the middle of the square, an obelisk topped with a bronze eagle, was erected in 1897. It commemorates the North American volunteers who joined the anti-royalist forces led by Francisco Miranda, but who were captured and hanged in 1806 by the Spaniards. The adjacent Parque Bicentenario was added in 1983, forming a spacious two-block open-air public ground. There are no colonial buildings left around either square, except for the cathedral.

Catedral

This fair-sized handsome church, on the eastern side of Plaza Girardot, was completed in 1743 (as the inscription over the side door reads) and not much has changed since. Recently whitewashed, the exterior is attractive, especially with late afternoon sunlight striking the façade.

Museos de Historia y de Arqueología

On the south side of Plaza Girardot is an

arcaded building, erected by Gómez as the seat of government. Today, there are two museums inside. The Museo de Historia has one room dedicated to Bolívar and one to Gómez, plus a handful of exhibits loosely related to Venezuelan history. The more inspiring Museo de Arqueología features local pre-Hispanic pottery. In the basement of this museum is the Sala de Etnología (the ethnological section) displaying crafts of some Indian groups living today, including the Maquiritare, Warao, Piaroa, Sanema, Guajibo and Guajiro. Both museums are open Tuesday to Friday from 8 am to noon and 2 to 6 pm, Saturday and Sunday from 9 am to 1 pm.

Casa de Dolores Amelia

Set on the northern side of Parque Bicentenario, this fine mansion was built in 1927-29 by Gómez for his favourite mistress, Dolores Amelia Núñez de Cáceres. Designed by Frenchman André Potel in the neo-Sevillan style, the building has been meticulously restored and is now occupied by an insurance company. It is not a tourist sight, but if you turn up during office hours, someone may let you in and show you around the patio and adjoining parts of the building, clad with *azulejos* (ornamental tiles) and reminiscent of the Alhambra in Granada. It's said that the house was linked by a tunnel with Gómez's office in Plaza Girardot.

Santuario de Madre María de San José

The Santuario, one block east of Plaza Girardot, is probably the most revered and visited city sight. Choroní-born Madre María (1875-1967) was venerated in 1992 by a papal decree, and solemnly beatified in 1995. Her remains were exhumed and, to everybody's surprise, the corpse was allegedly intact. You can see it in a crystal sarcophagus in the Santuario (though the face and hands are covered with masks). The Santuario is open Tuesday to Sunday from 8.30 to 11.30 am and 2.30 to 5 pm.

Plaza de Toros Maestranza

This large Spanish-Moorish bullring was designed by Carlos Raúl Villanueva, modelled on the one in Seville and built in 1933; it's possibly the most stylish and beautiful in the country. It was originally called Calicanto but renamed in memory of César Girón, Venezuela's most famous matador, who died in a traffic accident in 1971. The monument to him, which shows him fighting a bull, stands in front of the bullring. If you want to see the bullring from the inside, try getting in through the back door on the eastern side.

Museo Aeronáutico

This is the only aeronautical museum in the country. There are about 40 aircraft on display, including four helicopters. Many are war planes from the 1920s to the 1950s, which once served in the Venezuelan Air Force. The majority of the planes are displayed outdoors, but some valuable exhibits are kept indoors. Of these, the collection's gem is a beautifully restored French plane from the 1910s, which is reputedly in perfect working order. The museum also has a replica of the famous Jimmie Angel plane, but this one is yet to be restored.

In the middle of the exhibition grounds is the statue of Juan Vicente Gómez. This is the first and so far only monument to the caudillo, unveiled amidst great controversy in November 1995.

The museum is open only on Saturday and Sunday from 9 am to 6 pm. If you happen to come to Maracay on a weekday, enquire at the side gate at the end of Avenida Santos Michelena (best between 8 and 11 am or between 2 and 3 pm) and somebody may show you around.

Museo de Arte Contemporáneo

The entire block opposite the aeronautical museum is occupied by the Complejo Cultural (opened in 1983) which contains several cultural institutions, including the Casa de la Cultura, a library, music school and the contemporary art museum. The museum (open daily, except Monday, from

8.30 am to 5 pm) stages temporary exhibitions of modern art.

Galería Municipal de Arte

For more in the way of contemporary art, visit the Galería Municipal de Arte in the modern building of the Consejo Municipal, a five minute walk to the north. The gallery has changing exhibitions; from March to May, selected works from the so-called Salón Municipal de Pintura, the regional painting competition, are exhibited here.

Plaza Bolívar

Three blocks long and shady, this is the largest Plaza Bolívar in the country and, some claim, Latin America. It was laid out by Carlos Raúl Villanueva and opened in 1930. The monument to Bolívar is an exact replica of the Caracas statue.

Palacio de Gobierno

This large edifice, on the southern side of Plaza Bolívar, was once the splendid Hotel Jardín. Designed by Villanueva and inaugurated in 1930 by Gómez, the hotel overshadowed all other Venezuelan hotels of the day, and became a playground for the rich and beautiful. The place witnessed many important episodes of the country's political, social and cultural life, and even Carlos Gardel sang his nostalgic tangos here.

The hotel closed down in 1959 and was largely remodelled for its new function, yet you can still feel some of the charm of the cloisters and interior gardens. It's now the government house, not a tourist sight, but the police security guards may let you in. If they refuse you entry at the front door, try the back (south) gate, from Avenida Páez.

Teatro de la Opera

Commissioned by Gómez in 1934, the theatre was intended to be the best in the country, to match the capital status of the city. It was designed by Luis Malaussena, and a huge budget of two million bolívares was allotted for the structure alone. Planned to be opened in 1936, the work progressed swiftly and by December 1935 (the month

Gómez died) the theatre was almost ready; only the ceiling, imported from the USA, had to be fixed and the interior furnished. Nonetheless, the work was stopped by the new government and part of the imported decoration was moved to Caracas for use in theatres there. It wasn't until 1973 that the theatre finally opened. It can seat 860 and stages a variety of productions including opera, ballet, theatre, folkloric dance etc (performed mostly by visiting groups).

Mausoleo de Gómez

Also referred to as the Panteón de Gómez, the mausoleum is south of the city centre, just behind the cemetery. Interestingly, this was one of Gómez's earliest projects, built in 1919. A rather pretentious structure topped with a white Moorish dome, the pantheon houses the tomb of the general and members of his family. There are plenty of thanksgiving plaques placed on the interior walls. All have an almost identical inscription which reads thanks for the favours, but none is signed with a full name, only with initial letters.

Fresh flowers and lit candles are frequently left at the tomb, evidence that he is not forgotten. On the contrary, respect for Gómez seems to have been revived in Maracay over the past several years, partly as a result of the recent economic and political crisis. The mausoleum is open from 6 am to 3 pm, except Monday.

Parque Zoológico

At the northern city limits, the zoo is yet another of Gómez's achievements, established on one of his own estates. The zoo is well laid out with reasonable cage space for most of the animals, many of which are typical of Venezuela. It's open Tuesday to Sunday from 9 am to 5 pm. To get there from the city centre, take the Castaño/Zoológico buseta, which goes all the way along Avenida Las Delicias, and will deposit you right at the entrance to the zoo.

Special Events

The Fiesta de San José, Maracay's most important annual event, takes place over several days around 19 March, the city's patron saint's day. The major bullfight is celebrated during the feast, but other corridas are held on some Sundays during the year, mostly between Christmas and Easter.

Maracay's Teatro de la Opera invites some groups taking part in Caracas' International Theatre Festival to perform here.

Places to Stay
Maracay has a fair choice of accommodation, which is by and large fairly priced and conveniently located. This comes in handy, as you may want to start from here for nearby attractions, principally Rancho Grande (see the Parque Nacional Henri Pittier section).

Places to Stay – bottom end
There are several budget hotels right in the city centre. The *Hospedaje São Vicente* (☎ 45 61 89), across Avenida Bolívar from the cathedral, is perhaps the cheapest option, at US$5/6 for a matrimonial/double with fan but without private bath. One block east along Avenida Bolívar is the *Hotel Guayana*, which offers rooms with fan and bath for US$7/9.

You also have two quieter (but not better) cheapies on Avenida Santos Michelena: *Hotel Central* (☎ 45 28 34) and, 20m further down the street, *Hotel María Isabel*. Both have rooms with private baths and fans, and cost much the same as the Guayana. The Central also has triples for US$10. All these hotels have the odd loving couple passing through.

The *Hotel Canaima* (☎ 33 82 78), Avenida Bolívar Este No 53, one block west of Plaza Bolívar, is probably the cheapest option with air-conditioning but otherwise nothing special. A matrimonial/double with bath will cost US$8/10. The rundown *Hotel Bolívar* (☎ 45 02 53), Avenida Bolívar Este No 9, just off Plaza Girardot, is nothing special either and probably not worth its US$12/14 for doubles with baths and fan/air-conditioning. Appreciably better is the quiet *Hotel Mar del Plata* (☎ 46 43 13), Calle Santos Michelena Este No 23, which has

neat air-conditioned matrimoniales/doubles for US$11/13.

If you don't mind staying out of the city centre, the *Hotel Cristal* (☎ 54 06 68, 54 02 46), Avenida Bolívar Oeste No 206, is well worth its modest prices. Spacious and air-conditioned matrimoniales/doubles/triples are US$10/12/15. The hotel is four blocks west of Avenida Ayacucho, easily accessible by countless buses running along Avenida Bolívar.

Places to Stay – middle
Central options in this price bracket include the *Hotel Traini* (☎ 45 55 02), Avenida 19 de Abril, and the *Hotel Wladimir* (☎ 46 11 15, 46 25 66), Avenida Bolívar Este No 27. The Traini has air-conditioned singles/doubles/triples for US$15/17/20. The Wladimir costs about US$1 more per person.

The *Hotel Caroní* (☎ 54 18 17, 54 78 55), Avenida Ayacucho Norte No 19, just seven blocks west of Plaza Girardot, is good value for money. Clean air-conditioned singles/doubles/triples with private baths and hot water cost US$14/18/22.

Places to Stay – top end
The new *Hotel Princesa Plaza* (☎ 33 23 57, 33 25 71; fax 33 79 72) is on Avenida Miranda, next to the spanking 30-storey brick-and-glass Torre S, the highest and most modern addition to the cityscape. Both convenient and decent, the hotel costs just US$32 a double.

Other top-end hotels are outside the centre, mostly along Avenida Las Delicias in the northern residential districts. They include the modern high-rise *Hotel Byblos* (☎ 41 51 11; fax 41 03 35); the nostalgic 1950s-style *Hotel Maracay* (☎ 41 62 11; fax 41 08 65) set in vast grounds with a large swimming pool; and the closest to the city centre *Hotel Italo* (☎ 32 05 22; fax 32 04 43). All are three-star establishments. The four-star *Hotel Pipo Internacional* (☎ 41 31 11; fax 41 62 98) is on Avenida Principal El Castaño (the road to Choroní), on the city limits.

THE CENTRAL NORTH

Places to Eat
There are plenty of reasonably priced places to eat, scattered throughout the centre. Some of the cheapest typical meals are to be found in the *Mercado Principal* (built by Gómez in 1921), which has half a dozen food stands.

The *Caney Tropical* has tasty, inexpensive comida criolla, including arepas. *El Arepanito* is also good for local food and is open till late. The *Pizza Mía* has some of the better budget pizzas in the centre. The *Pepito Arturo*, across the road, specialises in parrillas and batidos. Next door, the *Chawarma King* serves felafel, kibbe and the like. The *Pollo en Brasas Friulana* is the place for chicken. All these places are marked on the city map.

The *Brasilandia*, Avenida Bolívar, close to the Hotel Cristal, is deservedly popular among locals for its hearty parrilla and chicken at good prices. Equally respectable is *La Ternera*, Avenida Ayacucho, next to the Mercado Libre Municipal (four blocks north of the Hotel Caroní), which has local-style cooked beef.

There are plenty of upmarket restaurants along Avenida Las Delicias; *El Riacho* and *El Bodegón de Sevilla* are reputedly among the best. Not so chic but cheaper is *La Terraza del Vroster*, also on Avenida Las Delicias, which serves a good range of pasta and pizza as well as Venezuelan cuisine.

Getting There & Away
Air Maracay's civil airport is in the airforce base. There are no regular commercial flights, but flights to Porlamar are planned.

Bus The bus terminal is on the south-eastern outskirts of the city centre. It's within walking distance of Plaza Bolívar, but it's quicker to take any of the frequent city buses.

The bus terminal is vast and busy, with frequent transport to most major cities. Buses to Caracas depart every 10 or 15 minutes (US$2.50, two hours), as do buses to Valencia (US$0.60, one hour).

There are at least a dozen departures a day to Barquisimeto (US$4.75, four hours), Maracaibo (US$9.25, nine hours) and San Cristóbal (US$13.50, 11½ hours). Half a dozen buses run to San Antonio del Táchira (US$14.50, 12½ hours) and Coro (US$6.50, 5½ hours). Three or four buses per day go to Mérida (US$13.50, 10 hours). There are direct buses to Puerto La Cruz (US$7.50, 6½ hours) and Ciudad Bolívar (US$10.50, 9½ hours), which bypass Caracas, saving time and money. The prices listed above are for air-conditioned services, but there are also the 25% cheaper ordinary buses on many routes. Several ordinary buses per day go to San Fernando de Apure (US$5, seven hours).

For transport to Ocumare de la Costa and Puerto Colombia, see the Parque Nacional Henri Pittier section.

SAN MATEO
The small town of San Mateo, 20km east of Maracay, is noted for a nearby hacienda which once belonged to the Bolívar family. It was granted to them in 1593, after they came to settle in Venezuela from their native Spain. At the beginning of the 18th century, the Bolívars built a sugarcane mill on their land and used African slaves to work the crops, a common practice throughout the region.

In 1814, Símon Bolívar set up a military camp on the hacienda, which predictably became the target of fierce attacks by the royalist troops. The camp was saved thanks to a heroic act of defence by patriot Antonio Ricaurte, one of Bolívar's lieutenants. Later on, Bolívar passed through San Mateo on various occasions, including a rest stop after the battle of Carabobo in 1821, when he freed the local slaves.

During the 19th century, the hacienda passed through the hands of various owners, until it was bought by the government of Juan Vicente Gómez in 1924 and turned into barracks. It was later transformed into a museum.

Things to See
Restored in the 1980s to its original state, the hacienda now houses two museums, both open Tuesday to Sunday from 10 am to 4 pm. The **Museo de la Caña de Azúcar** is centred

around the original sugarcane mill. Exhibits include the mill itself and a variety of tools, implements and objects related to sugar production.

On the opposite side of the road is the **Museo Histórico Militar**. The finely restored historic house, on the top of a hill, features a collection of period armour plus the usual Bolivariana, including documents and a number of Bolívar's portraits. The outbuildings, which served as the armoury during Bolívar's days, were intentionally left in a state of ruin, as they have been since 25 March, 1814. It was here that Antonio Ricaurte, a Colombian patriot in the service of Bolívar, sacrificed himself to save the battle almost lost to the Spaniards. Closely encircled by royalists, he led them into the armoury, then set fire to the gunpowder kegs, blowing up both the enemies and himself.

Getting There & Away

The hacienda is on the Maracay-La Victoria old road (not the freeway), a couple of km east of San Mateo town. The road is serviced by frequent buses and por puestos, which will put you off at the entrance to the museums. Ask the driver to drop you off at El Ingenio de Bolívar, as the place is commonly known. While you are in the area, consider stopping in San Mateo, to see the mid-18th century retable in the local church.

If you plan to visit San Mateo from Caracas, take a bus to La Victoria (from Nuevo Circo terminal) and change. There may also be some por puestos all the way to San Mateo through La Victoria.

LA VICTORIA

- *pop 110,000*
- *area code ☎ (044)*

Founded in 1593, La Victoria was an important commercial centre and the capital of Aragua state until 1917, when Juan Vicente Gómez moved the capital to Maracay 30km to the west.

Today it's a busy city surrounded with factories, but its historic centre retains some of its old architecture and flavour. Stroll around the central streets, between Plaza Ribas and Plaza Bolívar. Both plazas boast a church – the large 18th century neoclassical Iglesia de Nuestra Señora de la Victoria at Plaza Ribas, and the small Iglesia de Nuestra Señora de la Candelaria at Plaza Bolívar.

There are frequent buses to both Maracay (30km) and Caracas (77km). Buses to Maracay will drop you off at San Mateo (10km to the west). If you are heading from Maracay to Colonia Tovar (or vice versa), you need to change in La Victoria. Por puestos leave for Colonia Tovar (34km) a few times a day, and wind up along a spectacular mountain road offering dramatic views.

COLONIA TOVAR

- *pop 6000*
- *area code ☎ (033)*

This unusual mountain town sits at an altitude of about 1800m amidst the rolling forests of the Cordillera de la Costa, about 60km west of Caracas. It was founded in 1843 by a group of 376 German settlers from the Schwarzwald (Black Forest), recruited by Italian cartographer Agustín Codazzi (see boxed text entitled Agustín Codazzi on the following page). The town was named after Martín Tovar y Ponte, who donated these lands.

Effectively isolated from the outer world by the lack of roads and internal rules prohibiting marriage outside the colony, the village followed the mother culture, language and architecture for a century. It wasn't until the 1940s that Spanish was introduced as the official language and the ban on marrying outside the community abandoned. However, it was not until 1963 that a sealed road reached Colonia Tovar from Caracas marking a turning point in the history of the town, which by then had a mere 1300 inhabitants.

Today, Colonia Tovar has five times as many inhabitants and is a classic example of a tourist town, drawing in hordes of caraqueños on weekends, curious to see this bit of old Germany lost in Venezuelan cloudforest. They come to glimpse the traditional architecture, enjoy a German lunch or dinner, and to buy bread or sausage made

Agustín Codazzi

Adventurer, sailor, explorer, corsair, soldier, merchant, but primarily remembered as a cartographer, Agustín Codazzi was born in 1793 in Lugo, a town in northern Italy. At the age of 17 he enrolled in the Napoleonic army and was trained in mathematics, geometry, topography and the like to become a professional artillery officer (which, as it turned out, gave him a solid basis for cartography). Later, he took part in various battles under Napoleon, but then came Waterloo and there was nothing much for Codazzi to do.

He turned his hand to commerce, but his boat sank in the Mediterannean with all his merchandise on board. Codazzi, who miraculously survived, was financially ruined. His next endeavour was managing a casino in Constantinople (present-day Istanbul), but soon his passion for exploring overcame him and he took off to wander Europe and, in 1817, Baltimore in the USA.

When Codazzi heard that Bolívar was recruiting foreigners for a new Venezuelan army, he was the first to enrol. However, he met the French corsair Louis Aury and, on their way south, they landed on Old Providence (today Providencia, a Colombian island). From this island, the two adventurers regularly ransacked Spanish galleons, an activity which was not only profitable, but also contributed to the eventual defeat of the Spaniards. Based on the island for three years, Codazzi didn't miss the chance to explore large parts of Nueva Granada (now Colombia), and it was on Providence that he drew his first maps.

Once the Spanish were defeated by Bolívar's troops, there was not much left to ransack. Codazzi returned to his native Lugo to dedicate himself to agriculture, but before long his adventurous spirit took him back to the New World. Arriving in Cartagena in 1826, he made his way to Bogotá where he met Bolívar and Santander. The Independence heroes appreciated his military abilities more than his cartographic skills and sent him to Maracaibo to head the local military post in case of a Spanish return.

Four years later, Gran Colombia split into three separate countries. General José Antonio Páez, the first ruler of independent Venezuela, commissioned Codazzi to draft maps of various regions of the country. The job took him 10 years. Once completed, Codazzi went to Paris where, in 1841, he published the *Atlas Físico y Político de la República de Venezuela* and the corresponding *Resumen de la Geografía de Venezuela*. His work received wide recognition among French scientific circles and Codazzi was appointed an honorary member of the Académie Royale des Sciences in Paris.

At about this time the Venezuelan government began to look for European migrants eager to settle and work in Venezuela, to help revive an economy devastated by the Independence War, and proposed Codazzi devise a colonisation plan. First he went to Venezuela to select a place with acceptable climatic conditions for European migrants before returning to Europe. Here he collected a group of several hundred German peasants (the nationality he thought was the most adaptable to foreign life) and came with them to Venezuela. After an arduous hike from La Guaira, the landing point, up the coastal cordillera, they founded Colonia Tovar, in 1843. By then, the Venezuelan authorities had lost all enthusiasm for continuing the colonisation programme and Codazzi, again, dedicated himself to mapping.

The coup d'état of 1848, launched by Tadeo Monagas, brought Venezuela to the brink of civil war and Codazzi fled to Colombia. After arriving in Bogotá in 1849, he was appointed head of the Comisión Corográfica. Over the next 10 years, until his death, he drafted detailed maps, region by region, of six of the eight existing departments of Colombia.

At the beginning, when he had the interest and sponsorship of the government, his work advanced smoothly. Later on, however, internal political strife pushed cartographic concerns to one side and funds were cut off. It was only due to his personal dedication and enthusiasm that Codazzi set off north to complete mapping of the two missing coastal provinces. Disillusioned and abandoned, he died of malaria in 1859 in the obscure village of Espíritu Santo (present-day Agustín Codazzi) in northern Colombia. His name and work sank into obscurity for a century.

The man who created Venezuelan and Colombian cartography was forgotten by the two countries. It has only been over the last few decades that Codazzi has finally achieved the recognition he deserves, and his excellent maps have become the pride of national archives in both Colombia and Venezuela. ■

according to traditional recipes as well as delicious strawberries, apples, peaches and blackberries, cultivated locally thanks to the temperate climate. Other town assets are beautiful lush surroundings, and the cordiality and hospitality of the inhabitants, some of whom are descendants of the original settlers.

Call at the Museo de Historia y Artesanía (open Saturday, Sunday and holidays from 9 am to 6 pm) for a taste of the town's history. Don't miss the local church, a curious L-shaped building with two perpendicular naves (one for women, the other for men) and the high altar placed in the angle where the naves join. From there, the patron saint of the town, San Martín de Tours, overlooks both naves.

Colonia Tovar has a distinct dual personality. On weekends it may be virtually swamped with visitors and their cars (which effectively block the access roads), while on weekdays it is almost dead, and many restaurants are closed. Whichever time you come though, take some warm clothing – it's hard to imagine how much the temperature drops as you climb into these upper reaches of the cordillera. The town's average temperature is 16°C, but it's much lower at night.

Places to Stay & Eat

For most travellers, Colonia Tovar is a day trip from Caracas, but there are no problems if you want to stay longer. The town has more than a dozen hotels and cabañas, and most of them have their own restaurants. Private bath and hot water are the norm in most places, and some also have heated rooms. Some hotels offer full board, which may be convenient but means that you are stuck with the same kitchen for the duration of your stay.

By and large, accommodation in Colonia Tovar is good and stylish, but it's not cheap by Venezuelan standards. The room rates start at about US$16 per double, and more often than not are much higher than that.

The *Hotel Selva Negra* (☎ 51 415, 51 072), near the church, is the oldest and the best known lodge in town. Built in the 1930s, it now has about 40 cabañas of different sizes, from two to six guests, costing US$40 for two plus US$10 for each additional person. The old-style restaurant is in the original house.

Cheaper options include *Hotel Edelweiss* (☎ 51 260), *Hotel Drei-Tannen* (☎ 51 246) and *Hotel Bergland* (☎ 51 229, 51 994). Any

of these will cost about US$30 a double. For somewhere still cheaper, try the *Cabañas Breidenbach* (☎ 51 211), *Residencias Baden* (☎ 51 151) or *Cabañas Silberbrunnen* (☎ 51 490).

Getting There & Away

The usual departure point for Colonia Tovar is Caracas and the trip requires a change at El Junquito. Carritos to El Junquito depart from the corner just south of the Nuevo Circo bus terminal and cost US$0.50. From El Junquito, por puestos take you the remainder of the journey for US$0.60. The whole trip takes about two hours.

If you don't want to return to Caracas, you can take an exciting ride south down to La Victoria. Over a distance of only 34km, the road descends about 1250m. Por puestos depart from Colonia Tovar several times a day; the ride takes one hour and costs US$0.80.

PARQUE NACIONAL HENRI PITTIER

This is Venezuela's oldest national park, created in 1937. It occupies most of the north of Aragua state, stretching from the Caribbean coast in the north, almost as far south as the Valencia-Caracas freeway and the city of Maracay. The park was originally named Rancho Grande, but was later renamed in honour of the founder of Venezuela's national park system (see boxed text entitled Henri Pittier on the following page).

The park covers 1078 sq km of the Cordillera de la Costa, the coastal mountain range (considered the northern continuation of the great Andean system) which exceeds 2000m in some of the park's areas. From its ridge, the cordillera rolls dramatically down to the coast to the north, and south to Maracay.

Given the wide range in elevation, the park has a staircase of thermal zones and corresponding spheres of vegetation. Going from Maracay northwards (ie upwards), you pass through semi-dry deciduous woods, to ascend to evergreen rainforest and, further up, to dense cloudforest. All this can be found over a surprisingly short distance; it takes an hour to cover it in a bus or car. Over the crest and descending northwards towards the sea, you get the same sequence in reverse, with the difference being that, as you approach the coast, you also encounter arid coastal scrub, before you finally reach the beaches, mangroves and coconut groves. The descent also takes only an hour or so.

The animal world is also rich and diverse, including tapirs, deer, pumas, agoutis, peccaries, ocelots, opossums, armadillos, monkeys, snakes, frogs and bats. However, the park is most famous for its birds. About 580 species of birds have been identified in the park, which represents some 43% of the bird species found in Venezuela, and 7% of all the birds known in the world. Given the small area of the park, it's not a bad total, and hardly any other park of that size in the world can match it.

This diversity is the combined result of the variety of habitats and the unspoiled condition of these habitats. Additionally, the Paso Portachuelo, the lowest pass in the mountain

---

Henri Pittier

Henri François Pittier Dormond was born in Bex, Switzerland, in 1857. He graduated with a doctorate in Sciences and Civil Engineering, but it was botany that eventually became his real passion. Attracted by tropical nature, he explored Costa Rica and Panama before settling in Venezuela in 1917. His extensive travels throughout the country resulted in the collection and classification of more than 30,000 specimens of local plant, the basis for the creation of Herbario Nacional, or national herbariums.

The author of about 160 studies on forests, herbs, fruit and other aspects of botany, he realised the necessity for the protection of Venezuela's ecosystems, and proposed the creation of the national parks system to the government. The struggle took several years until, in 1937, President Eleázar López Contreras decreed the Parque Nacional Rancho Grande as Venezuela's first national park. It took another 15 years, until 1952, before the government declared a second protected area, Parque Nacional Sierra Nevada. In 1953, three years after Pittier's death, the Rancho Grande was renamed to commemorate the founder of Venezuela's national park system. ∎

---

ridge, is on a natural migratory route for birds and insects flying inland from the sea, and vice versa, from such distant places as Argentina and Canada.

Orientation

Two roads, both sealed, cross the park from north to south. Both originate in Maracay and go as far as the coast. The western road, the one built by Gómez as an escape route, leads from Maracay to Ocumare de la Costa and continues on to Cata; it ascends to 1128m at Paso Portachuelo. The eastern road heads from Maracay due north to Choroní and reaches the coast 2km further on at Puerto Colombia. It's narrower, poorer and more twisting, but it climbs up to 1830m and is more spectacular. Both roads are about 55km long and both may occasionally be blocked by landslides, particularly in the rainy season. There's no road connection between the coastal ends of these roads; a rented boat is the only way to get from one end to the other.

The coast has rocky cliffs in some parts, interspersed with bays filled with coconut groves and bordered by beaches. Some beaches are developed while others are virtually virgin. The town of Puerto Colombia is the major tourist destination on the coast. It offers the widest choice of hotels and restaurants, and boat-hire facilities.

The park has something for nearly everyone, including beachgoers, birdwatchers, hikers, architecture buffs and fiesta lovers. It's good for both day trips and longer stays. Unless you are particularly interested in bird-watching in Rancho Grande, it's better to take the eastern road, which provides access to more attractions and leads along a more spectacular route.

Coastal Towns

The coast has been inhabited for centuries, and some colonial towns have survived in the park. It's interesting to note that all these old settlements are set back from the waterfront; Cuyagua, Cata, Choroní and Chuao have all been founded several kilometres inland, back from the sea. This was to provide the towns with some protection against the pirates who roamed the coast.

The tiny 380-year-old **Choroní** is the finest colonial town in the park. It's just a few narrow streets in all, but they are lined with old pastel-coloured houses. Madre María de San José was born in one in 1875, and dedicated her life to the service for the poor. The house where she lived and worked is on the tree-shaded Plaza Bolívar. She later continued her work with the poor in Maracay, where she founded a religious congregation. She died at a respectable age of 92, and was beatified in 1995.

On Choroní's plaza there is a lovely parish church, Iglesia de Santa Clara, with a finely decorated ceiling. The wall over the high altar has been painted to look like a carved retable. The feast of Santa Clara, the patron saint of the town, is celebrated in August.

Puerto Colombia, on the coast just 2km north of Choroní, was Choroní's port. Over the recent decades, it has developed into the major travellers' haunt in the region. Unlike the sleepy and nostalgic Choroní, Puerto Colombia is full of young crowds, posadas and restaurants. It's an enjoyable enough place to hang around for a while, and a convenient base for excursions, eg to Chuao.

Chuao, about 8km east of Choroní as the crow flies, is a small old village, well known as a centre of cacao plantations. There is a very simple colonial church and the village is widely known for its Diablos Danzantes (Dancing Devils) celebrations. Villagers live in almost complete isolation: the only road is a rough 4km track between the village and the sea. Access to Chuao is by boat from Puerto Colombia followed by a one hour walk along the track.

Other old towns noted for their Diablos Danzantes tradition are **Ocumare de la Costa**, **Cata** and **Cuyagua**, though the celebrations here are not as famous as those in Chuao. All these towns are located in the western, coastal section of the park, and are connected to one another and to Maracay by road.

There's a significant black population in

these towns, especially in Chuao, so drumbeats are an integral part of life, and can be heard all year round on weekend nights and during holidays, and particularly during the Fiesta de San Juan on 23 and 24 June. The pulsating beat immediately sparks dancing and the atmosphere is great.

Beaches
For most tourists (particularly Venezuelans), beaches are the principal attraction of the park and, indeed, some of them are really beautiful. Since the coastal bays are relatively small, the beaches are not long, but they are often pretty wide and shaded by coconut palms.

Some beaches are accessible by road, but these are the most popular and crowded, and left covered with rubbish on weekends. Other beaches can only be reached by boat and these are usually solitary. Boat business is well developed and boats can take you to any isolated beach you wish. The charge is by boat, not by passenger, so the fare largely depends on how many people go with you on the trip (the boat's usual capacity is up to 10 passengers). Because the competition between boat operators is fierce, prices are negotiable, and you should always try to bargain. Puerto Colombia is the busiest tourist boat hub.

Before you go, decide which road to take, as you have to choose between beaches of either the Cata or Puerto Colombia areas. Boats can transfer you from one end to the other (Cata to Puerto Colombia, or vice versa) but this trip costs somewhere between US$60 and US$80 per boat.

In the Puerto Colombia area, the most popular beach is **Playa Grande**, a five minute walk by road east of town. It's about half a km long and is shaded by coconut palms, but is littered at weekends. There are several rustic shack restaurants at the entrance to the beach, serving good fried fish. You can camp on the beach or sling your hammock between the palms, but don't leave your stuff unattended.

If Playa Grande is too crowded or littered,

THE CENTRAL NORTH

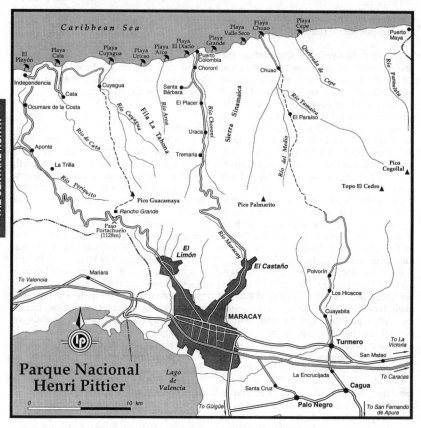

go to the wild **Playa El Diario**, on the op-posite (western) side of the town. To get there, take the side road, Calle El Ce-menterio, which branches off midway along the Choroní-Puerto Colombia road, next to a small bridge. The road passes a few hotels before it reaches the cemetery (500m from the turn-off), where the asphalt becomes concrete. Follow the road uphill for 200m and take a path branching off to the left. It climbs a bit then goes down to the small and shadeless El Diario beach (a 20 minute walk from the cemetery). If you take the concrete road to its end on the mountain top (crowned

with a CANTV communication mast), you'll get sweeping panoramic views (a 10 minute walk from the cemetery).

Other beaches in the area are normally visited by boat, though some of them can also be reached on foot, after a long and hot walk. Boats crowd at the river mouth in Puerto Colombia, and take tourists to iso-lated beaches farther down the coat, in-cluding **Playa Aroa** (US$30 return per boat, 15 minutes one way), **Playa Valle Seco** (US$25, 20 minutes), **Playa Chuao** (US$30, 30 minutes) and **Playa Cepe** (US$40, 45 minutes). The boat can pick you up at any time. The trip may be quite rough if the waves are high; be prepared to get wet.

In the Cata area, the first easily accessible beach is **El Playón**, a wide beach with facilities at the northern edge of the town of Independencia. Five km eastward is the area's most famous beach, **Playa Cata**, a postcard crescent of sand bordering the Bahía de Cata. Unfortunately, a couple of apartment towers have sprung up at the back. Boats from Cata take tourists to the smaller and quieter **Playa Catita**, on the eastern side of the same bay. It takes 10 minutes to get there, and the ride costs US$0.60 per person. You can also walk there – it takes longer but is worth it for interesting xerophytic vegetation on the way.

Further east is the unspoilt and usually deserted **Playa Cuyagua**, which is good for surfers. You can get there by a 2.5km sand track from the town of Cuyagua. Alternatively, boats from Cata can take you to the beach for about US$25 return.

Estación Biológica Rancho Grande

Far away from the coastal towns and beaches, this biological station is on the Maracay-Cata road, a few hundred metres from the Paso Portachuelo. At an altitude of 1100m and surrounded by cloudforest, the station is not visible from the road, but there's a sign.

The station is housed in an intriguing question-mark-shaped building. It was originally destined to be a posh country hotel, commissioned by Juan Vicente Gómez as one of his many grand projects. The building was only half-completed by the time Gómez died, and was left by the workers when they heard the news of the dictator's death. Two years later, after the national park was founded, Henri Pittier proposed to establish the research station here, which became fact in the mid-1940s. The station is run by the Facultad de Agronomía of the Universidad Central de Venezuela, based at El Limón, the north-western outer suburb of Maracay.

An ecologic path, known as the Sendero Andrew Field, has been traced through the forest behind the station, and it's open to the public. The loop, which is easy to walk in an hour, provides a good opportunity to watch the local flora and fauna, particularly birds. The best times for birds are early in the morning and late in the afternoon. September to November are the best months for viewing migratory birds. You may also see monkeys, agoutis, peccaries, snakes and butterflies. There are several other trails around the station.

Some more adventurous travellers may want to hike to the top of the Pico Guacamaya (see Hiking below). The station offers simple accommodation facilities, but no food (see Places to Stay & Eat). Remember that it rains quite a lot in the area, so bring along reliable rain gear.

Hiking

There are no marked trails prepared specifically for tourists but there are various rough paths, linking villages scattered throughout the area, which are used by the locals. Some paths were originally traced centuries ago, but many were abandoned and eventually disappeared when the roads were built.

The area along the coast, where most of the villages are located, has the best options for walkers and is relatively dry. It is possible, for example, to walk from Puerto Colombia west to Aroa (via Playa El Diario), and east to Chuao. The path to Chuao begins 6km up the road from Choroní, at the place known as El Mamón; the walk from here to Chuao will take five to seven hours. The route is confusing in parts because of various side paths, so you may want to look for a local guide – it's easy to find one.

Further up the mountains, where there are virtually no people living, trails are few and far between. The terrain is covered by thick forest and the rainfall is high. Remember that northern slopes of the cordillera receive more rain than the southern ones and the upper parts are pretty wet most of the year. The driest months are January to March.

One of the few trails that traverses the

cordillera from north to south is the path going from Chuao to Turmero, 14km east of Maracay. It's unmarked and not clear, and its upper reaches may be very wet and muddy in the rainy season. This hike can be done in two days but it may run to three. The trail goes from Chuao southward to the hamlet of El Paraíso and continues uphill to Hacienda La Azucena, the last point where you may get information about the rest of the route. It then climbs to about 1950m on the crest and descends gradually over the southern slope to Hacienda Portapán at around 1500m (where you are likely to see a human being again). From the hacienda, a jeep track goes down, then turns into a sealed road to Turmero. The trail can also be done in reverse, from Turmero to Chuao.

Another challenging cross-cordillera trail links the Rancho Grande biological station with Cuyagua, but it has become overgrown over recent years and is practically impassable. From the station, you can probably hike only as far as Pico Guacamaya (1828m), then return. The path is faint and easy to loose, and it will take you three to four hours uphill. Ask at the station for information and news on the condition of the trail.

Technically speaking, hikers who intend to camp overnight in the park should have the Inparques permit, obtainable at their office in Maracay.

Organised Tours

Ernesto Fernández, the chairman of the Sociedad Científica Amigos del Parque Nacional Henri Pittier, can arrange a full-day visit to the Rancho Grande biological station for US$10 to US$15 per person, depending on the number of people in the group. The visit includes bird-watching, breakfast, lunch and drinks, but doesn't cover the transport to/from the station. Ernesto can also organise three-day all-inclusive bird-watching trips around the park (around US$70 per person a day), as well as provide guides for the Chuao-Turmero trek (US$36 per group) and the Choroní-Chuao hike (US$18). Contact him on ☎ & fax (043) 45 34 70 or mobile ☎ 014 945 71 23.

Places to Stay & Eat

Accommodation and food are available in various areas. The telephone area code for the following listings is ☎ (043), the same as Maracay. You can camp free on the beaches, but never leave your tent unattended.

Puerto Colombia This tiny town already has two dozen places to stay – everything from rock bottom to luxury – and the number is growing swiftly. Locals also rent out their rooms if there's the demand. The prices usually rise at weekends and during major holiday periods (Christmas to early January, Carnaval, Holy Week, August). The rates listed below are for off-peak times. Restaurants, too, are in good supply, so starving is improbable; fried fish is the local staple.

One of the cheapest places to stay is the basic *Habitaciones La Abuela* (☎ 91 10 73), facing the Plaza San Juan. Rooms have fans but no private baths, and cost US$10/12 a double/triple.

Better budget places include the simple but friendly *Posada Los Guanches* (☎ 91 12 09), Calle Trino Rangel, close to the bus terminus; the *Posada Playa Grande* (☎ 91 10 54), above the *Tasca Bahía* (which serves reasonable food); the German-run *Posada Alfonso* (☎ 91 10 37), Calle Morillo (the access road) near the alcabala; and the unpretentious *Hostal Colonial* (☎ 91 10 87), opposite the bus terminus. All these places will cost around US$12 for a double with bath and fan.

The *Hotel Alemania* (☎ 91 11 57) and *Posada Don Miguel* (☎ 91 10 81), near to each other on Calle Morillo, are two slightly better options costing around US$16 a double. The colonial-style *Hospedaje La Montañita* (☎ 91 11 32), Calle Morillo just off the waterfront, has doubles for US$20. If you can afford US$25 for a double, go to the small and quiet *Posada La Parchita* (☎ 91 12 59), Calle Trino Rangel. The *Posada del Puerto* (☎ 91 12 39), Calle Los Cocos, has apartments with kitchen and fridge for 5/7 people for US$35/40.

Going up the price scale, you can stay in the pleasant *La Casa de Las García* (☎ 91 10

56), Calle El Cementerio (US$44 for a double with fan and breakfast), or in the small *Posada Pittier* (☎ 91 10 28, at the entrance to the town (US$60/70 for an air-conditioned double/triple with breakfast).

The long-established *Hotel Club Cotoperix* (☎ (02) 952 86 17), in an old colonial house on Calle Morillo, has doubles/triples with fan for US$40/44 and offers packages which include meals and boat excursions. The hotel has its own old-style restaurant. Cotoperix has been so successful that it has opened three other outlets in the town, but it now faces an increasing competition from the new, more attractive places.

One of these is the beautiful *Hacienda El Portete* (☎ 91 12 55; fax 91 12 73), Calle El Cementerio. Established in the meticulously refurbished old colonial mansion, the hotel has its own restaurant and swimming pool, and a charming atmosphere. It costs US$40 per person in air-conditioned doubles, breakfast included.

Another delightful place is the new *Estancia Akelarre* (☎ 014 916 77 65), on the southern outskirts of the town. Built in a colonial style, it has just six rooms and a small pool. A package including bed, three meals and excursions will cost around US$100 per person.

Finally, there's the posh *Posada Humboldt* (☎ 91 10 50, (02) 976 22 22), next door to the alcabala. Set in a colonial-style building, laid out around the flower-filled courtyard, it is a wonderful place to stay and eat (excellent food). It has no sign on the door and is by reservation only.

Budget eating is provided by a cluster of simple restaurants (including *Restaurant Araguaney* and *Cachapas Alvaro*) next to the pedestrian bridge leading to Playa Grande. Just over the bridge, the German-run *El Kiki* serves hearty food. *Pizzería Robin Hood*, Calle Morillo, is also good. Restaurants at Playa Grande cook inexpensive meals, mostly fried fish, for US$3 to US$5 per plate.

Choroní This oasis of peace is the place to escape the crowds of Puerto Colombia. The town has few tourist facilities apart from two pleasant colonial hotels on the main street: the *Hostería Río Mar* (☎ 016 631 26 19, (02) 941 19 45), which costs US$20 for a double and has a restaurant (the only reliable place to eat in town); and the *Posada Colonial Choroní*, operated by the Cacao Expediciones from Caracas (☎ (02) 977 12 34), which has just four rooms and costs US$30 per person, breakfast included.

You can also stay in the charming *Hacienda La Aljorra*, 2km inland from Choroní, on the road to Maracay. It costs a bit less than the Posada Colonial and has a restaurant.

Playa Cata & Around Many people camp on the Cata beach, either in tents or swinging in hammocks from the palms. There are toilets and changing rooms, and stalls on the beach sell cooked meals and drinks. There's a collection of dilapidated state-run cabañas beside the beach, but their days seem to be numbered.

In El Playón area, there are several hotels back from the beach, but they are more expensive than those in Puerto Colombia. The *Posada Los Bertis* is a good budget place, providing decent rooms with fan and bath, and can organise boat excursions. The *Hotel Montemar* (☎ 93 11 73), provides one of the better options; it has doubles with bath and air-conditioning.

In the nearby town of Ocumare de la Costa, there's the comfortable and pleasant *Posada María Luisa* (☎ 93 11 84), which costs about US$30 for bed plus breakfast and dinner.

Rancho Grande The biological station has simple dormitory-style lodging facilities, essentially destined for visiting researchers. Tourists can stay if there are vacancies, but are charged a hefty US$10 per head. No camping is allowed and no food is provided, but there are plans to open a café. It's cheaper and more comfortable to stay in a budget hotel in Maracay and make a day trip.

Getting There & Away
The departure point for the park is the Maracay bus terminal. Buses to Ocumare de

la Costa depart every hour, from 7 am to 5 pm (US$2, two hours). They can let you off at Rancho Grande, but will charge the full fare to Ocumare. From Ocumare, you catch a carrito to Playa Cata (US$0.60, 15 minutes). To Puerto Colombia, buses leave every two hours (US$2, 2¼ hours). The last bus to Maracay from both Ocumare and Puerto Colombia departs at 5 pm (later on weekends), but is not reliable.

Carabobo State

VALENCIA
- *pop 960,000*
- *area code ☎ (041)*

Valencia is Venezuela's third largest city, after Caracas and Maracaibo, and the capital of Carabobo state. It's a prosperous bustling urban sprawl sitting in the north-south valley of the Río Cabriales, and bordered by mountains on the north and west. At an altitude of 480m, the annual average temperature is about 25°C; hot days are refreshed by the evening breeze which comes down from the mountains. Valencia isn't at the top of the average traveller's list of not-to-be-missed destinations, yet it's a pleasant enough place to stop if you are coming this way.

History
Founded in 1555 and named after its Spanish mother town, Valencia has had a tumultuous and chequered history. It had not yet reached its seventh anniversary, when Lope de Aguirre, the infamous adventurer obsessed with finding El Dorado, sacked the town and burnt it almost to the ground. Twenty years later and not yet fully recovered, the town was attacked by Carib Indians who did much the same as Aguirre. A century later, in 1667, the town was seized and destroyed again, this time by French pirates.

The town's proximity to the Lago de Valencia didn't contribute to development either. The disease-breeding marshes brought about smallpox epidemics which decimated the population. Survivors were scared away and new settlers were few and far between. By the year 1800, ie after 250 years of existence, Valencia had barely 6000 inhabitants.

In 1812, a devastating earthquake shook the Andean shell, all the way from Mérida to Caracas, and left Valencia – as well as several other cities including Barquisimeto, Trujillo, San Felipe, Mérida and Caracas – in ruins yet again. Two years later the town was besieged by royalist troops under the command of José Tomás Boves (known as the Butcher) and taken 17 days later. The slaughter which followed left 500 people dead, including many innocent inhabitants. For the next seven years, no less than two dozen battles were fought around the town, until 24 June 1821 when Bolívar's decisive victory at the famous Battle of Carabobo clinched Venezuela's independence.

The victory seems to have been a turning point in the town's fortunes. In 1826, Valencia was the first town to oppose Bolívar's sacred union, Gran Colombia, and called for Venezuela to be declared a sovereign state. Four years later, this became fact after the Congress convened in Valencia and decreed the formal secession from Gran Colombia. At the same time Congress made Valencia the newborn country's capital. A year later, however, the newly elected government opted to move to Caracas.

Valencia experienced particularly rapid growth after WWII. It was then that Venezuela's industrial development accelerated, and Valencia caught the new economic winds in its sails. The Caracas authorities, deeply concerned about the over-industrialisation of the capital, pushed some industries out of the city, and Valencia, which already had a good transport infrastructure and other facilities, was one of the most blessed recipients.

Today, Valencia is Venezuela's most industrialised city, (except for heavy industry which is concentrated in Ciudad Guayana). Home to a thousand companies, producing everything from pots to cars, the city generates nearly a quarter of the country's national manufacturing product and it is

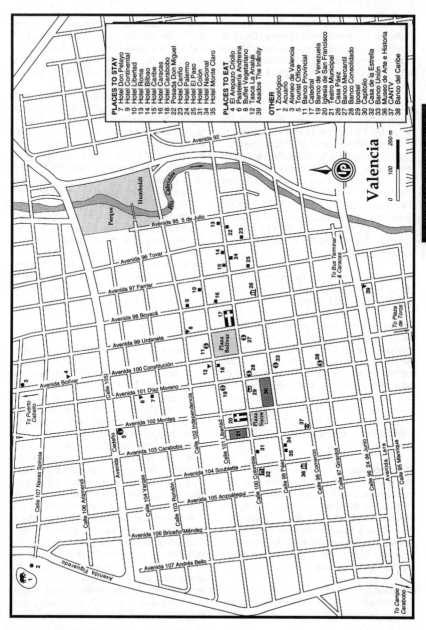

PLACES TO STAY
7 Hotel Don Pelayo
9 Hotel Continental
10 Hotel Libertad
13 Hotel Roma
14 Hotel Bilbao
15 Hotel Caribe
16 Hotel Caracas
18 Hotel Carabobo
22 Posada Don Miguel
23 Hotel Cariño
24 Hotel Palermo
25 Hotel El Paso
31 Hotel Colón
34 Hotel Nacional
35 Hotel Monte Claro

PLACES TO EAT
4 El Arepazo Criollo
6 Pastelería Andreina
8 Buffet Vegetariano
12 Tasca La Analus
39 Asados The Infinity

OTHER
1 Zoológico
2 Acuario
3 Ateneo de Valencia
5 Tourist Office
11 Banco Provincial
17 Catedral
19 Banco de Venezuela
20 Iglesia de San Francisco
21 Teatro Municipal
26 Casa Páez
27 Banco Mercantil
28 Banco Consolidado
29 Ipostel
30 Capitolio
32 Casa de la Estrella
33 Banco Unión
36 Museo de Arte e Historia
37 CANTV
38 Banco del Caribe

Valencia

0   100   200 m

justifiably called the Manufacturing Capital of Venezuela. It is also the centre of the most developed agricultural region, endowed with fertile soil and a favourable climate. Incidentally, like its mother city, Valencia is famous nationwide for its oranges.

Information

Tourist Office The main office, Dirección General de Turismo (☎ 57 75 01; fax 57 76 93), is in Torre Empresarial, Piso Bajo, Avenida Cedeño. They have an outlet, the Módulo de Información Turística El Vagón (☎ 58 95 90), in one of the old train carriages in Parque Humboldt. The carriages and the former train station are relics of the railway built by the Germans in 1894, which provided service to Caracas until the 1960s. Dazzled by cars and freeways, Venezuelans have abandoned passenger train transport altogether.

Inparques The Inparques office (☎ 57 46 09) is in the building of the former train station in Parque Humboldt.

Money Banco Consolidado handles Amex travellers cheque exchange. Other banks on the map are useful for cash advances on Visa and MasterCard. For changing cash, Italcambio is one of the very few casas de cambio; it's in Edificio Talia, Local 2, Avenida Bolívar, Urbanización Los Sauces, about 4km north of Plaza Bolívar. Turisol (☎ 22 70 57, 22 21 35; fax 22 92 59) is in Edificio Exterior, Local 3, Avenida Bolívar, Sector Las Acacias.

Plaza Bolívar

The heart of the historic town, the plaza has the monument to Bolívar at the centre. However, unlike the dozens of equestrian statues (often replicas of the Caracas monument) throughout the country, this one has a certain novelty. The bronze figure of Bolívar stands on a 15m-high white marble column which was brought from Italy.

Catedral

The cathedral, on the eastern side of the plaza, is reputedly 400 years old, but it has experienced so many alterations in its history that today it's an eclectic hotch-potch of styles. In the most recent restoration, carried out in the early 1950s for the city's 400th anniversary, the ceiling was changed to look like a wedding cake.

The most revered treasure in the cathedral, the figure of Nuestra Señora del Socorro, is kept in the chapel in the left transept. Carved in the late 16th century, the sorrowful Virgin in black was the first statue in Venezuela to be crowned (in 1910) by Rome. The gold crown is encrusted with innumerable precious stones and is stored in a safe. It is only taken out for very special celebrations.

The two large paintings, the *Last Supper* and the *Entry into Jerusalem*, which hang opposite one another on the side walls of the chapel, are the work of Antonio Herrera Toro, a Valencia-born artist, who left a number of murals and paintings in local churches and public buildings. Having studied in Rome, his art is strongly influenced by the great masters of the Italian Renaissance.

Casa Páez

This large historic mansion, on the corner of Calle Páez and Avenida Boyacá, was the home of Venezuela's first president, General José Antonio Páez. He distinguished himself by forging a formidable army of llaneros which fought under Bolívar on numerous fronts and largely contributed in achieving independence. In 1830, on the day when Venezuela split from Gran Colombia, Páez took power as the first acting president of the newborn sovereign country and established his residence in the new capital. A year later Páez was elected president of the republic and moved with the government to Caracas.

Restored and furnished with period fittings, the house is today a museum, open Tuesday to Friday from 9 am to noon and 3 to 5.30 pm, Saturday and Sunday from 9 am to 2 pm. The walls of the cloister lining the lovely central patio are graced with murals depicting the nine battles the general fought. The work was done by Pedro Castillo, and supposedly directed by Páez himself.

José Antonio Páez in 'plainsman' wear,
Fritz George Melbye (1867)

Capitolio
Built in 1772 as a convent, this large building takes up half of the block. It became the government house a century later after Guzmán Blanco expelled the former occupants, as he did with many other religious institutions throughout the country. It's not a regular tourist sight, but the guards at the door may let you in and show you around some of the formal rooms, including the Salón Bolívar assembly hall, boasting the famous portrait by Arturo Michelena of Bolívar mounted on his horse. The entrance to the building is from Plaza Sucre.

Teatro Municipal
Modelled on the Paris Opera House and inaugurated in 1894, the theatre was thoroughly renovated in the 1970s. Its 640-seat auditorium has a ceiling painted by Antonio Herrera Toro in 1892, depicting famous men of music and literature, including Rossini, Goethe, Shakespeare and Beethoven. If you want to see it during the day, enter through the back door (from Calle Libertad) which leads directly onto the stage; the guards should let you in.

Casa de la Estrella
In this large *casona*, the sovereign state of Venezuela was born on 6 May 1830, after Congress convened here and decreed secession from Gran Colombia. Reputedly built around 1660 as a hospital, the house was later remodelled and served as a college. At the time of writing, it was being extensively restored for a museum.

Museo de Arte e Historia
The museum is accommodated in the Casa de los Celis, possibly the most beautiful colonial mansion in the city, built in the 1760s and named after one of its owners, Colonel Pedro Celis. It closed for renovation in early 1997. Prior to this, there was a collection of colonial religious art and rooms dedicated to Antonio Herrera Toro (1857-1914) and Andrés Pérez Mujica (1873-1920), both artists born in Valencia.

Acuario & Zoológico
These are the favourite attractions for the *carabobeños*, as local inhabitants are known. The stars of the aquarium are the *toninas*, or freshwater dolphins, kept in a large central pool. Feeding and shows are at 10.30 am, and 1.30, 3 and 5 pm.

The aquarium-terrarium is next to the pool. It has a collection of Venezuelan freshwater fish and some typical snakes – electric eels, piranhas and anacondas. They're all here and highly worth visiting.

Beyond the aquarium is the small zoo, featuring some of Venezuela's typical animal species, including jaguar, tapir, caimán del Orinoco, turtles and a variety of birds.

Both the aquarium and zoo are open Tuesday to Sunday from 9 am to 6 pm (they may also open Monday in August), and the entrance fee is US$0.60 to each.

Plaza de Toros Monumental
The pride of Valencia, this bullring is indeed monumental, the second largest in the Americas after the one in Mexico City. Built

in 1967, it is capable of seating 27,000 spectators. It's not, however, a piece of great architecture. The bullring is on the southern edge of the city, at the end of Avenida Las Ferias, a southern extension of Avenida Constitución. Take the city bus (locally called *camionetica)* from the corner of Avenida Construcción and Avenida Lara, which will set you down a five minute walk from the plaza.

Museo Antropológico
Behind the bullring, in the Parque Recreacional Sur, this museum features a collection of fossils and artefacts related to pre-Hispanic cultures of the region. The area is not renowned for its safety, so take precautions if you decide to come here.

Special Events
The two major local events are the Semana de Valencia, in late March, and the Fiestas Patronales de Nuestra Señora del Socorro, in mid-November. The former features cultural events, an agricultural fair, parades, bullfights etc. The latter is essentially a religious feast in honour of the city's patron saint, in which the crowned Virgin is taken out of the church and paraded in a procession.

In September of every year, the prestigious Salón de Artes Visuales Arturo Michelena opens in the Ateneo de Valencia. This is Venezuela's oldest (and one of the most important) show of visual art.

Places to Stay
The cheapest accommodation is concentrated a few blocks east of Plaza Bolívar, but the hotels there are basic and do a lot of business renting rooms by the hour. The area itself is unpleasant and can be unsafe at night.

The *Hotel Caracas* (☎ 57 18 49), Avenida Boyacá No 100-84, just behind the cathedral, is clean and well kept, though it too sees passing couples. It has matrimoniales with bath and fan for US$7. One block north, the *Hotel Continental* (☎ 57 10 04), Avenida Boyacá No 101-70, has spacious rooms costing US$7/8 a matrimonial/double with bath and fan, US$9/13 with air-conditioning.

The area west of Plaza Bolívar seems to be a little safer, but don't venture here at night either. A reasonable cheapie here is the *Hotel Nacional* (☎ 58 36 76), Calle Páez No 103-51, which costs US$9/11/13 for a matrimonial/double/triple with bath and air-conditioning. The *Hotel Monte Claro* (☎ 58 12 14), next door, is basic.

The nearby *Hotel Colón* (☎ 57 71 05), Calle Colombia No 103-37, has doubles/triples with air-conditioning, TV, private bath and hot water for US$15/20. The *Hotel Carabobo* (☎ 58 88 60, 58 44 67), Calle Libertad 100-37, just off Plaza Bolívar, is a bit better and worth its US$19/24/27 for a double/triple/quad.

Top-end accommodation in the city centre is represented by the modern high-rise *Hotel Don Pelayo* (☎ 57 92 22, 57 93 52; fax 57 93 84), on the corner of Avenida Díaz Moreno and Calle Rondón. It has singles/doubles/triples with all facilities for US$30/33/36, as well as a choice of more expensive suites.

Other mid and top-range hotels are stranded out from the city centre. Some of them, such as *Hotel Le Paris* (☎ 21 56 55), *Hotel Palace* (☎ 21 89 22) and *Hotel Excelsior* (☎ 21 40 55), are on Avenida Bolívar. They all have air-conditioned rooms costing, at most, the same as the rooms of the Don Pelayo.

The best hotel in town is the expensive five-star *Hotel Inter-Continental Valencia* (☎ 21 10 33), Calle Juan Uslar, Urbanización La Viña, about 4km north of the city centre.

Places to Eat
The centre is OK for cheap eating but not so good for quality dining. There are plenty of budget eateries around the back streets, particularly in the area of basic hotels, which serve set lunches for at most US$3. Restaurants tend to close by 8 pm, except for tascas which by that time turn into mostly drinking venues. The *Hotel Nacional* and *Hotel Colón*, both have reasonable tascas; the former is cheaper though, and serves an

inexpensive menu del día at lunch time. The *Tasca La Analus*, which is opposite the Hotel Carabobo, is also OK.

For vegetarians, the best budget option in the centre is the *Buffet Vegetariano*, corner of Calle Independencia and Avenida Urdaneta. It offers hearty set meals for US$3 plus a variety of salads. It's open at lunch time only, Monday to Saturday.

The *Asados The Infinity*, Avenida Lara, is one of the better central outlets for chicken, parrillas, churrasco etc. *El Arepazo Criollo*, Avenida Bolívar, has a range of arepas and is open round the clock. The *Hotel Don Pelayo* has a good, reasonably priced restaurant. For a high-calorie desert, try the nearby *Pastelería Andreina*, which has a choice of rich cakes.

A better area for dining out is to the north of the centre. There are plenty of good places on Avenida Bolívar, including *El Toro Rojo* (parrillas), *Marisquería El Marchica* (fish and seafood), *La Trattoria Romana* (Italian), *La Villa de Madrid* (Spanish), *El Regio* (International) and *La Hostería del Rey* (French).

Getting There & Away

Air The airport is about 7km south-east of the city centre. There are direct flights to Caracas (US$44) by various airlines, from where you can continue to anywhere around the country. Sample destinations and fares from Valencia are: Barcelona (US$83), Maracaibo (US$109) and Porlamar (US$86). Servivensa has direct daily flights to Bogotá and Aruba.

Valencia is the home town of Aserca, a new, competitive Venezuelan airline.

Bus The bus terminal is about 4km northeast of the city centre, in the Disneyland-style Big Low Center, and is easily accessible by frequent local buses. The terminal is large, well organised and has a lot of facilities, including restaurants and snack bars.

Buses run regularly to all major cities. To Caracas, ordinary buses depart every 10 minutes or so (US$2.50, three hours) and

pass through Maracay (US$0.60, one hour). Frequent ordinary buses run to Puerto Cabello (US$1, 50 minutes), Tucacas (US$2, two hours), and Chichiriviche (US$2.50, 2½ hours).

Hourly buses run to Barquisimeto (US$3.75, three hours) and most of them continue on to Maracaibo (US$9.25, eight hours). There are about 10 buses a day to San Cristóbal (US$12.50, 10½ hours) and several of them go on to San Antonio del Táchira (US$13.50, 11½ hours). Four buses a day depart for the night trip to Mérida (US$12.50, nine hours). At least half a dozen buses go to Coro (US$5.50, 5½ hours). All fares are for air-conditioned buses; the ordinary service, available on many routes, is about 25% cheaper.

There are a dozen ordinary buses a day to San Fernando de Apure (US$6, eight hours), where you can change for the bus to Puerto Ayacucho.

CAMPO CARABOBO

Campo Carabobo, or the Carabobo Battlefield, is the site where, on 24 June 1821, the battle which sealed Venezuela's independence was fought between the Spanish royalist army and Bolívar's troops. Bolívar's regiments were strengthened by the lancers of Páez and the British legionnaires, and thanks to these two assisting forces El Libertador was able to win the battle. To commemorate the event, a complex of monuments has been erected on the site where the battle took place.

The approach is a wide entrance road, which turns into a formal promenade lined with bronze busts of the heroes of the battle. The promenade leads to the huge **Triumphal Arch** and the **Tomb of the Unknown Soldier** beneath it. Two soldiers keep guard of the tomb; their gala uniforms from the period seem more suitable for a Siberian winter than for the baking sun of Carabobo. Fortunately for them, the changing of the guard takes place every two hours.

A hundred metres beyond the arch is the **monument**, no doubt the largest in Venezuela. Designed by a Venezuelan sculptor,

Rodríguez del Villar, and revealed in 1930, the monument depicts the main heroes and allegoric figures, all made in stone and bronze. On the top is, you guessed it, an equestrian statue of Bolívar.

About 1km to the west is the **mirador**, from which Bolívar commanded the battle. It houses a large model of the battlefield, and provides a panoramic view over the whole site. The diorama cubicle, to the right of the access road, seems to have closed down.

Campo Carabobo is 32km south-west of Valencia, on the road to San Carlos. Frequent suburban buses (marked Campo Carabobo) go from Valencia to the battlefield. In Valencia, they go east along Calle Comercio and turn south into Avenida Carabobo; catch them on either of these streets, eg at the door of CANTV. They will leave you in Carabobo at the end of the entrance road. The trip takes an hour and costs US$0.25.

CERRO PINTADO

There are a number of petroglyphs in Carabobo state, the largest collection of which is at the site known as Cerro Pintado. Also called Parque Piedras Pintadas (though it's not a park), the site is 22km north-east of Valencia, near the village of Tronconero, and features dozens of weathered rocks and slabs scattered over a grassy slope. Many of the stones bear shallow engravings of mysterious designs and figures. Further on, there's a group of upright megalithic stones.

To get to the Cerro from Valencia, take the bus to Vigirima, which departs regularly and costs US$0.50. The bus passes through Guacara, 13km east of Valencia, then turns north to Vigirima, 12km further. You should get off midway along this stretch, by the Bodega Los Tres Samanes, at the Cruce de Tronconero. Here a dirt road, the Cerro Pintado, branches off to the left (west) and goes to the Río Tronconero, about 1.5km from the turnoff. Shortly past the bridge, take a rough track which branches off to the north. This track passes a rural school (soon after the turnoff, on your right), and continues north for another 1.5km, eventually getting to the

foothills of the Cerro. You can camp at the site if you wish. Bring food and water, as there is no water around.

There are other interesting groups of petroglyphs in the Montaña de Mataburro, several kilometres north of Vigirima; along the Río Chirgua, near the town of Chirgua, west of Valencia; in the area of Montalbán, still further west; and near the town of Güigüe, near the southern shore of Lago de Valencia.

LAS TRINCHERAS

The village of Las Trincheras, 18km north of Valencia, is noted for its hot springs. At about 92°C, the springs are among the hottest in the world, and they are also widely acclaimed for their curative properties. A large bath complex, Centro Termal Las Trincheras, has been built at the site, and includes a hotel, a restaurant, baths, mud bath and sauna.

The springs have been known for centuries and have attracted a number of explorers and naturalists, among them Alexander von Humboldt, who successfully boiled eggs in the hot water. In 1889, thermal baths were built that included a hotel and pools. The original hotel was reconstructed by General Gómez, who used to come here frequently. In 1980, the old hotel was restored, a new one was constructed beside it, and the pools were largely remodelled. There are three pools with temperatures ranging from 36°C to 42°C, and a mud bath.

The springs are renowned for their therapeutic properties, recommended in the treatment of a variety of ailments, including rheumatic, digestive, respiratory and allergic problems. They are also useful in helping you to lose weight, make the skin feel fresh and smooth, and help with general relaxation.

You can either come to the baths for the day (open from 7 am to 10 pm, mud bath until 6 pm only, entrance fee US$2.50), or you can stay in their hotel, using the baths and other facilities at the complex at no additional cost. The hotel has its own pool, for the exclusive use of guests.

Places to Stay & Eat

Centro Termal Las Trincheras offers comfortable air-conditioned singles/doubles/triples for US$16/21/23, and suites for US$25 to US$35. The price of the hotel includes the use of the baths, sauna and other facilities. The restaurant offers breakfast, lunch and dinner for both hotel guests and day visitors.

It's usually easy to get a room during the week but at weekends the hotel tends to fill up. Advance booking is available through their Caracas office (☎ (02) 661 36 26, 661 49 36; fax 661 35 02), Edificio Carini, Piso Bajo, Local A, Avenida Alma Mater, Los Chaguaramos.

Opposite the entrance to the baths complex is the *Hotel Turístico*, which has doubles/triples for US$15/18. It runs its own restaurant serving Venezuelan cuisine. The price doesn't include entrance to the baths.

Getting There & Away

There are city buses from Valencia to Las Trincheras, which you can catch on Avenida Bolívar, north of Avenida Cedeño. They go by the old Valencia-Puerto Cabello road and deposit you at the entrance to the baths. The trip takes half an hour to one hour and costs US$0.20. You can also get to the baths from the Valencia bus terminal by catching any of the frequent buses to Puerto Cabello. These buses go via the autopista (freeway) and charge the full fare to Puerto Cabello (US$1), but only take 20 minutes to get to Las Trincheras. They will put you down off the autopista, which is a 10 minute walk from the baths.

If you want to continue on from Las Trincheras north to Puerto Cabello, Tucacas or Chichiriviche, wave down the appropriate bus on the autopista.

PUERTO CABELLO

• *pop 140,000*
• *area code* ☎ (042)

Puerto Cabello began its life as a simple wharf built on the bank of an ample coastal lagoon, somewhere around the mid-16th century. The site was a perfect natural anchorage: it provided protection from winds and waves and was connected with the open sea by a convenient strait. In fact, there was hardly a better place for a port on the Venezuelan coast.

During the 17th century, the port grew on a busy contraband trade – mostly dealing in cacao – with Curaçao. At that time, it was under Dutch control. It wasn't until 1730 that the Spanish took over the port, after the Real Compañía Guipuzcoana had moved in. The company built warehouses and wharves, and an array of forts to protect the harbour. By the 1770s, Puerto Cabello came to be the most heavily fortified town on Venezuela's coast. Two forts remain from that period.

During the War of Independence, Puerto Cabello became an important royalist stronghold, from which attacks were launched against Bolívar's troops. After losing the battle of Carabobo, the Spanish retreated to Puerto Cabello and kept it until 7 November 1823; when they surrendered the town to General Páez. Puerto Cabello was the last place in Venezuela to be freed from Spanish rule.

In the 19th century, Puerto Cabello was Venezuela's busiest port, through which a good deal of cacao, coffee, indigo and cotton was shipped abroad. The port was modernised during the dictatorships of Gómez and Pérez Jiménez, and again over recent decades.

Today, the port handles 65% of the country's import and export cargo (except oil), and has the best natural conditions and technical facilities of all Venezuelan ports. Occupying an area of 200 hectares, it features 34 docks, a shipyard with a dry dock, large warehouses and extensive space for containers. Part of the harbour is taken by the naval base.

While the attention of governors was concentrated on the port and its infrastructure, the old town was largely neglected and was gradually falling into ruins. It wasn't until the 1980s that the government realised the value of the town's historic fabric, and launched an extensive restoration programme. Some streets have already been restored – with quite a remarkable result – and the work on others is in progress. Although there's still a long way to go, it's worth coming to see what has already been done. You can also visit the attractive surrounding area, including beaches to the east and lush forests to the south.

Orientation

Puerto Cabello has grown considerably over recent decades, stretching towards the west for about 7km along the freeway, as far as the airport. The central area, at the eastern end of the city, can be clearly divided in two parts: the colonial sector to the north and the new centre to the south. Plaza Bolívar roughly marks the borderline between the two areas. While the new centre is pretty dull and uninspiring, the partly renovated old town is attractive.

Information

Tourist Office The Dirección General de Turismo (☎ 61 39 21, 61 46 22; fax 61 32 55) is in the Edificio Gobierno de Carabobo, Calle Ricaurte, facing Plaza Bolívar. The office is open Monday to Friday from 8 am to 5 pm.

Money The main banks are scattered around the city centre, including the colonial sector. As elsewhere, the Banco Consolidado changes Amex travellers cheques. Other banks marked on the map handle Visa and Master-Card cash advances.

Old Town

The **Plaza Bolívar**, at the southern edge of the colonial sector, boasts yet another equestrian statue of Bolívar. A massive odd edifice built from coral rock, occupying the eastern side of the plaza, is the **Iglesia de San José**. It was begun in the mid-19th century and only completed some 100 years later, when the bell tower was added. At the time of writing, it was closed for restoration, but may reopen by the time you come.

The old town to the west of Calle Comercio have been largely restored and revived by painting the façades in bright colours. It's

now a pleasant area to stroll about, or watch the world go by from the open-air restaurants on the tree-shaded waterfront boulevard, **Paseo El Malecón**.

Don't miss walking along the two historic streets, **Calle de los Lanceros** and **Calle Bolívar**, and note the overhanging balconies and massive doorways which adorn some of the houses, including the fair-sized building of the **Museo de Historia**. Built in 1790 as a residence, it has a gracious internal patio and façades over both streets; the blue balcony facing Calle Bolívar is particularly impressive. The museum, which houses a collection related to the town's history, has been closed since the early 1990s.

At the northern end of Calle de los Lanceros is the **Iglesia del Rosario**, a handsome whitewashed church built in 1780. The wooden bell tower is unique in Venezuela. One block north of the church is the **Casa Guipuzcoana**, built in 1730 as the office for the Compañia Guipuzcoana. Today it's a public library which you can enter and look around.

The library faces a triangular square with the **Monumento del Aguila** in the middle. The monument, a tall column topped by a condor instead of an eagle, was erected in 1896 to the memory of North Americans who gave their lives for Venezuelan independence. Recruited by Francisco de Miranda, in 1806 they sailed from New York to Ocumare de la Costa, north of Maracay. Upon dropping anchor, however, two boats with Americans aboard were surprised and captured by Spanish guard boats. Ten officers were hung and the remaining 50-odd recruits were sent to prison. Miranda arrived in Coro a few months later with new recruits, but this expedition proved to be a failure as well.

Spanish Forts

North of the old town, separated from it by the entrance channel to the harbour, is the Fortín San Felipe, later renamed **Castillo Libertador** and commonly referred to as such. The fort was constructed in the 1730s by the Compañía Guipuzcoana to protect the

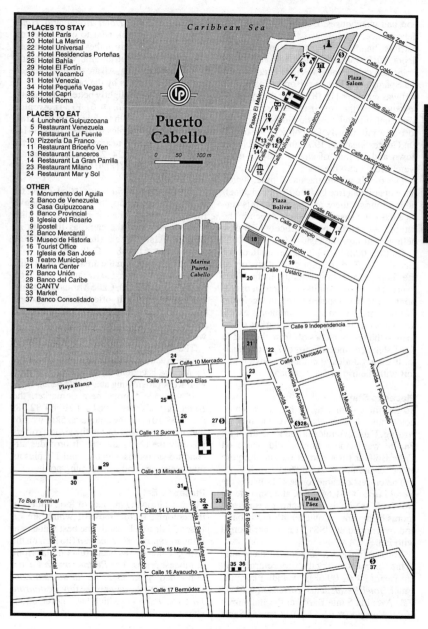

Caribbean Sea

PLACES TO STAY
19 Hotel París
20 Hotel La Marina
22 Hotel Universal
25 Hotel Residencias Porteñas
26 Hotel Bahía
29 Hotel El Fortín
30 Hotel Yacambú
31 Hotel Venezia
34 Hotel Pequeña Vegas
35 Hotel Capri
36 Hotel Roma

PLACES TO EAT
4 Lunchería Guipuzcoana
5 Restaurant Venezuela
7 Restaurant La Fuente
10 Pizzería Da Franco
11 Restaurant Briceño Ven
13 Restaurant Lanceros
14 Restaurant La Gran Parrilla
23 Restaurant Milano
24 Restaurant Mar y Sol

OTHER
1 Monumento del Aguila
2 Banco de Venezuela
6 Casa Guipuzcoana
8 Iglesia del Rosario
9 Ipostel
12 Banco Mercantil
15 Museo de Historia
16 Tourist Office
17 Iglesia de San José
18 Teatro Municipal
21 Marina Center
27 Banco Unión
28 Banco del Caribe
32 CANTV
33 Market
37 Banco Consolidado

Puerto
Cabello

0   50   100 m

Plaza
Salom

Calle Zea
Calle Colón
Calle Salom
Paseo El Malecón
Calle Comercio
Calle Arzobispo
Calle Municipio
Calle Democracia
Calle de los Lanceros
Calle Bolívar
Calle Heres

Plaza
Bolívar

Calle Ricaurte
Calle El Templo

Marina
Puerto
Cabello

Calle Girardot
Calle Ustáriz

Calle 9 Independencia
Calle 10 Mercado
Calle 11 Campo Elías
Playa Blanca
Calle 12 Sucre
Calle 13 Miranda

To Bus Terminal

Calle 14 Urdaneta
Calle 15 Mariño
Calle 16 Ayacucho
Calle 17 Bermúdez

Avenida 1 Puerto Cabello
Avenida 2 Municipio
Avenida 3 Anzoátegui
Avenida 4 Piasa
Avenida 5 Bolívar
Avenida 6 Valencia
Avenida 7 Santa Bárbara
Avenida 8 Carabobo
Avenida 9 Bárbula
Avenida 10 Juncal

Plaza
Páez

THE CENTRAL NORTH

port and warehouses. During the War of Independence, the fort was for a time in the patriots' hands, serving as the ammunition depot, but it was lost to the royalists in 1812. Francisco de Miranda was jailed here before the Spanish sent him to prison in Spain. The fort was recovered in 1823 after the eventual surrender of the royalists, and served the Venezuelan army. General Gómez used the fort as a jail, mostly for political prisoners. On Gómez' death in 1935, the prison closed down and 14 tons of chains and leg irons were thrown into the sea.

The fort is within the naval base, which once operated a free boat across the channel, taking tourists there and back, but this service has been suspended (it may open in the future). Ask at the tourist office which may help you arrange the visit.

On the 100m-high hill to the south of the city sits the **Fortín Solano**, another fort of the Guipuzcoana company, built in the 1760s to provide security for its commercial operations. This was reputedly the last colonial fort built in Venezuela. It commands excellent views of the city and the harbour. The road to the fort branches off from the road to San Esteban on the outskirts of Puerto Cabello. It's a good idea to combine a visit to the fort with the trip to San Esteban.

Places to Stay

So far, the colonial sector has not a single hotel, but this may change. At the time of writing, Fabio Morales of the Restaurant La Fuente was remodelling an old house on Calle Bolívar for a budget posada. Enquire at the restaurant (☎ 61 68 89).

The closest cheapie to the old town is the *Hotel París* (☎ 61 66 48), Calle Anzoátegui No 7-11, which is quiet and doesn't rent rooms by the hour. However, it's pretty basic and overpriced at US$12 for a matrimonial with fan.

You can find a cheaper room further south, in the central area. Try the very central *Hotel Universal* (☎ 61 09 68), Avenida Plaza; the small *Hotel Residencias Porteñas* (☎ 61 44 92), Avenida Santa Bárbara; the Italian-run *Hotel Venezia* (☎ 61 43 80), Avenida Santa Bárbara; and the *Hotel Roma* and *Hotel Capri* (☎ 61 34 82), next to each other on Calle Ayacucho. Any of these will cost about US$10/13 for a matrimonial with bath and fan/air-conditioning. All are on the basic side and may rent rooms by the hour.

There are some slightly better hotels in the area. The *Hotel Bahía* (☎ 61 40 34), Avenida Santa Bárbara, has air-conditioned matrimoniales/doubles with bath for US$16/20. Similar is the nearby *Hotel El Fortín* (☎ 61 43 56, 61 24 27), Calle Miranda, which costs US$16/18/20 for a matrimonial/double/triple.

The *Hotel Pequeña Vegas* (☎ 61 23 80, 61 57 69), Calle Mariño, looks more attractive from the outside than it really is. Its dim rooms cost much the same as those in El Fortín. Also check the cheaper *Hotel Yacambú* (☎ 61 03 82), Calle Miranda.

The best option in the area is probably the *Hotel Turístico Isla Larga* (☎ 61 37 41, 61 32 90; fax 61 44 16), Calle Miranda, close to the bus terminal. It offers air-conditioned matrimoniales/doubles/triples/quads for US$20/22/24/25. A new annex is being built which will add more rooms and a pool.

The city centre has no top-end hotels, until the construction of the massive 11-storey *Hotel La Marina* is completed (unlikely to be soon with work progressing at a snail's pace).

If you need somewhere upmarket, the *Hotel Suite Caribe* (☎ 64 30 79, 64 32 78; fax 64 39 10)), on the autopista, 5km west of the city centre (2km east of the airport) offers possibly the best standards. It provides air-conditioned rooms with bath and TV, plus its own restaurant and a swimming pool.

Places to Eat

There's a growing number of food outlets in the colonial sector, most of which are on Paseo Malecón. Possibly the best value here is the *Restaurant Briceño Ven* (no sign on the door), which serves beautiful comida criolla at modest prices. The *Restaurant La Fuente* is not bad either, as is the *Restaurant Lanceros*. Next to the latter is the tiny *Restaurant La Gran Parrilla*, which has unpretentious cheap parrillas.

The *Pizzería Da Franco* is a pleasant, inexpensive place with tables outside, which stays open until 11 pm. Further north, near the Monumento del Aguila, is the more up-market *Restaurant Venezuela*, good for fish and seafood. Just round the corner is the *Lunchería Guipuzcoana*, which serves cheap snacks.

In the city centre, there are several eating establishments in the Marina Center, which is a Disneyland-looking food centre, but they are poor value except for a small *Arepera La Mina* at the back of the building.

A few paces south of the Marina Center, on Calle Bolívar, is the good but not cheap *Restaurant Milano*, which specialises in pasta and seafood. The best place for seafood in the area is arguably the *Restaurant Mar y Sol*, overlooking the bay from the western end of Calle Mercado.

The food kiosks along Avenida Bolívar between the Marine Center and the theatre provide a variety of cheap snacks including hot dogs and hamburgers. There are also stalls selling elaborate wedding cakes.

Getting There & Away
Air The airport is 7km west of Puerto Cabello, next to the freeway. There are no scheduled flights.

Bus The bus terminal is on Calle Urdaneta, about 800m west of Avenida Bolívar. Frequent carritos run between the terminal and the centre, or you can walk the distance in 10 minutes. If you decide to walk, never go via the Playa Blanca beach, even if this seems to be a considerable shortcut. The beach is notorious for the armed robbery of tourists, especially due north of the bus terminal.

Buses to Valencia depart every 15 minutes (US$1, 50 minutes), where you change for equally frequent buses to Caracas. There are also regular buses to Tucacas (US$1, 1¼ hours) and San Felipe (US$1.50, 1¾ hours), and less frequent departures to Chichiriviche (US$1.50, 1¾ hours) and Barquisimeto (US$3.25, three hours). For transport to the nearby beaches and San Esteban, see the Around Puerto Cabello section.

Train Puerto Cabello is the terminus of the railway line to Barquisimeto, but it now only handles freight transport; the passenger service was suppressed in the mid-1990s.

Boat A ferry service is planned to Curaçao, Aruba and Bonaire (the Netherlands Antilles). Contact the tourist office for current information. The city has a small marina (☎ 61 72 77; fax 61 64 66).

AROUND PUERTO CABELLO
Beaches
There are several beaches to the east of Puerto Cabello, off the road to Patanemo. First comes **Balneario Quizandal**, about 7km by road from the city. This beach is quite developed, with a car park, showers, restaurants and a drive-in cinema.

From the beach, boats can take you to **Isla Larga**, an island popular with beachgoers, swimmers and snorkellers. There are two wrecks near the island, an additional attraction for snorkellers and scuba divers. Food stalls are open on the weekends (and sometimes on weekdays as well) and they can stuff you with fish. Take good sun protection, as there is no shade on the island. On weekends, when there are many holidaymakers, the boat ride will cost US$3 return, but during the week you'll probably have to pay the fare for the whole boat, US$20 return (negotiable).

The next exit off the Patanemo road, 1km beyond that to Quizandal, leads to the small **Playa Huequito**. In the same place another road branches off to the right and heads south to the small town of Borburata, which is widely known for its Fiestas de San Juan (23-24 June) and San Pedro (28 June). About 1.5km further on from the junction, the Patanemo road passes by the village known as **Rincón del Pirata**. This is the only place where the road runs close to the coast, but the place has little appeal and the beach is poor.

From this point, the road winds up a hill, then descends to yet another turnoff (6km beyond the Rincón), which leads 1.5km to the **Playa Patanemo**. This is the best beach in the area, wide and shaded by coconut

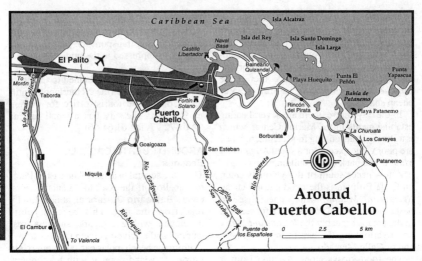

Around
Puerto Cabello

palms. Fish stalls open on the weekends, but on weekdays the beach is fairly solitary. You can pitch your tent amidst the palms; bring your own food and water.

At the turnoff is a pleasant hotel, *La Churuata*, with its own restaurant (about US$30 for a double with bath). The road continues half a km to the village of Los Caneyes, and 2.5km further on it eventually reaches the village of Patanemo. There's a budget place to stay, the family-run *Posada Chachita* in the village, and basic food is available. Patanemo is noted for the Diablos Danzantes celebrations on Corpus Christi, and for drumbeats on Fiesta de San Juan (23 and 24 June).

Carritos run regularly between the Puerto Cabello bus terminal and Patanemo, and will put you down at any turnoff of your choice, within reasonable walking distance of the beach. The ride to Patanemo village takes half an hour and costs US$0.40.

San Esteban

San Esteban is a pleasant village 7km south of Puerto Cabello. It's surrounded by lush vegetation, has a more enjoyable climate than the port and boasts a couple of attrac-

tions. It's also the starting point for the Camino Real, the old Spanish trail leading south to Valencia (see the following Parque Nacional San Esteban section). Carritos to San Esteban depart regularly from the bus terminal in Puerto Cabello (US$0.20, 15 minutes). They get to the bridge in San Esteban, where the road ends.

Walk south (600m from the bridge) along a path on the same side of the river, and you'll get to a large rock known as the Piedra del Indio, covered with petroglyphs. The rock is just next to the path, on your left.

San Esteban was the birthplace of Bartolomé Salom, one of the heroes of the War of Independence, who accompanied Bolívar all the way to Ayacucho. The house where he was born is 800m back along the road from the point where the carritos terminate. It has been left half-ruined, and is open for visitors from 9 am to 4 pm. Inside the main room is a life-sized statue of the general sitting in a hammock – quite an unusual sight.

A bit up the main road from the Salom's house is the inexpensive *Posada Mi Jaragual*, and there are also a few places to eat and drink, including the *Bar Club Popular* near the bridge, where you can try some of the typical alcoholic drinks such as the *leche de burra* or the *guarapita*.

Parque Nacional San Esteban

This national park, next to the west of Parque Nacional Henri Pittier, stretches from San Esteban southward almost to Naguanagua, on the northern outskirts of Valencia. Like its eastern neighbour, the park protects a part of the Cordillera de la Costa, noted for its rich and diverse flora and fauna.

There's a popular trail in the park, known as the Camino Real. In colonial times, it was the main route linking Puerto Cabello with Valencia, along which goods were transported. The trail leads north-south, passing over the ridge at an altitude of about 1400m.

You can still see traces of the cobbled Spanish road and even encounter the original Spanish bridge, the Puente de los Españoles from 1808. The trail is relatively easy, though side paths joining it may be confusing. Although the walking time between San Esteban and Naguanagua is about eight hours, count on two days to take it at a leisurely pace. There are some problems at the southern end, as the northern suburb of Naguanagua, Bárbula, is noted for armed robbery.

Many walkers departing from the northern end (San Esteban) make it just a one-day return trip by only going as far as the Spanish bridge. It's about a three hour walk up and a two hour walk back down.

THE CENTRAL NORTH

The North-West

Venezuela's north-west is a land of contrasts, with such diverse natural features as coral islands and beaches, rainforests and waterfalls, caves and chasms, the country's only desert, and South America's largest lake, Lago Maracaibo. The region combines the traditional with the contemporary, from living Indian cultures (such as that of the Guajiros) and colonial heritage (the best is found in Coro), to the modern city of Maracaibo. Administratively, the north-west, as described in this chapter, covers the states of Falcón, Lara, Yaracuy and Zulia.

Falcón State

CORO
- *pop 135,000*
- *area code ☎ (068)*

Set at the base of the curiously shaped Península de Paraguaná, Coro is a pleasant, peaceful city and the capital of Falcón state. Thanks to a large university it has a noticeably cultured air. More importantly, Coro has some of the best colonial architecture to be found in the country.

Founded by Juan de Ampiés in 1527, it was one of the earliest towns on the continent and the first capital of the Province of Venezuela. In the same year it was leased, along with the entire province, to the Welsers of Germany to conquer, settle and exploit. The contract was made by King Carlos I of Spain who was heavily in debt to German banking firms for loans he had used to buy the title of Holy Roman Emperor, Karl V (Charles V) in 1519. The Germans were eager to share in the reputedly fabulous riches of the just discovered continent. The Church was quick to follow and in 1531 it established the Episcopal See in Coro, the first archdiocese to be founded in the New World.

Despite this early and promising start,

HIGHLIGHTS

- Tramp around the colonial centre of Coro
- Experience the Sierra de San Luis
- Enjoy the beaches and coral reefs of Morrocoy national park
- Try bird-watching in Yacambú national park
- Visit the historic heart of Carora
- Marvel at the lightning phenomenon of Catatumbo

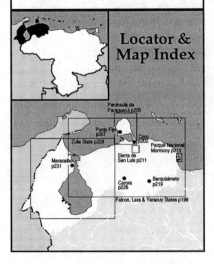

Locator & Map Index

Coro's development was bogged down right from the beginning. The town became not much more than a jumping-off point for repetitive expeditions in search of treasure, but El Dorado never materialised. In 1546 the contract with the Welsers was cancelled and the administrative seat of the province moved to El Tocuyo, 200km to the south. The Church was more patient but finally relocated the archdiocese to Caracas in 1637.

Having been looted and burned on various occasions in pirate attacks (in 1567, 1595

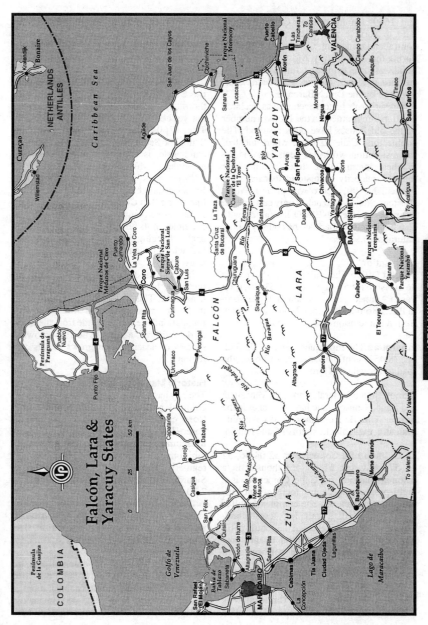

and 1659, among others), Coro struggled hard to survive and was only revived by contraband trade with Curaçao and Bonaire during the 18th century. Most of the historic buildings date from that time, and it's no surprise that their architectural detail is influenced by the Dutch Baroque.

Since Coro's historic centre was declared a national monument in the 1950s, a number of the old houses have been restored. The cobblestone Calle Zamora, where most of the restoration work has been done, is the loveliest colonial-style street, and it's here that the majority of historic mansions are located. In 1993, Coro was made a World Heritage Site – Venezuela's only cultural site to appear on the UNESCO list (along with Canaima national park as the country's only natural site).

Information

Tourist Office The tourist office, Secretaría de Turismo (☎ 51 11 32; fax 51 53 27), is on Paseo Alameda, a pedestrian mall just north of Plaza Bolívar. It is open Monday to Friday from 8 am to noon and 2 to 5 pm.

Inparques The Inparques office (☎ 78 582; fax 78 451) is in the Jardín Xerófilo, on the road to La Vela de Coro.

Money Banco Federal, Banco de Venezuela and Banco Consolidado have branches in the centre. The Banco Unión is on Avenida Manaure, eight blocks south of Calle Falcón.

La Colmena La Colmena (☎ 52 04 36, 52 20 57; ☎ & fax 51 14 46), housed in a colonial mansion on Calle Comercio, is a multi-programme centre focusing on culture, art, tourism etc. The complex features an exhibition hall, a craft shop, a restaurant, a travel agency, and tables in the central patio where meetings and cultural events take place. Live music is often performed on weekends.

Colonial Churches

The massive fortress-like **Catedral** was begun in the 1580s and concluded half a century later, making it the oldest surviving church in Venezuela. There are no reminders of its early history inside, yet the 1790 Baroque main retable is a good example of late colonial art.

Two blocks north, the 18th century **Iglesia de San Francisco** has been recently thoroughly restored, though the interior has not yet been fully furnished and decorated. The 1760s cupola of the Capilla del Santísimo Sacramento, at the top of the right-hand aisle, is considered one of the best examples of Mudejar art in Venezuela.

Just a stone's throw to the west of San Francisco is another 18th century church, the **Iglesia de San Clemente**. It was laid out on a Latin cross plan and is one of the very few examples of its kind in the country. Note the anchor hanging from the middle of the ceiling, which is commemorating St Clement's martyrdom.

In the barred pavilion on the plaza between the two churches is the **Cruz de San Clemente**. This is said to be the cross used in the first mass celebrated after the town's foundation. The cross is made from the wood of the *cují* tree, a xerophytic slow-growing species of acacia which grows in this arid region.

Historic Mansions & Museums

The city has a few good museums in restored colonial buildings. The **Museo de Arte Coro**, established in a beautiful mansion on Paseo Talavera, is a branch of the Caracas Museum of Contemporary Art. All the exhibitions are temporary and are changed regularly. The museum is open Tuesday to Saturday from 9 am to 12.30 pm and 3 to 7.30 pm, Sunday from 9 am to 4 pm.

Diagonally opposite, in another great historic casona, the **Museo de Arte Alberto Henríquez** is undergoing restoration. The museum features a collection of modern painting.

For an insight into the colonial past, go two blocks north to the **Museo de Coro Lucas Guillermo Castillo** (named after the bishop of Coro from 1923-48), in an old convent. An extensive collection of both religious and secular art from the region and beyond, including some extraordinary pieces, is displayed in 22 rooms. It's one of the best collections of its kind in the country. The museum is open Tuesday to Saturday from 9 am to noon and 3 to 6 pm, Sunday from 9 am to 1 pm; all visits are guided (in Spanish only) and the tour takes about an hour.

A short walk west is the **Casa de los Arcaya**, noted for its long, tile-roofed balconies. The mansion houses the **Museo de Cerámica Histórica y Loza Popular**, a small but interesting museum of pottery and ceramics; opening hours are the same as the Museo de Coro Lucas Guillermo Castillo.

Opposite Los Arcaya is the **Casa del Sol**, named for the decorative sun motif over its doorway. Next door is the more modest **Casa Nazaret**. Both buildings are now occupied by offices.

There are more great mansions on Calle Zamora. The **Casa de las Ventanas de Hierro** is noted for a splendid 8m-high plaster doorway and the wrought-iron grilles (imported from Spain) across the windows. It's now a private museum featuring a collection of historic objects (opening hours are the same as for the Museo de Cerámica). The **Casa del Tesoro** houses an art gallery. The **Casa de los Soto** is a private residence and cannot be visited.

Cementerio Judío
Established in the 1830s, this is the oldest Jewish cemetery still in use on the continent. Jews came to Coro from Curaçao in the early 19th century, a period of intensive trade with the Dutch islands. In the course of time, they formed a small but influential commercial community, despite the persecution of the post-independence caudillo governments. Today, there are perhaps at most half a dozen Jews still living in Coro.

The cemetery was founded by Joseph Curiel (1796-1886), a rich Jewish merchant who met Bolívar in Angostura and offered him Jewish help in the cause of independence. His tomb is one of the most elaborate, while the grave of his 10-year-old

daughter, dated 1832, is the oldest tomb in the cemetery. The Curiel family name occurs the most frequently in the cemetery.

The cemetery is normally locked and the keys are kept in the Museo de Coro Lucas Guillermo Castillo. Enquire there and someone will show you around the graveyard.

Médanos de Coro
Médanos de Coro is a national park north of the city, created in 1974 to protect the unusual environment of the isthmus of the Península de Paraguaná. The dominant feature of the isthmus' landscape are sand dunes, which rise up to 30m and give the impression of being in the middle of the Sahara. The most spectacular desert area is just north-east of the city, easily accessible by urban transport.

To get there from the city centre, take the Carabobo bus from Calle Falcón and get off 300m past the large Monumento a la Federación. From here it is a 10 minute walk north along a wide avenida to another public sculpture, Monumento a la Madre. A few paces north, there is nothing but sand. Armed robberies have been reported here, so don't go alone and keep on guard.

There's another, reputedly safer, access to the dunes from the highway to Punto Fijo. Take the urban bus to Plaza Concordia, from where it's a 10 minute walk north along the Punto Fijo road to the dunes.

Jardín Xerófilo
This beautiful, well-kept xerophytic botanical garden is about 4.5km west of the Monumento a la Federación, on the road to La Vela de Coro. It's officially open from 8.30 to 11.30 am and 2 to 3.30 pm, except Monday, but the doorkeeper lives on the premises and will probably let you in at other reasonable times of the day. To get to the garden, take the La Vela bus from Calle Falcón, anywhere east of Avenida Manaure.

Organised Tours
Camel Tours is the best adventure tour operator in town but was closed when we visited. It expects to be back in business by

PLACES TO STAY
3 Hotel Miranda Cumberland
6 Hotel Intercaribe
11 Hotel Capri
26 Hotel Roma
27 Hotel Martín
35 Hotel Colonial
44 Posada Turística Manena
46 Apart Hotel Sahara

PLACES TO EAT
2 Il Ristorante Da Vicenzo
4 Pizzería La Barra del Jacal
5 Panadería Costa Nova
7 Fuente de Soda Mi Casona
8 Comedor Popular
9 Pizzería Mersi
10 Restaurant Casavieja
15 Cafetín Alameda

32 Pub 1527
34 Hostería Colonial
37 La Tasca Española

OTHER
1 Airport Terminal
12 Kuriana Travel Agency
13 Museo de Coro Lucas
   Guillermo Castillo
14 Iglesia de San Francisco
16 Cruz de San Clemente
17 Iglesia de San Clemente
18 Casa de los Arcaya &
   Museo de Cerámica Histórica
   y Loza Popular
19 Casa del Sol
20 Casa Nazaret
21 Casa de los Soto
22 Casa de las Ventanas
   de Hierro

23 Casa del Tesoro
24 Teatro de Coro
25 Cementerio Judío
28 Ipostel
29 Museo de Arte Alberto
   Henríquez
30 Museo de Arte de Coro
31 Banco Federal
33 La Colmena
36 Banco de Venezuela
38 Tourist Office
39 Catedral
40 Ateneo de Coro
41 Statue of Juan de Ampiés
42 Public telephones
43 Iglesia de San Nicolás
   de Bari
45 Banco Consolidado

Coro

0   50   100 m

the time you read this with full-day tours to both Península de Paraguaná and to Sierra de San Luis for about US$30 per person per tour. Ask for Roberto Andara at the Pub 1527 (☎ 52 45 36), where Camel Tours will operate from.

Also check La Colmena travel agency (☎ 51 14 46), which may have some tours on offer, and the Kuriana travel agency (☎ 51 30 35).

Places to Stay
The recently opened *Posada Turística Manena* (☎ 51 66 15), Calle Garcés No 119, is the best central budget place to stay. It has just five rooms, all clean and with private bath. Matrimonial or triple with fan costs US$10 each; and matrimonial/triple with air-conditioning costs US$15/20.

There are four budget hotels right in the historic heart of the city: *Capri*, *Colonial*, *Martín* and *Roma*. All are basic, filthy and run down, so check a few before deciding. Expect a matrimonial with bath and fan to cost about US$7 to US$10. The Capri and Colonial also have noisy air-conditioned rooms for about US$10 to US$12.

The *Hotel Intercaribe* (☎ 51 18 11, 51 19 44; fax 51 14 34), Avenida Manaure, offers more comfort and facilities, including TV, for US$20/30/40 a single/double/triple. They require you to pay a security deposit equivalent to two nights regardless of the duration of your stay. Alternatively, try the new *Apart Hotel Sahara* (☎ 52 71 13, 52 82 46; fax 52 86 55), Calle Bolívar, which costs US$25/35/45.

The *Hotel Miranda Cumberland* (☎ 52 21 11, 52 30 22; fax 51 30 96), Avenida Josefa Camejo, opposite the airport, is the best place to stay in town. Air-conditioned doubles/triples cost US$60/75. The hotel has its own restaurant, bar, swimming pool and sauna.

Places to Eat
Some of the cheapest meals can be had (at lunch time only) in the *Comedor Popular*, though don't expect much. On a similar basic side is the unpretentious *Pizzería Mersi*, just

across the street. The *Hostería Colonial* is also quite a rudimentary eatery.

La Colmena, Calle Comercio, serves better food in more pleasant surroundings. The *Restaurant Casavieja*, Calle Zamora, has a charming setting in a colonial house with a fine patio, though the food quality seems to be running down.

The open-air *Pizzería La Barra del Jacal*, at its new enjoyable site on Calle Unión, does a good job and offers more than just pizzas.

Il Ristorante Da Vincenzo, opposite Hotel Miranda Cumberland, is one of the better restaurants in the city centre, specialising in Italian food.

For breakfast, try the *Panadería Costa Nova*, opposite the Hotel Intercaribe, which is good and popular with locals. Alternatively, go to the *Cafetín Alameda*, opposite San Francisco church. There are a few fast-food outlets on Paseo Talavera, plus the trendy *Pub 1527*, which is open till late.

Getting There & Away
Air The sleepy airport is just a five minute walk north of the city centre. Avensa has daily flights to Caracas (US$55) via Barquisimeto (US$40); for other domestic destinations you have to change at either of the two. You can also use the busier Las Piedras airport, near Punto Fijo on the Paraguaná Peninsula, about 90km from Coro. From Las Piedras, Servivensa has daily flights to Aruba and Curaçao (see the Punto Fijo section for details).

From Coro airport, two small local carriers, Aerocaribe Coro (☎ 52 18 37) and Aeroservicios Paraguaná (☎ 52 76 26), fly light planes to Aruba and Curaçao (US$80 to either) provided they collect a minimum of three passengers. You can charter their planes to take you on other routes as well.

Bus The bus terminal is on Avenida Los Médanos, about 2km east of the city centre, and is easily accessible by frequent city transport. Half a dozen buses run daily to Caracas (US$7 ordinary, US$8.75 deluxe, seven hours). There are a few direct buses a day to Mérida (US$11 ordinary, US$13.50

deluxe, 12 hours) and to San Cristóbal (US$12.25 ordinary, US$14.75 deluxe, 13 hours); all these buses go via Maracaibo. Buses to Punto Fijo (US$1.50, 1¼ hours) and Maracaibo (US$5.50, four hours) run every half an hour until 5 to 6 pm. There are also a few buses a day to Adícora (US$1) on the eastern coast of Península de Paraguaná, and por puesto jeeps to Curimagua (US$2).

Boat Coro isn't on the coast and its port, La Vela de Coro, is 12km north-east of the city. At the time of writing there were no ferries from La Vela to Curaçao and Aruba (the Netherlands Antilles), but plans were to reintroduce these services by 1998.

PENÍNSULA DE PARAGUANÁ
• *area code* ☎ (069)

Shaped vaguely like a human head, the Península de Paraguaná is intriguing for more reasons than just its shape. Its geography, history and culture are quite different from the mainland. It was once an island, but a sandbar was gradually built up by wind and waves, and linked it to the continent.

Stretching about 60km from north to south and 50km from east to west, Paraguaná is Venezuela's largest peninsula, covering an area of about 2500 sq km. It's flat except for an unusual mountain, the 830m Cerro Santa Ana, which juts out from the middle of the peninsula. The lowland vegetation is xerophytic, featuring a number of semi-desert plant species, the most noticeable of which is the *cardón*, a columnar cactus tree. Only in the upper reaches of the Cerro is the plant life lusher, including a variety of rainforest species.

The climate is dry, with a period of light rain extending from October to December. On average, there are only 40 rainy days per year. There are no permanent rivers on the peninsula.

The original inhabitants of Paraguaná were the Amuay, Guaranao and Caquetío Indians, all belonging to the Arawak linguistic family. Today these people are extinct. Europeans first saw Paraguaná in 1499, when Alonso de Ojeda landed at Cabo de San Román on the northern tip of the peninsula. Some 130 years later, the Dutch settled the nearby islands of Curaçao, Aruba and Bonaire, and since then there has been a steady mix of the Spanish, Dutch and indigenous cultural influences.

The region was never densely populated, the lack of precious fresh water effectively hindering development. Today, fresh water is piped from the mainland to the whole of the peninsula.

The earliest colonial towns emerged not on the coast but inland, at the foot of the Cerro Santa Ana, as that was the only source of fresh water. They still preserve some of their old urban fabric, including their churches. The most remarkable colonial churches are in Moruy, Santa Ana, Jadacaquiva and Baraived.

Another notable leftover from the colonial past is the number of large country mansions scattered around the region, outside the towns. These were once the farmhouses of the *hatos*, the country estates. Most of them were built in the late 18th century – the period of an intensive trade with the Dutch Antilles – and therefore reflect the Dutch-Caribbean architectural style. The Casa de las Virtudes near Buena Vista is one of the best examples of these mansions but it can only be viewed from outside.

Things began to change with the oil boom. In the 1920s an oil terminal was built in Punto Fijo, to ship oil from Lago Maracaibo overseas. Refineries were constructed in the 1940s and Punto Fijo boomed, becoming the largest urban centre on the peninsula; it continues to grow rapidly. The area around the city is dominated by the oil industry and criss-crossed by multi-lane highways. The rest of the peninsula, however, hasn't rushed into progress and modernity. It's still dotted with small, old towns with their colonial churches.

Orientation

The peninsula offers a variety of attractions, including colonial towns, nature reserves, beaches, salinas and flamingos, plus a

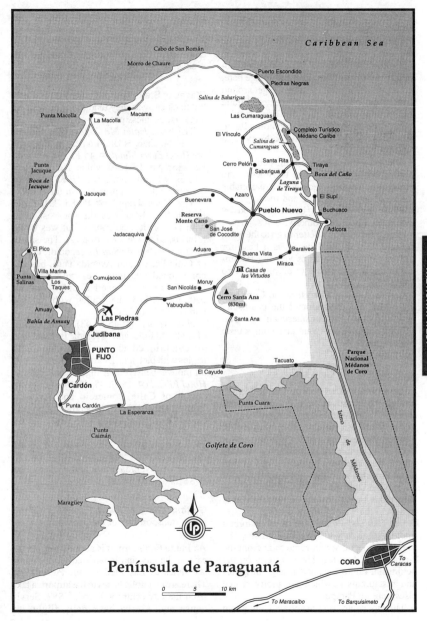

Caribbean Sea

Cabo de San Román
Morro de Chaure
Puerto Escondido
Piedras Negras
Salina de Baharigua
Punta Macolla
Macama
Las Cumaraguas
La Macolla
Complejo Turístico
Médano Caribe
El Vínculo
Salina de
Cumaraguas
Punta
Jacuque
Cerro Pelón
Santa Rita
Tiraya
Boca de
Jacuque
Sabarigua
Boca del Caño
Jacuque
Laguna
de Tiraya
El Supí
Buenevara
Azaro
Buchuaco
Reserva
Monte Cano
Pueblo Nuevo
Adícora
Jadacaquiva
San José
de Cocodite
El Pico
Aduare
Buena Vista
Baraived
Punta
Salinas
Villa Marina
Cumujacoa
Miraca
Los
Taques
San Nicolás
Moruy
Casa de
las Virtudes
Yabuquiba
Cerro Santa Ana
(830m)
Amuay
Las Piedras
Santa Ana
Bahía de Amuay
Judibana
PUNTO
FIJO
Parque
Nacional
Médanos
de Coro
Tacuato
Cardón
El Cayude
Punta Cardón
La Esperanza
Punta Cuara
Punta
Caimán
Istmo
de
Médanos
Golfete de Coro
Maragüey
CORO
To
Caracas
Península de Paraguaná
0   5   10 km
To Maracaibo
To Barquisimeto

general feeling of travelling through a semi-desert outback.

There's an array of sealed roads on the peninsula, except in the north-west which is almost uninhabited. Having an independent means of transport is a great advantage here, but if you don't you'll manage to get around using local buses and por puestos. Public transport is not frequent but does service most of the larger localities, including Punto Fijo, Santa Ana, Moruy, Pueblo Nuevo and Adícora.

The usual springboard for the peninsula is Coro, from where buses go to Adícora and Punto Fijo, the only places with a reasonable choice of accommodation and food.

Punto Fijo is much better serviced by public transport but otherwise it's an unremarkable place. It's better to go to the more pleasant Adícora and use it as a base for further excursions such as viewing flamingos at Laguna de Tiraya or hiking up Cerro Santa Ana.

Camel Tours of Coro (see the Coro section) have day trips around the peninsula, which may be worth considering if you're on a tough schedule and want just a quick taste of Paraguaná.

Punto Fijo

Punto Fijo appeared on maps in 1925, following the construction of an oil terminal serving Lago Maracaibo. The building of two refineries, in Amuay and Punta Cardón, boosted the development of the young town. Today it's an industrial city of about 110,000 inhabitants, approaching the size of Coro. In some aspects Punto Fijo has already outdistanced the state capital. Its airport, in Las Piedras, is busier than the one in Coro, as is trade and the way of life in general.

For tourists, Punto Fijo is of marginal interest, though you may need to stay the night here if you are en route to or from the Netherlands Antilles. The only city on the peninsula, Punto Fijo has a range of hotels and restaurants – which are pretty scarce elsewhere on Paraguaná.

The city centre is concentrated along two

north-south streets, Avenida Bolívar and Avenida Colombia. It's in this area that most of the hotels, restaurants, banks and bus company offices are located. Plaza Bolívar is several blocks east of the centre.

Places to Stay There are quite a lot of them, but book early as they tend to fill up with oil workers, business people, seamen etc.

The basic *Hotel Mi Cielo*, Calle Mariño No 19-24, charges US$4 a person. Better is the *Hotel Euzcalduna* (☎ 45 15 34), Avenida Ecuador No 18-160, which has doubles/triples without bath for US$8/10, and matrimoniales with private bath for US$9.

The *Hotel Miami* (☎ 45 85 35), Calle Falcón No 21-96, was the cheapest hotel with air-conditioned rooms, but was being refurbished as we went to press. The small, family-run *Pensión San Jorge*, on the corner of Calle Falcón and Avenida Perú, has air-conditioned matrimoniales with bath for US$15, air-conditioned doubles without bath for US$13 and triples with fan but without bath for US$12.

Hotel Venicia (☎ 45 57 43), on the corner of Calle Mariño and Avenida Bolívar, has air-conditioned matrimoniales/doubles/triples with bath and TV for US$15/17/19. A bit more expensive and slightly better is the *Hotel El Cid* (☎ 45 52 45, 45 19 67), on the corner of Calle Comercio and Avenida Bolívar. Other affordable central options include the *Hotel Caribe* (☎ 45 04 21, 45 63 54), Calle Comercio No 21-112 (US$15/20/25 a single/double/triple), and the *Hotel Presidente* (☎ 45 89 64, 45 51 56), on the corner of Avenida Perú and Calle Cuba (US$15/ 18/22).

Getting There & Away Punto Fijo is the major transport hub of the peninsula.

Air Punto Fijo's airport is about 10km northeast of the city and is labelled in all the air schedules as Las Piedras, not Punto Fijo. There are no public buses to the airport; a taxi from the city centre will cost US$7. Servivensa and Aserca have daily flights to

PLACES TO STAY
1 Hotel El Cid
6 Hotel Caribe
7 Hotel Presidente
10 Hotel Miami
11 Hotel Mi Cielo
12 Hotel Euzcalduna
13 Hotel Venicia
14 Pensión San Jorge

OTHER
2 Plaza del Obrero
3 Iglesia de Nuestra
  Señora de Coromoto
4 Expresos Occidente
5 Banco de Venezuela
8 Banco Unión
9 Banco Consolidado
15 Expresos Alianza
16 Banco Mercantil
17 Expresos San Cristóbal
18 Regional Bus Terminal
19 Market

Punto Fijo

THE NORTH-WEST

Caracas (US$59) and Aruba (US$68 one way, US$76 a 14-day return). Servivensa also flies direct to Maracaibo (US$43) and Curaçao (US$102 one way, US$150 a 14-day return).

Bus Punto Fijo has no central bus terminal; bus companies have their own offices scattered throughout the city centre. Expresos Occidente, Expresos Alianza and Expresos San Cristóbal service long-distance routes, including Caracas (US$10.50 deluxe, 8½ hours), Maracaibo (US$7 deluxe, 5½ hours) and Mérida (US$14.50 deluxe, 14 hours).

Regional buses depart from the market area, to the south of the centre. Buses to Coro (via a good 82km freeway) run every half an hour or less, until about 6 pm (US$1.50, 1¼ hours). There are also hourly buses to Pueblo Nuevo via the freeway and Santa Ana, and busetas to Pueblo Nuevo via Judibana and Moruy.

Boat Punto Fijo's port, Puerto del Guaranao, is about 2km south of the city centre. The Punto Fijo-Aruba ferries were not operating at the time of writing, but may recommence.

Santa Ana

Santa Ana is the oldest town on Paraguaná and its ancient capital. A Caquetío Indian settlement is reputed to have existed here since at least the 1540s. The church was originally built in the 16th century – thus being the first church on the peninsula – and extended and remodelled at the end of the 17th century. The unusual bell tower was added around 1750. Since then the church has hardly changed and remains one of the prettiest country churches in Venezuela. It also has an amazing retable, a curious piece of popular art graced with naive elements, dating from the mid-18th century.

Except for mass on Sunday at 9 am and the occasional cleaning, the church stays locked. The priest in the Casa Parroquial, on the northern side of Plaza Bolívar, may open it up for you.

There are several basic places to eat in town but nowhere to stay for the night. The Inparques office is just north of the church, opposite Restaurant El Cují. Buses between Pueblo Nuevo and Punto Fijo pass by on the main road every hour or so.

Moruy

The small village of Moruy, 7km north-west of Santa Ana, has another lovely colonial church – this one built around 1760 – though its internal furnishing and decoration are very modest. The village (along with the nearby hamlet of San Nicolás) is also noted for manufacturing *silletas paraguaneras*, chairs made from cactus wood of the cardón.

Moruy is a popular starting point for a hike up the Cerro Santa Ana (see the following section). There's nowhere to stay overnight in the village and not much to choose from as far as lunch or dinner go. Busetas or/and buses run regularly to Punto Fijo, Pueblo Nuevo and Santa Ana.

Cerro Santa Ana

This mountain, 830m above the plains, is visible from almost any point on the peninsula. The Cerro actually has three peaks; the highest is also the westernmost and it is dramatic from almost every angle. The mountain along with the surrounding area (19 sq km altogether) has been decreed a monumento natural and is under the control of Inparques.

The vegetation is stratified according to altitude, going from xerophytic species at the foot of the mountain to a type of cloudforest above 500m. There are even some orchids and bromeliads in the upper reaches.

There are two routes to the top. The main route begins at Moruy and heads eastwards for 800m along an unsealed road to the Inparques post and a bivouac area. From there, a proper trail heads to the highest peak. It used to be possible to go up to the summit, but Inparques has restricted tourist traffic to prevent excessive damage to the habitat. You can only walk as far as La Planicia, at about 550m.

Another starting point is the town of Santa Ana from where a rough road from Inparques office heads north to another bivouac site (a 30 minute walk). The trail which begins there leads to the lowest, eastern peak of the Cerro, then continues up westwards along the crest to the main peak. Here, too, there are restrictions which allow you only as far as La Hierbita at 550m.

Both Inparques posts at the foot of the mountain allow tourists to head uphill until 9 or 10 am. Hikers need to return by 3 pm and register with the respective office.

The peak is windy and frequently shrouded in cloud. Occasionally it rains in the upper reaches, especially between September and January, the wet months. Take a sweater and waterproof gear, just in case.

Pueblo Nuevo

Home to about 8000 people, Pueblo Nuevo is the largest town in the inland portion of Paraguaná. There are still some fine colonial houses and a church dating from 1758, but it was remodelled this century with modern fittings added.

Pueblo Nuevo has two or three family homes that work as informal posadas, and several restaurants serving inexpensive meals. Buses and busetas to Punto Fijo (via

Moruy) depart regularly, and there are also por puestos to Adícora.

Reserva Monte Cano

Monte Cano is a 16 sq km biological reserve, about 15km west of Pueblo Nuevo. The reserve was created to protect the only remaining lowland forest on the peninsula. Surprisingly enough, this small area features 62% of the plant species of Falcón state. The reserve's research station is in San José de Cocodite, accessible via a side road branching off to the west from the Pueblo Nuevo-Buena Vista road 2km south of Pueblo Nuevo. There's no public transport on this side road.

The reserve was run by Bioma ecological foundation, but since its recent closure the reserve's status remains unclear. Check for news with the Inparques offices.

Adícora

The small town of Adícora (population 4500), on Paraguaná's eastern coast, is one of the most popular tourist destinations on the peninsula. The town has quite a bit of old architecture, a beach, accommodation, food and a few local operators offering windsurfing and excursions around the peninsula. Founded on a small headland jutting into the sea, Adícora was used in the 18th century by the Compañía Guipuzcoana as one its trading bases, turning it into a prosperous town. Strolling around the streets, you'll still find brightly coloured Dutch-Caribbean houses characterised by barred windows with pedestals and decorated caps.

Windsurfing Over recent years, Adícora has been gaining fame as a windsurfing centre, with some of the best wave and wind conditions on Venezuela's coast. The winds are strongest and most consistent from January to June, and the calmest from September to November.

There are a few windsurfing operators in town, including Carlos Windsurfing Place (☎ 014 68 06 60) and Windsurfing Adícora (☎ 88 045). Both offer windsurfing courses, equipment rental and simple lodging. The

latter also has bicycles and diving gear for rent, and organises excursions around the peninsula.

Places to Stay & Eat Adícora has a better choice of hotels than any other town on the peninsula, except for Punto Fijo. Accommodation prices tend to vary from weekdays to weekends, and seem to be negotiable in some places on slow days, when there are few tourists around. On the other hand, hotels can be packed out with beachgoers on weekends and holidays.

The *Posada La Carantoña*, in a fine old house in the town's centre, one block back from the beach, is a pleasant place to stay and one of the cheapest at US$15 a double with bath and fan. Another good budget choice is the *Conjunto Residencial Montecano* (☎ 88 174), half a km from the waterfront along the road towards Pueblo Nuevo. Run by a friendly Italian-Venezuelan couple, the place offers doubles/triples with bath and fan for US$12/15 and has hearty inexpensive food in its own restaurant.

The *Posada Kitzberger* (☎ 88 004) on the Malecón (beach promenade) has rooms to sleep five people for US$30, and a restaurant. There are more restaurants along the beach, though most of them are only open on the weekends.

Possibly the most spectacular place to stay is the *Campamento Vacacional La Troja* (☎ 88 048), occupying an entire block in the middle of the town. This walled complex, built in the traditional style and set in a lush garden (quite unusual on the peninsula), offers comfortable accommodation and food. A package including breakfast and dinner will cost around US$35 per person. It can be booked in Caracas on ☎ (02) 952 83 52.

Getting There & Away Adícora is linked to Coro by several daily buses, the last departing at around 4 pm. There are also por puestos to Pueblo Nuevo (12km).

Lagunas & Salinas

The **Laguna de Tiraya**, about 6km north of Adícora, is the area where flamingos feed, mostly from November to January, but you can be pretty sure of finding smaller or larger numbers of them almost all year round. There is no public transport to the lagoon, but you can walk or try to hitch (the traffic is mainly on weekends, at other times it's pretty sporadic).

From Adícora, take the road to El Supí and turn left onto the recently sealed road that branches off to the west 4km north of Adícora. This road leads to Santa Rita, and skirts the lagoon. The flamingos may be quite close to shore or off in the distance, on the opposite, eastern side of the lagoon.

Further north, between Santa Rita and Las Cumaraguas, is the **Salina de Cumaraguas**, where salt is mined using rudimentary methods. Several kilometres north-west of Las Cumaraguas is the **Salina de Bajarigua**, which is also a feeding ground for flamingos; at times it attracts an even larger colony of them than Laguna Tiraya. There's public transport on a sealed road from Las Cumaraguas to Pueblo Nuevo via El Vínculo.

Be prepared for the heat; take sufficient water, sunscreen, sunglasses and a hat. If you have your own transport, you can explore the region further north as far as **Cabo de San Román**, which is the northernmost point of Venezuela.

Beaches

The beaches on Paraguaná don't perhaps match those of Morrocoy or Henri Pittier, and usually lack shade because coconut palms are a rare sight here. Like all other beaches in Venezuela, they are quiet on weekdays, and swamped with people on the weekends.

The beaches on the eastern coast stretch almost all the way from Adícora to Piedras Negras. **Adícora** is the most popular beach resort, though **El Supí** and **Buchuaco**, farther north, have arguably finer beaches. **Tiraya** is less popular with holidaymakers because it's harder to get there. On the west coast, the popular beaches include **Villa Marina** and **El Pico**, both serviced by local transport from Punto Fijo.

SIERRA DE SAN LUIS
* *area code* ☎ (068)

The Sierra de San Luis is the belt of verdant mountains stretching just to the south of the arid coast of Coro. It is a vital source of water for the whole coastal area, including the Península de Paraguaná. About 200 sq km of the rugged terrain was made into a national park in 1987. Elevations within the park range from 200m up to 1501m at the Cerro Galicia, the park's highest point. Average temperatures range between 25°C and 15°C, respectively. Annual rainfall is moderate, not exceeding 1500mm, and the wettest months are October to December.

The Sierra boasts a few picturesque towns, several waterfalls, about 20 caves and a dozen *simas* (deep vertical holes in the earth). It offers a fresh pleasant climate, exotic forests full of birds, an adequate array of hotels and restaurants, reasonable public transport and a good choice of walking paths.

Orientation

San Luis, Cabure and Curimagua are the major towns of the Sierra. All three are accessible by public transport from Coro, but each one by a different route. Curimagua is the closest to Coro (45km) and has the most frequent transport. Curimagua and its environs also have the best choice of accommodation, and provide the most popular and convenient base to explore the region.

Of the three towns, San Luis is possibly the most picturesque. Founded in 1590, it's the oldest Spanish settlement in the area and has preserved some of its colonial architecture, including a fine church. Of the waterfalls, the Cataratas de Hueque are the largest and perhaps the most spectacular. Among the caves, the Cueva de Zárraga and Cueva del Encanto are the most frequent tourist destinations. The Haitón de Guarataro is the most impressive local sima. It's 305m deep, but the mouth is only about 12m in diameter. There's also the Camino de Los Españoles, an old Spanish trail between Cabure and La Negrita; its best preserved part is near Acarite, where there's a brick bridge from around 1790.

PLACES TO STAY
1 Posada El Conuquero
2 Casa de Campo
3 Finca El Monte Santiago
4 Posada El Trapichito
5 Hotel Falconés
6 Hotel Apolo
7 Caravan
8 Posada El Gigante del Sabor
9 Posada La Soledad
10 Posada Paraguariba
11 Posada El Duende
12 Hotel La Montaña
13 Club Campestre Camino Viejo

THE NORTH-WEST

Sierra de
San Luis

0   2.5   5 km

Scattered dwellings

Places to Stay & Eat

With few exceptions, the places to stay in the region are clean, pleasant and friendly. They don't offer excessive luxuries, but are adequate, comfortable and inexpensive. Most are family-run posada-style places, operated directly by the owners. Many of the hotel owners/managers will offer excursions around the sights in the area, or at least will provide information on how to get there.

Curimagua & Around There are at least four places in the town alone. The Dutch-owned *Hotel Falconés* (☎ 51 82 71) has seven triples with bath and hot water for US$24 each, plus a restaurant serving reasonable food, including set lunch for US$7.

The nearby Argentine-run *Hotel Apolo* (☎ 51 76 34) is bigger, provides similar standards for much the same price, and has a slightly cheaper restaurant.

The *Posada El Gigante del Sabor*, at the western end of the town, is the cheapest place around: US$9/12 a matrimonial/triple. It also serves some of the cheapest meals. Across the road, a Lithuanian family rents out a *caravan* which can sleep four people, for US$20.

About 5km west of Curimagua, on the slope of the Cerro Galicia, is the colonial-style *Posada La Soledad*. This is the most isolated and highest hotel in the Sierra. Built with traditional techniques and materials, this typical house with a central patio may become one of the loveliest hotels in the region, when it opens. The owner, Pol Acosta (☎ 51 24 84 in Coro), is one of the best guides to the region and plans to run horse riding excursions.

Two km east of Curimagua, off the road to Coro, is the *Posada El Trapichito*, which offers four simple matrimoniales at US$18 each, and has a pleasant restaurant. Three km farther on along the road to Coro, is the *Finca El Monte Santiago*, a nine hectare farm owned and run by a friendly Swiss couple, Ernst and Ursula. They have just two double rooms, at US$16 each, but expect to finish another two by 1998. They prepare rich meals for guests, with just about everything home grown and home made, and organise hikes in the area.

San Luis The family-run *Posada Paraguariba* (☎ 63 110), Calle San Antonio, is the only place to stay in town. Rooms with bath and hot water are good value at US$12/14/16 a double/triple/quad, and meals are available at the posada's own restaurant, which provides attractive sweeping views over the valley.

Cabure The loveliest place to stay here is the *Posada El Duende* (☎ 61 10 79), about 1.5km up a steep rough road from the town. Built in a traditional rustic style, the posada has simple but comfortable doubles with bath for US$14 and a six-person dorm for US$20, plus an appealing restaurant.

The *Club Campestre Camino Viejo* (☎ 61 10 43), next to the local cemetery, has four matrimoniales for US$18 each and two eight-bed cabañas for US$30, plus a restaurant and a swimming pool. The Spanish bridle path begins here.

The *Hotel La Montaña* (☎ 61 11 77) has matrimoniales for US$10 (also rented by the hour), a restaurant and a disco.

Other Areas The *Casa de Campo*, halfway between Coro and Curimagua, is the most upmarket accommodation in the region. This large hillside holiday complex offers a variety of rooms, suites and cabañas plus a restaurant and bar service. Expect a double to cost US$40 to US$80. Information and booking is available through their Coro office (☎ 52 63 46).

Further to the north, in the village of Santa María de la Chapa, is the pleasant and comfortable *Posada El Conuquero*, which costs US$18/20 for a matrimonial/double with bath and hot water, and has its own restaurant.

Getting There & Away
The usual point of departure for the Sierra is Coro's bus terminal. Por puesto jeeps to Curimagua (via La Chapa) depart from 5 am till mid afternoon (US$2, 1½ hours). There are also infrequent carritos to San Luis (via El Tigre) and Cabure (via Pueblo Nuevo de La Sierra).

PARQUE NACIONAL MORROCOY
At the eastern edge of Falcón state, Morrocoy national park comprises a strip of the coast and the offshore area dotted with islands, islets and cays, many islands skirted with white-sand beaches and surrounded by coral reefs. Morrocoy is one of the most spectacular littoral environments on Venezuela's coast.

The park is also well known for its variety of wading and water birds including ibis, herons, cormorants, ducks, pelicans and flamingos. They inhabit, either permanently or seasonally, some of the islands and coastal mangroves, especially the Golfete de Cuare, which is one of Venezuela's richest bird breeding grounds and has been declared a wildlife refuge.

The park is a popular destinations for Venezuelan beachgoers, who come en masse on holidays and weekends and leave the islands badly littered. The fragile island environment is beginning to suffer from human interference, though you can still enjoy deserted and apparently virgin beaches on weekdays.

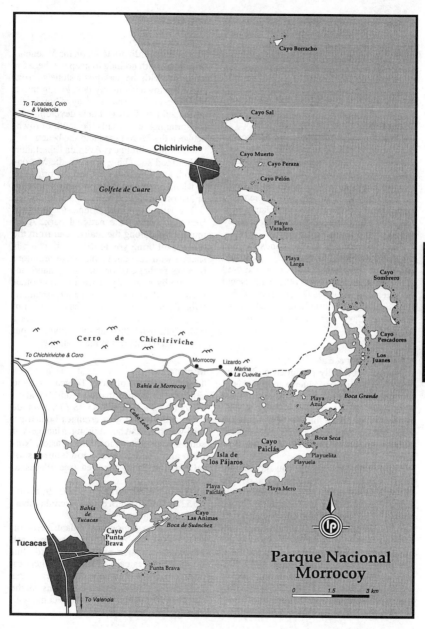

Cayo Borracho

To Tucacas, Coro
& Valencia

Cayo Sal

Chichiriviche

Cayo Muerto
Cayo Peraza

Golfete de Cuare

Cayo Pelón

Playa
Varadero

Playa
Larga

Cayo
Sombrero

Cerro de Chichiriviche

Cayo
Pescadores

To Chichiriviche & Coro

Morrocoy
Lizardo
Marina
La Cuevita

Los
Juanes

Bahía de Morrocoy

Playa
Azul

Boca Grande

Caño León

Boca Seca

**Cayo
Paiclás**

Playuelita
Playuela

**Isla de
los Pájaros**

Playa
Paiclás

Playa Mero

*Bahía
de
Tucacas*

Cayo
Las Ánimas
Boca de Suánchez

Tucacas

Cayo
Punta
Brava

Punta Brava

To Valencia

**Parque Nacional
Morrocoy**

0   1.5   3 km

More significantly, some of the coral has died recently, believed to be the result of a chemical leak from a nearby oil refinery in early 1996. Official sources are silent on the issue, but independent biologists are monitoring the damage and claim that up to half of the coral is dead.

Orientation

The park lies between the towns of Tucacas and Chichiriviche (detailed in the following sections), which are its main gateways. Both these towns have well organised boat services to the islands, as well as an array of places to stay and eat. You can use them as a springboard for day trips to the islands or, if you have a tent or a hammock, you can stay on the islands themselves.

The most popular of the islands is Cayo Sombrero, which has fine coral reefs and some of the best beaches. It's more exposed to the open sea than most other islands and the breeze means it has fewer insects. Other places good for snorkelling include Cayo Borracho, Cayo Peraza, Playa Mero and Playuela.

Places to Stay & Eat

Camping is officially permitted on four islands: Sal, Sombrero, Muerto and Paiclás. If you plan on staying in a hammock, make absolutely sure you take along a fine mosquito net. All the four islands have beach restaurants and/or food kiosks, but some of them may be closed on weekdays in the slow season.

Before you go camping, you should contact Inparques office in Tucacas, and pay the camping fee of US$2.50 per person a night at the Banco Unión in Tucacas or Banco Industrial de Venezuela in Chichiriviche.

When camping on the islands, take food, sufficient fresh water, snorkelling gear, good sun protection and a reliable insect repellent. The insects – small biting gnats known locally as the *puri-puri* – are most annoying in windless months, usually November to February. You can use camping gas stoves but no open fire is permitted.

TUCACAS
* *pop 15,000*
* *area code* ☎ (042)

This is a hot, ordinary town on the Valencia-Coro road, with nothing to keep you here for long. Yet, with the park just a stone's throw away, the town is quickly developing into a holiday centre, and has an array of hotels and other facilities. Plenty of new developments are springing up towards the south of town, between the Morón road and the beach.

The town's lifeline is Avenida Libertador, a 1km road stretching between the Morón-Coro highway in the west and the bridge to an island in the east. Many businesses are on or just off this street.

The island over the bridge, Cayo Punta Brava, is part of the national park. A 15 minute walk along the sealed road from the bridge will bring you to the beach which is shaded with coconut palms; there are more beaches farther east on the same island, accessible by road. If you want to visit other islands of the park, go to the *embarcadero* (wharf), in the town close to the bridge, from where boats can take you for a trip along *caños* (channels) through mangroves, or put you down on one of the many islands.

Information

There's no tourist office in Tucacas, but you can get some information from Varadero Tours (☎ 83 47 45; fax 83 38 81), Avenida Libertador, which also arranges boat trips, bird-watching and horse riding. Managers of some budget hotels, including Carlos, Norbert and André, are good sources of information about the area (see Places to Stay & Eat).

The Inparques office (☎ 83 00 69; fax 83 00 53) is at the eastern end of Avenida Libertador, close to the bridge.

The Banco Unión, Avenida Libertador, just off the Coro-Morón highway, gives cash advances on Visa and MasterCard, but doesn't changes cash or travellers cheques. Varadero Tours, Submatur and other places may change your dollars and cheques but the rates can be poor, so it's better to come with enough bolívares.

Diving & Snorkelling

Submatur (☎ 83 00 82; fax 83 10 51), Calle Ayacucho No 6, between Plaza Bolívar and the bridge, is a diving centre and shop owned by Mike Osborn. It sells everything you could possibly need for snorkelling and diving, and some of the equipment can be rented. The centre is run by professional licensed diving instructors and offers diving courses and guided dives.

Beginners can take a one day course, including a short theoretical introduction and exercises, followed by a half-hour dive for US$70. Each following day includes two dives and costs US$60. The centre also offers a four day PADI diving course which consists of theory (in English or French on request) and eight dives, for US$330, and you get an international PADI certificate. In both courses, the cost of equipment and boats to the diving spots are included in the price (but not accommodation or food). Submatur also organises boat excursions to Los Roques and Las Aves (US$130 per person a day, all-inclusive) and can design a programme to suit your needs. You can pay in US dollars.

Snorkelling gear can be rented from many boat operators and hotel managers (about US$7 per day), as well as from the Submatur diving shop.

Places to Stay & Eat

Most of the budget hotels are together on Avenida Libertador, halfway between the Morón-Coro road and the bridge. The cheapest is the *Hotel La Esperanza* (☎ 83 09 50), Avenida Libertador No 6, managed by a German guy, Norbert. Matrimoniales with bath and fan cost US$6, and rooms with two double beds go for US$8. You can drink till late in the adjacent tasca, and eat in the reasonably priced *Restaurant La Esperanza*, next door.

Right across the road is the Hotel Las Palmas (☎ 83 14 93), better known as the *Posada de Carlos*, after the name of the owner. Neither name is on the door; the place is recognisable by the si hay habitación inscription. The hotel offers matrimoniales/

doubles with bath for US$8/12, and you can use the kitchen and fridge at no extra cost.

Other budget places in the same area include *Hotel Oti Daly Mar* (☎ 83 14 78), the *Hotel La Suerte* (☎ 83 13 32) and the *Posada Johnatan* (☎ 83 02 39). All three have rooms with bath and fan for much the same as the Posada de Carlos. The Johnatan and La Suerte establishments also have matrimoniales with air-conditioning for around US$16.

Belgian André Nahon, one of the Submatur instructors, runs the 10-room *Submar Inn* (☎ 83 17 54), built in a pleasant garden behind his house. Good doubles/triples with bath and fan cost US$10/13, or you can sling your hammock for US$4. The place is beyond the Hospital of Tucacas, on the unsafe side of the road, and is unmarked. Don't try to look for it if you arrive after dark; call him from the bus stop and he'll probably come and accompany you to his hotel.

The centrally located *Hotel Gaeta* (☎ 83 04 14), Avenida Libertador No 34, appears to be overpriced at US$35/40/42 for an air-conditioned matrimonial/double/triple with bath and TV. Better value is offered at the nearby *Hotel Turístico Manaure* (☎ 83 06 11; fax 83 06 12), Avenida Silva, which has spacious singles/doubles/triples/quads for US$45/50/ 60/72, breakfast included. The hotel has its own restaurant and a swimming pool with a tobogán (water slide).

Budget restaurants (apart from La Esperanza, listed above) include *Nuevo Tito*, on Calle Sucre close to the Hotel Johnatan, and *El Timón*, diagonally opposite Banco Unión. For somewhere more upmarket, try the *Venemar*, close to the bridge.

Getting There & Away

Bus As Tucacas is on the main Valencia-Coro road there are frequent buses to both Valencia (US$2, two hours) and Coro (US$4, four hours). Buses from Valencia pass through regularly on their way to Chichiriviche (US$0.60, 40 minutes).

Getting Around

Boats to the islands normally take up to seven or eight people and charge a flat rate per trip. Prices to all the islands and beaches are posted next to the ticket office close to the wharf. They are return fares per boat, not per person. The fare to the farthest islands such as Cayo Sombrero or Cayo Pescadores is around US$55 return. The closer (and cheaper) destinations include Playa Paiclás (US$25), Playa Mero (US$30), Playuela (US$33) and Playa Azul (US$38). The boatman will pick you up from the island in the afternoon or at a later date, depending on when you want to return. On weekdays during the off-season, you can usually beat the price down.

Some hotels have their own boats (or have contracts with boat owners) and offer excursions. These are mostly full day trips around the islands with stops for snorkelling and relaxing on beaches, usually including Cayo Sombrero. These excursions can work out cheaper than those arranged at the boat wharf.

CHICHIRIVICHE
- *pop 6000*
- *area code* ☎ (042)

Chichiriviche is the northern gateway to the park, providing access to half a dozen neighbouring cays. The town is smaller than Tucacas but equally undistinguished and unattractive. Accommodation here is more expensive than in Tucacas, but boat fares are cheaper.

The access to the town is from the west, by the 12km road which runs along a causeway through mangrove swamps. The area along this road is a favourite feeding ground for flamingos, which mostly gather here between August and January, but a small community can remain up to March or even April, as long as there's sufficient water. November is usually the peak month, when up to 5000 birds can stay in the area.

Upon entering the town, the road divides. Its main branch, Avenida Zamora, continues straight ahead to the bus terminus and the town's centre, and ends at the waterfront next to the northern wharf. The southern branch, Avenida Cemento, goes to the cement plant south of the town, passing on the way

through several hotels and providing access to the southern wharf.

Information
Varadero Tours (☎ 86 919), Avenida Zamora, can provide some tourist information, organise tours and exchange cash and travellers cheques (poor rates). The Banco Industrial de Venezuela, Avenida Zamora, changes cash dollar bills (but not travellers cheques) at reasonable rates and gives advances on Visa (but not on MasterCard).

Diving
The Swiss-run Agua-Fun Diving (☎ & fax 86 265), Calle El Sol, in the southern part of the town, is a professional and well equipped diving school. It offers diving services similar to those of Submatur of Tucacas, at roughly the same prices.

Places to Stay & Eat
There are several pleasant budget places to stay close to the bus terminus. The *Guest House América Mía* (☎ & fax 86 547), above the Banco Industrial, costs US$7 per person in doubles with bath and fan, and you can use the kitchen and fridge. The place is run by a helpful Argentine couple, Enrique and Silvia, who also organise boat trips and offer laundry service.

The nearby *Residencia La Perrera* (☎ & fax 86 372), run by an Italian couple, Innocente and Elisabetta, is also a good and friendly place and costs much the same as the América Mía.

Another pleasant family option in the area is the Spanish-run *Villa Gregoria* (☎ 86 359), Calle Mariño, one block north of Avenida Zamora. Singles/doubles/triples with bath and fan are rated at US$10/15/20; rooms on the 1st floor are more attractive. The *Residencias Delia* (☎ 86 089), a few paces west along the same street, is also friendly, but only has rooms with shared baths. It's marginally cheaper than the Gregoria.

If you're hunting for the cheapest place in town, check the basic *Hotel El Centro* (☎ 86 906), near the waterfront. The entrance is at the back of the *Panadería El Centro* (which does good breakfast) on Avenida Zamora. Claustrophobic rooms cost US$5 per person. Next door is the *Habitaciones Rigoberto* (no sign), which offers better rooms with bath for the same US$5 a person price.

The *Hotel Capri* (☎ 86 026), Avenida Zamora opposite the Panadería El Centro, is a reasonable air-conditioned option. Matri-moniales/doubles/triples with bath and hot water are US$17/22/27. The new *Hotel Caribana* (☎ 86 837), a few hundred metres inland along the same road, offers similar standards and prices.

In the southern part of the town are the German-run *Posada Alemania* (☎ 86 979), set in a pleasant coconut-palm garden (US$7 per person), and the dearer *Hotel Náutico* (☎ 86 024) on the waterfront.

The town's most expensive options include the *Hotel La Garza* (☎ 86 711; fax 86 347) on Avenida Zamora at the corner of Avenida Cemento, and the *Hotel Mario* (☎ 86 811; fax 86 096), just across the road. Doubles in either of these will cost around US$50; both have swimming pools.

For cheap food try *El Juncal* or *Taberna de Pablo*, both on Avenida Zamora, or *Pizzería Casamare* on the waterfront. Among the best places are *Txalupa*, on the waterfront, and *Il Ristorante*, at the Hotel Capri.

Getting There & Away

Chichiriviche is about 22km off the main Morón-Coro highway, and is serviced by half-hourly *busetas* (small buses) from Valencia (US$2.50, 2½ hours); keep an eye on your bags on this route.

There are no direct buses to Chichiriviche from Caracas or Coro. To get there from Caracas, take any of the frequent buses to Valencia (US$3, three hours) and change there. From Coro, take any bus to Valencia, get off in Sanare, the turn-off for Chichiriviche (US$3.75, 3¾ hours), and catch the Valencia-Chichiriviche buseta.

Getting Around

The town has two wharves: the Embarcadero Playa Norte, near the eastern end of Avenida Zamora; and the Embarcadero Playa Sur, about 1km south, near the Hotel Náutico. Boat fares are the same at both wharves. As in Tucacas, the boat takes a maximum of seven to eight passengers and the fare is per boat. The return fare to the closest cays, such as Cayo Muerto, Cayo Sal or Cayo Pelón, is about US$20, whereas the return fare to the farthest cays, such as Cayo Borracho, Cayo Sombrero or Cayo Pescadores, is about US$42. The return time is up to you, and haggling over the price is also possible here.

Lara & Yaracuy States

BARQUISIMETO
- *pop 800,000*
- *area code* ☎ (051)

Barquisimeto is Venezuela's fourth largest city, after Caracas, Maracaibo and Valencia. It's the capital of Lara state and an important commercial, industrial and transport centre. At an altitude of 550m, the city has a warm, relatively dry climate with a mean temperature of 24°C.

Originally founded in 1552 on the Río Buría, Barquisimeto moved three times before it was eventually established at its present-day location in 1563. Its growth was slow, as the Indian tribes in the region were particularly fierce in defending their territory. The 1812 earthquake destroyed much of the town and its colonial architecture.

As in almost every other large city in Venezuela, the rush to modernise in recent decades has been intensive and indiscriminate and carried out at the expense of those Spanish structures which had survived the earthquake.

Today Barquisimeto is a predominantly modern city dotted with a number of shady parks and plazas. It's not a major travellers' destination, but it has some minor sights and a developed tourist infrastructure. There are also some rather interesting places around Barquisimeto.

Information

Tourist Office Dirección de Turismo (☎ 53 75 44) is in Edificio Fundalara on Avenida Libertador, near the Complejo Ferial. It's over 2km north-east of the centre, beyond Parque Bararida. It's open Monday to Friday from 8 am to noon and 2.30 to 6 pm.

Inparques The Inparques office (☎ 54 81 18; ☎ & fax 54 91 03) is in the south-eastern corner of the Parque del Este, on Avenida Libertador. It's open Monday to Friday from 8 am to noon and 2 to 5.30 pm.

Money Most of the major banks are on or just off Avenida 20 (the main commercial street in the centre). Turisol (☎ 51 86 34, 51 87 34) is in Edificio Hotel Hevelín, Planta Baja, Local 1, Avenida Vargas between Carreras 21 and 22.

Things to See

The **Plaza Bolívar**, the original centre of the city, adorned with yet another replica of the Bolívar statue in Caracas, is now lined with modern edifices except for the **Iglesia de la Concepción** on the southern side of the square. This was Barquisimeto's first cathedral, but it was destroyed in the earthquake of 1812 and rebuilt 30 years later in a different style.

A few steps south of the church is the **Museo de Barquisimeto**, located in a large building with a rectangular courtyard and a chapel in the middle. It was built in the 1910s as a hospital. From 1954 until 1977 it was used for various purposes, until authorities decided to demolish it to make way for modern buildings. Thanks to public protests it was restored and turned into a museum which now features temporary exhibitions. It's open Tuesday to Friday from 9 am to 5 pm, Saturday to Sunday from 10 am to 5 pm.

Plaza Lara, two blocks east of Plaza Bolívar, is the city's only area with colonial character, thanks to the restored historic buildings lining the square. The **Iglesia de San Francisco**, on the southern side of the plaza, was built in 1865 and did the honours as the second cathedral, until the modern **Catedral** was constructed in the 1960s on the

corner of Avenida Venezuela (Carrera 26) and Avenida Simón Rodríguez (Calle 29). Quite an innovative design, the curving paraboloidal concrete roof has unfortunately already heavily blackened. The cathedral is only open for mass (several times on Sunday, at 6 pm on weekdays) so plan accordingly if you want to see its centrally located high altar.

The **Parque Bararida**, on the north-eastern outskirts of the centre, has small botanical and zoological gardens.

Special Events

The city's biggest annual event is the Fiestas Patronales de la Divina Pastora. Although the patron saint's day is 14 January (when the image of the Virgin Mary is paraded from the shrine in Santa Rosa village into the city), the celebrations go for several days before and after the official day, and the Complejo Ferial (fairgrounds) stages an agricultural fair, band concerts, sports events etc.

Places to Stay

If you're just in transit, there are half a dozen budget hotels on the northern side of the bus terminal. For somewhere better in the area, try the *Hotel Villa Lara* (☎ 46 16 21, 46 43 54), on the corner of Avenida Rómulo Gallegos and Carrera 21. Expect to pay US$15/18/20 for air-conditioned matrimoniales/doubles/triples with bath and hot water.

In the city centre, one of the cheapest is the simple *Hotel del Centro* (☎ 31 45 24, 31 53 46), Avenida 20 near the corner of Calle 26. Doubles/triples with fan and bath cost US$6/8 while air-conditioned doubles/triples/quadruples go for US$8/9/10.

Hotel Lido (☎ 31 55 68, 31 52 79) at Carrera 16 No 26-92, one block west of Plaza Bolívar, is a small, family-run place with air-conditioning and TV. Matrimoniales/doubles/triples cost US$12/15/17. Similar in price and standards, and owned by the same people, is *Hotel Savoy* (☎ 31 51 34) on Carrera 18 between Calles 21 and 22. Slightly better and more expensive is the *Hotel Florida* (☎ 32 98 04) on Carrera 19 between Calles 31 and 32 (US$13/17/19 a

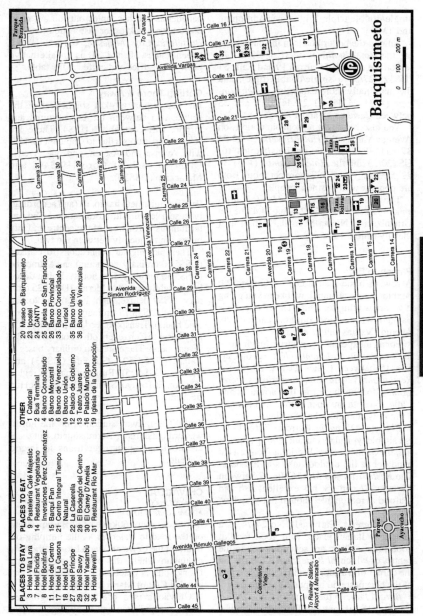

Barquisimeto

0   100   200 m

THE NORTH-WEST

PLACES TO STAY
3   Hotel Villa Lara
7   Hotel Florida
8   Hotel Bonifrán
11 Hotel del Centro
17 Hotel La Casona
18 Hotel Lido
27 Hotel Príncipe
29 Hotel Savoy
32 Hotel Yacambú
34 Hotel Hevelín

PLACES TO EAT
9   Pastelería Café Majestic
14 Restaurant Vegetariano
    Inversiones Pérez Colmenárez
15 Barquí Pan
21 Centro Integral Tiempo
    Natural
22 La Caserella
28 El Bodegón del Centro
30 El Caney D'Amelia
31 Restaurant Río Mar

OTHER
1   Catedral
2   Bus Terminal
4   Banco Consolidado
5   Banco Mercantil
6   Banco de Venezuela
10 Banco Unión
12 Palacio de Gobierno
13 Teatro Juares
16 Palacio Municipal
19 Iglesia de la Concepción
20 Museo de Barquisimeto
23 Ipostel
24 CANTV
25 Iglesia de San Francisco
26 Banco Provincial
33 Banco Consolidado &
    Turisol
35 Banco Unión
36 Banco de Venezuela

single/double/triple with air-conditioning and TV).

Among the better hotels in the city centre are the *Hotel Bonifrán* (☎ 31 68 09, 31 75 09) on the corner of Carrera 19 and Calle 31 (US$25/27/30 a single/double/triple), and the marginally more expensive *Hotel Príncipe* (☎ 31 21 11, 31 25 44) on Calle 23 between Carreras 18 and 19.

You also have two reasonable options on Avenida Vargas: the *Hotel Hevelín* (☎ 52 24 87, 51 37 29) with doubles/triples for US$20/23 and the *Hotel Yacambú* (☎ 51 30 22, 51 32 29) for US$2 more per room. Both are popular with business people.

The best is the five-star *Hotel Barquisimeto Hilton* (☎ 53 60 22; fax 54 43 65) in Urbanización Nueva Segovia, 2km east of the city centre.

Places to Eat

A row of basic restaurants on Carrera 24, next to the bus terminal, will keep you going if you're waiting for a bus. The city centre is packed with eating outlets, particularly Avenida Vargas and its environs.

For an inexpensive vegetarian lunch, go to the *Centro Integral Tiempo Natural* on Carrera 15 between Calles 24 and 25, or the *Restaurant Vegetariano Inversiones Pérez Colmenárez* on the corner of Carrera 18 and Calle 26. Both are open from about noon to 3 pm only, and closed on Sunday.

El Caney D'Amelia, Carrera 17 No 20-74, is a simple typical restaurant serving appetising, inexpensive comida criolla. You can eat inside or at the outdoor tables at the back. The *Restaurant Río Mar*, Calle 17 between Carreras 17 and 18, has excellent fish and seafood at reasonable, though not very low, prices.

La Caserella, Carrera 15 No 24-74, is a new cosy Italian place, with good food at good prices. There are several tascas in the centre, of which *El Bodegón del Centro*, on the corner of Carrera 19 and Calle 21, is one of the cheapest and is open till midnight.

Barqui Pan, on the corner of Calle 26 and Carrera 18, is one of the better central

panaderías and has tables outside – a good place for a breakfast or just a cup of coffee. *Pastelería Café Majestic*, Carrera 19 between Calles 30 and 31, is an alternative place for pastries and coffee at the table.

Getting There & Away

Air The airport is 4km south-west of the centre; taxi between the bus terminal and airport will cost about US$4. There are several departures a day to Caracas (US$58) with Avensa and Aserca, and one Avensa flight to each of Coro (US$40) and Maracaibo (US$50).

Bus Barquisimeto has roads (and accordingly buses) leading in all directions. The bus terminal is north-west of the centre and city buses run frequently between the two.

There are regular connections to Caracas (US$5.50 ordinary, six hours) and Maracaibo (US$5.50 ordinary, five hours). Half a dozen buses nightly depart to Mérida (US$7.25 ordinary, US$9 deluxe, eight hours) and to San Cristóbal (US$8.75 ordinary, US$11 deluxe, nine hours). Transporte Federación runs ordinary buses to Coro every other hour (US$6.25, seven hours). There are also ordinary buses to Valera (US$3.50), Guanare (US$3) and Barinas (US$4.25). Buses within the region (Quíbor, El Tocuyo, Sanare, Chivacoa etc) run frequently.

Train The railway station is on the north-western outskirts of Barquisimeto, but there are no longer passenger trains to Puerto Cabello.

CHIVACOA
- *pop 45,000*
- *area code* ☎ (051)

Chivacoa, about 60km east of Barquisimeto on the road to Valencia, is the jumping-off point for the Cerro de María Lionza, the holy mountain where the para-religious María Lionza cult is practised (see the boxed text entitled Cult of María Lionza).

Chivacoa is a pretty undistinguished town, except for an unusually large number

Cult of María Lionza

Venezuela's most curious quasi-religious phenomenon, the Cult of María Lionza is an amalgam of pre-Hispanic indigenous creeds, African voodoo and Christian practices. It involves magic, witchcraft, esoteric rites and trance rituals.

There are few serious studies of the cult, so many of its aspects, such as its origins or doctrines, are still obscure. What is clear, however, is that the cult attracts more and more followers every year and spiritual centres proliferate in cities throughout the country. The 'guides', or intermediaries, who run these centres, claim to be able to communicate with deities and spirits, heal the sick, tell the future and the like.

In search of new inspirations – or in order to give more colour and mystery to the cult – some guides adopt ideas and rites from other parts of the world such as India, Japan and the Philippines. Consequently, the cult vocabulary is dotted with a plethora of exotic terms like 'karma', 'reincarnation', 'yoga', 'transmigration of souls' etc. This makes the María Lionza cult even more confusing, obscure and difficult to investigate.

The cult is pantheistic and involves a constellation of deities, spirits and other personalities with very diverse origins, the number of which is growing year by year. At the top of the hierarchy is María Lionza, a female deity, usually portrayed as a beautiful woman riding a tapir. La Reina, or Queen – as she is commonly referred to – is followed by countless divinities: historical or legendary personages, saints, powers of nature etc, usually grouped into *cortes* or courts. The list of the most popular deities includes Cacique Guaicaipuro, Negro Primero, Virgen de Coromoto, Negro Felipe and Dr José Gregorio Hernández. For many followers, Hernández is the second in importance after the Reina.

Although the María Lionza cult is practised throughout Venezuela, its most sacred area and the focus for pilgrimages is the mountain range commonly referred to as the Cerro de María Lionza, south of the town of Chivacoa in Yaracuy state. Devotees come here all year round, mostly on weekends, to practice their rites. The biggest celebrations, drawing in thousands, are held on 12 October, El Día de la Raza (Discovery of America), and during the Semana Santa, or the Holy Week. ■

of *perfumerías* selling everything imaginable related to the cult. It's an interesting experience to browse through these shops, to get a taste of what the María Lionza phenomenon is. Here you'll find an extensive collection of books and brochures dealing with magic, witchcraft, reading the future and the like, cigars and candles (indispensable ritual accessories), as well as an unbelievable range of essences, perfumes, lotions etc. Here you can also familiarise yourself with the cult's pantheon, as every perfumería has a complete stock of plaster figures of the deities in every size and colour.

Places to Stay

Chivacoa has a range of places to stay, including *Hotel Abruzzese* (☎ 83 04 19), Avenida 9 No 10-25; *Hotel Venezia* (☎ 83 05 44), on the corner of Calle 12 and Avenida 9; and *Hotel Leonardo* (☎ 83 08 66), on the corner of Calle 11 and Avenida 9. All are reasonably priced and within a couple of blocks of Plaza Bolívar.

Getting There & Away

There are plenty of buses between Barquisimeto and Valencia, and between Barquisimeto and San Felipe, which will put you off on the main road on the northern outskirts of Chivacoa, a 10 minute walk to Plaza Bolívar.

There are also buses from Barquisimeto to Chivacoa (marked Chivacoa Directo) which will deposit you a couple of blocks south of Plaza Bolívar (US$0.80, one hour), as well as por puestos which go up to Plaza Bolívar and stop next to the church (US$1, 50 minutes).

CERRO DE MARÍA LIONZA

This is the most sacred mountain for followers of the María Lionza cult. The mountain outcrop stretches east-west, several kilometres south of Chivacoa and is part of a much larger mountain formation known as the Macizo de Nirgua. The range is covered with thick rainforest and is rich in endemic species. It is the source of the state's largest river, Río Yaracuy. Inparques declared the 117 sq km area of the mountain the Monumento Natural María Lionza in 1960 in an attempt to protect the region from overuse by thousands of the cult's followers. However, the religious significance of the mountain overshadows its natural wealth.

Several sanctuaries have emerged along the northern foothill of the mountain, where pilgrims flock before heading up the hills. The most important of these are Sorte and Quibayo (or Quiballo). Both have their own Altar Mayor where the initial celebrations are performed before the group and its medium head off to the shrine of their choice, one of any number that are scattered all over the forest. It's at these shrines that the proper rites are performed, and they may last the whole night or longer, and usually include a trance seance.

Quibayo

Quibayo is just a collection of several dozen shabby shacks which are either perfumerías or basic places to eat. The Altar Mayor on the riverbank houses a bizarre collection of figures which you'll already have seen in Chivacoa – portraits of Bolívar, various Indian caciques, and numerous images of María Lionza herself. The faithful light candles and sit in front of the Altar to smoke cigars. The Inparques office is 30m from the altar.

Quibayo is larger than Sorte (so it has more frequent transport) and seems to be more accustomed to casual visitors. Yet, it's not a tourist spot by any definition. Behave sensibly and modestly, and don't openly use your camera, which may easily arouse hostile reactions from cult believers.

Hiking up the Mountain

From the Quibayo altar, a path goes over the bridge to the other bank of the river (in which the faithful perform ritual ablutions) and then up to the top of the mountain. All the way along the path are *portales* (literally gates), shrines dedicated to particular deities or spirits. On the top, there are Las Tres Casitas (the Three Little Houses) of Cacique

Guaicaipuro, Reina María Lionza and Negro Felipe. A sketch map of the route and portales is posted on the side of the Altar Mayor. Technically, the trip to the top takes three hours, but there are some dangers.

Dangers

Followers of the cult point out that the trip to the top is full of drawbacks. At each portal you have to ask the respective spirit for permission to pass by. This is done by smoking cigars, lighting candles and presenting offerings. Permission may or may not be granted. One of the devotees commented that he had tried on various occasions and hadn't succeeded. Those who continue on without a permit may be punished by the spirits. Some, so local stories claim, have never returned.

Inparques staff have a far more rational standpoint. They don't recommend the trip to the summit because of muddy paths, snakes and because you might get lost in the maze of paths.

An additional drawback is that like any place with crowds of people it attracts thieves; robberies have been reported by travellers. Try not to venture too far on your own and keep your wits about you. The question of how much or how little you are going to comply with the spirits' wishes is up to you.

Wandering around, especially on weekends, you may come across a group of faithful practising their rituals. Keep away unless you're invited or unless you are with a guide who will introduce you.

Places to Stay & Eat

There are no hotels in either Sorte or Quibayo, but you can camp in the forest, as many pilgrims do. If this is the case, never leave your tent and belongings unattended. You won't starve at the shack restaurants, but their offerings are mostly basic and prices inflated.

Getting There & Away

Jeeps to Quibayo depart when full from Plaza Bolívar (US$0.75, 20 minutes). They run regularly on weekends but there may be only a few departures on weekdays. Jeeps to Sorte (US$0.60, 15 minutes), are even less frequent. The jeeps travel 4km south on a good sealed road to a large ceiba in the middle of the road, then turn right onto a rough road and continue through sugarcane plantations for another 4km to Quibayo. The road to Sorte branches off to the left 1km past the ceiba.

QUÍBOR
* *pop 55,000*
* *area code* ☎ (053)

Quíbor, about 35km south-west by freeway from Barquisimeto, is a pretty large and swiftly growing satellite town of the state capital. It was founded in 1620, but there's little colonial past left. However, it may still be worth stopping if you're wandering around the region.

Things to See
One of the oldest colonial relics, dating from the times of the town's foundation, is the **Ermita de Nuestra Señora de Altagracia**, a fortress-like church on Calle 13 between Avenidas 19 and 20, on the northern edge of the town. The large **Iglesia de Nuestra Señora de Altagracia**, on Plaza Bolívar, is also named after the patron saint, but was only built in 1808 and reconstructed after the earthquake of 1881.

In the north-western corner of the plaza is the **Cementerio Indígena de Quíbor**, a pre-Hispanic cemetery excavated in the 1960s. Most of the finds from the cemetery are now part of the collection of the **Museo Arqueológico**, on the corner of Calle 12 and Avenida 10, two blocks north of Plaza Bolívar. The museum was closed for years, but its extensive reconstruction in 1997 would suggest it might open by the time this guide is published, si Dios quiere.

Places to Stay
The best place to stay in town is the *Hostería Valle de Quíbor* (☎ 42 601), which costs US$15/18 for an air-conditioned double/triple with bath and TV. The place is three blocks south-east of Plaza Bolívar on the

corner of Avenida 5 and Calle 7 and has its own restaurant, piano bar and swimming pool. A marginally cheaper alternative is the *Hotel Gran Duque* (☎ 42 149), next to the Estación de Servicio La Ceiba, on Avenida Florencio Jiménez, at the eastern entrance to the town (from Barquisimeto).

Getting There & Away
Buses between Barquisimeto and Quíbor run frequently from 6 am to 6 pm (US$0.50, 45 minutes). There are also por puestos (US$0.75, half an hour). In Barquisimeto, they depart from the bus terminal; in Quíbor, they queue at the corner of Avenida 6 and Calle 12, one long block from Plaza Bolívar. Buses to El Tocuyo run along Avenida 7, lining Plaza Bolívar.

EL TOCUYO
* *pop 48,000*
* *area code* ☎ (053)

The town of Nuestra Señora de la Pura y Limpia Concepción del Tocuyo was founded in 1545 in a verdant valley of the Río Tocuyo. Two years later it became the capital of the Province of Venezuela, after the authorities moved here from Coro, following the revocation of the contract with the Welsers and the departure of the Germans. El Tocuyo remained the capital until 1577 (when the capital was transferred to Caracas), and over that time it evolved into a graceful colonial town. Despite its political downgrading, the town continued to grow, taking advantage of its fertile soil, ideal for growing sugarcane and a variety of vegetables. Over the colonial period, seven churches and a number of splendid mansions were built.

Unfortunately, a serious earthquake in 1950 ruined a good number of the buildings. The job was completed by Colonel Marcos Pérez Jiménez, Venezuela's dictator of the time. On his orders, most of the damaged structures were demolished and a new town was built on the site. In effect, El Tocuyo is an ordinary modern town with just a handful of restored or reconstructed historic buildings.

Things to See

The most important monument related to colonial times is the **Iglesia de Nuestra Señora de la Concepción**, two blocks west of Plaza Bolívar. It shared the fate of most other buildings and was bulldozed (despite the fact that it could have been repaired), but was later reconstructed.

The church's exterior is noted for its exceptional bell tower and fine façade. Inside, the splendid retable from the 1760s (which fortunately survived the earthquake) takes up the whole wall behind the high altar. Like almost all altarpieces of the period, it was carved entirely out of wood but, unusually, it was not painted or gilded, and is the only one of its kind in the country. Look around the interior and you'll see other relics from the colonial past, among them the original pulpit.

None of the other colonial churches was restored or reconstructed, but two were left in ruins, untouched from the day of the earthquake: the **Iglesia de Santo Domingo**, on the corner of Carrera 10 and Calle 19; and the **Iglesia de Belén**, at Carrera 12 between Calles 15 and 17.

The town has two small museums. The **Museo Arqueológico J M Cruxent** (open Wednesday to Friday from 3 to 6 pm, Saturday and Sunday from 9 am to 2 pm), on the northern side of Plaza Bolívar, has some pre-Columbian ceramics found in the region. The **Museo Lisandro Alvarado** (named after the locally born politician, doctor and anthropologist), at Calle 17 near the corner of Carrera 11, features historic objects related to the town. It's open Tuesday to Friday from 9 am to noon and 2.30 to 5 pm, Saturday and Sunday from 10 am to 4 pm.

You can enter the **Casa de la Cultura**, a former convent on the Plaza Bolívar, to see its spacious courtyard and photos depicting the damage by the 1950 earthquake it somehow withstood.

Places to Stay

The most attractive place to stay is the *Posada Colonial* (☎ 63 24 95), Avenida Fraternidad between Calles 17 and 18 near Plaza Bolívar. It has a fine location, a restaurant and a swimming pool, and costs US$12/14/16 for an air-conditioned matrimonial/double/triple. Other budget (but less stylish) lodging options include the *Hotel Venezia* (☎ 63 12 67) on the corner of Calle Comercio and Carrera 9, and the *Hotel Nazaret* (☎ 63 24 34), on Avenida Fraternidad between Calles 7 and 8.

Getting There & Away

Buses between Barquisimeto and El Tocuyo run at least every half an hour till about 6 pm (US$1, 1¼ hours). There are also por puestos (US$1.50, one hour).

SANARE
- *pop 12,000*
- *area code ☎ (053)*

With its steep streets winding over hillsides, Sanare is pleasant town with a distinctly mountain atmosphere. Founded in 1620, historic relics include the three-nave Santa Ana church. At an altitude of about 1400m, the climate is fresh with an average temperature of 20°C. The town is a gateway to the Parque Nacional Yacambú.

Places to Stay & Eat

The most charming place to stay is the well-kept *Posada Turística El Cerrito* (☎ & fax 49 00 16), about half a km south of Plaza Bolívar (take Calle 17 from the square). Built in a colonial style, the posada has singles/doubles/triples/quads with bath and hot water for US$11/14/17/22.

Half a km up the road, on the way to Yacambú national park, is the *Posada Los Sauces* (☎ 49 08 53), which costs much the same but isn't as good. Alternatively, you can stay for the same price in the very central *Hotel Taburiente* (☎ 49 01 48), on Avenida Miranda, 40m from the church.

All three hotels have their own restaurants, of which the one in El Cerrito is probably the best in town. There are more restaurants scattered throughout the town's centre.

A: Colonial façade, Coro
B: Colonial house, Coro
C: Médanos de Coro

D: Cerro de Santa Ana, Península de Paraguaná
E: Church in Santa Ana, Península de Paraguaná

Left: Old street, Maracaibo
Right: Capilla del Calvario, Carora
Bottom: Image of María Lionza, Quiballo

Getting There & Away
Por puesto minibuses run between Barquisimeto and Sanare until mid afternoon (US$1, 1¼ hours).

PARQUE NACIONAL YACAMBÚ
This park was created in 1962 to protect a 145 sq km chunk of a mountain range known as the Sierra de Portuguesa, just south-east of Sanare. This is actually the northern part of the Andean massif, reaching elevations of up to 2200m within the park's boundaries. The park has Venezuela's only active volcano, locally called La Fumarola, named after the cloud of smoke which floats over it.

Most of the park's area is covered with cloudforest featuring plant species typical of the Andes, many of which are endemic. About 60 species of orchid have been recorded. There haven't been any detailed studies of the fauna, but it is remarkably rich and includes rare endangered mammals such as the spectacled bear *(oso frontino)* and jaguar. The park is particularly good for birdwatchers.

Yacambú is an important water resource for the region, and there's a large reservoir, the Embalse Yacambú, formed by a dam built just south of the park. The rainy period is from April to November. The mean annual rainfall in some upper areas reaches 3000mm.

Orientation
The access to the park is from Sanare, by the 30km road which goes to the dam. This road crosses the park and passes by the Inparques administrative centre at El Blanquito. The rangers here can give you information about the walks and sights, including miradores (viewpoints), waterfalls and the Cañón de Angostura (gorge of the Río Yacambú).

Places to Stay
The park has dorm-style accommodation in El Blanquito, at US$1.50 a bed (bring your sheets). You should book this several days in advance at Inparques office in Barquisimeto. Camping is allowed in determined areas in

the park, and can be arranged directly with the rangers.

Getting There & Away
There doesn't seem to be a regular form of public transport to the park other than occasional por puestos from Sanare. Negotiate the lift with drivers in Sanare.

CARORA
- *pop 90,000*
- *area code ☎ (052)*

Carora, about 100km west of Barquisimeto, on the road to Maracaibo, is the second largest town in Lara state, after Barquisimeto. Founded in 1569 on the banks of the Río Morere, the town has experienced several serious floods, the last one in 1973. Despite considerable damage, Carora has preserved a good deal of its colonial architecture. The historic centre has recently been extensively restored, and it's well worth a visit.

The town's main thoroughfares are Avenida Francisco de Miranda and Avenida 14 de Febrero, and most of the shops, offices, hotels and restaurants are here. The historic sector is about 1km to the north-west, close to the river. The town is small enough to get around on foot, or you can use micros which link its old and new sectors.

Information
The Banco Unión is on the corner of Carrera Lara and Calle Rivas. The Banco Consolidado is on Avenida Francisco de Miranda, half a km south-east from Avenida 14 de Febrero, and the Banco de Venezuela is one block further.

Carora Viajes travel agency (☎ 21 59 81; fax 21 43 95), Calle San Juan, can provide some tourist information and organise regional tours.

Old Town
The historic part of the town, around Plaza Bolívar, is neat, well kept and colonial in style, though not all the buildings date from that period. Some of the most interesting houses have been clearly labelled. Have a

THE NORTH-WES

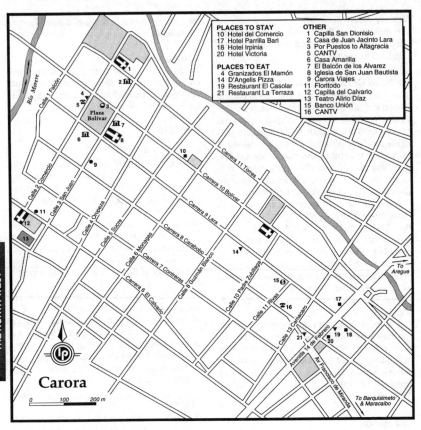

PLACES TO STAY
10 Hotel del Comercio
17 Hotel Parrilla Bari
18 Hotel Irpinia
20 Hotel Victoria

PLACES TO EAT
4 Granizados El Mamón
14 D'Angelis Pizza
19 Restaurant El Casolar
21 Restaurant La Terraza

OTHER
1 Capilla San Dionisio
2 Casa de Juan Jacinto Lara
3 Por Puestos to Altagracia
5 CANTV
6 Casa Amarilla
7 El Balcón de los Alvarez
8 Iglesia de San Juan Bautista
9 Carora Viajes
11 Floritodo
12 Capilla del Calvario
13 Teatro Alirio Díaz
15 Banco Unión
16 CANTV

Carora

0   100   200 m

To Argue

To Barquisimeto & Maracaibo

THE NORTH-WEST

look at the **Casa Amarilla**, the oldest surviving house in town (mid-17th century), now a public library, and **El Balcón de los Alvarez**, a house from the 18th century where Bolívar stayed in 1821. The **Casa de Juan Jacinto Lara** (1778-1859) was the birthplace of this hero of the War of Independence, who gave his name to the state.

The town has some fine colonial churches. The main one, **Iglesia de San Juan Bautista** (raised in 1992 to the rank of a cathedral), on Plaza Bolívar, was built in the middle of the 17th century and has preserved its original external form intact. Its beautiful,

richly gilded main retable dates from 1760. The church is open early in the morning and late afternoon.

The **Capilla San Dionisio**, one block north-east of Plaza Bolívar, has recently been thoroughly renovated. It's only used for special ceremonies, including funerals, and is closed in other times. About 300m north-east of San Dionisio is the striking ruin of the **Iglesia de la Purísima Concepción**, commonly referred to as the Portal de la Pastora. You'll have a good view of the ruin from the dyke at the end of Calle Comercio.

On the opposite, south-western end of

Calle Comercio stands the **Capilla del Calvario**. It has one of the most amazing façades in Venezuela, an extraordinary example of local Baroque. Its simple interior boasts an interesting main retable plus two side retables on both walls. The chapel is often open in the morning, but if it's locked the keys are kept in the Floritodo, a flower shop diagonally opposite the church.

The modern Teatro Alirio Díaz, next to the chapel, has an archaeological collection displayed in its foyer. The guards will let you in during the day.

Bodegas Pomar

Venezuela's best wines are produced here, marketed under the label of Viña Altagracia and distributed throughout the country. Depending on the variety, a bottle of wine will cost about US$4 to US$6 in a wine shop or supermarket.

Venezuela has almost no wine tradition. Viña Altagracia only started its experimental phase in 1985, and it wasn't until 1990 that the commercial production began. A dozen varieties of wine are currently produced, including whites and reds.

Bodegas Pomar, on the southern outskirts of Carora, 3km from the town's centre, feature the installations where the whole production process takes place: everything from sorting the grapes to packing the final product into cardboard boxes and sending them away. The vineyards themselves are in the village of Altagracia (hence the wine's brand name), 24km north-west of Carora by a sealed road. They cover about 125 hectares in all. Altagracia's climate has a harmonious blend of low humidity, good sunlight, warm days and fresh nights all the year round, so the crop can be harvested twice a year (in March and September).

Bodegas Pomar can be visited, but you should arrange this one or two days in advance. Call them on ☎ 21 21 91, 21 18 89 or 21 79 21; fax 21 70 14, and they will show you around the installations (commentary in Spanish only). They may also organise a visit to the vineyards in Altagracia in their or, preferably, your means of transport. If you want to go there on your own (por puestos to Altagracia depart infrequently from Plaza Bolívar), contact them to arrange your visit to the vineyards.

Places to Stay

There are three hotels on Avenida 14 de Febrero, near Avenida Francisco de Miranda, in the town's new centre. The cheapest is *Hotel Victoria,* on the corner of Carrera Carabobo. It's simple but well kept and costs US$6/8 for doubles/triples with bath and fan.

If you need air-conditioning try the *Hotel Parrilla Bari* (☎ 21 67 45), where matrimoniales with bath go for US$11. The best of the lot is *Hotel Irpinia* (☎ 21 63 62), where comfortable singles/doubles with bath and air-conditioning cost US$12/15.

There are no hotels in the historic quarter. The closest is the basic *Hotel del Comercio*, Carrera Bolívar No 5-47, where doubles with bath and fan/air-conditioning cost US$6/8. But be warned: the hotel's cervecería (bar) likes to play music at full volume until late.

There are two better places to stay on Avenida Francisco de Miranda, south-east of the centre. The closer to the centre is the *Posada Madre Vieja* (☎ 21 25 90, 21 37 87), in the spacious garden-like grounds. Air-conditioned singles/doubles/triples with bath cost US$20/25/30, and there are also some cheaper rooms with fan instead of air-conditioning. The other place, the *Hotel Katuca* (☎ 21 33 10, 21 33 02), is 1.5km farther south-east along the road.

Places to Eat

There are several places to eat on and around Avenida 14 de Febrero. Some of the cheapest meals are to be found at the restaurant of the *Hotel Parrilla Bari* and the *Restaurant La Terraza*. Better food is served in the *Restaurant El Casolar* and in the pleasant *D'Angelis Pizza*. The *Granizados El Mamón*, on Plaza Bolívar, has good fruit juices, snacks and delicious granizados (a cross between an ice cream and a juice). Both the *Posada Madre Vieja* and *Hotel Katuca* have their own restaurants.

THE NORTH-WEST

Getting There & Away

Carora lies a couple of km north off the Barquisimeto-Maracaibo highway. At the time of writing, a bus terminal was being built on Avenida Francisco de Miranda, on the south-eastern outskirts of the town, about half a km north off the highway for all the buses which currently enter the town's centre.

Carora has half-hourly buseta connections with Barquisimeto (US$1, 1½ hours), and there are also por puestos (US$1.25, 1¼ hours). It's an interesting trip on a good autopista across arid, hilly countryside. Buses to Maracaibo come through from Barquisimeto every hour or so (US$4, 3½ hours). There are also hourly buses to Cabimas (US$3, 3½ hours).

Zulia State

MARACAIBO

- *pop 1.3 million*
- *area code ☎ (061)*

Although the region was explored as early as 1499 and Maracaibo was founded in 1574 (after several previous unsuccessful attempts), the town only really began to grow in the 18th century as the port servicing trade between the Andean region and the Netherlands Antilles and beyond. The republicans' naval victory over the Spanish fleet, fought on Lago de Maracaibo on 24 July 1823, brought the town some political importance. It was not, however, until 1914 that the first oil well, Zumaque No 1, was sunk in the area. The oil boom took off and the city developed into Venezuela's oil capital, with two-thirds of the nation's output coming from beneath the lake.

Maracaibo is today the country's largest urban centre after Caracas, and a predominantly modern, prosperous city. It's the capital of Zulia, Venezuela's richest state, and it's also an important port. Its climate is hot, humid and often windless, with an average temperature of 30°C – among the highest in the country.

Maracuchos, as local inhabitants are called, have a more regional outlook than other Venezuelans, with some separatist tendencies apparent in local government circles and influential groups. They feel that the state produces the money that the rest of the country spends.

The region around the city preserves some of its original culture and way of life. The Guajiros to the north and the Yukpa and the Barí to the west are among the most traditional Indian groups in the country. Maracaibo is probably the only city in Venezuela where you can still see Indians in their native dress, particularly the Guajiro women in their traditional *mantas* (colourful long loose dresses), their *alpargatas* (sandals with giant pompoms), and sometimes with their faces painted with a dark pigment.

Maracaibo has no absolute must see attractions, and few tourists bother to come here. However, you may need to stop in the city on the way to the Colombian coast, or you may just want to catch a glimpse of what an oil capital is really like. Like any city of its size, Maracaibo offers developed tourist facilities, and you may even find it interesting and agreeable, despite the unbearable heat.

With more time, you can explore the surrounding region which offers a range of attractions, from a community living in houses built on stilts on Sinamaica Lagoon to forests of oil derricks on Lago Maracaibo. The Around Maracaibo section details some of the regional sights.

Information

Tourist Offices The Corpozulia tourist office (☎ 92 18 11, 92 18 40, 92 18 76) is on the 9th floor of the high-rise Edificio Corpozulia on Avenida Bella Vista between Calles 83 and 84. It's about 2km north of the city centre; the Bella Vista por puestos from Plaza Bolívar will take you there. The office is open Monday to Friday from 8 am to noon and 2 to 4 pm.

The Dirección de Turismo tourist office (☎ & fax 51 25 61) is on the 4th floor of the Edificio Lieja, Avenida 18 off Avenida 5 de Julio.

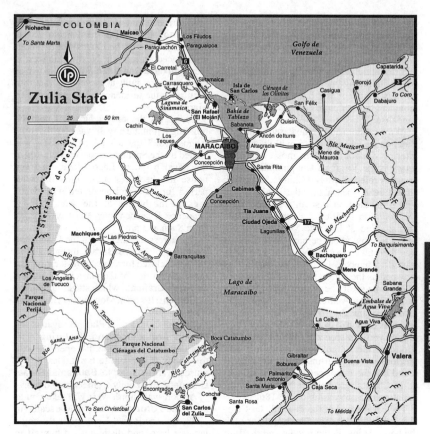

Zulia State

0   25   50 km

Inparques The Inparques office (☎ 61 92 98) is in Parque Paseo del Lago, Avenida El Milagro.

Money Some of the useful banks are marked on the maps. The Casa de Cambio Maracaibo, Avenida 9B just south of Avenida 5 de Julio, changes cash – one of the few places to do so. Turisol (☎ 92 18 33, 92 18 61) is in Edificio La Guajira, Torre Norte, Planta Baja, Locales 2 and 3, Avenida Bella Vista, on the corner of Calle 67 (Cecilio Acosta).

There are several casas de cambio in the bus terminal, which change Venezuelan bolívares into Colombian pesos, and vice versa, and some also exchange US dollars.

Old Town
If you are caught in Maracaibo en route, you probably won't go far beyond the central area, the oldest part of the city. Most of the tourist sights are here, a short walk apart. The axis of this sector is the **Paseo de las Ciencias**, a seven-block-long and one-block wide green belt made after demolishing old buildings to establish a park on the site. This controversial plan was executed in 1973 and

effectively cut the very heart out of the old town. The only structure not pulled down is the **Iglesia de Santa Bárbara** in the middle of the Paseo. The park itself has been graced with fountains and works by contemporary artists, including one by Jesús Soto. Unfortunately, none of the fountains work any more and the sculptures are gradually being vandalised.

At the western end of the Paseo stands the **Basílica de Chiquinquirá**, with its opulent interior decoration. The most venerated image is the Virgin of Chiquinquirá, affectionately referred to as La Chinita, in the high altar. Legend has it that the image of the Virgin, painted on a small wooden board, was found in 1709 by a humble campesina on the shore of Lago de Maracaibo and it began to glow after she brought it home. It was then taken to the church and miracles started to happen. In 1942 the Virgin was crowned as the patron saint of Zulia state.

The image of the Virgin Mary, accompanied by San Andrés and San Antonio, is hardly recognisable from a distance. Special access is provided to allow you to get close to it so you can appreciate the crown of the Virgin, made of gold and encrusted with precious stones. Pilgrims gather here all year round but the major celebrations, the Feria de la Chinita, are held in November, culminating in a procession on the 18th.

The eastern end of the Paseo de las Ciencias is bordered by the **Plaza Bolívar** with the hero's statue in the middle and the 19th century **Catedral** on the eastern side. The most revered image in the cathedral is the Cristo Negro or Cristo de Gibraltar, so called as it was originally in the church of Gibraltar, a town on the southern shore of Lago de Maracaibo. The town was overrun and burnt by Indians in 1600 but the Christ miraculously survived, even though the cross to which the statue was nailed was burnt. Blackened by smoke, Cristo Negro is also known, like La Chinita, for his miraculous powers and attracts pilgrims from the region and beyond. The image is in the chapel to the left of the high altar.

On the northern side of the plaza is the large, arcaded mid-19th century **Palacio de Gobierno**, also called the Palacio de las Aguilas (Palace of the Eagles) for two condors placed on its roof. Next to the west is the **Casa de la Capitulación**, also known as Casa Morales, built at the end of the 18th century as the residence of the governor of Maracaibo.

Today it's the only residential colonial building left in the city. It was here that on 3 August 1823 the act of capitulation was signed by the Spanish, who were defeated in the naval battle of Lago Maracaibo. The house has been restored, fitted out with period furniture and decorated with paintings of the heroes of the War of Independence. It can be visited Monday to Friday from 8 am to 3 pm.

Just across the street from the Casa is the monumental **Teatro Baralt**, inaugurated in 1883, but closed for years for restoration. On the southern side of the plaza is the **Museo de Artes Gráficas**, which stages temporary exhibitions. It's open Monday to Friday from 8 am to 4 pm.

One block north of Plaza Bolívar is the **Museo Arquidiocesano**, featuring religious art from the region. It's open Tuesday to Sunday from 9 am to 6 pm. Next to the museum is the **Templo Bautismal Rafael Urdaneta**, open daily from 9 am to 6 pm.

A short walk north-west will take you to the **Museo Urdaneta**. Born in Maracaibo in 1788, General Rafael Urdaneta is the city's greatest hero, and distinguished himself in numerous battles in the War of Independence. The museum, built on the site where Urdaneta was born, features a variety of objects, documents, paintings and other memorabilia. It's open Tuesday to Friday from 9 am to noon and 2 to 5 pm, Saturday and Sunday from 10 am to 1 pm.

Three blocks to the east is the **Museo Antropológico**, Avenida Bella Vista No 91-37, but it was closed for refurbishing when this book was researched.

Calle 94 has been partly restored to its former appearance, characteristic for the brightly coloured façades and grilled windows of the houses. The most spectacular

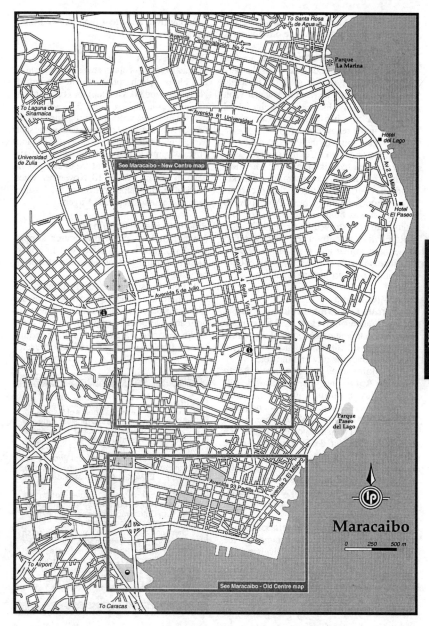

Maracaibo

0   250   500 m

THE NORTH-WEST

part of the street is between Avenidas 6 and 8. Another area noted for fine old houses is around the Iglesia de Santa Lucía.

The **Capilla de Santa Ana**, on the corner of Avenida El Milagro and Calle 94, is the only chapel which has preserved some of its colonial decoration, namely the retable, Mudejar vault and pulpit. Today, the Capilla is the lateral chapel of the church in the Hospital Central. It's currently under renovation.

The sector south of the Paseo is a wonder of heat, dirt and chaos. Countless street stalls make the area feel like a market. The most striking sight here is the imposing old market building, overlooking the docks. A curious metal structure with certain Art Nouveau features, it was built on the site of the previous market destroyed by fire in 1927. The building has recently been wholly refurbished and turned into the **Centro de Arte de Maracaibo**. It stages temporary exhibitions and has an art and craft gallery.

Other Attractions

The **Parque La Marina** on the lakeshore, at the confluence of Avenida El Milagro and Avenida Bella Vista, 5km north of the centre, has a tower **El Mirador**, which provides a good view over the city and the lake.

A few kilometres farther north is **Santa Rosa de Agua**, once a small lakeside village, today a suburb within the city boundaries. There are some *palafitos* (houses built on stilts) on the shore, which might be worth a visit if you don't plan on a trip to the Laguna de Sinamaica (see the Around Maracaibo section). Perhaps it was in Santa Rosa that in 1499 the Spaniards first saw these houses and gave Venezuela its name. There is a bust of Amerigo Vespucci, who took part in the expedition, on the plaza near the waterfront.

The **Museo de Arte Contemporáneo** is currently being built in the grounds of the Universidad de Zulia on Avenida Universidad. Some of the exhibition space may be open by 1998.

On the northern outskirts of Maracaibo, on the road to Sinamaica, is the **Planetario Simón Bolívar**, which is open Tuesday to Saturday from 8 am to 4 pm, Sunday from 8 am to 6 pm.

Special Events

Maracaibo's major annual event is the Feria de la Chinita, which springs to life around 10 November and goes on until the coronation of the Virgin on 18 November. This week-long festival includes, apart from religious celebrations, various cultural and popular events such as bullfights, toros coleados, street parades and, obviously, music, above all the gaita, the typical local rhythm. The best time to listen to the gaita is on the eve of 18 November when musical groups gather in front of the Basílica to play the Serenata para la Virgen.

Places to Stay – bottom end

Maracaibo has notorious water supply problems, which may affect you in hotels, particularly the budget ones. Check before booking in.

If you're just trapped for the night in the city, there are several basic hotels on the western side of the bus terminal. They are poor and overpriced, yet you'll save on a trip to the centre in search for a similarly primitive shelter. Try the *Hotel San Diego* or *Hotel*

Gaita

Gaita is the typical musical genre of Maracaibo. This lively percussion-based music is sung and accompanied by a band using a variety of typical instruments such as the *cuatro*, *maracas*, *furruco* and *charrasca*. Lyrics are mostly either religious or political and are largely improvised. Ricardo Aguirre (1939-69), nicknamed El Monumental, is considered one of the greatest gaita singers.

Gaita is particularly popular during the Christmas period, but the season usually extends from October to January. It can be heard less frequently in other months.

Gaita came to Venezuela with the Spanish but its origins are older and some scholars claim that it has Persian roots. Gaita hasn't been overshadowed by the nationwide *joropo*; on the contrary it is has made its way well outside Zulia to become the second most popular national beat. ■

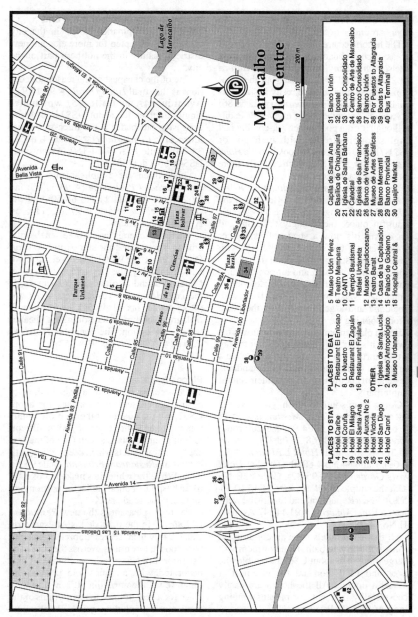

Maracaibo - Old Centre

Lago de Maracaibo

0   100   200 m

PLACES TO STAY
4   Hotel Caribe
17 Hotel Coruña
19 Hotel El Milagro
23 Hotel Santa Ana
24 Hotel Aurora No 2
35 Hotel Victoria
41 Hotel San Diego
42 Hotel Caroní

PLACES TO EAT
7   Restaurant El Enlosao
8   Lo Nuestro
9   Restaurant El Zaguán
16 Restaurant Fñulana

OTHER
1   Iglesia de Santa Lucía
2   Museo Antropológico
3   Museo Urdaneta
5   Museo Udón Pérez
6   Teatro Mampara
10 CANTV
11 Templo Bautismal
    Rafael Urdaneta
12 Museo Arquidiocesano
13 Teatro Baralt
14 Casa de la Capitulación
15 Palacio de Gobierno
18 Hospital Central &
19 Capilla de Santa Ana
20 Basílica de Chiquinquirá
21 Iglesia de Santa Bárbara
22 Catedral
25 Iglesia de San Francisco
26 Banco de Venezuela
27 Museo de Artes Gráficas
28 Banco Mercantil
29 Banco Provincial
30 Guajiro Market
31 Banco Unión
32 Ipostel
33 Banco Consolidado
34 Centro de Arte de Maracaibo
36 Banco Consolidado
37 Banco Unión
38 Por Puestos to Altagracia
39 Boats to Altagracia
40 Bus Terminal

Caroní which are more acceptable than the others around.

The historic centre has very little to offer as far as accommodation goes. The cheapest hotels, such as *Santa Ana*, *Coruña* and *Aurora No 2*, are behind the cathedral but they rent rooms by the hour and are really basic. Marginally better is the *Hotel Caribe* (☎ 22 59 86) on Avenida 7 near the corner of Avenida Padilla, though it's not good either. Air-conditioned singles/doubles/triples with bath go for US$11/13/15. It's better to book into the *Hotel El Milagro* (☎ 22 89 34), which costs a bit more but is cleaner and better kept.

The old-style *Hotel Victoria* (☎ 22 96 97, 22 94 66), overlooking Plaza Baralt and the old market building, must once have been a beautiful place. Increasingly unkempt and run down, it's now a shade of its former glory, yet it's the only central hotel with character and still not bad value. It has spacious rooms with bath and air-conditioning which cost US$10/13/15/17 a single/double/triple/quad. Make sure to choose a room with a balcony and a good view over the plaza before booking in.

If you plan on hanging around in town for a while, it's probably better and safer to stay farther north of the centre, where there are a number of budget hotels and their standards are generally better than those of their central counterparts.

Going from south to north, you have the older-style *Hotel Nuevo Montevideo* (☎ 22 27 62), Calle 86A No 4-96; the 200-room *Hotel Roma* (☎ 22 08 68, 22 08 77), Calle 86 No 3F-76; the small *Hotel La Unión* (☎ 92 40 68), Calle 84 No 4-60; the familiar *Hotel Oasis Garden* (☎ 97 95 82), Calle 82B No 8-25; the simple *Hotel Astor* (☎ 91 45 10, 91 45 30), Plaza República; and finally the well-located *Hotel Almeria* (☎ 91 44 24), Avenida 3H No 74-78.

All the listed hotels have air-conditioned rooms with private bath. None of them will charge more than about US$15 a double; the Astor and La Unión are the cheapest at US$10 a double. All the hotels are easily accessible by frequent por puestos running along Avenida Bella Vista.

Places to Stay – middle & top end
There are no upmarket hotels in the city centre; they all opted for more elegant, new districts, mainly in the northern part of the city.

One of the cheapest of the reasonable options is the small *Hotel Doral* (☎ 98 17 92), Avenida 14A at Calle 75, which has singles/doubles for about US$24/28. More expensive but better is the three-star *Hotel Maracaibo Cumberland* (☎ 22 29 44; fax 21 38 26), Calle 86A No 4-150, which costs US$48/56 a double/triple.

Other three-star establishments include the *Aparthotel Presidente* (☎ 98 31 33; fax 98 24 85), Avenida 11 No 68-50; and the *Gran Hotel Delicias* (☎ 97 61 11), on Avenida Las Delicias.

There are several classier hotels in the city, among them the four-star *Hotel Kristoff* (☎ 97 29 11; fax 98 07 96), Avenida 8 No 68-48. Possibly the best place to stay in Maracaibo, and also the most expensive, is the large lakeside five-star *Hotel del Lago* (☎ 92 40 22; fax 91 45 51) on Avenida El Milagro. One km to the south is a cheaper waterfront option, the four-star *Hotel El Paseo* (☎ 92 40 84; fax 91 94 53).

Places to Eat
There are a lot of cheap eateries in the city centre, which serve set lunches for about US$2, but the quality of the food often mirrors the price. After 6 pm or so it's difficult to find a budget place to eat. One of the few cheap central outlets which keeps going until 8 pm is the *Restaurant Friulana*, Calle 95 No 3-06. While the white tiles make it look a bit like a hospital or public toilet the portions are large and the food is OK.

Far more pleasant is the new *Restaurant El Enlosao* in the Casa de los Artesanos on Calle 94, which serves unpretentious but tasty food at low prices. Across the street, the 1st-floor *Lo Nuestro* is a charming bar decorated with antiques, old photos and other town memorabilia. It's a nostalgic place for a beer or three to the rhythms of the local music (including gaita). By the time you read this the menu may feature some traditional local dishes.

A few paces away, on the corner of Calle 94 and Avenida 6, is another attractive eating establishment, the *Restaurant El Zaguán*. The place consists of a restaurant serving good comida criolla at reasonable prices, a bar, and an open-air café shaded by a beautiful old ceiba. The place is open until 11 pm but closed on Monday.

Like the hotels, the cream of the restaurants have gathered in the northern sector of the city. Many of them are concentrated around Avenida 5 de Julio and Avenida Bella Vista, Maracaibo's new centre. To name a few: *Mi Vaquita* (steaks), on the corner of Calle 76 and Avenida 3H; *El Carite* (fish and seafood), on the corner of Calle 78 and Avenida 8A; *Tasca Torremolinos* (Spanish), on the corner of Calle 75 and Avenida 9B; and *Da Maurizio*, Avenida Bella Vista at Calle 68. It's also easy to find somewhere cheap to eat in this area. Many of the city's restaurants don't open on Sunday.

For something different, go to the revolving rooftop *Restaurant Girasol* in the Hotel El Paseo. It's not cheap but the food is good and the views excellent.

Entertainment
Have a look in *Panorama*, Maracaibo's major daily paper, for what's going on in the city.

Check the programme of the *Centro de Bellas Artes (CBA)*, Avenida 3F No 67-217, which has a multi-purpose auditorium used for concerts, art film and theatre performances. CBA is home to the Orquesta Sinfónica de Maracaibo and the Danza Contemporánea de Maracaibo. The *Centro de Arte de Maracaibo (CAM)* also hosts musical and stage events, and art films. The *Teatro Baralt* may finally be open by the time you read this, after a snail-pace restoration.

The restored Calle 94 is slowly coming to life. Pop into the *Galería de Artes Visuales Emerio Darío Lunar* (also known as the Museo Udón Pérez), which stages temporary arts and crafts exhibitions. The nearby house accommodates the *Teatro Mampara* and also has an exhibition space.

There are several night spots in Maracaibo which present gaita bands, either regularly or from time to time. Check the *Palacio de la Gaita* on Calle 77 between Avenidas 13 and 13A, which is one of the better gaita haunts in town.

Spectactor Sports
The baseball games are played at the stadium of the Complejo Polideportivo, south-west of the Universidad de Zulia. The basketball matches are played in the nearby gym in the same sports complex.

The horse racing track, the Hipódromo de Santa Rita, is on the eastern side of Lago de Maracaibo, across the Rafael Urdaneta Bridge from the city. Races are held on Wednesday starting at 5.30 pm.

Getting There & Away
Air La Chinita airport is about 12km south-west of the city centre. There's no public transport; a taxi will cost about US$8.

There are plenty of flights to the main cities in the country, including more than a dozen flights daily to Caracas serviced by most major airlines (US$68). Air Venezuela and Oriental de Aviación fly direct to Mérida (US$45). Aeropostal and Air Venezuela service San Antonio del Táchira (US$49). Zuliana de Aviación and Aserca go to Porlamar (US$82). Avensa/Servivensa has direct daily flights to Barquisimeto (US$50) and Las Piedras (US$44). To other domestic destinations you'll usually have to change in Caracas. On the international front, Avensa flies direct to Miami, while Servivensa services Aruba and Curaçao. Zuliana de Aviación's flights to Bogotá, Medellín and Miami have been suspended undefinitely.

Bus The large and busy bus terminal is about 1km south-west of the city centre. Frequent local transport links the terminal to the centre and other districts.

Ordinary buses to Coro (US$5.50, four hours) run every half an hour, and to Barquisimeto (US$5.50, five hours) depart

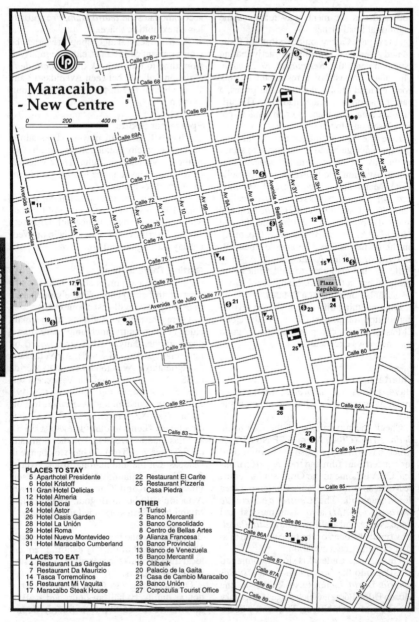

Maracaibo - New Centre

PLACES TO STAY
5 Aparthotel Presidente
6 Hotel Kristoff
11 Gran Hotel Delicias
12 Hotel Almeria
18 Hotel Doral
24 Hotel Astor
26 Hotel Oasis Garden
28 Hotel La Unión
29 Hotel Roma
30 Hotel Nuevo Montevideo
31 Hotel Maracaibo Cumberland

PLACES TO EAT
4 Restaurant Las Gárgolas
7 Restaurant Da Maurizio
14 Tasca Torremolinos
15 Restaurant Mi Vaquita
17 Maracaibo Steak House

22 Restaurant El Carite
25 Restaurant Pizzería
    Casa Piedra

OTHER
1 Turisol
2 Banco Mercantil
3 Banco Consolidado
8 Centro de Bellas Artes
9 Alianza Francesa
10 Banco Provincial
13 Banco de Venezuela
16 Banco Mercantil
19 Citibank
20 Palacio de la Gaita
21 Casa de Cambio Maracaibo
23 Banco Unión
27 Corpozulia Tourist Office

every hour or so. There are regular departures to Caracas (US$13.50 deluxe, 11 hours). Four or five buses depart nightly for San Cristóbal (US$11 deluxe, US$8.75 ordinary, eight hours).

There are half a dozen night buses to Mérida (US$7 ordinary, nine hours); they go via the Pan-American Highway along the northern base of the Andes. There are no direct buses to Mérida on the Trans-Andean mountain road via El Aguila. You must go to Valera (buses every half an hour, US$4.75, four hours) and change there for another one to Mérida (four buses a day, US$4, five hours).

To Colombia To Maicao in Colombia, there are buses early in the morning (US$6.50, four to five hours) and shared taxis operating regularly from about 5 am to 3 pm (US$10, three hours). All passport formalities are done in Paraguachón on the border. The Venezuelan immigration in Paraguachón may charge an exit tax of US$5 to US$10.

Wind your watch back one hour when crossing from Venezuela to Colombia. If you enter from Colombia, expect a search of your luggage by Venezuelan officials.

Maicao is widely and justifiably known as a lawless town and is far from safe – stay there as briefly as possible. Several companies operate buses from Maicao to Santa Marta; buses depart frequently until about 5 pm (US$9, four hours).

AROUND MARACAIBO

Maracaibo is on the strait linking Lago Maracaibo to the Caribbean Sea. The lake, at 12,870 sq km, is the largest on the continent. More than that, it is also the richest; enormous deposits of oil discovered in the 1910s beneath the lake bed have made Venezuela one of the world's major oil exporters.

Although oil is the most obvious feature of the Maracaibo region, there's much more to see around the city. The region boasts a variety of attractions, some of which are detailed below.

Puente Rafael Urdaneta

Named after the greatest local hero, the Rafael Urdaneta Bridge spans the neck of Lago Maracaibo just south of the city. It was built in 1959-62 to provide a short cut to the centre of the country and, at 8679m, it is perhaps the longest prestressed concrete bridge in the world. A great achievement of local engineers, the bridge is the pride of Maracuchos and appears in every local tourist brochure.

You'll cross the bridge if arriving in Maracaibo from anywhere in the east or south-east. There's a good view of Maracaibo from the bridge and vice versa.

Altagracia

Altagracia is a town facing Maracaibo from the opposite side of the strait. The town has preserved some of its old architecture, particularly the charming, typical houses, recently painted in much the same style as those in Maracaibo.

The most interesting area is around Plaza Miranda, the square just one short block up from the lakefront. A stroll about the town, together with a pleasant boat trip from Maracaibo, justifies a half-day trip from the city.

Getting There & Away Boats from Maracaibo to Altagracia depart every hour or two until about 6 pm from the wharf off Avenida Libertador. The trip takes 30 minutes and costs US$1. In Altagracia, the boats anchor at the pier, one block below Plaza Miranda.

There are also por puestos which leave when full from next to either wharf. The ride (via the Rafael Urdaneta Bridge) takes 45 minutes and costs US$1.50.

Boats are a much more pleasant means of transport but sometimes break down, leaving por puestos as the only option.

Ciénaga de los Olivitos

Ciénaga de los Olivitos, about 20km northeast of Altagracia, is one of the major habitats of the flamingos in Venezuela. These lovely birds live there (mainly on the edge of Bahía de Tablazo) all year round, though some fly

THE NORTH-WEST

temporarily to other regions, such as the Península de la Guajira and the Península de Paraguaná. The mangroves growing on the Ciénaga are home to many other bird species as well; about 110 species have already been recorded in the area. The Ciénaga was decreed a wildlife refuge in 1986.

Getting There & Away The Ciénaga is not easy to get to as it is not accessible by road. Ask the fishermen in Guarico (port of Altagracia) or (better) Sabaneta, who might take you across the Bahía de Tablazo to the Ciénaga. Alternatively, take a bus or por puesto from Altagracia to Quisiro, get off in the village of Ancón de Iturre, and talk to the local fishers. Before you set off, contact the Inparques office in Maracaibo for more specific and detailed information.

Castillo de San Carlos de la Barra
This fort lies about 30km due north of Maracaibo, on the eastern tip of Isla de San Carlos. It was built in the second half of the 17th century to guard the entrance of the lake from pirates. Even though the mouth was largely protected by a sandbar, there were many marauders eager to cross over and sack Maracaibo. The fort was in Spanish hands until the naval battle of Lago Maracaibo in 1823, and after their defeat it passed to the republicans.

In 1903, the fort was bombarded by a fleet of warships sent by Germany, Italy and Great Britain to blockade Venezuelan ports after the country failed to pay its foreign debts. During the dictatorship of Juan Vicente Gómez, the fort served as a jail for political prisoners, after which it was used as an arms depot. Finally decreed a national monument, it was extensively restored in the late 1980s to become a tourist attraction.

Castillo de San Carlos is similar to the forts in Cumaná and those on the Isla de Margarita. It's built on a four-pointed star plan with circular watchtowers on each corner and a square courtyard in the middle.

Getting There & Away The fort is accessible by regular passenger boats from the town of San Rafael (El Moján). San Rafael, about 40km north of Maracaibo, is serviced by a number of buses from the city's terminal. San Rafael is a fairly undistinguished town except for a huge, somewhat macabre sculptured head of Bolívar in the middle of the central plaza.

Laguna de Sinamaica
This is the most popular tourist sight around Maracaibo. The lagoon is noted for several hamlets whose inhabitants live in palafitos on or off the lake's shore. Sinamaica is famous nationwide as the place where one can see roughly what Alonso de Ojeda and Amerigo Vespucci saw in 1499 and named the place Venezuela.

A boat will take you around the lagoon and the side caños, passing scattered palafitos along the shores. However, don't expect too much. Some of the houses are still traditionally built of *estera*, a sort of mat made from a papyrus-like reed that grows in the shallows. If you ignore the TV antennas – sticking out from the roof of almost every house – they probably don't look much different from their predecessors 500 years ago. Many houses, though, are now built from modern materials, including timber, brick and tin, which spoil the overall impression. Electric power lines over the lagoon don't add to the sense of authenticity either. A Parador Turístico was built by Corpozulia in the middle of the lagoon, and has a restaurant, craft shop and toilets. This is an obligatory stop for every boat trip.

Originally the lagoon was inhabited by the Paraujano (or Añú) Indians, but they are now extinct. Today the local population, estimated at 2300, is almost exclusively mestizo.

Getting There & Away Laguna de Sinamaica is an easy day trip from Maracaibo. First you have to get to the town of Sinamaica, 60km north of Maracaibo, 19km past San Rafael. Take a bus to Guane or Los Filudos, whichever departs first, from the Maracaibo bus terminal. The trip to Sinamaica takes up to two hours and costs US$0.80. Get off one block past the main square (just behind the police station). From there, por puestos do the 5km run on a sealed road to Puerto Cuervito, which is on the edge of the lagoon (US$0.20, 10 minutes).

In Puerto Cuervito, a fleet of pleasure boats is waiting all day long to take tourists around the lagoon. A boat normally takes six passengers and costs about US$25 (per boat). Bargaining is possible when there are not many tourists around. The tour takes about an hour, but longer if you feel like having lunch in the Parador (the boat will wait for you without any additional charge). There are two cheaper restaurants by the wharf in Puerto Cuervito.

Los Filudos

Los Filudos, on the northern outskirts of the town of Paraguaipoa, 95km north of Maracaibo, has a large Guajiro Indian market on Monday morning. By dawn of that day, Guajiros from all over the region (including Colombian Guajira) come here to sell their products and buy supplies. Although it runs until the afternoon, most of the business is done early in the morning and by 11 am or so most of the shoppers are gone.

Getting There & Away The Filudos bus from the Maracaibo terminal will take you to the market for US$1 in two to 2½ hours, but start very early if you want to get a feel for the place.

Oil Towns

Although Maracaibo is considered the oil capital, most oil drilling is undertaken along the north-eastern shore of Lago de Maracaibo. Here is where genuine oil towns have sprung up, all the way from Cabimas to Bachaquero. Cabimas, with about 180,000 inhabitants, is the largest of them, followed by Ciudad Ojeda with a population of 110,000. There's little to attract tourists in these towns, even though accommodation is

available. What is interesting is the forest of old off-shore oil derricks spread along the shore for some 50km or more. There's a number of good viewpoints for these derricks; amongst others the waterfronts of Tía Juana and Lagunillas. Although the Corpozulia tourist office says its OK to take photos the local Guardia Nacional may have a different idea, so be discreet.

Getting There & Away Half-hourly buses go from Maracaibo to Cabimas (US$1, 1½ hours), where you change for a por puesto to Lagunillas (US$1.25, 45 minutes). The road doesn't skirt the lakeside, and only occasionally will you catch distant views of the derricks. The views of the lake are further obstructed by the containing dyke built to protect the area which has sunk about 9m as a result of decades of oil exploitation. To get a closer look, walk onto the dyke. Alternatively, ask a local taxi driver to take you to the best viewpoints.

Río Catatumbo

There are plenty of rivers emptying into Lago Maracaibo, but the Río Catatumbo is exceptional. A unique electrical phenomenon occurs near its mouth – almost uninterrupted lightning, which is bright but silent. The phenomenon, referred to as Faro de Maracaibo (Maracaibo Beam) or Relámpago de Catatumbo (Catatumbo Lightning), can be observed at night from all over the region, from hundreds of kilometres away. It's visible, for example, from Maracaibo and San Cristóbal. Travelling by night on the Maracaibo-San Cristóbal or San Cristóbal-Valera roads, you'll get a glimpse of it, weather permitting. Obviously, the closer to the mouth of the Río Catatumbo you get, the more impressive the spectacle. Towns on the western and southern shores of Lake Maracaibo (such as Barranquitas, San Antonio, Bobures or Gibraltar) are good observation points.

The Andes

South America's spinal column, the Andes, runs the whole length of the continent, from Tierra del Fuego to the Caribbean Sea. In Venezuela, the Andes extend from the Táchira depression, near the Colombian border, north-east to Trujillo and Lara states. This part of the range is roughly 400km long and about 70 to 100km wide, and is Venezuela's highest outcrop.

Strictly speaking, this range continues further to the north-east (past another depression in the Barquisimeto region) to the Caribbean coast, and then winds eastward. Although this coastal section is a structural continuation of the Andean cordillera, it's not commonly regarded as part of the Andes, but referred to as the Cordillera de la Costa. Venezuela has another part of the Andes along its border with Colombia, west of Maracaibo Lake. This range is called the Serranía de Perijá.

The state of Mérida is in the centre of the Venezuelan Andes. The mountains here are not a single ridge, but two roughly parallel chains separated by a verdant mountain valley. The southern chain culminates at the Sierra Nevada de Mérida, crowned by a series of snowcapped peaks. The country's highest summits are here, including Pico Bolívar (5007m), Pico Humboldt (4942m) and Pico Bonpland (4883m). All this area was declared Parque Nacional Sierra Nevada in 1952, thus making it Venezuela's second national park. The northern chain, the Sierra La Culata, directly opposite the Sierra Nevada, reaches 4660m and is also a national park. In the deep valley between the two ranges sits the city of Mérida, the region's major urban centre and the country's mountain capital. The Andes continue into the neighbouring states of Táchira and Trujillo, and merge into single ridges, which gradually descend to the lowlands.

The mountains are dotted with small towns whose inhabitants continue the traditions of their predecessors, the roots of which

HIGHLIGHTS

- See Good Friday's Passion play in Tostós
- View the unique retables of the church in San Miguel
- Gaze upon the high mountain scenery of the Sierra Nevada
- Take a cable car ride to Pico Espejo
- Go mountain trekking around Mérida
- Savour the beauty of the austere páramos
- Visit the village of Los Nevados
- Experience the old mountain towns of Jajó and Jají
- Try jungle hiking down the cloudforested slopes of the Andes

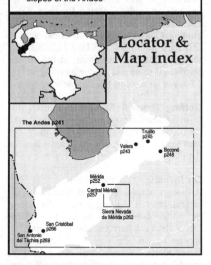

Locator & Map Index

The Andes p241

Trujillo p245

Valera p243

Boconó p248

Mérida p252

Central Mérida p257

Sierra Nevada de Mérida p262

San Cristóbal p266

San Antonio del Táchira p269

go back to the Timote-Cuica Indians, the most advanced pre-Hispanic culture of Venezuela. The land appears to be more actively cultivated here than elsewhere in the country, and the local campesinos seem to work harder than their lowland counterparts.

The Andes are popular hiking territory,

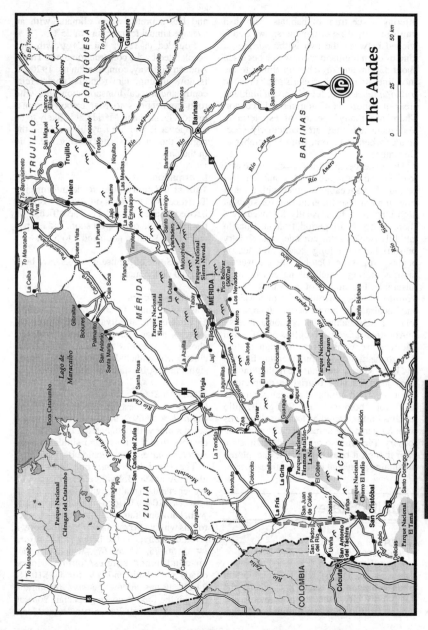

The Andes

THE ANDES

offering a spectrum of habitats from lush rainforest up to permanent snow. Sandwiched between the two is the *páramo*, a kind of open highland moor which begins at about 3300m and stretches up almost to the snowline. Its most characteristic plant is the *frailejón* (espeletia), found only in highland areas of Venezuela, Colombia and Ecuador. There are many species of espeletia in Venezuela and they are particularly spectacular when in bloom, from September to December.

The Venezuelan Andes have a dry season from December to April. May and June is a period of changeable weather with a lot of sunshine but also frequent rain (or snow at high altitudes). It is usually followed by a short, relatively dry period, from late June to late July (which some consider a second dry season) before a long, really wet season begins. August to October are the wettest months, during which hiking can be truly miserable. The amount of rain varies locally; Trujillo state is generally drier than Mérida and Táchira. The snowy period (June to October) may be dangerous for mountaineers.

Administratively, Trujillo, Mérida and Táchira are considered Andean states, though the mountains spill over into Barinas and Lara. Mérida state has the highest mountains and the best tourist infrastructure; consequently it attracts the greatest number of visitors, both local and foreign. Trujillo remains undiscovered by tourism, despite its colonial gems and some splendid mountain scenery. Táchira also seems underestimated, even though it boasts beautiful, unexplored mountains protected by four national parks.

Trujillo State

VALERA
- *pop 130,000*
- *area code* ☎ (071)

Valera is the largest and most important urban centre in the state; it's actually the state's only city, twice as populous as the capital, Trujillo. It lies at an altitude of 540m,

and has a pretty warm climate, with an average annual temperature of 25°C.

Founded in 1820, Valera's growth was accelerated by the construction of the Trans-Andean highway, completed in the 1920s. It is now an important regional commercial centre and a local transportation hub, with road connections to Maracaibo, Barquisimeto, Guanare and Mérida. It is likely to be a stopover if you are travelling around the region, though there's not much to see or do in the city.

Information
Tourist Office The Centro de Información Turística (☎ 54 286) is on Avenida Bolívar between Calles 10 and 11. The office is on the 1st floor, above a craft shop, and is open daily from 9 am to noon and 2 to 5 pm.

Money Some of the useful banks have been marked on the map.

Organised Tours
Casanova Tours (☎ 21 16 54, 53 865), Centro Comercial Edivica, Calle 8, is one of Valera's major tour companies. It offers a choice of *circuitos turísticos* (tourist circuits), which include natural and cultural sights in Trujillo state and beyond.

Places to Stay
One of the cheapest places is the basic *Hotel Central* (☎ 53 697), on Plaza Bolívar, which has doubles with bath and fan for US$7. It's cheaper than the noisy and similarly basic *Hotel Primavera*, on Avenida Bolívar.

The *Hotel Marcelino*, one block south along Avenida Bolívar, offers marginally higher standards, although it too is noisy. It costs US$10/13/15 for a single/double/triple with bath and fan, and has some cheaper rooms without private bath. One block down Avenida Bolívar is the better *Hotel Aurora* (☎ 31 56 75, 31 59 67), which provides air-conditioned singles/doubles/triples/quads with bath and TV for US$10/18/24/28. It has an inexpensive restaurant, though the food is nothing special. You can also try the small Italian-run *Hotel Monte*

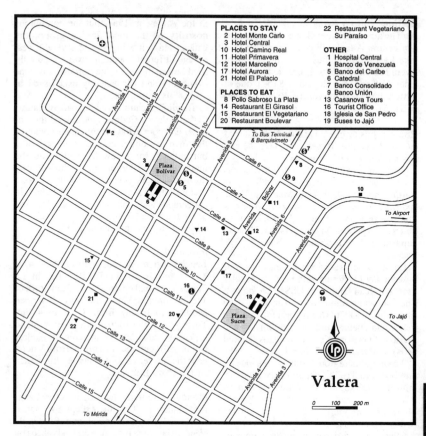

PLACES TO STAY
2 Hotel Monte Carlo
3 Hotel Central
10 Hotel Camino Real
11 Hotel Primavera
12 Hotel Marcelino
17 Hotel Aurora
21 Hotel El Palacio

PLACES TO EAT
8 Pollo Sabroso La Plata
14 Restaurant El Girasol
15 Restaurant El Vegetariano
20 Restaurant Boulevar

22 Restaurant Vegetariano
     Su Paraíso

OTHER
1 Hospital Central
4 Banco de Venezuela
5 Banco del Caribe
6 Catedral
7 Banco Consolidado
9 Banco Unión
13 Casanova Tours
16 Tourist Office
18 Iglesia de San Pedro
19 Buses to Jajó

Valera

0   100   200 m

THE ANDES

Carlo, on Avenida 13, which has simple doubles with bath and fan for US$13.

Appreciably better is the *Hotel El Palacio* (☎ 52 923, 55 850; fax 52 019), in the Centro Comercial Miami Center on Calle 12, which costs US$30/34/36 a single/double/triple and has a reasonable restaurant.

The best place in the city centre is the three-star *Hotel Camino Real* (☎ 21 21 77, 51 704) on Avenida Independencia. This multicoloured tower offers decent doubles for US$50, and has a top-floor piano bar (open from 6 pm on) providing good views all around.

Places to Eat
The city centre is packed with commercial centres, many of which have fast-food outlets, cafés etc. A good example of these is the Centro Comercial Edivica, which occupies an entire block and has several eating outfits, among them the vegetarian *El Girasol*. Other good, budget vegetarian eateries include *Su Paraíso* on Calle 13 (closed Sunday) and *El Vegetariano* on Calle 11 (closed Saturday).

For chicken, try the *Pollo Sabroso La Plata* on Avenida Bolívar. The *Restaurant Boulevar*, also on Avenida Bolívar, serves local food, including arepas.

Getting There & Away

Air The airport is about 4km north-east of the city centre. A taxi will cost about US$7, or take La Cejita minibus from the corner of Avenida 6 and Calle 6. There are two flights a day to Caracas with LAI (US$57), one of which has a stopover in Barquisimeto (US$45).

Bus The bus terminal is about 1.5km north-east of the centre. To get there, take the city bus marked Plata 3 Terminal.

There are several buses a day to Caracas (US$11 deluxe, 9½ hours), and all go via Barquisimeto, Valencia and Maracay. These apart, there are ordinary buses to Barquisimeto every two hours (US$3.75, four hours). Expresos Valera has half-hourly departures to Maracaibo (US$4.75, five hours).

Empresa de Transporte Barinas has four buses a day to Mérida along the spectacular Trans-Andean Highway (US$4, five hours). The road winds almost 3500m up to the Paso El Aguila at 4007m (the highest road pass in Venezuela), before dropping 2400m down to Mérida. There are also por puestos (shared taxis) to Mérida (US$7, four hours).

Among the regional routes, por-puesto minibuses to Trujillo depart every 10 to 15 minutes (US$0.60, 45 minutes), and to Boconó every half hour (US$2, two hours). There are also hourly minibuses to Timotes (US$1, one hour).

Buses to Jajó depart from the corner of Calle 8 and Avenida 4 in the centre (not from the bus terminal) every hour or so, from about 7 am to 5 pm (US$1, 1½ hours). There's also one direct bus a day to Tuñame.

TRUJILLO

- *pop 55,000*
- *area code* ☎ (072)

Trujillo is just 35km from Valera (by the recently built autopista), but it seems a world apart. Unlike Valera, it has agreeable climate, fine setting, some colonial architecture and the unhurried air of days gone by. It has traditionally been the state's capital.

Trujillo was the first town to be founded in the Andes, in 1557, but the continuous hostility of the local Indian group, the Cuicas, led to it being moved several times. Seven different locations were reputedly tried before the town, the portable city, was eventually and permanently established in 1570 at its present site.

Trujillo's location in a long narrow valley, El Valle de los Cedros, determined the unusual and somewhat inconvenient layout of the town. It's only a couple of blocks wide, but extends for a few kilometres up the mountain gorge. Despite new suburbs along the Río Castán, at the foot of the historic sector, Trujillo remains a small town, both in appearance and feeling. Set on an elevation of around 800m, it enjoys a pleasant climate, with a mean temperature of 22°C.

Information

Tourist Office The tourist office (☎ 34 411, 36 14 55) is not in Trujillo, but in La Plazuela, a small colonial town 3km north of Trujillo on the Valera freeway. It's open Monday to Friday from 8 am to 4 pm. There's also the tourist information stand (open the same hours) on Avenida Andrés Bello, at the entrance to Trujillo from Valera, near the bus terminal. It's about 1km north-east of Plaza Bolívar.

Money There aren't many options for changing money in Trujillo, except for Banco Unión, Banco Provincial and Banco de Venezuela which may give cash advances on Visa and MasterCard.

Old Town

Trujillo's historic quarter stretches along two east-west parallel streets, Avenida Independencia and Avenida Bolívar. Bordered by these streets, at the eastern, lower end of the sector, is **Plaza Bolívar**, the historical heart of the town and still the nucleus of the city's life today. The **Catedral**, completed in 1662, has a lovely white-washed façade, but the refurbished interior has almost nothing left of its colonial fittings, except for the stone baptismal font.

There are still some graceful old buildings

THE ANDES

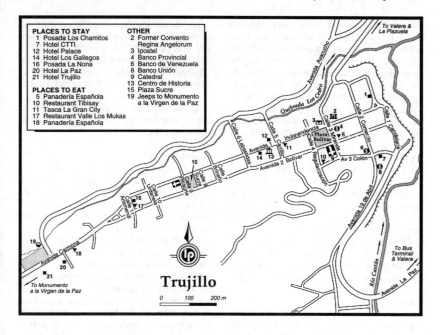

PLACES TO STAY
1 Posada Los Chamitos
7 Hotel CTTI
12 Hotel Palace
14 Hotel Los Gallegos
16 Posada La Nona
20 Hotel La Paz
21 Hotel Trujillo

PLACES TO EAT
5 Panadería Española
10 Restaurant Tibisay
11 Tasca La Gran City
17 Restaurant Valle Los Mukas
18 Panadería Española

OTHER
2 Former Convento
  Regina Angelorum
3 Ipostel
4 Banco Provincial
6 Banco de Venezuela
8 Banco Unión
9 Catedral
13 Centro de Historia
15 Plaza Sucre
19 Jeeps to Monumento
  a la Virgen de la Paz

Trujillo

0   100   200 m

around the plaza. The finest in the area is the carefully restored, fair-sized mansion on the corner just north of the plaza. Built in 1598-1617 as the Convento Regina Angelorum, it's now the public library. You'll find more surviving colonial houses west of the plaza, on both Avenida Independencia and Avenida Bolívar. Perhaps the best approach to sightseeing is to take either of the two streets uphill and return back down by the other one. They merge 10 blocks further up to become Avenida Carmona, but the best architecture is within a few blocks of the plaza.

The **Centro de Historia**, in a beautifully restored colonial mansion at Avenida Independencia No 5-29, houses the museum of the town's history. The various exhibits include old maps, armour, period furniture, pre-Columbian pottery and even a fully equipped kitchen with an old stove. It was in this house on 15 June 1813, that Bolívar signed his controversial Decreto de Guerra a Muerte, or War to the Death, under which all

royalists captured were to be summarily executed. The table on which the proclamation was signed and the bed in which Bolívar slept are part of the exhibition. The museum is open Monday to Friday from 9 am to noon and 2.30 to 5 pm, Saturday and Sunday from 9 am to noon and 3 to 5 pm.

Monumento a la Virgen de la Paz
This gigantic monument was erected in 1983 on top of the mountain overlooking Trujillo, several kilometres to the west of town. The 46m-high, 1200-tonne statue of the Virgen stands on the 1603m top of the Cerro Peña de la Virgen. From several miradores (viewpoints), accessible by staircase, one can enjoy views over much of Trujillo state and beyond. On a clear day, the snowcapped peaks of the Sierra Nevada de Mérida and a part of Lago de Maracaibo are visible. The monument is open daily from 8 am to 4 pm, and the admission fee is US$1.25.

Jeeps to the monument go from the upper

THE ANDES

end of Trujillo, next to the park opposite Hotel Trujillo. They depart when they have collected at least four passengers and charge US$0.60 per head either way. There may be quite a long wait on some weekdays, but you can pay for four seats and have the jeep to yourself. It's best to start early, as later on the Virgen is often shrouded by clouds, even in the dry season. If you feel like going there on foot, it'll be a two-hour walk uphill.

La Plazuela

This small colonial town, 3km north of Trujillo on the Valera autopista, has been partly rebuilt and partly restored to its former form. It's not much more than one cobbled street, complete with a church and houses. In one of them is the tourist office.

Getting to La Plazuela is very easy – just get off the Valera-Trujillo por puesto. Getting away may be a bit harder, as most por puestos come through full and won't stop.

Places to Stay

Probably the most pleasant budget place is the *Posada Los Chamitos* (☎ 32 898), Calle Candelaria, two blocks downhill from Plaza Bolívar. It's just a private house, whose owner rents out three rooms, charging US$6/9/12 for a single/double/triple. The posada is often full.

The *Posada La Nona* (☎ 32 009), Calle Arismendi, is another informal and unmarked place to stay, whose owner, Señora Reyna, has five rooms for rent. Each room has one double bed and one bunk (up to four people) and costs US$10.

The *Hotel Palace* (☎ 31 936), Avenida Independencia No 5-12, offers simple singles/doubles/triples with bath and fan for US$8/11/12, and serves inexpensive meals. Nearby is the *Hotel Los Gallegos* (☎ 33 193), Avenida Independencia No 5-65, which has air-conditioned rooms costing US$15/20 a double/triple, plus some slightly cheaper rooms with fan. The *Hotel CTTI* (☎ 31 412), on the 4th floor of the modern building on the corner of Avenida Colón and Avenida 19 de Abril, costs US$17/22 for an air-conditioned double/triple.

There are two reasonable options on Avenida Carmona at the upper end of town. The cheaper *Hotel La Paz* (☎ 34 864, 35 157) has spacious doubles/triples/quads for US$22/24/26. The *Hotel Trujillo* (☎ 33 576, 33 646; fax 33 942) is the best in town. It has air-conditioned doubles/triples (US$32/36), a restaurant, bar and swimming pool. The pool can be used by nonresidents from 10 am to 4 pm, for US$2.

Places to Eat

The *Restaurant Tibisay*, just behind the cathedral, is one of the cheapest places in town. It can be entered from both Calle Regularización and Avenida Colón. Straightforward and very cheap meals are served until about 8 pm.

The *Restaurant Valle los Mukas*, set in a historic house at Calle Arismendi No 1-43, specialises in local food, has good trout and the food is reasonably priced. There are plans for a posada to open here.

El Rincón de los Abuelos (the restaurant of the Hotel CTTI) has inexpensive food, including some Arab dishes. One of the best places in town is the restaurant of the *Hotel Trujillo*.

The *Panadería Española*, at its two locations, on both Plaza Bolívar and Avenida Camona, has excellent bread, pastries, cakes and coffee.

Getting There & Away

Air The city has no airport and uses the one in Valera, 30km from Trujillo.

Bus The bus terminal is on Avenida La Paz, north-east of the town's centre, beyond Río Castán. Urban minibuses link the terminal to the centre.

The terminal is rather quiet, and the only really frequent connection is with Valera (US$0.60, 45 minutes). There are a couple of night buses to Caracas (US$9 ordinary, 9½ hours). Transport to Boconó (US$1.75, two hours) thins out in the afternoon. It may be more reliable and faster to go to Valera, from where minibuses to Boconó are supposed to depart regularly until 5 to 6 pm.

THE ANDES

BOCONÓ
- *pop 45,000*
- *area code* ☎ (072)

Boconó is 50km south-east of Trujillo as the crow flies, but it's twice that distance by a spectacular, winding mountain road. The town sits at an altitude of about 1225m, and thus enjoys a pleasant temperature of around 20°C. The favourable climate and fertile soil of the region contributed to the development of agriculture. A variety of crops, including coffee, potatoes and chickpeas, are cultivated in the surrounding hills.

Boconó was founded as early as 1560. Its location is actually one of the previous foundation sites of Trujillo, which later moved. Some of the inhabitants, however, decided to stay and take their lives into their own hands. Isolated for centuries from the outside world, Boconó grew painfully slowly and remained largely self-sufficient. It wasn't until the 1930s that the Trujillo-Boconó road was built, thus linking the town to the state capital and areas to the north and west. The construction of the Guanare-Boconó road has provided access from the south and east.

Despite easy access by sealed roads, Boconó still maintains a sense of isolation, even though tourism has recently begun to increase. Agriculture apart, the town has developed into a regional craft centre, specialising mostly in weaving, basketry and pottery. Furthermore, Boconó is a jumping-off point for San Miguel, Tostós and Niquitao (see the following sections).

Information
Tourist Office The Oficina Municipal de Turismo, in the Alcaldía on Plaza Bolívar, may be able to provide some information.

Money It's better to come with local currency, though Banco Unión and Banco Provincial may give advances on credit cards.

Things to See
The **Ateneo de Boconó**, on Calle Páez, runs art and craft exhibitions and has a craft workshop which can be visited (Monday to Friday from 8.30 am to noon and 2 to 5.30 pm). The **Trapiche de los Clavo** is going to be opened in the 19th-century sugarcane mill, on Calle Jáuregui opposite the hospital. It will contain a museum dealing with sugarcane and coffee.

There are several home workshops in the town and its environs. One of the best known is the pottery workshop of the Briceño family, on the outskirts of Boconó, off the road to Guanare.

The Casa Artesanal, on the road to Valera, about a km from the centre, is one of the better craft shops in Boconó. In the centre proper, check the Artesanía Antojitos Andinos on Avenida Colombia.

Places to Stay
There's quite a choice of budget accommodation in the town's centre, including the *Hotel Italia* (☎ 52 25 65), Calle Jáuregui No 1-40; the *Posada Turística Los Andes* (☎ 56 15 42), Calle Páez No 1-08; the *Hotel Antero* (☎ 52 08 18), Avenida Colombia No 2-47; the *Hotel Colonial* (☎ 52 27 50), Avenida Miranda No 5-28 (Plaza Bolívar); the *Hotel Venezia* (☎ 52 27 78), Calle Bolívar No 4-39; and the *Hotel Boconó*, Avenida Miranda No 8-45. They all charge much the same – around US$7/10 for a single/double with bath – and standards are similar. The Venezia and Boconó are marginally better than the rest, so check them first.

The *Hotel Vega del Río* (☎ 52 24 93, 52 29 92) and *Hotel Campestre Las Colinas* (☎ 52 26 95, 52 19 60), both on the north-western outskirts of Boconó, on the road to Trujillo, are appreciably better than those listed above, and have their own restaurants.

You can also stay in the pleasant *Estancia de Mosquey* (☎ 56 15 55, 56 18 86), 10km from Boconó on the road to Guanare, though it's only convenient if you have your own transport. The place has a fine restaurant and a swimming pool.

Places to Eat
There's a number of budget places to eat in the central streets, including some in the cheap hotels. Better restaurants include *La Alameda* on Avenida Ricaurte, and *Las*

THE ANDES

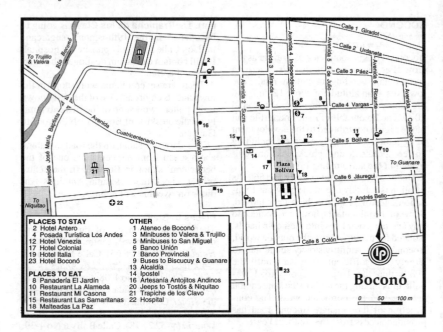

PLACES TO STAY
2 Hotel Antero
4 Posada Turística Los Andes
12 Hotel Venezia
17 Hotel Colonial
19 Hotel Italia
23 Hotel Boconó

PLACES TO EAT
8 Panadería El Jardín
10 Restaurant La Alameda
11 Restaurant Mi Casona
15 Restaurant Las Samaritanas
18 Malteadas La Paz

OTHER
1 Ateneo de Boconó
3 Minibuses to Valera & Trujillo
5 Minibuses to San Miguel
6 Banco Unión
7 Banco Provincial
9 Buses to Biscucuy & Guanare
13 Alcaldía
14 Ipostel
16 Artesanía Antojitos Andinos
20 Jeeps to Tostós & Niquitao
21 Trapiche de los Clavo
22 Hospital

Boconó

0   50   100 m

Samaritanas on Avenida Sucre. *Mi Casona* on Calle Bolívar is also OK.

The *Malteadas La Paz* on Plaza Bolívar serves excellent batidos, merengadas and malteadas. The *Artesanía Antojitos Andinos* on Avenida Colombia has delicious local snacks and drinks, such as the leche de burra, chicha andina and torta de pan.

Getting There & Away

There's no bus terminal in Boconó; transportation companies have their own offices scattered throughout the central sector of town (see the map for locations), from where their vehicles depart.

Minibuses to Valera (US$2, two hours) depart as soon as they get full (roughly every half an hour) until about 6 pm. From the same spot there are minibuses to Trujillo (US$1.75, two hours), but they are not as regular and stop running earlier. If there's none due to depart, take a minibus to Valera, get off in La Concepción and change.

Buses to Guanare depart until 3 pm (US$2, 3½ hours). If you miss the last one, take one of the half-hourly buses to Biscucuy, which operate until 5 pm (US$1.50, two hours). From there you may be able to catch a por puesto to Guanare (US$1.25, one hour).

Minibuses to San Miguel run every hour or so (US$0.50, 40 minutes).

Jeeps to Niquitao depart every half hour or so until 5 to 6 pm on weekdays (US$0.75, 50 minutes). On weekends, they leave when they get full (every one to two hours). The road to Niquitao is sealed all the way, but steep in parts and full of potholes, especially beyond Tostós. The Niquitao jeeps don't enter Tostós, but there are jeeps direct to Tostós (US$0.30, 20 minutes) departing from the same place in Boconó.

Also from the same place there are jeeps to Las Mesitas. In theory, there are three jeeps a day, but only the first one, at about 1 pm, is reliable. There are also three jeeps from Las Mesitas back to Boconó, but again, only the first one, at 7 am, is reliable.

SAN MIGUEL

A tiny town 27km north of Boconó, San Miguel is well known for its colonial church. It's an austere, squat, white-washed construction, reputedly built around 1760. The unusual features of the structure include roofed external corridors on both sides of the church and a Latin cross floor-plan layout, a design rarely used in Venezuela. However, the highlight is inside; the church has one of the most beautiful folksy retables in the country.

The retable, dating from the time of the church's construction, is a striking, colourful composition, notable for its naive style. In the central niche, above the tabernacle, there was a statue of San Miguel, the patron saint of the church and the town, but it was stolen a few years ago. Eight other niches – each occupied by a winged archangel – are distributed symmetrically on two tiers, while the whole remaining surface of the retable is painted with decorative motifs in bright colours, mostly in red, green and yellow.

There are several statues of saints in the transept and on either side of the decorative arch leading to the chancel. The statue of the blind Santa Lucía holding her eyes on a plate is particularly impressive. Side retables in the transept are also worth a look.

The church is open daily, except Wednesday, from 9.30 am to noon and 2 to 5 pm. Mass is at noon on Sunday.

About 1km outside San Miguel, on the only road to the town, is the cemetery. Some of the curiously shaped tombstones have been painted with extremely bright colours.

The town's main event is the Romería de los Pastores y los Reyes Magos, celebrated annually from 4 to 7 January.

Places to Stay & Eat

The *Hostería San Miguel*, the state-owned hotel built during the fat years of the oil boom, is the only place to stay. It's pleasant, comfortable, reasonably priced and has its own restaurant. The Hostería is on the opposite side of the plaza from the church.

Getting There & Away

San Miguel lies 4km off the Boconó-Trujillo road. The narrow, sealed side road to the town branches off 23km from Boconó.

San Miguel only has a public transport link with Boconó. Minibuses run between the two towns every hour or so (US$0.50, 40 minutes). In San Miguel, they stop at the plaza in front of the church.

TOSTÓS

The small town of Tostós, about 10km southwest of Boconó, is famous nationwide for its Easter celebrations, during which the Passion play is re-enacted on Good Friday. On that day, the town fills up and the crowd's emotions reach fever pitch when Christ is being crucified. The rest of the year, Tostós is a quiet town, picturesquely stuck to a hillside, as it has been for 380 years.

The town can be easily reached by sealed road from Boconó, from where it's serviced by regular por-puesto jeeps (US$0.30, 20 minutes).

NIQUITAO

- *pop 5000*
- *area code ☎ (072)*

About 25km beyond Tostós is the larger town of Niquitao. It's also a colonial settlement, founded in the 1620s, and still has some of its historic architecture in place. The area around Plaza Bolívar, complete with the church, is particularly well preserved. The town sits on an altitude of nearly 2000m, so it has a typical mountain climate, with warm days but chilly nights.

Niquitao is a convenient springboard for trips into the surrounding páramos and mountains, including the highest top in the area, La Teta de Niquitao, at 3977m. You can walk there, but it's a two day return trip, so you need to be prepared for camping. You can also go by jeep; the trip to La Teta will include a two to three-hour jeep ride uphill plus a short walk to the top. Jeep excursions are easy to arrange through hotel managers,

THE ANDES

who will suggest the most interesting destination in the region. Horse riding trips are also possible.

Places to Stay & Eat

The town has several accommodation options, of which the friendly, familiar *Posada Mama Chepy*, 400m south of Plaza Bolívar, is the cheapest. It has seven simple double rooms with own bath, costing US$7 each. You can use the family kitchen to cook your food, or they can prepare meals for you.

The *Posada Turística Guirigay*, on Avenida Bolívar, one block south of the plaza, provides doubles/triples with bath for US$9/11, and also has its own restaurant. The *Posada Don Jerez*, on Plaza Bolívar, is slightly more expensive though no better. Just across the road is the reasonable *Tasca La Estancia de Don Ramón*.

Getting There & Away

Jeeps (taking up to 12 passengers) service the Boconó-Niquitao road every half hour on weekdays, and every one to two hours on weekends.

From Niquitao, there's a road (partly sealed but in bad shape) to Las Mesitas. There are a couple of jeeps servicing this route, all departing from Boconó (the most reliable is the jeep leaving Boconó at 1 pm). Beyond Las Mesitas, there's a rough road over a mountain pass to the town of Tuñame (no public transport on this stretch), from where a better road (and por-puesto jeeps) continue downhill to Jajó.

JAJÓ
- *pop 4000*
- *area code ☎ (071)*

Jajó, 48km south of Valera, off the road to Mérida, is a small old mountain town with a long history. It was founded in 1611 by Sancho Briceño Graterol in a remote place amid verdant mountains. Although sealed roads now link the town with both Valera and Mérida, Jajó is still a tiny, sleepy place. It's possibly the finest small colonial town in Trujillo state.

Its prettiest part is around Calle Real, the street which runs northward from Plaza Bolívar. About 100m up this street is the Museo Casa Colonial, which resembles a charming antique shop rather than a museum.

Places to Stay & Eat

Jajó has three hotels and all are pleasant. The cheapest is *La Pensión de Jajó*, on the southern side of Plaza Bolívar. It has no sign but you can recognise it by its balcony. Installed in an old house with a patio, there are only a few rooms, all with one double and one single bed and private bath with hot water. A room costs US$10 regardless of the number of people – up to three. La Señora can provide home-cooked meals if you wish, but let her know in advance.

On the western side of the plaza is the *Hotel Turístico Jajó* (☎ 57 581), the only modern building on the square, which spoils the appearance of the plaza. It's comfortable but doesn't have the charm of the Pensión, and costs US$12 for a single or couple, US$15 for triple and US$18 for a quad. The hotel has its own restaurant which serves good trout.

The friendly *Posada Turística Marisabel* (☎ 56 999), Calle Páez (the northern continuation of Calle Real), two blocks north of the square, has clean (though dark) rooms, which cost much the same as those in the Hotel Turístico. It also has its own restaurant.

Getting There & Away

The usual point of departure for Jajó is Valera. There are hourly buses between Valera and Jajó (US$1, 1½ hours) which operate until about 5 pm. They don't go by the Valera-Mérida Trans-Andean Highway through La Puerta, but along a shorter, eastern road. These buses don't depart from the Valera bus terminal, but from the corner of Calle 8 and Avenida 4.

If you want to get to Jajó from Mérida, take the morning bus to Valera, get off next to the petrol station at the turnoff to Jajó and try to hitch the remaining 11km stretch to Jajó, though there are not many vehicles using this road.

THE ANDES

Mérida State

MÉRIDA
- *pop 240,000*
- *area code* ☎ (074)

Mérida is arguably Venezuela's most popular destination among foreign backpackers. It has an unhurried and friendly atmosphere, plenty of tourist facilities, the famous teleférico and beautiful mountains all around, with the country's rooftop, Pico Bolívar, just 12km away. It's the country's major centre for outdoor activities.

Home to the large Universidad de los Andes (the second oldest university in the country, founded in 1785), the city has a sizeable academic community, which gives it a cultured and bohemian air. Furthermore, Mérida is inexpensive and relatively safe by Venezuelan standards.

Although generally considered by Venezuelans as a cold city (at 1625m, it's the highest state capital in the country), Mérida enjoys a pleasant, mild climate, with an average temperature of 19°C. The tourist season is at its peak here around Christmas, Carnaval and Easter, and from late July to early September.

History
La Ciudad de Santiago de los Caballeros de Mérida was founded in 1558 by Juan Rodríguez Suárez from Pamplona, in Nueva Granada (now Colombia). It's interesting to note that most early towns in the region, including San Cristóbal and Barinas, were founded by expeditions sent from Pamplona, an important political and religious centre of the day, and that they remained under Colombian jurisdiction for a long time after. It was not until 1777 that Mérida (as well as San Cristóbal) became part of Venezuela. The association with Colombia can still be felt today, and is noticeable in the people, culture and language.

Mérida was born illegally, since Rodríguez Suárez had no required Spanish approval to found a new city. Consequently, he was hunted down and taken to Bogotá where he was placed on trial. Facing the death sentence, he miraculously escaped and fled to Trujillo, Venezuela, where he was granted political asylum, reputedly the first case of its kind in the New World.

The foundation controversy ended two years later, after Juan de Maldonado, again from Pamplona, was sent with all the paperwork in order, and Mérida was legally founded. However, the Rodríguez Suárez adventure has eventually come to be commonly recognised as the city's foundation.

Separated by high mountains from both Colombia and Venezuela, Mérida grew very slowly during colonial times. The 1812 earthquake devastated most of the urban fabric, and further hindered development. Two years later, the ruined town gave a warm welcome to Bolívar who passed through, leading his troops on to Caracas. In 1820, Mérida saw Bolívar again, this time on his march to Colombia.

The isolation that had retarded Mérida's progress for centuries, suddenly proved to be its ally. During the federation wars in the mid-19th century, when Venezuela was plunged into full-blown civil war, the city's isolation attracted refugees, and the population began to grow. It was not, however, until the 1920s that access roads were constructed and later sealed, which smoothed the way for Mérida's development. Mérida's transition from a town into a city really only took place over the last few decades.

Orientation
Mérida sits on a flat *meseta*, an alluvial terrace which stretches for 12km between two parallel rivers; the edges of the terrace drop abruptly to the riverbanks. The historic quarter is in the north-eastern end of the plateau, easily recognised by the typically Spanish chessboard grill of the street layout. Having filled the meseta as densely as possible, Mérida is now expanding beyond it.

Information
Tourist Office The Cormetur (Corporación Merideña de Turismo) has its main office (☎ 63 48 77, 63 08 14; fax 63 27 82) on

THE ANDES

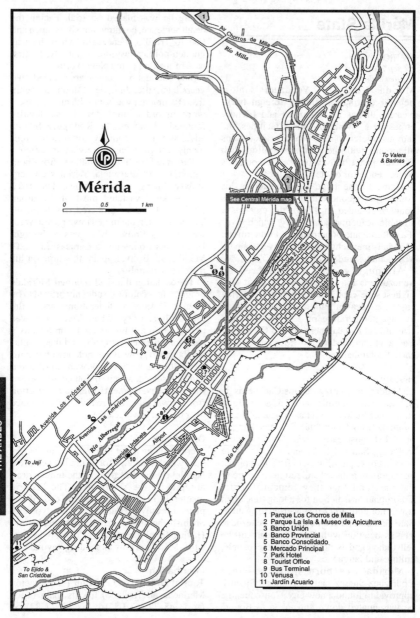

THE ANDES

1 Parque Los Chorros de Milla
2 Parque La Isla & Museo de Apicultura
3 Banco Unión
4 Banco Provincial
5 Banco Consolidado
6 Mercado Principal
7 Park Hotel
8 Tourist Office
9 Bus Terminal
10 Venusa
11 Jardín Acuario

Avenida Urdaneta, near the airport. The office is open Monday to Friday from 8 am to noon and 2 to 6 pm, and provides city maps and good information. Cormetur also operates several *módulos de información* throughout the city, including one at the airport (☎ 63 93 30), one at the bus terminal (☎ 63 39 52) and another one at Plaza Las Heroínas, next to the cable-car station.

Most of the major tour companies (see Organised Tours) will provide information about trekking, mountaineering and other activities.

Inparques The Inparques office (☎ 52 98 76, 52 82 84; fax 52 87 85), Calle 19 No 5-44 (open Monday to Friday from 8.30 am to noon and 2 to 5 pm), issues permits for trekkers. There's also the convenient Inparques outlet at the cable-car station (open Wednesday to Sunday from 7.30 am to 2 pm), which does the same. You need a permit if you are going to stay up in the mountains overnight. It's issued on the spot (you have to show your passport) and costs US$0.25 per person per night. The permit should be returned after completing your hike – this is intended to make sure nobody is left wandering lost up in the mountains.

Money Banks which could possibly handle foreign-exchange transactions are marked on the map. The Banco Consolidado is on Avenida Las Américas, outside the centre.

It's unlikely that any bank will exchange cash. The only official place to do this is at the Italcambio office at the airport, which also changes travellers cheques (bring the purchase receipt with you). There may be some other places to change cash and tour companies should know of them.

Post & Communications Both CANTV and Ipostel are next door to each other on Calle 21. Ipostel has a post restante facility. Letters sent here to you should be addressed with your name, Lista de Cartas Sobrantes, Ipostel, Calle 21 entre Av 4 y 5, Mérida, Estado Mérida, Venezuela.

Laundry Many budget hotels and posadas offer this service, and if not, they will direct you to a nearby lavandería automática. There are plenty of them throughout the central area, including the Minelly, Avenida 6 No 17-55; the Márquez, Avenida 2 No 14-64; and the Acuario, Avenida 7 No 25-27. All offer service washing and drying for around US$2 for a 5kg load.

Medical Services Mérida has an array of clinics and hospitals, including Clínica Milla (☎ 52 11 38, 52 22 27), Avenida 2 No 12-17; Clínica Mérida (☎ 63 90 11, 63 90 16), Avenida Urdaneta; and Clínica Santa Filomena (☎ 44 66 33, 44 66 38), Avenida Los Próceres. If you have dental problems, try Dr Ruth de Castillo, Calle 19 between Avenidas 2 and 3 (Monday, Wednesday and Friday from 2 to 6 pm).

Things to See
The city centre is quite pleasant for leisurely strolls, though there's not much in the way of colonial architecture or outstanding tourist attractions. Plaza Bolívar is the city's heart, but it's not a colonial square. Work on the **Catedral** was begun in 1800, based on plans of the 17th-century cathedral of Toledo in Spain, but was not completed until 1958, and probably only then because things speeded up to meet the celebration for the 400th anniversary of the city's foundation. The end result is different from the initial design.

Next to the cathedral is the **Museo Arquidiocesano**, with a collection of religious art, open Tuesday to Friday from 9 am to noon. Note the bell cast in 909, thought to be the world's second-oldest surviving bell. Across the square, the **Casa de la Cultura** has various temporary exhibitions of local artists and craftspeople. It's open weekdays from 8 am to noon and 2 to 6 pm.

The Universidad de los Andes building, just off the square, houses the **Museo Arqueológico**, open Tuesday to Friday from 9 am to noon and 3 to 6 pm, and on weekends from 3 to 7 pm. A small but interesting collection supported by extensive

THE ANDES

background information (in Spanish only) gives an insight into the pre-Hispanic times of the region.

The recently completed large and sparkling Complejo Cultural, one block north of the plaza, accommodates the **Museo de Arte Moderno**, open Tuesday to Friday from 9 am to noon and 2.30 to 6 pm, and on weekends from 10 am to 6 pm.

The **Museo de Arte Colonial**, two blocks north-east of the plaza, has a collection of mostly sacred art. It's open Tuesday to Friday from 8 am to noon and 2 to 6 pm, and weekends from 9 am to 4 pm.

Seven blocks north-east, at the end of Avenida 4, you'll find the small **Parque de las Cinco Repúblicas**, boasting the oldest monument to Bolívar, dating from 1842.

Activities

While the city cultural attractions listed above may not seem extremely fascinating, Mérida is easily Venezuela's major centre of active tourism. The region provides excellent conditions for a range of activities as diverse as rock climbing, bird-watching and rafting, and local operators have been quick to make them easily accessible for visitors – see Organised Tours for what's on offer. Also see Around Mérida for more details about activities.

Language Courses

Mérida is an ideal place for travellers to study Spanish. Firstly, it has a lot to offer visitors, so you won't be bored staying here while studying. Secondly, Spanish spoken in the Andes is slower and easier to understand than that spoken in other parts of Venezuela, so it's a good place for practising. Finally, Mérida is well prepared to teach you Spanish, and the prices of language courses are lower here than just about anywhere else in the country.

The city has several language schools plus plenty of students and tutors offering private lessons. They advertise through posadas, bars, tour companies etc. The major institutions offering Spanish courses include:

Instituto Latino-Americano de Idiomas
 Centro Comercial Mamayeya, Piso 4, Oficina 26, Avenida Las Américas (☎ & fax 44 78 08)
Iowa Institute
 Avenida 4 con Calle 18 (☎ 52 64 04; email iowainst@ing.ula.ve)
Venusa
 Avenida Urdaneta No 49-49 (☎ 63 39 06; fax 63 35 25)

All the listed schools run courses of various length (from one week onward) at different levels. They are flexible at accommodating travellers' needs, and you usually don't have to wait long before the course starts.

Organised Tours

There are plenty of tour companies in Mérida and prices are generally reasonable. Understandably, mountain trips feature most prominently on the operators' lists, and include treks to the highest peaks such as Pico Bolívar and Pico Humboldt; expect to pay about US$30 to US$50 per person a day, all-inclusive.

The village of Los Nevados is probably the most popular destination among those who don't attempt to climb the peaks. Most companies offer this trip, but you can easily do it on your own; all the tour companies listed below will give you details on how to do it, and can arrange a jeep to Los Nevados without charging commission. Refer to the Around Mérida section for more about this trip.

The Sierra de la Culata is a relatively new but easy and attractive destination, available as a tour from most agents. It's usually a two to three day trip, costing around US$30 per person a day, all-inclusive.

A worthwhile excursion out of Mérida is a wildlife safari in Los Llanos, Venezuela's greatest repository of wildlife, particularly birds. There's a number of ecotourist camps in Los Llanos which offer tours in their ranches (known as *hatos*), but they are expensive (US$100 to US$150 per person a day). Mérida's companies (including those listed below), will organise a similarly fascinating excursion for around US$35 to

THE ANDES

US$50 a day. It's offered as a three to five day all-inclusive package.

The companies offer a lot of other destinations and activities including mountain biking, paragliding, rock climbing, fishing and horse riding. Some also handle rental of mountaineering equipment, camping gear, bikes etc. Finally, most will provide tourist information even if you don't plan on buying their services.

Like elsewhere in the country, Mérida's tour companies normally accept cash payment for their services in US dollars, and most will also accept travellers cheques, but no credit cards.

Tour Companies The most responsible, knowledgeable, stable and competitive operators at the time of writing included:

Bum Bum Tours
    In the new Posada Las Heroínas, Calle 24 No 8-301 (☎ & fax 52 58 79; email raquele@bolivar. funmrd.gov.ve; website jvm.com/bumbum). One of Mérida's most progressive and innovative operators, opening new routes and destinations. Apart from a wide range of standard tours, the company offers some challenging, savage treks through total wilderness and is the best (and original) operator for rafting trips. Kayaking and floating are also available. Bum Bum runs a cybercafé and sells mountain maps and travel publications including, occasionally, Lonely Planet guidebooks. It has excellent reports from travellers of its Los Llanos tours, some of which are conducted by Alan Highton, possibly the best bird and wildlife guide around. By and large, good value for money on all tours.
Guamanchi Expeditions
    Calle 24 No 8-39 (☎ & fax 52 20 80; email geca@bolivar.funmrd.gov.ve; website www. ftech.net/geca). One of Mérida's established companies, with a wide range of tours up to the mountain peaks and down to Los Llanos. It has good bicycles for rent (but expensive), bike tours and good information about do-it-yourself bike trips. Similar prices as Bum Bum.
Natoura Adventure Tours
    Calle 24 No 8-237 (☎ & fax 52 42 16; email natoura@telcel.net.ve). Also with a long history and sound reputation, the company is particularly good in mountain trekking and climbing, though it runs a range of other tours as well, including bird-watching in Mérida region and Los Llanos. It has recently introduced rafting and fishing trips. It uses good camping and mountaineering equipment on its tours, and some of it can be rented. Prices are a little higher than those of the companies listed above.

There are plenty of other companies in town, which may be as good and reliable, and will cost much the same or even marginally less. Shop around, talk to other travellers and check things thoroughly before you commit yourself.

Special Events
The region is rich in feasts and festivities, many of which are confined to a particular small area or even a single town. The year begins with the Paradura del Niño, observed throughout the region during the whole of January. This traditional festival involves 'stealing' the infant Jesus from his crib, then searching for him and celebrating his 'finding'.

The Reyes Magos (Epiphany), on 6 January, is particularly solemn in the town of Santo Domingo. On 2 February, the Vasallos de La Candelaria brings ritual dances to La Parroquia, Mucuchíes, Bailadores and La Venta.

The Feria del Sol is Mérida's Carnaval and the city's main annual party, replete with music, popular dance, sports events, major bullfights and beauty pageant. It goes for nearly a week preceding Ash Wednesday.

Given the strong traditional character of the region, the Semana Santa (Holy Week) is celebrated quite solemnly in many towns and villages, particularly so in La Parroquia, Lagunillas, Santo Domingo, Chiguará and La Azulita.

On 15 May there's the Fiesta de San Isidro Labrador. It's a sort of agrarian rite in honour of the patron saint of farmers, celebrated with processions featuring domestic animals and crops. It's most elaborate in Apartaderos, Mucurubá, Bailadores and La Azulita.

The Fiesta de Santiago Apóstol is held on 25 July in Lagunillas, Ejido and Jají. Los Negros de San Gerónimo is celebrated in Santo Domingo on 30 September. The Fiesta

THE ANDES

de San Rafael takes place on 24 October in San Rafael.

The town of Mucurubá observes the Fiesta de la Inmaculada Concepción, on 7 December, with a spectacular display of some 20,000 candles which are lit in the evening in the main plaza.

Christmas is essentially a family feast, celebrated at home. The Fiesta de San Benito springs to life on 29 December in Timotes, La Venta, Apartaderos and Mucuchíes. On this day the locals take to the streets in black and red costumes and sometimes black-coloured faces, in honour of the only black saint in Venezuela, and spend the day dancing to the rhythm of drums and parading from door to door.

The Despedida del Año Viejo (Farewell to the Old Year), at midnight on 31 December, features the burning of life-size human puppets, often stuffed with fireworks, which have been prepared weeks before and placed in front of the houses.

Places to Stay – bottom end

Mérida has heaps of places to stay and most are good value for money. A good part of them are posadas, or small, family-run guest-houses, often with a friendly atmosphere. Many provide kitchen and laundry facilities.

Perhaps the most popular backpacker haunt over recent years has been the *Posada Las Heroínas* (☎ 52 26 65), Calle 24 No 8-95, in Parque Las Heroínas. You pay US$4 per person in neat rooms with shared facilities, and can use the kitchen and laundry. The posada was run by a polyglot Swiss, Tom, and his wife Raquel, but they have moved to a new place nearby, at Calle 24 No 8-301 (☎ 52 58 79), and are turning it into another posada, which may be operating by the time you read this. They own and run Bum Bum Tours which is based here. The place has a unique location, with fabulous views over the cable car and the Chama Valley.

Other cheap posada-style places include: *Posada La Joya Andina* (☎ 52 60 55), Calle 24 No 8-51; *Residencia San Pedro* (☎ 52 27 35), Calle 19 No 6-36; *Posada Mucumbarí*

(☎ 52 60 15), Avenida 3 No 14-73; *Posada Calle 18* (☎ 52 29 86), Calle 18 No 3-51; *Posada Turística Marianela* (☎ 52 69 07), Calle 16 No 4-33, and *Residencia Araure* (☎ 52 51 03), Calle 16 No 3-34. All are clean and pleasant and cost US$4 to US$5 per head in doubles or triples with shared facilities.

The cheapest posada offering rooms with private bath (for about US$5 per person) is the *Posada Mara* (☎ 52 55 07), Calle 24 No 8-215.

For a little more, you have a wide choice of pleasant posada-style options, all with private bath and hot water. They include: the *Posada Encanto Andino* (☎ 52 69 29), Calle 24 No 6-53 (US$12/15/18 a double/triple/quad); *Hotel Español* (☎ 52 92 35), Avenida 2 No 15-48 (spotlessly clean doubles for US$11); *Posada Luz Caraballo* (☎ 52 54 41), Avenida 2 No 13-80 (US$10/15/20 a single/double/triple); *Posada Los Compadres* (☎ 52 28 41), Avenida 4 No 15-05 (US$12/16/20 a matrimonial/double/triple); *La Casona de Margot* (☎ 52 33 12), Avenida 4 No 15-17 (US$16/22/25 a matrimonial/triple/quad); *Posada Alemania* (☎ 52 40 67), Avenida 2 near the corner of Calle 18 (US$13/15 a double/triple); *Posada Turística La Merideña* (☎ 52 57 38), Avenida 3 No 16-39 (US$14/20 a double/triple); and *Posada Doña Pumpa* (☎ 52 72 86), Calle 14 No 5-11 (US$16/20/24 a double/triple/quad).

One of the cheapest hotels in the city centre is the *Hotel Italia* (☎ 52 57 37), Calle 19 No 2-55. It has small, basic singles/doubles without bath for US$4/6 and rooms with bath for US$7/10. Another ultra-budget option is *Hotel Panamá* (☎ 52 91 56), Avenida 3 No 18-31, which has all rooms with private bath and hot water and costs US$4/6/8/10 a single/matrimonial/double/triple. Both hotels are popular with travellers but face increasing competition from the more enjoyable posadas.

The *Hotel Frontino* (☎ 52 75 55, 52 82 49), Avenida 3 No 24-19, has been recently refurbished and is OK. It has singles/doubles/triples with TV, bath and hot water for US$10/14/18.

Top: View of the Andean páramo with Pico Humboldt & Pico Bolívar in the background
Left: Juan Félix Sánchez chapel, San Rafael
Right: Laguna Mucubají, The Andes

Left: Stained glass window of the Santuario de la Virgen de Coromoto, near Guanare
Right: Los Llanos landscape
Bottom: Religious statues in the Museo de Anzoátegui, Barcelona

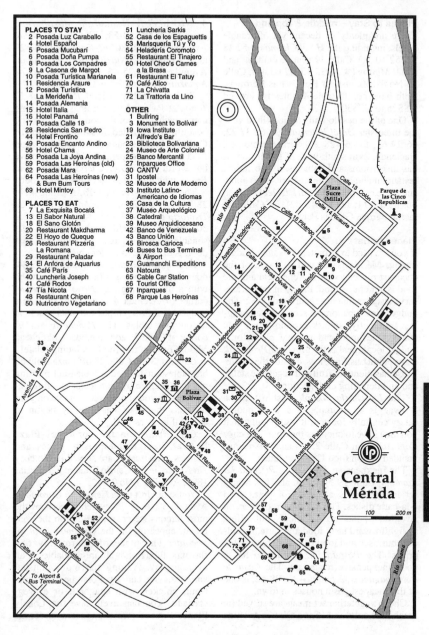

PLACES TO STAY
2 Posada Luz Caraballo
4 Hotel Español
5 Posada Mucubarí
6 Posada Doña Pumpa
8 Posada Los Compadres
9 La Casona de Margot
10 Posada Turística Marianela
11 Residencia Araure
12 Posada Turística La Merideña
14 Posada Alemania
15 Hotel Italia
16 Hotel Panamá
17 Posada Calle 18
28 Residencia San Pedro
44 Hotel Frontino
49 Posada Encanto Andino
56 Hotel Chama
58 Posada La Joya Andina
59 Posada Las Heroínas (old)
62 Posada Mara
64 Posada Las Heroínas (new) & Bum Bum Tours
69 Hotel Mintoy

PLACES TO EAT
7 La Exquisita Bocatá
13 El Sabor Natural
18 El Sano Glotón
20 Restaurant Makdharma
22 El Hoyo de Queque
26 Restaurant Pizzería La Romana
29 Restaurant Paladar
34 El Anfora de Aquarius
35 Café París
40 Lunchería Joseph
41 Café Rodos
47 Tía Nicota
48 Restaurant Chipen
50 Nutricentro Vegetariano
51 Lunchería Sarkis
52 Casa de los Espaguettis
53 Marisquería Tú y Yo
54 Heladería Coromoto
55 Restaurant El Tinajero
60 Hotel Cheo's Carnes a la Brasa
61 Restaurant El Tatuy
70 Café Atico
71 La Chivatta
72 La Trattoria da Lino

OTHER
1 Bullring
3 Monument to Bolívar
19 Iowa Institute
21 Alfredo's Bar
23 Biblioteca Bolivariana
24 Museo de Arte Colonial
25 Banco Mercantil
27 Inparques Office
30 CANTV
31 Ipostel
32 Museo de Arte Moderno
33 Instituto Latino-Americano de Idiomas
36 Casa de la Cultura
37 Museo Arqueológico
38 Catedral
39 Museo Arquidiocesano
42 Banco de Venezuela
43 Banco Unión
45 Birosca Carioca
46 Buses to Bus Terminal & Airport
57 Guamanchi Expeditions
63 Natoura
65 Cable Car Station
66 Tourist Office
67 Inparques
68 Parque Las Heroínas

Central Mérida

THE ANDES

Places to Stay – middle & top end

There are plenty of decent yet affordable hotels, including the *Hotel Chama* (☎ 52 48 51, 52 10 11), Calle 29 near Avenida 4, and *Hotel Mintoy* (☎ 52 35 45, 52 03 40), Calle 25 No 8-130, just off Parque Las Heroínas. Both have comfortable doubles for around US$25 to US$30.

One of the best lodging options in town is the three-star *Hotel Belensate* (☎ 66 37 22, 66 29 63; fax 66 28 23), Urbanización La Hacienda, 2km south-west of the airport. It has nice rooms and cabañas, a fine Italian restaurant and a swimming pool. Also good, and more central, is the *Park Hotel* (☎ 63 48 66, 63 70 14; fax 63 45 82), on Calle 37, facing Parque Glorias Patrias.

Places to Eat

If you are used to unpretentious, low-budget dining, Mérida is for you. It's one of the cheapest places to eat in Venezuela and the food is generally good. Plenty of restaurants serve tasty set lunches for around US$2. The budget dining panorama seems to be changing frequently, so ask around when you come. One good and reliable place for a budget local meal is the *Mercado Principal*, on Avenida Las Américas, outside the centre. It also has plenty of fruit and vegetable stalls, and an interesting craft section.

The *Lunchería Joseph*, just off Plaza Bolívar, is an example of a good budget eatery centrally located; it's so popular that you may have to queue at the door. The cosy *Café Atico*, on Calle 25, is another recommended option for a US$2 set lunch.

The inexpensive *Restaurant Pizzería La Romana*, Calle 19 No 5-13, also has hearty set lunches, plus a variety of pizzas and à-la-carte dishes. The *Restaurant Chipen*, on Avenida 5, has no set meals but offers straightforward tasty food à la carte, including churrasco and lomito, at very reasonable prices. The *Posada Luz Caraballo* has a good inexpensive restaurant. The *Casa de los Espaguettis*, Avenida 4 No 28-52, is one of the cheapest pasta houses in town.

Cheap vegetarian set meals are served (at lunch time only) in *El Sano Glotón*, Avenida

4 No 17-76; *Restaurant Makdharma*, Avenida 4 No 18-58; *El Sabor Natural*, Avenida 3 No 16-80; *El Tinajero*, Calle 29 near Avenida 4; *Nutricentro Vegetariano*, Avenida 5 No 25-46; and *El Anfora de Aquarius*, Avenida 2 No 23-18.

The reasonably priced *Restaurant El Tatuy*, at Parque Las Heroínas, has a long menu including local food. The cosy and beautifully decorated *Restaurant Paladar*, Calle 21 No 5-68, has a short menu but good food and is not expensive. More expensive but worth it is *Hotel Cheo's Carnes a la Brasa*, which serves good steaks and trout.

The *Marisquería Tú y Yo*, Avenida 4 No 28-70, has excellent fish and seafood. *La Trattoria da Lino*, Pasaje Ayacucho No 25-30, serves wonderful Italian food at reasonable prices, whereas *La Chivatta*, next door, is the place to go for chicken.

La Exquisita Bocatá, Avenida 4 No 15-24, does delicious bocatás (a sort of sandwich with a meat filling). *El Hoyo de Queque*, corner of Avenida 4 and Calle 19, offers budget breakfasts, crêpes and other snacks at its outdoor tables. The *Lunchería Sarkis*, corner of Calle 26 and Avenida 5, has cheap Middle Eastern fast food, including felafel.

Café París, on Calle 23 off Plaza Bolívar, has tables outside and is a pleasant meeting place frequented by both locals and foreigners, though you should keep an eye on your bags, as the place has recently begun to attract thieves as well.

Café Rodos, on the corner of Plaza Bolívar, has good espresso, juices and pastries. Great cakes are served in the cosy *Tía Nicota*, in the Centro Comercial Galerías 1890, Avenida 3 No 25-42.

You shouldn't miss *Heladería Coromoto*, Avenida 3 No 28-75, which is perhaps the most famous ice-cream parlour on the continent, appearing in the *Guinness Book of Records*. The place offers roughly 650 flavours, though not all are available on an average day. Among the more unusual varieties, you can try Polar beer, shrimp, trout, chicken with spaghetti or el vegetariano. You can even have the Lonely Planet flavour (which appears under its

Spanish name, Planeta Solitario). The place is open 2 to 10 pm (closed Monday).

Entertainment

For an evening beer with dance music in a 'student' atmosphere, go to the *Birosca Carioca*, Calle 24 No 2-04, which is one of the most popular nightspots in the city centre. Or try the noisy *Alfredo's Bar*, on the corner of Calle 19 and Avenida 4.

La Jungla, Parque Glorias Patrias (Calle 36 con Avenida 4), has good music and a bigger dance floor than the Birosca. Alternatively, try *El Bodegón de Pancho*, in Centro Comercial Mamayeya on Avenida Las Américas.

Getting There & Away

Air The airport is on the meseta, right inside the city, 2km south-west of Plaza Bolívar. Frequent urban busetas pass by the airport. The runway is short, and the proximity of high mountains doesn't make landing an easy task, especially in bad weather. Consequently, particularly in the rainy season, flights are often diverted elsewhere, usually to El Vigía (accessible from Mérida, by a new road via a tunnel). If this is the case, the airline should provide free transport to/from Mérida – be sure to insist.

Avensa/Servivensa, LAI and Air Venezuela all fly daily to Caracas (US$63). Oriental de Aviación has flights to Maracaibo. Air Venezuela flies to San Antonio del Táchira via Maracaibo and to Porlamar via Caracas. For other destinations, you usually have to change in Caracas.

Bus The bus terminal is 3km south-west of the city centre; it's linked by frequent public transport, or you can take a taxi (US$2). Half a dozen buses a day run to Caracas (US$12 ordinary, US$15 deluxe, 12 hours) and to Maracaibo (US$7 ordinary, US$9.25 deluxe, nine hours). Busetas to San Cristóbal depart every two hours from 8 am to 6 pm (US$5, 5½ hours), or you can take a por puesto (US$6.50, 4½ hours); all go via El Vigía and La Fría (not via the Trans-Andean route). A new road leading through a chain of channels

between Mérida and El Vigía should be open by now, cutting down travel time by about an hour.

Four buses a day run to Valera via the Trans-Andean highway (US$4, five hours), and five buses go to Barinas (US$3.50, four hours). Both roads are spectacular. Both routes are also serviced by por-puesto cars, which are about an hour faster but cost nearly twice as much as the bus. Por puestos also operate on many shorter, regional routes, including Apartaderos and Jají.

Getting Around

Teleférico This is the world's highest and longest cable car ride and the highlight of a visit to Mérida. It was constructed in the late 1950s by a French company and runs the 12.6km from Mérida to the top of Pico Espejo (4765m), covering the 3188m climb in four stages. There are five stations: Barinitas (1577m), La Montaña (2436m), La Aguada (3452m), Loma Redonda (4045m) and Pico Espejo.

Unfortunately, the cable car is often out of order, operating for less than a year over the past five years. It was running up to Loma Redonda as we went to press, but don't be surprised if you find it closed again.

The cable car normally operates from Wednesday to Sunday, though in the tourist season it may run every day. The first trip up is at 7.30 am and the last at noon (2 pm in peak season). The last trip down is at 1.30 pm (4 pm in peak season). The ascent to Pico Espejo takes about an hour if you go straight through. Don't forget to take warm clothes.

It's best to go up as early as possible, as clouds usually obscure views later on. There may be long queues during peak holiday periods. You can book in advance at the ticket office or reserve a ticket by phone (☎ 52 50 80).

Apart from splendid views during the trip itself, the cable car provides easy access for high mountain hiking (see Around Mérida for details on hikes), saving you a day or two of puffing uphill. Bear in mind, however, that acclimatisation problems can easily occur by quickly reaching high altitudes.

THE ANDES

Bus & Taxi The city is well serviced by small buses and minibuses, or you can move around by taxi. This may be particularly convenient for trips to and from the bus terminal and airport, when you're carrying all your bags with you. The taxi trip between the city centre and the bus terminal or airport will cost about US$2 each.

Línea Tele-Cars (☎ 63 95 89, 63 56 49, 63 88 34) is a reliable and honest taxi company with radio service. Apart from services within the city, the company organises taxi trips around the region including Lagunillas and Jají (a half-day tour for US$25 per taxi), El Aguila and Mucubají (US$45 full day), and Tovar and Bailadores (US$55 full day). A taxi takes up to four passengers.

Car Rental Several car-rental companies have desks at the airport. Dávila (☎ 63 45 10) is possibly the most popular among travellers, but check others as well and compare. Look for Lada Niva, which is perhaps the cheapest car you can get (about US$35 a day including free 250km), and it's a 4WD.

AROUND MÉRIDA
The region surrounding Mérida offers plenty of attractions, both natural and cultural. You could easily spend a month here, and still only see a little of what the mountains have to offer. Many sights are accessible by road, so you can get around cheaply by public transport. This particularly refers to towns and villages which dot the Trans-Andean Highway and surrounding mountain slopes and valleys. Many of them have preserved their historic architecture and yesteryear's atmosphere.

Exploring the region is quite easy, as transport and accommodation along the Trans-Andean Highway are in good supply. Virtually every sizeable village on the road has at least one posada, and there's a satisfactory number of roadside restaurants.

If you plan on hiking, you can get to many more attractions, mostly natural ones: mountain tops, verdant valleys, glacial lakes, waterfalls, hot springs and páramos among them. You don't necessarily need a tent, as some routes are one day walks, or have accommodation facilities on the way.

Jají & Around
Jají, about 38km west of Mérida, is the best known of dozens of traditional mountain towns and villages that dot the region. It's easily accessible by por puestos from Mérida's bus terminal (US$0.60, 50 minutes). Jají was extensively reconstructed in the late 1960s to become a manicured, typical *pueblo andino* (Andean town), and is pretty touristy. Its Plaza Bolívar has a choice of handicraft shops which enjoy particularly good trade on weekends, when most visitors come. There are two budget posadas at the plaza.

Eight km before Jají, beside the road, is the Chorrera de los González, a series of five waterfalls. You can stop here to bathe in the falls' ponds, or just to have a look. You can climb three of the waterfalls by taking side paths.

Mucuchíes & Around
Mucuchíes, about 48km north-east of Mérida, is a more authentic pueblo andino than Jají. This 400 year old town has a fine parish church on Plaza Bolívar and a choice of accommodation, including the good, inexpensive *Hotel Los Andes*.

Several kilometres further down the road is the village of San Rafael, noted for an amazing small stone chapel built by a local artist, Juan Félix Sánchez (1900-97), who is buried inside. This is his second chapel; the first, in similar style, was constructed two decades ago in the remote hamlet of El Tisure, a five to seven-hour walk from San Rafael (there is no access road).

CIDA Astronomical Observatory
North of San Rafael, at an altitude of about 3600m, is the Centro de Investigaciones de Astronomía (CIDA), an astronomical observatory which has a museum of astronomy. It's normally open to the public only one weekend a month, but in peak holiday seasons (Christmas, Carnaval, Easter) it's open daily. Information can be obtained at

☎ 71 27 80, 71 38 83; email mace@cida.ve; website www.cida.ve. The centre is off the main road and there is no public transport on the access road which branches off the Mérida-Apartaderos road between Mucuchíes and San Rafael. Some Mérida companies may organise tours to the observatory.

Theme Parks
There are three theme parks in the vicinity of Mérida. They have become favourite attractions for Venezuelan tourists, though they may look somewhat pretentious for some foreign travellers. Put aside at least three hours to visit any of the parks. Don't enter them if it's raining because much of the action takes place outdoors. All the parks are open daily from about 9 am to 4 pm (longer on weekends); admission is US$5 to US$8.

Los Aleros, on the road to Mucuchíes, shortly past Tabay, was opened in 1984. It's a re-creation of a typical Andean village from the 1930s, brought to life with period events, crafts and food, plus a few extra surprises. Por puestos from the corner of Calle 19 and Avenida 4 in Mérida will take you there.

The **Venezuela de Antier** was opened in the early 1990s, following the success of Los Aleros. Here, the same entrepreneur, Romer Alexis Montilla, has created a sort of Venezuela in a capsule, by reproducing its landmarks, costumes and traditions. You'll find the Plaza Bolívar of Caracas, the Puente Urdaneta of Maracaibo and the oldest monument to Bolívar from Mérida. You'll see Amazonian Indians, Guajiro women in their traditional dresses, and even General Juan Vicente Gómez will show up in his uniform. The old trapiche serves sugarcane juice for guests, and cockfights may be held at weekends. There's also a collection of old cars. The park is several kilometres from Mérida on the Jají road; take a por puesto from Calle 26.

The most recent park, **Xamú – Pueblo Indígena**, is based on an Indian theme. Built on a hillside near the town of Lagunillas, it's a re-creation of an Indian settlement typical of the groups which once populated the region. Visitors are guided around rustic dwellings, lectured on traditional farming methods and shown weaving techniques and other activities, to gain an insight into the lifestyle of the indigenous people before the Spanish conquest.

Hiking & Mountaineering
Possibilities are almost unlimited. Some of the more popular destinations are detailed below, but there are plenty of other options. Except for the Pico Bolívar climb, the other listed trips can be made without a guide, though it's more comfortable and safer to go on an organised tour. If you prefer to go on your own anyway, most of Mérida's tour operators, including Bum Bum, Guamanchi and Natoura, will provide information free of charge about these and other do-it-yourself tours. Don't ignore their comments about safety measures. Some companies, including Bum Bum, sell trekking maps of the area.

Bear in mind that weather can change frequently and rapidly even in the dry season. Rain can occur anytime and visibility can drop dramatically within an hour, leaving you trapped high up in the mountains for quite a while. Be careful and hike properly equipped, with good rain gear and warm clothing, and some extra food and water. Particular care should be taken on remote trails where you may not meet anyone for days. Also keep in mind the altitude sickness risk (see Health in the Facts for the Visitor chapter).

Pico Bolívar This is possibly the most popular peak to climb, mostly because it's Venezuela's highest point (5007m). Given the country's mania for Bolívar monuments, it probably shouldn't come as a surprise that a bust of the hero has been placed on the summit.

The climb is not technically difficult, but requires a rope and you shouldn't do it without a guide (particularly in the wet season) unless you have sound mountaineering experience. Virtually every major tour company in Mérida organises trips to Pico

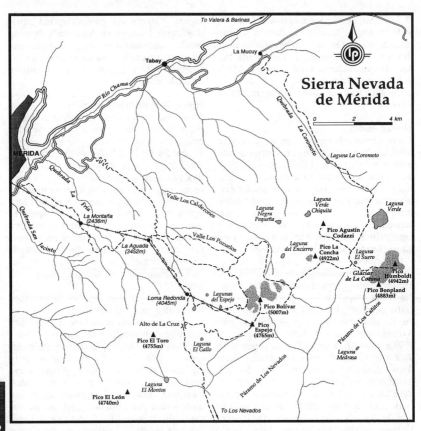

To Valera & Barinas

La Mucuy

Tabay

Río Chama

Sierra Nevada de Mérida

Quebrada La Coromoto

0   2   4 km

MÉRIDA

Quebrada La Fría

Laguna La Coromoto

Quebrada San Jacinto

La Montaña (2436m)

Valle Los Calderones

Valle Los Pozuelos

Laguna Negra Pequeña

Laguna Verde Chiquita

Laguna Verde

La Aguada (3452m)

Laguna del Encierro

Pico Agustín Codazzi

Pico La Concha (4922m)

Laguna El Suero

Loma Redonda (4045m)

Lagunas del Espejo

Pico Bolívar (5007m)

Glaciar de La Corona

Pico Humboldt (4942m)

Pico Bonpland (4883m)

Alto de La Cruz

Pico El Toro (4755m)

Laguna El Gallo

Pico Espejo (4765m)

Páramo de Los Cañitos

Laguna Medrasa

Páramo de Los Nevados

Laguna El Montos

Pico El León (4740m)

To Los Nevados

Bolívar, usually offering a range of options, including combination trips to Pico Bolívar, Los Nevados, Pico Humboldt etc.

Pico Humboldt This is perhaps the second most popular peak among climbers and high-mountain trekkers, and Venezuela's second highest summit (4942m). There's not much here in the way of mountaineering, but the hike itself is marvellous.

The starting point for the trek is La Mucuy, accessible by road from Mérida. Take a carro to Tabay, from the corner of Calle 19 and Avenida 4. From Tabay's Plaza Bolívar, por puesto jeeps go to La Mucuy; Inparques has its post here.

A four to six-hour walk will take you up to the small Laguna La Coromoto (3200m), where trekkers normally camp the first night. The next day, it's a three to four-hour walk to reach Laguna Verde (4000m), one of the largest lakes in the area. Some hikers stay here the second night, but if it's still not too late, you can walk for another hour to Laguna El Suero, a tiny lake at about 4200m, almost at the foot of the glacier. It gets freezing at night, so have plenty of warm clothes.

Pico Humboldt is a two to four-hour ascent, depending on the weather. You reach the snowline at about 4700 to 4800m. Further up, crampons and an ice axe are recommended, and keep an eye out for crevices. Again, this climb is best done with an experienced local guide, particularly in the rainy (snowy) season.

Back at Laguna El Suero, you can return the same way to La Mucuy or continue along the route known as La Travesía to Pico Espejo (4765m). After an initial 500m ascent from the lake, the trail to Pico Espejo (four to six hours) goes for most of the way at roughly the same altitude, nearly 4700m. You then can climb Pico Bolívar, before returning to Mérida by foot or teleférico (if it works). The whole loop will take four to seven days, or even longer, depending on how many peaks you climb and the weather conditions.

The mountain-tour operators in Mérida can provide full equipment and guides for these treks.

Los Nevados If you are not up to scaling the peaks, there's an easy and spectacular (and therefore very popular) trip to Los Nevados, a charming mountain pueblo set at an altitude of about 2700m (accommodation and food available). The trip is normally done as a two to three day loop, and includes a jeep, mule rides and the use of the cable car if operational.

The usual way of getting to the village is by jeep along a breathtaking mountain track hugging the cliffside (US$50 per jeep for up to five people, four to five hours). You stay the night in Los Nevados, from where you walk, or ride on muleback to Loma Redonda cable-car station. You can then return by cable car to Mérida, or walk downhill to the beautiful Valle Los Calderones for another night, and return to Mérida on the third day.

You can also do the trip the other way round: go by cable car to Loma Redonda and walk to Los Nevados (four to five hours) for the night. From Los Nevados, you can walk back the same way (six hours) and return by

cable car, or take one of the sporadic jeeps to Mérida (63km). Some hikers continue walking for seven hours (24km) over to the village of El Morro (rooms and meals available), from where there are more jeeps to Mérida.

Sierra La Culata This national park, to the north of Mérida, also offers some amazing hiking territory, and is particularly noted for its desert-like highland landscapes. Take a por puesto to La Culata (departing from Calle 19 between Avenidas 1 and 2), from where it's a three to four-hour hike uphill north-east to a primitive shelter known as El Refugio at about 3700m. Continue the next day for about three hours to the top of Pico Pan de Azúcar (4660m). Return before 4 pm, the time the last por puesto tends to depart back to Mérida.

Some guided tours don't return the same way but descend south-east through a deserted, moonscape-like terrain to a chain of mountain lakes and on via the natural hot springs down to Mucuchíes. Trails are faint on this route and it's easy to get lost if you don't know the way; don't wander too far unless you're an experienced trekker.

Pico El Aguila & Around This is another interesting area for hiking. Take a morning bus to Valera and get off at Venezuela's highest road pass (4007m), at the foot of the **Pico El Aguila** (4118m), about 60km from Mérida. Bolívar marched this way on one of his campaigns, hence the monument dedicated to the hero on the pass. It's the statue of a condor.

There's a roadside restaurant where you can have a hot chocolate before setting off. Take the side road up to El Aguila peak (a 20-minute walk), crowned with a CANTV mast, for beautiful páramo and great panoramic views around. Here you may find the bearded helmetcrest, living at the highest altitude of the hummingbird species.

Locals with mules often wait on the pass opposite the restaurant to take tourists to **Laguna Mucubají** (3540m), 5km due south,

THE ANDES

but it's perhaps better to walk there, so as to get a closer look at the splendid páramo filled with frailejones. The walk, downhill all the way, will bring you to the Barinas road and the laguna, just off the road. It's one of the largest lakes in the Sierra Nevada national park.

You can walk from here (for one hour) up the reforested pine slope to **Laguna Negra**, a small but beautiful mountain lake with amazingly dark water. A 45 minute walk further uphill is another fine lake, **Laguna Los Patos**.

If you want to camp, get a permit from Inparques at Laguna Mucubají. The office is open from 8 am to 6 pm, and the staff can provide information on other sights in the area. There are two hotels by the road near the lake, including the excellent Spanish-run *Parador Turístico Sierra Nevada* (US$15 a double with a fireplace).

A trail from Laguna Mucubají goes 7km south to the top of **Pico Mucuñuque** (4672m), the highest peak in this range, known as the Serranía de Santo Domingo. The round trip will take you a good part of the day. It's a rather difficult hike, as the trail is not clear in the upper reaches and you have to ascend over 1100m from the laguna. Ask for detailed instructions at the Inparques post.

Mountain Biking

Biking is becoming increasingly popular in the region. Several tour companies in Mérida organise bike trips and rent bikes. Shop around as bicycle quality and rental prices may differ substantially between tour companies.

One of the most popular bike routes is the loop around the remote mountain villages south of Mérida, known as Pueblos del Sur. The loop normally includes the villages of San José, Mucutuy, Mucuchachí, Canaguá, Chacantá, El Molino, Capurí and Guaraque. It's a beautiful trip – provided you've got legs of iron.

Paragliding

Paragliding is another popular new activity

in the region. Most tour operators offer tandem flights with a skilled pilot, so no previous experience is necessary. The usual starting point for flights is Las González, an hour's jeep ride from Mérida, from where you fly for about 20 to 30 minutes over an 850m altitude difference. The cost of the flight is much the same with all agencies (US$60), jeep transport included.

Some agencies offer paragliding courses which take five to eight days, cover theory (available in English) and practice (including three solo flights) and cost US$300 to US$350. The course allows you to fly solo, but you'll still have to rent a paraglider (US$50 a flight, US$200 a week) plus transport.

One of the most experienced local gliding pilots and instructors is Raúl Penso, who runs tandem flights and conducts courses. He can be contacted through Bum Bum.

Rafting

This is the newest craze. It was introduced in 1996 by Bum Bum, and other companies (including Natoura) are eager to go on with it as well. Rafting is done on some of the rivers at the southern foothills of the Andes, and is usually included in the tour to Los Llanos. Rafting is a wet-season activity, normally from May to November, but climate anomalies over the past few years make it difficult to determine the season.

Fishing

Anglers may be interested in trout fishing. The most popular places to fish are Laguna Mucubají and Laguna La Victoria, and, to a lesser extent, Laguna Negra and Laguna Los Patos. The fishing season runs from April to September. You need a permit from the Ministerio de Agricultura y Cría (☎ 63 29 81), Avenida Urdaneta, near the airport in Mérida. The permit costs next to nothing and allows for angling in the national park.

Fishing equipment can be hired from some tour companies or, if you plan on serious angling, buy your own gear in Mérida.

Táchira State

SAN CRISTÓBAL
* *pop 320,000*
* *area code* ☎ (076)

The capital of Táchira state, San Cristóbal is today a thriving commercial centre fuelled by the proximity of Colombia just 40km away. Spread over a mountain slope at an altitude of about 800m, the city has an attractive location and agreeable climate, with an average temperature of 21°C. However, San Cristóbal has no extraordinary attractions, therefore for most travellers it's just a place to pass through. It is a transit point on the Pan-American route between Venezuela and Colombia, and you'll surely pass through if you come from or go to Cúcuta in Colombia.

Founded in 1561 by Juan de Maldonado, the town grew slowly, and three centuries after its birth it was still not much more than an obscure settlement. This is why the city has almost no colonial architecture.

For over 200 years, San Cristóbal was ruled from Nueva Granada (present-day Colombia). In 1777, with the rest of Táchira, it came under Venezuelan administration. Even then, though, because of the lack of roads to Caracas, the town was linked more to Colombia than to Venezuela. It wasn't until 1925 that the winding Trans-Andean road reached San Cristóbal from Mérida, and when the Pan-American highway was completed in the 1950s, it provided a fast, lowland link with the centre of the country.

Information
Tourist Office The Cotatur tourist office (☎ 56 28 05, 56 59 56; fax 56 24 21) is in the Complejo Ferial (Fair Complex), on the corner of Avenida España and Avenida Universidad, in Pueblo Nuevo district, about 3km north-east of the city centre. It's open Monday to Friday from 8 am to noon and 2 to 5.30 pm. To get there, take the white bus marked Pueblo Nuevo heading northbound along Avenida 7.

Cotatur has unreliable módulos de información at the airport terminals of Santo Domingo and San Antonio, and plans to open one in San Cristóbal's bus terminal.

Inparques The Inparques office (☎ 46 52 16; fax 47 01 83) is in Parque Metropolitano, Avenida 19 de Abril.

Money Some of the useful central banks have been marked on the map.

Things to See
San Cristóbal began its life around what is now Plaza Maldonado. The monumental **Catedral** wasn't completed until the early 20th century, after the previous church had been wrecked by an earthquake. It houses the venerated statue of San Sebastián, the city's patron saint. Next door to the cathedral is the fine **Palacio Episcopal**. On the northern side of the plaza is the massive **Edificio Nacional**, now home to courts of law.

Plaza Bolívar is not a colonial square either. The oldest building here is the 1907 **Ateneo de San Cristóbal**, recently thoroughly restored. Opposite, the large modern Centro Cívico houses the **Museo de Artes Visuales**.

There are other historic buildings on and around Plaza Sucre. The large **Palacio de Gobierno**, also known as the Palacio de los Leones after the stone lions placed on the roof, was built in the 1910s as a government house. The nearby decorative building accommodates the **Universidad Nacional Abierta**.

The **Complejo Ferial**, 3km north-east of the centre, is a large fair and sports complex, complete with exhibition halls, multiple sports stadium, velodrome and Venezuela's second largest bullring. Two km north of the complex along Avenida Universidad is the **Museo del Táchira**, in an old hacienda. It features archaeology, history, art and craft collections, and is open Tuesday to Sunday from 9 am to noon and 2 to 5 pm.

Special Events
San Cristóbal's major annual bash is the Feria de San Sebastián, which is held in the

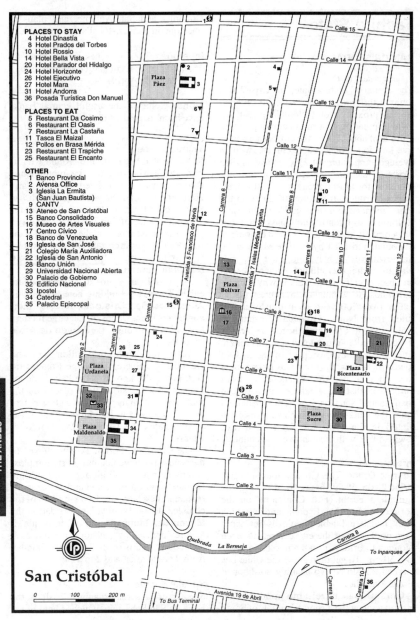

PLACES TO STAY
4 Hotel Dinastía
8 Hotel Prados del Torbes
10 Hotel Rossio
14 Hotel Bella Vista
20 Hotel Parador del Hidalgo
24 Hotel Horizonte
26 Hotel Ejecutivo
27 Hotel Mara
31 Hotel Andorra
36 Posada Turística Don Manuel

PLACES TO EAT
5 Restaurant Da Cosimo
6 Restaurant El Oasis
7 Restaurant La Castaña
11 Tasca El Maizal
12 Pollos en Brasa Mérida
23 Restaurant El Trapiche
25 Restaurant El Encanto

OTHER
1 Banco Provincial
2 Avensa Office
3 Iglesia La Ermita
  (San Juan Bautista)
9 CANTV
13 Ateneo de San Cristóbal
15 Banco Consolidado
16 Museo de Artes Visuales
17 Centro Cívico
18 Banco de Venezuela
19 Iglesia de San José
21 Colegio María Auxiliadora
22 Iglesia de San Antonio
28 Banco Unión
29 Universidad Nacional Abierta
30 Palacio de Gobierno
32 Edificio Nacional
33 Ipostel
34 Catedral
35 Palacio Episcopal

THE ANDES

San Cristóbal

0   100   200 m

second half of January. It includes agricultural and industrial fairs, bullfights, bicycle races and other sports events, craft fair, popular music, dance and parades, plus a lot of food and drink. Many events take place at the Complejo Ferial.

Places to Stay
If you're coming by bus and just need shelter for the night, there are several basic hotels directly south of the bus terminal. Alternatively, go to the city centre (a 10 minute ride by local bus) where there are plenty of budget hotels (some double as love hotels).

The *Hotel Andorra*, Carrera 4 No 4-67, near the cathedral, is one of the cheapest central options, rated at US$6/8 for a single/double. Set in an old house with a fine patio, it has some charm but basic rooms. The nearby *Hotel Mara* (☎ 43 82 18) is also on the basic side and costs about a dollar more. Another budget choice in the same area is the *Hotel Ejecutivo* (☎ 44 62 98), Calle 6 No 3-25, which offers marginally better standards, and costs US$8 for a matrimonial with bath. The *Hotel Horizonte* (☎ 43 00 11), also in this area, is appreciably better and costs US$12/14/17 a single/double/triple.

Five blocks towards the east, the *Hotel Parador del Hidalgo* (☎ 43 28 39), Calle 7 No 9-35, is simple and lacks style, but has clean rooms with private baths and hot water, for US$10 a double. More prepossessing is the *Hotel Rossio* (☎ 43 23 30), Carrera 9 No 10-98, which charges US$8/10/12 for a matrimonial/double/triple with bath and fan. The nearby *Hotel Prados del Torbes* (☎ 43 90 55) costs US$12/15/18.

For more style and comfort, try the *Hotel Bella Vista* (☎ 43 78 66, 43 81 58), on the corner of Carrera 9 and Calle 9, which has spacious singles/doubles/triples with bath for US$16/22/25. Possibly the best place to stay in the centre is the *Hotel Dinastía* (☎ 44 13 66; fax 44 89 95), Avenida 7 at Calle 14, which has air-conditioned singles/doubles/triples for US$32/38/40.

San Cristóbal has several posadas – a good budget alternative to hotels, worth considering, particularly so if you are in town for

more than just one night. The closest to the centre is the *Posada Turística Don Manuel* (☎ 47 80 82), Carrera 10 No 1-63, off Avenida 19 de Abril. It has just four rooms, costing US$10/12/14 a single/double/triple with bath, TV and fridge, and you can use the kitchen. Other posadas include *La Montagnola* (☎ 56 52 76), Avenida ULA, Quinta Antoniana, near the Complejo Ferial; *La Fuente* (☎ 44 46 26), Avenida Principal Pueblo Nuevo, Sector El Paraíso; and the more expensive, air-conditioned *Los Pirineos* (☎ 55 56 28), Avenida Francisco Cárdenas, Quinta El Cerrito, Urbanización Pirineos.

The poshest place to stay in town is the *Hotel El Tamá* (☎ 55 83 66, 56 12 47; fax 55 04 46), Avenida 19 de Abril, Urbanización Los Pirineos. It has a restaurant, bar, gym and swimming pool.

Places to Eat
There are many restaurants throughout the centre, including numerous greasy spoons which serve set lunches for US$2 (eg *La Castaña* or the restaurant in the *Hotel Parador del Hidalgo*). Just round the corner from the latter, the *Restaurant El Trapiche* is slightly better and more enjoyable. More decent central eateries include the *Restaurant Da Cosimo*, Avenida 7 No 13-51, and the restaurant of the *Hotel Dinastía*.

Vegetarians can get budget lunches at *El Encanto*, Calle 6 No 3-57, and *El Oasis*, Avenida 5 at Calle 13.

Getting There & Away
Air San Cristóbal's airport is in Santo Domingo, about 35km south-east of the city, but there's not much air traffic going through here. The airport in San Antonio del Táchira is far busier and just about the same distance from San Cristóbal.

Bus The bus terminal is about 2km south of the city centre, linked by frequent city bus services. There are about 10 buses daily to Caracas (US$12.50 ordinary, US$15.75 deluxe, 13 hours). Most depart in the late afternoon/early evening for an overnight trip via El Llano highway. Busetas to Barinas run every hour or so between about 6 am and 6 pm (US$5, five hours).

In theory, busetas to Mérida go every two hours from 8 am until 6 pm (US$5, 5½ hours); in practice, however, they depart as soon as all seats are taken. The 6 pm buseta is unreliable if fewer than 10 passengers show up. There are also por-puesto cars to Mérida (US$6.50, 4½ hours).

Por-puesto minibuses to San Antonio del Táchira, on the Colombian border, run every 10 or 15 minutes (US$1, 1¼ hours); it's a quite spectacular road. Por-puesto minibuses and busetas to La Grita depart pretty regularly (US$2.50, two hours), and there's reasonable transport to other regional destinations.

SAN PEDRO DEL RÍO
- *pop 3000*
- *area code* ☎ (077)

San Pedro del Río is a tiny old town about 40km north of San Cristóbal. It has been extensively restored and has some fine architecture. It's colonial-looking, well cared for and clean, and has become a popular weekend haunt among visitors from the region, mostly from San Cristóbal. On these days, food and craft stalls open and the town blossoms. During the rest of the week, by contrast, San Pedro is an oasis of peace and tranquillity.

There are perhaps four calles and four carreras altogether, all cobblestoned and lined with single-storey whitewashed houses. Calle Real is the nerve centre of the town, and it's here that most craft shops and restaurants are nestled.

Places to Stay & Eat
The town's first and best known place to stay is the *Posada Turística La Vieja Escuela* (☎ 93 720), Calle Real No 3-61. Located in a fine historic house which once was a school, the posada has spotlessly neat matrimoniales/quads for US$14/20 and its own restaurant serving regional specialities. You can sample some local alcoholic drinks, including leche de burra, calentado, piñita and fresa mora.

Alternatively, you can stay in the *Posada Turística Paseo La Chirirí*, Calle Los Morales No 1-27, which has matrimoniales/triples for US$15/20. There's also the *Posada Valparaiso* (☎ 91 10 32), on the road to San Juan de Colón, about 3km out of San Pedro. It has its own restaurant.

There has been an impressive growth of eating outlets in San Pedro over recent years, though most of them only open on weekends. The major restaurants include *La Casona de los Abuelos* and *Río de las Casas* on Calle Real, and *El Refugio de San Pedro* on Plaza Bolívar.

Getting There & Away
San Pedro del Río lies just off the unfinished San Cristóbal-La Fría freeway. There are still two large sections of the freeway to be built and traffic uses the old winding mountain roads.

From San Cristóbal, take the half-hourly Línea Colón bus to San Juan de Colón (US$0.80, 1¼ hour) and ask the driver to let you off at the turnoff to San Pedro (about 10km before San Juan), from where it's a 10 minute walk to the town. To return from San Pedro to San Cristóbal, take the Expresos Ayacucho bus to San Juan de Colón (US$0.25, 20 minutes) and change for the Línea Colón bus to San Cristóbal (US$1, 1½ hours). There may be one or two direct buses a day from San Pedro to San Cristóbal.

If you are coming from the north (eg from Mérida or Maracaibo), get off at the turnoff to San Pedro, about 10km past San Juan de Colón (driver will know where to let you off). To go to Mérida from San Pedro, go by Expresos Ayacucho bus to San Juan de Colón, then change for one of the frequent buses to La Fría (US$0.50, 50 minutes), change there for a bus to El Vigía and change again for a bus to Mérida.

SAN ANTONIO DEL TÁCHIRA
- *pop 50,000*
- *area code* ☎ (076)

San Antonio is a Venezuelan border town of some 50,000 people, living off trade with neighbouring Colombia. You will pass through it if taking this route between the two countries. Wind your watch back one hour when crossing from Venezuela to Colombia.

Information

Tourist Office There's no tourist office in town, but any of several travel agencies on Carrera 4 (marked on the map) should solve transport problems.

Immigration The DIEX office is on Carrera 9, between Calles 6 and 7, and is theoretically open daily from 6 am to 8 pm, though it

may close earlier. You must get an exit or entry stamp in your passport here. There's a departure tax of some US$5 to US$10 (it seems to change frequently), paid in bolívares, required from all tourists leaving Venezuela via this border crossing.

Nationals of most countries don't need a visa for Colombia, but all travellers must get an entry stamp from DAS (Colombian immigration). The DAS office is just behind the bridge over Río Táchira (the actual border), and has similar opening hours to DIEX.

It's a short walk from San Antonio, but it's

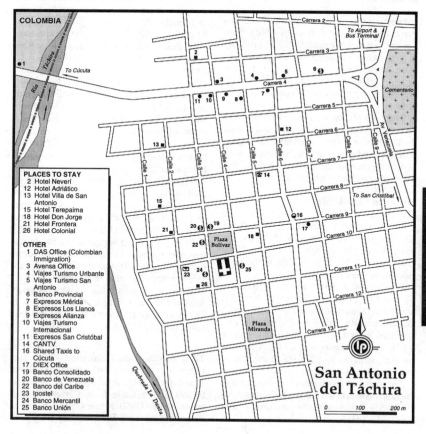

PLACES TO STAY
2 Hotel Neverí
12 Hotel Adriático
13 Hotel Villa de San Antonio
15 Hotel Terepaima
18 Hotel Don Jorge
21 Hotel Frontera
26 Hotel Colonial

OTHER
1 DAS Office (Colombian Immigration)
3 Avensa Office
4 Viajes Turismo Uribante
5 Viajes Turismo San Antonio
6 Banco Provincial
7 Expresos Mérida
8 Expresos Los Llanos
9 Expresos Alianza
10 Viajes Turismo Internacional
11 Expresos San Cristóbal
14 CANTV
16 Shared Taxis to Cúcuta
17 DIEX Office
19 Banco Consolidado
20 Banco de Venezuela
22 Banco del Caribe
23 Ipostel
24 Banco Mercantil
25 Banco Unión

San Antonio del Táchira

0   100   200 m

THE ANDES

perhaps better not to walk over the bridge, as some cases of robbery have been reported. The scam is that someone 'accidentally' bumps into you, throwing you off balance, while your backpack is ripped off you and thrown over the bridge, and accomplices below take care of it from there. Instead of walking, take a bus or a colectivo (that's what por puestos are called in Colombia) which will let you off in front of DAS.

There's another DAS office in Cúcuta, in the suburb of San Rafael, Avenida 1 No 28-57, and also a DAS office at Cúcuta airport, but the latter only deals with air passengers.

Money There are more than half a dozen banks in San Antonio, none of which changes cash. Banco Consolidado will probably change American Express travellers cheques, while Banco Unión, Banco de Venezuela, Banco Mercantil and Banco Provincial may service Visa/MasterCard cardholders.

There are plenty of casas de cambio in the centre, particularly on Carrera 4 and around the DIEX office. They all change US dollars, bolívares and pesos, at rates similar to those in Cúcuta across the border. None of the casas changes travellers cheques.

Places to Stay & Eat

Hotel Frontera (☎ 71 52 45), Calle 2 No 8-70, is possibly the cheapest in town (US$4/6 a double without/with bath), but basic. *Hotel Villa de San Antonio* (☎ 71 10 23), Carrera 6 No 1-61, is also on the basic side but is more expensive.

Probably the best budget bet is *Hotel Colonial* (☎ 71 26 79), Carrera 11 No 2-51, which has clean matrimoniales/doubles with fan and private bath for US$7/9. It has its own inexpensive restaurant. Quite similar is the *Hotel Terepaima* (☎ 71 17 63), Carrera 8 No 1-37, which costs US$10 a double. It also has a cheap restaurant.

The cheapest air-conditioned rooms are in the *Hotel Nevarí* (☎ 71 50 02), Carrera 3 No 3-13. Singles/doubles/triples/quads cost US$10/12/14/15.

The best accommodation in town is at *Hotel Don Jorge* (☎ 71 40 89; fax 71 19 32), Calle 5 No 9-20, and *Hotel Adriático* (☎ 71 03 97; fax 71 57 57), Calle 6, corner of Carrera 6. Either costs about US$18/25/32 a single/double/triple, and both have their own restaurants.

Getting There & Away

Air The airport is a couple of km north-east of town, reached by local transport. Avensa/Servivensa has four flights daily to Caracas (US$86) and Aserca has a further two flights. Aeropostal and Air Venezuela fly to Maracaibo (US$49), and there are flights to other domestic destinations. Servivensa flies daily to Medellín in Colombia (US$45) and to Bogotá (US$50). These are the cheapest onward tickets out of Venezuela, and a rather convenient way of getting to these two Colombian destinations at a price only marginally higher than you'd pay by bus.

All the local travel agencies will book and sell air tickets for flights within Venezuela and to Colombia (but not for Colombian domestic flights).

Bus San Antonio has a new bus terminal, halfway to the airport. Four bus companies – Expresos Mérida, Expresos Los Llanos, Expresos Alianza and Expresos San Cristóbal – operate buses to Caracas, with a total of seven buses daily. All depart between 4 and 7 pm and use El Llano route (US$13.25 ordinary, US$16.75 deluxe, about 14 hours). Bus companies still maintain their offices in the town centre, close to each other on Carrera 4, where they also sell tickets.

There are no direct buses to Mérida; go to San Cristóbal and change. Por puestos to San Cristóbal leave frequently from the bus terminal (US$1, 1¼ hours).

To Colombia Buses and shared taxis run frequently to Cúcuta in Colombia, about 12km from San Antonio. Catch buses (US$0.30) on Calle 6 or Carrera 4, and shared taxis (US$0.50) on Calle 6 near the corner of Carrera 9. Both will deposit you at the Cúcuta bus terminal, passing through the centre. You can pay in bolívares or pesos.

The Cúcuta terminal is dirty, busy and unsafe – one of the poorest in Colombia. So watch your belongings closely. You may be approached by very well-dressed English-speaking characters who will offer help in buying your bus ticket for you. Ignore them – they are con-men. Buy your ticket directly from the bus office.

There are frequent buses to Bucaramanga (US$12, six hours). Approximately a dozen air-conditioned buses run daily to Bogotá (US$32, 16 hours). If you plan on staying in Cúcuta, don't go all the way to the terminal, but get off in the centre.

Los Llanos

Occupying the entire central part of Venezuela, roughly a third of the national territory, Los Llanos (literally the plains) are billiard-table-flat, low-lying savannas. They extend south-westwards, well into Colombia, taking up just about as vast an area of that neighbouring country as they do of Venezuela.

In administrative terms, Venezuelan Llanos comprises the states of Barinas, Apure, Portuguesa, Cojedes and Guárico. Sometimes the southern parts of Anzoátegui and Monagas are also regarded as the Llanos (and called Llanos Orientales, or Eastern Llanos). The Llanos are at their best down south, in Apure state, which is referred to as the Llano Bajo (Lower Llano).

A result of the accumulation of sand, clay and mud deposited by rivers over millions of years, these eerie expanses really lack any distinguishing topographic features. They are mostly covered with grass, with ribbons of gallery forest along the rivers, and scattered islands of woodland here and there. Rivers are numerous and, in the wet season, voluminous; the main ones are the Apure, Meta, Arauca and Capanaparo – all of which are left-bank tributaries of the Orinoco, which itself is the south-eastern border of the Llanos.

The climate of Los Llanos has a clearly defined pattern, and is extreme in both wet and dry seasons. The former (referred to as *invierno*, or literally winter) lasts from May to November and is characterised by frequent and intense rains. The rivers overflow, turning much of the land into shallow lagoons. Humboldt, who was here in this season, compared Los Llanos to an ocean covered with seaweed. In December, the rains stop and rivers return to their normal courses, steadily getting narrower as the dry season (called *verano*, or summer) progresses. The sun beats down upon the parched soil and winds blow the dust all around.

The Llanos are sparsely populated. Except

HIGHLIGHTS

- Go on wildlife safaris in the *hatos*
- Visit the Santuario de la Virgen de Coromoto
- Experience the unique sounds of *joropo*

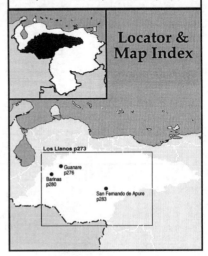

Locator & Map Index

Los Llanos p273

Guanare p276

Barinas p280

San Fernando de Apure p283

for San Fernando de Apure, in the heart of the region, all the significant urban centres developed in the more hospitable environment at the northern outskirts of the plains. Roads are few, but the state, in an attempt to open up the plains, has built a few access roads. San Fernando de Apure is accessible by paved roads from Maracay/Caracas in the north, and Barinas/Guanare in the northwest. The road from San Fernando southwards to Puerto Páez, on the Colombian frontier, is in large part surfaced.

The inhabitants of the plains, the *llaneros*, are tough and resistant people, used to a hard life. Not without reason, Bolívar employed them in his army to fight against the Spaniards, with great success. As the soil is not all

Los Llanos
0
25
50 km
TRUJILLO
PORTUGUESA
COJEDES
GUÁRICO
BARINAS
APURE
BOLÍVAR
COLOMBIA
San Carlos
Tinaco
Guanare
Barinas
San Fernando de Apure
Calabozo
Valle de la Pascua
Acarigua
Araure
Biscucuy
Boconó
Trujillo
Valera
Sabana Grande
La Puerta
Timotes
Santo Domingo
Parque Nacional Sierra Nevada
Barinitas
Barrancas
Boconoito
Santuario de la Virgen de Coromoto
Sanare
Guanarito
Libertad
San Silvestre
San Rafael de Canagua
Puerto de Nutrias
Bruzual
Mantecal
La Ye
Hato El Frío
Apurito
Achaguas
Camaguan
Cazorla
El Baúl
Hato Piñero
Galeras
Dos Caminos
El Sombrero
Barbacoas
El Calvario
Chaguaramas
Las Mercedes
Lezama
Las Piedras
San Antonio de Tamanaco
Embalse Playa de Riecito
Tucupido
El Socorro
Mejo
Santa Rita
Cabruta
Caicara de Orinoco
Las Bonitas
Santa Rosalía
Mantecal
Parque Nacional Aguaro-Guariquito
Embalse del Guárico
Parque Nacional Cinaruco-Capanaparo
Hato San Leonardo
Guachara
Hato La Trinidad de Arauca
Hato El Cedral
Elorza
Guasdalito
El Amparo de Apure
Arauca
Puerto Carreño
Puerto Páez
El Burro
Río Orinoco
Río Apure
Río Apure Viejo
Río Portuguesa
Río Guárico
Río Chirgua
Río Cojedes
Río San Carlos
Río Guanare
Río Masparro
Río Santo Domingo
Río Canagua
Río Anaro
Río Sipapo
Río Arauca
Río Capanaparo
Río Cinaruco
Río Meta
Río Manapire
Río Espino
Río San Bartolo
Río Zuata
Río Macaira
Río Maniapure
Río Suapure
Río Cuchivero
Río Guaniamo
Caño Tortuga
Caño Guaritico
Río Arichuna
Río Apurito
To Barcelona
To Ciudad Bolívar
To Maracay & Caracas
To Valencia
To San Cristóbal
To Puerto Ayacucho

LOS LLANOS

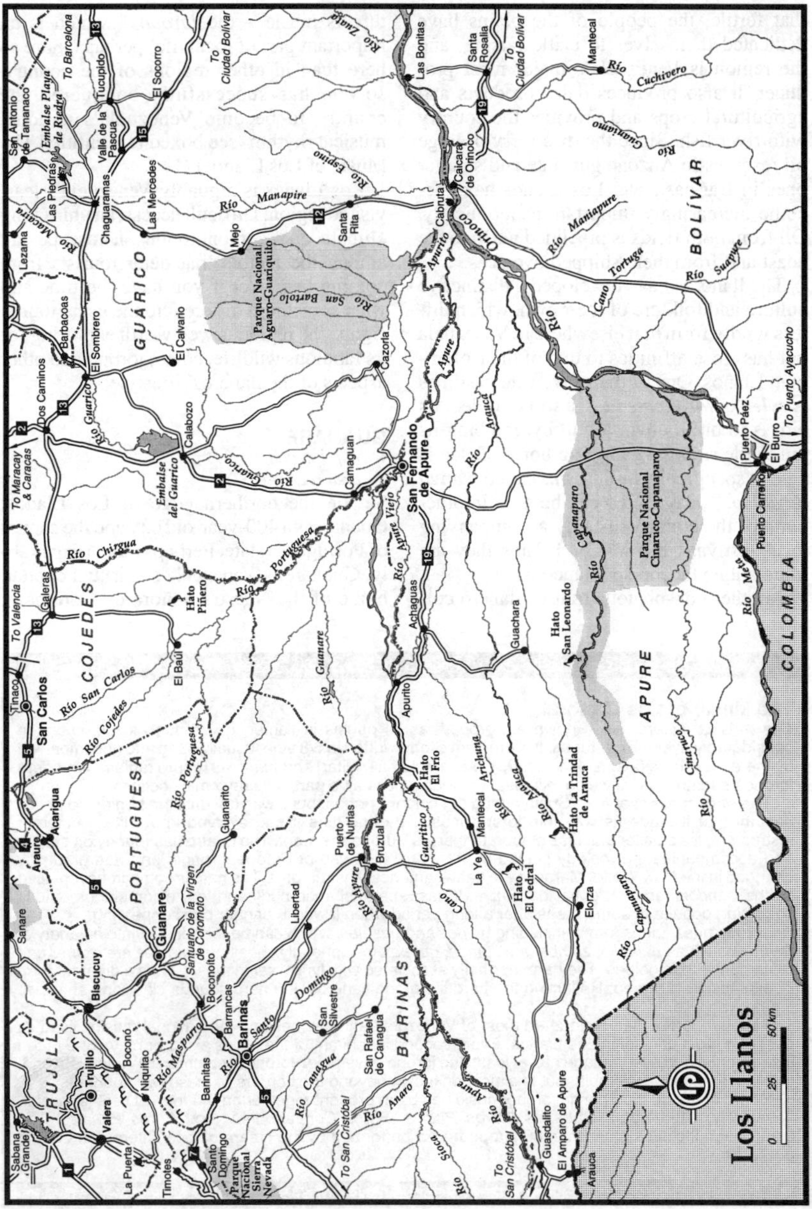

that fertile, the people of the plains have dedicated themselves to cattle raising, and the region is Venezuela's major meat producer. It also produces dairy products and agricultural crops and provides the country with river fish. Since the discovery of large oil reserves in Anzoátegui state and smaller ones in Barinas state, Los Llanos have become increasingly important economically. Oil from both fields is pipelined north to the coast and from there shipped overseas.

The llaneros have developed a distinctive culture and folklore of their own, which differs wildly from that elsewhere in Venezuela but has close affinities to that of the Colombian Llanos. One of their favourite pastimes is *coleo* or *toros coleados*, a sort of rodeo. Its aim is to bring down a bull by grabbing its tail while riding a galloping horse. Coleo is held at specifically built tracks called *manga de coleo*. Today, coleo can be seen in other parts of the country, usually accompanying local festivals, but in Los Llanos they are more authentic and spontaneous.

Another conspicuous trait of llanero culture is music – the *joropo* – which is an important part of local life, perhaps more so here than in other regions of the country. Joropo has successfully conquered the country to become Venezuela's national musical rhythm (see boxed text entitled The Music of Los Llanos).

Los Llanos is arguably Venezuela's least visited region. Difficult access, an uninviting climate and a monotonous landscape are among the factors that deter tourists from coming here. Yet if you have the time and want something different to the usual tourist sights, the region is well worth exploring for its fabulous wildlife, coleo, joropo and other aspects of the llaneros' lifestyle.

GUANARE
- *pop 130,000*
- *area code ☎ (057)*

Set on the northern edge of Los Llanos, Guanare is a 400-year-old city and the capital of Portuguesa state. Perhaps more remarkably, Guanare is Venezuela's spiritual capital, home of the Nuestra Señora de Coromoto,

The Music of Los Llanos
The *música llanera*, also known as *joropo*, has its origins in flamenco, although it has changed considerably over the centuries. It's a rhythmic form written in 6/8 time, usually sung and accompanied by the *arpa llanera* (a sort of local harp), a *cuatro* (small guitar) and *maracas* (gourd rattles). A modern joropo ensemble usually also includes the double bass as a part of its rhythmic section.

The harp came over from Spain during the colonial period, but it was not until the beginning of this century that it made its way into joropo music. By that time it had evolved into quite a different instrument; it's smaller and less elaborate than its European parent. The cuatro has four nylon strings and accompanies the melody played by the harp. It is also of European origin and has gradually changed in the New World. Maracas are native American instruments. The harp is sometimes replaced by the *bandola*, another guitar derivative. It has a pearl-shaped body and four nylon strings, and is becoming popular in some areas after a long period when it was in danger of disappearing.

Joropo has various forms, including *golpes* and *pasajes*, which can be further split into a variety of rhythms such as *pajarillo*, *zumba que zumba*, *quirpa* etc. Generally speaking, pasajes are slower and more gentle than golpes. The harp, normally associated with lyrical salon music, finds a different form of expression in joropo. Reflecting the hard life of the llaneros, the harp sounds clear and sharp, at times even wild.

Although joropo has conquered most of Venezuela and has become the national music, it's at its best and most original in Los Llanos. Every second inhabitant of the plains sings or plays one of the instruments, and every village has at least one joropo ensemble. Joropo is common in Venezuela and, to a lesser extent, Colombia, but is almost unknown beyond the borders of these two countries.

Some of the best authentic joropo music has been brought together on the four-CD set (available separately) titled *Puros Gabanes, Puros Recios, Puros Contrapunteos* and *Puros Pasajes*. The compilation includes more than 80 joropo tracks performed by the cream of local interpreters of the genre. ■

the country's patron saint. Predictably, the city is Venezuela's major pilgrimage centre, attracting some half a million visitors each year.

Founded in 1591 by Juan Fernández de León, La Ciudad del Espíritu Santo del Valle de San Juan del Guanaguanare is one of the few towns in Venezuela whose original act of foundation document has been preserved (it is kept in Seville, Spain). Like most early towns, Guanare's development was precarious and hindered by Indians inhabiting the region. Things began to change on 8 September 1652, when the Virgen de Coromoto allegedly miraculously appeared before an Indian cacique on the Río Guanaguanare, near the town (see boxed text entitled Virgen de Coromoto). As with all miracles of that kind, the place soon became a destination for pilgrims from the region and beyond.

A fair-sized church was built for the Virgin, and the town steadily developed around the cult. A serious earthquake in 1782 damaged many buildings, the church included, but the miraculous powers of the Virgin continued to draw in the faithful in increasing numbers. By that time, the town's population had already reached 13,000. The coronation of the Virgin as the patron saint of Venezuela, in 1949, contributed to even larger floods of pilgrims. Its religious status apart, Guanare has also developed into an important regional centre for cattle raising.

Information
The tourist office (☎ 51 03 24) is at Calle 17 No 3-14. There's also a tourist information desk in the bus terminal.

Some of the central banks useful for cash advances on Visa and/or MasterCard are marked on the map. Changing cash or travellers cheques may prove difficult in Guanare.

Basílica de la Virgen de Coromoto
This is by far the most important monument in the city, and the destination for every pilgrim. The church, on Plaza Bolívar, was constructed in 1710-42, but the 1782 earth-

quake almost completely destroyed it. The image of the Virgin, which had been kept inside, was saved and temporarily guarded in the hospital chapel while the church was reconstructed in a different style; the work was completed in 1807.

Inside the church, the showpiece is the large, three-tier main retable, an excellent piece of colonial baroque art made by Pantaleón José Quiñones de Lara in 1739. It later took 16 months for Romualdo Antonio Vélez to gild it. In front of the retable stands the 3.4m-high elaborate *sagrario* (tabernacle), made entirely of silver in 1756. A painting on the dome over the high altar depicts the legend of the Virgen de Coromoto. The stained glass windows were commissioned in Munich, Germany.

At the head of the right-hand aisle is a statue of the Virgen de Coromoto. Climb a few steps to the feet of the Virgin to have a look through the magnifying glass at the tiny image of the Virgin, though the picture is pretty faint and indistinct. Another statue of the Virgin is at the opposite end of the same aisle. Note the number of commemorative plaques on the wall behind the statue.

Other Attractions
The mid-18th century **Convento de San Francisco**, on the corner of Carrera 3 and Calle 17, no longer serves its original purpose. In 1825, it was turned into a college, the first institution of its kind in Venezuela. Today, the building accommodates the offices of the Universidad Nacional Experimental de los Llanos. You can enter its spacious courtyard which has retained much of its old style and charm. The church has a beautiful façade, but its interior lacks decoration; it's now used for university meetings and symposiums.

Directly opposite the church is the **Museo de la Ciudad de Guanare**. Housed in one of the few remaining colonial buildings, the museum presents a small collection related to the town's history.

Two blocks north from here is the **Parque Los Samanes**, named after a species of the spreading trees which grow in the park.

Guanare

LOS LLANOS

To Acarigua
To Bus Terminal
To Airport
To Hotel Táchira, Hotel El Llanero & Barinas

Plaza Coromoto

Plaza Bolívar

Parque Los Sumanes

Calle 8
Calle 9
Calle 10
Calle 11
Calle 12
Calle 13
Calle 14
Calle 15
Calle 16
Calle 17
Calle 18
Calle 19
Calle 20
Calle 21
(Calle 22)
Avenida Sucre

Carrera 1
Carrera 2
Carrera 3
Carrera 4
Carrera 5
Carrera 6
Carrera 7
Carrera 8
Carrera 9
Carrera 10
Carrera 11

0   100   200 m

PLACES TO STAY

6 La Posada del Reo
18 Hotel Italia

PLACES TO EAT

2 Panadería Cleopatra
3 Panadería Altamira
11 Pizzería La Focaccia
14 La Arepa Recondita
14 Trattoria da Vanna
17 Restaurant Centro II

OTHER

1 Banco Mercantil
4 Banco del Caribe
5 Basílica de la Virgen de Coromoto
7 Former Convento de San Francisco
8 Museo de la Ciudad de Guanare
9 Tourist Office
12 Centro de Cultura
13 Banco de Venezuela
15 Banco Unión
16 CANTV
19 Buses to Santuario de la Virgen de Coromoto

You'll find the first impressive specimen in front of the entrance. It's thought that Bolívar's troops camped here in 1813.

There are several monuments dedicated to the Virgen de Coromoto in town, including the 1928 statue on Plaza Coromoto, seven blocks east of Plaza Bolívar along Carrera 5. On the same square you'll find a charming sculptured scene depicting the miraculous appearance of the Virgin to the Indian cacique and his family.

Special Events

As might be expected, Guanare's annual celebrations revolve around the Virgen de Coromoto. Most pilgrims flock to the city in time for the Fiesta de la Virgen de Coromoto on 8 September, the anniversary of the Virgin's appearance. There may also be crowds of believers on 2 February, the anniversary of the day when the image of the Virgin was moved from the actual site of the apparition to the city.

Guanare is also noted for its Mascarada, the three-day-long colourful Carnaval celebration, which culminates in a parade of *carrozas* (floats).

Places to Stay

The city centre is almost a hotel desert, except for two good, budget places, gracias a Dios. One of these is the *Hotel Italia* (☎ 53 12 13, 51 42 77), Calle 20, off the corner of Carrera 5. Run by a friendly Italian, it offers good air-conditioned singles/doubles/triples with private bath and TV for US$12/15/18. The other option is the new *La Posada del Reo* (☎ 51 03 24), on the corner of Calle 16 and Carrera 3, which costs much the same.

Marginally cheaper but not as good and central is the *Hotel Táchira* (☎ 51 68 49), Avenida Juan Fernández de León No 29-66. It's on the western continuation of Carrera 5, about half a km west of Avenida Sucre. Another half a km west along Avenida Juan Fernández de León is the still slightly cheaper *Hotel El Llanero* (☎ 51 68 89).

There are several reasonable motels on the outskirts of Guanare, including *Motel La Fontana* (☎ 51 35 42, 51 37 83) and *Motel*

La Sultana (☎ 53 17 23, 51 41 22), both on Avenida Circunvalación, and *Motel Portuguesa* (☎ 53 07 57, 51 11 02) on Avenida 23 de Enero.

Places to Eat

Pizzería La Focaccia, on Plaza Bolívar, is a pleasant place with tables outside, and is open until 10.30 pm. It has simple pizzas, spaghetti and some popular local dishes. Better pizzas and pastas are served in the *Trattoria da Vanna*, on the corner of Carrera 6 and Calle 15, which also has some reasonably priced local food.

La Arepa Redonda, on Plaza Bolívar, does arepas and does them well. The *Restaurant Centro II*, Calle 18 off Carrera 5, offers inexpensive comida criolla. *La Posada del Reo* runs its own restaurant, as does the *Hotel Italia* and many motels.

Getting There & Away

The bus terminal is on Calle 8, 2km southeast of the city centre, and is serviced regularly by local transport. To get there from the centre, take eastbound buseta No 14 or 24 from Carrera 5.

Guanare sits on the El Llano highway, so there is a fair bit of traffic heading south-west to San Cristóbal (US$6 ordinary, US$7.75 deluxe, 6½ hours) and north-east to Caracas (US$6.50 ordinary, US$8.25 deluxe, seven hours). There are several departures a day to Barquisimeto (US$3, three hours) and to Boconó (US$2, 3½ hours). Buses to Barinas run frequently until 6 pm (US$1.50, 1½ hours). If you are heading to Mérida, go to Barinas and change.

SANTUARIO DE LA VIRGEN DE COROMOTO

This is the place where the Virgen de Coromoto allegedly appeared in 1652. A cross was placed here after the event, and was later replaced with a chapel, but the site was isolated and rarely visited. Instead, the pilgrims flocked to Guanare's church, which for centuries boasted the holy image and effectively acted as the Virgin's shrine, as it still does today.

Now things are changing. The construction of a huge church at the actual site of the apparition commenced in 1976, and was completed for the papal visit in February 1996, when 300,000 faithful attended the mass. It's planned that the image of the Virgin be brought here from Guanare and placed in the high altar.

The Templo Votivo – as the church is called – is monumental, strikingly modern and truly impressive. Designed by the Venezuelan architect Erasmo Calvani, the irregular concrete structure is laid out on a floor plan of a 4000-sq-metre heart. The high altar is believed to be at the exact location of the Indian cacique's hut where the Virgin appeared. The walls behind the altar are graced with marvellous stained glass windows.

The church has two unequal bell towers (75m and 68m high), both accessible by stairs up to their top balconies, which are expected to open to the public. Currently, you can go up to a viewing platform (at 32m) between the towers, which is accessible by lift for a small fee. A museum is planned in the basement of the church.

Getting There & Away

The Santuario is 25km south of Guanare; 10km by the main road towards Barinas plus 15km by the sealed side road branching off to the south. Small buses, operated by Línea Los Cospes, depart regularly from the corner of Carrera 9 and Calle 20 in Guanare (US$0.40, 45 minutes), and will deposit you right at the church's entrance.

BARINAS

- *pop 225,000*
- *area code ☎ (073)*

Barinas was founded in 1576 by Spanish conquerors from Pamplona in Nueva Granada, and developed right from its birth. At the beginning of the 17th century, tobacco gave the town an economic base and overseas fame. Barinas was the only region in the province allowed by the Crown to grow tobacco. Other crops, including sugar cane, bananas and cacao, were subsequently introduced to the region, as was cattle raising. By the end of the 18th century, Barinas was the second largest town in Venezuela, after Caracas.

Virgen de Coromoto

The Virgen de Coromoto allegedly appeared on 8 September 1652 to the cacique of the Cospes Indians, some 20km south of Guanare. As legend has it, the Virgin not only appeared, but also talked to the Indian chief in his own language, trying to convince him to have holy water poured over his head so that he would be able to enter heaven. The Virgin also left the cacique an image of herself, radiating with rays of brilliant light.

Astonished and confused, the chief ignored the Virgin's advice and fled into the mountains. As soon as he entered the woods, however, he was bitten by a venomous snake. Only then, moments before his death, did he ask to be baptised, telling his tribe to do likewise.

On 2 February 1654, the Spanish brought the image to Guanare and placed it in a small sanctuary. News of the miracle spread throughout the region and beyond, and Guanare began to attract believers. As its fame spread far and wide, a good-sized church was commissioned, and completed in 1742 after 30 years of work, to provide a more decent shelter for the image.

In 1942, the Virgen de Coromoto was declared the patron saint of Venezuela and solemnly crowned by Pope Pius XII in 1949. A year later a statue of the Virgin and an open-air chapel were erected at the site of the apparition, and a huge church has recently been completed there. The image will be moved from Guanare to the new church.

The image itself is tiny. It's an oval painting, measuring 22mm by 27mm, made on papyrus-like paper. Today its colours have almost totally washed out. ■

LOS LLANOS

The War of Independence and the civil wars which plagued Venezuela during the 19th century seriously affected the town's and the state's development, and many inhabitants fled, mostly to the Andes. In that period a lot of colonial architecture was lost, either destroyed during the struggles or abandoned.

Once the civil wars ended, a steady revival began. Agriculture and cattle raising were joined by a short-lived timber industry, which took advantage of extensive rainforest in the western part of the state, indiscriminately and rapidly logging it until it was almost completely destroyed. Meanwhile, oil was discovered in the region, 50km south of Barinas, and is now pipelined to the coast near Morón.

Today Barinas is the capital of the state of the same name, and the thriving centre of a vast agricultural and ranching region. The climate is hot and damp, with an average temperature of 27°C and frequent rains from May through to November. There's not much to see or do in the city and, accordingly, few travellers bother to stop here.

Information

Tourist Office The Corbatur (Corporación Barinesa de Turismo) tourist office (☎ 27 091; ☎ & fax 28 162) is on Avenida Marqués del Pumar, half a block back from Plaza Bolívar, and is open Monday to Friday from 8 am to noon and 2 to 6 pm. There are also three *módulos de información turística* (theoretically open daily), at the airport, in the Parque Los Mangos on Avenida Cuatricentenaria, and in the Ciudad Deportiva on Avenida Adonay Parra Jiménez.

Money Most major banks are scattered between Calle Cruz Paredes and Plaza Bolívar (see the map).

Things to See

The unusual, two-block-long Plaza Bolívar still boasts some colonial buildings. The **Catedral** dates from the 1770s, except for the bell tower which wasn't added until the present century. The church's interior was being renovated at the time of writing.

Opposite the cathedral, across the plaza, is the **Palacio del Marqués**, which occupies the entire side of the square. Commissioned by the Marqués de las Riberas de Boconó y Masparro as his private residence, and constructed at the end of the 18th century, the palace reflected the owner's wealth and the town's prosperity at the time. It was partly ruined during the Wars of Federation in the mid-19th century, but was restored in the 1940s. It now houses the municipal council and the police station.

On the north-eastern side of the plaza is the **Casa de la Cultura**, built during the final decades of the 18th century as the town hall and jail. José Antonio Páez was imprisoned here, but managed to escape, liberating 115 of his fellow prisoners on the way. The building was the town jail until 1966. Today it's a cultural centre, running art exhibitions and various other events. The finely restored house on the south-western side of the square, which is now the Escuela de Música, was originally the masonic lodge.

The city has two small museums. The **Museo Alberto Arvelo Torrealba** (named after a local poet), on the corner of Calle 5 de Julio and Avenida Medina Jiménez, presents some aspects of the life and culture of the llaneros. It's open Tuesday to Saturday from 9 am to noon and 3 to 6 pm, and Sunday from 9 am to noon. The **Museo San Francisco de Asís**, Avenida Medina Jiménez No 2-89, has a collection of colonial (mostly religious) objects.

The **Jardín Botánico** and the small **Zoológico** are located on the campus of the Universidad Nacional Experimental de los Llanos, 3km south-west of the centre, on the road to San Cristóbal.

Places to Stay

If you are in Barinas for one or two nights only, it's probably best to look for a budget room around the bus terminal. There are half a dozen inexpensive hotels on the street just west of the terminal. Among them, the *Motel San Marino* (☎ 22 351) is one of the cheapest

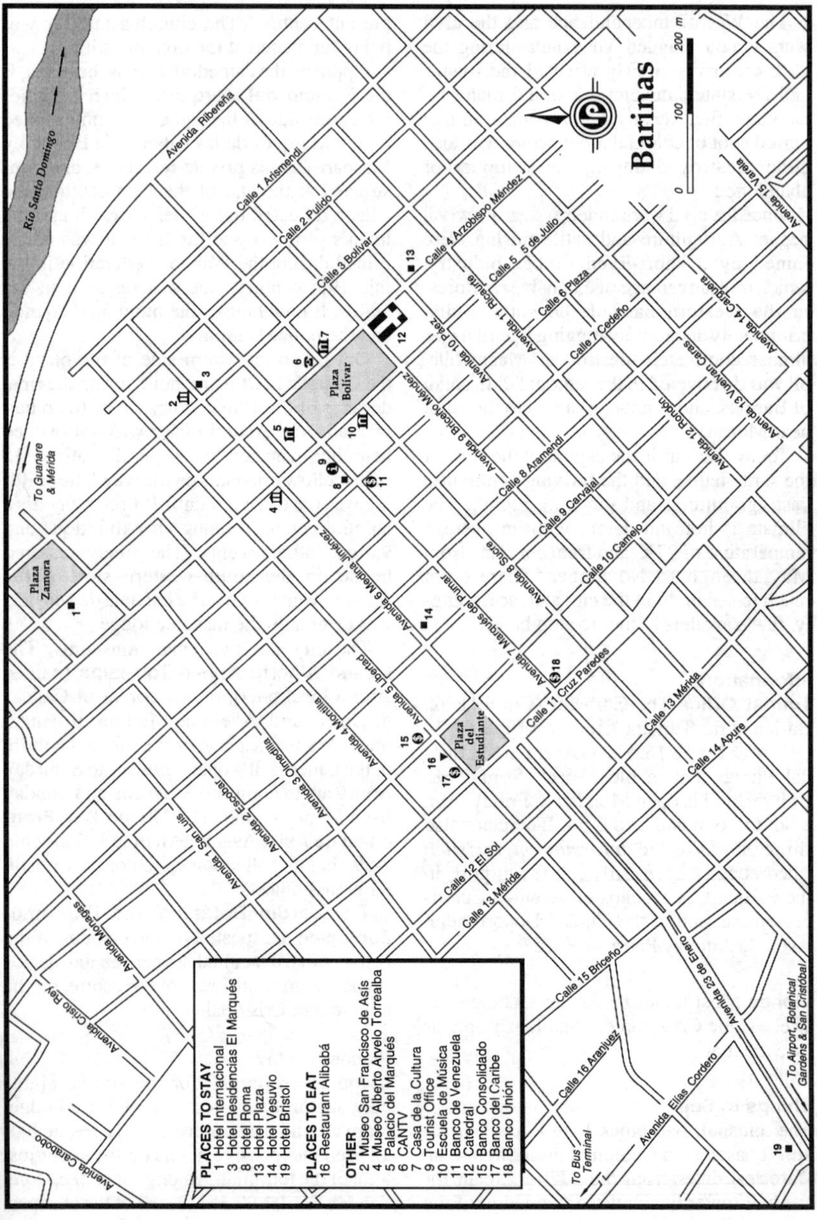

Barinas
0
100
200 m
Río Santo Domingo
To Guanare & Mérida
To Airport, Botanical Gardens & San Cristóbal
To Bus Terminal
Plaza Zamora
Plaza Bolívar
Plaza del Estudiante
Avenida Ribereña
Calle 1 Arismendi
Calle 2 Pulido
Calle 3 Bolívar
Calle 4 Arzobispo Méndez
Calle 5 5 de Julio
Calle 6 Plaza
Calle 7 Cedeño
Calle 8 Aramendi
Calle 9 Carvajal
Calle 10 Camejo
Calle 11 Cruz Paredes
Calle 12 El Sol
Calle 13 Mérida
Calle 14 Apure
Calle 15 Briceño
Calle 16 Aranjuez
Avenida Cristo Rey
Avenida Carabobo
Avenida Monagas
Avenida 1 San Luis
Avenida 2 Escobar
Avenida 3 Olmedilla
Avenida 4 Montilla
Avenida 5 Libertad
Avenida 6 Medina Jiménez
Avenida 7 Marqués del Pumar
Avenida 8 Sucre
Avenida 9 Briceño Méndez
Avenida 10 Páez
Avenida 11 Ricaurte
Avenida 12 Rondón
Avenida 13 Vuelvan Caras
Avenida 14 Carguera
Avenida 15 Varela
Avenida 23 de Enero
Avenida Elías Cordero
PLACES TO STAY
1 Hotel Internacional
3 Hotel Residencias El Marqués
8 Hotel Roma
13 Hotel Plaza
14 Hotel Vesuvio
19 Hotel Bristol
PLACES TO EAT
16 Restaurant Alibabá
OTHER
2 Museo San Francisco de Asís
4 Museo Alberto Arvelo Torrealba
5 Palacio del Marqués
6 CANTV
7 Casa de la Cultura
9 Tourist Office
10 Escuela de Música
11 Banco de Venezuela
12 Catedral
15 Banco Consolidado
17 Banco del Caribe
18 Banco Unión

LOS LLANOS

and good value for money. Doubles with private bath and fan/air-conditioning cost US$6/8.

In the city centre, the cheapest place is the basic *Hotel Roma* (☎ 24 624), Avenida Marqués del Pumar, on the corner of Calle Plaza. It costs US$8/9 for a matrimonial/double with bath and fan; add a dollar for air-conditioning. The *Hotel Plaza* (☎ 24 918), Calle Arzobispo Méndez No 10-20, has air-conditioned rooms with bath for US$10/12 a single/double. The *Hotel Vesuvio* (☎ 24 294), Avenida Medina Jiménez No 8-38, charges much the same. The *Hotel Residencias El Marqués* (☎ 26 576), Avenida Medina Jiménez No 2-88, is slightly cleaner and better, and charges US$12/15/18 for air-conditioned singles/doubles/triples.

The three-star *Hotel Internacional* (☎ 22 343, 23 303), Calle Arzobispo Méndez, facing Plaza Zamora, is the oldest hotel operating in town. It was built by Pérez Jiménez around 1950, when there was still no reliable road connection with Caracas. It offers singles/doubles/triples for US$22/30/40.

Other three-star options are outside the centre and include the *Hotel Bristol* (☎ 20 911, 20 840; fax 20 229)), *Hotel Turístico Varyná* (☎ 33 50 94, 33 39 84; fax 33 32 49) and *Hotel Valle Hondo* (☎ 33 51 77, 23 606). They all are on Avenida 23 de Enero, south-west of the old centre, near the airport. All are comfortable and provide reasonable standards and facilities like a TV and hot water, and each has its own restaurant and bar.

Places to Eat

There's a good collection of basic restaurants in the bus terminal area. The vicinity around Plaza Bolívar doesn't have much to choose from, except for a few fast-food outlets. The *Hotel Plaza* has a restaurant serving cheap set meals. A tiny cubbyhole proudly named the *Restaurant Alibabá*, Avenida Libertad No 10-09, serves delicious felafel. Avenida Marqués del Pumar is the main commercial street in the centre and there are some res-

taurants along it. Several better restaurants can be found on Avenida 23 de Enero.

Getting There & Away

Air The airport is 1.5km south-west of Plaza Bolívar. Both Servivensa and LAI have several flights a day to Caracas (US$74) via Acarigua (US$38).

Bus The bus terminal is 2km west of Plaza Bolívar and is serviced by local transport. Barinas has regular bus services south-west to San Cristóbal (US$5 ordinary, US$6 deluxe, five hours), and north-east to Caracas (US$8 ordinary, US$10 deluxe, 8½ hours), and all points in-between such as Guanare, Valencia and Maracay. Transporte Barinas has five departures a day to Mérida (US$3.50, four hours). Several companies, including Expresos Los Llanos and Expresos Zamora, operate buses south-east into Los Llanos, with a total of half a dozen departures a day to San Fernando de Apure (US$7 ordinary, eight hours).

SAN FERNANDO DE APURE
- *pop 90,000*
- *area code ☎ (047)*

The capital of Apure state, San Fernando de Apure is the largest city of the Llano Bajo; it's actually the only city of any size for a couple of hundred miles around. Sitting on the southern bank of the Río Apure, in the very heart of Los Llanos, it is an important regional trading centre for most of the Río Apure basin. Cattle raising and, to a lesser extent, farming are the two major activities in the region. Crops and livestock are funnelled through San Fernando and trucked north to the central states of Aragua, Carabobo, Miranda and Distrito Federal.

San Fernando was born as a missionary outpost at the end of the colonial era and its development was for a long time hindered by its isolation. It wasn't until the road from Calabozo was extended south to the Río Apure that the town began to grow more swiftly. Today the city also has a sealed road link with the western states of Barinas, Mérida and Táchira.

San Fernando is not a tourist attraction in itself and has little to keep you in the city. On the other hand, the vast region all around boasts some of the best of what Los Llanos have to offer, including several ecotourist ranches (see the Hatos section further on). San Fernando is the usual jumping-off point for trips to the hatos.

Information

Tourist Office The Coratur (Corporación Apureña de Turismo) tourist office is in a free-standing building in the middle of Paseo Libertador, about 700m south of the Monumento a Los Llaneros.

For information about the hatos, you can also try the Agencia de Viajes y Turismo Doña Bárbara (☎ 41 34 63; fax 41 22 35), Edificio Hotel La Torraca, Piso Bajo, Paseo Libertador. The company runs the Campamento Doña Bárbara in the Hato La Trinidad de Arauca (for which its staff can book and arrange transport) and may provide information about other hatos in the region, including El Frío and El Cedral.

Money See the map for locations of potentially useful banks.

Things to See

Walk along Paseo Libertador, the city's main thoroughfare. At its northern end is a circular square with a large fountain adorned with concrete caymans. Beside the fountain is the **Monumento a Pedro Camejo**, an equestrian statue of one of the bravest lancers to have fought under General José Antonio Páez in Bolivar's army. Camejo, who died in the Battle of Carabobo, is commonly known as Negro Primero, as he was the first black person to distinguish himself in the War of Independence.

Just east of the fountain is **Palacio Barbarito**, possibly the most interesting architectural relic in the city. It was built by Italian merchants at the turn of the century. At that time the Río Apure used to pass just a few metres from the palace pier, and boats came directly from Europe, up the Orinoco and Apure. Most of the trade was related to

egret feathers and cayman leathers, and was initially very profitable. Later on the business deteriorated and the Italians sold the palace and left. It then passed through the hands of various owners who divided and subdivided it repeatedly, so much of the original internal design has been lost.

About 600m south along Paseo Libertador is the large **Monumento a Los Llaneros**, dedicated to the tough and brave people who made up the backbone of Bolívar's army. Another 600m down the Paseo stands **Monumento a San Fernando**, the largest and tallest monument in the city. The tourist office is 100m further south.

The **Plaza Bolívar**, six blocks west of Paseo Libertador, boasts a modern cathedral and an old masonic lodge, and is pleasantly shaded with trees.

Places to Stay

One of the cheapest places in town is *Hotel Neyla* (☎ 23 347), Carrera Sucre, four blocks east of Paseo Libertador. It's basic but costs just US$4/5/6 for a single/double/triple with bath and fan.

If you need air-conditioning, the cheapest option is the *Hotel Roma* (☎ 23 652), Calle Ricaurte No 4, but it only has matrimoniales (US$8 for a room with bath) and is pretty basic. The *Hotel Los Llanos* (☎ 41 27 95), Carrera Páez No 118, has marginally better matrimoniales for US$10. Other budget options include the *Hotel El Río* (☎ 41 19 28), Avenida María Nieves, and the *Hotel Boulevard* (☎ 23 122), Paseo Libertador. Both offer simple air-conditioned singles/doubles/triples with bath for US$9/11/12.

For somewhere better, try either the *Hotel La Torraca* (☎ 22 777, 22 676), on Paseo Libertador, or the *Hotel Trinacría* (☎ 23 578, 23 778), on Avenida Miranda. Both have fairly decent air-conditioned matrimoniales/doubles/triples with bath and TV for US$14/15/17. Also check the slightly more expensive *Nuevo Hotel Apure* (☎ 41 44 83).

The best in town is the *Gran Hotel Plaza* (☎ 41 49 68), on Plaza Bolívar. Comfortable air-conditioned doubles/triples are rated at

San
Fernando
de Apure

0   50   100 m

Río Apure

To Caracas

To Barinas

To Monumento
a San Fernando
& Tourist Office

To Airport

Plaza
Bolívar

PLACES TO STAY
2 Hotel El Río
5 Nuevo Hotel Apure
11 Hotel Trinacría
12 Hotel La Torraca &
Agencia de Viajes y
Turismo Doña Bárbara
13 Hotel Neyla
15 Hotel Roma
16 Gran Hotel Plaza
19 Hotel Los Llanos
23 Hotel Boulevard

PLACES TO EAT
3 Pizzería La Olla
22 Restaurant Beirut
25 Restaurant Independencia
26 Arepera La Estación
27 La Taberna de Don Juan

OTHER
1 Bus Terminal
4 Petrol Station
6 Fountain
7 Monumento a Pedro Camejo
8 Palacio Barbarito
9 Banco Provincial
10 Banco Consolidado
14 Banco Unión
17 Catedral
18 Templo Masónico
20 CANTV
21 Banco Mercantil
24 Monumento a los Llaneros

Avenida María Nieves
Avenida Miranda
Carrera 2
Carrera 3 Comercio
Carrera 4 Bolívar
Carrera 5 Sucre
Carrera 6 Páez
Carrera 7 Muñoz
Carrera 8 Aramendi
Carrera 9 Colombia
Carrera 3 Comercio
Carrera 4 Bolívar
Carrera 7
Muñoz
Carrera 8 Aramendi
Paseo Libertador
Avenida 1 de Mayo
Avenida 1 de Mayo
Calle 21 Independencia
Calle 20 Negro Primero
Calle 19 Madariaga
Calle 18 Piar
Calle 17 Girardot
Calle 16 Boyacá
Calle 15 Ricaurte
Calle 14
Calle 9
Calle 10 Miranda
Calle 11

LOS LLANOS

US$25/30. Choose one of the upper-floor rooms which looks over the plaza.

Places to Eat

San Fernando has a satisfactory array of eating outlets around its central area; many places are on Paseo Libertador. As you might expect, the carne llanera, the local beef, appears on menus of many restaurants, as does fish from the local rivers.

The *Pizzería La Olla*, Avenida María Nieves, is popular with locals for its good-value pizza, spaghetti and chicken. The *Restaurant Beirut*, Paseo Libertador, does tasty Middle Eastern sandwiches, including felafel and chawarma. The *Arepera La Estación*, Avenida 1 de Mayo, serves inexpensive arepas and is open till late. Across the street, *La Taberna de Don Juan* is one of the best places to eat and drink in town.

Getting There & Away

Air The airport is about 3km east of the city centre; a taxi there shouldn't cost more than US$3. San Fernando is a regular stopover for Avensa flights between Caracas and Puerto Ayacucho. There's one flight a day in each direction; the airfare to Caracas is US$59 and to Puerto Ayacucho is US$48.

Bus The bus terminal is on the northern outskirts of the city, near the river. You can either walk there (five minutes from Plaza Bolívar) or take a taxi (US$1).

There are three or four buses a day directly to Caracas (US$6.25 ordinary, US$8.25 deluxe, eight hours), and about 10 buses to Maracay (US$5 ordinary, 6½ hours). Five or six buses a day travel to Barinas (US$7 ordinary, eight hours) and one of them continues on to San Cristóbal (US$11.50, 13 hours).

Half a dozen buses a day (all in the morning) set off for an interesting ride south to Puerto Ayacucho (US$8.50 ordinary, eight hours), via Puerto Páez. The road is now sealed almost all the way (except for about 30km), but the bridges on the Capanaparo and Cinaruco rivers are incomplete, so the trip includes *chalana* (ferry) crossings across

these two rivers and, obviously, across the Orinoco between Puerto Páez and El Burro. The route is transitable all year round.

Boat Despite its location on a large river, the Río Apure (which was once the region's transport lifeline), San Fernando has no regular passenger boat service, either up or downstream.

HATOS

Most of Los Llanos is divided into large ranches known as hatos. They are principally dedicated to cattle raising – as they have been for a century or more – but some of them have turned to ecotourism. The owners have built lodges equipped with reasonable facilities, which they call *campamentos*, and run excursions to show guests the local wildlife. Some hatos dealing with tourists have taken quite a serious approach to environmental issues, introducing the protection of wildlife within their ranches, installing research stations, contributing to ecological funds and the like.

A visit to an ecotourist hato is usually only available through an all-inclusive package, which has to be booked and paid for beforehand. Packages are normally three day/two night visits, which include full board and one or two excursions each day.

Excursions are like safaris, in a jeep or boat. There's usually one trip in the morning and another in the afternoon, the best times to observe the wildlife and, coincidentally, to avoid the unbearable midday heat. There will be more boat trips in the rainy period and more jeep rides in the dry season. Whichever means of transport is used, however, you are taken into wilderness areas where animals, mostly birds, are plentiful and easy to see. Among the mammals and reptiles, capybaras and caymans are particularly common. Read the boxed text entitled The Wildlife of Los Llanos for more information about local fauna.

The wildlife is abundant in both rainy and dry seasons. The main difference is that in the dry season most animals flock to scarce sources of water, which makes them easy to watch. In the wet season, on the other hand, when most of the land is half-flooded, animals are virtually everywhere.

The dry season is generally considered as the peak season, and in most hatos this is reflected by higher tour prices. This is a good time to come, as you can expect good weather and there are usually more trip options to choose from, as a greater area is accessible by land.

If you go in the dry season, take a hat, sunglasses and sunscreen. In the wet season, make sure to have wet weather gear. Whenever you come, don't forget a torch, good binoculars and plenty of film. Mosquito repellent is essential during the rainy season, but it is also very useful in the dry period.

So far, there are perhaps a dozen ecotourist hatos, but new ones spring up here and there. Some of the more established and perhaps most reputable hatos are detailed below, though they are probably not the cheapest ones. Their approximate locations are shown on the Los Llanos map.

Most hatos offer pretty much the same services, and the fauna is similar across the region. For example, El Frío, El Cedral and La Trinidad are relatively close to each other, so you can expect similar wildlife habitats in each of them. You may consider factors such as price and facilities (eg El Cedral has a tiny swimming pool and air-conditioning), but otherwise there is no great difference between the ranches.

The Wildlife of Los Llanos

Los Llanos are one of Venezuela's greatest repositories of wildlife, especially birds, which live here permanently or gather seasonally to breed and feed. About 350 bird species have been recorded in the region, which accounts for over a quarter of all the bird species found in Venezuela. Water and wading birds predominate, and the list includes ibis, herons, cormorants, egrets, jaçanas, gallinules and darters. The *corocoro*, or scarlet ibis *(Eudocimus ruber)*, noted for its bright red plumage, is a spectacular sight when it appears in large colonies in the dry season. Three-quarters of the world's corocoro population lives in Venezuela.

Among the more than 50 mammal species that inhabit the region is the *chigüire*, or capybara *(Hydrochoerus hydrochaeris)*. This is the world's largest rodent, growing up to about 60kg. It has a guinea-pig face, bear-like coat and is equally at home on land and in the water, feeding mainly on aquatic plants. It's the most visible mammal in Los

Capybara *(chigüire)*

Llanos (apart from ubiquitous zebu herds) and is often seen in families of two adults and several young, or in large groups.

Other local mammals include armadillos, peccary, opossums, anteaters, tapirs, ocelots and the occasional jaguar. Two interesting aquatic mammals are the *tonina*, or freshwater dolphin *(Inia geoffrensis)*, and the *manatí*, or manatee *(Trichechus manatus)*, which inhabit the larger tributaries of the Orinoco. Both are endangered species, but numbers of the latter are dangerously low.

Also threatened with extinction is the largest American crocodile, the *caimán del Orinoco*, or the Orinoco cayman *(Crocodylus intermedius)*. Populations of these huge reptiles, which once lived in large numbers and measured up to 8m from head to tail, have been decimated by ranchers killing them for their skins. Far more numerous is the *baba*, or the spectacled cayman *(Caiman crocodylus)*, the smallest of the family of local crocodiles, growing up to 3m in length.

Two large national parks, Cinaruco-Capanaparo (also known as Santos Luzardo) and Aguaro-Guariquito, protect important wildlife habitats of Los Llanos. A third, smaller park, Río Viejo, has recently been established in the extreme western part of the region. ■

Since many campamentos require advance booking and pre-payment, plan ahead. Tours to some hatos have to be arranged in Caracas. Refer to the Organised Tours section in the Caracas chapter for relevant tour operators.

Tours in the ecotourist hatos are not cheap. They cost somewhere between US$80 and US$150 per person a day, which adds up to some US$240 to US$450 for the whole tour. Some hatos are well off the beaten track, so you may need to pay extra for transport to and from the campamento.

Cheaper wildlife safaris in Los Llanos are available from Mérida. Several of Mérida's tour companies have put together their own llano circuits and seem to do a good job. The companies don't use ecotourist hatos' services but have arrangements with selected local families and use their informal lodging and eating facilities. Conditions are usually rustic and the whole trip is more casual, but you will see the same plethora of wildlife for roughly a third of the hato tour price. Travellers consistently recommend these tours. See the Mérida section for further information.

Otherwise, you can explore Los Llanos on your own, particularly if you have your own transport, ideally a 4WD. The Barinas-San Fernando road cuts through an interesting part of the plains and is serviced by regular transport (about six buses a day in either direction). The section of road between Bruzual and Apurito is perhaps the most spectacular as far as animal-watching is concerned. Plenty of birds can be seen from the road itself. There is a choice of simple accommodation in Bruzual and Mantecal, either of which can serve as jumping-off points for excursions around the area.

Hato El Frío

Occupying about 800 sq km, Hato El Frío lies on both sides of the Mantecal-San Fernando road, and has around 45,000 head of cattle. Its campamento is located 2km north of the road, 187km west of San Fernando (42km east of Mantecal). It has a lodge with 10 double rooms (with the capacity for 20 guests), a pleasant dining room and a biological station where caymans, turtles and other endangered species are bred.

There are boats and jeeps that take visitors for two four-hour excursions at 8.30 am and 3.30 pm. There's a choice of about 10 excursions in *verano* and five in *invierno*. It's estimated that about 13,000 chigüires and 25,000 *babas* live in the hato.

So far, El Frío seems to be pretty tolerant of individual travellers, and will probably accept you if you turn up unexpectedly, as long as there are vacancies. The price per day per person is US$90 from 1 April to 30 June, US$110 from 1 July to 15 September and US$130 from 16 September to 31 March. El Frío has an office in Achaguas (☎ & fax (047) 81 223), 89km towards San Fernando, where you can book a tour. Various Caracas tour companies (including Orinoco Tours) organise tours to El Frío.

El Frío is easily accessible by public transport; the San Fernando-Mantecal buses will drop you off at the main gate, a 20-minute walk to the campamento.

Hato El Cedral

Hato El Cedral is about 70km south-west by sealed road from El Frío. It covers 560 sq km and has around 20,000 head of cattle. The campamento is 7km west off the road. It provides comfortable lodging in cabañas, which are equipped with air-conditioning and private baths with hot water, and there is a tiny swimming pool.

There are half a dozen different excursions, by boat or specially prepared minibus, but the trips seem to be shorter than those in El Frío. More than 250 bird species have been recorded on the ranch (much the same as in El Frío), as well as 14,000 capybaras, not to mention numerous representatives of other species.

El Cedral is quite rigorous about tours, which have to be booked beforehand from Caracas (see the Caracas chapter for details). If you come without a booking, you are likely to be turned away. The price in the peak season (15 November to 15 April) is US$120 per person a day in a double room, and US$155 in a single room. In the off season, it's US$80 and US$115, respectively. This price doesn't include transport to/from the hato. It can be arranged for an extra fee, when you book your package; the return trip from San Fernando airport to El Cedral costs US$25.

Hato La Trinidad de Arauca

Better known by the name of its campamento, Doña Bárbara, this hato is pretty close to El Cedral, but it's accessible via a roundabout route through Elorza. In the dry season, the campamento can be reached by road, but in the wet season, the only access is by river (two hours from Elorza).

With 360 sq km, La Trinidad is smaller, but has as equally rich and diverse wildlife as El Frío and El Cedral, except for capybaras, which are not so numerous here. Its campamento is pleasant and well organised, and offers horse riding excursions. Bookings should be made through the Doña Bárbara travel agency in San Fernando de Apure (see this section for details). La Trinidad charges about US$110 per person a day.

The campamento was named after Rómulo Gallego's classic novel, for which the hato provided the setting and principal character. The grave of Francisca Vásquez de Carrillo (the real name of the owner of the hato, on whom Doña Bárbara was based) is in the hato, as is a replica of her house, a modest, thatched adobe structure, with some old objects inside. Today the campamento is run by the friendly Estrada family.

Hato San Leonardo

This 180-sq-km hato is located on the Río Capanaparo, some 80km south of Achaguas as the crow flies. Access in the dry season is by dirt roads, but in the rainy months you can only get there by boat (a 3½ hour trip) or a light plane.

The campamento has simple but comfortable cabañas with bath and fan, a restaurant, bar and a swimming pool. The three day/two night package includes accommodation, full board and excursions, and will cost US$240 per person from December to April, and US$200 in the remaining months. Add US$60 per person extra for the return transfer between San Fernando and the hato. Packages can be booked and bought from the hato's Caracas office (see the Caracas chapter for details), and are also sold by some major tour companies. San Leonardo also offers fishing tours.

Hato Piñero

The best known ranch in the Llano Alto (Upper Llano), Hato Piñero is in Cojedes state, close to the town of El Baúl. It's easily accessible by road from anywhere in the central states. If you are coming from Caracas, go to Valencia, from where it's about 210km south.

Given its location, Piñero has a somewhat different spectrum of wildlife to that of the hatos in the Llano Bajo. The topography of this ranch (about 800 sq km) is more diverse, and forests cover part of the hato. The wet season comes later (in late May or early June) and ends earlier (in September). Although capybaras and caymans are not so ubiquitous here, there is a variety of other animals, including ocelots, monkeys, anteaters, agoutis, foxes, tapirs and iguanas. This is largely the effect of hunting and logging bans, which were introduced as early as the 1950s.

There are tourist facilities for about 25 guests, and packages should be booked in Caracas (see that chapter for details). The package including full board and excursions will cost US$120 a day from May to November and US$150 from December to April.

The North-East

Venezuela's north-east is essentially for outdoor activities; this is the region for sunbathing, snorkelling, diving, sailing, walking and the like. The coast has some amazing stretches, including the marvellous Mochima national park. The region also boasts Venezuela's best cave, the Cueva del Guácharo.

Most of the cultural and historic attractions are close to the sea, for it was principally the coast that the Spanish conquered and settled. However, although they arrived here as early as 1498 and soon founded their first towns, there's not much of the colonial legacy left, except for the partly preserved old quarters of Barcelona and Cumaná, and some old churches and forts scattered over the region.

Administratively, the north-east covers the states of Anzoátegui, Sucre and Monagas, plus the insular state of Nueva Esparta, which comprises the islands of Margarita, Coche and Cubagua.

Anzoátegui State

BARCELONA
- *pop 270,000*
- *area code ☎ (081)*

Barcelona was founded in 1671 by a group of Catalan colonists and named after their home town in Spain. It was set on the Río Neverí, 5km back from its outlet to the Caribbean. Its centre is still there, but the city has expanded dramatically, and is gradually merging into a single urban sprawl with its dynamic young neighbour, Puerto La Cruz. Barcelona remains the capital of Anzoátegui state, but is has already lost ground as a tourist and commercial centre to Puerto La Cruz.

Central Barcelona is a pleasant enough place, with several leafy plazas and some colonial architecture. The historic quarter has been partly restored and whitewashed

HIGHLIGHTS

- Enjoy the beaches and coral reefs in Mochima national park
- Visit the Salinas de Araya
- Discover secluded beaches east of Río Caribe
- Explore the magnificent Guácharo cave
- View mountain scenery around Caripe

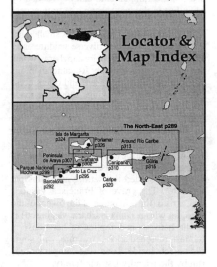

Locator & Map Index

throughout, and this gives it a pleasant general appearance, even though the urban fabric is a mishmash of houses dating from different periods. The city doesn't seem to have rushed into modernity at the pace of Puerto La Cruz, and the yesteryear feel is still noticeable within the old town.

Information
Tourist Office The main tourist office, Coranztur (☎ 74 11 42, 74 36 46), is on the ground floor of the building of the Gobernación, on Avenida 5 de Julio. It's open

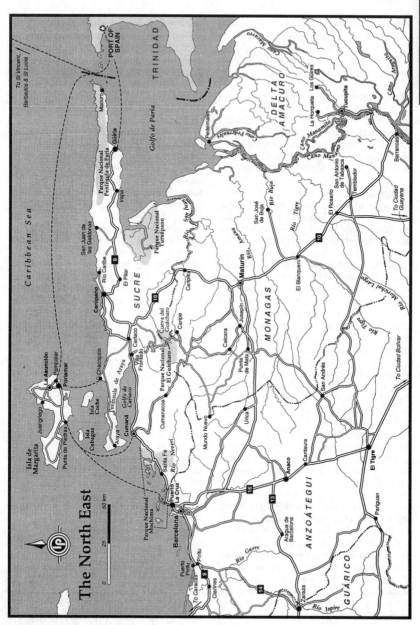

The North East

0   25   50 km

Caribbean Sea

To St Vincent,
Barbados & St Lucia

PORT OF
SPAIN

TRINIDAD

Isla de
Margarita

La Asunción
Pampatar
Porlamar

Juangriego

Punta de Piedras

Isla Cubagua

Isla Coche

Golfo de Cariaco

Araya

Cumaná

Parque Nacional
Mochima

Barcelona

Puerto
La Cruz

Santa Fe

Río Neverí

Mundo Nuevo

Cumanacoa

Parque Nacional
El Guácharo

Cueva del Guácharo

Caripe

Villa
Frontado

Cariaco

Chacopata

Peninsula de Araya

San Juan
de las Galdonas

Río Caribe

El Pilar

Carúpano

SUCRE

Parque Nacional
Turuépano

Parque Nacional
Península de Paria

Irapa

Güiria

Macuro

Golfo de Paria

Federales

CANO Pedernales

Pedernales

Caño Macareo

DELTA
AMACURO

Los Güires

Tucupita

La Horqueta

Caño Manamito

Caño Manamo

Barrancas

San Antonio
de Tabasca

El Rosario

Temblador

To Ciudad
Guayana

Río Morichal Largo

To Ciudad Bolívar

MONAGAS

Maturín

San José
de Buja

Río Buja

Río Tigre

El Blanquero

Juspín

Caicara

Punta
de Mata

Utica

San Andrés

Cantaura

Anaco

Aragua de
Barcelona

ANZOÁTEGUI

El Tigre

Pariguan

Río Guere

Clarines

Piritu

Puerto
Piritu

To Caracas

Zaraza

Río Ispire

GUÁRICO

Cariaco

Caripito

Río San Juan

Araya

Río Aragua

9

10

10

9

9

13

16

10

16

Monday to Friday from 8 am to noon and 2 to 5 pm. You may also try the Dirección de Cultura y Turismo (☎ 74 29 78), just off Plaza Boyacá, which is open half an hour longer in the afternoon.

Money There are only a few banks in central Barcelona, and they are unlikely to do anything more than advance cash on Visa and/or MasterCard. If you don't have a credit card, you'd better come with sufficient bolívares, or you may need to go to Puerto La Cruz to change your travellers cheque or cash.

Things to See
The city's historic centre is **Plaza Boyacá**, with a statue of General José Antonio Anzoátegui, the Barcelona-born hero of the War of Independence, in its middle. On the western side of this tree-shaded square stands the **Catedral**, built a century after the town's foundation. The most venerated object in the church is the glass reliquary in a chapel off the left aisle, where the embalmed remains of the Italian martyr San Celestino are kept. The richly gilded main retable dates from 1744, but the images of saints were made in modern times.

On the southern side of the plaza is the **Museo de Anzoátegui**. Housed in the carefully restored, oldest surviving building in town (1671), the museum features a variety of objects related to Barcelona's history. Note the collection of unusual religious statues equipped with movable limbs; only their faces, hands and feet have been properly finished. They were dressed in robes according to the occasion and their pose adjusted to the situation. The museum is open Tuesday to Friday from 8 am to noon and 2 to 5 pm, Saturday and Sunday from 9 am to 3 pm. There may be a guide who can explain the collection (in Spanish only).

An extension to the museum is housed in the **Ateneo de Barcelona** (same opening hours), two blocks east. On the 1st floor of this colonial building is a 44-piece collection of paintings (most of which date from the 1940s and 1950s) by some of the prominent modern Venezuelan artists. The collection

belonged to Miguel Otero Silva, a well-known novelist; after his death the paintings were donated to the state. The Ateneo also presents temporary exhibitions on the ground floor and conducts various cultural activities. There's a small handicraft shop attached, but a far larger selection of crafts is offered by the Gunda Arte Popular craft shop on Carrera Bolívar.

The **Plaza Rolando** is lined by more recent buildings, including the **Iglesia del Carmen** and the **Teatro Cajigal**, both dating from the 1890s. The latter is an enchanting, small theatre which seats 300 people, still used for theatre performances and musical concerts; the security guards may let you in during the day.

There are a few more plazas farther to the north-west, including Plaza Miranda and Plaza Bolívar, just one block from each other. The western side of the latter is occupied by the **Casa Fuerte**, which was once a Franciscan hospice but was destroyed by the royalists in a heavy attack in 1817. Over 1500 people, both defenders and the civilians who took refuge here, lost their lives in the massacre which followed the takeover. The surviving parts of the walls have been left in ruins as a memorial.

The Palacio Legislativo, two blocks south of Plaza Boyacá, has the **Galería de Arte** featuring temporary exhibitions.

Places to Stay
Barcelona is not an accommodation paradise; if you need somewhere upmarket or trendy, go to Puerto La Cruz. On the other hand, Barcelona has a reasonable range of budget hotels, which are usually better value than their Puerto La Cruz counterparts. Furthermore, hotels in Barcelona don't fill up as fast as those in Puerto La Cruz, so you may sometimes need to come here in search for a room.

The *Hotel Plaza* (☎ 77 28 43), on Plaza Boyacá, is one of the most pleasant budget places in town. It's in a fine colonial house with a patio, and has rooms of different standards and prices. Some front doubles don't have private bath, but they are spacious and overlook the plaza and the cathedral, and are excellent value at US$8. There are also some less attractive air-conditioned doubles with bath for around US$12.

Another good inexpensive option is the *Hotel Canarias* (☎ 77 10 34), on Carrera Bolívar. Matrimoniales with fan and bath are US$10, while matrimoniales/triples with air-conditioning and bath cost US$12/15. You can also try the simple *Hotel Madrid* (☎ 77 40 43) at the back of the cathedral, which has a variety of rooms, from primitive singles without bath for US$5 to reasonable doubles with bath for US$10.

The *Hotel Nacional* (☎ 77 12 43), on Calle Zamora, has long-term accommodation contracts with an oil company, so it's almost always full, but you can occasionally grab a vacant matrimonial with bath for just US$6. Still cheaper is the very basic *Hotel Cultura*, which has matrimoniales with shared bath for US$5.

The 70-room high-rise *Hotel Barcelona* (☎ 77 10 65, 77 10 87; fax 77 12 98) has passed its best times but it's still not bad value at just US$18/22 for air-conditioned doubles/triples with bath and TV. Probably better cared for but noisy is the *Hotel Neverí* (☎ 77 23 73), on Avenida Miranda, which costs US$15 for an air-conditioned double. One of Barcelona's best central options is the *Hotel Oviana* (☎ 76 16 71, 76 41 47; fax 76 49 53), on Avenida Caracas, five blocks west of Plaza Bolívar. It costs US$25/28/32 a single/double/triple.

Places to Eat

Like accommodation, dining out is better in Puerto La Cruz, but Barcelona does have an array of acceptable eateries and the prices are more reasonable.

A cheap and good place to eat is the market, the *Mercado Municipal La Aduana*, next to the bus terminal, south-east of the city centre. It has more than a dozen popular restaurants, which serve a variety of typical food from around 6 am to 2 pm.

In the centre, Avenida 5 de Julio is the main culinary artery, lined with budget restaurants, snack luncherías, fuentes de soda

and street food vendors. The self-service *Gran Palacio Gastronómico*, near the Gobernación, offers a choice of inexpensive fast food and snacks.

Next door, the *Gran Fraternidad Universal* serves cheap vegetarian meals at lunchtime, Monday to Friday. One block south, the *Arepera El Gran Sabor* does good arepas and some popular Venezuelan dishes at low prices. The 1st-floor *Restaurant Piazza*, next to the Hotel Barcelona, has pizzas and steaks at reasonable prices and is open till 11 pm, ie longer than most of the central restaurants.

There are also some places to eat on Avenida Miranda, including *El Castillo de Oriente*, which does parrillas. The *Hotel Neverí* runs its own restaurant offering international and local cuisine, as does the *Hotel Oviana*, whose restaurant has some Italian cooking.

Getting There & Away

Air The airport is 2km south of the city centre and is accessible by urban transport. Avensa/Servivensa has three flights a day to Caracas (US$56) and one to Puerto Ordaz (US$45). Aserca services Maracaibo (US$107), San Antonio del Táchira (US$119), Las Piedras (US$92) and Barquisimeto (US$91), all via Caracas. Several airlines, including Laser, Oriental de Aviación and Rutaca flies direct to Porlamar on Isla de Margarita (US$33).

Bus The bus terminal is about 1km south-east of the city centre, next to the market. To get there, take a buseta south along Avenida 5 de Julio, or walk 15 minutes.

The terminal handles mostly regional routes, including hourly buses to Píritu and Clarines. Few long-distance buses originate from here, but some (not many) buses from Puerto La Cruz call here on their way to Caracas (US$6.25 ordinary, 4½ hours) and Ciudad Bolívar (US$5 ordinary, four hours). The terminal in Puerto La Cruz is far busier, so it's often better to go there instead of waiting here for an infrequent and unreliable bus to come through.

To Puerto La Cruz, catch a city bus going

THE NORTH-EAST

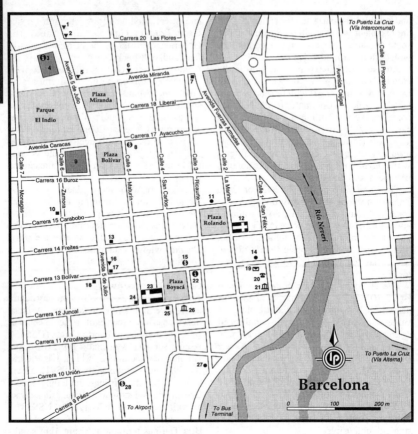

Barcelona

0   100   200 m

PLACES TO STAY
7 Hotel Neverí
10 Hotel Nacional
13 Hotel Cultura
17 Hotel Barcelona
18 Hotel Canarias
24 Hotel Madrid
25 Hotel Plaza

PLACES TO EAT
1 Gran Fraternidad
   Universal
2 Gran Palacio
   Gastronómico

5 Arepera El Gran
   Sabor
6 El Castillo de
   Oriente
16 Restaurant Piazza

OTHER
3 Coranztur Tourist
   Office
4 Gobernación
8 Banco Mercantil
9 Casa Fuerte
11 Teatro Cajigal
12 Iglesia del Carmen

14 Gunda Arte
   Popular
15 Banco de
   Venezuela
19 Ipostel
20 CANTV
21 Ateneo de
   Barcelona
22 Dirección de Cultura
   y Turismo
23 Catedral
26 Museo de
   Anzoátegui
27 Galería de Arte
28 Banco Unión

north on Avenida 5 de Julio (US$0.20). They use two routes, Vía Intercomunal and Vía Alterna. Either will set you down in the centre of Puerto La Cruz. There are also por puesto minibuses, which depart from Avenida 5 de Julio, two blocks south of the Banco Unión, and are faster than the buses.

PUERTO LA CRUZ
- *pop 160,000*
- *area code* ☎ (081)

Puerto La Cruz is a young, dynamic and expanding city. Until the 1930s it was no more than an obscure village, but it boomed after rich oil deposits were discovered in the region to the south. Port facilities have been built in Guanta and Guaraguao, just east of town; the latter serves as a main oil terminal, to ship oil piped from the wells overseas.

The city has become popular among Venezuelan holiday-makers, and is very touristy. It's the major gateway to Isla de Margarita, Venezuela's No 1 mass-tourist beach destination, and it's also a jumping-off point to the beautiful Mochima national park, which stretches just north and east of the city. Taking advantage of its strategic position, Puerto La Cruz has grown into Venezuela's major water sports centre, with half a dozen marinas and yacht clubs, sailing and diving schools, yacht rental facilities, diving and fishing tours etc.

The city has quite a lively 10-block-long waterfront boulevard, Paseo Colón, packed with hotels, tour agencies, bars and restaurants. It comes to life in the late afternoon and evening, when plenty of craft stalls open and a gentle breeze refreshes the heat of the day. This apart, however, the city has little to show tourists: a block or two back from the beach and it's just an ordinary place. Some travellers may be disappointed.

Information
Tourist Office The Coranztur tourist office (☎ 68 81 70) is midway along Paseo Colón and is open daily from 8 am to 9 pm. City maps can be bought at Kiosko El Universal. Pick up *Boulevard*, the free what's on weekly

brochure, distributed through hotels, travel agencies etc.

Money Most major banks are within a few blocks south of Plaza Colón (see the map for locations). There are also several casas de cambio which exchange cash and travellers cheques. Some of them are in the hotels on Paseo Colón, including the Oficambio in the Hotel Rasil, the Asecambio in the Hotel Gaeta, and the Viajes Venezuela in the Hotel Riviera. Some casas may charge commission, so shop around. Turisol (☎ 66 88 59, 66 88 06; fax 66 99 10) is next door to Banco Consolidado.

Complejo Turístico El Morro
This large, modern residential/tourist complex, is being constructed on the waterfront 4km west of the city centre. It is one of the most ambitious urban projects ever to be carried out in the country.

Set on a coastal stretch of land, roughly in the form of a 1.5 by 2km rectangle, the complex is a model district, designed in its entirety and built from scratch. The area has already been crisscrossed by a maze of canals, on the banks of which a city of apartment blocks and houses is being built. Many of the inhabitants will have direct access to the waterfront with their own piers and slipways. The complex will boast commercial centres, hotels, parks, gardens and golf courses.

The project began in the 1970s and some residential areas, the marina and a few of the planned chain of seaside hotels, including the Hotel Doral Beach and Hotel Maremares, have been completed. Also finished is the Centro Comercial Plaza Mayor, on the southern side of the complex, which has a multiscreen cinema. There's still a long way to go, but it's worth seeing if you are interested in urban planning or architecture. Night boat excursions around the canals are organised on weekends from the Centro Comercial Plaza Mayor.

To get to the complex from either Puerto La Cruz or Barcelona, take the Avenida Intercomunal bus and get off one block north of the Cruzero de Lecherías, at the place where five 20-storey residential towers, known as the Conjunto Residencial Vistamar, loom. From there, por puestos go north, skirting the western, then northern side of the complex, and take you to the marina.

Organised Tours

A score of travel agents have mushroomed in the city, taking advantage of the tourist dollar. Many can be found on Paseo Colón: some have their own offices, while others nestle in handicraft shops, hotel lobbies etc. They offer tours to anywhere in the country, from the Gran Sabana to the Andes, but it's far cheaper to arrange one from the local centre (Santa Elena de Uairén and Mérida, respectively). It may be, however, worth giving some thought to regional tours, principally around the Parque Nacional Mochima. One-day tours are standard, but longer trips can be arranged with some operators. Tours usually include snorkelling (equipment provided), but may also include fishing, scuba diving, water sports and the like.

Boat excursions to the nearby islands of Mochima park have become popular with visitors (mostly Venezuelans) and depart regularly every morning from the three central piers, between the tourist office and Plaza Colón. The full-day trips normally include visits to three or four beaches, an hour of snorkelling, plus lunch and drinks, for about US$20 per person. There are also transport-only boat trips to some of the more popular beaches (US$5 return). Boats depart regularly in the holiday season and on weekends. See the Parque Nacional Mochima section for more information on these trips.

The Explosub (☎ 65 36 11 ext 3347; ☎ & fax 67 32 56), in the Hotel Meliá, and Lolo's Diving Center (☎ 68 30 52; fax 68 28 85) in the Guanta Marina, are major local diving schools which organise diving courses and tours. Lolo receives better comments from travellers than does Explosub.

Places to Stay

Puerto La Cruz is an expensive place to stay by Venezuelan standards, and hotels fill up fast in the tourist season. It's difficult to find anything reasonable for below US$12 a double. Many hotels have gathered on Paseo Colón and the adjoining streets, and this is the most lively and enjoyable area in which to stay. All the hotels listed below have rooms with private bath and either fan or air-conditioning, as indicated.

Places to Stay – bottom end & middle

The cheapest options on Paseo Colón include the *Hotel Montecarlo* (☎ 68 56 78), *Hotel Neptuno* (☎ 65 32 61), *Hotel Diana* (☎ 65 00 17) and *Hotel Margelina* (☎ 68 75 45). All have rooms with air-conditioning, but are otherwise nothing special. Check a few of them and inspect rooms before deciding. Expect a double to cost US$12 to US$16. The Diana has some cheaper rooms with fan (US$10 for a matrimonial), and offers laundry service.

The small, eight-room *Hotel Guayana* (☎ 65 21 75), on Plaza Bolívar, one block back from the Paseo, is one of the cheapest places in town. It has doubles/triples with fan for US$8/10 (air-conditioned for US$12/14), but they are not spotlessly clean or good. Somewhat better is the nearby *Hotel Rey* (☎ 68 68 10), which costs US$15/20 for an air-conditioned double/triple. There are more budget places a few blocks to the southwest, including the friendly *Hotel Luna y Sol* (☎ 68 66 62), at Calle Ricaurte No 5. The cost is US$12 for a good matrimonial with air-conditioning, and there are laundry facilities.

If you are prepared to spend a bit more, the *Hotel Europa* (☎ 65 00 34, 68 81 57), off Plaza Bolívar, is good value. It's clean, well run and costs just US$20/24/28 for an air-conditioned double/triple/quad. You may also try the *Hotel Sorrento* (☎ 68 67 45; fax 65 22 12), Avenida 5 de Julio, which offers doubles for US$24 and is not bad value either.

Places to Stay – top end

More comfortable yet still affordable options include the *Hotel Gaeta* (☎ 65 04 11; fax 65 00 65) and *Hotel Senador* (☎ 67 35 22; fax

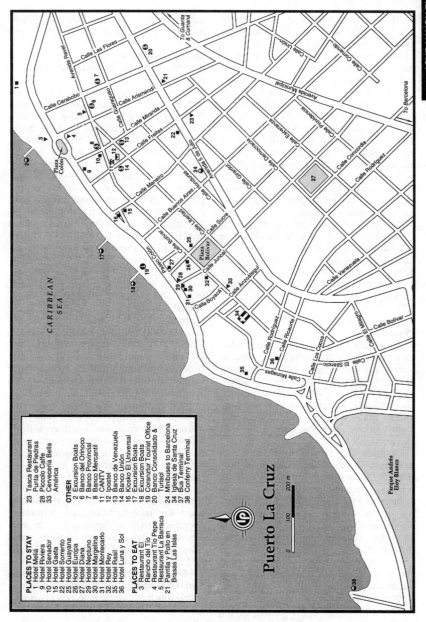

PLACES TO STAY
1 Hotel Meliá
9 Hotel Riviera
10 Hotel Senador
15 Hotel Gaeta
22 Hotel Sorrento
25 Hotel Guayana
26 Hotel Europa
27 Hotel Diana
29 Hotel Neptuno
30 Hotel Margelina
31 Hotel Montecarlo
32 Hotel Rey
35 Hotel Rasil
36 Hotel Luna y Sol

PLACES TO EAT
3 Restaurant El
   Rancho del Tío
4 Restaurant Tío Pepe
5 Restaurant La Barraca
21 Parrilla y Pollo en
   Brasas Las Islas

23 Tasca Restaurant
   Punta de Piedras
28 Piccolo Caffe
33 Cervecería Bella
   América

OTHER
2 Excursion Boats
6 Banco del Orinoco
7 Banco Provincial
8 Banco Mercantil
11 CANTV
12 Ipostel
13 Banco de Venezuela
14 Banco Unión
16 Kiosko El Universal
17 Excursion Boats
18 Excursion Boats
19 Corantur Tourist Office
20 Banco Consolidado &
   Turisol
24 Minibuses to Barcelona
34 Iglesia de Santa Cruz
37 Bus Terminal
38 Conferry Terminal

CARIBBEAN
SEA

Puerto La Cruz

0   100   200 m

Parque Andrés
Eloy Blanco

65 23 38). A double with a sea view in either will cost around US$40. The waterfront high-rise *Hotel Riviera* (☎ 67 21 11; fax 65 13 94) is probably a more attractive option and costs much the same.

Top-end accommodation is well represented in Puerto La Cruz; the smartest hotels on the central waterfront are the four-star *Hotel Rasil* (☎ 67 25 35; fax 67 31 21) and the five-star *Hotel Meliá* (☎ 67 29 93; fax 65 31 17), both expensive. The Meliá has a good swimming pool fronting the beach, open to nonresidents for US$3. Cheaper and almost as good is the *Cristina Suites* (☎ 67 47 12, 67 14 10), a few blocks back from the Paseo Colón. Its suites cost around US$60/70/80 for one/two/three persons.

You also have some classy options in the Complejo Turístico El Morro, including the *Hotel Maremares* (☎ 81 10 11; fax 81 30 28), the *Hostería El Morro* (☎ 81 13 11; fax 81 42 26), and the *Hotel Doral Beach* (☎ 81 11 11, 81 35 21, 81 26 11), all on Avenida Américo Vespucio.

Places to Eat

The waterfront is essentially the upmarket area, but there are also some cheaper places, including *Piccolo Caffe*, which does good breakfasts and pastas and is open until late. Just outside, a few street stalls serve delicious Middle Eastern fast food, such as felafel and chawarma. The top-floor restaurant of the *Hotel Neptuno* is OK and inexpensive.

For more budget eating, comb the streets back from the beach. Try, for example, *Parrilla y Pollo en Brasas Las Islas*, which has good chicken and grilled beef, or the *Tasca Restaurant Punta de Piedras*, Calle Freites No 46, which serves hearty fish and meat dishes. And don't miss popping in to the nostalgic archetypal old-time *Cervecería Bella América* at Calle Bolívar No 143.

The cream of the city's restaurants and bars is in the area of Plaza Colón and along the beach; some are included on the map. This area is alive until late, when fresh breezes cool the heat of day and people gather in the numerous open-air establishments which overlook the beach.

Getting There & Away

Air The airport is in Barcelona (see that section for details).

Bus The busy bus terminal is conveniently sited in the middle of the city, just three blocks from Plaza Bolívar. Frequent buses run west to Caracas (US$6.25 ordinary, US$7.75 deluxe, five hours) and east to Cumaná (US$1.50, 1½ hours); some of the latter continue east to Carúpano (US$4, 3½ hours) and a few go as far as Güiria (US$6.50, 5½ hours). If you go eastwards (to Cumaná or farther on), grab a seat on the left side of the bus as there are some spectacular views over the islands of Parque Nacional Mochima. There are also por puesto cars to Caracas (US$13.50, four hours), Cumaná (US$3.25, 1½ hours) and Santa Fe (US$1.25, 40 minutes), and por puesto jeeps to Los Altos (US$0.75, 40 minutes).

Half a dozen buses run daily to Ciudad Guayana (US$6.25 ordinary, US$7.50 deluxe, six hours), and all go via Ciudad Bolívar (US$4.75 ordinary, US$6 deluxe, 4½ hours). There are also buses to Maturín (US$3.50 ordinary, US$4.25 deluxe, three hours), a few of which continue on to Tucupita (US$8, 6½ hours).

To Barcelona, take a city bus from Avenida 5 de Julio. They go either by Avenida Intercomunal or Vía Alterna. Both will deposit you in Barcelona's centre in 45 minutes to one hour, depending on the traffic. There are also por puesto minibuses to Barcelona.

Boat Puerto La Cruz is the major departure point for Isla de Margarita. Conferry operates ferries to the island, with four departures a day (there may be fewer in the off-peak season). The passenger fare is US$9/6 in 1st/tourist class and the trip takes 4½ hours. Conferry also operates their comfortable *Margarita Express* boat, two times a day, which does the trip in two hours and costs US$30 per head. The Conferry terminal is accessible by por puestos from the centre. Do this trip in the daytime – it's a spectacular journey between the islands of Parque Nacional Mochima.

CLARINES & PÍRITU
There are several colonial churches in small towns throughout the northern part of Anzoátegui state. Among them, those in Clarines and Píritu have been restored and are the most interesting. Both towns are on the Caracas-Barcelona highway.

Clarines, founded in 1694, is about 1km south of the highway. Its church, Iglesia de San Antonio, is at the upper end of the old town. Built in the 1750s, the church is a massive, squat construction laid out on a Latin cross floor plan, and is one of only a few examples of its kind in Venezuela. The austere façade is bordered by square twin towers. Perhaps the most unusual features of the structure are the two external arcades running between the towers and the transepts on both sides of the church.

The single-nave interior is topped with a wooden cupola and is refreshingly well-balanced in both proportion and decoration. Over the high altar is a three-tier main retable from around 1760. It is placed against the wall, which still bears its original painting depicting a curtain. The church is open from approximately 9.30 to 11.30 am and 3 to 6 pm.

Píritu is 16km east of Clarines, just north of the highway (but the access road branches off from the highway 2km before the town and rejoins it 2km beyond it). The town was founded in 1656, and about half a century later the Iglesia de Nuestra Señora de la Concepción was built. It also looks a bit like a fortress, though the structure's design is quite different: there's only one bell tower, no transept and no arcades.

This three-nave church has quite a number of remarkable colonial altarpieces. The main retable and the two side retables date from about 1745 and, like most of the others, are richly gilded. Note the painted decoration of the vault in the chancel.

Getting There & Away
As both towns are situated just off the Caracas-Barcelona highway, access is easy and the transport frequent. Apart from the long-distance buses running between these two cities, there are regional hourly buses from Barcelona to both Píritu and Clarines.

PARQUE NACIONAL MOCHIMA
Straddled roughly half-half across the border of Anzoátegui and Sucre states, the 950 sq km Mochima national park covers the offshore belt of the Caribbean coast between Puerto La Cruz and Cumaná, including a wealth of islands and islets, plus a strip of the hilly coast noted for deep bays and white-sand beaches.

The main groups of islands include, from west to east, Las Borrachas, Las Chimanas and Las Caracas. There are also a number of islands closer to the mainland, including Isla de Plata and Isla de Monos. Most of the islands are barren, rocky in parts and quite spectacular, but some have fine beaches. Some islands are surrounded by coral reefs and offer good snorkelling. The waters are warm and usually calm, and abound in marine life. The weather is fine for most of the year, with moderate rainfall mainly between July and October.

Orientation
For most visitors the springboard for Mochima is Puerto La Cruz, for exploration of the park by water or road. The insular part of the park can only be reached by boat, so trips can be expensive because they are monopolised by boat operators. See the Getting Around the Islands section for details. On the other hand, the mainland coastal part of the park is very easy to explore, as it's accessible from the Puerto La Cruz-Cumaná road. The road is serviced frequently by buses and por puestos, and there are lots of accommodation and food facilities along the way.

Parts of the road skirt the seafront, so you'll have some spectacular glimpses of the islands. There are a dozen beaches off the road, possibly the most popular of which are Playa Arapito, about 23km from Puerto La

Cruz, and Playa Colorada, 4km farther east. On weekends, popular beaches swarm with holiday-makers, some of whom seem to come just to drink beer and listen to loud music. On the other hand, some deserted beaches can be unsafe, particularly at night – use common sense. Camping on solitary beaches is not always safe either; there have been reports of robberies on both the islands and mainland beaches.

About 10km east of Playa Colorada is an ordinary town of Santa Fe, which has become a gringo haunt thanks to a fine beach and tourist facilities. Another 10km east along the Cumaná road, a side road branches off to the north and goes 5km downhill to the village of Mochima, which is a jumping-off point for nearby beaches.

For some panoramic views of the park, complete with its islands, bays and beaches, you can take a trip to Los Altos de Santa Fe, a mountain village about 30km east of Puerto La Cruz. A completely different visual approach is from the ferry between Puerto La Cruz and Isla Margarita, which sails between some of the park's islands, providing good views on either side.

Isla de Plata

This is one of the popular islands among Venezuelan tourists, thanks to its beach and coral reefs, and the proximity to the mainland, which makes boat access frequent and cheap. There are food and drink stalls on the island but no fresh water. Enjoy a startling, surreal view of the nearby huge cement plant.

Isla de Plata is about 10km east of Puerto La Cruz and is accessible by boat from the pier at Pamatacualito, the eastern suburb of the port of Guanta (serviced by por puestos from Puerto La Cruz). Boats run regularly, especially during weekends, taking 10 minutes to get to the island (US$1.50 return). The island can also be reached by excursion boats directly from Puerto La Cruz, but these are more expensive and less regular.

Playa Colorada

This beach is not long or wide, but has fine orange sand and is charmingly shaded with coconut groves. It's very popular – try to avoid coming here on weekends, when its swamped with visitors and left littered. The beach is just 200m off the road, and you'll get a good view of it (particularly attractive at sunset) while approaching by road from the east.

There are several places to stay nearby, among them the *Villas Turísticas Playa Colorada* (also known as El Tucusito), which offer trailers (caravans) with kitchen (US$30 for up to four people) and double rooms (US$20), complete with a small pool and a restaurant.

A few blocks uphill from El Tucusito is the cheaper *Quinta Jaly* (☎ 016 681 81 13), run by friendly French Canadians, Lynn and Jacques. Just opposite, the equally friendly Swiss woman named Rita offers two rooms and two studios with bath and fan and prepares fabulous breakfasts.

Santa Fe

Santa Fe is a drab fishing town where few travellers would bother to stop, going by the general appearance of the place. However, the town has a beach which has become popular with foreign backpackers, who come here and stay for days. This is thanks to the grass-roots initiative of some residents, inspired by an interesting artist and writer, José Vivas, to make the place a small ecotourist resort.

The project has gone ahead with such enthusiasm and determination that there are now a dozen posadas along the 1km-long beach, and most will also serve meals. The conditions are simple but the prices are very modest, and various facilities and activities are available (laundry, billiards, Spanish lessons, boat excursions, snorkelling, horse riding etc), that make the place an attractive and lively travellers' hangout. Some Venezuelans come here on weekends, but for the rest of the week this is essentially a gringo stronghold, much favoured by Germans. The beach itself is nothing special, but it's regularly cleaned and the water is clear and sheltered.

If you're looking for a budget place to

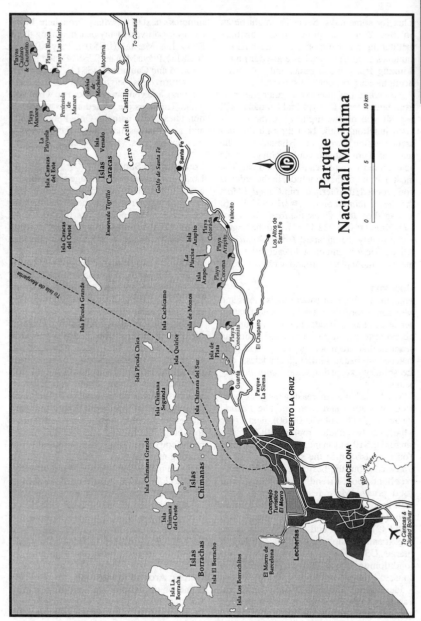

Parque Nacional Mochima

relax for some days, Santa Fe might be an option. You can spend your mornings meditating in a hammock, your days taking launches to nearby beaches and your nights drinking fruity merengadas and cold beer. Bring insect repellent and sunscreen.

Buses and por puestos (regular transport from both Puerto La Cruz and Cumaná) will deposit you on the highway at the town's main junction. Walk 1km through this unprepossessing town to the fish market on the seafront. Turn left and you'll soon get to the beach lined with places to stay and eat. The most popular of these include, in the order as you proceed, the German-run *Café del Mar*; the *Residencia La Sierra* (☎ 014 993 31 16) managed by José Vivas; the *Residencia Los 7 Delfines* (☎ 014 922 42 41); and the largest and possibly the cheapest *Hotel Cochaima*. All are friendly and close to each other, and there are more places around to choose from.

Mochima

The small village of Mochima is clean and well cared for. It's not a tourist destination per se and has no beach, but it is a jumping-off point to half a dozen isolated mainland beaches that are inaccessible by road. The beaches are beautiful though shadeless, and are solitary except for some major holiday peaks.

Mochima has an increasing range as far as accommodation and food go. The *Posada Puerto Viejo* (☎ 014 993 00 60), next to the wharf, has two double rooms with bath and fan for US$10 and an inexpensive restaurant. You can also eat in the similarly priced *El Guayacán*, but the best is *El Mochimero* – excellent food, friendly atmosphere and good prices. More restaurants open temporarily during holiday peaks. The *Posada Gaby* (☎ 014 993 27 25; ☎ in Cumaná (093) 31 08 42) at the far end of the village, is the largest and perhaps the best place to stay. It charges US$15/18 for a double with fan/air-conditioning. Locals also rent out rooms and houses.

Jeeps from Cumaná (there's no direct transport from Puerto La Cruz) will bring you to the village's centre (US$0.80, 40

minutes), next to the wharf. From here, boats can transport you to any beach, among them Playa Las Maritas (US$10), Playa Blanca (US$11), Playa Manare (US$14), and Playas Cautaro and Cautarito (US$14). The figures are return fares per boat (up to five passengers), and you can be picked up when you want. The fares are posted at the wharf but don't hesitate to bargain. Only Playa Blanca and Las Maritas have food facilities, and they are the most visited beaches.

Los Altos de Santa Fe

Los Altos is a mountain village accessible by a winding sealed road from the coast, and serviced regularly throughout the day by jeeps from Puerto La Cruz (US$0.75, 45 minutes). At an altitude of about 900m, it has a pleasant climate about 5°C cooler than that on the coast. It's a typical one-street village, snaking up and down the rugged terrain for almost 5km, without any pronounced centre. It's surrounded by verdant highlands sprinkled with coffee and cacao haciendas, some of which can be visited.

Although Los Altos is only 4km back from the coast as the crow flies, it doesn't provide many panoramic bird's-eye views of the coast and the islands beyond. The best vistas are actually from the access road, as you approach the village. Once you enter it, which is roughly by the Bodega El Progreso, the road gradually descends inland and there are few reasonable lookouts. Jeeps continue for about 5km to their terminus on the opposite end of the village, but it's probably not worth going that far.

If you plan to stay overnight, get off at the *Posada El Paraíso*, 2km down the road from El Progreso. This is just about the only place to stay, with 10 matrimoniales at US$10 and three doubles at US$12. It's simple but agreeable and has its own restaurant. There are a couple of more restaurants nearby, and one of the very few lookouts to the sea.

Getting Around the Islands

Some of the islands are easy to reach by full-day boat excursions organised from Puerto La Cruz. One of the most popular tours includes Playa El Saco (on Isla Chimana Grande) and Playa El Faro (on Isla Chimana Segunda), both with food facilities. An additional attraction of El Faro beach are iguanas. Another standard tour goes to Islas Arapo and Arapito and includes an hour's snorkelling in La Piscina between the two islands (equipment provided). The boats depart from Puerto La Cruz's waterfront from 9 to 10 am and return about 5 pm, and tours cost around US$20 per person, including a lunch and soft drinks.

Some of the most popular insular beaches (including El Saco and El Faro) have boat services, so you don't need to take a tour but can choose to stay on one beach. Boats depart between about 8 am and noon from the city waterfront and return in the afternoon up to about 4 or 5 pm. The return fare to El Faro or El Saco is US$4 to US$5 per person. There may also be some boats to Isla de Plata, but you can get there more cheaply from Guanta.

Sucre State

CUMANÁ
- *pop 270,000*
- *area code ☎ (093)*

Founded by the Spaniards in 1521, Cumaná takes pride in being the oldest existing town on South America's mainland. There's not much colonial architecture, however; several earthquakes, including three serious ones in 1684, 1765 and 1929, reduced the town each time to little more than a pile of rubble, and its historic character largely disappeared in the subsequent reconstructions. Today, the city is the capital of Sucre state and an important port for sardine fishing and canning.

Cumaná is noted more for its attractive environs rather than for the city itself. There are some beaches nearby, the closest being Playa San Luis, on the south-western outskirts of the city. Some better beaches are in the Mochima national park, a little farther down the coast. Cumaná is one of the

gateways to Isla de Margarita and a convenient jumping-off point for the Península de Araya, the village of Mochima and the Cueva del Guácharo (see these sections).

Information
Tourist Office The Dirección de Turismo (☎ 31 60 51) is on Calle Sucre, close to the Iglesia de Santa Inés. The office is open Monday to Friday from 8 am to noon and 2.30 to 5.30 pm. There's also a tourist stand at the airport.

Inparques The regional Inparques office (☎ & fax 31 15 70) is in the Parque Guaiquerí, Avenida Arismendi. It deals with the parks in Sucre and Anzoátegui (including Mochima).

Money Most major banks are on Calle Mariño and Avenida Bermúdez. Banco Consolidado is on the corner of Avenida Bermúdez and Avenida Aristides Rojas. Just about the only casa de cambio, Oficambio, Calle Mariño, 10 block west of Plaza Miranda, changes cash and travellers cheques and is open on weekdays from 8.15 to 11.45 am and 2.15 to 5 30 pm, Saturday from 9 to 11.30 am.

Things to See
Some streets around the **Iglesia de Santa Inés** retain some of their former appearance. The church itself dates from 1929, and has few objects of an earlier date inside, apart from the 16th-century statue of the patron saint, on the right-hand wall near to the high altar. The **Catedral**, on Plaza Blanco, is also relatively young, and has a hotchpotch of altarpieces in its largely timbered interior.

Perhaps the best restored colonial structure in town is the **Castillo de San Antonio de la Eminencia**, overlooking the city from a hill just south-east of the centre. Originally constructed in 1659 on a four-pointed star plan, it suffered pirate attacks and earthquakes, but the coral rock walls have survived and are in pretty good shape. The fort commands good views over the city and the bay.

The city has three modest museums. The

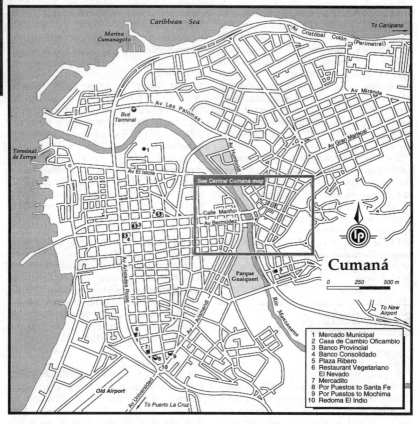

Cumaná

0   250   500 m

1 Mercado Municipal
2 Casa de Cambio Oficambio
3 Banco Provincial
4 Banco Consolidado
5 Plaza Ribero
6 Restaurant Vegetariano
   El Nevado
7 Mercadito
8 Por Puestos to Santa Fe
9 Por Puestos to Mochima
10 Redoma El Indio

Casa Natal de Andrés Eloy Blanco is the
house where this poet, considered one of
Venezuela's most extraordinary literary
talents, was born in 1896. It's open Monday
to Saturday from 9 am to noon and 3 to 8 pm,
Sunday from 3 to 8 pm. The **Museo Gran
Mariscal de Ayacucho** is dedicated to the
Cumaná-born hero of the War of Independence, General Antonio José de Sucre
(1795-1830), best remembered for liberating
Peru and Bolivia. It's open Monday to Saturday from 9 am to noon and 3 to 6 pm. The
Museo del Mar is at the old airport, 2km
south-west of the city centre.

There are two pleasant parks in the centre,
the **Parque Ayacucho** and **Parque Guaiquerí**, and several tree-shaded plazas.

Places to Stay
The city has over 30 hotels and there's
generally no problem finding somewhere to
stay. Most budget places are conveniently
located in the city centre, within a few blocks
of Plaza Bolívar. All the hotels listed below
have rooms with private bath and either fans
or air-conditioning.

There are several inexpensive places on
Calle Sucre, including the *Hotel Vesuvio*

(☎ 31 40 77), the *Hotel Cumaná* (☎ 31 05 45) and the *Hotel Italia* (☎ 66 36 78). They are all pretty simple and will cost about US$8 a double with bath and fan. The Italia also has some more expensive rooms with air-conditioning. The best budget option in this street appears to be the *Hotel Astoria* (☎ 66 27 08), which charges US$8/10/12 for air-conditioned singles/doubles/triples.

You may also want to try the small *Hospedaje Lucila* (☎ 31 18 08), on Calle Bolívar, which is clean and quiet, though there will probably be some loving couples passing through. Matrimoniales with fan/air-conditioning cost US$7/9. Another cheap option in the area is the *Hotel América* (☎ 32 19 55), Calle Comercio, which costs US$8/10 a matrimonial/double with fan. Finally, the cheapest place around seems to be the basic *Hospedaje La Gloria* (☎ 66 42 43), on Calle Sucre, which costs just US$5 for a matrimonial, and as a result is often full.

There are also some inexpensive hotels just west across the river from Plaza Miranda, the cheapest of which is the unremarkable *Hotel Dos Mil* (☎ 32 34 14) at US$6/8/10 a single/double/triple with fan. Appreciably better is the nearby *Hotel Regina* (☎ 32 25 81, 31 10 73) at US$13/18/ 23 for an air-conditioned single/double/triple. Choose an east-facing room on the top floor, for a good view over the city centre including its two churches and the fort.

A few blocks west of the Regina, you'll find two more reasonable (if lacking in style) options: the *Hotel Turismo Guaiquerí* (☎ 66 34 44, 31 08 21) and the *Hotel Mariño (*☎ 32 07 51, 32 23 11). Either will cost about US$16/20/24 a single/double/triple.

The just opened *Bubulina's Hostal* (☎ & fax 31 40 25), around the corner from the tourist office, is far more pleasant and stylish than anything listed above. Housed in a fine historic building in a restored colonial street, this sort of upmarket posada offers six matrimoniales and six doubles, all with air-conditioning, TV, bath and hot water, for US$48 each, breakfast included.

Upmarket hotels are away from the centre, mainly on Avenida Perimetral and Avenida Universidad, both near the waterfront. The most expensive place to stay in town is the four-star *Hotel Los Bordones* (☎ 51 31 11, 51 08 64; fax 51 53 77), at the end of Avenida Universidad, near the beach but a long way from the centre.

Places to Eat

The city centre has few classy establishments, but budget eating is no problem. For arepas, you have several central areperas, such as *19 de Abril* (possibly the best), *El Punto Criollo* or *El Consulado*. Some of the cheapest parrillas can be found at the food kiosks at Plaza Ribero, one long block south of Santa Inés church. Central panaderías include *Mister Pan* (which has some tables to sit and eat at), *Super Katty* and *La Catedral*.

The restaurant in the *Hotel Italia* serves unpretentious inexpensive meals, as does *Restaurant El Polo Norte*. For better food in more pleasant surroundings check the *Restaurant El Colmao* (closed on Sunday), though it's not that cheap. Better still, go to *Bubulina's Restaurant*, in the hotel of the same name. It does delicious traditional local dishes at fair prices.

Outside the centre, some of the best budget food is available at the *Mercadito* (literally small market), Avenida Aristides Rojas, which has at least 15 restaurants. Fish and seafood are particularly good here. Two blocks north-west from the Mercadito is the cheap *El Nevado* vegetarian restaurant. The *Mercado Municipal*, off Avenida El Islote, is also a good and cheap place to eat.

Entertainment

The informal open-air *Bar Restaurant Jardín Sport*, on Plaza Bolívar, serves inexpensive snacks, but it's essentially the cheap beer that draws people in. The place is popular with both locals and foreigners and is open late. The old jukebox has broken down, but now there are musical videos on a TV screen.

Getting There & Away
Air The old airport, 2km south-west of the

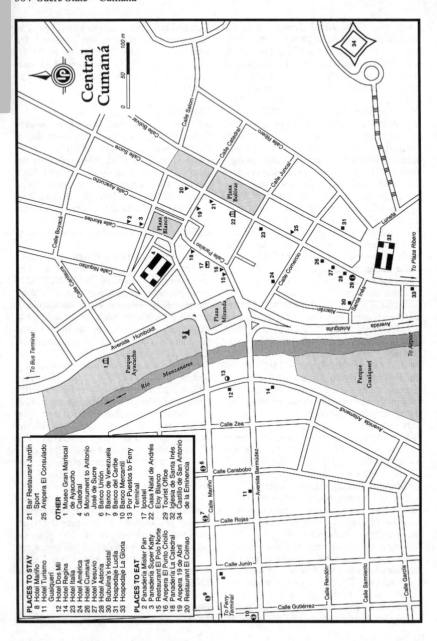

Central
Cumaná

PLACES TO STAY
8 Hotel Mariño
11 Hotel Turismo
   Guaiquerí
12 Hotel Dos Mil
14 Hotel Regina
23 Hotel Italia
24 Hotel América
26 Hotel Cumaná
27 Hotel Vesuvio
28 Hotel Astoria
30 Bubulina's Hostal
31 Hospedaje Lucila
33 Hospedaje La Gloria

PLACES TO EAT
2 Panadería Mister Pan
3 Panadería Super Katty
15 Restaurant El Polo Norte
16 Arepera El Punto Criollo
18 Panadería La Catedral
19 Arepera 19 de Abril
20 Restaurant El Colmao

21 Bar Restaurant Jardín
   Sport
25 Arepera El Consulado

OTHER
1 Museo Gran Mariscal
   de Ayacucho
4 Catedral
5 Monument to Antonio
   José de Sucre
6 Banco Unión
7 Banco de Venezuela
9 Banco del Caribe
10 Banco Mercantil
13 Por Puestos to Ferry
   Terminal
17 Ipostel
22 Casa Natal de Andrés
   Eloy Blanco
29 Tourist Office
32 Iglesia de Santa Inés
34 Castillo de San Antonio
   de la Eminencia

city centre, has closed and a new airport has opened about 4km south-east of the city. Servivensa, Air Venezuela and Oriental de Aviación service Cumaná, with six direct flights daily to Caracas (US$59) and three to Porlamar on Isla de Margarita (US$33).

Bus The bus terminal is 1.5km north-west of the city centre and linked by frequent urban buses.

There is a regular bus service to Caracas available, operated by a number of companies (US$7.25 ordinary, US$9 deluxe, 6½ hours). All buses go through Puerto La Cruz (US$1.50, 1½ hours), and there are also frequent por puesto cars to Puerto La Cruz (US$3.25, 1½ hours).

Half a dozen buses daily depart for Ciudad Bolívar (US$6 ordinary, six hours) and continue on to Ciudad Guayana (US$7.50, eight hours). Five or six buses go daily to Güiria (US$4.50 ordinary, 4½ hours). Buses to Carúpano run regularly throughout the day (US$2.75, 2½ hours), as do por puesto cars (US$4.50, two hours).

For Cueva del Guácharo, take the Caripe bus (US$3, 3½ hours) which will let you off at the cave's entrance; there are two departures daily, at 7.15 am and 12.30 pm. There are also infrequent por puestos.

Por puesto cars to Santa Fe (US$1, 45 minutes) depart from near the Mercadito, one block off the Redoma El Indio. Por puesto jeeps to Mochima (US$0.80, 35 minutes) depart from the same street.

Boat All ferries and boats to Isla de Margarita depart from the docks next to the mouth of Río Manzanares and arrive at Punta de Piedras. There is no urban bus service from the city centre to the ferry docks but por puestos go there frequently from the door of the Hotel Dos Mil (US$0.20).

Conferry runs two ferries a day, at 7 am and 5 pm. The passenger fare is US$7 and the trip takes about 3½ hours. Naviarca sails the same route on the fast *Gran Cacique II* boat, daily at 7 am and 2 pm. Tickets are US$15/7.50 in the 1st/tourist class, and the trip takes two hours. Check the departure

times when you come, as they tend to change frequently. Some departures may be suspended or cancelled in the slow season.

From the same docks, Naviarca operates ferries to Araya, on the Península de Araya, theoretically at 6 and 9 am and 12.30 and 3.30 pm, Monday to Friday, and at 9 am on Saturday and Sunday, but their schedule is, as they say, flexible. It's better to go by a small boat popularly called *tapadito*; they run from the same docks approximately every hour or two until about 4 pm (US$1, one hour). The area around the ferry docks is not famous for its safety, so use a por puesto instead of walking.

Cumaná has the good Marina Cumanagoto (☎ 31 14 23), which is purpose-built, well-organised and one of the cheapest in the country. It's a 10 minute walk from the bus terminal.

PENÍNSULA DE ARAYA

This 70km-long and 10km-wide peninsula stretches east-west along the mainland's coast, with its tip lying due north of Cumaná. Punta Arenas, on the peninsula's end, is just 5km from Cumaná as the crow flies, but it's some 180km by road. The peninsula is hilly, arid and infertile. Its eastern part is higher and more rugged, with the highest peak reaching 596m. The small population is scattered in a handful of coastal villages, mostly on the northern coast, along which the only peninsular road runs. Sandwiched between the peninsula and the mainland is the Golfo de Cariaco, a quiet, deep, intensely blue body of water.

History

The Spaniards first landed on the peninsula in 1499. After the unexpected discovery of fabulous pearl fisheries around the islands of Cubagua and Coche, Pedro Alonso Niño and Cristóbal de la Guerra sailed down to the western tip of the peninsula to find another, quite different treasure – extensive *salinas*, or saltpans. These salt beds still are Venezuela's largest salt deposits.

At that time, salt was increasingly sought after in Europe as an indispensable means for the preservation of food, mainly fish. The Dutch, who by then already had a well-developed fishing industry but only a scarce supply of salt, were the first to realise the value of the Spanish discovery, and soon began to take advantage of it. The Spaniards, on the other hand, who had some salt reserves at home, blindly concentrated on the pearl harvesting of Cubagua and Coche islands. It wasn't until the pearl beds were wiped out, around the mid-16th century, that the Crown eventually turned to the saltpans.

By that time, however, the salinas of Araya were being furtively exploited by the Dutch and English, and the Spanish couldn't do much about it. Various battles were fought by the Spaniards in an attempt to get control of their treasured possession, but the indiscriminate plundering of the salt continued. To prevent further attempts of theft, the Crown eventually set about constructing a fortress.

After carefully selecting the location, work on the fort began in 1618 and took almost 50 years to be completed. Progress was interrupted by pirates and storms, and hindered by the heat, which was so extreme that most of the work had to be carried out at night. The fortress ended up being the most costly Spanish project to be realised in the New World up to that time, however it was also the most powerful and magnificent. Equipped with 45 cannons and defended by a 250-man garrison, La Real Fortaleza de Santiago de León de Araya successfully repelled all attempts to take it.

A turning point in the fort's fortunes came in 1726 with a wild hurricane. The storm produced a tide which broke over the salt lagoon, flooding it and turning it into a gulf. Salt could no longer be exploited so the fort lost its role and the Spanish decided to abandon the peninsula. Before leaving, however, they determined to blow up the fort, to prevent it falling into foreign hands. Despite using all the available gunpowder, the structure largely resisted the efforts to destroy it. Damaged but not ruined, the mighty bulwarks still proudly crown the waterfront cliff.

Meanwhile, as the years passed, the salinas slowly returned to their old state, and mining was gradually reintroduced. Today they provide a good part of the salt produced by Venezuela.

Araya

The fort and the salinas – the peninsula's two major attractions – are both in the town of Araya at the western end of the peninsula. Araya, the largest settlement on the peninsula, is the easiest point to get to and the major destination for ferries and boats from Cumaná. The town is on the Bahía de Araya, with its *muelle* (wharf) in the middle. The fort is half a km to the south, while the salinas spread outwards to the north.

Salinas de Araya These are Venezuela's largest salinas and a good part of the country's salt comes from here. The salt mining is operated by ENSAL company, which has built installations on the seafront and produces half a million tons of salt per year. Until recently, ENSAL organised tours around the salt works, but there were no tours when this book was researched. They may be reintroduced in the future. Check with the Cumaná tourist office for news. Even if there are no organised tours, the trip to Araya is worth considering for the boat ride itself and for the fort. You can still see quite a bit of the salinas from outside the installations and restricted areas.

Upon arrival in Araya, check for tours at the Gerencia, the company's main office. It's at the northern end of the town, in what once was the Hotel Araya, a 15 minute walk from the ferry landing.

Previously, the tours included three areas to visit: the salinas naturales (technically called Unidad 1), salinas artificiales (Unidad 2) and the main complex of buildings where the salt is sorted, packed and stored. The salinas naturales, about 1km east of town, is an intriguingly pink salt lagoon, from which the salt is dragged to the shore by specially constructed boats and then put into piles for drying.

The salinas artificiales, a couple of km

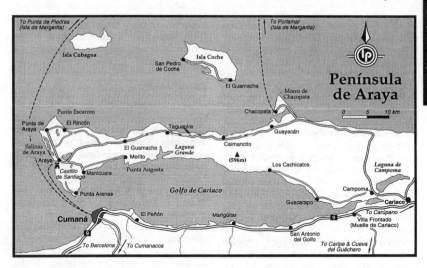

north of the town, is an array of rectangular pools which are filled in with salt water and left to dry out. Thanks to the intense strength of the sun, the water evaporates leaving behind pure salt. The salt is then dragged out, the pool refilled, and the whole process starts again. What is particularly amazing here is the unbelievable pink of the water. Since pools are in different stages of evaporation, there's an incredible variety of tones, ranging from creamy pink to deep purple. The water coloration is due to the artemia, a microscopic saltwater shrimp.

A *mirador* (lookout) has been built on the hill to the east of the salinas, and provides a panoramic view over the whole chessboard of pools. It's on the road to Punta de Araya, 2km north of Araya.

Start early in the morning to allow sufficient time, in case tours are available. Previously, the tours took up to three hours and were free. Be prepared for baking heat: sunscreen, sunglasses and a hat is a must. It's wise to carry a large bottle of water or other drink.

Castillo de Santiago Commonly referred to as the Castillo (castle), the fort stands on the waterfront cliff at the southern end of the bay, a 10 minute walk along the beach from the wharf. It's ruined, but the mighty walls give a good impression of what the fort looked like, despite the damage. You can wander freely around the place, as there's no gate.

Places to Stay There are four or five simple posadas in town, including the *Posada Araya's Wind* (☎ (093) 71 442), near the fort, which is possibly the best of the lot. Alternatively, try the nearby *Posada Helen* (☎ 71 101), which is clean and friendly, or the pleasant *Posada Guacaraya* (☎ 71 087), near Plaza Bolívar.

Getting There & Away
There are ferry and boat services between Cumaná and Araya. In theory, the ferry is scheduled to sail four times a day (once on weekends), but sometimes a day will pass without there being a single departure. Boats are more reliable, and go to Cumaná every hour or two, until 4 or 5 pm (US$1, one hour). Upon arrival at Araya, check the schedule for boats back to Cumaná and keep in mind that the last boat may depart earlier than scheduled, or sometimes not at all.

Although there's a sealed road between Araya and Cariaco (95km), there's not much travelling along it. There are few por puestos that run all the way from Araya to Cariaco. You can try hitching but the traffic is minimal. It dies completely after 3 or 4 pm.

There's a busy boat service between Chacopata and Porlamar on Isla de Margarita. Boats run from 7 or 8 am until about 4 pm, departing as soon as they get filled with passengers (you shouldn't normally have to wait more than an hour or two). Boats vary in size, capacity (from about 30 to 70 passengers) and quality – some look ready to sink at any moment. The trip takes between one and two hours, depending on the particular crate, but the fare is the same with all of them – US$3.75. There's a frequent por puesto transport service between Chacopata and Cariaco (US$1.50, 45 minutes), and there are also direct por puestos between Chacopata and Carúpano (US$3.75, 1½ hours).

Around the Peninsula

Given the scarcity of roads and public transport, you are likely to limit your visit to Araya, making it a lovely one-day trip out of Cumaná. If you have more time to spend, you may like to go to the sleepy fishing village of Punta Arenas, 10km south of Araya. It has a good beach and two posadas, the *Villa Arenas* and *Shailili-Ko*. Another nearby village, Manicuare, is known for its pottery, which has been produced here since time immemorial, but there's nowhere to stay for the night. Infrequent por puestos go from Araya to both Punta Arenas and Manicuare.

The peninsula has some attractive natural areas and a varied wildlife, including lizards, snakes and a diversity of birds. The lagoon near Chacopata is favoured by pink flamingos and scarlet ibis. Incidentally, Chacopata is the peninsula's only village linked by regular road transport with Cariaco (see above).

For any off-the-road walks on the peninsula, wear sturdy shoes, not so much for the snakes but to protect feet against cacti, an important component of the local flora. Don't forget there's almost no shade on the peninsula, so adequate protection against the sun is essential.

CARÚPANO
* *pop 95,000*
* *area code* ☎ (094)

Set on the coast 137km east of Cumaná, Carúpano is the last city of any size on Venezuela's Caribbean coast. It has an airport where large jets can land, and it is linked by sealed roads with Cumaná to the west and Maturín and Ciudad Guayana to the south. It's an active port for cacao which is cultivated in the region before it's shipped overseas.

Despite its regular chessboard layout, suggesting its colonial origins (indeed, it was founded in 1647), the town has no outstanding historic monuments. Of the minor sights, you might want to visit the two main churches, Iglesia de Santa Catalina and Iglesia de Santa Rosa de Lima, the modest Museo Histórico de Carúpano, and the unusually large Mercado Municipal. Carúpano is centred around Plaza Colón, while Plaza Bolívar is stranded in a south-western suburb.

Information

Corpomedina (☎ 31 97 24, 31 22 83; fax 31 20 67), Plaza de Santa Rosa de Lima, has details about their tourist programmes and facilities in the area, collectively referred to as Proyecto Paria. The Agencia de Viajes Venezuela Evasión (☎ 31 21 57, 31 95 77), Avenida Independencia No 172, sells air tickets and may also provide some general information.

Most major banks are located around Plaza Colón. Apart from the Banco Consolidado which changes Amex travellers cheques, the other banks shown on the map are only useful for credit card transactions.

Special Events

Carúpano springs to life for the four days (Saturday to Tuesday) before Ash Wednesday, when Carnaval is held. There are dances, parades and a lot of music and rum, making this a good time to visit.

Places to Stay

If you come by bus for just an overnight stay, the cheapest bet around the bus terminal is the *Pensión Venezuela*. It's clean and quiet, even though it only has shared bathrooms, and costs US$4 per person. Next to the Pensión is the *Residencia Virgen del Valle*, but it's unfriendly, basic and overpriced.

The *Residencia Hotel Ecuador* (☎ 31 34 55), Avenida Independencia No 185, has acceptable matrimoniales/triples with private bath and fan for US$8/18. The *Hotel Bologna* (☎ 31 12 41), Avenida Independencia No 47, has matrimoniales with bath and fan/air-conditioning for US$8/10, but they are basic and unkempt. Better rooms for a bit more are available at the *Residencia Hotel El Centro* (☎ 31 36 73), Avenida Carabobo. You can also try the *Hotel María Victoria* (☎ 31 11 70), on Avenida Perimetral, at the north-east end of the town near the port, which offers air-conditioned doubles/triples with bath for US$15/18.

For more comfort, try the *Hotel San Francisco* (☎ 31 10 74, 31 32 84; fax 31 51 76), Avenida Juncal No 87A, which provides reasonable air-conditioned doubles/triples with bath, for around US$22/30. Alternatively, try the marginally better *Hotel Lilma* (☎ 31 13 41, 31 13 61; fax 31 24 24), Avenida Independencia No 161, for US$30/35. Probably even better is the *Hotel Victoria* (☎ 31 39 10, 31 15 54; fax 31 17 76), on Avenida Perimetral, a 10 minute walk east of the bus terminal. It costs US$32/36 a double/triple and has a small pool.

The Corpomedina's new *Posada La Colina* (☎ 32 05 27; fax 32 29 15), just behind the Hotel Victoria, is the most enjoyable place to stay in town, for US$40 a double, breakfast included.

There are some posadas outside Carúpano, including two good and pleasant places on Playa Copey, about 5km west of the city: the *Posada Nena* (☎ 31 72 97) and the *Posada Casa Blanca* (☎ 31 68 96).

Places to Eat

There are plenty of eateries scattered throughout the city. The market is, as elsewhere, one of the cheapest options for unsophisticated local dishes, and Carúpano's *Mercado Municipal* is quite large. The *Pastelería Challa* has good cheese and ham pasteles and coffee, though there are no tables for you to sit down and eat.

The *Restaurant La Flor de Oriente*, Avenida Libertad, serves hearty comida criolla at low prices. The *Lunchería El Oasis*, on Plaza Bolívar, is a tiny Middle Eastern cubbyhole serving beautiful felafel, cafta, chawarma and the like. There are a few similar Arab eateries nearby, including *El Rey del Faláfel* and *El Farahon*, both on Avenida Juncal. In the same area is the *Pizzería El Rincón de Italia*, which does some of the better pizzas in town. Another good, inexpensive Italian outfit, the *Trattoria La Madriguera* is at Avenida Independencia No 12.

The *Restaurant El Kiosco*, Avenida Perimetral, is not that cheap but has well prepared food, especially fish and seafood dishes. The restaurant in the *Hotel Lilma* is particularly good, as is the one in the *Posada La Colina*. The *Posada Nena* and *Posada Casa Blanca* also have their own restaurants.

Getting There & Away

Air The airport is 1.5km west of the city centre. There are two flights a day to Porlamar on Isla de Margarita (US$33) and one to Caracas (US$64).

Bus The bus terminal is a short walk north of the centre, on the Avenida Perimetral. Buses to Caracas go regularly throughout the day (US$9.75 ordinary, US$12 deluxe, 8½ hours), and they all pass via Cumaná (US$2.75, two hours) and Puerto La Cruz (US$3.75 ordinary, US$4.25 deluxe, 3½ hours). There are also frequent por puestos to Cumaná (US$4.50, two hours).

There are half a dozen buses to Güiria (US$3, 2½ hours) en route from Caracas/Puerto La Cruz; por puestos go to Güiria regularly (US$4.50, two hours). Three

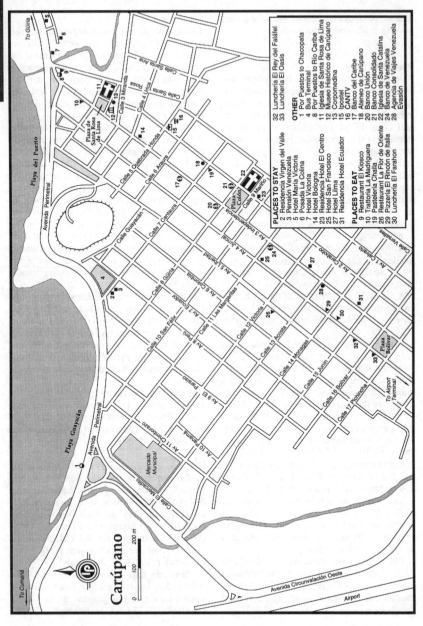

PLACES TO STAY
2 Residencia Virgen del Valle
3 Residencia Virgen del Valle
5 Pensión Venezuela
6 Hotel María Victoria
7 Posada La Colina
14 Hotel Victoria
14 Hotel Bologna
23 Residencia Hotel El Centro
25 Hotel San Francisco
27 Hotel Lilma
31 Residencia Hotel Ecuador

PLACES TO EAT
9 Restaurant El Kiosco
18 Restaurant Madriguera
19 Pastelería Challá
26 Restaurant La Flor de Oriente
29 Pizzería El Rincón de Italia
30 Lunchería El Farahon

32 Lunchería El Rey del Faláfel
33 Lunchería El Oasis

OTHER
1 Por Puestos to Chacopata
4 Bus Terminal
8 Por Puestos to Río Caribe
11 Iglesia de Santa Rosa de Lima
12 Museo Histórico de Carúpano
13 Corpomedina
15 Ipostel
16 CANTV
17 Banco del Caribe
18 Ateneo de Carúpano
20 Banco Unión
21 Banco Consolidado
22 Iglesia de Santa Catalina
24 Banco de Venezuela
28 Agencia de Viajes Venezuela
     Evasión

Carúpano

To Cumaná

To Güiria

To Airport
Terminal

To Airport

Avenida Circunvalación Oeste

Airport

0   100   200 m

morning buses go to Ciudad Guayana, (US$6, seven hours). Por puestos to Río Caribe depart from outside the Restaurant El Kiosco (US$0.60, 30 minutes).

For Cueva del Guácharo, take the Caracas/ Cumaná bus, get off by the petrol station at Villa Frontado, also called Muelle de Cariaco (US$1.50, one hour), and catch one of the two buses coming through from Cumaná to Caripe (passing through about 8.30 am and 1.30 pm) which will drop you down at the cave (US$1.75, two hours); or hitch, though the traffic is sporadic.

For Isla de Margarita, the shortest and cheapest way is via Chacopata. Por puestos direct to Chacopata depart from Avenida Perimetral near the market (US$3.75, 1½ hours), where you change for a boat to Porlamar (US$3.75, one to two hours). See the Península de Araya section for more about these boats.

RÍO CARIBE
- *pop 30,000*
- *area code* ☎ (094)

Río Caribe is a seaside town 25km east of Carúpano. It has no beaches or great attractions, but nonetheless is a pleasant, easy going place, fairly popular with holiday makers, and dotted with tourist facilities. It can be a useful springboard for beaches farther east, and perhaps a more attractive place to stay than Carúpano. If you happen to come here, visit the Museo Histórico on Avenida Bermúdez, and the 18th century church on Plaza Bolívar.

Places to Stay
The town has quite a developed range of accommodation, including several posadas. One of the cheapest is the *Posada Don Chilo* (☎ 61 212), Calle Mariño 27, which charges US$4 a person. It's basic and only has shared facilities.

The *Pensión Papagayos* (☎ & fax 61 868), Calle 14 de Febrero, costs US$6 per person and is probably the best value among the cheapies. Rooms don't have private baths, but are clean and pleasant, and you can

use the kitchen and fridge. The friendly owner speaks German and organises excursions in her own jeep.

The *Posada de Arlet* (☎ & fax 61 290), Calle 24 de Julio, is also good and pleasant, even though it's more expensive. Owned and managed by a polyglot Swiss woman, this quiet place charges US$25 for a matrimonial with bath, fan and breakfast. Here, too, the owner offers trips around the region, though they are more expensive that those in the Papagayos.

Should you need an air-conditioned room, then the *Hotel Evelín* (☎ 61 759), Avenida Bermúdez No 39, is the cheapest at US$18/ 20/25 a matrimonial/double/triple. Nearby on the same road, at Nos 70 and 78, are two simple and inexpensive posadas (no signs on the doors).

The largest and most comfortable place in town is the *Hotel Mar Caribe* (☎ & fax 61 494), near the waterfront. It boasts 50 air-conditioned rooms, a restaurant and a swimming pool, and costs US$22/25/30 a single/double/triple.

Places to Eat
The *Tasca Mi Cocina*, one block south from Plaza Sucre, is popular among locals and visitors for good food at good prices. Also popular, the *Tasca de Luis*, Avenida Bermúdez, is a bit more expensive, though probably not better.

The new, German-run *Pizzeria Ecco*, on Avenida Rómulo Gallegos facing the waterfront, does pizzas and does them well. The *Abasto Independencia*, an ordinary looking grocery on Avenida Bermúdez, sells delicious pastelitos. The restaurant of the *Hotel Mar Caribe* is one of the best and most expensive eateries in town.

Getting There & Away
The best transport link is with Carúpano; por puesto cars depart frequently from the Plaza Bolívar (US$0.60, 30 minutes), and there are also buses.

There are infrequent pick up trucks to the villages of Medina (US$1.25), Puy Puy (US$1.50) and San Juan de las Galdonas

(US$4), which operate on a por puesto principle. They don't get as far as the beaches of Medina and Puy Puy; to get there, you have to rent the vehicle *(pagar expreso)*, which will cost at least 10 times more than the por puesto fare. The trucks depart from the south-eastern end of Río Caribe, opposite the petrol station. The best chances for a short wait are early in the morning. The traffic thins out gradually from the early afternoon.

AROUND RÍO CARIBE

The coast east of Río Caribe has some of the country's loveliest beaches. There are perhaps two dozen named beaches on the 40km coastal stretch between Río Caribe and San Juan de Unare, the last seaside village accessible by road. The best known (and arguably among the nicest) are Playa Medina and Playa Puy Puy, but you're likely to find other amazing patches of sand.

The trend of establishing posadas has been particularly strong in the region, to the extent that there are now at least a dozen posadas on or near the beaches. Most are small and inexpensive and also serve meals, so you can easily stay longer and on the cheap.

On the other hand, roads in the area are few, largely unsealed and often in bad shape, and transport services infrequent at best (see the Río Caribe section for transport details). This makes getting around inconvenient and time consuming which, paradoxically, has some advantages; the region remains largely undeveloped and is not swamped with tourists. There are no classy high-rise beach hotels and mass tourism is unknown.

Orientation

Beginning from Río Caribe along the road to Bohordal, you'll find the enjoyable *Posada La Ruta del Cacao* (☎ 014 994 01 15) in the village of Guayabero, just 3km away. Another 3km down the road, a side sealed road branches off to the left and runs for about 6km to the **Playa Chaguaramas de Loero**. It's a pleasant if not particularly memorable beach with no food, accommodation or toilet facilities, though you can

string your hammock under the roof of the *churuata*.

Back on the main road, 6km beyond the turn-off to Chaguaramas is the three-room rustic *Posada Tierra de Gracia*, and 2km farther on you'll get to the *Hacienda Bucare* (☎ 014 994 00 54). The latter hadn't been completed at the time of writing, but looks like it will easily be one of the loveliest posadas in the area. The owner, Billy Esser, is a good guide to the region.

Proceeding east, the road to **Playa Medina** branches off 4km beyond the hacienda. It goes 5km to the village of Medina, where you can stay in the large and good *La Posada del Angel* (☎ in Carúpano (094) 31 28 12), for US$10 per person. The manager provides transport to the nearby beaches. The road continues north-eastwards for 1km to a fork, where a beautiful small *Posada El Milagro* offers rustic rooms for US$10 per head.

The left branch goes for 2km to the postcard Playa Medina, and you'll get a fantastic bird's-eye view of this tranquil, crescent-shaped beach from the road as it descends to the sea. The golden-sand beach is beautifully set in a deep bay and shaded with a forest of coconut palms. Amidst the palms is a collection of stylish cabañas and a restaurant, both operated by Corpomedina as part of the Proyecto Paria, an ecotourist development project of the region. Packages including accommodation, three meals and transfer from/to Carúpano cost US$90/145/190/240 per one/two/three/four persons; they can be bought in Corpomedina office in Carúpano. Camping is not allowed on Playa Medina.

The right branch leads 6km over a heavily potholed road to the village of Puy Puy (where you can stay in the fine *Posada de Joel* for US$12 a person) and continue for 2km to the **Playa Puy Puy**, where Corpomedina runs a collection of cabañas and a restaurant. Accommodation costs US$35/48/52/57 per 1/2/3/4 persons; the restaurant serves inexpensive meals. Camping is permitted for US$1 per tent.

Few travellers venture farther east, though beaches dot the coast as far as the eye can

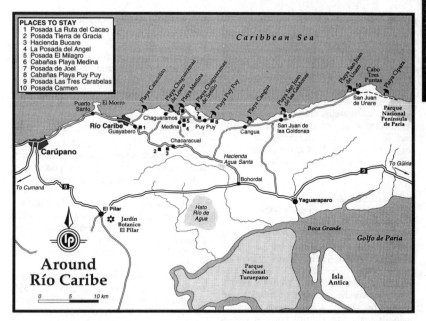

Around
Río Caribe

0   5   10 km

PLACES TO STAY
1 Posada La Ruta del Cacao
2 Posada Tierra de Gracia
3 Hacienda Bucare
4 La Posada del Angel
5 Posada El Milagro
6 Cabañas Playa Medina
7 Posada de Joel
8 Cabañas Playa Puy Puy
9 Posada Las Tres Carabelas
10 Posada Carmen

see. The most frequently visited place in the area is the seaside village of **San Juan de las Galdonas**, noted for its fine beaches. The village has a few simple posadas, including the pleasant beachfront *Posada Las Tres Carabelas*. The usual access to San Juan is by the partly sealed 24km side road which branches off the Río Caribe-Güiria highway, 11km east of Bohordal. Another, poorer access road branches off 8km north of Bohordal and leads through the village of Cangua, next to a beach of the same name.

From San Juan de las Galdonas, a rough road goes for about 20km to the village of **San Juan de Unare**, which has a small beach and the basic *Posada Carmen*. You can walk a couple of hours east to the **Playa Cipara**, where two rustic rooms and basic meals are available. Just a few kilometres east of here, the Parque Nacional Península de Paria begins and stretches 100km along the coast right to the eastern tip of the peninsula.

Apart from the Medina and Puy Puy beaches, Corpomedina manages several inland projects as part of its Proyecto Paria. They include the **Hacienda Agua Santa** (cacao hacienda), the **Jardín Botánico El Pilar** (botanical gardens) and the **Hato Río de Agua** (buffalo ranch).

The buffalo ranch is the major attraction and has a *campamento* where a package costs US$55/85/110 for one/two/three persons a day. The package includes accommodation and three meals (excellent food), plus excursions around the ranch (watching buffalos, bathing in hot springs, sightseeing of local wildlife by jeep and canoe). Day visits (without accommodation and food) are also possible. For details, enquire at Corpomedina office at Carúpano. If you set off from Caracas, you can get the information from the Fundación Proyecto Paria (☎ (02) 762 22 48, 762 72 34; fax 762 50 30), Edificio Galerías Bolívar, Piso 2, Oficina 22-A, Boulevard de Sabana Grande.

IRAPA

- *pop 12,000*
- *area code* ☎ (094)

Irapa is an old port on the Golfo de Paria that grew fat on cacao cultivated in the region and shipped overseas. Today it's a sleepy place which still bears some traces of its former glory, namely some large houses influenced by Trinidadian architectural style. The town lies 2.5km south of the Carúpano-Güiria road, so it doesn't have much through traffic, nor many visitors. This gives it the air of isolation and tranquillity, where not much seems to be going on.

Places to Stay & Eat

The cheapest of a few options is the friendly *Posada Chuchú Domínguez* (☎ 97 810), Calle Carabobo, which costs US$5 for a simple room with bath (double or triple). More comfortable is the *Posada Tierra de Gracia* (☎ 97 863; fax 97 756), Calle Bermúdez, one block back from the beach. It has air-conditioned matrimoniales and doubles for US$25 a room, and a pleasant open-air restaurant. Finally, you can stay in the central *Hotel Maryoli* (☎ 97 315), Calle Anzoátegui, which provides air-conditioned matrimoniales/doubles/triples for US$14/15/16 and some cheaper rooms with fan. It too has a restaurant, and you can also eat in the nearby *La Posada de Hilario*, Calle Monagas.

Getting There & Away

Por puestos depart from the town's centre to Carúpano (US$3.50, 1½ hours), and Güiria (US$1.25, 40 minutes).

GÜIRIA

- *pop 25,000*
- *area code* ☎ (094)

Güiria is the easternmost point on Venezuela's coast that you can reach by road, after a 275km ride from Cumaná. It's the largest town on the Península de Paria and an important fishing port. The town itself is rather an ordinary place with no significant tourist attractions. On the other hand, the neighbouring region, particularly the rugged

Parque Nacional Península de Paria, stretching along the peninsula's northern coast, is attractive.

Güiria has a ferry connection with Trinidad and other islands of the Lesser Antilles. The town is also a possible back door to the Orinoco Delta.

Information

The Acosta Asociados (☎ 81 679, 81 112, 92 09 64, 014 980 14 84), Calle Bolívar No 33, are representatives of Windward Lines; they sell tickets for the ferry to Trinidad (see below) and also arrange all the necessary formalities.

The Librería Las Novedades, next door at No 31, has not much to do with books but will provide information about ferries, if the Acosta office is closed. They change US dollars (low rate) or at least will know where to change money.

The Banco del Orinoco usually changes travellers cheques but charges a hefty US$5 commission on each transaction. The Banco de Venezuela and Banco Unión may give advances on Visa and MasterCard.

Places to Stay & Eat

At the low-budget end, the most popular place to stay is the *Hotel Plaza* (☎ 82 00 22), on the corner of Plaza Bolívar. It costs US$7/10 for a double with a bath and fan/air-conditioning, and has its own restaurant, the best inexpensive eatery in town.

For a similar price, you can stay in the rustic *Hotel Fortuna*, Calle Bolívar No 10, 50m from the plaza, or in the *Hotel Miramar* (☎ 82 07 32), Calle Turipiari, a little bit farther towards the port.

The *Posada Gran Puerto* (☎ 81 085), Calle Vigirima, doesn't offer much more but is a bit more expensive. Its sibling, the *Hotel Gran Puerto* (☎ 81 343), Calle Pegallos, provides slightly better standards in air-conditioned matrimoniales/doubles/triples for US$12/15/20. You can also try the new *Hotel El Milagro* (☎ 81 218), Calle Valdéz on the corner of Calle Vigirima, which is cheaper and has its own restaurant.

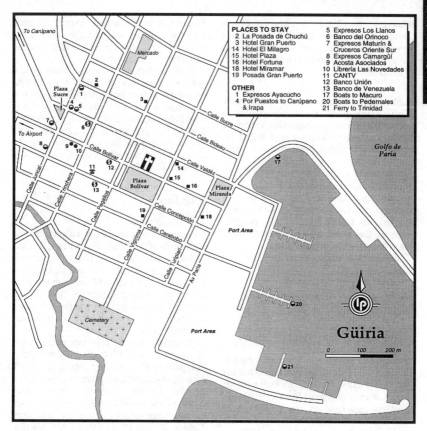

PLACES TO STAY
2 La Posada de Chuchú
3 Hotel Gran Puerto
14 Hotel El Milagro
15 Hotel Plaza
16 Hotel Fortuna
18 Hotel Miramar
19 Posada Gran Puerto

OTHER
1 Expresos Ayacucho
4 Por Puestos to Carúpano
& Irapa

5 Expresos Los Llanos
6 Banco del Orinoco
7 Expresos Maturín &
Cruceros Oriente Sur
8 Expresos Camargüi
9 Acosta Asociados
10 Librería Las Novedades
11 CANTV
12 Banco Unión
13 Banco de Venezuela
17 Boats to Macuro
20 Boats to Pedernales
21 Ferry to Trinidad

Golfo de Paria

Güiria

0   100   200 m

One of the best central places to stay is *La Posada de Chuchú* (☎ 81 266, 82 02 51), Calle Bideau No 35, which can provide air-conditioned doubles and triples for US$20. Its own restaurant, *El Timón de Máximo*, will have opened by the time you get there. You'll find more eating outlets around the central streets, including a few tascas on Calle Bolívar.

If you prefer to stay in more bucolic surroundings, the beachfront *Hotel Playa Paraíso* (☎ 82 03 50, 82 04 51), Carretera Las Salinas, a few kilometres north of town, is a reasonable option.

Getting There & Away

Air The airport is a 15 minute walk west of the town's centre. There are no scheduled flights but there may be irregular flights on light planes to Porlamar on Isla de Margarita and elsewhere. Enquire at Acosta Asociados.

Bus There's no bus terminal. Several bus companies servicing Güiria have their offices close to each other on Calle Juncal, near the triangular Plaza Sucre where the Carúpano highway enters the town.

There are half a dozen buses a day to Caracas (US$12.50 ordinary, US$15.50

deluxe, 11 to 12 hours). They all go via Cumaná and Puerto La Cruz. Por puestos run frequently to Carúpano (US$4.50, two hours) and, less regularly, to Irapa (US$1.25, 40 minutes).

Boat Windward Lines operate a ferry on the Güiria-Trinidad-St Vincent-Barbados-St Lucia route. The whole loop takes a week, as the ferry spends several hours in each port. The Güiria-Trinidad portion takes seven hours.

Theoretically, the ferry arrives at Güiria from Trinidad every second Tuesday at 10 pm and departs back to Trinidad on Wednesday at 11 pm. On alternate weeks it goes to Pampatar on Isla de Margarita. In practice, however, this is not always the case; check beforehand for the next departure.

Approximate deck fares (in US$) from Güiria are:

Destination	One Way	Return
Trinidad (Port of Spain)	60	80
St Vincent (Kingstown)	92	150
Barbados (Bridgetown)	102	163
St Lucia (Castries)	108	174

Payment can be made in US dollars cash or travellers cheques or in bolívares, but not with credit cards. Tickets are valid for six months. Passengers must have a return ticket, unless they have an onward ticket with another carrier. There also are optional air-conditioned cabins available for US$20 a double per night. Acosta Asociados (see Information) provides information and sells tickets. The ferry docks at the southern side of the harbour. The passport formalities are conducted on board before departure or upon arrival.

There are also boats to Port of Spain, which depart when they have collected enough passengers eager to pay a US$500 to US$600 fee per boat. Up to around 15 people fit on the boat. Enquire at the Acosta Asociados office for boats before hunting for one in the harbour.

Peñeros (open fishing boats) leave from the northern end of the Güiria port to Macuro, every morning, except Sunday, without a fixed schedule, but normally around 11 am. They charge US$2.50 and the trip takes 1½ to two hours.

Irregular fishing and cargo boats (a few per week) go to Pedernales, at the northernmost mouth of the Orinoco Delta. The trip takes four to five hours and the fare is largely negotiable; you shouldn't probably pay more than US$10 per person. You can also hire a boat to Pedernales, but this will be far more expensive. From Pedernales, there are boats south to Tucupita.

MACURO
- *pop 2000*
- *area code* ☎ (094)

Macuro is a remote fishing village near the eastern tip of the Península de Paria, that has claims to more fame than its size suggests. It was reputedly somewhere here that Columbus landed in August 1498, though there are no records stating the exact landing site. What is known is that this was the only place on South America's mainland where Columbus came ashore.

Although Macuro is a poor place, it has lots of character. While the village itself is not particularly inspiring, being in such a historically significant place may be. If you decide to come, visit the little history museum and consider a hike to Uquire (see the following section). The nice and friendly *Posada Beatriz* (☎ 81 699), Calle Mariño, will provide a budget shelter, and there's one or two other places to stay.

Macuro is accessible only by water (there's no access roads). Boats depart from Güiria to Macuro daily, except Sunday, somewhere between 10 am and noon (US$2.50, 1½ to two hours). Boats depart Macuro for Güiria early in the morning, between 5 and 6 am.

PARQUE NACIONAL PENÍNSULA DE PARIA
This 375 sq km park stretches for 100km along the northern coast of the peninsula, right up to its eastern tip. It encompasses a

coastal mountain range, which looms up almost right from the sea and reaches its maximum elevation at Cerro Humo (1257m). The coast is graced with several coves, in which some tiny fishing villages have nestled. Going from west to east they include Santa Isabel, Mejillones, Uquire and Don Pedro.

The mountain is largely covered with forest, and the higher you go the wetter it is. The upper reaches of the outcrop (roughly above 800m) form a typical cloudforest habitat, with characteristic epiphytes, lianas, ferns and the like. This part is largely unexplored and intact, and there hasn't been a comprehensive inventory of the wildlife, though it's certainly rich and diverse.

On the other hand, the southern foothills of the range, along the park's border areas, are increasingly affected by local farmers who clear the forest and claim the land for agriculture. The new danger to the peninsula is the discovery of offshore oil, the exploitation of which may change this remote bucolic corner of Venezuela altogether.

Orientation

The park has no tourist facilities and is rarely visited by travellers. The access is not straightforward either, despite the proximity of human settlements. The villages on the northern coast are best (or only) accessed by boat, the closest points of departure being Macuro and San Juan de Unare. Yet boat trips are irregular and expensive. The access from the south is from the Carúpano-Güiria highway, but there are few gateways here which lead into the park.

There are a few trails crossing the park north to south, and these are the best way to get deeper into the wilderness. Ideally, you should take a local guide, because the trails are not always easy to follow. There may also be some danger from snakes – watch as you walk and wear appropriate footwear.

Walking Trails

One of the trails goes between the villages of Manacal and Santa Isabel, in the western end of the park. The rough road to Manacal

branches off the Carúpano-Güiria highway 20km east of Yaguaraparo and winds uphill to the village at 750m. There are few vehicles along this road, so you may need to walk (three hours). There are no hotels in Manacal, but some sort of informal accommodation, eg in the school, can usually be arranged. It's still easier if you have a hammock, as you'll be allowed to sling it under the roof in some homes.

The trail from Manacal goes uphill to the crest at almost 1000m, then down to Santa Isabel on the coast. Guides can be found in Manacal and the hike will take five to seven hours. The trail goes close to the park's highest peak, Cerro Humo, and you can walk to the top from the crest along a side path.

There's an informal posada in Santa Isabel and meals are available. There's no way out by road from the village, so you can either choose to walk back or negotiate a boat to San Juan de Unare, from where you can continue overland.

A variation of the previous route is the Las Melenas to Santa Isabel trail. The road to Las Melenas branches off 8km east of the turnoff to Manacal (5km west of the turnoff to Irapa) and goes to the village of Río Grande Arriba (4km). It then continues uphill as a poor jeep track to Las Melenas (8km), where you're likely to find a guide. The trail which goes from here to Santa Isabel is shorter than the trail from Manacal and the ascent is shorter. The trails join near the crest to form one path.

On the opposite, eastern end of the park, there's a path from Macuro to Uquire on the northern coast (a five to six-hour walk). Guides for this hike can be found in Macuro. Uquire has a good beach, and you may be able to arrange a room or hammock for the night (or take your own hammock). Like other routes, you can either walk back or hunt for a boat to bring you back to Macuro around the peninsula's tip, but it's expensive. If you don't plan on walking much, you can hire a boat in Macuro to take you to Uquire and back, and the return fare won't be much more than the one-way trip.

Monagas State

MATURÍN
- *pop 310,000*
- *area code* ☎ (091)

Founded in 1760 as a Capuchin mission, Maturín has grown into a pole of the agro-industrial development of the eastern Llanos. Large deposits of oil found and exploited in the region has made the city's status even more important. It is also a busy regional transport hub, connecting routes from the north-eastern coast to the Orinoco Delta and the Gran Sabana.

Maturín is the capital of Monagas state and a modern industrial city of wide avenues and thrilling commerce. Although the city has little to offer tourists, you are likely to pass through if you're travelling around the region, and usually will need to change buses here. Occasionally, you'll end up staying the night in the city.

Organised Tours
Maturín's major operator of Morichal Largo tours (see the following section) is Sergio Córdova (☎ 41 41 22, 42 47 89; ☎ & fax 42 66 74), Edificio Banco Unión, Oficina 3-A, Avenida Juncal, right in the city centre. All-inclusive full-day tours include transfer from/to Maturín, boat trip and a lunch, and cost US$60 per person for a minimum of two people. Discounts are provided for larger parties.

Places to Stay
If you're coming by bus and are trapped in Maturín for the night, there's hardly a more convenient budget place than the *Hostería El Portal del Terminal*, inside the bus terminal building. It's simple but clean and well run, and just about the cheapest you can find in town: US$7/8 a matrimonial/double with bath and fan, US$8/9 with air-conditioning.

In the city centre there's a good range of budget hotels around Plaza Ayacucho, which are easily accessible from the bus terminal by frequent city buses, or take a taxi (US$2). One of the cheapest here is the *Hotel La*

Trinidad (☎ 42 93 56), Carrera 8A No 37. It has matrimoniales with bath and fan for US$8 and matrimoniales/doubles/triples with bath and air-conditioning for US$10/13/15. The hotel is well managed and kept, and was so successful that it has opened two branch outlets just around the corner: at Calle 18 No 6 (☎ 41 06 26) and Calle 18 No 13 (☎ 42 24 76). Both are much the same as the original.

The *Hotel Europa* (☎ 42 82 92) and *Hotel Galicia* (☎ 41 30 80), next door to one another on Plaza Ayacucho, are slightly more expensive. Alternatively, try the *Hotel Iruna* (☎ 42 94 86), Carrera 7 No 64, two blocks east of Plaza Bolívar, which costs US$18 a double.

The *Hotel Colonial* (☎ 42 11 75; fax 42 53 16), Avenida Bolívar No 58, is a more up-market central option. It costs US$40/50 a double/triple and has a choice of suites for marginally more. Still better is the high-rise *Hotel Monagas Internacional* (☎ 51 88 11), Avenida Libertador, next to the bus terminal. One of the largest and poshest places in the area is the *Hotel Morichal Largo* (☎ 51 61 22, 51 42 22; fax 51 55 44), 3km out of town on the road to La Cruz.

Getting There & Away
Air The airport is 2km east of the city centre; eastbound buses Nos 1 and 5 from Avenida Bolívar will let you off near the terminal. Servivensa, Air Venezuela, Aeropostal and Aserca operate flights to Caracas (US$64). Rutaca, LAI and Aereotuy flies to Porlamar (US$33). Rutaca has flights on weekdays to Port of Spain, Trinidad (US$60 one way, US$105 return).

Bus The bus terminal is on Avenida Libertador, near Avenida Orinoco. It's about 2km south-west of the city centre, and the two are linked by frequent urban transport.

Several buses a day run to Caracas, mostly in the evening (US$9.25 ordinary, US$11.50 deluxe, 8½ hours). There are buses to Ciudad Guayana (US$3, 3½ hours), Tucupita (US$3.50, four hours) and Caripe (US$1.75, three hours), and all these regional routes are also serviced by por puestos for roughly double the fare of the bus.

For the Cueva del Guácharo, take the Caripe bus or por puesto, get off at the turnoff to Cariaco at the village of El Guácharo (9km before Caripe), and walk or hitch to the cave (2.5km).

RÍO MORICHAL LARGO

The lower course of the Río Morichal Largo, south-east of Maturín, near the Orinoco Delta, has beautiful lush vegetation (including the *moriche* palm after which it has been named), rich wildlife and Warao Indian settlements. This prompted the development of tourist infrastructure, which includes a pleasure boat service on a stretch of the river. The embarkation point is on the highway to Ciudad Guayana, about 90km south-east of Maturín, where excursion boats await tourists to take them down the river.

The boat trips give a taste of the wildlife and the Indian communities typical of the Orinoco Delta, without actually penetrating into the delta proper. They are becoming popular as an easier, shorter and cheaper alternative to the delta tours out of Tucupita. An increasing number of tour companies in Maturín (see that section) and elsewhere offer tours along the river. You can also go on your own to the embarkation point and negotiate a trip directly with the boat operators.

The village of San José de Buja, 85km south-east of Maturín, is becoming another springboard for a delta-like experience, down along the Río Buja, and is already used by various tour companies.

CARIPE
- *pop 12,000*
- *area code ☎ (092)*

Set in a verdant mountain valley midway between Maturín and the Caribbean coast, Caripe is a pleasant, easy-going town renowned for its agreeable climate, its attractive environs, its coffee and orange plantations and its proximity to Cueva del Guácharo, Venezuela's most magnificent cave.

The town is clean and quite prosperous looking, with fine villas and well kept gardens. The place is quite touristy, and on weekends it's full of people escaping the steamy lowlands which dominate the region. The town is little more than two parallel streets, around which most activities and services are centred.

Information

Local tour agencies (see the Organised Tours section) may provide some information about the town and the region.

Banco Unión and Banco de Venezuela give advances on Visa and MasterCard. Banco del Orinoco doesn't provide credit card services, but changes travellers cheques at an appreciably good rate and doesn't charge a commission on Amex.

Things to See & Do

Save for a beautiful colonial high altar in the modern parish church there's nothing particular to see in town, but the rugged surroundings are amazing and pleasant for walks. The No 1 attraction in the region is certainly the Cueva del Guácharo, 12km from the town (see the following section).

El Mirador (1100m), to the north of the town, commands sweeping views over the Valle del Caripe. It's an hour's walk from town, or you can go there by road. Among other sights, there are two nice waterfalls: **Salto La Payla**, near the Guácharo cave, and the 80m **Salto El Chorrerón**, an hour's walk from the village of Sabana de Piedra. Numerous longer trips are possible, including the hike to the highest peak in the region, **Cerro Negro**.

Organised Tours

The Trekking Travelers Tours (☎ 51 352; fax 51 843), Calle Guzmán Blanco, offers jeep, hiking, caving and horse riding trips. Their comprehensive full-day jeep tour includes most major sights in the area plus three meals, and costs around US$60 per person (negotiable) in a group of two to six people. They also do two-day treks to the top of the Cerro Negro, and longer trips around the

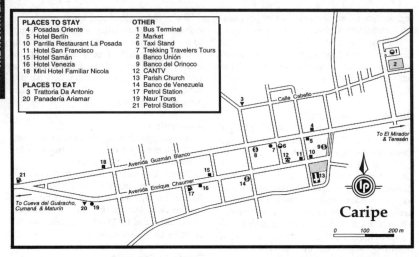

PLACES TO STAY	OTHER
4 Posadas Oriente	1 Bus Terminal
5 Hotel Berlín	2 Market
10 Parrilla Restaurant La Posada	6 Taxi Stand
11 Hotel San Francisco	7 Trekking Travelers Tours
15 Hotel Samán	8 Banco Unión
16 Hotel Venezia	9 Banco del Orinoco
18 Mini Hotel Familiar Nicola	12 CANTV
	13 Parish Church
PLACES TO EAT	14 Banco de Venezuela
3 Trattoria Da Antonio	17 Petrol Station
20 Panadería Ariamar	19 Naur Tours
	21 Petrol Station

Caripe

local caves. They can put together a tour according to your interests, and provide transport and camping equipment.

The Viajes y Turismo Caripe (☎ & fax 51 246), at the entrance to the Hotel Berlín at Avenida Guzmán Blanco, has four-hour minibus tours around some of the nearby attractions, including the Cueva del Guácharo and Salto La Paila, for US$30 per person (a minimum of four people required). Other trips can be organised on request.

The Naur Tours (☎ 51 845; fax 51 330), Avenida Enrique Chaumer No 70, can be useful if you need a vehicle (jeep, minibus etc) with a driver for regional excursions. This can work out pretty cheaply if you are travelling in a large party and split the rental costs. They may also offer some packages.

Places to Stay & Eat

Caripe is becoming increasingly popular with tourists, and there's a score of places to stay in and around the town. Hotel prices tend to rise on weekends.

The *Parrilla Restaurant La Posada*, opposite the church, has some simple but acceptable rooms at the back, which makes it perhaps the cheapest place to stay in town

(US$7 a double without bath). The restaurant itself is also very cheap and OK, as is the *Trattoria Da Antonio* on Calle Cabello.

Across the street from La Posada, the *Hotel San Francisco* (☎ 51 018) has rooms with own bath rated at US$9/10/11 a single/double/triple. Rooms cost much the same in the *Posadas Oriente* (☎ 51 971), on Avenida Guzmán Blanco.

Better options include the German-run *Hotel Berlín* (☎ 51 246) for US$18 a double; the *Hotel Venezia* (☎ 51 875) for US$13/15/17 a single/double/triple; and the *Hotel Samán* (☎ 51 183) for US$13/18/21. The Venezia has one of the best restaurants in town. You could also try the *Mini Hotel Familiar Nicola* (☎ 51 489), which costs US$13/15 a double/triple.

There are also many more places to stay and eat around the town, particularly along the road between Caripe and the village of El Guácharo. Some of them have cabañas, which may work out cheaply if you are in a large party. There's also the pleasant, inexpensive *Hacienda Campo Claro* (☎ 55 10 13) in Teresén, 5km east of Caripe. Most of the hotels and cabañas have their very own restaurants.

Left: Salinas de Araya
Right: Parque Nacional Mochima
Bottom: Pleasures of outback travel in Guayana

Top: Venezuelan beach in peak season
Bottom: Isla de Margarita in sunset mood

Getting There & Away

The bus terminal is at the north-eastern end of the town, behind the market. There's an evening bus direct to Caracas via Maturín (US$12.50, 11 hours). Buses to Maturín depart every two hours until about 5.30 pm (US$1.75, three hours) and there are also por puestos (US$3, two hours).

There are two buses daily to Cumaná, at 6 am and at noon (US$3, 3½ hours). They pass the Guácharo cave on the way. There are also infrequent por puestos to Cumaná (most reliable in the morning). A return taxi trip from Caripe to the Guácharo cave (including a wait to visit the cave) shouldn't cost more than about US$16.

CUEVA DEL GUÁCHARO

The Guácharo cave, 12km from Caripe on the road towards the coast, is Venezuela's longest, largest and arguably most magnificent cave. It had been known to the local Chaima Indians long before Columbus crossed the Atlantic, and was later explored by Europeans. The eminent scientist Alexander von Humboldt penetrated 472m into the cave in September 1799, and it was he who first classified its unusual inhabitant,

the guácharo, or oilbird (see the boxed text entitled The Guácharo), after which the cave has been named. In February 1835, Agustín Codazzi explored 1200m into the cave, much the same depth as tourists go today.

The guácharo apart, the cave has an impressive variety of other wildlife, such as fish, crabs, crickets, mice, rats, spiders, ants, centipedes and bats. It also shelters some amazing natural formations including a maze of stalactites and stalagmites. Some speleologists consider that this is one of the most complete cave ecosystems to be found anywhere in the world.

The cave became Venezuela's first natural monument, Monumento Natural Cueva del Guácharo, in 1949. In order to protect the habitat where the birds feed, a 627 sq km area around the cave was decreed the Parque Nacional El Guácharo in 1975.

All visits to the cave are by guided tours, in groups of up to 10 people; tours depart from the reception building and take about 1½ hours. A 1200m portion of the total 10.2km length of the cave is normally visited, though occasionally water rises in August and/or September and can limit sightseeing to half a km of the cave. Bags

The Guácharo

The guácharo, or oilbird (Steatornis caripensis), is a nocturnal, frugivorous (fruit eating) bird, the only one of its kind in the world. It inhabits caves in various parts of tropical America, living in total darkness and leaving the cave only at night for food, principally the fruit of some species of palms. The guácharo has a radar-location system similar to that used by bats, which enables it to get around in the dark.

The adult bird is about 60cm long, with a wingspan of a metre. It has reddish-brown feathers and a curved beak. The bird played an important part in the religion of some Indian civilisations, including Nazca and Inca.

In Venezuela, the guácharo has been seen in over 40 caves in various regions of the country; by far the biggest colony is in the Guácharo Cave. From August to December, the population in this single cave is estimated at about 15,000 birds, and occasionally even up to 18,000. In the dry season the colony diminishes, but at least 8000 birds remain in March and April, the least populated months. The birds inhabit only the first chamber of the cave, the 750m-long Humboldt's Hall. ■

have to be left in the building by the ticket office, but cameras with flash are permitted in the cave beyond the area where the guácharo live.

The reception building has a small museum and a cafeteria. These have the same opening hours as the cave, daily from 8 am to 4 pm. The admission fee for foreigners is a hefty US$5 and there are no student discounts.

You can camp next to the building at the entrance to the cave, but only after closing time; it costs US$2.50 per tent and you can use the bath, open 24 hours. If you camp here, be sure to watch the hundreds of birds pouring out of the cave mouth at around 7 pm and returning at about 4 am. There's a 30m-high waterfall, Salto La Payla, a 25 minute walk from the cave.

Speleologists and other interested people, who want to visit the cave's galleries beyond the usual public access, will need a special permit from the Inparque head office in Caracas. A local guide will then take you around. The strenuous trip is quite an adventure, and takes at least 12 hours to visit the whole cave, so you need to be physically fit. To start, access is through a pond where you'll get totally wet. The guide's fee should be negotiated directly.

Getting There & Away

The possible jumping-off points for the cave include Cumaná, Carúpano, Caripe and Maturín. See these sections for transport details.

Isla de Margarita

With an area of about 940 sq km, Isla de Margarita is Venezuela's largest island, 67km from east to west and 32km from north to south. It lies some 40km off the mainland, due north of Cumaná. It's composed of what were once two neighbouring islands, now linked by a narrow, crescent-shaped sandbank, La Restinga.

The eastern part of Margarita is the larger and more fertile, and contains 95% of the island's total population of 330,000. The thriving city of Porlamar and all the major towns are here, connected by quite a well-developed array of roads. The western part, known as the Península de Macanao, is arid and sparsely populated, with its 15,000 or so people living in a dozen villages located mostly along the coast. Both sections of the island are mountainous, their highest peaks approaching 1000m.

Generally speaking people are drawn to the island for two reasons. The first is the beaches which skirt its coast. Thanks to them, Margarita has become the prime destination for Venezuelan holiday-makers seeking white sand and sunbathing with decent facilities at hand. The islands are also popular with international visitors, most brought here on charter flights. The tourism infrastructure is well developed, and Margarita has a collection of posh hotels comparable only to that in Caracas.

The island's other magnet is shopping. Margarita is a duty-free zone, so the prices of consumer goods are supposed to be lower than on the mainland, though in many cases there's no significant difference. Despite that, local shops are packed with bargain-seekers.

Margarita is much more than just beaches and shopping, even though few Venezuelans would perhaps think about coming here for any other reasons. The island's geography makes for quite a colourful spectrum of habitats, including mangrove swamps, cloud- forest and semi-desert. No less than five nature reserves, among them two national parks, have been established on Margarita.

The island is also interesting culturally, featuring some important historic monuments, including two fine Spanish forts and just about the oldest church in the country. The island is sprinkled with small old towns, some of which have preserved much of their traditional culture and are vivid centres of craftwork. Finally, since Margarita has become a touristy place, it has a wide range of facilities, plenty of comfortable hotels, fine restaurants, experienced tour operators, good road infrastructure and reasonable transport, all of which makes travel easy.

The island's climate is typical of the Caribbean; average temperatures range between 25°C and 28°C, and the heat of the day is agreeably cooled in the evening by breezes. The rainy period lasts from November to January, with rain falling mostly during the night. Peak seasons for Venezuelan tourists include Christmas, Easter and the August holiday period.

Administratively, Isla de Margarita and the two small islands of Cubagua and Coche make up the state of Nueva Esparta. Although Porlamar is by far the largest urban centre on the island, the small, sleepy town of La Asunción is the state capital.

Getting There & Away
Air Margarita's airport is in the southern part of the island, 20km south-west of Porlamar, reached by por puestos (US$1.75). A taxi on this route will cost about US$9. The airport is identified in all the flight schedules as Porlamar.

The island is a busy and lucrative market, so all the major national airlines fly here and fight for passengers. There are about 20 flights a day to Caracas; Servivensa has five flights (US$45), but other carriers such as Air Venezuela, Aserca and Laser may offer better fares. There are scheduled direct flights with various carriers to Barcelona (US$33), Carúpano (US$33), Cumaná (US$33), Maturín (US$33) and Puerto Ordaz (US$55), and indirect flights to just about anywhere else in the country. Servivensa and Rutaca have direct daily flights to Canaima (US$106), while Aereotuy and Aeroejecutivos fly to Los Roques (US$90).

Aeropostal flies twice weekly to Port of Spain, Trinidad (US$90). There are no direct flights to Miami; all go via Caracas.

Boat – International There's an international ferry service between Pampatar and Trinidad, operated by Windward Lines. The ferry is supposed to arrive at Pampatar from Trinidad every other Wednesday at 6 am, and depart back to Trinidad the same day at 6 pm.

The ferry then continues to St Vincent, Barbados and St Lucia.

Approximate deck fares (in US$) from Pampatar are:

Destination	One-way	Return
Trinidad (Port of Spain)	65	90
St Vincent (Kingstown)	97	160
Barbados (Bridgetown)	107	173
St Lucia (Castries)	113	184

On Wednesday of alternate weeks the ferry goes to Güiria. See the Güiria section for further details.

Boat – Domestic Isla de Margarita has links with the mainland via Puerto La Cruz and Cumaná (both from Punta de Piedras, some 29km west of Porlamar) and Chacopata (from Porlamar).

The Puerto La Cruz route is operated by the Conferry car/passenger ferries, with four departures a day (up to six in holiday peaks). Passengers fares are US$9 in 1st class and US$6 in tourist class. Cars go for US$17, jeeps for US$19 and motorcycles for US$5. The trip takes about 4½ hours. Conferry also operates its 1996-built ultra-modern *Margarita Express* boat on this route, which takes up to 500 passengers and 150 cars and runs up to 36 knots per hour. It does two sailings a day and takes just two hours. It's a comfortable but expensive trip: US$30 per passenger, US$50 per car, US$60 per jeep and US$12 per motorcycle.

The Cumaná route is also serviced by Conferry, with two departures a day. Fares are US$7 per passenger, US$16 per car, US$18 per jeep and US$5 per motorcycle, and the trip takes 3½ hours. Additionally, the route is operated by Naviarca's *Gran Cacique II* hydrofoil, with two departures a day (US$15 1st class, US$7.50 tourist class, two hours).

In the off season, there may be fewer departures than listed. Tickets for the Conferry ferries can be bought at their office in Porlamar (☎ 61 92 35, 61 67 80) or at the ferry terminal in Punta de Piedras (☎ 98 148). Tickets for Naviarca are only available

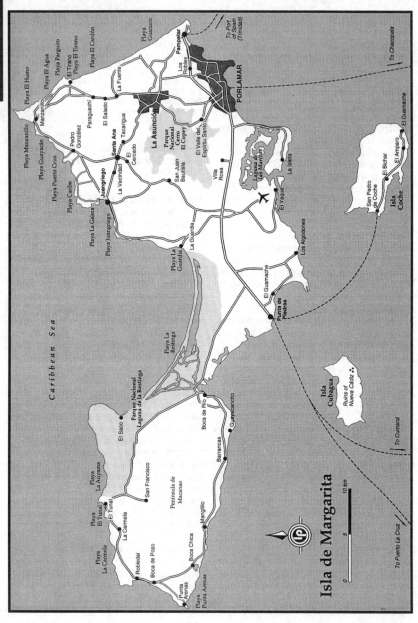

Isla de Margarita

at Punta de Piedras (☎ 98 072, 98 339). There are frequent small buses (US$0.75) between Punta de Piedras and Porlamar, or go by taxi (US$10).

The Chacopata route is operated by small passenger-only boats from the old market area in Porlamar (US$3.75, one to two hours). The boats depart as soon as they fill up (practically every hour or so). There's frequent onward por puesto transport from Chacopata to Cariaco (US$1.50, 45 minutes). See the Península de Araya section for further details.

There's also a ferry service between Punta de Piedras and Isla de Coche, operated once a day by Conferry (US$1, one hour).

Getting Around

Porlamar is the island's transport hub, from where frequent small buses (locally called *micros*) service towns and beaches around the main, eastern part of the island. Public transport on Macanao is poor.

A rented car may be an interesting proposition, especially if there are a few people in your party to share the cost. There are at least a dozen car rental companies in the oval building opposite the airport international terminal, and most have another office in Porlamar. Rental rates are lower than those on the mainland; you can get a small car from about US$40 a day. Scooters and bicycles can be hired at several places in Porlamar.

If you prefer a more comfortable form of sightseeing, there are plenty of travel agencies-cum-tour operators, which will happily show you around the island and beyond. Most companies are in Porlamar, but there are also some in Juangriego and elsewhere. They offer general-interest tours around the island as well as more specific trips (eg La Restinga) and activity tours (horse riding, fishing, snorkelling, scuba diving). The Archipiélago Los Frailes, north-east of Margarita, has become a popular destination for snorkelling. A day tour to Los Frailes, including snorkelling and fishing (equipment provided), will cost around US$50 per person with most operators.

PORLAMAR

- *pop 200,000*
- *area code ☎ (095)*

Porlamar is the largest population centre on the island and is likely to be your first stop when coming from the mainland. It's a modern bustling city replete with shopping centres, hotels and restaurants. Tree-shaded Plaza Bolívar is Porlamar's historic centre, but the city is progressively expanding eastward, with new suburbs and tourist facilities being built all the way along the coast up to as far as Pampatar.

Porlamar offers little sightseeing, other than wandering around trendy shops packed with imported goods. The most elegant and expensive shopping areas are on and around Avenidas Santiago Mariño and 4 de Mayo. Two central pedestrian malls, Boulevard Guevara and, to a lesser extent, Boulevard Gómez, south of Plaza Bolívar, trade mostly in clothing at more affordable prices.

Information

Tourist Offices The government-run Corporación de Turismo (☎ 62 25 14, 62 36 38) is based at the Centro Artesanal Los Robles, in Los Robles, which is midway between Porlamar and Pampatar. The office is open Monday to Friday from 8.30 am to noon and 1.30 to 5.30 pm.

The private corporation Cámara de Turismo (☎ 63 56 44), on Avenida Santiago Mariño in Porlamar, is open weekdays from 8 am to noon and 2 to 6 pm. It also has a stand at the airport (open irregularly).

Pick up a copy of *Margarita La Guía*, a useful quarterly guide published in Spanish, English and German. Also get hold of *Mira!*, an English-language monthly paper which features practical details and background information about the island and beyond. Both are distributed free through some travel agencies, upmarket hotels and other tourist establishments.

Money Banks that handle some foreign currency transactions are marked on the map. There are also casas de cambio, in both the old centre (eg Casa de Cambio La Precisa)

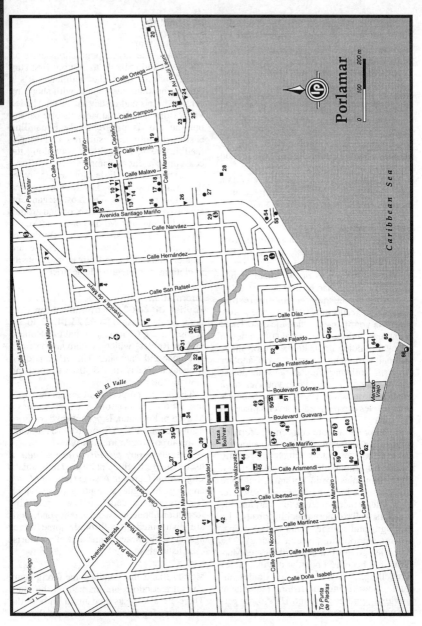

Porlamar

PLACES TO STAY
4   Hotel Internacional
6   Stauffer Hotel
15 Hotel Gran Avenida
20 Hotel Ancla
21 Hotel Imperial
22 Hotel Tama
23 Hotel María Luisa
28 Hotel Bella Vista
32 Hotel Porlamar
34 Hotel Boulevard
43 Hotel Plaza
44 Hotel Nuevo
    Paraíso
51 Hotel Central
58 Hotel Torino
60 Hotel Malecón
61 Hotel España

PLACES TO EAT
2   Gran Café Corleone
8   Pizzas Pastas
9   Restaurant El Faro
    de Julio
10 Max's Restaurant
11 Restaurant Flor de
    Margarita
13 Restaurant El Chipi
14 Restaurant II
    Castello Romano
24 Bar Restaurant
    Bahía

25 Rancho Mandinga
26 Paris Croissant Café
33 Restaurant Punto
    Criollo
36 Restaurant Rancho
    Grande
40 El Pollo de Carlitos
41 Dino's Grill
42 Tasca La Cueva de
    la Rioja
46 Restaurant Beirut

OTHER
1   Banco Unión
3   Banco Provincial
5   Casa de Cambios
    Cafyca
7   Hospital
12 Lavandería Wash
    Quick
16 Discoteca Village
    Paradise
17 Eye Discoteca
18 Conferry Office
19 Lavandería Edikö's
27 Car Rental
    Companies
29 Banco Consolidado
30 Museo de Arte
    Contemporáneo
    Francisco
    Narváez

31 Micros to La
    Asunción
35 Micros to Playa El
    Agua
37 Micros to El Valle
38 Micros to
    Juangriego
39 Por Puestos & Taxis
    to Airport
45 Ipostel
47 Banco Mercantil
48 Banco de Venezuela
49 Banco Consolidado
50 CANTV
52 Lavandería La
    Burbuja
53 Cámara de Turismo
    Tourist Office
54 Aereotuy
55 Mosquito Coast
56 Micros to Pampatar
57 Casa de Cambio La
    Precisa
59 Micros to Punta de
    Piedras
62 Micros to La
    Restinga
63 Banco Principal
64 Tickets for the Boat
    to Chacopata
65 Old Lighthouse
66 Boats to Chacopata

and the new centre around Avenida Santiago Mariño (eg Casa de Cambios Cafyca). They change cash and travellers cheques, and some don't charge a commission on cheques. There are also a few casas de cambio in the airport terminal. Some stores will exchange cash dollars and/or will accept them for payment. Credit cards are widely accepted in shops, upmarket hotels and restaurants.

Turisol (☎ 63 15 06, 63 11 29; fax 63 11 23), Calle Fermín, is the American Express representative.

Laundry There are plenty of them, including the Lavandería Edikö's and the Lavandería Wash Quick, both in the new centre, and the Lavandería La Burbuja in the old quarter.

Things to See
One of the few real tourist sights is the **Museo de Arte Contemporáneo Francisco Narváez**, in a large, modern building on the corner of Calles Igualdad and Díaz. On the ground floor is a collection of sculptures and paintings by this Margarita-born artist (1905-82), while the salons on the upper floor are used for temporary exhibitions. The museum is open Tuesday to Friday from 9 am to 5 pm, and on weekends from 10 am to 4 pm.

A small but colourful **Mercado Viejo** (old market) is held in the morning on the waterfront end of Boulevard Gómez. As might be expected, there are plenty of fish, including some sharks.

Places to Stay
Porlamar has loads of hotels for every budget. As a general rule, the price and standard rise from west to east. Accordingly, if you're after a budget shelter, the best choice of these is in the area of Plaza Bolívar, but if fancy lodging is what you need, look for it around Avenida Santiago Mariño and farther east.

Places to Stay – bottom end

There are a score of budget hotels within the few blocks south-west of Plaza Bolívar. All the hotels listed below have private facilities, unless indicated otherwise.

One of the popular traveller haunts is the basic *Hotel España* (☎ 61 24 79), Calle Mariño No 6-35, near the waterfront. It has a variety of rooms, some better than others, so be sure to inspect a few before deciding. Expect to pay about US$8/10 for a double/triple with bath and fan, a dollar less without bath.

The nearby *Hotel Malecón* (☎ 64 25 79), Calle La Marina, has just recently been revamped and is good value. Run by a friendly Mexican, Luis, it charges US$9/11 a double/triple with fan, US$12/14 with air-conditioning. Choose a room overlooking the sea. A restaurant is planned on the top floor.

The *Hotel Plaza* (☎ 63 03 95), Calle Velázquez No 15-42, a block west of Plaza Bolívar, offers reasonable standards and costs much the same as the Malecón. Another budget option is the new *Hotel Nuevo Paraíso* (☎ 63 96 52), which has neat if dim rooms that cost US$8/10 a double/triple with fan.

The *Hotel Central* (☎ 614757) is nothing very special but it's conveniently located on Boulevard Gómez, and has air-conditioned doubles/triples for US$15/18. Much the same cost, but better, is *Hotel Torino* (☎ 61 07 34), Calle Mariño No 7-33.

There are also some reasonable budget hotels towards the east of Plaza Bolívar, including the *Hotel Porlamar* (☎ 63 02 71), Calle Igualdad, which costs US$15/16 a double/triple with fan, US$17/19 with air-conditioning. The *Hotel Internacional* (☎ 61 89 12), on Calle Patiño at Avenida 4 de Mayo, has spacious air-conditioned triples for US$18.

Among the few budget places to stay in Porlamar's new suburbs east of Avenida Santiago Mariño, the *Hotel Tama* (☎ 61 16 02; fax 63 30 17), Avenida Raúl Leoni at Calle Campos, is the most popular gringo haunt, and deservedly so. Clean rooms cost US$9/

10 a single/double with fan, US$12/15/16 a single/double/triple with air-conditioning, and the hotel has its own restaurant and a bar with a great atmosphere. If it's full (which happens often), you'll find the undistinguished but acceptable and cheap *Hotel Ancla* (☎ 64 23 26), on Callejón Ancla, two blocks to the east. It costs US$10/13 for a double/triple.

Places to Stay – middle & top end

Porlamar has plenty of hotels in this category. Most of them, particularly the top-end establishments, are in the eastern part of the city. The old centre has no plush hotels but it does have a collection of middle-range businesses, and some of these are good value. The *Hotel Boulevard* (☎ 61 05 22, 61 07 32; fax 63 21 84), Calle Marcano, is a good example, with decent singles/doubles/triples for US$25/28/32.

There are some upmarket hotels on the trendy Avenida Santiago Mariño, including the respectable *Stauffer Hotel* (☎ 61 32 22, 61 29 11; fax 61 87 08), which costs US$60 a double with breakfast. Otherwise, try the *Hotel Gran Avenida* (☎ 61 74 57), Calle Cedeño, which is nowhere as good but one of the cheaper options around Avenida Santiago Mariño. Air-conditioned doubles/suites with TV cost US$25/36.

The large high-rise four-star *Hotel Bella Vista* (☎ 61 41 57; fax 61 25 57) is one of the poshest options in the area. It offers all facilities including a swimming pool, five restaurants and a nightclub, for about US$75 a double. The nearby three-star *Hotel María Luisa* (☎ 61 05 64, 63 67 37; fax 63 59 78) is much cheaper (US$36/44/48 a single/double/triple) and not much worse.

The five-star establishments, including the *Hotel Marina Bay* (☎ 62 52 11; fax 62 41 10) and the *Margarita Hilton* (☎ 62 33 33; fax 62 08 10), are farther east.

Places to Eat

The old centre has a wide choice of budget eateries. Some of the cheapest meals are served in the basic *Restaurant España*, in the hotel of the same name (open from 7 am to

8 pm, Monday to Saturday). The *Restaurant Punto Criollo*, Calle Igualdad, is deservedly popular with locals and visitors for its solid Venezuelan food and reasonable prices. *Pizzas Pastas* offers just what the name says and is good value; take away or eat in (open Monday to Saturday from noon to 4 pm only).

The *Dino's Grill*, Calle Igualdad, serves inexpensive parrillas, fish and seafood, indoor and in a charming garden at the back, and is open till late. Set meals at US$2.50 are available at lunch time. Directly opposite is a cosy tasca, *La Cueva de la Rioja*, which is not expensive either. One block north, on Calle Marcano, *El Pollo de Carlitos* does chicken and does it well. The *Restaurant Rancho Grande*, Calle Guevara, offers some Colombian and Venezuelan typical cuisine, while the *Restaurant Beirut*, Calle Mariño, has reasonably priced Lebanese food.

Most of the finer restaurants are in the eastern sector of the city. On Calle Cedeño alone, just east of Avenida Santiago Mariño, there are half a dozen good restaurants, including *El Chipi*, *Il Castello Romano*, *Max's* and *El Faro de Julio*.

The *Hotel Tama* boasts a charming front-garden restaurant serving good food at good prices, and there are several upmarket places around, including the *Bar Restaurant Bahía* and the *Rancho Mandinga*, both with live music nightly.

The *Paris Croissant* café has tables outside and serves breakfast, crêpes, ice cream, pastries etc. The *Gran Café Corleone* is open 24 hours, as are a few other panaderías on Avenida 4 de Mayo.

Entertainment

Discotheques appear and disappear frequently, so you may find quite a different scene to the one described here. One of the few discos that has kept going for years with invariable popularity is the waterfront *Mosquito Coast*, near the Hotel Bella Vista. It has an American slant, attracts mostly a younger clientele and has an adjacent outfit serving Tex Mex food.

The *Eye Discoteca*, Calle Marcano, is, by contrast, the most recent addition to the city nightlife and enjoys the location of what once was an opulent Italian restaurant. It now serves Indonesian food. Just around the corner, the *Village Paradise* has pool tables and plenty of drinks but no food. Other disco-type places to check include *Subsuelo*, *Buccaneers* and *Nikel*, all on Avenida 4 de Mayo.

Getting There & Away

There's frequent transport to most of the island, including Pampatar, La Asunción and Juangriego, operated by small buses locally called micros. They leave from different points in the city centre; the departure points for some of the main tourist destinations are indicated on the map.

PAMPATAR
- *pop 12,000*
- *area code* ☎ (095)

Pampatar is 10km north-east of Porlamar, but the two urban centres are gradually merging into a single conurbation. Founded in the 1530s, Pampatar was one of the earliest settlements on Margarita, and within 50 years it grew into the largest shipping centre in what is now Venezuela. It still has some colonial buildings and a nostalgic hint of bygone days, yet it's increasingly circled by new constructions.

Things to See

Pampatar's fort, the **Castillo de San Carlos Borromeo**, built in the 1660s on the site of the previous stronghold (which was destroyed by pirates), is the best preserved and restored construction of its type on the island. It's a classic example of Spanish military architecture, similar to other forts built around the colony. There is a small exhibition of period weapons, paintings and coats of arms in the rooms surrounding the central courtyard. The fort is right in the centre of town, on the waterfront, and can be visited daily from 9 am to noon and 2 to 5 pm.

Opposite the fort is the **parish church**, a sober whitewashed construction dating from the mid-18th century. Go inside to see the crucifix, Cristo del Buen Viaje, over the high altar. The legend has it that the ship which carried the crucifix from Spain to Santo Domingo called en route at Pampatar, but despite repeated efforts couldn't depart until the Christ image had been unloaded. It has remained in Pampatar since and is much venerated by local fishers.

A hundred metres east of the church is a neoclassical building from 1864, known as **Casa de la Aduana**. It's now home to Fondene, the state's development foundation, which holds temporary exhibitions on the ground floor.

The beach, which extends for a km east of the fort, has some old-world charm, with rustic boats anchored in the bay and on the shore, and fishers repairing nets on the beach. The large community of pelicans adds colour to this picture postcard scene. The beach is more suitable for watching fishing activities than for sunbathing or swimming, because the water isn't crystal clear. The cape at the far eastern end of the bay is topped with another fort, the ruined **Fortín de la Caranta**, which provides better views than the Castillo.

Places to Stay & Eat
Few travellers stay in Pampatar, but if you want, there's quite a choice of places. Many of them are the so-called *apart-hoteles*, offering studio apartments including a fully-equipped kitchenette.

Some of the cheaper places are on Calle Almirante Brion, one block back from the beach. The simplest here is the *Hotel Apache* (☎ 62 40 30), which has matrimoniales/triples with bath and fan for US$10/20. The nearby *Aparthotel Don Juan* (☎ 62 36 09), has double rooms for US$18 and suites for up to four people for US$25; all have air-conditioning, private bath, fridge and gas stove. Across the street, the *Posada La Bufonera* (☎ 62 84 18, 62 99 77) is the best and most attractive of the lot, but also the most expensive: its fully equipped suites cost US$40/50 for two/three people.

The *Restaurant Trimar* on the beach, next to La Bufonera, has good, reasonably priced food, and there are several other open-air eateries along the beach.

There are more places to stay on Calle El Cristo, a five minute walk eastwards, including *Los Chalets de la Caranta* (☎ 62 12 14), with its own restaurant, and *Aparthotel Pampatar* (☎ 62 19 35). Farther east is the five-star *Hotel Flamingo Beach* (☎ 62 45 94; fax 62 26 72).

Getting There & Away
Micros between Porlamar and Pampatar run every five to 10 minutes (US$0.25, 20 minutes).

LA ASUNCIÓN
- *pop 15,000*
- *area code ☎ (095)*

La Asunción, set in a fertile valley in the inland portion of the island, is the capital of the Nueva Esparta state, even though it's far smaller than Porlamar. It's distinguished for its tranquillity and its verdant environs. There's virtually no duty-free commerce here, and hotels and restaurants are scarce.

Things to See
Built in the second half of the 16th century, the **catedral** on the tree-shaded Plaza Bolívar is one of the oldest surviving colonial churches in the country, possibly the second after Coro's cathedral. It has an unusual bell tower at the back corner, a delicate Renaissance portal on the façade and two more doorways on the side walls.

On the northern side of the plaza is the **Museo Nueva Cádiz**, named after the first Spanish town in South America, established around 1500 (but officially founded in 1519) on Isla Cubagua, south of Margarita. An earthquake in 1541 completely destroyed the town. It wasn't until an excavation in 1950 that the town's foundations were uncovered, along with some architectural details and various period objects. The museum displays a small collection of exhibits related to the region's history, including two huge anchors recovered from shipwrecks. It's open daily, except Monday, from 9 am to 5.30 pm.

On the western side of the plaza is the modern **Casa de la Cultura**, which stages changing exhibitions.

Just outside town, a 10 minute walk southward up the hill, is the **Castillo de Santa Rosa**, one of the seven forts built on the island to protect it from pirate attacks. It provides a good view over the town and the valley, and has some old armour on display. The opening hours are the same as the museum.

Places to Stay & Eat

The *Hotel de la Asunción* (☎ 42 06 66), Calle Unión, two blocks east of Plaza Bolívar, is one of the very few places to stay in town. It costs US$10/14/15 for an air-conditioned matrimonial/double/triple with bath, and you can have a TV set and a fridge for a few extra dollars. At the time of writing, the hotel was about to open its own tasca.

Getting There & Away

Micros from Porlamar will let you off on the tree-shaded Plaza Bolívar of La Asunción (US$0.40, 20 minutes). After having a look around, you can return to Porlamar or continue on to Juangriego (US$0.40, 20 minutes) – there is frequent transport to both these destinations. If you are going to the latter, you can stop in Santa Ana to see its church which is similar to the La Asunción cathedral but two centuries younger. In the nearby village of El Cercado, typical Venezuelan pottery is made.

JUANGRIEGO
- *pop 14,000*
- *area code* ☎ (095)

Set on the edge of a fine bay in the northern part of Margarita, Juangriego is a pleasant enough and relaxing backwater sort of town. It has become popular with tourists, even though there's really not much to see or do here except for watching the marvellous sunsets.

The town is swiftly spreading inland from the waterfront, but the place to hang around is the beach along the bay, with the rustic fishing boats and visiting yachts. Far away on the horizon, the peaks of Macanao are

visible, and are particularly spectacular when the sun sets behind them.

The Fortín de la Galera, the fort crowning the hill just north of town, is today nothing more than stone walls with a terrace and a refreshment stand on the top. At sunset it is packed with tourists who come for the view, though a similarly attractive vista can be had from the beach.

Places to Stay & Eat

Juangriego is increasingly catering to tourism and already has a dozen hotels and even more restaurants. In the middle of the beach is the simple Dutch-operated *Hotel Nuevo Juangriego* (☎ 53 24 09). Doubles with bath and fan on the waterfront side go for US$20, while those at the back are US$15. If you choose a room facing the bay you'll enjoy a postcard snap of the sunset from your window. Downstairs is the slightly overpriced restaurant, with some umbrella-shaded tables outside on a terrace and others right on the beach.

The basic *Hotel El Fortín* (☎ 53 00 92), a few hundred metres north along the beach, costs US$10 a matrimonial with bath and has equally attractive sunset views if you choose the right room, although there are only three rooms facing the bay. Its restaurant, and *El Búho*, next door, are pleasant places to eat, even though there appears to be an unmentioned sunset-view tax in the food prices. *El Viejo Muelle*, a few paces away, is yet another romantic place for a meal or beer at sunset, though again, the prices seem to be inflated because of the location.

Just back from the beach, in the Centro Comercial Juangriego on Calle La Marina, are two acceptable budget hotels: the *Hotel La Coral* (☎ 53 24 63), rated at US$12/15 a double/triple; and the *Hotel Gran Sol* (☎ 53 32 16) at US$15/20. There are several other accommodation and food options in the same area and farther back from the beach.

Getting There & Away

Frequent micros run between Porlamar and Juangriego (US$0.60, 40 minutes); all pass via La Asunción.

PARQUE NACIONAL LAGUNA DE LA RESTINGA

Laguna de la Restinga is one of two national parks on the island (the other is Cerro El Copey, near La Asunción). The park covers the lagoon and a mangrove area at its western end. This is a habitat for a variety of birds including pelicans, cormorants and scarlet ibis.

Micros from the waterfront in Porlamar go regularly to La Restinga (US$0.80) and will deposit you at the entrance to the embarkation pier. From there, five-seat motorboats will take you for a trip (US$12 per boat) along the *caños* (channels) that cut through the mangroves. The excursion includes a stop on a fine shell beach, where you can grab a fresh fried fish in one of the open-air restaurants before returning.

BEACHES

Isla de Margarita has 167km of coastline endowed with some 50 beaches big enough to name, not to mention smaller bits of sandy coast. Many beaches have been developed, with a range of services such as restaurants, bars, and deckchairs and sunshades for hire. Though the island is no longer a virgin paradise, you can still find a relatively deserted strip of sand.

On the whole, Margarita's beaches have little shade, and some are virtually barren. The beaches on the northern and eastern coasts are better than those skirting the southern shore of the island. You can camp on the beaches, but use common sense and be cautious. Don't leave your tent unattended. Swimmers should be aware of the dangerous undertows on some beaches, including Playa El Agua and Playa Puerto Cruz.

Playa El Agua

This wonderful 3km-long stretch of white sand is the most heavily promoted and developed beach on the island. Effectively, it has become Margarita's trendiest beach, full of Venezuela's beautiful and arty people, their chocolate bodies finely contrasting with lobster-coloured gringos. It may be a sardine-can experience in the short holiday peaks, but at other times it's quite OK, especially if you walk to the northern, less developed part of the beach.

The beach is shaded with coconut groves and densely dotted with palm-leaf thatched restaurants and bars offering a good selection of food, cocktails and frequent live music. Various beach and watersports services are available, including flights along the coast in ultralight planes (US$30/50 for a 15/30 minute flight).

Behind the beach is a collection of hotels and holiday homes, though not much of that would really fall into the bottom-end price bracket. The *Hostería El Agua* (☎ & fax 49 12 97), on the Manzanillo road, half a km back from the beach, is one of the cheapest places around. Run by a friendly French couple, the hotel has 15 air-conditioned rooms for US$25/30 a single/double, and offers a variety of services, including tours, money exchange and bicycle and motorcycle rental.

The beach has a regular micro transport from Porlamar (US$0.50, 45 minutes), so you can easily come here for the day if you can't afford to stay overnight.

Other Beaches

Other popular destinations include Playa Guacuco and Playa Manzanillo. Perhaps Margarita's finest beach is Playa Puerto Cruz, which arguably has the widest, whitest stretch of sand and still isn't overdeveloped. If you want to escape from people, head for the northern coast of Macanao, which is the wildest part of the island. In the main, eastern section of Margarita, one of the most deserted beaches is the small and shadeless Playa La Boquita, next to the wide and long Playa Caribe, north of Juangriego.

Guayana

Guayana encompasses the whole of Venezuela's south-east, everything that lies to the south of the Orinoco River, including its delta. Geographically, it's composed of several wildly diverse regions, including the Guiana Highlands dotted with massive table mountains known as *tepuis*, the basins of the upper Orinoco and Amazon carpeted with a thick rainforest, and the swampy Orinoco Delta with its extensive mangroves. In administrative terms, Guayana lies within the states of Bolívar, Amazonas and Delta Amacuro.

Guayana covers approximately half of the country's area, yet it is home to only 1.2 million people, a mere 6% of the nation's population. Three-quarters of that population is concentrated in the only two important cities of the region, Ciudad Bolívar and Ciudad Guayana, while the rest are scattered over a vast area without any significant urban centres.

Guayana is home to the majority of Venezuela's Indian groups. Although the most numerous group, the Guajiro, live in Zulia state, all the other main communities, including the Warao, Pemón, Yanomami and Piaroa, inhabit Guayana. They constitute about 10% of the total population of the region.

Guayana is rich in natural resources, with considerable deposits of iron ore and bauxite (from which aluminium is made), and two particular treasures – gold and diamonds. Almost all these riches are in Bolívar state. The Lower Orinoco is Guayana's most industrialised area; Ciudad Guayana has become Venezuela's major centre of heavy industry.

From a tourist point of view, Guayana is one of Venezuela's most attractive and amazing regions, renowned for its mysterious tepuis, spectacular waterfalls, wild jungles and sweeping savannas. The region boasts seven national parks (covering about 20% of

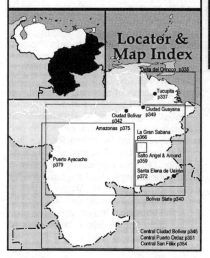

HIGHLIGHTS

- Enjoy a boat trip to the Orinoco Delta
- Savour the old-time charm of Ciudad Bolívar
- Try a trip up the Caura River to Pará Falls
- Visit spectacular Angel Falls by air or boat
- Climb to the mesa of the Roraima tepui

Locator & Map Index

Delta del Orinoco p335

Tucupita p337

Ciudad Guayana
Ciudad Bolívar p349
p342

Amazonas p375

La Gran Sabana p366

Salto Angel & Around p359

Puerto Ayacucho p379

Santa Elena de Uairén p372

Bolívar State p340

Central Ciudad Bolívar p345
Central Puerto Ordaz p351
Central San Félix p354

Guayana), including Venezuela's three largest nature reserves (Parima-Tapirapecó, Canaima and Serranía La Neblina).

Most parts of the region are barely explored and large areas have hardly ever been penetrated. The roads are few and far between, so most transport is by jeep, boat or light plane.

Exploring the region on your own is not easy or cheap, except for more developed areas. Organised tourism has developed considerably over the past decade, cutting further and further into the wilderness. However, it's not cheap.

Delta del Orinoco

Covering an area of about 25,000 sq km, the Orinoco Delta is the second largest on the continent, after the Amazon. In its lower course the river reaches a width of 20km and splits into about 40 major *caños* (channels) which carry the waters down into the Atlantic. Their *bocas* (mouths) are distributed along 360km of coast. The southernmost channel, Río Grande, is the main one and is used by ocean-going vessels sailing upriver to Ciudad Guayana.

The delta formed over the millennia as sediments were brought down by the river and accumulated. As the process continues, the delta is slowly extending out into the ocean. In the course of the last century alone, about 900 sq km of new land appeared. The delta consists of a maze of islands separated by caños. A good part of the banks of the channels are lined by mangroves. The land is largely covered by mixed forest, which includes a variety of palms, of which the *moriche* is the most typical of the region. It has traditionally provided the basic food of the delta's inhabitants, the Warao Indians, as well as material for their dwellings, crafts, tools and household implements.

The climate of the delta is hot and humid. The average annual temperature is around 26°C and changes little throughout the year. However, temperature variation between day and night can be considerable. The annual rainfall is relatively high, exceeding 2000 mm in many areas, and, in general, the closer you get to the coast the more it rains. The driest period is from January to March; the remaining part of the year is wet or very wet.

This rainfall pattern doesn't exactly correspond with the water level of the Orinoco, which essentially depends on the climate in the upper reaches of the river and its major tributaries. The water level is usually at its lowest in March, and highest from August to September; in that time, parts of the delta become marshy or flooded.

Curiously enough, the state is not named after the Orinoco, but after Río Amacuro, a small river which runs along a part of the Guyana border and empties into Boca Grande, the main mouth of the Orinoco. Tucupita is the state capital and its largest town.

This is the major point of departure for organised tours to the delta, and the place to arrange a tour. However, the nondescript town of Barrancas (not to be confused with Los Barrancos, opposite San Félix) is the delta's busiest port, from which non-tourist boats run through to most delta destinations, particularly towards the Lower Delta to the east.

The delta has long been one of Venezuela's wildest and best preserved regions. Yet this is now being changed, following the discovery and subsequent exploitation of large oil reserves in the area of Pedernales. Another dangerous addition to the delta's traditional life is drug smuggling. The delta is increasingly used for trafficking of cocaine from Colombia via the

The Warao

The Orinoco Delta is inhabited by the Warao (or Guarao) Indians, the second largest indigenous group in Venezuela (after the Guajiro), numbering about 24,000. They live along the caños, constructing their *palafitos* (houses on stilts) on riverbanks and live mostly off fishing. Water is pivotal in their lives, as indicated by the tribe's name ('wa' in the local language means canoe, 'arao' means people).

Many of the Waraos still use their native language (classified as independent, or not belonging to any of the major language families); only half the indigenous population speaks Spanish. Two-thirds of the Waraos live in the eastern part of the delta, between Caño Mariusa and Río Grande, distributed across about 250 tiny communities.

The Waraos are very skilful craftspeople. They are renowned for their basketry and woodcarvings, especially *curiaras* (dugouts) and animal figures carved from balsawood. Their *chinchorros* (hammocks), made from the fibre of the moriche palm, are also widely known. ■

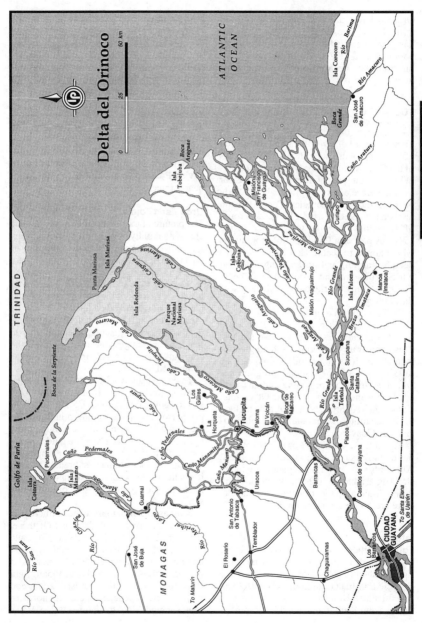

Delta del Orinoco

GUAYANA

Orinoco River and out into the Caribbean through the maze of delta waterways. It may have an irreversible impact on the local population and the safety of the region. So far, there has been no reports of incidents involving tourists.

TUCUPITA
- *pop 60,000*
- *area code* ☎ (087)

Tucupita is a hot river town and the capital of Delta Amacuro state. It sits on the banks of the Caño Manamo, the westernmost channel of the delta, which flows northwards for 110km before emptying into Golfo de Paria near the town of Pedernales. Caño Manamo has been blocked by a dyke built 22km south of Tucupita. The dyke was erected in the 1960s as part of a flood-control programme which aimed to secure land in the northern delta for farming and stock raising. The road which runs on the top of the dyke is Tucupita's only overland link with the rest of the country.

Tucupita evolved in the 1920s as one of a chain of Capuchin missions that were founded in the delta to convert the Indians. This opened up the region for both governmental activities and criollo colonists. The missions established social programmes which focused on providing Indians with education and health services. Other missions scattered throughout the region include the Araguaimujo, Nabasanuka and San Francisco de Guayo.

Tucupita is essentially a base for exploring the delta rather than an attraction in itself. Although you may find it pleasant enough strolling around the central streets or along Paseo Manamo, the riverbank esplanade, there are no special sights in town.

Information
Tourist Office The Diturda (Dirección de Turismo del Estado Delta Amacuro) municipal tourist office (☎ 21 68 52) is in the Edificio San Juan (2nd floor), Calle Bolívar, just off Plaza Bolívar. It's open Monday to Friday from 8 am to noon and 3 to 6 pm.

Money Banco de Venezuela and Banco Unión might give cash advances on Visa and MasterCard but that's about it. Cash dollars and travellers cheques may prove to be difficult to change in Tucupita. Most of the tour agencies will accept cash payments, not credit cards or travellers cheques.

Things to See
The **Iglesia de San José de Tucupita**, the Capuchin mission church built in 1930, is the oldest building in town. It served as a parish church until the monumental **Catedral de la Divina Pastora** was completed in 1982 after nearly three decades of painstaking work.

Organised Tours
The picture of tour companies in Tucupita is changing rapidly, with new agencies appearing on the market and others going out of business. At the time of writing, there were half a dozen tour operators in town and all focused on trips into the delta. The tourist office keeps track of the current situation and has a list of registered companies. It may be useful to consult the staff before you strike a deal with an unregistered operator, as you won't be able to get your money back if the company doesn't provide the services it has committed itself to.

Tours are usually all-inclusive two to four-day trips (there are hardly any one day tours) and the going rate is about US$50 to US$90 per person a day, depending principally on the number of people in the group. Most agencies say they can provide a guide speaking English and sometimes other languages such as German, Italian or French, though it's better to check this by asking to meet the guide personally before you commit yourself.

Most agents offer tours to the northern part of the delta, towards Pedernales. Of these, Aventura Turística Delta (☎ 21 08 35), Calle Centurión No 62, receives possibly the best comments from travellers. The agency is run by a helpful couple, Nicolás and Vidalig, and their tours are well organised and good value. Other agencies operating northern routes include Trip to Nature (☎ 21 01 44),

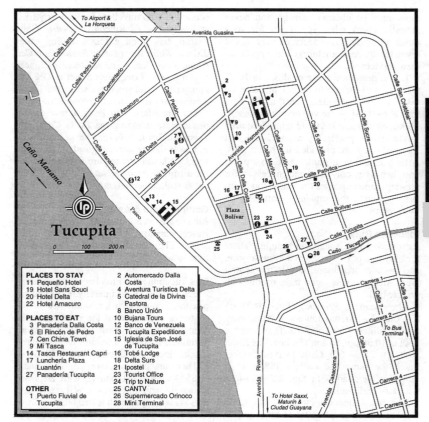

Tucupita

0   100   200 m

PLACES TO STAY
11 Pequeño Hotel
19 Hotel Sans Souci
20 Hotel Delta
22 Hotel Amacuro

PLACES TO EAT
3 Panadería Dalla Costa
6 El Rincón de Pedro
7 Cen China Town
9 Mi Tasca
14 Tasca Restaurant Capri
17 Lunchería Plaza
   Luantón
27 Panadería Tucupita

OTHER
1 Puerto Fluvial de
  Tucupita

2 Automercado Dalla
  Costa
4 Aventura Turística Delta
5 Catedral de la Divina
  Pastora
8 Banco Unión
10 Bujana Tours
12 Banco de Venezuela
13 Tucupita Expeditions
15 Iglesia de San José
   de Tucupita
16 Tobé Lodge
18 Delta Surs
21 Ipostel
23 Tourist Office
24 Trip to Nature
25 CANTV
26 Supermercado Orinoco
28 Mini Terminal

Calle Bolívar No 18; Bujana Tours (☎ & fax 21 27 76), Calle Dalla Costa; and Tucupita Expeditions (☎ 21 29 86; ☎ & fax 21 08 01), Calle Manamo No 26.

Delta Surs (☎ 21 26 66; ☎ & fax 21 38 77), Calle Mariño at Calle Pativilca, is one of the few operators offering tours to the far eastern area of the delta, which is arguably more interesting due to its more diverse wildlife and more numerous Indian population. These tours are more expensive. Delta Surs have a campamento in San Francisco de Guayo.

Also in Guayo is the French-run camp-

amento Tobé Lodge, which offers accommodation (in beds and hammocks), meals and tours around the area. Tobé Lodge has its office at Plaza Bolívar in Tucupita (☎ & fax 21 07 09), where its packages can be bought (though most are distributed and sold through selected travel agencies around the country). Transport to the camp is provided by the company's own fast boat departing from El Volcán.

Despite tourist office efforts to eliminate pirate guide services, there are quite a few independent guides who descend like vultures as soon as you arrive in town. Their tours may be cheaper, though you never actually know what you'll get for your money; Lonely Planet received very mixed (even totally contradictory) comments about their services.

If you decide on these guides, clarify all the details of the trip (duration, places to be visited, food and lodging etc), and have a look at the boat before you commit yourself. Make sure the boat has two engines (required by law) and preferably a roof, and that mosquito nets are provided for hammocks. After you and your guide agree on a price, you should pay only the money necessary for pre-departure expenses (gasoline, food). Insist on paying the remaining part only on your return.

Places to Stay

Accommodation is scarce in Tucupita. There are only four or five hotels in the town centre, and two or three more outside the central area. All the hotels listed have rooms with private baths.

The cheapest, *Pequeño Hotel* (☎ 21 05 23), Calle La Paz, has doubles with fan/noisy air-conditioning for US$8/10. They lock the door at 10.30 pm, so don't be late. The *Hotel Delta* (☎ 21 24 67), Calle Pativilca, offers much the same and costs US$8/10/15 a double/triple/quad with fan, US$12/14/18 with air-conditioning.

The *Hotel Amacuro* (☎ 21 04 04), Calle Bolívar, is a little bit better and has quieter air-conditioning. Its singles/doubles/triples cost US$10/12/14. The best of the central options is the recently opened *Hotel Sans Souci* (☎ 21 01 32), Calle Centurión, which costs US$10/13 a matrimonial with fan/air-conditioning, and has its own restaurant.

The *Hotel Saxxi* (☎ 21 21 12, 21 01 75), in Paloma, 6km south of Tucupita on the main road, is the best place to stay in the area. It costs US$25/28/32 for an air-conditioned matrimonial/double/triple, and has a swimming pool, restaurant and bar.

Places to Eat

There's a range of simple places to eat in town, of which *Mi Tasca*, Calle Dalla Costa,

is popular with travellers for its hearty food at low prices. *El Rincón de Pedro*, Calle Petión, has good chicken among other dishes, while the nearby *Restaurant Cen China Town* does some reasonable Chinese cooking. The *Tasca Sans Souci* is OK and inexpensive, and you can also try the *Tasca-Restaurant Capri*, on Calle Manamo.

For breakfast, you have a few central panaderías, including the *Dalla Costa* and *Tucupita*. The *Lunchería Plaza Luantón*, on Plaza Bolívar, serves good coffee and snacks. Should you require food provisions for a trip try *Automercado Dalla Costa* or, better still, *Supermercado Orinoco*.

Getting There & Away

Air The airport is 3km north of town; the San Rafael carrito goes there from the town centre. There are flights to Porlamar a few times a week (US$47).

Bus Tucupita has a brand new bus terminal, which handles all the intercity buses and por puestos. It's about a km south-east of the centre; a taxi between the centre and the terminal will cost about US$1. The Mini-Terminal, on Calle Tucupita in the centre, handles local and suburban bus traffic.

There are two buses nightly to Caracas (US$14 deluxe, 11 hours), with Expresos Camargüí and Expresos Los Llanos. Expresos La Guayanesa has two buses daily to Ciudad Guayana (US$3, 3½ hours), but por puestos service this route regularly (US$6, two hours). The trip includes a ferry ride across the Orinoco from Los Barrancos to San Félix (no extra charge).

There are several buses a day to Maturín (US$3.50, four hours), or you can go by a more frequent por puesto (US$7, three hours).

Boat Passenger boats are supposed to depart daily from Puerto Fluvial de Tucupita to Pedernales (US$16, four to five hours). There are no boat services from Tucupita to the eastern part of the delta. There may be some boats from El Volcán, the port near the dyke, 22km south of Tucupita. However, most boats to the eastern delta (Curiapo, Misión San Francisco de Guayo, Misión Araguaimujo, San José de Amacuro etc) depart from Barrancas.

The Lower Orinoco

The Lower Orinoco is the industrial heart of Guayana. This is the most densely populated part of the region, and the only one which has a road network to speak of. Here are Guayana's only two cities, Ciudad Bolívar and Ciudad Guayana, both of which sit on the right bank of the Orinoco, in Bolívar state (Venezuela's largest state, occupying over a quarter of the country's territory).

While Ciudad Bolívar is an important historic city with character and charm, Ciudad Guayana is not much more than a vast urban sprawl dotted with industrial installations. Either of the two cities makes a convenient starting point for exploring Bolívar state, especially its most attractive south-eastern part, which includes Salto Angel (Angel Falls), the Gran Sabana and Roraima. The state is bisected by an excellent and spectacular highway, which runs from Ciudad Guayana south to Santa Elena de Uairén on the Brazilian border.

CIUDAD BOLÍVAR
- *pop 280,000*
- *area code ☎ (085)*

Ciudad Bolívar is a hot city set on the southern bank of the Orinoco, about 420km upstream from the Atlantic. Founded in 1764 on a rocky elevation at the river's narrowest point, the town was appropriately named Angostura (literally narrows), and grew slowly as a sleepy river port hundreds of miles from any important centres of population. Then, suddenly and unexpectedly, Angostura became the place where much of the country's (and the continent's) history was forged.

It was here that Bolívar came in 1817, soon after the town had been liberated from Spanish control, and set up the base for the

military operations that led to the final stage of the War of Independence. The town was made the provisional capital of the yet to be liberated country. It was in Angostura that the British Legionnaires joined Bolívar before they all set off for the battle of Boyacá that secured the independence of Colombia. The Angostura Congress convened here in 1819 and gave birth to Gran Colombia, a unified republic comprising Venezuela, Colombia and Ecuador. In honour of Bolívar, the town was renamed Ciudad Bolívar in 1846.

Today, Ciudad Bolívar is the capital of Bolívar state, and a fair-sized city with quite a number of tourist attractions. Its centre has retained the flavour of an old river town and still conserves some of the architecture dating from its 50-year-long colonial era. It's a popular stop for travellers, partly for the city itself, and partly as a jumping-off point for Salto Angel.

Information
Tourist Office The CIAT (Centro de Información y Atención al Turista) tourist office (☎ 22 771, 24 803) is on Avenida Táchira, two blocks north-west of the airport terminal, and is open Monday to Friday from 8 am to noon and 2 to 5.30 pm.

Inparques The Inparques office (☎ 29 908) is in the Edificio de la CVG, on the corner of Avenida Germania and Avenida Andrés Bello. It's no longer necessary to come here to get a permit for camping in Canaima.

Money The Banco Unión, Banco Mercantil and Banco de Venezuela give advances on credit cards. The Banco Consolidado, corner of Avenida Aeropuerto and Avenida Andrés Bello, near the airport, changes Amex travellers cheques at good rates. Across the road, in the Hotel Laja Real, is the only authorised casa de cambio in town, which exchanges cash and cheques, but charges a 2% commission on transactions.

Moneychangers hang around the entrance of the Hotel Colonial, on Paseo Orinoco, and change dollars and travellers cheques,

GUAYANA

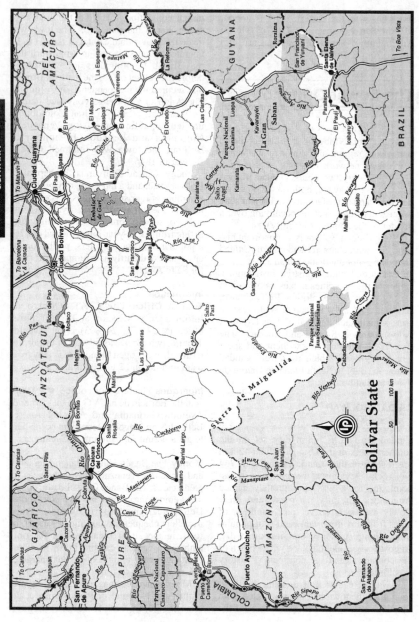

though the rates are rather poor. They actually don't change money themselves, but take you to a nearby shop (most often a jeweller), where the transaction takes place and seems to be safe.

Paseo Orinoco

This lively waterfront boulevard is lined with arcaded houses, some of which date back to Bolívar's days. Midway along the Paseo is the **Mirador Angostura**, a rocky headland that juts out into the river at its narrowest point. If you happen to be here in August, when the water is at its highest, you may have the river just below your feet. This is also the time to watch fishermen with their *atarrayas* (fishing nets), trying to catch the delicious *sapoara* (or *zapoara*), which appear only during this short period. In March, by contrast, the water level may be over 15m lower.

The lookout commands good views up and down the Orinoco. Five km upriver you'll see a suspension bridge, **Puente de Angostura**, constructed in 1967; it's the only bridge across the Orinoco. It's 1678m long, and its central, highest section is over 50m above water. Walkers are not allowed on the bridge – you can only cross in a vehicle.

Close to the lookout is a restored 18th-century prison building, which functioned as a jail until 1952. It's now home to the **Instituto de Cultura del Orinoco** (open daily, except Monday, from 9.30 am to noon and 3 to 5 pm), which features the crafts of Indian communities from Venezuela's south. Note the aquarium with fish species typical of the Orinoco, including the sapoara.

Two blocks west along the Paseo is the **Museo de Ciudad Bolívar**, in a spacious colonial residence known as the Casa del Correo del Orinoco. It was here that the republic's first newspaper was printed from June 1818 until 1821, and you can see the original press on which it was done, along with other objects related to the town's history and a collection of modern painting. The museum is open Tuesday to Saturday from 9 am to noon and 2 to 5 pm, and Sunday from 9 am to noon.

Colonial Quarter

The historic heart of the city is on a hillside to the south of the river, and is centred around the finely restored and tranquil **Plaza Bolívar**. Apart from the usual monument to Bolívar in the middle, there are five allegorical statues on the square which personify the five countries Bolívar liberated. To the east looms the massive **Catedral**, begun right after the town's foundation and completed 80 years later.

Half of the western side of the plaza is taken up by the **Casa del Congreso de Angostura**, built in the 1770s. It housed lengthy debates of the 1819 Angostura Congress. You can have a look around the interior.

On the northern side of the square is the **Casa Piar**, where General Manuel Piar was kept prisoner in October 1817, before having been placed in front of a firing squad against the wall of the cathedral and executed. Piar liberated the city from the Spanish control, but rejected Bolívar's authority and was sentenced to death in a controversial and much criticised trial.

Other historic buildings around the plaza include the **Casa Parroquial** and the **Gobernación**. Just one block south is the **Alcaldía de Heres**, a pair of fine old buildings on both sides of Calle Igualdad, linked by an intriguing aerial walkway.

Don't miss visiting the **Parque El Zanjón**, a most unusual city park, replete with massive boulders (called the lajas). The fine old-style **Casa de Tejas**, picturesquely set on one of the boulders, houses a small art exhibition.

On the southern edge of the colonial sector is the pleasantly shaded **Plaza Miranda**. A sizeable building on its eastern side was constructed in 1870 as a hospital, but it never served that purpose. In 1892, it was turned into barracks and served the army until 1954, only to become a police station afterwards. Eventually, after an extensive refurbishing, it reopened in 1992 as the **Centro de las Artes**, which stages temporary exhibitions (open Tuesday to Friday from 9 am to noon and 3 to 5 pm, Saturday from 10 am to 4 pm, and Sunday from 9 am to 1 pm). Go upstairs

GUAYANA

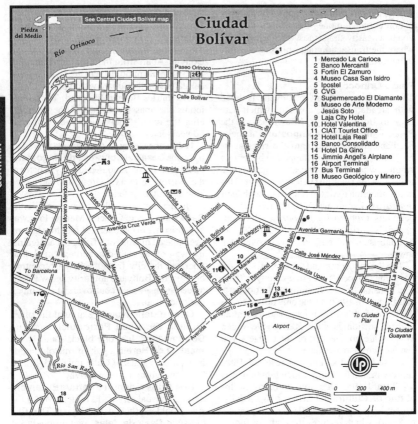

Ciudad
Bolívar

1 Mercado La Carioca
2 Banco Mercantil
3 Fortín El Zamuro
4 Museo Casa San Isidro
5 Ipostel
6 CVG
7 Supermercado El Diamante
8 Museo de Arte Moderno
    Jesús Soto
9 Laja City Hotel
10 Hotel Valentina
11 CIAT Tourist Office
12 Hotel Laja Real
13 Banco Consolidado
14 Hotel Da Gino
15 Jimmie Angel's Airplane
16 Airport Terminal
17 Bus Terminal
18 Museo Geológico y Minero

to the mirador on the roof, for a good view of the **Fortín El Zamuro**, crowning the top of the highest hill in the city, half a km to the south. The fort is open to visitors (the entrance is from Paseo Heres) and provides fine views over the old town.

Other Attractions
Beyond the fort, on Avenida Táchira, is the **Museo Casa San Isidro**, in a beautiful colonial mansion of the coffee hacienda which once stretched as far as the airport. Bolívar stayed here for 29 days and reputedly constructed his vehement speech for the

Angostura Congress. The house interior is maintained in the style of Bolívar's era, and has the same opening hours as the Centro de las Artes.

Proceed 1km south on Avenida Táchira and take the perpendicular Avenida Briceño Iragorry to the left, which will lead you to the **Museo de Arte Moderno Jesús Soto**. The museum has a good collection of works by this renowned kinetic artist (who was born in Ciudad Bolívar in 1923), as well as works by other national and international modern artists. The museum is open Tuesday to Sunday from 10 am to 5 pm.

In front of the airport terminal, a 10 minute walk from the museum, stands the legendary **airplane of Jimmie Angel** (read the Salto Angel section for more about him). This is the original plane, which was removed from the top of Auyantepui in 1970 and restored in Maracay.

In the south-western suburb of the city is the **Museo Geológico y Minero**, which introduces Guayana's mines, mining techniques, machinery etc.

Organised Tours

There are plenty of tour operators in the city, most of which are grouped around Paseo Orinoco and the airport. In the former area, start by checking the offers of three companies nestled in riverfront hotels: Neckar Tour (☎ 24 402, 28 350) in the Hotel Colonial; Expediciones Dearuna (☎ 014 985 13 60; ☎ & fax 26 089) in the Hotel Caracas; and Cunaguaro Tours (☎ 22 041; fax 27 810) in the Hotel Italia. In the airport area, Turi Express (☎ 28 910), in the airport terminal, is one of the better agencies.

Tour companies in Ciudad Bolívar have quite mixed comments among travellers. It's recommended you talk to other travellers who've just returned from a tour, before striking a deal. The restaurant in the Hotel Italia is the main rendezvous for tourists and guides, so it's an excellent place for getting information.

Probably none of the tour operators and airlines listed here will accept payment by credit cards, or will charge about 10% more if you pay with one. While the usual form of payment is cash (US dollars or bolívares), some of the agents may also accept travellers cheques. The prices listed below are for orientation purpose only; they may vary between the companies and largely depend on the number of people in the group, conditions and your bargaining skills.

Tours to Salto Angel Ciudad Bolívar is the main gateway to Salto Angel, and tours to the falls are the staple of most tour operators in the city. The most common tour on offer is a one day trip which includes a return flight to

Canaima, a flight over Salto Angel, lunch in Canaima and a short boat excursion to other nearby falls (usually Salto El Sapo). Tours depart from Ciudad Bolívar around 7 to 8 am and return at 4 to 5 pm, and cost about US$150 to US$170 per person. Some agents may offer Kavac as an alternative to Canaima, in which case the tour will include, apart from the Salto Angel flyover, an excursion to the Cueva de Kavac, and will cost around US$160 to US$180.

A Canaima-Kavac two-day tour which combines all the attractions of the two one-day trips is available from some agencies for about US$220 to US$250. Three-day tours are also offered, particularly in the rainy season when they will include a boat trip to the foot of Salto Angel (but no flight over the falls), for roughly US$220 to US$250. There are also likely to be some longer tours on offer, usually including other regional sights along with Salto Angel. Also, most agents will be able to tailor tours to suit your particular requirements.

The tour companies use the services of small regional airlines, all of which are based at the airport. There are half a dozen of them, including Aero Servicios Caicara (☎ 23 463), Rutaca (☎ 22 195), Ciaca, Transmandú (☎ 21 462) and Aerobol (☎ 28 686), and most have offices at the terminal. The first three seem to be more reliable than the others. Free luggage allowance is 10kg.

The airlines can fly you to Canaima (US$50 either way) and to Kavac (US$60), and can also include a flight over Salto Angel for about US$35 extra. In other words, they can put together a no-frills tour to Salto Angel (without lunch or side trips) for around US$135, which is probably the minimum you have to pay for the pleasure of seeing the falls.

The usual scenario of these tours is as follows. You depart in the morning, heading towards Canaima. If the pilot expects the sky over Salto Angel to be clear, he flies first to the waterfall and then puts you down at Canaima, picking you up later in the afternoon after he has completed his scheduled flights for that day. If the pilot predicts bad weather, he flies you straight to Canaima and tries the falls in the afternoon after he's finished his rounds. See the Salto Angel section for more information. The prices of tours to Salto Angel don't include the US$5 entrance fee to the national park, which is collected by Inparques upon landing at Canaima.

Other Tours All the tour companies offer a range of other tours, of which trips to La Gran Sabana are possibly the most popular among travellers, even though they can be organised more cheaply from Santa Elena de Uairén. They are normally offered by agents as four-day jeep trips, for about US$200 per person, all-inclusive.

Another tour appearing on the menu of various operators is Río Caura, which is normally scheduled as a five day trip, costing US$300 to US$360 per person. A minimum of four people is usually necessary for these tours. Soana Travel (☎ 22 536; fax 22 030), Calle Bolívar, is perhaps the most reliable operator on this route.

Roraima is another destination, but it's an expensive proposition (roughly US$300 to US$400 a person for a six to eight day tour). It's much cheaper to do this trip on your own, contracting a guide in Paraitepui (see the Roraima section).

Special Events
The city's major annual bash is the Feria del Orinoco, held in late August to correspond with the massive appearance of the sapoara in the river. The celebrations include – you've guessed it – a competition in sapoara fishing, a lot of sapoara on local menus, aquatic sports, an agriculture fair, plus a range of cultural and other popular events. The Fiesta de Nuestra Señora de las Nieves, the patron saint of the city, is held on 5 August.

Places to Stay – bottom end
There's a good choice of budget hotels on or just off Paseo Orinoco, which is arguably the most pleasant area to stay within the city. All the hotels listed provide rooms with both private bath and fan (or air-conditioning where indicated).

The *Hotel Caracas* (☎ 26 089), Paseo Orinoco No 82, and *Hotel Italia* (☎ 27 810), Paseo Orinoco No 131, have long been popular travellers' haunts. The Caracas is quite simple but pretty cheap (US$8/9 a matrimonial/double) and has a lovely large terrace overlooking the Paseo, where you can sit with a bottle of beer, watch the world go by and enjoy the evening breeze. The Italia doesn't offer much luxury either and has problems with cleanness and security. It costs US$8/9 a matrimonial/double with fan, US$11/12 with air-conditioning. The hotel has a good budget restaurant which, in contrast to the hotel standards, hasn't run down, gracias a Dios.

The *Hotel Unión* (☎ 23 374), Calle Urica No 11, is clean if styleless, and has rooms with fan and air-conditioning for slightly less than those in the Italia. The Brazilian-run *Hotel Ritz* (☎ 23 886), Calle Libertad No 3, offers air-conditioned doubles with bath for US$12, and doubles with fan but without bath for US$8. If price is more important to you than location, check the *Hotel Roma* (☎ 27 389), Avenida Cumaná No 31, five blocks south of the river, which costs just US$5/8 a matrimonial/double with bath. The rooms are dim but otherwise OK.

Places to Stay – middle & top end
The best place to stay on Paseo Orinoco is the old-style *Hotel Colonial* (☎ 24 402, 28 167; fax 23 080), where quite spacious air-conditioned singles/doubles/triples cost US$18/21/24. Grab a room at the front side, overlooking the river. You can eat in one of the two hotel restaurants.

Most of the middle and top-end hotels are away from the river. Some of them are near the airport, which may be convenient if you plan on catching a morning flight to Canaima. *Hotel Da Gino* (☎ 20 313; fax 25 454) is just a two-minute walk from the airport terminal and charges US$22/25 for an air-conditioned double/triple.

The nearby *Hotel Laja Real* (☎ 27 911; fax 28 778) is about the best hotel in town

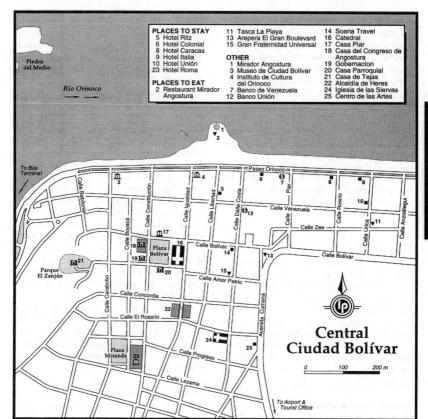

Central Ciudad Bolívar

PLACES TO STAY
5 Hotel Ritz
6 Hotel Colonial
8 Hotel Caracas
9 Hotel Italia
10 Hotel Unión
23 Hotel Roma

PLACES TO EAT
2 Restaurant Mirador Angostura
11 Tasca La Playa
13 Arepera El Gran Boulevard
15 Gran Fraternidad Universal

OTHER
1 Mirador Angostura
3 Museo de Ciudad Bolívar
4 Instituto de Cultura del Orinoco
7 Banco de Venezuela
12 Banco Unión
14 Soana Travel
16 Catedral
17 Casa Piar
18 Casa del Congreso de Angostura
19 Gobernación
20 Casa Parroquial
21 Casa de Tejas
22 Alcaldía de Heres
24 Iglesia de las Siervas
25 Centro de las Artes

GUAYANA

and charges US$35/42/45 for a single/double/triple. There's a cheaper outlet of the same business, the *Laja City Hotel* (☎ 29 910), on Avenida Bolívar, which charges US$22/25/28 a double/triple/quad. Midway between the two, on Avenida Maracay, is the small, quiet and good *Hotel Valentina* (☎ 22 145; fax 27 919), rated at US$20/24/28 a single/double/triple. It has a decent restaurant.

Places to Eat

The best choice of inexpensive local food is at the *Mercado La Carioca* (popularly called La Sapoara), which is a purpose-built and well-organised market, at the eastern end of Paseo Orinoco. It has a row of restaurants lining the riverfront and is a good, clean and pleasant place to eat, from about 6 am until mid-afternoon.

In the central waterfront area, the restaurant of the *Hotel Italia* is the most popular budget place to eat among travellers. Alternatively, try the *Restaurant Mirador Angostura*, which is even cheaper and is popular with locals.

El Gran Boulevard is the best central arepera, where you can get arepas with a score of fillings. The *Gran Fraternidad Universal*, on Calle Amor Patrio, has good, cheap vegetarian meals, at weekday lunch time only. Get there just after noon, as they run out of food quickly. The *Tasca La Playa*, Calle Urica, has good food and atmosphere. The two restaurants in *Hotel Colonial* have some Italian dishes at affordable prices.

Further away from the river, the *Tasca Restaurant Ankares* in the Hotel Valentina is good, and the restaurant in the *Hotel Laja Real* is not bad either.

Should you need some food provisions for an off-the-beaten-track trip (eg Roraima), the *Supermercado El Diamante*, Avenida Germania, is possibly the best stocked place in town.

Things to Buy

Ciudad Bolívar is an important centre of the gold trade. It may be worth checking local jewellers if you plan to buy gold and are not going to El Callao (which is arguably the cheapest place in the country to buy gold – see that section). Many of the gold shops nestle in two passageways off Paseo Orinoco – Pasaje Bolívar and Pasaje Trivigno-Guayana, both of which are near the Hotel Colonial.

Getting There & Away

Air The airport is 2km south-east of the riverfront and is linked to the city centre by frequent busetas. Busetas (marked Ruta 1) going eastbound along Paseo Orinoco will take you there.

Ciudad Bolívar has few links with the country's other major cities (the nearby Ciudad Guayana is a much more important air transport hub). Servivensa has one flight a day to Caracas (US$72) via Maturín (US$41). Servivensa no longer uses Ciudad Bolívar as a stopover for its flights between Caracas and Canaima. Now it flies via Porlamar. However, the city remains the major jumping-off point for Canaima, serviced by light planes of half a dozen small carriers (see Organised Tours above).

Bus The bus terminal is on the junction of Avenida República and Avenida Sucre, about 2km south of the centre. To get there, take the westbound buseta (marked Terminal) from Paseo Orinoco. Busetas heading to further southern suburbs will also drop you at the terminal.

Buses to Caracas run regularly throughout the day, though most depart in the evening for an overnight trip (US$10.50 ordinary, US$13.25 deluxe, nine hours). There are a dozen departures a day to Puerto Ayacucho (US$12.25 ordinary, US$14 deluxe, 10 to 11 hours); the road is now fully sealed (though it still hasn't been marked on some of the local maps). Buses to Puerto La Cruz depart every hour or two (US$5, four hours).

Turgar, Línea Orinoco, Travircán and Expresos Guayana service the route to Santa Elena de Uairén, with a total of nine departures daily (US$11.25 ordinary, US$14 deluxe, 10 to 11 hours). To Ciudad Guayana, buses depart every 15 to 30 minutes (US$1.50, 1½ hours).

Six buses a day depart for Ciudad Piar (US$2, two hours), three of which continue up to La Paragua (US$4.50, four hours). There are also por puestos to both Ciudad Piar (US$3.50, 1½ hours) and La Paragua (US$6, 3½ hours).

Boat Boats go regularly across the Orinoco to the town of Soledad, but there is no regular passenger boat service further up or down the river.

RÍO CAURA

Caura River is a right-bank tributary of the Orinoco, about 200km south-west of Ciudad Bolívar. It's a singularly beautiful and picturesque river, graced with islands, beaches and huge granite boulders. It's cut by rapids and falls, of which Pará Falls are among Venezuela's most spectacular waterfalls. For a good part of its course, Caura flows through the rainforest, which is rich in wildlife. The river banks are inhabited by Indian communities, of which the Yekuana is the major group. They are renowned for particularly fine basketry.

All in all, Caura offers a variety of nature and culture experiences few other rivers can match. Furthermore, Caura is one of Venezuela's least polluted rivers. Gold mining hasn't yet affected the river, though prospectors have been combing the region for a while. Boat trips on Caura can be run year round, unlike excursions on some other rivers, which are only possible during the rainy season. Caura is known as the blackwater river (see boxed text entitled River Coloration), so mosquitoes here are scarce.

Not surprisingly, Caura is swiftly becoming a popular destination, and an increasing number of tour companies include a boat trip on this river in their programme. Doing the trip on your own is not easy or cheap, as you need to hire a boat anyway, which may be almost as expensive as a tour.

Organised Tours

Various travel operators in Caracas (including Cacao Expediciones), Ciudad Bolívar (Soana Travel among others), Ciudad Guayana (Keyla Tours) and other cities offer Caura tours. It's most often a five day package, which costs US$60 to US$90 a day, all-inclusive (accommodation in hammocks). Tour operators in Ciudad Bolívar are likely to be the cheapest.

The usual starting point for tours is Ciudad Bolívar, from where tourists are driven west for 205km along Puerto Ayacucho road, then by a small side road branching off to the south and running for about 50km to Las Trincheras. There are several campamentos in the area, where tours stay the first (and last) night. The next day, boats take tourists 130km upriver (a five to six hour ride) to a sandbank known as El Playón, where another night is spent. The following day a two hour walk uphill takes visitors to the amazing Pará Falls, consisting of five 50m-high falls.

CIUDAD GUAYANA
* *pop 520,000*
* *area code ☎ (086)*

Set on the southern bank of the Orinoco at its confluence with the Río Caroní, Ciudad Guayana is quite an unusual city. It was officially founded in 1961 to serve as an industrial centre for the region, and took into its metropolitan boundaries two quite different urban components – the colonial town of San Félix on the eastern side of the Caroní, and the newborn Puerto Ordaz on the opposite bank.

At the time of its foundation the total population of the area was about 40,000.

GUAYANA

River Coloration

An interesting aspect of rivers is their colour, which can range from light-greyish or yellowish *(ríos blancos*, or white rivers), to dark coffee or even ink *(ríos negros*, or black rivers). The coloration is a complex response to chemical components of the rock and soil of the riverbed and shores, the flora along the banks, the climate, the season, and many other factors. Generally speaking, the dark colour of the water is the result of scarce organic decomposition caused by poor nutriments in the soils (such as in the Amazon rainforest), or the acids generated in the slow process of decay of organic substances which is hindered by the lack of calcium (which is common when igneous rock prevails in a region). Interestingly enough, black rivers are almost free of mosquitoes and other insects, and caymans are virtually unknown there. In contrast, all these creatures abound in white rivers.

As for the Orinoco tributaries, Río Caroní, Río Atabapo and Río Sipapo are examples of dark rivers, while most of the rivers of Los Llanos (eg Río Apure or Río Arauca) have a light coloration. Understandably, the colour of the Orinoco itself largely depends on the colours of its affluents. Broadly speaking, the lower its course, the lighter the colour. Río Negro, as its name suggest, is a black river.

The best place to see the colour difference of any two rivers is, naturally, their confluence. The waters of the tributary don't usually mix with the main river immediately, but gradually, over a longer or shorter distance, down from the confluence, initially forming two parallel flows of different colours. This phenomenon is clearly visible at the confluence of the Caroní and Orinoco rivers. ■

Thirty five years later, the two parts have virtually merged together into a 20km-long urban sprawl populated by more than half a million people. In effect, Ciudad Guayana is Venezuela's fastest growing city, and may be for a while until the population reaches its one million target.

Three bridges have been built across the Caroní River to unify the two sections of the city which apparently still can't come to terms with its Ciudad Guayana name. The inhabitants persistently refer to their hometown as either San Félix or Puerto Ordaz, depending on which part they are talking about. Similarly, businesses label their addresses with either component, without bothering to include the united name. And don't look for Ciudad Guayana in air and bus schedules, because there's no such destination. The airport and bus terminal appear under the name of the sector of the city where they are located.

San Félix was founded in the 16th century but don't let this date confuse you – there's nothing old about the town, apart perhaps from the chessboard layout on which it was planned. The town's centre is today a busy, dirty commercial sector with rather nondescript architecture. It's essentially a workers' suburb, and can be unsafe.

Puerto Ordaz is quite a different story; it's modern, well planned, and has a good infrastructure of roads, supermarkets, and services. The centre is quite clean and pleasant, and it's here that the cream of restaurants and trendy shops are located. It's basically the executive zone, as you can easily tell from the people, their cars and the general atmosphere. Yet there's something eerie about the place; it lacks the feel of older cities that have evolved in a natural way over centuries.

The city was named after Diego de Ordaz, the Spanish explorer who, in 1531-32, first sailed up the Orinoco as far as Raudales de Atures, near what is now Puerto Ayacucho. He was searching for gold, as it was thought that the Orinoco was one of the gateways to the mythical land of El Dorado. However, it wasn't until the mid-19th century that gold

was found in the region around El Callao, and this is today the main area for gold mining. It's estimated that the total gold reserves of Guayana are about 8000 tonnes.

Puerto Ordaz is the seat of the CVG, or Corporación Venezolana de Guayana. This is the regional government body founded in 1960 to run and integrate industrial development of the region with ecological protection and conservation.

Save for three scenic parks, there's not much to see or do in the city. For most travellers, it's a transit point between Caracas/Ciudad Bolívar and Gran Sabana/Brazil, rather than a destination in its own right. On the other hand, like any city of that size, Ciudad Guayana has well-established tourist facilities, so you can eat and sleep well, change money easily, arrange a tour or buy any provisions you need for further travel, and while you're there you can see the parks.

Information

Tourist Offices In Puerto Ordaz, the tourist office is at the airport terminal. In San Félix, the office is on the riverfront, on the corner of Calle 1 and Carrera 1. Both offices are open Monday to Friday from 8 am to noon and 2 to 5.30 pm.

Money Most of the potentially useful central banks are marked on the Puerto Ordaz and San Félix maps.

Brazilian Consulate The consulate (☎ 23 52 43) is in Edificio Amazonas, Avenida Las Américas. The only other consulate on the way to Brazil is in Santa Elena de Uairén, on the border.

Parque Cachamay

This pleasant riverside park is just 1km south of Puerto Ordaz's centre. The showpiece here is the view of Caroní River which turns into a series of rapids and eventually into a spectacular 200m-wide line of waterfalls. The park is open Tuesday to Sunday from 5.30 am to 5.30 pm and there's a small admission fee.

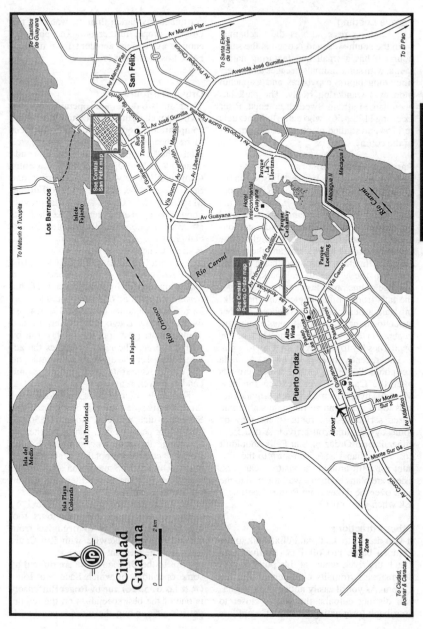

GUAYANA

Ciudad Guayana

To Castillos de Guayana

To El Pao

To Maturín & Tucupita

Los Barrancos

Islote Fajardo

Río Orinoco

Isla Fajardo

Isla Providencia

Isla del Medio

Isla Playa Colorada

0   1   2 km

To Ciudad, Bolívar & Caracas

Matanzas Industrial Zone

Av Manuel Piar

San Félix

To Santa Elena de Uairén

Av Principal Chirca

Av Manuel Piar

Avenida José Gumilla

See Central San Félix map

Av Antonio de Berrío

Bus Terminal

Av José Gumilla

Av Leopoldo Sucre Figarella

Av N Guayana

Av Centurión

Av Mendoza

Via Sucre

Av Libertador

Av Guayana

Parque La Llovizna

Hotel Intercontinental Guayana

Parque Cachamay

Av Guayana

Parque Loefling

Macagua

Macagua II

Río Caroní

Río Caroní

Av Principal de Castillito

See Central Puerto Ordaz map

Av Las Américas

Alta Vista

Las Américas

Paseo Caroní

Paseo Caroní

CVG

Vía Caroní

Puerto Ordaz

Av Guayana

Bus Terminal

Airport

Av Monte Sur 2

Av Atlántico

Av Monte Sur 04

C Caroní

Parque Loefling

The Loefling park adjoins the Cachamay from the south-west and is open at the same hours. It has a small zoo featuring native fauna, with some animals in cages and others (including tapirs, capybaras and Capuchin monkeys) wandering freely. The park has been named after a Swedish botanist, Peter Loefling (1729-56), who came to Venezuela in 1754 and studied plants in the eastern part of the colony.

Parque La Llovizna

La Llovizna Park has been established on the group of islands on the Caroní River, about 5km upstream from where it spills into the Orinoco. The 30-odd islands are separated by narrow water channels and interconnected by footbridges. The highlight is the 20m-high Salto La Llovizna, and the drizzle (literally llovizna) it produces has given the name to the waterfall and park. Several vantage points provide dramatic views over the falls from various angles, and the walking trails around the park give access to other attractions, including small lakes, exuberant vegetation and even a beach. The park is open Tuesday to Sunday from 9 am to 3 pm.

The recently opened freeway, Avenida Leopoldo Sucre Figarella, which crosses over the Caroní River next to the new Macagua hydroelectric scheme, provides access to the park, but so far there's no urban buses servicing this route (there may be some by the time you arrive). A taxi from either Puerto Ordaz or San Félix shouldn't cost more than US$6. To return to the city, hunt for a lift around the visitors' car park. There are plans to open a walking trail to the park over the dykes from Parque Loefling – ask when you come.

Other Attractions

If you decide to visit San Félix, walk to the Orinoco bank, just off Plaza Bolívar, and watch the river, which at this point is 7km downstream from its confluence with the Caroní. As you'll easily notice, the river has two distinct colours; the waters closer to your bank (originating from the Caroní) are conspicuously darker than the waters of the Orinoco proper further out. The phenomenon is even more apparent from the San Félix-Los Barrancos ferry.

Organised Tours

There are two dozen tour operators in town – virtually all of them in Puerto Ordaz – and competition is fierce, but don't expect prices to be cheaper than elsewhere. Some well established companies, such as Anaconda Tours (☎ 22 31 30; fax 22 65 72), Centro Comercial Anto, Avenida Las Américas, and Selva Tours (☎ & fax 62 24 80), Edificio Monterrey, Calle Caura, Alta Vista, provide good service but are expensive. Keyla Tours (☎ 23 18 67; fax 23 12 01), Centro Comercial Guayana, Avenida Monseñor Zabaleta, is slightly cheaper.

Aventura Gran Sabana (☎ 62 65 82, 014 986 82 63), run by Marcos Alberto Pérez, was recommended by some travellers. Other newer and smaller operators include Ivarkarima Expediciones (☎ 22 26 19, 014 986 49 13), run by Diego Rizzo Guerrero, and Waika Safari (☎ & fax 22 77 73), run by Alfredo Jorge. The latter organises the adventurous La Paragua-to-Canaima and Karuai-to-Kamarata overland trips and handles bicycle rental.

The staple offer of most operators is the three to five day tour around the Gran Sabana, which will cost around US$90 to US$90 per person a day. It may be cheaper to arrange this tour with some of Ciudad Bolívar's companies, but the cheapest option is to go by bus to Santa Elena and buy the tour there (see the Santa Elena de Uairén section for details).

Another standard package offered by agents is Salto Angel, and these tours, too, are probably cheaper to organise from Ciudad Bolívar. Likewise with Río Caura tours (see the relevant section).

Trips to the Orinoco Delta are offered by some operators, of which Sacoroco Tours (☎ & fax 61 55 26), run by Roger Ruffenach, is one of the best specialists on the region, yet it's also among the most expensive. If

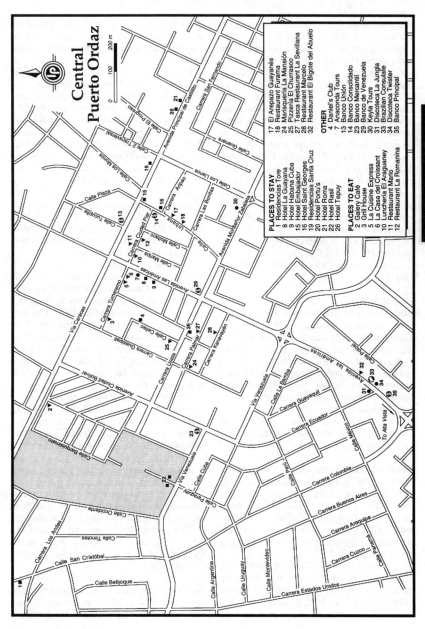

Central Puerto Ordaz

0   100   200 m

GUAYANA

PLACES TO STAY
1 Residencias Tore
8 Restaurant Furama
9 Hotel La Guayana
15 Hotel Embajador
16 Hotel Saint Georges
19 Residencias Santa Cruz
20 Hotel Portu's
21 Hotel Roma
22 Hotel Rasil
26 Hotel Tepuy

PLACES TO EAT
2 Galeri Café
3 Grill House
5 La Cuisine Express
6 La Casa del Croissant
10 Lunchería El Araguaney
11 Restaurant Mario
12 Restaurant La Romanina

17 El Arepazo Guayanés
18 Restaurant Furama
24 Marisquería La Mansión
25 Pizzería El Churrasco
27 Tasca Restaurant La Sevillana
28 Restaurant Marcelo
32 Restaurant El Bigote del Abuelo

OTHER
4 Daniel's Club
7 Anaconda Tours
13 Banco Unión
14 Banco Consolidado
23 Banco Mercantil
29 Banco de Venezuela
30 Keyla Tours
31 Discoteca La Jungla
33 Brazilian Consulate
34 Discoteca Twister
35 Banco Principal

you want to do this trip more cheaply, go to Tucupita and shop around there.

Among the shorter regional tours, some companies offer half-day trips to the Castillos de Guayana, and day trips to Represa de Guri and Cerro Bolívar (all these places are detailed in separate sections later in this chapter). Waika Safari is refurbishing the rustic Campamento El Mono, near the spectacular 70m Salto El Mono, in the wild forested mountains three hours by jeep south-east of Ciudad Guayana. It offers two-day jeep tours (US$90 a person) and plans to run budget bicycle trips to the camp.

CVG organises tours to its industrial establishments in the city, including the steel mill and aluminium plant. It will also have updated information about visiting Represa de Guri and Cerro Bolívar. The CVG headquarters (☎ 22 61 55) are in Edificio CVG, Calle Cuchiveros, Alta Vista Norte, Puerto Ordaz.

Places to Stay

Both Puerto Ordaz and San Félix have a range of hotels. As might be expected, the accommodation in San Félix is poorer but, paradoxically, no cheaper than in Puerto Ordaz. It's advisable to stay in Puerto Ordaz, not only for the better value, but also for the convenience, nicer surroundings and security. All hotels listed below have private bath (unless indicated otherwise) and either fan or air-conditioning. Only the top-end hotels have hot water, but it's hardly necessary in this steamy climate.

Puerto Ordaz The main budget hotel area is in the centre, around Avenida Principal de Castillito. One of the cheapest establishments here is *Hotel Portu's*, which costs US$5 a matrimonial with fan but without bath, US$6/8 a matrimonial with bath and fan/air-conditioning. The hotel has a budget restaurant attached.

The *Hotel Roma* (☎ 22 37 80), next door, is basic but acceptable and costs much the same as the Portu's. At first sight, you might think the hotel has been demolished, but it hasn't. Look out for the steps and go

downstairs (watch your head). There are more cheapies in the same area, including the very basic and unpleasant *Residencias Santa Cruz*.

It's more pleasant to stay farther to the west and south of Avenida Principal de Castillito. The cheapest places in this area include the *Hotel Saint Georges* (☎ 22 00 79), *Hotel Habana Cuba* (☎ 22 49 04) and *Hotel La Guayana* (☎ 22 73 75); none of them should cost more than about US$15/17 for an air-conditioned double/triple. La Guayana is perhaps the best of the lot and has a reasonable restaurant.

A few blocks to the south, on Carrera Upata, is the more decent *Hotel Tepuy* (☎ 22 01 11, 22 01 20; fax 23 32 20), which costs US$20/24/36 an air-conditioned single/double/triple, and is possibly the cheapest place in town that has hot water.

The *Hotel Embajador* (☎ 22 55 11, 22 57 65; fax 22 61 23), on the corner of Avenida Principal de Castillito and Calle Urbana, is a good central place to stay, for US$32/36 a single/double room and US$48/52 a double/triple suite. One of the best in the city centre is the huge *Hotel Rasil* (☎ 22 02 30, 23 33 48; fax 22 77 03), at US$40/45/50 for a single/double/triple. Its older section, in a smaller building on the other side of Calle Paraguay, is cheaper.

Not far from the Rasil is the *Residencias Tore* (☎ 23 17 80, 23 13 89; fax 23 17 43), Calle San Cristóbal at Carrera Los Andes, a posada-like place, quite different in style and atmosphere to the regular hotels. Set in a quiet and leafy back street (yet a manageable walking distance from the centre), it's a small and enjoyable family-run guesthouse. Simple but comfortable air-conditioned doubles are US$26, and guests can have meals in the hotel's own open-air restaurant.

The *Hotel Intercontinental Guayana* (☎ 22 22 80, 23 00 11; fax 23 19 14), on the bank of the Caroní River, is the best hotel in Puerto Ordaz.

San Félix There are about a dozen hotels in the town centre, all of which are budget establishments. Most are basic and double as

A	
B	C
	D

A: Hacha Falls, Canaima   C: Salto Yuruaní
B: Salto Angel   D: Quebrada de Jaspe

Landscapes of Roraima and its peculiar plants

sex hotels. The few more tolerable places include the *Hotel Yoli* (☎ 43 341), on Carrera 3; the *Hotel Aguila* (☎ 44 291), on Calle 4; and the *Hotel Excelsior* (☎ 41 375), on Calle 3. Any of them will cost about US$15/18 a double/triple, and none is anything special.

The *Hotel Miranda*, on Plaza Miranda, may be a bit better than that lot, if and when it's open, si Dios quiere.

Places to Eat

There are lots of restaurants in both San Félix and Puerto Ordaz and you can eat quite well. Most of the upmarket establishments are in Puerto Ordaz, which is a much more pleasant area for dining, while San Félix abounds in rather ordinary eateries. On Sunday, many restaurants close, especially in Puerto Ordaz.

In Puerto Ordaz, the bottom end of the gastronomic scene is represented by street stalls along Avenida Principal de Castillito and Calle Los Llanos, around the budget hotels area. There are several chicken outlets there, where half a chicken with yucca and salad can be bought for less than US$3 and makes a filling meal. *El Arepazo Guayanés*, on Calle Urbana, serves arepas filled with everything from cheese to seafood, for US$1.25 each. Some other inexpensive places in the area include the *Restaurant La Guayana* in the hotel of the same name, *Lunchería El Araguaney*, *Restaurant Mario*, *Grill House*, *Pizzería El Churrasco* and *Restaurant Marcelo*.

For more upmarket places, try the *Restaurant La Romanina* (Italian food and steaks), the *Marisquería La Mansión* (fish and seafood) and the *Restaurant Furama* (Chinese cuisine). The *Tasca Restaurant La Sevillana* is a pleasant chic place open till late, and it's not too expensive.

The *Galery Café* is a beautiful new arty café, which has quickly become a trendy place. It has live music most of the days, lovely salads, sandwiches and fondue, and is open till late.

La Cuisine Express and *La Casa del Croissant*, next door to each other on Carrera Tumeremo, are two enjoyable cafés.

Entertainment

For night-time dancing, try *La Jungla* or *Twister*, two popular discos opposite each other on Avenida las Américas. Or, try the *Pool Discoteque*, in the Centro Comercial Caura in Alta Vista, which has pool tables, cheap beer and usually a good atmosphere. If playing pool and drinking are all you're after, check the cheap *J & J Pool*, Carrera Necuima next to Pizza Hut in Alta Vista, or the more upmarket *Daniel's Club* on Calle Callao.

Getting There & Away

Air The airport is at the western end of Puerto Ordaz, on the road to Ciudad Bolívar. Buses (marked Sidor Directo) from Alta Vista will leave you at the terminal's entrance. Note that the airport appears in all schedules as Puerto Ordaz, not Ciudad Guayana.

Puerto Ordaz is the busiest air hub in eastern Venezuela. Avensa/Servivensa has direct flights to Caracas (US$68), Porlamar (US$55), Barcelona (US$45) and Maturín (US$41) and has connections to other destinations. Several other airlines, including Aserca, Aeropostal and Rutaca, service Ciudad Guayana and may be cheaper.

Servivensa has daily flights on DC-3s to Canaima (US$71) and on to Santa Elena de Uairén (another US$71, but if you don't stop in Canaima it's US$71 for the whole Puerto Ordaz-Santa Elena route). The planes fly at low altitudes, thus providing some spectacular views over the Gran Sabana and its tepuis.

Bus Ciudad Guayana has two bus terminals. The main one is in San Félix, on Avenida Gumilla, about 1.5km south of the town centre. The environs of the terminal can be unsafe, particularly after dark, so don't walk there; get there by carrito or taxi, which will drop you off at the entrance. Plenty of carritos pass the bus terminal on their way between Puerto Ordaz and San Félix.

The other terminal is in Puerto Ordaz, on Avenida Guayana, about 1km east of the airport. It's smaller, cleaner, quieter and safer, and handles far fewer buses than that

GUAYANA

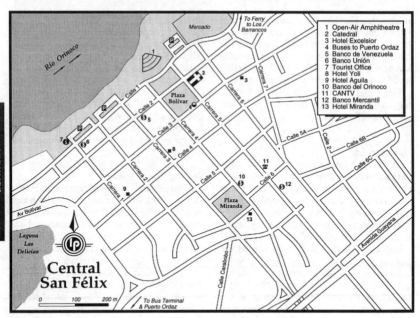

Río Orinoco

Mercado

To Ferry
to Los
Barrancos

1   Open-Air Amphitheatre
2   Catedral
3   Hotel Excelsior
4   Buses to Puerto Ordaz
5   Banco de Venezuela
6   Banco Unión
7   Tourist Office
8   Hotel Yoli
9   Hotel Aguila
10 Banco del Orinoco
11 CANTV
12 Banco Mercantil
13 Hotel Miranda

Plaza
Bolívar

Calle 1
Calle 2
Calle 3
Carrera 7
Carrera 6
Carrera 5
Carrera 4
Carrera 3
Carrera 2
Carrera 1
Calle 4
Calle 5
Calle 5A
Calle 2
Calle 6
Calle 6B
Calle 6C

Plaza
Miranda

Av Bolívar

Laguna
Las
Delicias

Calle Carabobo

Avenida Guayana

**Central
San Félix**

0   100   200 m

To Bus Terminal
& Puerto Ordaz

in San Félix. It's essentially a transit point rather than a destination, but not all the buses pass through here.

There are regular departures from San Félix's terminal to Caracas (US$12 ordinary, US$15 deluxe, 10½ hours), and most of these buses call en route at Puerto Ordaz's terminal. Buses to Ciudad Bolívar depart from both terminals every half hour or so (US$1.50, 1½ hours).

Nine buses daily arrive from Ciudad Bolívar on their way to Santa Elena (US$9.75 ordinary, US$12 deluxe, nine to 10 hours); they all call at San Félix, but only a few in Puerto Ordaz.

Expresos Maturín has buses from San Félix to Maturín every hour or two (US$3, 3½ hours) and also a few buses a day travelling further north to the coast, to Carúpano (US$6, 6½ hours) and Güiria (US$8, nine hours). Expresos La Guayanesa has two buses a day from San Félix to Tucupita (US$3, 3½ hours), but por puestos go there

regularly (US$6, two hours). All these trips involve a ferry ride across the Orinoco from San Félix to Los Barrancos.

Most buses going to Ciudad Guayana are labelled San Félix, since it's here that they terminate. You'll rarely find Puerto Ordaz or Ciudad Guayana in bus schedules throughout the country.

CASTILLOS DE GUAYANA

About 38km east of San Félix, two old forts sit on the hilly right bank of the Orinoco, overlooking the river. They were built to protect Santo Tomás, the first Spanish settlement founded on the riverbank in 1595.

The older fort, the **Castillo de San Francisco** (named after the monastery of San Francisco de Asís which stood on the site before the fort was built) dates from the 1670s. As pirate raids continued unabated, a second fort, the **Castillo de San Diego de Alcalá**, went up in 1747 on a nearby higher hill. However, this didn't provide adequate protection either. The settlement was eventually moved upriver in 1762, and refounded two years later as Santo Tomás de la Guayana de Angostura (present-day Ciudad Bolívar), while the forts were abandoned. At the end of the 19th century, the forts were remodelled and used to control river traffic, which they did until 1943. In the 1970s, they were restored to their original condition and became tourist attractions. The higher fort commands fine views over the Orinoco and beyond.

Getting There & Away

The forts are accessible by road from San Félix. Por puestos take you there from the place known as El Mirador, at the eastern end of San Félix, which can be reached by city buses. The ride to the forts costs US$1.25 and takes 1¼ hours.

Alternatively, take a tour. Several travel agencies (Anaconda Tours, among others) operate half-day tours to the Castillos, for around US$25 per person.

REPRESA DE GURI

Due south of Ciudad Guayana is a large lake, Embalse de Guri. This is the reservoir of the second largest hydroelectric project in the world (the recently completed Itaipú on the frontier of Brazil and Paraguay is the largest).

The Represa Raúl Leoni – as it is officially named, though commonly referred to as Represa de Guri (Guri Dam) – was built in the lower course of the Río Caroní, about 100km upstream from its inlet into the Orinoco. The work was carried out in stages, from 1963 to 1986. Eight million cubic metres of concrete were used to build a gigantic 1304m-long dam, which is 162m high at its highest point. Covering an area of about 4250 sq km, the reservoir created by the dam is Venezuela's largest lake after Lago Maracaibo. It now abounds in fish, mainly *pavón* (peacock bass) and its equally ferocious cousin, the *payara*. The lake has grown in popularity as a good sport-fishing destination.

With a potential of 10 million kilowatts,

the complex satisfies over half of the country's electricity demand. The Guri Dam provides power not only for the giant industrial plants of the region, but also supplies electricity to central Venezuela, Caracas included. The dam and some of the installations can be visited.

Organised Tours

The EDELCA (Electrificación del Caroní), the state company which operates the dam, runs free tours, daily at 9 and 10.30 am and 2 and 3.30 pm. From the visitors' centre, you are taken by bus for a one-hour trip around the complex. Although you don't see much of the installations, you get to realise how enormous the project is.

The tour includes a stopover at a lookout, from where you get a good general view of the dam and of a large kinetic sculpture by Alejandro Otero. You are then shown one of the units of the powerhouse, embellished with a geometrical decoration by Carlos Cruz Díez. Finally you go to the Plaza del Sol y la Luna, noted for a huge dial showing months, hours and minutes.

Places to Stay & Eat

There's the *Hotel Guri* in the Guri compound, which has its own restaurant and a pool. The hotel was closed down at the time of writing, but may reopen by the time you arrive. Before the closure a double room was around US$30.

Getting There & Away

This is a bit complicated, as there's no public transport to the dam. The entrance to the complex is at the north-western end of the Embalse de Guri, about 80km by road from Puerto Ordaz. You first go along the Ciudad Guayana-Ciudad Piar highway, then along the Guri side road which branches off and goes to the alcabala at the entrance to the Guri complex. No public buses go along this road, so a taxi or hitching are the options.

EDELCA vehicles run regularly from Puerto Ordaz to the dam, so it may be worth checking its office. Otherwise, take the bus going along the old road (not the autopista) between Ciudad Guayana and Ciudad Bolívar and get off at the place called Km 70. From here, hitch the remaining bit. At the alcabala, you will be given a permit; the visitors' centre is 5km further inside the compound, so again you have to rely on someone's vehicle.

Tours to Guri Dam (usually combined with a visit to Cerro Bolívar) are available from a few travel agents in Ciudad Guayana. Expect to pay US$60 to US$80 for this tour.

CERRO BOLÍVAR

Jutting 600m out of the surrounding plains, some 100km south of Ciudad Bolívar, Cerro Bolívar is a huge, oval, iron-ore mountain, 11km long and 3km wide. The mountain has intrigued explorers since the early days of the Spanish conquest. Around the mid-18th century, Capuchin missionaries set up the first forges here, but it actually was not until 1947 that US geologists confirmed the unusually high grade of the ore (up to 60% pure iron in some parts), which led the way for large-scale exploitation. Since then, the ore has been systematically stripped from the mountain by men and machines, and now the Cerro is terraced all around. The ore is then loaded onto rail cars and transported to the steel mill at Ciudad Guayana.

About 10km east of the Cerro is Ciudad Piar, a town founded in the 1950s to provide the operational and administrative centre for the mining company (Ferrominera) and accommodation for the workers. Today, it's a town of 22,000 inhabitants. The Ferrominera administration building is at the western end of the town, at the entrance to the mine's restricted area. This is where you get a permit to visit the mine.

Getting There & Away

Ciudad Piar is accessible by bus from Ciudad Bolívar (US$2, two hours); there are no buses from Ciudad Guayana.

If you fly from Ciudad Bolívar to Canaima, you'll get a bird's-eye view of the Cerro, as planes normally pass over it.

EL CALLAO
- *pop 11,000*
- *area code ☎ (088)*

El Callao is an old gold town set on the Yuruarí River, about 180km south-east of Ciudad Guayana, in what has been Venezuela's richest gold region. This enormous basin spreads from El Callao southwards for 200km right up to the edge of the Gran Sabana, and is dotted with hundreds of gold mines.

The gold rush hit the region in 1849, when prospectors found exceptionally rich lodes in the Río Yuruarí. Fortune seekers from all corners of Venezuela, as well as Trinidad, British Guiana and beyond were quick to rush in and take part in what was one of the world's greatest gold rushes in modern history. El Callao was the early product of that rush, and developed dramatically.

Today, El Callao is a quiet and tidy town, the gold-shopping mecca of the region. It boasts a spectacular number of gold jewellers – possibly as many as 20 on Plaza Bolívar alone – and many more down side streets. The jewellery is not renowned for any particular artistic quality, but it's arguably the cheapest in the country.

The jewellery is produced locally in numerous small workshops, using rudimentary manual techniques. Some of them can be visited; just walk around the central streets and look for signs saying Taller de Oro.

The town's other distinctive feature is its Trinidad-influenced Carnaval, accompanied with calypso, steel bands and floats – a palpable mark of the substantial Antillan migration during the gold rush.

There are several gold mines around the town, of which the Mina Colombia, operated by the Minerven state company, is the largest. It's the deepest gold mine in Venezuela, with galleries spread over seven levels, from 157 to 479m below the ground surface. It produces 4.5 tons of gold per year, with plans for 6.5 tons by 2001. The mine is 3km from El Callao, and is serviced by por puestos, but it can't be visited. Check when you arrive as this may change.

Places to Stay

There are several budget hotels within a few blocks north-west of Plaza Bolívar, including *Hotel Italia* (☎ 61 147), *Hotel Ritz*, *Residencia Guarauno* (☎ 61 401) and *Residencias Piar*. There's also *Hotel El Callao* (☎ 61 915) one block north of Plaza Bolívar, next to the bus terminus. None of these hotels should cost more than US$8 per matrimonial. The *Hotel Venecia*, one block south of Plaza Bolívar, is a bit better, and the *Hotel Isidora* (☎ 61 290), further south, is perhaps the best place in town.

Getting There & Away

El Callao has a regular bus service to/from San Félix (US$3.50, three hours). The town sits a couple of km off the main highway and long-distance buses bypass it. If you plan on going to La Gran Sabana, walk to the highway and wave down the Santa Elena bus.

EL DORADO

- *pop 4000*
- *area code ☎ (088)*

Appropriately named El Dorado (The Golden One), this is another gold town, on the Cuyuní River, 108km south of El Callao. It grew fat on the 19th-century gold rush, and there are still a number of mines operating in the area. In the 1950s, a maximum-security prison was built across the river from the town and it's still in use today. The famous French convict Papillon stayed here for a while. The jail can no longer be visited after a couple of tourists, under military guidance, were taken hostage by prisoners in 1992.

Unlike the orderly and tranquil El Callao, El Dorado looks wild and chaotic, and has much of the gold-rush atmosphere. It seems a tough town, with filthy streets and a busy triangular square, around which much of the town's life concentrates.

There are a number of rudimentary gold mines in the El Dorado area and it's possible to visit some. Jeeps and pick-up trucks park on the square and go to the mines on demand, usually with miners early in the morning. Talk to the drivers, some of whom will be eager to take you for a trip around the mines.

A day trip will cost anywhere between US$40 and US$100 per jeep.

Places to Stay

There are three budget hotels on the triangular square: *Hotel Edgar*, *Hotel El Dorado* and the worst, *Hotel San Antonio*. All have rooms with private baths and fans, and cost US$8/10 a single/double. There are some more basic hotels on the street going from the square to the river.

Getting There & Away

El Dorado is 6km off the Ciudad Guayana-Santa Elena highway. The turnoff (marked km 0) is a point of reference from which road distances are measured and signed every kilometre all the way south to the Brazilian border.

Santa Elena buses don't normally call at El Dorado, but buses to Ciudad Guayana run every two to three hours from the triangular square (US$5, five hours). There are also por puestos to Tumeremo, from where there are more buses to Ciudad Guayana.

Salto Angel & Around

Commonly known to the English-speaking world as Angel Falls, this is the world's highest waterfall. Its total height is 979m, recorded by a National Geographic Society expedition in 1949. It also has the world's greatest uninterrupted drop – 807m, which is 16 times the height of Niagara Falls. The waterfall has clearly become Venezuela's No 1 promotional landmark, and you will find photos of it in just about every tourist brochure.

Salto Angel spills from the heart-shaped Auyantepui (meaning Mountain of the God of Evil in the Pemón language), one of the largest of the tepuis, with a flat top of about 700 sq km. The waterfall is in the central part of the tepui and drops into what is known as Cañón del Diablo (Devil's Canyon).

The waterfall is not named, as one might expect, after a divine creature, but after an

GUAYANA

American bush pilot, Jimmie Angel (1899-1956), who landed on the boggy top of Auyantepui in 1937 in a four-seater airplane, in search of gold. The plane stuck in the marshy surface and Angel couldn't take off again. He, his wife and two companions trekked through rough virgin terrain to the edge of the plateau, then descended over a km of almost vertical cliff, to return to civilisation after an 11 day odyssey.

Orientation
Salto Angel is in a distant wilderness, without any road access. The village of Canaima, about 50km north-west of Salto Angel, is the major gateway to the falls. Canaima doesn't have any overland link to the rest of the country either (except for a couple of adventurous, seasonal trails), but it does have an airport. The small Indian settlement of Kavac, at the south-eastern foot of Auyantepui, is becoming another jumping-off point for the falls, mostly for organised tours. It's also isolated, but it has its own airstrip.

A visit to Salto Angel is usually undertaken in two stages, with Canaima (or Kavac) as the stepping-stone. Most tourists fly into Canaima, from where they take a light plane or boat to the falls. No walking trails go all the way from Canaima (or Kavac) to the falls.

There are a number of other attractions in the Canaima area, mostly waterfalls, of which the most popular is Salto El Sapo. In Kavac's area the most frequently visited sight is the Cueva de Kavac.

Salto Angel, Auyantepui, Canaima and the surrounding area lie within the boundaries of the Parque Nacional Canaima, Venezuela's second largest national park, covering 30,000 sq km. The park stretches east and south almost up to the national border and encompasses most of La Gran Sabana (detailed later in this chapter). All visitors coming to Canaima pay the US$5 national park entrance fee, which is collected upon arrival at the airport (if you haven't paid it when buying your flight ticket).

Planning
When to Go The dry season in the region normally lasts from January to May; rains tend to begin in late May or early June and continue until November. They gradually ease in December and stop by January. Recent climatic anomalies throughout the world were also felt in the Salto Angel region; in both 1996 and 1997 the rainy season continued well into February.

Understandably, the season determines the volume of Salto Angel (and other waterfalls). At times in the dry season, it can be pretty faint – just a thin ribbon of water fading into mist halfway down its drop. In the rainy months, on the other hand, it's often voluminous and spectacular.

The waterfall is at its most impressive after heavy rains, which occur frequently in August and September. Unfortunately, this is precisely the period when it is hardest to see, as it's often covered by clouds. In general, the best time of the day as far as the waterfall's visibility is concerned is between 10 am and 1 pm. Morning hours are the best for taking photos of the waterfall, as it faces east and is in direct sunlight until around noon.

The rainy season is certainly a better time to come to admire Salto Angel and other waterfalls, though, of course, it's more risky. One of the other advantages of coming in the wet period is that you can take a boat tour to Salto Angel, which is only organised when the water level of local rivers is sufficiently high (roughly from June to December or January).

What Kind of Trip Numerous tour operators in virtually every corner of the country offer trips to Salto Angel – this is after all one of Venezuela's major tourist attractions – so there's no problem whatsoever getting there. If there's any problem it may be money, as none of these trips is cheap; you need at least about US$140 for a glimpse of the falls.

The cheapest way to get to Salto Angel is to take a no-frills day trip with one of the small airlines from Ciudad Bolívar (see Organised Tours in the Ciudad Bolívar section).

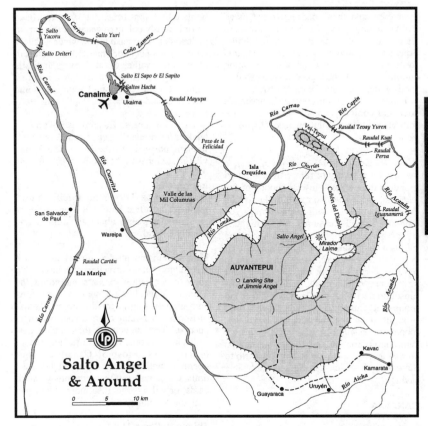

Salto Angel
& Around

0   5   10 km

GUAYANA

However, you may end up not seeing the waterfall, especially in the rainy season. The airlines offering these trips are essentially commercial passenger carriers which fly people (mainly miners and their families) between the scattered towns and villages of the region, on a more or less regular schedule. Flying around Salto Angel is for them only a part of their activity, and not necessarily the major one. The pilots will fly you there, but according to their schedule, ie on the way to Canaima or another regional destination in the morning or on the way back to Ciudad Bolívar in the afternoon. If

the waterfall happens to be visible you are lucky; if not, you've paid for nothing.

The second cheapest option (about US$150 to US$170) is a day tour organised by Ciudad Bolívar's tour operators, which add some other local attractions to Salto Angel plus a lunch. The tour companies use the same local airlines but charter the whole flight, so they are less dependent on the carriers' schedules.

Some travellers prefer to fly to Canaima on their own and arrange the flight over Salto Angel (or the boat trip to the falls, or both) from there with local operators. This can be more expensive than a package from Ciudad Bolívar and will involve shopping around in Canaima, yet it gives you more flexibility, especially if you plan on staying in Canaima for a while. To keep costs down, camping equipment would be a good idea, as well as food brought in from Ciudad Bolívar.

If money is not a problem, Hoturvensa's packages come in handy – they are a comfortable and easy solution (see Organised Tours below).

What to Bring Bring waterproof gear, a swimsuit and plenty of film. Efficient insect repellent is essential – insects abound on the savanna, though not so much in the jungle. A long-sleeved shirt will further protect you from insects and occasional chills at night. A hat or other head protection from sun and rain is a wise idea. A torch can be useful. If you plan on boat excursions, make sure to have a plastic sheet or bag to protect your gear. A tent or hammock (preferably with a mosquito net) will save you having to spend money at Canaima's hotels, while food brought from the outside will save you money on restaurants. Also, with your own camping equipment and food, you may be able to arrange a transport-only boat trip to Salto Angel, which can be a considerable saving.

CANAIMA
- *pop 1200*
- *area code* ☎ (086)

Canaima is a mixed tourist-Indian village which serves as a springboard for Salto Angel. It appeared on the tourist map in the 1960s, after a large holiday camp named the Campamento Canaima, and an airport capable of receiving commercial jets, were built here. Today, it's a blend of an Indian settlement of some 150 Pemón families and a rapidly developing tourist resort.

Without a doubt, Canaima's location is spectacular. It sits on a peaceful, wide stretch of the Río Carrao, known as Laguna de Canaima, just below the point where the river turns into a line of magnificent falls, Saltos Hacha. The rose-coloured lagoon is

bordered by a pink beach. The falls, too, have conspicuously coloured water, ranging from yellowish to brownish tones, which vaguely remind you of beer or brandy. The colouring of these (as well as of other rivers and falls in the region) is caused by the *tanino*, or tannin, a solid compound found in some local trees and plants, especially in the Bonnetia tree.

The Campamento Canaima is right on the bank of the romantic lagoon. The airport is a five minute walk to the west. The Indian village stretches to the south of the camp.

Information
Tourist Office There's no specific tourist information office here, but tour operators are knowledgeable about the region and usually helpful.

Money Campamento Canaima changes cash US dollars (but not travellers cheques), as do some other establishments including the Tienda Quincallería Canaima (souvenir-cum-grocery shop) near the airport. Tomás of Bernal Tours may change your travellers cheques. The rate is lower than in the cities, so it's best to come with a sufficient amount of bolívares. Most of Canaima's tour operators will accept payment in US cash dollars, but will refuse payment by credit cards, or will charge 10% more if you pay with plastic money.

Things to See & Do
Most regional attractions are inaccessible on your own, so you'll have to use the services of tour operators (see below). What you can do are short walks in the environs of Canaima, such as a hike to the top of the hill just east of the village. It's a steep 20 minute ascent (ask for directions), rewarded with great views. You can also stroll around the dusty streets of the village. There's an interesting thatched Pemón church at the southern end of Canaima.

Like most visitors, you'll probably spend some time in the Campamento Canaima, enjoying the beach and views of the falls. The lagoon looks wonderfully calm, but there are treacherous undercurrents caused by the waterfalls. Some people have drowned trying to swim from the camp to the island opposite. Be careful and find out where it's safe to swim before you go into deep water. Also, the beach may have some chigoes *(niguas)*, small sand fleas which tend to burrow into skin.

Organised Tours

Canaima is a hive of tour-business activity, with half a dozen tour operators and their planes, boats and jeeps. They offer tours to Salto Angel, other nearby falls, Indian villages and whatever other interesting sights they have discovered in the area.

Tour Operators Hoturvensa (Hoteles y Turismo Avensa), a travel offspring of Avensa/Servivensa airlines, runs Campamento Canaima. The agency offers packages which include accommodation and full board in its camp, Servivensa's flight over Salto Angel (weather permitting), a short boat trip on the Laguna de Canaima and a complimentary drink on arrival. Two kinds of packages are available: a two day/one night stay for US$374, and a three day/two night stay for US$724 (single or double occupancy).

The packages don't include the flight into and out of Canaima, so keep US$150 in reserve. Also keep in mind that if you don't see the falls because of bad weather, Hoturvensa won't give you any money back; it's just your bad luck. The packages can be bought from any Avensa office in Venezuela and from most travel agencies. This is the most expensive form of visiting Canaima and Salto Angel. Hoturvensa doesn't offer any tours other than these two packages.

There are several other tour operators in Canaima, including Canaima Tours, Tiuna Tours, Kamaracoto Tours and Bernal Tours. Canaima Tours (☎ 62 55 60, 61 69 81; fax 62 05 59) is the agent of Hoturvensa and has its office in Campamento Canaima. The remaining companies are cheaper and their advertised prices can be negotiated to some extent. They all wait for incoming flights at

the airport, and this is the right place and the time to shop around for a tour.

The reliable Tiuna Tours offers a wide choice, all of which are conducted by bilingual guides. The company runs tours for packaged groups flown in by Aereotuy, as well as servicing individual travellers who arrive at Canaima independently. Kamaracoto Tours has roughly similar tours and comparable prices, and it provides local services for some of Ciudad Bolívar's tour companies.

Bernal Tours, run by Tomás Bernal, offers slightly different tours, which most travellers consider good value. Tomás lives on the island on Laguna de Canaima, opposite the Campamento Canaima. Tour participants stay in his house and sleep in hammocks. Facilities are quite simple, but there's great charm about the place, plus a fantastic pink beach in front of the Hacha Falls. If Tomás is not waiting at the airport, you'll probably find him at the fuente de soda, his favourite place to sit with a bottle of beer. Alternatively, enquire at Tienda Quincallería Canaima.

Obviously, Salto Angel is the main attraction, and the major focus of the tour companies. As there are no trails to the waterfall you have to take a tour, either by plane or boat.

Salto Angel by Plane Flights to the waterfall are serviced by light (usually five-seat) planes of various small airlines which come to Canaima, mostly from Ciudad Bolívar. The pilots fly two or three times back and forth over the face of the falls, circle the top of the tepui and then return. The return trip out of Canaima takes about 40 minutes and costs roughly US$40. These trips can be arranged directly with the pilots at the airport or with local tour operators.

Servivensa flies the guests of Campamento Canaima to Salto Angel in its 22-seater DC-3s. These planes – which hark back to WWII – have been remodelled by enlarging the windows to provide better views. Non-guests can use Servivensa's services if there are vacancies, for US$45 per person. Canaima Tours handles information and bookings.

Salto Angel by Boat This is a memorable experience – arguably even more fascinating than the flight – which allows you to see the waterfall from a different perspective, and, more importantly, to enjoy it at a more leisurely pace.

Motorised canoes only operate in the rainy season, usually from June to December or January. The boats depart from Ucaima, above Hacha Falls, and go up the Carrao and Churún rivers to Isla Ratoncito at the foot of Salto Angel. From there, an hour's walk will take you uphill to Mirador Laime, the outcrop right in front of the falls.

All Canaima-based tour companies (except Hoturvensa) offer all-inclusive boat trips to the falls. A minimum of five to six persons is usually required (boats have a capacity of 10 to 12 passengers), but some operators may be satisfied with just four. The shortest and cheapest is a full day return trip, which requires an early start at around 5 am and gives you about 30 minutes to an hour face to face with Salto Angel. The package usually includes a trip to Salto El Sapo and the whole tour costs US$110 to US$150. The more relaxing three day/two night tours (all-inclusive) are offered for US$180 to US$240, and they also include Salto El Sapo. Transport-only trips can be arranged with some operators, for about 20% to 40% less than all-inclusive tours.

Other Tours The most popular short trip is to Salto El Sapo. It's usually included in the Salto Angel boat package, but can be an excursion in its own right (US$20 per person, two to three hours). It's a 10 minute boat trip from Canaima plus a short walk. You can't get to the falls on foot from Canaima (it's on the other side of the Río Carrao), so you'll have to take a tour (unless you're staying at Tomás' camp on the island).

Salto El Sapo is beautiful and unusual in that you can walk under it. Be prepared to get drenched by the waterfall in the rainy season, so take a swimsuit. A few minutes

walk from El Sapo is Salto El Sapito, another attractive waterfall which is normally included in the same excursion.

Salto Yuri is another popular nearby destination. It's a half-day jeep and boat trip, offered by most local operators (US$30 to US$40 per person).

In the dry season, when the water level in local rivers is low, the choice of boat excursions can be limited, though trips upstream on the Río Carrao to Isla Orquídea may still be possible. Another boat excursion available in the dry season is the trip up the Río Cucurital to Wareipa, a standard offer of Tiuna Tours (US$100 one day, US$150 three days/two nights).

Canaima Tours organises tours to Kavac, if there are sufficient people justifying the flight. This is a day package which includes Servivensa's DC-3 return flight to Kavac (flying over Salto Angel), an excursion to Cueva de Kavac and lunch (US$120 per person).

Places to Stay & Eat
Canaima's main lodging/eating venue is the *Campamento Canaima*, operated by Hoturvensa. The camp consists of about 35 palm-thatched cabañas (109 rooms in all, with bath and hot water), its own restaurant, bar and fuente de soda. The cabañas, scattered along the lagoon bank, are built in a traditional style; the elevated restaurant offers an excellent view over the lagoon and falls; the fuente de soda is right on the beach.

Accommodation is only available as part of a package (see Tour Companies above), but the camp's restaurant, bar and fuente de soda are open to all. The restaurant is expensive (breakfast US$10, lunch US$12, dinner US$12), but the food is good and you can eat as much as you want.

Some potential travellers to Canaima may be put off by the apparent monopoly of the camp, but don't worry as there are cheaper options for both accommodation and food. There are now more than half a dozen other campamentos and posadas in Canaima, some of which also serve meals. Some camps service organised tours, but usually

have vacancies which they rent out to individual tourists. At most places expect to
pay US$6 to US$10 for a hammock, and
US$12 to US$25 for a bed. Some campamentos will let you string up your own
hammock under their roof (and use their
facilities) for US$3 to US$5.

The *Campamento Churún Vená*, opposite
the soccer pitch in the southern part of the
village, is one of the cheaper places, at
US$7/15 a hammock/bed. The nearby *Res-
taurant Imabarí* (popularly known as Los
Simons) is reasonably cheap by Canaima
standards – US$7 for lunch or dinner. In the
same area, the *Campamento Weytüpü* (☎ 62
59 55), opposite the school, provides a more
comfortable lodging, for US$55/80 a
double/triple.

In the northern part of the village, the
cheapest hammock-type accommodation is
in the *Campamento Hermanos Jiménez*, for
US$6 per hammock. About 250m further
north along the road you'll come across three
places to stay: the *Posada Kusarí* (US$15
per bed), the *Posada Kaikusé* (US$20) and
the expensive and overpriced *Campamento
Parakaupa*.

Tiuna and Kamaracoto may have some
hammock and/or bed accommodation – ask
their agents at the airport upon arrival.

If you have your own tent, you can camp
free in Canaima, but get a permit from the
Inparques officer at the airport. The usual
place to camp is on the beach next to the
helpful Guardia Nacional post, just off Campamento Canaima. You may be able to
arrange with the Guardia to leave your stuff
at the post while you are away.

There are a few shops in Canaima which
sell basic supplies such as bread, pasta,
canned fish, biscuits etc, but prices are rather
high. If you plan on self-catering, it's best to
bring your own food with you.

Getting There & Away

Servivensa has one jet flight a day from
Caracas to Canaima, via Porlamar. If you
buy either of Hoturvensa's packages, it will
sell you a discount ticket (about US$150
return from either Caracas or Porlamar).

Otherwise it will charge its normal fare
(US$106 one way, US$212 return), but may
not want to sell tickets in advance, hoping to
fill flights with package-tour passengers.
Even if you succeed in buying a ticket, there
may still be difficulties at the airport. Some
travellers have reported that they had to be
forceful before they were allowed on the
plane.

Servivensa has daily flights on DC-3s
from Puerto Ordaz (US$71) and Santa Elena
de Uairén (US$71). Tickets for these flights
can apparently be bought with less hassle.
Whichever route you're travelling, though,
make sure to book your onward ticket otherwise you may have to wait for several days
for a seat to become available.

Servivensa's DC-3 flies from Canaima to
Kavac at about 10 am and returns around
2.30 pm. These flights only operate if there
are sufficient passengers for the Kavac tour
(see Other Tours above), but when they do
go, you can buy a ticket for the flight only
(US$45 each way).

Several small regional carriers fly from
Ciudad Bolívar to Canaima on a semi-
regular or charter basis (US$50). See
Organised Tours in the Ciudad Bolívar section for details.

KAMARATA

Kamarata is an old Pemón village on the Río
Acanán, at the south-eastern foot of Auyantepui. Some decades ago, it was discovered
as a possible alternative jumping-off point
for Salto Angel, and since then has been
slowly attracting adventurous travellers.
There are a few simple places to stay and eat,
and you can camp next to the Capuchin
mission.

In order to attract tourists, the locals built
the village of Kavac (see below), which has
since taken over most of Kamarata's tourist
traffic. It's a hot two-hour walk from Kamarata, or a short drive on a dirt road.

KAVAC

Kavac is the tourist outlet of Kamarata. It
consists of 20-odd churuatas built in traditional style, making it a fine example of a

typical Pemón settlement. It's neat, quiet and almost devoid of people. It sits on the plain savanna close to Auyantepui.

Organised Tours

There are three small tour/hotel operators in Kavac – Asociación Civil Kamarata Kavac, Makunaima Tours and Excursiones Pemón – which organise tours in the region, though most tourists come in package groups put together by tour companies from outside, mostly from Ciudad Bolívar.

The major attraction in the area is the Cueva de Kavac, which despite its name is not a cave but a deep gorge with a waterfall plunging into it. There's a natural pool at the foot of the waterfall, which you reach by swimming upstream in the canyon – so bring your swimsuit with you. You actually don't need any guide to get to the falls – it's a pretty straightforward half an hour walk from Kavac. If in doubt, discreetly follow any of the tour groups.

Boat trips to Salto Angel are organised in the rainy season only. The boats go from Kamarata down the Acanán and Carrao rivers, then up the Churún to Isla Ratoncito. Following a walk to the Mirador Laime, the boats then sail down the Churún and Carrao rivers to Canaima, where the tours conclude. It's normally a four day tour which costs US$200 to US$300.

Kavac is a starting point for a trip (or rather, an expedition) to the top of Auyantepui. Guides for this long and adventurous hike can be contracted through local tour agencies in Kavac or Kamarata. The trail leads from Kavac via Santa Marta to Guayaraca, from where it approaches the foot of the tepui before snaking uphill, following roughly the same route Jimmie Angel used for his descent in 1937. In three days (from Kavac) you'll get to a place called El Libertador, so named after Bolívar's bust was placed here. You need another week or so to get to the point from where Salto Angel plunges. Count roughly US$20 a day per guide for the group plus another US$20 per porter.

Places to Stay

The *Hotel Kavaikoden* is the only place in Kavac which has beds, but it's often full with incoming tours. There are more places offering accommodation in hammocks (US$6 to US$10 per head) and these are fairly easy to come by.

Getting There & Away

Kavac has an airstrip where light planes land several times a week from Ciudad Bolívar and Santa Elena de Uairén (about US$70 to/from either). There are also flights to/from Canaima (US$45).

La Gran Sabana

La Gran Sabana, a rolling grassy highland in Venezuela's far south-eastern corner, is vast, wild, beautiful, empty and silent. In geographical terms, it's the upland region lying in the basin of the upper Caroní River at an elevation of over 800m. Its area is put at some 35,000 sq km, and much of it lies within the limits of the Parque Nacional Canaima. Correctly speaking, La Gran Sabana doesn't include the Kamarata Valley and the Sabanas of Urimán and Canaima.

The only town in the region is Santa Elena de Uairén, close to the Brazilian frontier. The remaining part of the sparse population, mostly Pemón Indians, the traditional inhabitants of this land, live in scattered villages and hamlets. It's estimated that there are about 15,000 Indians living in some 270 settlements.

The most striking natural feature dominating the skyline of the Gran Sabana are gigantic flat-topped mountains called the tepuis (see boxed text entitled Tepuis & Simas on the following page). The best known of all the tepuis is Roraima, the first to be climbed and increasingly popular among travellers, although the trip to the top and back will take at least five days.

There are many other sights in La Gran Sabana that are easier to visit and some of them are conveniently located on the main road. Particularly amazing are the many waterfalls.

Orientation

Until not long ago, the Gran Sabana was virtually inaccessible. It wasn't until 1973 that a road between El Dorado and Santa Elena was completed, and it was not until 1990 that the last stretch of this road was sealed. Today, it's one of the best highways in the country, and one of the most spectacular. The entire length of the road is signposted with kilometre marks, telling you how far you are from El Dorado. The El Dorado fork is km 0 and Santa Elena is km 316. These are a great help and are often included in tourist publications to help you determine the location of the sights.

Travelling southward from El Dorado, you'll find the fine *Campamento La Montañita* at km 70 just by the road, which has several inexpensive cabañas, a restaurant and a camp site.

At km 85, you reach **Las Claritas**, a particularly dirty and busy ramshackle town, and 3km further south is **San Isidro** (often simply called km 88), another unsavoury collection of tin and rubbish shacks. Both settlements have grown as gold mining supply centres for what is today one of Venezuela's major gold-rush areas. Both of these localities rekindle memories of the old American gold outposts you've seen on the movies, with prospectors much in evidence and noisy bars crammed with tipsy miners. Both places offer a choice of accommodation; the comfortable and reasonably priced *Campamento Turístico Anaconda*, in Las Claritas, is arguably the best option.

Proceeding south, at km 95 the road begins to wind up the so-called **La Escalera** (literally stairway). This portion of road, snaking through lush rainforest and ascending about 800m over 40km, is reputed to be one of the best bird-watching roads on the continent.

At km 99 you'll be passing a huge sandstone boulder, **Piedra de la Virgen**, which marks the entrance to the Parque Nacional Canaima. At km 120 is a 40m-high

Tepuis & Simas

Tepuis are flat-topped cliff-edged mountains typical of southern Venezuela. There are over a hundred such plateaux, dotting the vast region from the Colombian border in the west up into Guyana and Brazil in the east. Their major concentration is in the Gran Sabana.

Tepui (also spelled tepuy) is the Pemón Indian word for mountain, and has been adopted as the term to identify this specific type of table mountain. Interestingly, the term tepui is only used in the Pemón linguistic area, ie in the Gran Sabana and its neighbourhood. Elsewhere, the table mountains are called either cerros or montes.

Geologically, these sandstone mesas are the remnants of a thick layer of Precambrian sediments (some two billion years old) which gradually eroded leaving behind only the most resistant rock 'islands'. Effectively isolated over millions of years from each other and from the eroded lower level, the tops of tepuis saw the independent evolution of flora and fauna. Developing in such a specific environment, many species have preserved features of their remote ancestors, and outside tepuis can only be seen in fossilised remains.

Every tepui has a characteristic plant life, different from any of its neighbours. Scientific explorations show that roughly half of a total of some 2000 plant species found on top of the tepuis are endemic, that is, they grow only there. This is about the highest percentage of endemic flora found anywhere in the world. Yet, only a handful of tepuis have been researched, and there are still many virtually untouched by humans.

Another geological curiosity of southern Venezuela are huge round holes in the ground known as simas. They have vertical walls and flat bottoms – you might say they are a mirror image of tepuis. They were explored for the first time in 1974, and are unique. Only a few of them, so far, have been found, the largest of which is about 350m in diameter and 350m deep. They all are in the Parque Nacional Jaua Sarisariñama, some 400km west of La Gran Sabana. The region is only accessible by helicopter. ■

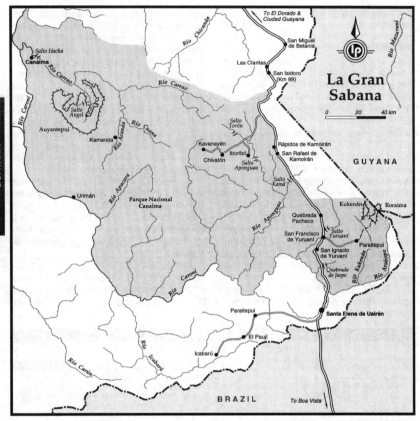

waterfall called **Salto El Danto**. It's not visible from the road but is very close to it.

The road continues to wind uphill to km 135, where the rainforest suddenly ends and you enter a vast flat grassland. This is the beginning of La Gran Sabana, which stretches south for nearly 200km. You are now at an altitude of about 1200m which can be clearly felt by more moderate temperatures, particularly during cloudy days, and by chilly nights.

At km 141 is the Inparques office, and 2km further on you'll be passing by a military outpost at Luepa. At km 147 a side

road branches to the west and runs for 70km to the village of **Kavanayén**. Midway down this road, a dust track departs south to the Indian hamlet of Iboribó, from where you will be able to walk to the marvellous **Salto Aponguao**.

The main road continues south to **Rápidos de Kamoirán**, at km 172, where there's a hotel, restaurant and petrol station, and small rapids behind the complex. At km 195 is the **Salto Kawí**, a small but lovely cascade spilling onto red jasper rock, and at km 202 you'll find the frequently visited **Salto Kamá**.

The **Quebrada Pacheco**, noted for yet another waterfall, is at km 237, and the **Balneario Soruapé**, a km off the road at km 244, is a popular place to bathe in natural pools. Just 3km further south you'll find the amazing **Salto Yuruaní**, before reaching the village of **San Francisco de Yuruaní** at km 250. Here a side road runs east to the Indian village of Paraitepui, from where a fascinating hike will take you to the even more fascinating top of **Roraima** tepui.

The main road proceeds south to the impressive **Quebrada de Jaspe**, at km 273, one of the most popular attractions in the region. Five km down the highway, a rough jeep track branches off to the east and runs for 3km to two picturesque waterfalls, **Salto Agua Fría** and **Salto Puerta del Cielo**.

At km 316, you'll finally reach **Santa Elena de Uairén**, the region's only town to speak of. The highway heads south to the Brazilian border, at km 331, and continues to Boa Vista, 223km beyond the frontier.

There's an unsealed road heading west from Santa Elena to the mining settlement of **Icabarú**, 115km away. Tours around this part of La Gran Sabana are available from Santa Elena, though some more adventurous travellers may want to go on their own to the friendly village of **El Paují**, at km 73, which offers a reasonable choice of simple places to stay and eat, and use it as a base for exploring the area. Nearby attractions include the **Salto Catedral**, **Pozo Esmeralda**, **Salto El Paují** and **El Abismo**.

Some of the major attractions mentioned in this section are detailed separately below.

Getting Around
Getting around the Gran Sabana is not all that easy, as public transport only operates along the highway and is infrequent (nine buses a day in each direction, but half of them run at night). Given time, you can visit the sights on the main road using a combination of hitching and buses. Heading towards Kavanayén, however, may prove difficult, as there are no buses on this road and traffic is sporadic. A comfortable solution is a tour

from Santa Elena (see that section for details).

Whichever way you choose to explore the region, bring plenty of good insect repellent. The Gran Sabana is infested by a kind of gnat known as *jején*, commonly (and justifiably) called *la plaga*, or the plague. They are ubiquitous and voracious, especially so in the morning and late afternoon, and their bites itch for days.

SALTO APONGUAO
Salto Aponguao, also known by its Indian name of Chinak-Merú (merú means waterfall in the Pemón language), is one of the most impressive and photogenic waterfalls in the Gran Sabana, though it's not all that easy to get to on your own. The waterfall is off the highway, 30km along an unsealed road towards Kavanayén plus another 10km south to the Indian hamlet of Iboribó. The villagers offer rustic lodging in hammocks under a roof and serve simple meals.

The locals will take you in a *curiara* (dugout canoe) to the other side of the Río Aponguao and provide a compulsory guide for a trip to the falls (though the path is so clear that no guide is necessary). It's a half-hour walk to the falls. The fee for the return boat ride and the guide has recently been raised to a hefty US$5 per person.

The Salto is about 105m high, and even in the driest season is pretty spectacular. In the wet season it can be a wall of water nearly 100m wide. There's a well-marked path leading downhill to the foot of the falls where you can bathe in natural pools and take excellent pictures of the falls; sunlight strikes the falls from mid-morning until very early afternoon.

Getting There & Away
See the Kavanayén section for information.

KAVANAYÉN
Kavanayén is a small Indian village lost in the middle of the Gran Sabana, about 70km west of the highway, and accessible by a rough road. It developed around the Capuchin mission established here half a

century ago. The missionaries erected a massive stone building for themselves and apparently assumed that the Indians wanted to live in a similar type of dwelling; almost all houses in the village are heavy stone constructions – a striking contrast to the thatched adobe churuatas you'll see elsewhere in the region.

Kavanayén enjoys a spectacular location. Set on the top of a small mesa, the village is surrounded by tepuis and one can see at least half a dozen of these mountains, including the unique cone-shaped Wei Tepui, or Mountain of the Sun.

A rough jeep track leads from Kavanayén to the Karuai-Merú, a fine waterfall at the base of Ptari Tepui, 20km away. The road is so bad the trip may take up to 1½ hours. Otherwise, it's a five hour walk each way. The scenery is fabulous.

There's an adventurous trail from Karuai to Kamarata, which takes a week to complete. One of the most competent guides for this trek is Carlos Enrique Calcaños – ask for him in Kavanayén.

Places to Stay & Eat
The mission provides basic dorm-type accommodation for around US$5 per hard bed. There are two informal restaurants in the village (recognised by the names of their owners as Señora Guadalupe and Señora Rosa) which serve unsophisticated but cheap and filling meals.

There is also accommodation (US$25 for four persons) and food available in Chivatón, 17km before Kavanayén. The place is frequently used by tours as an overnight stop, but it's not convenient for individual travellers without their own transport.

Getting There & Away
The road leading to Kavanayén is almost traffic-free, so it may take a long time to hitch. Quicker options include tours (but not all tours go as far as Kavanayén) or taxis. The nearest place to hire a taxi is San Isidro (km 88). Count on roughly US$100 per taxi for the return journey to Kavanayén. In the wet season not many taxi drivers are eager to go

this way as the last 10km stretch is tortuous, with all kinds of potholes, and sometimes the road is only passable by jeep. For a little extra money you can include Salto Aponguao in the trip to Kavanayén. Taxis from San Isidro to the waterfall (without visiting Kavanayén) shouldn't cost more than US$60 return.

SALTO KAMÁ
Salto Kamá, or Kamá-Merú, is a lovely 50m-high waterfall, just 200m west of km 202. Don't miss walking down the right (northern) bank to its base (for a small fee). The locals can take you for a boat trip (US$1.25) around the waterfall's pool and behind its water curtain; be prepared to get completely wet. For photographers, sunlight strikes the falls from mid-morning to mid-afternoon.

Places to Stay & Eat
There are two cheap, basic campamentos next to the falls, and each has its own simple restaurant. You can also pitch your tent in the camps for a small fee.

Rápidos de Kamoirán, at km 172, has a restaurant and a hotel (US$16 a double), which is one of the usual overnight stops for tours around the Gran Sabana.

Getting There & Away
If you're travelling on your own, just stay on the road and flag down anything that is heading in your direction. Keep an eye on parked cars belonging to tourists visiting the falls.

QUEBRADA PACHECO
Also known as Arapán-Merú, this is a handsome multi-step cascade, just 100m to the east of the road at km 237. It's much nicer up close than you'd imagine from the road. The best light for photos is in the afternoon.

There are basic tourist facilities, including lodging in hammocks in a churuata (US$4 per person) and meals (US$4).

SALTO YURUANÍ
Ten km south of Quebrada Pacheco, at km 247, you pass over a bridge across the Yuruaní River. From the bridge you'll see the waterfall, about a km to the east, with the

Yuruaní Tepui in the background. The way to the falls is along both the southern and northern banks of the river. It's a wonderful waterfall, about 7m high and 100m wide, with an amazing water coloration reminiscent of beer. The best sunlight strikes the falls in the afternoon. There's a place for camping next to the falls but bring a lot of insect repellent as this waterfall is notorious for jejenes.

RORAIMA

Roraima, on the tripartite border of Venezuela, Guyana and Brazil, is one of the largest and highest tepuis; its plateau is at about 2700m and the highest peak at 2810m. It was the first of the tepuis on which a climb was recorded (in 1884) and has been much explored by botanists. Interestingly, although Roraima is a classic example of a tepui and lies within the Pemón linguistic area, it is not called a tepui but a monte – nobody knows why.

Roraima is the easiest table mountain to ascend, and is increasingly popular among travellers. The climb doesn't require any particular skills and can be done by anyone reasonably fit and healthy. There are no elements of technical climbing on the route, no ropes, ladders etc. Perhaps 200 people trek to the top every month, more than 80% of whom are foreigners.

Yet it's not an easy or short walk. You need a minimum of five days to do this trip, camping equipment and food. Be prepared for a hard trek and some discomfort, including plenty of rain and la plaga. Still you'll be rewarded by some of the most unusual and memorable experiences you will have in Venezuela. The hike is fascinating and the top of the mesa is a dream.

San Francisco de Yuruaní

The starting point for the trip is the small village of San Francisco de Yuruaní, 66km north of Santa Elena de Uairén by the highway.

There are two small tour operators, Roraima Tours and Arapena Tours, which offer expensive all-inclusive tours, or can

just arrange guides and porters. Guides charge US$25 a day per group. Porters, should you need one, charge US$30 per day and can carry up to about 17kg. Both guides and porters can also be hired in the village of Paraitepui, your next stop on the way to Roraima.

Some travellers recommend Kendall Donald Mitchell as a good English-speaking guide, even though he charges around US$40. He can be found at San Francisco or Quebrada Pacheco, though he's often out on a tour.

Accommodation options in San Francisco include the roadside *Hospedaje Minina*, 100m north of the bus stop (US$10 a triple), and an unmarked house next to Roraima Tours (US$4 per person). There are a few basic places to eat, including *Restaurant Roraima*, at the central junction, which will keep you going. The restaurant also provides accommodation in hammocks (US$2).

Paraitepui

Paraitepui is about 25km east of San Francisco. To get there, hire a jeep from the tour operators in San Francisco (US$50, regardless of the number of passengers, up to about eight) or walk. The road to Paraitepui branches off the highway 1km south of San Francisco. It's a hot, steady seven-hour walk, mostly uphill, to Paraitepui (back to San Francisco, it's six hours).

The road is not difficult to follow, except for one point (about five hours walk from San Francisco), where it divides. The road which goes straight ahead leads to the hamlet of Chirimatá, while the Paraitepui road proper (which you should follow), branches off sharply to the right. Don't worry too much if you miss this turn-off; there's a path from Chirimatá to Paraitepui.

You may be lucky enough to hitch a jeep ride on this road, but traffic is sporadic and drivers will probably charge you for the lift (a more reasonable fare than jeep rental in San Francisco).

Paraitepui is a nondescript Indian village of about 250 people, whose identity has been largely shattered by tourists and their money.

GUAYANA

Upon arrival, you will invariably be greeted by one of the village headmen, who will show you the list of guides (apparently every adult male in the village is a guide) and inform you about prices. They are much the same as in San Francisco. Although you don't really need a guide to follow the track up to the tepui, the village headmen won't let you pass through without one.

There are no hotels in the village, but you can camp on the square near the school, under a thatched roof (US$3 per person). Overpriced hot meals are available in the house behind the school. A few shops in the village sell basic food (canned fish, biscuits, packet soups) at exorbitant prices.

Climbing Roraima

Once you have arranged your guide, you can set off for Roraima. The trip to the top takes two days (the total walking time is about 12 hours uphill and 10 hours down). There are several good places to camp (with water) on the way. The most popular camp sites are on the Río Tek (four hours from Paraitepui), the Río Kukenán (30 minutes farther on) and the so-called *campamento base* (base camp) at the foot of Roraima (three hours uphill from Río Kukenán). The steep and tough four hour ascent from the base camp to the top is the most spectacular part of the hike.

The volume of the Río Kukenán depends on the highly changeable and unpredictable rainfall on the Kukenán and Roraima tepuis, and the river level can change substantially in an hour or less. The river can be impassable after rains and you may need to wait for several hours or even a day until the level drops. As a rough rule, the water level is lower in the evening than it is in the morning. Also, don't camp immediately on the shore, unless you don't mind taking an unexpected bath.

Once you reach the top, you walk for some 15 minutes to the place known as El Hotel, one of the few good camping sites. It's actually a patch of sand large enough for about four small tents, partly protected by an overhanging rock. There are several other, smaller 'hotels' in the area.

The scenery that surrounds you is a moonscape, evocative of a science-fiction movie: impressive blackened rock of every imaginable shape, gorges, creeks, pink beaches, and gardens filled with unique flowering plants. Frequent and constantly changing mist and fog add to the mysterious air.

It's here that a guide finally becomes handy, as it's very easy to get lost on the vast plateau. Your guide will take you to some attractions, including El Foso, a curious round pool in a deep rocky hole. It's about a three hour walk north from El Hotel. On the way, you'll pass the amazingly lush Valle Arabopo. Beyond the pool is the Valle de los Cristales and the Laberinto, both well worth a trip. Another fascinating area is the southwestern part of Roraima, where attractions include La Ventana (Window), El Abismo (Abyss) and La Piscina (Swimming Pool). Plan on staying at least two days on the top, though it's better to allow longer.

When to Go

The dry season is from December to April, but the tops of the tepuis receive rain off the Atlantic all year round. The weather changes in a matter of minutes, with bright sunshine or heavy rain possible at any time.

What to Bring

A good tent, preferably with a fly sheet, is a must. It gets bitterly cold at night on the top, so bring a good sleeping bag and warm clothes. You also need reliable rain gear, sturdy shoes, a cooking stove and the usual hiking equipment. Bring enough food to share with your guide and to last you one or two days more than planned; you may not be able to resist the temptation of staying longer on the top, or you may be stuck at Río Kukenán, unable to cross. A rope may be useful for crossing the river.

There's no plaga atop Roraima, but you'll have plenty of these nasty biting gnats on the way, so take an effective insect repellent. Don't forget a good supply of film. A macro lens is a great help in photographing the unique small plants. Make sure to bring along plastic bags, to take *all* your garbage back down to civilisation. However, don't remove anything that belongs to the mountain – no plants, rocks, crystals etc. Searches are often conducted on returning travellers, and crystals are subject to heavy on-the-spot fines.

Getting There & Away
San Francisco de Yuruaní is on the Ciudad Guayana-Santa Elena highway, and nine buses a day run in either direction. Buy all food at either starting point; don't count on shopping in San Francisco, let alone in Paraitepui.

QUEBRADA DE JASPE
Between San Francisco and Santa Elena, at km 273, is yet another Gran Sabana waterfall. This one is small and faint, but what is truly amazing is the intense orange-red colour of pure jasper rock over which the creek flows. The Quebrada is 200m to the east of the highway, hidden in a stretch of woodland.

SANTA ELENA DE UAIRÉN
* *pop 12,000*
* *area code* ☎ (088)
Founded in 1924, Santa Elena began to grow when diamonds were discovered in the 1930s in Icabarú region, 115km to the west. However, isolated from the centre of the country by a lack of roads, it remained a small village. The second development push came with the opening of the highway from El Dorado.

Today, Santa Elena is a pleasant, easy-going border town with an agreeable if damp climate and a Brazilian air thanks to the significant number of residents from across the border.

The Carnaval here has a distinctly Brazilian feel, with samba rhythms and a parade of *carrozas* (floats). Small as it is, Santa Elena is the main town of the Gran Sabana and the biggest before you reach Tumeremo, 385km to the north.

Information
Tourist Office Tour agencies (see Organised Tours) are good sources of information about the region.

Money So far, it's impossible to get cash advances on credit cards, though this may change. Banco del Orinoco is the only bank at which you can change Amex travellers cheques, but it charges a hefty US$5 commission on transactions.

Various establishments, including shops, travel agencies and hotels, may change cash and occasionally travellers cheques. La Boutique Zapatería is one of the most reliable places to change both travellers cheques and cash (including Brazilian currency), and offers reasonable rates. Moneychangers hang around the corner of Calle Bolívar and Calle Urdaneta and deal with cash.

If you are heading north into Venezuela, keep in mind that the nearest place you can change money is likely to be Ciudad Guayana, 600km away. If you're heading south for Brazil, get rid of all your bolívares in Santa Elena and buy Brazilian currency.

Brazilian Consulate The consulate is at the north-eastern end of town and is open on weekdays from 8 am till noon. It's a good idea to get your visa beforehand, because if this consulate fails to issue a visa, you'll have a long way to go to get one (the nearest Brazilian consulate is in Ciudad Guayana).

Immigration The DEX office, behind the large new building of the Prefectura, is open Monday to Saturday from 7.30 to 11.30 am and 2 to 5 pm, and Sunday from 8 to 11.30 am. Be sure to have your passport stamped here before leaving, or upon arrival in Venezuela. Brazilian passport formalities are done at the border itself. A yellow fever vaccination certificate may be required by officials if you're entering Brazil.

Organised Tours
There are half a dozen tour agencies in Santa Elena (see the map for locations). Their staple is a two or three day jeep tour around

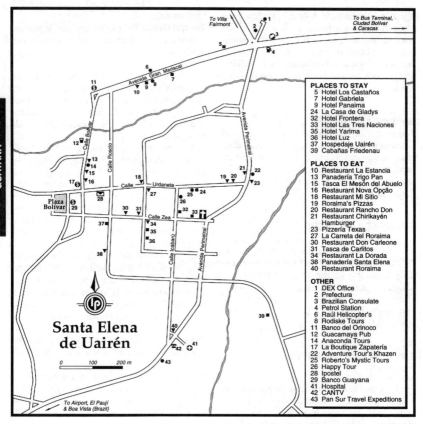

PLACES TO STAY
5 Hotel Los Castaños
7 Hotel Gabriela
9 Hotel Panaima
24 La Casa de Gladys
32 Hotel Frontera
33 Hotel Las Tres Naciones
35 Hotel Yarima
36 Hotel Luz
37 Hospedaje Uairén
39 Cabañas Friedenau

PLACES TO EAT
10 Restaurant La Estancia
13 Panadería Trigo Pan
15 Tasca El Mesón del Abuelo
16 Restaurant Nova Opção
18 Restaurant Mi Sitio
19 Roraima's Pizzas
20 Restaurant Rancho Don
21 Restaurant Chirikayén
    Hamburger
23 Pizzería Texas
27 La Carreta del Roraima
30 Restaurant Don Carleone
31 Tasca de Carlitos
34 Restaurant La Dorada
38 Panadería Santa Elena
40 Restaurant Roraima

OTHER
1 DEX Office
2 Prefectura
3 Brazilian Consulate
4 Petrol Station
6 Raúl Helicopter's
8 Rodiske Tours
11 Banco del Orinoco
12 Guacamaya Pub
14 Anaconda Tours
17 La Boutique Zapatería
22 Adventure Tour's Khazen
25 Roberto's Mystic Tours
26 Happy Tour
28 Ipostel
29 Banco Guayana
41 Hospital
42 CANTV
43 Pan Sur Travel Expeditions

Santa Elena
de Uairén

La Gran Sabana, with visits to the most interesting sights. They can bring you back to Santa Elena, or drop you on the road at the northernmost point of the tour if you plan to continue north. Count on roughly US$30 to US$35 per day per person in a group of three or four, and about US$5 less than this in a larger party. These prices include transport and a guide, but no accommodation or food. However, tours normally stop in budget places, where beds and meals don't usually cost more than about US$5 each. Shop around, as prices and routes vary.

Some operators can take you to Paraitepui,

the starting point for the Roraima trek, for around US$90 per jeep for up to six or seven people (plus another US$90 if you want them to pick you up on a prearranged date and take you back). It works out cheaper to go by bus to San Francisco, and hire a jeep there (US$50) or walk.

The new Roberto's Mystic Tours (☎ 95 11 71), in La Casa de Gladys at Calle Urdaneta No 187, is run by Roberto Marrero, the author of various guidebooks and maps of La Gran Sabana, and an experienced guide who conducted tours for the now defunct Alfonso Tours. Apart from the standard Gran Sabana trips, he offers tours to the gold and diamond mines in El Paují area.

Another recommended agency is Tayuk-asen Tours (☎ & fax 95 10 50), in the Hotel Luz on Calle Lucas Fernández Peña, which offers good service and reasonable prices. It's particularly experienced in tours to the top of Roraima, providing guides, porters, equipment and transport. A six day tour will cost US$200 to US$300 per person, depending on the conditions and the number of people in the group. The company also rents out camping equipment.

The Adventure Tour's Khazen (☎ & fax 95 13 71), Avenida Perimetral, which is run by Frank Khazen, also offers a choice of tours and can arrange your camping equipment rental. Other tour companies include Anaconda Tours (☎ 95 10 16), Happy Tour (☎ 95 13 39), Rodiske Tours (☎ 95 14 67) and Pan Sur Travel Expeditions (☎ 95 14 11; fax 95 13 86).

Raúl Helicopter's (☎ & fax 95 11 57, 95 10 49), Avenida Gran Mariscal, provides air services in light planes and helicopters. This is not exactly a proposition for backpackers, but if money is no problem it can take you anywhere, eg put you on the top of Roraima (around US$1000 per four persons).

Places to Stay

There's no shortage of accommodation in Santa Elena, and it's easy to find a room, except perhaps in mid-August, when the town celebrates the feast of its patron saint. The town has a problematical water supply, so check whether your hotel has water tanks. Few hotels in Santa Elena have single rooms; obviously, you can be accommodated in a double room but you'll have to pay the double room price. All hotels listed here have rooms with private bath.

The favourite travellers' lodge is the friendly La Casa de Gladys (☎ 95 11 71). Neat doubles are US$7 (which makes it just about the cheapest place in town), and you can use the kitchen and fridge. Good coffee is served free all day. Gladys offers laundry facilities for guests and handles rental of tents, sleeping bags etc for Roraima.

Other budget places (costing a bit more than La Casa) include the Hotel Las Tres Naciones (no sign outside), Hotel Panaima (☎ 95 14 74), Hospedaje Uairén and the basic Hotel Luz (☎ 95 10 50). Next door to the latter is the similarly basic Hotel Yarima, but it doubles as a love hotel.

For a little more (say, US$10 to US$12 a double), you have several reasonable options, including Hotel Gabriela (☎ 95 13 79) and Hotel Los Castaños (☎ 95 14 50), both pleasant and good value.

One of the best in the town's centre is the Hotel Frontera (☎ 95 10 95), which has doubles with TV for US$18. Another good choice is the Cabañas Friedenau (☎ 95 13 53), which offers cabañas to sleep 3/5/9 people for US$22/44/66. In the northern Akurima suburb, the Villa Fairmont (☎ 95 10 22), is possibly the most comfortable place, for US$20/25/30 for a large single/double/triple, and has its own restaurant.

Frank (of Adventure Tour's Khazen) has a few budget rooms for rent at his tour office, on Avenida Perimetral. The disco next door, however, may turn nights into torture. Check before booking if and when the disco operates. When this book was being researched, Frank was planning to build a campamento near the new bus terminal, which would provide budget accommodation in cabañas and a camping ground.

Places to Eat

There are plenty of inexpensive eateries all around the central streets. They include: Restaurant Mi Sitio, Tasca de Carlitos, Restaurant Don Carleone and Restaurant Chirikayén Hamburger. For pizza, choose between Pizzería Texas and Roraima's Pizzas. Restaurant La Dorada is the place for cheap chicken. La Carreta del Roraima does some vegetarian dishes.

Better places include Restaurant La Estancia, Restaurant Roraima, Restaurant Rancho Don, Restaurant Nova Opção and Tasca El Mesón del Abuelo.

Panadería Santa Elena opens at 6 am and is a good place for an early breakfast, while Panadería Trigo Pan has tables outside to sit

GUAYANA

with a cup of coffee and watch the unhurried world go by.

Getting There & Away

Air The airport is 7km south-west of town, off the road to the frontier. There's no public transport; a taxi will cost around US$3. Tour operators are often waiting for incoming flights and will usually give you a free lift to town, hoping you might be interested in their tours.

Servivensa has daily flights to Puerto Ordaz (US$71), with a stopover in Canaima (US$71). These flights are serviced by old DC-3s. It's a good opportunity for picture shooting since the plane flies at only about 1000m and close to the tepuis. Anaconda Tours and some other agencies will book and sell tickets.

Light planes, usually five-seaters, service regional destinations, including El Paují and Icabarú (US$20 to either, providing the plane is full).

Bus The new bus terminal is on the Ciudad Guayana highway, about 2km east of the town centre. There are nine buses daily to Ciudad Bolívar (US$11.25 ordinary, US$14 deluxe, 10 to 11 hours), and they all pass through Ciudad Guayana (US$9.75 ordinary, US$12 deluxe, nine to 10 hours). A jeep to El Paují departs around 6 am (US$10, three hours).

There are four buses a day to Boa Vista, Brazil (US$14, three to four hours). The road is now sealed all the way. Remember to get an exit stamp in your passport from DEX beforehand. The border, locally known as La Línea, is 15km south of Santa Elena. The bus calls at the Brazilian border immigration post for passport formalities. The border is open from 7 am to 10 pm.

Amazonas

Venezuela's southernmost state, Amazonas, covers an area of 175,000 sq km, or approximately one-fifth of the national ter-

ritory, yet it has, at most, 1% of the country's population. Despite its name, most of the region lies in the Orinoco drainage basin, while the Amazon basin takes up only the south-western portion of the state. The two basins are linked by the unusual Brazo Casiquiare, a natural channel which sends a portion of the water of the Orinoco to Río Negro and down to the Amazon.

The region is predominantly a thick tropical forest crisscrossed by a maze of rivers and sparsely populated by a mosaic of Indian communities. The current Indian population is estimated at 40,000, half of what it was in 1925. The three main Indian groups, Piaroa, Yanomami and Guajibo, make up about three-quarters of the indigenous population, while the remaining quarter is composed of the Yekuana (Maquiritare), Curripaco, Guarekena, Piapoco and a number of smaller communities. Approximately 20 Indian languages are used in the region.

In contrast to the central Amazon basin in Brazil, Venezuelan Amazonas is quite diverse topographically, its most noticeable feature being the tepuis. Though not as numerous nor as classical as in La Gran Sabana, they do give the green carpet a distinctive and spectacular appearance.

The best known of the Amazonas tepuis is Cerro Autana, about 80km south of Puerto Ayacucho. It is the sacred mountain of the Piaroa Indians, who consider it the birthplace of the universe. The tepui is reminiscent of a gigantic tree trunk which looms about 700m above the surrounding plains. There's a unique cave about 200m below its top, which cuts right through the tepui.

At the far southern end of the region, along the border with Brazil, is the Serranía de la Neblina, or Misty Mountain, hardly ever explored and virtually unknown. At 3014m, it's the tallest mountain on the continent east of the Andean chain. It has a canyon running through its middle which is considered to be one of the world's deepest. It's also thought that La Neblina has some of the richest endemic plant life anywhere in the world.

Puerto Ayacucho, situated at the north-western tip of Amazonas, is the only town of

GUAYANA

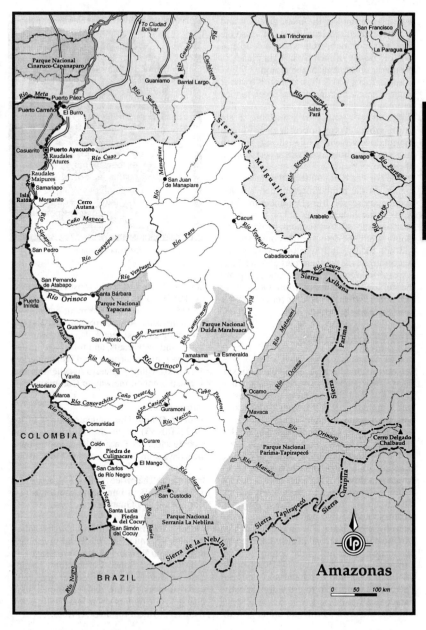

Amazonas

0   50   100 km

GUAYANA

significance, and is the main gateway and supply centre for the entire state. It's also the chief transport hub, from where a couple of small regional airlines fly in light planes to the major settlements of the region.

As there are no roads, transport is by river or air. There's no regular passenger service on virtually any stretch of any river, which makes travel on your own difficult, if not impossible. Tour operators in Puerto Ayacucho have swiftly filled the gap and can take you just about everywhere – at a price, of course.

The climate is not uniform throughout the region. At the northern edge, there's a distinctive dry season from December to April. April is the hottest month. The rest of the year is marked by frequent heavy rains. Going south, the dry season becomes shorter and not so dry, and eventually disappears. Accordingly, the southern part of Amazonas is wet all year round. The best time to explore the region is reputedly from October to December, when the river level is high but rains are already easing.

PUERTO AYACUCHO
- *pop 70,000*
- *area code ☎ (048)*

Set on the middle reaches of the Orinoco, Puerto Ayacucho is by far the largest town in the region and the capital of Amazonas. It was founded in 1924, together with another port, Samariapo, 63km upriver.

The two ports have been linked by road to each other, to bypass the unnavigable stretch of the Orinoco cut by a series of rapids, enabling timber to be shipped from the upper Amazonas down to the centre of the country.

For a long time, and particularly during the oil boom, Amazonas was a forgotten territory and the two ports were little more than obscure villages. The link between them was the only sealed road in the whole region; connection to the rest of the country was by a rough track. Only in the late 1980s, when this track was improved and surfaced, did Puerto Ayacucho start to grow dramatically. Paradoxically, the port, which was responsible for the town's birth and initial growth,

Yanomami Indian

has lost its importance as most cargo is now trucked by road.

Puerto Ayacucho is the main gateway to the Venezuelan Amazon region and is swiftly becoming a tourist centre. There's a range of hotels and restaurants, and travel agents can take you up the Orinoco and its tributaries, deep into the jungle. Puerto Ayacucho is also a transit point on the way to Colombia.

Information
Tourist Office The Cadetur tourist office (☎ 21 00 33) is in the building of the Gobernación, on Plaza Bolívar, and is open weekdays from 8 am to noon and 2 to 5.30 pm.

Inparques The office (☎ 21 47 71; fax 21 37 15) is in Edificio Funeraria Amazonas (1st floor), Calle La Guardia.

Money The Banco Unión changes Amex travellers cheques and cash and gives cash advances on Visa and MasterCard. Banco de Venezuela and Banco Caroní don't change cash or cheques but they do service credit card holders. Some tour agencies may change your dollars or at least will accept them as payment for their services.

Immigration The DIEX office is on Avenida Aguerrevere and is open weekdays from 8 am to noon and 2 to 6 pm, though it doesn't seem to keep to these hours very strictly. Get your passport stamped here when leaving or entering Venezuela.

Things to See

Puerto Ayacucho is hot, but is pleasantly shaded by luxuriant mango trees and has some attractions. The **Museo Etnológico de Amazonas**, Avenida Río Negro, gives an insight into the culture of the main Indian groups of the region, including the Piaroa, Guajibo, Yekuana and Yanomami. It has a good selection of exhibits with interesting background information, in Spanish only. The museum is open Tuesday to Friday from 8.30 to 11 am and 2.30 to 6 pm, Saturday from 9 am to noon and 3.30 to 7 pm, and Sunday from 9 am to 1 pm.

The **Mercado Indígena**, held every day in the morning (busiest Thursday to Saturday) on the square opposite the museum, sells Indian crafts, though you may find more interesting artefacts in the handicraft shops, Artesanías Amazonas and Bazar Corotería La Colmena. Visit the **Catedral** on Plaza Bolívar to see its colourful interior.

The **Cerro Perico**, south-west of the town centre, provides views over the Río Orinoco and the town. Another hill, Cerro El Zamuro, commonly known as **El Mirador**, is 1.5km south of the centre and overlooks the Raudales Atures, the spectacular rapids that block river navigation (the other rapids, the Raudales Maipures, are near Samariapo). Both are more impressive in the rainy season, when the water level is high. The difference between the water level in the dry and rainy periods can surpass 15m.

There are some attractions around Puerto Ayacucho. The **Parque Tobogán de la Selva** is a picnic area developed around a large, steeply inclined smooth rock with water running over it – a sort of natural slide. It's 30km south of town along the Samariapo road, then 6km off to the east. There's no transport directly to the park. You can either take a por puesto to Samariapo, get off at the turn-off and walk the remaining distance, or negotiate a taxi in Puerto Ayacucho. The rock is a favourite weekend place among the townspeople, who, unfortunately, leave it pretty littered (watch out for broken glass). There's a less well known natural waterslide farther upriver.

The **Cerro Pintado** is a large rock with pre-Columbian petroglyphs carved high above the ground in a virtually inaccessible place. It's 17km south of town and a few kilometres off the main road to the left. The best time to see the carvings is early in the morning or late in the afternoon.

Organised Tours

The tour business has flourished over the past decade, and probably as many as a dozen operators are now hunting for your money. Tour agents have some standard tours, but most can arrange a tour according to your interests and time. Be sure to carry your passport and tarjeta de ingreso on all trips.

Among the popular shorter tours are a three day trip up the Sipapo and Autana rivers to the foot of Cerro Autana, and a three day trip up the Río Cuao. You can expect to pay US$40 to US$60 per person per day, all-inclusive.

If you're looking for a longer and more adventurous journey, consider the so-called Ruta Humboldt, following the route of the great explorer. The trip goes along the Orinoco, Casiquiare and Guainía rivers up to Maroa. From there, the boat is transported overland to Yavita, and you then return down the Atabapo and Orinoco to Puerto Ayacucho. This trip takes eight to 10 days and will cost around US$80 to US$100 per person a day.

The far south-eastern part of Amazonas, where the Yanomami live, is a restricted area requiring special permits which are almost impossible to get.

Probably the most reputable agency in town is Expediciones Guaharibo (☎ 21 06 35), but it is also the most expensive. Its tours are well prepared and provide a VIP service, including plastic chairs and tablecloths; it

GUAYANA

may be too much luxury for some travellers. The company's main office is in Caracas (☎ (02) 952 69 96; fax 953 00 92), where most tours are put together and sent to Puerto Ayacucho.

Of the cheaper local companies, it's difficult to heartily recommend any particular one. It seems that Coyote Expeditions (☎ 21 20 27) is currently one of the cheapest and most popular companies with travellers. Autana Aventura (☎ 21 26 19) was one of the major operators, but there have been a number of complaints about it. The relatively new Siapa Amazonas Expeditions (☎ 21 49 58) also has received a mixed reaction from some travellers. Before you make a final decision, it may be worth checking out two of the most established companies, Turismo Yutajé (☎ 21 06 64) and Tobogán Tours (☎ 21 48 65).

If there's a serious discrepancy between what an agency promises and what it actually provides, complain to the tourist office and insist on receiving part of your money back.

Aguas Bravas (☎ 21 05 41) offers rafting over the Atures rapids. It runs two trips a day (about three hours long), at US$35.

Places to Stay

The town has two dozen hotels, some of which have already become popular with foreign travellers. All those listed have private baths, and fan or air-conditioning.

The most popular choice with backpackers has long been the simple *Residencia Internacional* (☎ 21 02 42), at Avenida Aguerrevere No 18. However, perhaps encouraged by recommendations in guidebooks, it has almost doubled its prices, up to US$10/15 a double/triple, which no longer makes the place great value. The *Hotel Maguarí* (☎ 21 31 89), Calle Evelio Roa No 35, is probably less pleasant but more central and cheaper (US$8/11). Still cheaper is the basic *Residencias Ayacucho* (☎ 21 07 79), which has doubles with bath for US$6.

The *Residencias Río Siapa* (☎ 21 01 38) is a good place with friendly management. Air-conditioned matrimoniales/doubles/triples with bath cost US$11/13/15. There's

no sign at the entrance, so keep your eyes open when walking down the street. Even better is the new, small *Residencias La Cueva* (☎ 21 05 63), which has swiftly become popular with travellers. Its spotlessly clean air-conditioned doubles/triples cost US$14/18.

The *Gran Hotel Amazonas* (☎ 21 03 28, 21 01 55) was perhaps the best hotel in town when built, but its good days have long gone. Yet it's still probably worth US$18/20/25 for a double/triple/suite, and it's the only city hotel with a swimming pool.

Other reasonable options include the *Hotel Orinoco* (☎ 21 02 85), on the northwestern fringes of town (US$17/18 a double/triple), and the *Hotel Apure* (☎ 21 05 16), at the southern end (US$26/32). Both have comfortable air-conditioned rooms.

Places to Eat

There's quite a choice of eating outlets in town, but most are closed on Sunday. *Fuente de Soda El Capi*, Calle Evelio Roa, has savoury food, including vegetable salads, at very moderate prices. For tasty chicken and parrillas, try the cheap *Pollos y Parrillas El Cordero*, in the market area on Avenida Orinoco. The *Restaurant El Angoleño* doesn't look very elegant, but the food is good and cheap. Hearty felafel, chawarma and the like are served at the *Centro Recreativo La Gran Vía* on Avenida Orinoco. The *Restaurant Las Palmeras* is a quite pleasant palm-thatched place that cooks some of the better pizzas in town.

One of the favourite budget places to eat among locals is the Mercadito (literally little market), which boasts half a dozen rudimentary eateries, including *Restaurant El Rincón Llanero*, *Restaurant El Punto Criollo* and *Fritanga Negro Felipe*.

Among some more decent places, the *Restaurant La Estancia*, Avenida Aguerrevere, maintains good food and prices, as does the *Hostería Río Negro*, Avenida Río Negro. The *Restaurant El Sherazad* specialises in Middle Eastern cuisine. *Tasca El Arbolito*, Avenida Aguerrevere, is one of the few

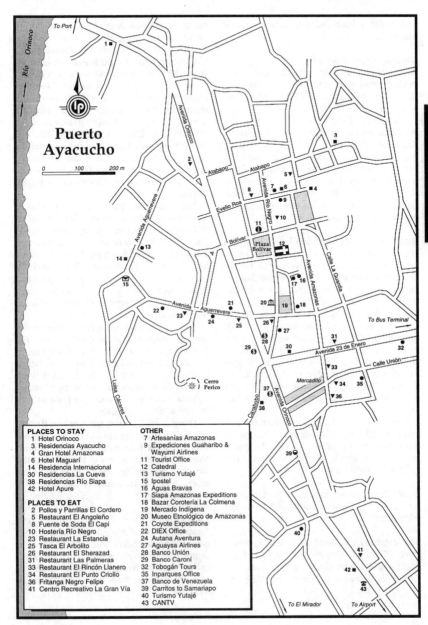

Puerto Ayacucho

To Port

Río Orinoco

0   100   200 m

Avenida Orinoco

Atabapo

Atabapo

Avenida Río Negro

Evelio Roa

Bolívar

Plaza Bolívar

Avenida Aguerrevere

Avenida Amazonas

Calle La Guardia

Avenida Aguerrevere

To Bus Terminal

Avenida 23 de Enero

Calle Unión

Mercadito

Luisa Cáceres

Carabobo

Avenida Orinoco

Cerro Perico

To El Mirador   To Airport

PLACES TO STAY
1 Hotel Orinoco
3 Residencias Ayacucho
4 Gran Hotel Amazonas
6 Hotel Maguarí
14 Residencia Internacional
30 Residencias La Cueva
38 Residencias Río Siapa
42 Hotel Apure

PLACES TO EAT
2 Pollos y Parrillas El Cordero
5 Restaurant El Angoleño
8 Fuente de Soda El Capi
10 Hostería Río Negro
23 Restaurant La Estancia
25 Tasca El Arbolito
26 Restaurant El Sherazad
31 Restaurant Las Palmeras
33 Restaurant El Rincón Llanero
34 Restaurant El Punto Criollo
36 Fritanga Negro Felipe
41 Centro Recreativo La Gran Vía

OTHER
7 Artesanías Amazonas
9 Expediciones Guaharibo &
   Wayumi Airlines
11 Tourist Office
12 Catedral
13 Turismo Yutajé
15 Ipostel
16 Aguas Bravas
17 Siapa Amazonas Expeditions
18 Bazar Corotería La Colmena
19 Mercado Indígena
20 Museo Etnológico de Amazonas
21 Coyote Expeditions
22 DIEX Office
24 Autana Aventura
27 Aguaysa Airlines
28 Banco Unión
29 Banco Caroní
32 Tobogán Tours
35 Inparques Office
37 Banco de Venezuela
39 Carritos to Samariapo
40 Turismo Yutajé
43 CANTV

places for a beer and music on weekend nights.

Getting There & Away

Air The airport is 6km south-east of the town centre; taxis cost US$4. Avensa has one flight daily to Caracas (US$76) via San Fernando de Apure (US$48).

Two small local carriers, Aguaysa and Wayumi, operate flights within Amazonas. There are daily flights (except Sunday) to San Fernando de Atabapo (US$50) and San Juan de Manapiare (US$50), and one flight a week (usually on Friday) to San Carlos de Río Negro (US$80) and Maroa (US$80). Other, smaller localities are serviced irregularly on a charter basis.

Bus The bus terminal is 6km east of the centre, on the outskirts of town. To get there, take the city bus from Avenida 23 de Enero, or a taxi (US$1.50). Buses to Ciudad Bolívar depart at regular intervals throughout the day (US$12.25 ordinary, US$14 deluxe, 10 to 11 hours). There are half a dozen departures a day to San Fernando de Apure (US$8.50 ordinary, eight hours), from where you get buses to Caracas, Maracay, Valencia, Barinas and San Cristóbal. There are also direct buses from Puerto Ayacucho to Caracas, Maracay and Valencia, but they go via a longer route through Caicara del Orinoco.

Por puestos to El Burro run from the terminal (US$2.50, 1½ hours). Carritos to Samariapo depart from Avenida Orinoco, two blocks south of Teatro Don Juan (US$1.75, 1½ hours).

Boat There is no passenger boat service down the Río Orinoco, and cargo boats are infrequent.

To Colombia The nearest Colombian town, Puerto Carreño, is at the confluence of the Meta and Orinoco rivers and is accessible from Puerto Ayacucho in two ways. Remember to get an exit stamp in your passport at DIEX before setting off.

The first way leads via Casuarito, a Colombian hamlet right across the Orinoco from Puerto Ayacucho. A boat between Puerto Ayacucho's wharf (at the north-eastern end of town) and Casuarito shuttles regularly throughout the day (US$1). From Casuarito, the *voladora* (high-speed boat) departs in the afternoon to Puerto Carreño (US$6, one hour); in the opposite direction, the voladora leaves Puerto Carreño at 6 am. In the dry season (December to April), there may also be some jeeps from Casuarito to Puerto Carreño.

The other way goes via Puerto Páez, a Venezuelan village about 95km north of Puerto Ayacucho. Get there by San Fernando bus (US$2.50, two hours); the trip includes a ferry crossing of the Orinoco from El Burro to Puerto Páez. The bus will drop you off in the centre of the village. Go to the wharf and take a boat across the Río Meta to Puerto Carreño (US$1); they run regularly between 6 am and 6 pm.

Puerto Carreño is a long, one-street town with an airport, half a dozen hotels (*El Vorágine*, near the Venezuelan consulate, is perhaps the best budget bet) and a number of places to eat. Go to the DAS office, one block west of the main square, for an entry stamp in your passport. A number of shops will change bolívares to pesos.

There are two flights per week to Bogotá (US$110). Buses go only in the dry season, approximately from mid-December to mid-March. They depart once a week for the two-day journey by rough road to Villavicencio (US$60), which is four hours by bus from Bogotá.

To Brazil Take a flight from Puerto Ayacucho to San Carlos de Río Negro, from where irregular boats will take you to San Simón de Cocuy, on the frontier. Take a bus to São Gabriel (Brazil) and search there for cargo boats down the Río Negro to Manaus.

Glossary

abasto – grocery store

acure – a hare-sized rodent, species of agouti

AD – Acción Democrática, or Democratic Action Party; populist party, created in 1941 by Rómulo Betancourt and one of the two major traditional parties

adeco – a member or follower of the Acción Democrática party

adobe – sun-dried brick made of mud and straw, used in traditional rural constructions

alcabala – road checkpost operated by the Guardia Nacional

alcaraván – stone curlew, large shore birds

andino/a – inhabitant of the Andes

araguaney – *Tabebuia chrysantha*, the trumpet tree, a large tree with yellow flowers (Venezuela's national tree)

atarraya – a kind of traditional, circular fishing net, used on the coast and rivers

ateneo – cultural centre

autopista – freeway

azulejos – ornamental hand-made tiles brought to South America from Spain and Portugal in colonial times

baba – the spectacled cayman, the smallest of the family of local crocodiles

balneario – seaside, lake or river bathing place with facilities

bandola – four-string guitar-type instrument used by some *joropo* bands instead of the harp

Baré – also referred to as *Bale*, an Indian group living in southern Amazonas

barrio – a shantytown built of *ranchos* by the poor around the big city centres; particularly numerous and extensive in Caracas, they are found throughout South America, though are named differently in different countries: *tugurios* in Colombia, *favelas* in Brazil, *villas miserias* in Argentina, *cantegriles* in Uruguay, *barriadas* in Peru and *callampas* in Chile

bodega – warehouse; also used to mean grocery, especially in small localities and rural areas

bolo – informal term for the bolívar (currency), see *real*

bonche – party (informal)

bongo – large dugout canoe; traditionally hand-hewn, today usually equipped with outboard motor

bora – aquatic plant with mauve or white flowers and leaves that look like small balloons; capybaras' favourite dish

broma – literally joke; a problem, or an object or entity that need not be precisely named (informal)

bucare – *Erythrina poeppigiana*, a large tree with red flowers which often provides shade to coffee or cacao plantations; its branches house orchids and bromeliads

buhonero – street vendor

buseta – small bus

cabaña – cabin, found mostly on the coast or in the mountains

cachicamo – armadillo

caimán – American crocodile, similar to alligators but with a more heavily armoured belly

caminata – trekking

campamento – countryside accommodation, usually with its own food facilities and often a tour programme; may be available as an all-inclusive package only

campesino – rural dweller, usually of modest economic means; a peasant

canoa – a dugout canoe

CANTV – national telephone company

caño – natural water channel

carabobeño/a – inhabitant of Carabobo state, particularly Valencia

Caracazo – the violent street riots of 27-29 February 1989 in Caracas in which more than 300 died

caraqueño/a – person born and/or residing in Caracas

cardón – columnar type of cactus, typical of Península de Paraguaná

casa – house; the term can be used for anything from a rustic hut to a rambling colonial mansion

casa de cambio – money exchange office

cascabel – rattlesnake

caserío – hamlet

casona – large, usually historic mansion; stately home

catire – a person of light complexion

caudillo – South American dictator, normally a military man who assumes power by force and is noted for autocratic rule; caudillos governed Venezuela from 1830 to 1958

Causa R – the Causa Radical, a left-wing political party founded by unionists in opposition to the traditional parties

cédula – identity document of Venezuelan citizens and residents

ceiba – a common tree of the tropics; can reach a huge size

chalana – river ferry for people and vehicles

chaguaramo – popular term for royal palm

chamo/a – boy/girl, young person, mate (informal)

chapaletas – fins, flippers (rubber paddle-like devices used for swimming, snorkelling etc)

chévere – good, fine (informal)

chigüire – capybara; the world's largest rodent

chimó – tobacco tar used by people in the Amazon, the Andes and other regions; a ball of chimó is placed under the tongue or between the gum and cheek until it dissolves; a 'nicotine candy'

chinchorro – a hammock woven of cotton threads or palm fibre like a fishing net; typical of many Indian groups, including Warao and Guajiro

chiripa – a crawling insect; also used to describe a small newly born political party (informal)

churuata – a traditional palm-thatched circular Indian hut

cinemateca – art cinema which focus on screening films of a higher artistic quality

cogollos – the top ranks of the political parties

cola – literally 'tail'; also used in the sense of 'lift' as in *dar una cola* (to give a lift) and

pedir una cola (to ask for a lift); useful expressions when hitchhiking

coleo – a form of rodeo practised in Los Llanos; the aim is to overthrow a bull by grabbing its tail from a galloping horse

colibrí – hummingbird

cónchale – informal tag word; used on its own or added to the beginning of a sentence to emphasise emotional involvement

conuco – a small cultivated plot, usually obtained by slash burning

Copei – Partido Social Cristiano, or Social Christian Party, founded by Rafael Caldera in 1946 in opposition to the leftist AD party; initially conservative and catholic-oriented, since the 1970s it has gradually moved leftward to become the essentially populist party; until the 1993 election, Copei and AD almost monopolised the popular vote

copeyano – a member of the Copei party

corrida – bullfight

criollo – Creole, a person of European (especially Spanish) ancestry but born in the Americas

cuadra – city block

cuatro – a sort of small four-stringed guitar, used in *joropo* music

cuñado – literally 'brother-in-law'; mate, friend (informal)

curiara – a small dugout canoe

danta – tapir; large hoofed mammal of tropical and subtropical forests which is a distant relative of the horse

denuncia – an official report/statement to the police

DIEX or **DEX** – Dirección Nacional de Identificación y Extranjería (Venezuelan immigration authorities)

embalse – reservoir formed by a dam built for hydroelectric or water supply purposes

E'ñepá – see *Panare*

esquina – street corner

estacionamiento (vigilado) – (guarded) car park

farmacia – pharmacy

flamenco – flamingo

flor de mayo – the species of orchid which is Venezuela's national flower

flux – suit

fortín – a small fort

fósforos – matches

frailejón – *espeletia*; a species of plant typical of the *páramo*

franela – literally 'flannel'; commonly used for T-shirt

fuerte – fort

fundo – country estate

furruco – musical instrument consisting of a drum and a wooden pole piercing the drumhead, and the sound is produced by striking the drumhead by moving the pole up and down; used in some kinds of popular music including the *gaita*

gaita – popular music played in Zulia state

gallera – cockfight ring

garimpeiro – illegal gold miner

garza – heron

gavilán – sparrow hawk

gringo/a – any white foreigner, not only a Yankee; sometimes, not always, derogatory

guacamayo – macaw

guácharo – oilbird, a species of nocturnal bird living in caves

Guajibo – or *Guahibo* (*Hiwi* in the native language), an Indian group living in parts of Los Llanos and Amazonas along the frontier with Colombia

Guajiro – often referred to by their native name of Wayú, Venezuela's most numerous Indian group, living in Zulia state (Venezuela) and Península de la Guajira (Colombia)

guardaequipaje – left-luggage office; checkroom

guardaparque – national park's ranger

Guardia Nacional – the militarised police responsible for security

guarupa – jacaranda, a tall tropical tree with lavender-blue blossoms

hacienda – a country estate

hato – large cattle ranch, typical of Los Llanos

Hiwi – see *Guajibo*

hospedaje – cheap hotel

invierno – literally 'winter' but refers to the rainy season

Ipostel – the state company operating a network of post offices

IVA – the impuesto de valor agregado, a value-added tax (VAT)

jején – a species of small biting flies which infest La Gran Sabana and, to a lesser extent, some other regions

jíbaro – drug dealer (informal)

joropo – typical music of Los Llanos, today widespread throughout the country; considered Venezuelan national rhythm

lapa – a species of agouti, a rabbit-sized rodent whose brown skin is dotted with white spots

libre – taxi

liqui liqui – men's traditional costume, typical of most of the Caribbean; a white or beige suit comprising trousers and a blouse with a collar, usually accompanied by white hat and shoes

llanero/a – inhabitant of Los Llanos

(Los) Llanos – literally plains; Venezuela's vast central region

loro – parrot

malecón – waterfront promenade

manatí – manatee; a cetaceous herbivore living in calm rivers, and can reach 5m in length

manga de coleo – track where *coleo* is held

mapanare – a venomous snake common in Venezuela

Maquiritare – see *Yekuana*

maracas – gourd rattles; an indispensable accompanying instrument of the *joropo*

maracucho/a – person from Maracaibo, often extended to mean anyone from the Zulia state

margariteño/a – person from the Isla de Margarita

MAS – Movimiento al Socialismo; leftist political party created by the former guerrilla leaders after the insurgent forces had been dismantled in the early 1970s

matrimonial – a hotel room with a double bed intended for married couples

médanos – sand dunes near Coro

merengue – musical rhythm orginated from the Dominican Republic, today widespread throughout the Caribbean

merú – Pemón Indian word for waterfall

mestizo – a person of mixed European-Indian blood

mirador – lookout, viewpoint

monedero – originally, term referring to public telephone operated by coins, but now extended to any public phone

moriche – a palm common in Los Llanos and the Orinoco Delta, and used by Indians for construction, food, household items, handicrafts etc

morocho – person of dark complexion; usually a mix of black and white ancestry

morrocoy – tortoise, typical of some regions including Los Llanos and Guayana

mosquitero – mosquito net

muelle – pier, wharf

mulato – a person of mixed European-black ancestry

musiú – old-fashioned term for foreigner, derived from the French 'monsieur' and used by elderly locals in some rural areas

Navidad – Christmas

nevado – a snow-capped peak

orquídea – orchid

oso hormiguero – anteater

palafito – a house built on stilts over the water; a typical Warao dwelling in the Orinoco Delta but also found in Zulia state, especially in the Laguna de Sinamaica

palos – drinks (informal)

pana – mate (informal)

Panare – Indian group living in Bolívar and Amazon states, also known by their native-language name of *E'ñepá*

paño – small towel, the one you'll get in cheap hotels

parada – bus stop

páramo – open highlands above about 3300m, typical of Venezuela, Colombia and Ecuador

parapente – paraglider

pardo – mulatto; person of mixed European-African descent

paují – a black bird which inhabits cloud-forest in the north and west of Venezuela

Pemón – Indian group inhabiting La Gran Sabana and neighbouring areas

peñero – open fishing boat made from wood

pereza – sloth

Piaroa – originally called Wóthuha, an Indian group living in Amazonas state

plaza de toros – bullfight ring

por puesto – a popular means of transport, a cross between a bus and taxi which plies fixed routes and departs when full

posada – a small family-run guesthouse

primo – literally 'cousin'; mate, brother (informal)

propina – tip

Pumé – see *Yaruro*

puri-puri – small biting flies, similar to *jején*

quinta – a house with a garden; originally a fifth of the block, hence its name

ranchería – Indian hamlet

rancho or **ranchito** – a ramshackle dwelling built of waste materials by the poor

raudales – rapids

real – an informal term for the bolívar (currency)

redoma – roundabout (circular road junction)

refugio – a rustic shelter in a remote area, mostly in the mountains

residencias – cheap hotel or, more often, apartment building

rústico – jeep

salinas – seaside saltpans or shallow lagoons used for extraction of salt

salsa – a type of Caribbean dance music of Cuban origin, evolved and matured in New York, from where it has conquered the whole Caribbean basin and the surrounding countries

Semana Santa – Holy Week, the week before Easter Sunday

shabono – a large circular house typical of the Yanomami Indians

SIDA – AIDS

sifrino/a – yuppie (informal)
simas – sinkholes
soroche – altitude sickness

tapara – cup-like vessel which is made from a hollowed-out pumpkin cut in half, traditionally used in some rural areas for drinking, washing etc
tarjetero – public telephone operated by phone cards
teleférico – cable car
telenovela – TV soap opera
tepui – also spelled tepuy, a flat-topped sandstone mountain with vertical flanks; the term is derived from the Pemón Indian word for mountain
terminal de pasajeros – bus terminal
tigre – jaguar
tonina – fresh-water dolphin
toros coleados – see *coleo*
trapiche – traditional sugarcane mill
turpial – a small black, red and yellow bird; Venezuela's national bird

urbanización – suburb

vallenato – typical Colombian music, widespread in Venezuela's north-west
vaquero – cowboy of Los Llanos

vená – Pemón Indian word for high waterfall
verano – literally 'summer' but used in the sense of dry season

Warao – Indian group living in the Orinoco Delta
Wayú – see *Guajiro*
viaje expreso – literally 'express trip', when you pay the whole trip in a car, jeep, boat etc, like a taxi
Wóthuha – see *Piaroa*

yagrumo – a tree with large palmate silver-coloured leaves
Yanomami – Indian group living in the Venezuelan and Brazilian Amazon
Yaruro – known in their native-language as Pumé, an Indian group living in Apure state (Venezuela) and Arauca and Casanare states (Colombia)
Yekuana – also referred to as *Maquiritare*, an Indian group inhabiting parts of Amazonas and Bolívar states
yoppo – hallucinogenic powder inhaled through the nostrils using a long pipe and is traditionally used by Yanomami shamans

zamuro – vulture

Food & Drink Glossary

aceite – oil
aceituna – olive
agua – water
aguacate – avocado
aguardiente – sugarcane spirit flavoured with anise, typical of Colombia, similar to *miche*
ají – red chilli pepper
ajo – garlic
ajoporro – leek
alcaparra – caper
aliño – combination of spices
almeja – clam
almendra – almond
almuerzo – lunch
arepa – a small maize pancake, which in itself is plain and comes as an accompaniment to some dishes; more popularly, it's served as a snack in its own right, stuffed with a variety of fillings including cheese, beef, ham, octopus, shrimps, sausage, eggs, salad, avocado and just about anything you might think of; in the Andean region, there's also the quite different *arepa de trigo*, which is made from wheat
arepera – eating place that serves arepas; it can be just a self-service arepa snack bar, but also a restaurant with table service which, apart from arepas, offers other typical dishes such as *mondongo*, *hervido*, *pabellón* etc
arroz – rice
arveja – green peas
atún – tuna
auyama – pumpkin
avellanas – hazelnuts
azúcar – sugar

bagre – catfish
batata – sweet potato
batido – fresh fruit juice (pure or watered down)
bebida – drink, beverage
berenjena – eggplant
bienmesabe – sponge cake with coconut flavour
brócoli – broccoli

cachapa – a round juicy pancake made of fresh corn, usually served with cheese and/or ham
cachito – a sort of croissant filled with chopped ham and served hot
calabacín – zucchini, courgette
calabaza – squash
calamar – squid
calentado – typical drink of the Andean highlands, made from *miche* and milk, sweetened with *papelón*, seasoned with herbs and served hot
camarón – small shrimp
cambur – banana
canela – cinnamon
cangrejo – crab
carabina – Mérida version of *hallaca*
caracol – snail
caraota – black bean
carite – kingfish
carne – meat
carne de cochino – pork
carne de res – beef
carne guisada – stewed beef
carne mechada – shredded beef
carne molida – mince meat
casabe – a very large, dry flat bread made from *yuca amarga* (bitter yucca, grated, pressed and dried) which has traditionally been an important part of the diet of the Indian communities
cazón – baby shark
cebolla – onion
cebollín – scallion, spring onion
céleri – celery
cereza – cherry
cerveza – beer
champiñón – mushroom
charcutería – pork butcher's shop selling hams, sausages, salamis etc
chayote – christophene, chayote; a light green pear shaped vegetable
chicha – a thick, filling nonalcoholic drink made from corn or rice; it also has an alcoholic variety
chicharrón – pork crackling

chimbombo – okra, ladies fingers, gumbo
chivo – goat
chorizo – seasoned sausage
chuleta – chop, rib steak
churro – fried pastry tubes sprinkled with sugar; often sold on the street
cilantro – coriander
ciruela – plum
cocada – blended drink made from coconut milk
cochino – pork
coco – coconut
coctel – cocktail
cocuy – a kind of liqueur made from sugar cane
codorniz – quail
coliflor – cauliflower
contorno – accompaniment to the main dish
cordero – lamb
corocoro – grunt (fish)
corvina – blue fish
costilla – rib
cotufa – popcorn
crema agria – sour cream

dátil – date
desayuno – breakfast
dorado – dolphin fish
dulce – small cake
durazno – apricot

empanada – a crescent-shaped deep-fried cornmeal turnover stuffed with ground beef *(empanada de carne)*, chicken *(empanada de pollo)* or cheese *(empanada de queso)*; a ubiquitous snack found throughout the continent, with numerous local varieties
ensalada – salad
espárrago – asparagus
espinaca – spinach

falda – flank
frambuesa – raspberry
fresa – strawberry
frijoles – red beans
fruta – fruit
frutería – fruit shop or place that serves fruit salads, fruit juices, fruit milk shakes etc
fuente de soda – budget eating place serving snacks and drinks

galleta – biscuit, cracker
gallina – hen
garbanzo – chickpea
grasa – fat
guacuco – clam
guanábana – soursop
guarapita – drink made from a sugarcane spirit and fruit juice
guasacaca – a piquant sauce made of capsicum, onions and seasoning; the red-coloured varieties are hotter than the green ones; the sauce is served with chicken, *parrillas*, *empanadas* etc, and you'll often find it on restaurant tables
guayaba – guava
guayoyo – weak black coffee
guisante – pea

haba – broad bean/large lima bean, common in the Andes
hallaca – chopped pork, beef and/or chicken with vegetables and olives, all folded in a maize dough, wrapped in banana leaves and steamed; particularly popular during Christmas
helado – ice cream
hervido – a hearty soup made of beef *(hervido de res)* or chicken *(hervido de gallina)* with potatoes, carrots and a variety of local root vegetables
hielo – ice
hígado – liver
higo – fig
hongo – mushroom, fungus
huevo – egg
huevos fritos – fried eggs
huevos revueltos – scrambled eggs

jamón – ham
jamón serrano – cured ham that is sliced paper thin
jengibre – ginger
jojoto – kernel corn, fresh corn
jugo – juice
jurel – a type of fish similar to saurel or scad

langosta – lobster
langostino – large shrimp, large prawn
lebranche – black mullet
leche – milk

leche de burra – a thick alcoholic beverage made of *miche*, egg and milk which is common in the Andes
leche descremada – skimmed milk
lechón – a pig carcass stuffed with its own meat, rice and dried peas and then baked
lechosa – papaya, pawpaw
lechuga – lettuce
lenguado – sole, flounder
lenteja – lentil
lima – lime
limón – lemon
limonada – lemonade
lisa – silver mullet, grey mullet
lomito – tenderloin
lunchería – cheap restaurant serving staple food and snacks

maíz – corn, maize
maíz pelado – unleavened corn
mamón – grape-sized fruit, with green skin and reddish edible flesh you suck until you get to the core
mandarina – mandarin, tangerine
maní – peanuts
mantecado – vanilla or dairy ice cream
mantequilla – butter
manzana – apple
margarina – margarine
mariscos – shellfish, seafood
masa – dough
mayonesa – mayonnaise
mejillones – mussels
melocotón – peach
melón – cantaloupe, rockmelon
merengada – fruit milk shake
merey – cashew
mero – grouper (groper) or sea bass
miche – anise-flavoured spirit made from sugarcane, similar to Colombian *aguardiente*, and so called in some areas
milanesa – thin steak
mondongo – a seasoned tripe cooked in bouillon with maize, potatoes, carrots and other vegetables
mora – blackberry
mostaza – mustard
muchacho – roast beef served in sauce

nabo – turnip

naranja – orange
nata – thick sweat cream
natilla – sour-milk butter
níspero – fruit of the medlar tree
nuez – nut, walnut

ñame – a type of yam, edible tuber

ocumo – root vegetable with dark skin and white meat; basic food for many Indian groups
ostra – oyster

pabellón criollo – a main course consisting of shredded beef, rice, black beans, cheese and *tajada*; it's Venezuela's national dish
paella – Spanish dish of rice, pork, chicken and seafood
pámpano – pompano (fish)
pan – bread
panqueca – pancake, crêpe
papa – potato
papas fritas – chips, French fries
papelón – crude brown sugar, sold in solid blocks in cubic or pyramid shape
parchita – passion fruit
pargo – red snapper
parrilla – also called *parrillada*, a mixed grill of different kinds of meat, usually including steak, pork, chops, chicken and a variety of sausages; originally an Argentine speciality but now widespread in Venezuela
pasapalos – hors d'oeuvres, small snacks, finger food
pastel – pastry
pasticho – lasagne
paticas – pig's feet
patilla – watermelon
pato – duck
pavo – turkey
pavón – peacock bass, a tasty freshwater fish, common in the Los Llanos
payara – a type of peacock bass, common in the Orinoco River and its tributaries
pechuga – breast (poultry)
pepino – cucumber
pepitona – ark-shell clam
pera – pear
perejil – parsley
pernil – leg of pork

perro caliente – hot dog
pescado – fish that has been caught to eat
pez – a live fish
pimentón – capsicum
pimienta – pepper
piña – pineapple
plátano – plantain (green banana)
pollo – chicken
pulpo – octopus
punta trasera – top rump

quesillo – caramel custard
queso – cheese

rábano – radish
raspao – snowcone, shaved ice with flavoured sugar syrup, sold only on the street
refresco – soft drink
refresquería – place serving soft drinks and snacks
reina pepiada – chicken with avocado, a tasty stuffing for *arepas*
remolacha – beetroot
repollo – cabbage
riñones – kidneys
róbalo – snook, bass
ron – rum
rosbif – roast beef
rueda – fish steak

sal – salt
salchicha – sausage
salmón – salmon
salsa – sauce
salsa de tomate – tomato sauce, ketchup
sancocho – a vegetable stew with fish, beef or chicken
sangría – red wine diluted with soda water with chunks of fruit
sardina – sardine
sierra – king mackerel, sawfish
solomo – sirloin
sopa – soup

tajada – fried ripe plantain

tamarindo – tamarind
tapas – typical Spanish hors d'oeuvres, a staple offering of the *tascas*; the most common include *empanadas, tortillas, jamón serrano, calamares, camarones, chorizos a la plancha* (grilled sausage) and *pimientos fritos* (fried peppers); some are served cold, others hot, and some of the latter variety may be a core of a main course
tasca – Spanish-style bar-cum-restaurant, ubiquitous in Venezuela which serves Spanish snacks *(tapas)* and dishes plus a variety of drinks
té – tea
tequeño – white cheese strips wrapped in pastry and deep-fried
teta – iced fruit juice in a plastic wrap, which is eaten by sucking
tizana – a variety of chopped fruit in fruit juice, it usually includes pieces of pawpaw, banana, watermelon, cantaloupe, pineapple and orange
tocineta – bacon
tomate – tomato
toronja – grapefruit
torta – cake
tortilla – omelette
tostón – fried plantain
trago – alcoholic drink
trigo – wheat
trucha – trout

uva – grape
uva pasa – raisin

vieira – scallop
vinagre – vinegar
vino blanco – white wine
vino espumoso – sparkling wine
vino rosado – rosé
vino tinto – red wine

yuca – yucca (edible root)

zanahoria – carrot

Index

LONELY PLANET PHRASEBOOKS

Building bridges,
Breaking barriers,
Beyond babble-on

Listen for the gems

Speak your own words

Ask your own questions

Master of your own image

- handy pocket-sized books
- easy to understand Pronunciation chapter
- clear and comprehensive Grammar chapter
- romanisation alongside script to allow ease of pronunciation
- script throughout so users can point to phrases
- extensive vocabulary sections, words and phrases for every situation
- full of cultural information and tips for the traveller

'...vital for a real DIY spirit and attitude in language learning' – Backpacker

'the phrasebooks have good cultural backgrounders and offer solid advice for challenging situations in remote locations' – San Francisco Examiner

'...they are unbeatable for their coverage of the world's more obscure languages' – The Geographical Magazine

---

Arabic (Egyptian)
Arabic (Moroccan)
Australia
  Australian English, Aboriginal and Torres Strait languages
Baltic States
  Estonian, Latvian, Lithuanian
Bengali
Brazilian
Burmese
Cantonese
Central Asia
Central Europe
  Czech, French, German, Hungarian, Italian and Slovak
Eastern Europe
  Bulgarian, Czech, Hungarian, Polish, Romanian and Slovak
Ethiopian (Amharic)
Fijian
French
German
Greek

Hindi/Urdu
Indonesian
Italian
Japanese
Korean
Lao
Latin American Spanish
Malay
Mandarin
Mediterranean Europe
  Albanian, Croatian, Greek, Italian, Macedonian, Maltese, Serbian and Slovene
Mongolian
Nepali
Papua New Guinea
Pilipino (Tagalog)
Quechua
Russian
Scandinavian Europe
  Danish, Finnish, Icelandic, Norwegian and Swedish

South-East Asia
  Burmese, Indonesian, Khmer, Lao, Malay, Tagalog (Pilipino), Thai and Vietnamese
Spanish (Castilian)
  Basque, Catalan and Galician
Sri Lanka
Swahili
Thai
Thai Hill Tribes
Tibetan
Turkish
Ukrainian
USA
  US English, Vernacular, Native American languages and Hawaiian
Vietnamese
Western Europe
  Basque, Catalan, Dutch, French, German, Irish, Italian, Portuguese, Scottish Gaelic, Spanish (Castilian) and Welsh

---

LONELY PLANET JOURNEYS

JOURNEYS is a unique collection of travel writing – published by the company that understands travel better than anyone else. It is a series for anyone who has ever experienced – or dreamed of – the magical moment when they encountered a strange culture or saw a place for the first time. They are tales to read while you're planning a trip, while you're on the road or while you're in an armchair, in front of a fire.

JOURNEYS books catch the spirit of a place, illuminate a culture, recount a crazy adventure, or introduce a fascinating way of life. They always entertain, and always enrich the experience of travel.

'Idiosyncratic, entertainingly diverse and unexpected . . . from an international writership'
– The Australian

'Books which offer a closer look at the people and culture of a destination, and enrich travel experiences'
– American Bookseller

FULL CIRCLE
A South American Journey
Luis Sepúlveda
Translated by Chris Andrews

Full Circle invites us to accompany Chilean writer Luis Sepúlveda on 'a journey without a fixed itinerary'. Whatever his subject – brutalities suffered under Pinochet's dictatorship, sleepy tropical towns visited in exile, or the landscapes of legendary Patagonia – Sepúlveda is an unflinchingly honest yet lyrical storyteller. Extravagant characters and extraordinary situations are memorably evoked: gauchos organising a tournament of lies, a scheming heiress on the lookout for a husband, a pilot with a corpse on board his plane . . . Part autobiography, part travel memoir, *Full Circle* brings us the distinctive voice of one of South America's most compelling writers.

Luis Sepúlveda was born in Chile in 1949. Imprisoned by the Pinochet dictatorship for his socialist beliefs, he was for many years a political exile. He has written novels, short stories, plays and essays. His work has attracted many awards and has been translated into numerous languages.

'Detachment, humour and vibrant prose' – **El País**

'an absolute cracker' – **The Bookseller**

Australia Council
for the Arts

This project has been assisted by the Commonwealth Government through the Australia Council, its arts funding and advisory body.

LONELY PLANET TRAVEL ATLASES

Lonely Planet has long been famous for the number and quality of its guidebook maps. Now we've gone one step further and in conjunction with Steinhart Katzir Publishers produced a handy companion series: Lonely Planet travel atlases – maps of a country produced in book form.

Unlike other maps, which look good but lead travellers astray, our travel atlases have been researched on the road by Lonely Planet's experienced team of writers. All details are carefully checked to ensure the atlas corresponds with the equivalent Lonely Planet guidebook.

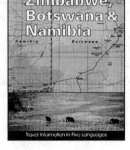

The handy atlas format means no holes, wrinkles, torn sections or constant folding and unfolding. These atlases can survive long periods on the road, unlike cumbersome fold-out maps. The comprehensive index ensures easy reference.

- full-colour throughout
- maps researched and checked by Lonely Planet authors
- place names correspond with Lonely Planet guidebooks
  – no confusing spelling differences
- legend and travelling information in English, French, German, Japanese and Spanish
- size: 230 x 160 mm

Available now:
Chile & Easter Island • Egypt • India & Bangladesh • Israel & the Palestinian Territories •Jordan, Syria & Lebanon • Kenya • Laos • Portugal • South Africa, Lesotho & Swaziland • Thailand • Turkey • Vietnam • Zimbabwe, Botswana & Namibia

---

LONELY PLANET TV SERIES & VIDEOS

Lonely Planet travel guides have been brought to life on television screens around the world. Like our guides, the programmes are based on the joy of independent travel, and look honestly at some of the most exciting, picturesque and frustrating places in the world. Each show is presented by one of three travellers from Australia, England or the USA and combines an innovative mixture of video, Super-8 film, atmospheric soundscapes and original music.

Videos of each episode – containing additional footage not shown on television – are available from good book and video shops, but the availability of individual videos varies with regional screening schedules.

Video destinations include: Alaska • American Rockies • Australia – The South-East • Baja California & the Copper Canyon • Brazil • Central Asia • Chile & Easter Island • Corsica, Sicily & Sardinia – The Mediterranean Islands • East Africa (Tanzania & Zanzibar) • Ecuador & the Galapagos Islands • Greenland & Iceland • Indonesia • Israel & the Sinai Desert • Jamaica • Japan • La Ruta Maya • Morocco • New York • North India • Pacific Islands (Fiji, Solomon Islands & Vanuatu) • South India • South West China • Turkey • Vietnam • West Africa • Zimbabwe, Botswana & Namibia

The Lonely Planet TV series is produced by:
Pilot Productions
The Old Studio
18 Middle Row
London W10 5AT UK

For video availability and ordering information contact your nearest Lonely Planet office.

Music from the TV series is available on CD & cassette.

PLANET TALK

Lonely Planet's FREE quarterly newsletter

We love hearing from you and think you'd like to hear from us.

When...is the right time to see reindeer in Finland?
Where...can you hear the best palm-wine music in Ghana?
How...do you get from Asunción to Areguá by steam train?
What...is the best way to see India?

For the answer to these and many other questions read PLANET TALK.

Every issue is packed with up-to-date travel news and advice including:

- a letter from Lonely Planet co-founders Tony and Maureen Wheeler
- go behind the scenes on the road with a Lonely Planet author
- feature article on an important and topical travel issue
- a selection of recent letters from travellers
- details on forthcoming Lonely Planet promotions
- complete list of Lonely Planet products

To join our mailing list contact any Lonely Planet office.

Also available: Lonely Planet T-shirts. 100% heavyweight cotton.

LONELY PLANET ONLINE

Get the latest travel information before you leave or while you're on the road

Whether you've just begun planning your next trip, or you're chasing down specific info on currency regulations or visa requirements, check out Lonely Planet Online for up-to-the minute travel information.

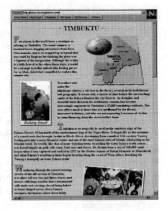

As well as travel profiles of your favourite destinations (including maps and photos), you'll find current reports from our researchers and other travellers, updates on health and visas, travel advisories, and discussion of the ecological and political issues you need to be aware of as you travel.

There's also an online travellers' forum where you can share your experience of life on the road, meet travel companions and ask other travellers for their recommendations and advice. We also have plenty of links to other online sites useful to independent travellers.

And of course we have a complete and up-to-date list of all Lonely Planet travel products including guides, phrasebooks, atlases, Journeys and videos and a simple online ordering facility if you can't find the book you want elsewhere.

www.lonelyplanet.com
or
AOL keyword: lp

LONELY PLANET PRODUCTS

Lonely Planet is known worldwide for publishing practical, reliable and no-nonsense travel information in our guides and on our web site. The Lonely Planet list covers just about every accessible part of the world. Currently there are nine series: *travel guides, shoestring guides, walking guides, city guides, phrasebooks, audio packs, travel atlases, Journeys* – a unique collection of travel writing and *Pisces Books* - diving and snorkeling guides.

EUROPE

Amsterdam • Austria • Baltic States phrasebook • Britain • Central Europe on a shoestring • Central Europe phrasebook • Czech & Slovak Republics • Denmark • Dublin • Eastern Europe on a shoestring • Eastern Europe phrasebook • Estonia, Latvia & Lithuania • Finland • France • French phrasebook • Germany • German phrasebook • Greece • Greek phrasebook • Hungary • Iceland, Greenland & the Faroe Islands • Ireland • Italian phrasebook • Italy • Lisbon • London• Mediterranean Europe on a shoestring • Mediterranean Europe phrasebook • Paris • Poland • Portugal • Portugal travel atlas • Prague • Romania & Moldova • Russia, Ukraine & Belarus • Russian phrasebook • Scandinavian & Baltic Europe on a shoestring • Scandinavian Europe phrasebook • Slovenia • Spain • Spanish phrasebook • St Petersburg • Switzerland •Trekking in Spain • Ukrainian phrasebook • Vienna • Walking in Britain • Walking in Switzerland • Western Europe on a shoestring • Western Europe phrasebook

Travel Literature: The Olive Grove: Travels in Greece

NORTH AMERICA

Alaska • Backpacking in Alaska • Baja California • California & Nevada • Canada • Deep South• Florida • Hawaii • Honolulu • Los Angeles • Mexico • Miami • New England • New Orleans • New York City • New York, New Jersey & Pennsylvania • Pacific Northwest USA• Rocky Mountain States • San Francisco • Southwest USA • USA phrasebook • Washington, DC & the Capital Region

CENTRAL AMERICA & THE CARIBBEAN

• Bahamas and Turks & Caicos • Bermuda • Central America on a shoestring • Costa Rica • Cuba •Eastern Caribbean •Guatemala, Belize & Yucatán: La Ruta Maya • Jamaica

SOUTH AMERICA

Argentina, Uruguay & Paraguay • Bolivia • Brazil • Brazilian phrasebook • Buenos Aires • Chile & Easter Island • Chile & Easter Island travel atlas • Colombia Ecuador & the Galápagos Islands • Latin American Spanish phrasebook • Peru • Quechua phrasebook • Rio de Janeiro • South America on a shoestring • Trekking in the Patagonian Andes • Venezuela

Travel Literature: Full Circle: A South American Journey

ISLANDS OF THE INDIAN OCEAN

Madagascar & Comoros • Maldives• Mauritius, Réunion & Seychelles

AFRICA

Africa - the South • Africa on a shoestring • Arabic (Moroccan) phrasebook • Cape Town • Central Africa • East Africa • Egypt • Egypt travel atlas• Ethiopian (Amharic) phrasebook • Kenya • Kenya travel atlas • Malawi, Mozambique & Zambia • Morocco • North Africa • South Africa, Lesotho & Swaziland • South Africa, Lesotho & Swaziland travel atlas • Swahili phrasebook • Trekking in East Africa • West Africa • Zimbabwe, Botswana & Namibia • Zimbabwe, Botswana & Namibia travel atlas

Travel Literature: The Rainbird: A Central African Journey • Songs to an African Sunset: A Zimbabwean Story

THE LONELY PLANET STORY

Lonely Planet published its first book in 1973 in response to the numerous 'How did you do it?' questions Maureen and Tony Wheeler were asked after driving, bussing, hitching, sailing and railing their way from England to Australia.

Written at a kitchen table and hand collated, trimmed and stapled, *Across Asia on the Cheap* became an instant local bestseller, inspiring thoughts of another book.

Eighteen months in South-East Asia resulted in their second guide, *South-East Asia on a shoestring*, which they put together in a backstreet Chinese hotel in Singapore in 1975. The 'yellow bible', as it quickly became known to backpackers around the world, soon became *the* guide to the region. It has sold well over half a million copies and is now in its 9th edition, still retaining its familiar yellow cover.

Today there are over 240 titles, including travel guides, walking guides, language kits & phrasebooks, travel atlases and travel literature. The company is the largest independent travel publisher in the world. Although Lonely Planet initially specialised in guides to Asia, today there are few corners of the globe that have not been covered.

The emphasis continues to be on travel for independent travellers. Tony and Maureen still travel for several months of each year and play an active part in the writing, updating and quality control of Lonely Planet's guides.

They have been joined by over 70 authors and 170 staff at our offices in Melbourne (Australia), Oakland (USA), London (UK) and Paris (France). Travellers themselves also make a valuable contribution to the guides through the feedback we receive in thousands of letters each year and on our web site.

The people at Lonely Planet strongly believe that travellers can make a positive contribution to the countries they visit, both through their appreciation of the countries' culture, wildlife and natural features, and through the money they spend. In addition, the company makes a direct contribution to the countries and regions it covers. Since 1986 a percentage of the income from each book has been donated to ventures such as famine relief in Africa; aid projects in India; agricultural projects in Central America; Greenpeace's efforts to halt French nuclear testing in the Pacific; and Amnesty International.

'I hope we send people out with the right attitude about travel. You realise when you travel that there are so many different perspectives about the world, so we hope these books will make people more interested in what they see. Guidebooks can't really guide people. All you can do is point them in the right direction.'

– Tony Wheeler

LONELY PLANET PUBLICATIONS

Australia
PO Box 617, Hawthorn 3122, Victoria
tel: (03) 9819 1877 fax: (03) 9819 6459
e-mail: talk2us@lonelyplanet.com.au

USA
Embarcadero West, 155 Filbert St, Suite 251,
Oakland, CA 94607
tel: (510) 893 8555 TOLL FREE: 800 275-8555
fax: (510) 893 8563
e-mail: info@lonelyplanet.com

UK
10a Spring Place,
London NW5 3BH
tel: (0171) 428 4800 fax: (0171) 428 4828
e-mail: go@lonelyplanet.co.uk

France:
71 bis rue du Cardinal Lemoine, 75005 Paris
tel: 1 44 32 06 20 fax: 1 46 34 72 55
e-mail: 100560.415@compuserve.com

**World Wide Web: http://www.lonelyplanet.com
or *AOL keyword: lp***

MAIL ORDER

Lonely Planet products are distributed worldwide.They are also available by mail order from Lonely Planet, so if you have difficulty finding a title please write to us. North American and South American residents should write to Embarcadero West, 155 Filbert St, Suite 251, Oakland CA 94607, USA; European and African residents should write to 10a Spring Place, London NW5 3BH; and residents of other countries to PO Box 617, Hawthorn, Victoria 3122, Australia.

NORTH-EAST ASIA

Beijing • Cantonese phrasebook • China • Hong Kong • Hong Kong, Macau & Guangzhou • Japan • Japanese phrasebook • Japanese audio pack • Korea • Korean phrasebook • Mandarin phrasebook • Mongolia • Mongolian phrasebook • North-East Asia on a shoestring • Seoul • Taiwan • Tibet • Tibet phrasebook • Tokyo

Travel Literature: Lost Japan

MIDDLE EAST & CENTRAL ASIA

Arab Gulf States • Arabic (Egyptian) phrasebook • Central Asia • Central Asia phrasebook • Iran • Israel & the Palestinian Territories • Israel & the Palestinian Territories travel atlas • Istanbul • Jerusalem • Jordan & Syria • Jordan, Syria & Lebanon travel atlas • Lebanon • Middle East • Turkey • Turkish phrasebook • Turkey travel atlas • Yemen

Travel Literature: The Gates of Damascus • Kingdom of the Film Stars: Journey into Jordan

ALSO AVAILABLE:

Travel with Children • Traveller's Tales

INDIAN SUBCONTINENT

Bangladesh • Bengali phrasebook • Delhi • Goa • Hindi/Urdu phrasebook • India • India & Bangladesh travel atlas • Indian Himalaya • Karakoram Highway • Nepal • Nepali phrasebook • Pakistan • Rajasthan • Sri Lanka • Sri Lanka phrasebook • Trekking in the Indian Himalaya • Trekking in the Karakoram & Hindukush • Trekking in the Nepal Himalaya

Travel Literature: In Rajasthan • Shopping for Buddhas

SOUTH-EAST ASIA

Bali & Lombok • Bangkok • Burmese phrasebook • Cambodia • Ho Chi Minh City • Indonesia • Indonesian phrasebook • Indonesian audio pack • Jakarta • Java • Laos • Lao phrasebook • Laos travel atlas • Malay phrasebook • Malaysia, Singapore & Brunei • Myanmar (Burma) • Philippines • Pilipino phrasebook • Singapore • South-East Asia on a shoestring • South-East Asia phrasebook • Thailand • Thailand's Islands & Beaches • Thailand travel atlas • Thai phrasebook • Thai audio pack • Thai Hill Tribes phrasebook • Vietnam • Vietnamese phrasebook • Vietnam travel atlas

AUSTRALIA & THE PACIFIC

Australia • Australian phrasebook • Bushwalking in Australia • Bushwalking in Papua New Guinea • Fiji • Fijian phrasebook • Islands of Australia's Great Barrier Reef • Melbourne • Micronesia • New Caledonia • New South Wales • New Zealand • Northern Territory • Outback Australia • Papua New Guinea • Papua New Guinea phrasebook • Queensland • Rarotonga & the Cook Islands • Samoa • Solomon Islands • South Australia • Sydney • Tahiti & French Polynesia • Tasmania • Tonga • Tramping in New Zealand • Vanuatu • Victoria • Western Australia

Travel Literature: Islands in the Clouds • Sean & David's Long Drive

ANTARCTICA

Antarctica